The Middle Ages

A CONCISE ENCYCLOPÆDIA

A map of the known world, centred on the city of Jerusalem, from an English psalter of the early 13th century (British Library, London).

General editor: H. R. Loyn

The Middle Ages

A CONCISE ENCYCLOPÆDIA

With 250 illustrations

THAMES AND HUDSON

Sources of the illustrations

Numbers refer to the page on which the illustration is to be found.

A READER'S GUIDE TO THE USE OF THIS BOOK

The Middle Ages have long been dominated in the public mind by images of knightly prowess and courtly ritual, by the noble zeal and bloody violence of the Crusaders. Such colourful concepts have tended to obscure the true value of the period as an age of real advance in every field, of political and social evolution, of intellectual and artistic creativity, and of commercial and scientific progress.

It is a daunting task to do justice to this broad panorama, and we have had, of necessity, to be selective. The overriding aim throughout has been to provide both beginner and specialist with a single volume that presents a summary of current thought on the key protagonists, events and themes relating to the history of Europe – from Scandinavia to the Middle East – from *c*.400 to *c*.1500. Within this vast geographical and historical sweep, we have tried to strike a balance between concise, factual entries on the major battles, treaties, individuals and locations, and a more discursive treatment of topics of lively background interest. The encyclopaedia should therefore prove useful both to students and scholars, as an *aide-mémoire*, for checking essential facts quickly and easily; and as a stimulating guide and companion to the enquiring reader with a more general interest in the period.

An encyclopaedia should be more than an inert collection of key facts, and, to enable the reader to follow a creative line of enquiry from entry to entry, the *cross-references* have been specially designed to aid freedom of movement within the text without impeding readability. Most proper names have not been cross-referenced, and many may be assumed to have entries of their own. Those subjects listed at the end of an entry, in small capitals, refer the reader to connected topics not already mentioned that will prove of further interest.

General works of reference are suggested in the *Bibliographical note* on p.352, but more specific titles have also been given with virtually every entry, to provide a thorough and up-to-date bibliography. We have aimed to give easily accessible, recent titles, except where older publications remain the standard scholarly works. For entries where no bibliographical reference is given, cross-references should lead you to a longer associated entry, where relevant titles will be found.

The illustrations have been specially chosen for their documentary interest; figures in *square brackets* at the end of an entry indicate pages elsewhere in the encyclopaedia where relevant illustrations can be found. There are also two general *maps* on pp.6 and 7, and several smaller maps and *genealogical tables* may be found throughout the text. The more substantial entries are attributed to their authors according to the key given on p.8, with the *List of contributors*. Foreign names have largely been anglicized, except where no common English version exists – especially in the case of Arab names, for example. For the order of entries we have followed the *Cambridge Medieval History*.

My debt as general editor is great to numerous friends, colleagues and research students, who have helped with entries appropriate to their expertise. Dr Anne Dawtry, the late Miss Jane Herbert, and Mrs Sara-Jane Webber acted as sub-editors for some sections in the early stages of the enterprise; Mrs Michelle Brown, Dr Elizabeth M. Hallam, Mrs Elizabeth Lockwood and Dr Cathy Harding helped greatly in the later stages. Mrs Miriam van Bers, Mrs Helena Reid and Miss Anne Markinson kept the word-processing under control, ensuring that the inevitable complications did not get out of hand. My thanks go to all, and especially to the editorial staff at Thames and Hudson. **Henry Loyn**

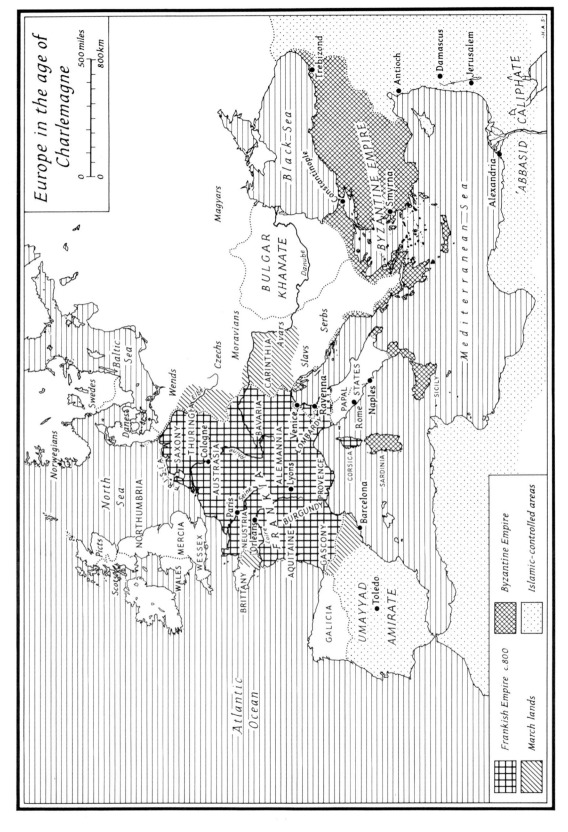

Europe in the age of
Charlemagne

500 miles
800 km

0
0

— H. A. S. —

Trebizond

Antioch   Damascus

BYZANTINE EMPIRE   Jerusalem

CALIPHATE

ABBASID

Alexandria

Mediterranean Sea

Constantinople   Smyrna

Black Sea

Magyars

BULGAR
KHANATE

Danube

Moravians

Avars

Serbs
Slavs

CARINTHIA

SICILY

Czechs

Wends

Elbe

Baltic
Sea

Norwegians

Swedes

Danes

North
Sea

NORTHUMBRIA

Picts

Scots

WALES

MERCIA

WESSEX

BRITTANY

Atlantic
Ocean

SAXONY

THURINGIA

AUSTRASIA

Cologne

Rhine

BAVARIA

ALEMANNIA

Venice   Ravenna

LOMBARDY

PAPAL
STATES

Rome   Naples

CORSICA

SARDINIA

Barcelona

GALICIA

UMAYYAD
AMIRATE

Toledo

GASCONY

AQUITAINE

Lyons

BURGUNDY

PROVENCE

F R A N K I A

Orléans

NEUSTRIA

Paris

Seine

Loire

Byzantine Empire

Islamic-controlled areas

Frankish Empire c.800

March lands

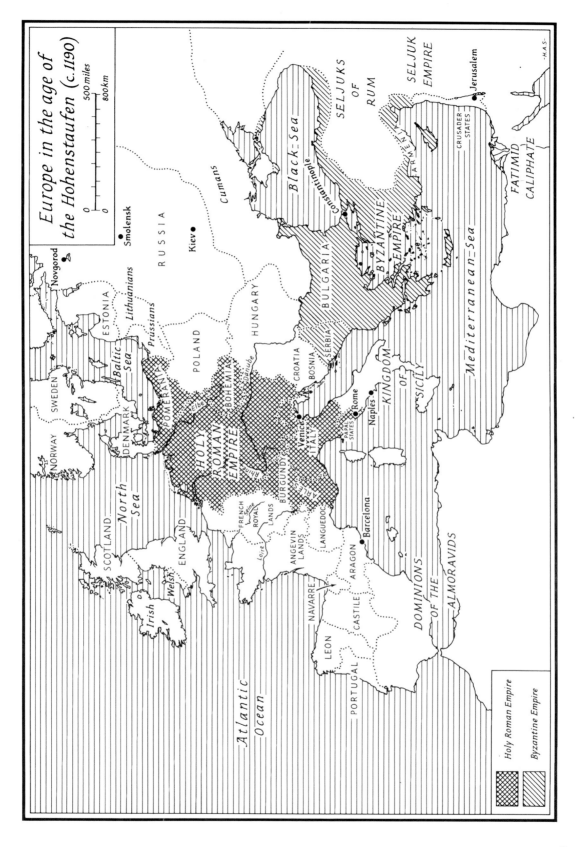

Europe in the age of
the Hohenstaufen (c.1190)

500 miles
800 km
0

Novgorod
Smolensk
Kiev
RUSSIA
Cumans
SWEDEN
NORWAY
ESTONIA
Lithuanians
Prussians
Baltic Sea
North Sea
SCOTLAND
Irish
Welsh
ENGLAND
DENMARK
POMERANIA
POLAND
HUNGARY
Black Sea
SELJUKS OF RUM
SELJUK EMPIRE
Jerusalem
Elbe
BOHEMIA
Danube
CROATIA
BOSNIA
SERBIA
BULGARIA
Constantinople
BYZANTINE EMPIRE
ARMENIA
CRUSADER STATES
FATIMID CALIPHATE
HOLY ROMAN EMPIRE
Rhine
BURGUNDY
Rome
PAPAL STATES
Venice
ITALY
Naples
KINGDOM OF SICILY
Mediterranean Sea
Seine
FRENCH ROYAL LANDS
Loire
ANGEVIN LANDS
LANGUEDOC
Barcelona
ARAGON
NAVARRE
CASTILE
LEON
PORTUGAL
DOMINIONS OF THE ALMORAVIDS
Atlantic Ocean

-H.A.S.-

Holy Roman Empire
Byzantine Empire

LIST OF CONTRIBUTORS

DB **Dr David Bates** Senior Lecturer in History, University College, Cardiff

CB **Christopher Brooke** Dixie Professor of Ecclesiastical History, Gonville and Caius College, Cambridge

RB **Dr Rosalind Brooke** Faculty of History, University of Cambridge

MB **Michelle Brown** Research assistant, Department of Manuscripts, British Library, London

SB **Sarah Brown** Architectural Staff of the Royal Commission on the Historical Monuments of England, London

RAB **R. Allen Brown** Professor of History, King's College, University of London

TJB **T. Julian Brown** Professor of Palaeography, King's College, University of London

DC **David F.L. Chadd** The Dean, School of Art History and Music, University of East Anglia

WD **Wendy Davies** Professor of History, University College London

AD **Dr Anne Dawtry** Lecturer in History, Chester College, Chester

PD **Dr Peter Denley** Lecturer in History, Queen Mary and Westfield College, University of London

ADD **Alan Deyermond** Professor of Spanish, Queen Mary and Westfield College, University of London

GE **Dr Gillian Evans** Fellow of Fitzwilliam College, Cambridge

JF **Jill Franklin** University of East Anglia

PG **Philip Grierson** Emeritus Professor and Fellow of Gonville and Caius College, Cambridge

EMH **Dr Elizabeth M. Hallam** Assistant Keeper, Public Record Office, London

CH **Dr Catherine Harding** Department of Art, Queen's University, Kingston, Canada

JH **Jane Herbert** Queen Mary and Westfield College, University of London

RH **Rosalind Hill** Professor Emerita of History, Queen Mary and Westfield College, University of London

GK **Dr Gillian Keir** Queen Mary and Westfield College, University of London

CHK **Dr Clive Knowles** Senior Lecturer in History, University College, Cardiff

CHL **C. Hugh Lawrence** Emeritus Professor of History, Royal Holloway and Bedford New College, University of London

EL **Elizabeth Lockwood** Queen Mary and Westfield College, University of London

HRL **Henry Loyn** Emeritus Professor of History, Queen Mary and Westfield College, University of London

DL **David Luscombe** Professor of Medieval History, University of Sheffield

GM **Professor Geoffrey Martin** Keeper of the Public Record Office, London

RIM **Robert I. Moore** Senior Lecturer in Medieval History, University of Sheffield

JLN **Dr Janet Nelson** Lecturer in History, King's College, University of London

DN **Donald M. Nicol** Koraës Professor of Modern Greek and Byzantine History, Language and Literature, King's College, University of London

CP **Ciaran Prendergast** Royal Holloway and Bedford New College, University of London

JR-S **Jonathan Riley-Smith** Professor of History, Royal Holloway and Bedford New College, University of London

NR **Nicolai Rubinstein** Emeritus Professor of History, Queen Mary and Westfield College, University of London

DJS **Dr D. Justin Schove** Headmaster of St David's School, Beckenham

IS **Ian Short** Professor of French, Birkbeck College, University of London

JS **Jane Symmons** Queen Mary and Westfield College, University of London

TSS **Mr T.S. Smith**

RT **Dr Rodney Thomson** Department of History, University of Tasmania

S-JW **Sara-Jane Webber** Queen Mary and Westfield College, University of London

SW **Steven Wilson** School of Oriental and African Studies, University of London

GZ **George Zarnecki** Emeritus Professor, Courtauld Institute of Art, London

A

'Abbādid dynasty Founded by the vizir and qādī Abū 'l-Qāsim Muhammad Ibn 'Abbād (1023–42), who was of mixed Arab and Spanish blood, the 'Abbādid dynasty ruled Seville between the fall of the caliphate of Cordoba and the Almoravid conquest of Muslim Spain. Under its rule, Seville became the most prosperous of the *taifa* kingdoms that were the successor states to the caliphate, absorbing a number of smaller *taifas* and conquering Cordoba in 1070. The 'Abbādid court was the centre of a brilliant poetic culture; the kings were themselves poets. The last of the line, al-Mu'tamid, was deposed and imprisoned by the Almoravids in 1091.
□ D. Wasserstein *The Rise and Fall of the Party-Kings* (1986)

'Abbāsid dynasty The 'Abbāsid caliphs or successors of Muhammad exercised authority over a large part of the Muslim world, their period of greatest triumph in the arts of civilization and politics coinciding with the reign of Hārūn ar-Rashīd (786–809), a contemporary of Charlemagne. They rose to power at the head of Shi'ite factions opposed to the Umayyads, but after their victories in the late 740s, when the entire Muslim world except Spain (which remained loyal to the Umayyads) submitted to them, they adopted the Sunnite rites of the majority and moved their capital from Damascus further east, building the great new city of Baghdad. Persian influence, with its traditions of oriental absolutism, became paramount in their administration; the interests of the dynasty became increasingly focused on the East, looking to the great trade routes to India and China. A separate caliphate was set up for Egypt and Palestine under the Fātimids in the 10th c., and the 'Abbāsids found their role reduced to that of religious and ceremonial leaders, the reality of power passing to the Seljuk Turks, who conquered Baghdad in the mid-11th c., and ultimately to the Mongols, who abolished the caliphate in 1258. [*185*]
□ *The Cambridge History of Islam* vol. 1, ed. P. Holt, A. Lambton and B. Lewis (1970)

Abbo of Fleury, St (954–1004) One of the most learned men of his day, Abbo wrote treatises on papal authority, astronomy and mathematics. Trained in the schools of Fleury, Rheims and Paris, he supported the Cluniac reformers and, after a period of exile in England, was elected abbot of Fleury in 988. He had already won a reputation as an active monastic reformer, intent on keeping monasteries free from episcopal and secular control, and

had played a prominent part in the English Benedictine revival, especially at Ramsey Abbey.
□ D. Knowles *The Monastic Order in England* (1950); P. Cousin *Abbon de Fleury-sur-Loire* (1954)

'Abd al-Malik Caliph 685–705 (b. 647) The true consolidator of the power of the Umayyad dynasty. Known to historians as 'the father of kings', he and his four sons dominated the caliphate to the 740s, and under their guidance, from their base at Damascus, the Muslim faith was spread from the uplands of Spain to the province of Sind in India. 'Abd al-Malik's personal contribution lay in reconciling rival factions and in encouraging military control both to the west (Carthage fell in 698) and to the east. Conspicuous consumption and the building of the great mosque, the Dome of the Rock at Jerusalem, highlighted the imperial attributes of the dynasty.

Gold dinar of the caliph **'Abd al-Malik.**

'Abd ar-Rahmān I Umayyad ruler of Andalusia 756–88 (b. 731) Last remaining member of the Umayyad dynasty after their overthrow by the 'Abbāsids; in 756 he established himself as independent amir of Cordoba in Spain. During his reign he was able to control the various factions within Spain and even won the support of the Christian Basques against Frankish incursions. The attempt by Charlemagne in 778 to conquer Spain aided by Ibn al-'Arabī of Saragossa, for example, was unsuccessful owing to an alliance between 'Abd ar-Rahmān and the Christian Berbers of the Basque country. The Franks were defeated and their rearguard wiped out at Roncesvalles in the Pyrenees, a battle which gave rise to the famous epic poem, the *Chanson de Roland*, since Roland, the warden of Brittany, was among those killed there. Following 'Abd ar-Rahmān's death civil war again broke out under his son Hishām I (788–96) and continued for almost a century.
□ P. Hitti *History of the Arabs* (1951)

Abelard, Peter

Abelard and Heloise on a 14th-c. carved capital at the Concièrgerie, Paris.

Abelard, Peter (1079–1142) Philosopher and theologian, born at Le Pallet near Nantes. His career was unusually varied for a master of the schools: he was educated at Loches or Tours under Roscelin of Compiègne, at Paris under William of Champeaux and at Laon under Anselm of Laon. With all these teachers he quarrelled violently. He taught in schools at Paris, Melun and Corbeil until *c.*1119 when he secretly married Heloise, niece of Canon Fulbert of Paris. Following the birth of their son, Astrolabe, Abelard was forcibly castrated by agents of Fulbert. Having arranged Heloise's profession as a nun at Argenteuil, Abelard became a monk of Saint-Denis nearby. But he soon returned to teaching and in 1121 suffered his first condemnation as a heretic at Soissons.

From 1122 he taught in a rural retreat at Quincey in Champagne and from *c.*1127 was abbot of Saint-Gildas-de-Rhuys in his native Brittany. In both places Abelard was plagued with difficulties, but while abbot he arranged for Heloise to start a new convent at Quincey, dedicated to the Paraclete. From *c.*1136 he reappeared in the schools of Paris, where his hearers included John of Salisbury. A second and more damaging condemnation occurred at a council held at Sens in 1140, and this was confirmed by Pope Innocent II. The defeat followed heated debates between, on the one side, Abelard and his sympathizers, who included Arnold of Brescia, and, on the other, Bernard, the influential abbot of Clairvaux, and many bishops of France. Abelard retired into the abbey of Cluny where he was befriended by Abbot Peter the Venerable. He died at the priory of Saint-Marcel at Chalon-sur-Saône in, or shortly after, 1142. Peter the Venerable transferred Abelard's remains to the Paraclete where Heloise remained as abbess until her death in 1164.

To portray Abelard as a fighter for intellectual emancipation from the dominance of monks who were enemies of learning and enquiry, is to simplify the tensions that led to Abelard's two condemnations for heresy. His critics included highly articulate men of genius, not only Bernard of Clairvaux but also William of Saint-Thierry and Hugh of Saint-Victor, while Abelard (himself a monk for much of his life) undoubtedly revelled in provocative disputes. In the *Historia Calamitatum* ('History of my Troubles') Abelard blames both the envy of his rivals and his own pride for his failures. But he captured the interest and devotion of more than one generation of students for making Aristotle's logic clear and for exploring brilliantly the functions and limitations of language.

As a philosopher Abelard has been correctly described as a non-realist. In his early career he turned away from the prevalent realist view of universals (e.g., genus, species) as existent things (*res*). He distinguished himself for his penetrating glosses on Aristotle's texts, rather than for the creation of a philosophical synthesis. In theology Abelard examined critically the received traditions of Christian thought; his *Sic et Non* ('Yes and No') is an attempt to resolve the apparent contradictions within Christian teaching through the application of dialectic. His methods were not unusual for his time, but his conclusions were judged incautious by many. His theological teaching reflected his dialectical non-realism; he presented the Trinity in terms of divine attributes (power, wisdom and love) rather than of divine persons. He saw the redemptive work of Christ less as an objective fact (the liberation of man from sin or the devil), than as an example of teaching and sacrifice which arouses a subjective response to divine love. In ethics he turned away from concern with actions towards the study of intention and consent. This interiorizing tendency is evident also in the substantial literary, legislative and liturgical contributions he made to the establishment of the convent of the Paraclete under Heloise as abbess: the nuns were exhorted to study and pray, and not to be bound more than necessary by external observances. Abelard admired contemplative figures who had been models of wisdom and virtue, whether they were pagans, such as Plato or Socrates, Cicero or Seneca, prophets, such as Elijah or John the Baptist, or early Christian monks such as Anthony and Jerome. All these loved wisdom and all, therefore, like Christ, deserved the name of philosopher.

Assessments of Abelard's overall achievement are inescapably too sympathetic or too critical. His original contributions to the rise of Paris university and of the medieval scholastic movement have sometimes received exaggerated attention, but he did make a strong impression upon the schoolmen of his time, however quickly his interests and books were rejected or, at best, pruned by his successors. His principal writings are, in logic, his *Dialectica* and commentaries on Aristotle's logic, and, in theology, his *Sic et Non* and his *Theologia* (both of which underwent successive revisions), his *Ethics* or *Know*

Thyself, commentaries on the opening of Genesis and on the Epistle to the Romans, and the *Dialogue between a Philosopher, a Jew and a Christian*. Today he is most popularly known through his correspondence with Heloise. The letters may not have circulated before the mid-13th c. and their authenticity is sometimes contested, largely because of the difficulty in interpreting the characters of the authors. But their love affair aroused considerable interest both immediately and throughout the Middle Ages. Abelard was also a gifted poet and musician.　　DL
□ E. Gilson *Heloise and Abelard* (1953); D. E. Luscombe *The School of Peter Abelard* (1969); *Abélard en son Temps* ed. J. Jolivet (1981)

Abū Bakr Caliph 632–34 The first caliph, or successor to Muhammad, and father-in-law of the Prophet. He overcame factions inside Arabia, extended Islam throughout the Arabian peninsula and in the last year of his life won great victories over the Byzantine forces which opened the way to the conquest of Palestine. His chief instrument in his military ventures was the general Khalid ibn al-Walīd, 'Sword of Allah', ultimate conqueror of Damascus (635).
□ P. Hitti *History of the Arabs* (1951)

Accursius the Glossator (*c*.1182–1260) A native of Florence and professor of law at Bologna university, he is particularly famous for his commentaries on the *Code, Institutes* and *Digest* of Justinian, which became the most widely used companion to these works in the medieval universities. He died at Bologna and was buried in the churchyard of S. Francesco (the Church of the Cordeliers). His son Francis was also a jurist of considerable renown, taking his doctorate in law at the early age of 17.
□ W. Ullmann *Law and Politics in the Middle Ages* (1975)

Adam of Bremen (d. *c*.1081) Canon of Bremen who became head of the cathedral school there in 1066. He wrote an ecclesiastical history in four books in which he described the spread of Christianity in Northern Europe, especially in the dioceses of Bremen and Hamburg. The work ends with a valuable treatise on the state of Denmark in the third quarter of the 11th c.
□ B. Schmiedler *History of the archbishops of Hamburg-Bremen* (1959)

Adelaide, St (931–99) Second wife of Otto the Great and daughter of Rudolf II of Burgundy. In 947 she was betrothed to Lothar, son of Hugh, king of Italy. After Lothar's death in 950 she was captured and imprisoned by Berengar, margrave of Ivrea, because she refused to marry his son. She escaped in

951, taking refuge at Canossa. In the same year she married Otto the Great and was crowned empress in 962. She accompanied Otto on his third Italian campaign in 966, and after Otto's death she remained active in government until she quarrelled with her son Otto II. In 983 she was reconciled with him and was appointed viceroy in Italy. She played an important part in government during the minority of Otto III with Otto II's widow Theophano, and was a prominent supporter of the Cluniac reform movement.
□ K. J. Leyser *Rule and Conflict in an Early Medieval Society* (1979)

Adelard of Bath (1090–1150) English monk, mathematician and scientist who translated into Latin some of the work of the 9th-c. Islamic mathematicians, Al-Khwārizmī and Abu-Ma'shar. He is also believed to have introduced into the Western world knowledge of the astrolabe, a scientific instrument (inherited through the Arabs from the Greeks) for telling the time through observation of the sun, and for finding latitudes and calculating altitudes. His translation of an Arabic version of Euclid became a standard textbook of geometry in the Western world.
□ F.J.P. Bliemetzrieder *Adelhard von Bath* (1935); M. Clagett *Dictionary of Scientific Biography* ed. C. C. Gillespie (1970)

Adhemar (d. 1098) Bishop of Le Puy. Appointed apostolic legate to the First Crusade, he accompanied the crusaders to the East. He negotiated with the Emperor Alexius Comnenus at Nicaea, restored some discipline amongst the crusaders and died soon after the capture of Antioch.
□ G.J. d'Adhémar Labaume *Adhémar de Monteil, évêque du Puy* (1910)

Adoptionist heresy Belief which held that Christ as man could not possibly be God's son by birth, but only by adoption through his baptism. Prevalent in Spain in the late 8th c., it was chiefly expounded by Elipandus, archbishop of Toledo, was attacked by Alcuin in his writings and condemned at the Councils of Frankfurt (792–94), Friuli (796), Rome (799) and Aix-la-Chapelle (800). Despite this, the Spanish bishops never broke formally with the church. The controversy arose again during the scholastic debates of the 12th c., Abelard and Gilbert de la Porée teaching that since God's nature was unchangeable, his humanity could only be external and accidental and not substantial to his very nature. This belief was condemned by Pope Alexander III on 18 February 1177, but Adoptionism continued to be a prime question for theological debate throughout the Middle Ages.

An 11th-c. Canterbury manuscript of **Aelfric**'s writings, showing agricultural labourers at work.

Adrian I (Hadrian) Pope 772–95 One of the most influential popes of the early medieval period, Adrian invited Charlemagne and the Franks to support him against Lombard pressure. The intervention proved decisive: the Lombard kingdom was overwhelmed and Charlemagne took on the title of king of the Lombards. Adrian very skilfully kept alive papal control in the centre of Italy in the new political situation, repaired and reconstructed the city of Rome itself and eased the way, by a series of delicate negotiations with Constantinople, for a new order in the West that was ultimately symbolized by the imperial coronation of Charlemagne in 800 at the hands of Adrian's immediate successor, Leo III.
□ D. Bullough *The Age of Charlemagne* (1966)

Adrian IV (Nicholas Breakspear) Pope 1154–59 (b. *c.*1100) The only Englishman ever to have become pope. Born at Abbot's Langley near St Albans, he became a canon of the abbey of Saint-Ruf near Arles in France and was elected abbot there in 1137. He was appointed cardinal-bishop of Albano by Pope Eugenius III (1148–53) and subsequently served as a papal legate to Scandinavia. He organized the affairs of the Norwegian archbishopric of Trondheim and made arrangements which resulted in the recognition of Uppsala as the seat of the Swedish metropolitan. Upon his return, Breakspear was well received by Eugenius' successor Anastasius IV, and at the latter's death Nicholas was elected pope. Although he crowned Frederick Barbarossa as Holy Roman Emperor in 1155, his pontificate was seriously marred by his disputes with Frederick, which had not been resolved at the time of Adrian's death.
□ W. Ullmann, 'The Pontificate of Adrian IV', *Cambridge Historical Journal* (1955); R. Southern, 'Pope Adrian IV', *Medieval Humanism and other Studies* (1970)

Aelfric (955–1020) Abbot of Eynsham. English monastic reformer and grammarian. Aelfric owed his reforming instincts to his education at Winchester under its reforming bishop, Aethelwold. In 981 he was sent to Cerne in Dorset to supervise the monastic school and in 1005 was appointed abbot of Eynsham. His chief works, which form a most important contribution to late Anglo-Saxon literature, include a collection of homilies, a metrical version of the Lives of the saints and a Latin grammar.
□ M. McGatch *Preaching and Theology in Anglo-Saxon England: Aelfric and Wulfstan* (1977)

Aethelbert King of Kent *c.*560–616 or 618 His birth date, early career and date of accession are obscure. Bede tells that he succeeded to the kingdom of Kent in 560, while the Anglo-Saxon Chronicle gives the date as 565, but there may have been early confusion between the date of his birth and the date of his accession. It is certain that he married Bertha, a Christian princess, daughter of King Charibert of Paris, before 589.

By 597 he was nominally supreme over all the Anglo-Saxon kingdoms south of the Humber, and in full command of the Thames estuary, exercising lordship over the kingdom of Essex where his nephew Saeberht was king. His powerful position enabled Aethelbert to guarantee the safety of St Augustine and his fellow missionaries when they embarked on their task of converting the English to Christianity in 597. He allowed them to make converts in Kent and to set up sees at Canterbury, Rochester and London. Among the immediate benefits that he gained as a result of the presence of the missionaries was intensified contact with the Continent and the ability, as Bede informs us, to issue laws (the earliest law code to survive from Anglo-Saxon England, *juxta Romanorum exempla*). By the time of his death, however, the position of Aethelbert as bretwalda or high king was already being undermined by the growing power of Raedwald, king of the East Angles.

Bede, who is our chief source for his life, paints a picture of a powerful, but cautious and superstitious king, unwilling to receive the missionaries in an enclosed building for fear of witchcraft, and hesitant about giving up the faith of his forbears. He is said to have compelled no one to accept Christianity, though after his own conversion he came to favour his fellow Christians. In his comment on Aethelbert's death Bede describes him as the third English king to rule all the southern kingdoms but the first to enter the kingdom of heaven.

□ H. Mayr-Harting *The Coming of Christianity to Anglo-Saxon England* (1972)

Silver penny of **Aethelred II** minted *c.*997-1003. The moneyer's name appears on the reverse.

Aethelflaed (d. 918) Lady of the Mercians. Eldest daughter of Alfred the Great. In *c.*886, she married Aethelred, who became ealdorman of Mercia, and together they undertook the defence of Mercia from the Danes. When Aethelred fell ill and eventually died in 911, Aethelflaed continued to govern Mercia in her own right, playing the Danes, Norwegians, Scots and Welsh against one another. In 916 she led an expedition against the Welsh and in 917 captured Derby from the Danes; Leicester and York also submitted to her rule in 918. Working closely with her brother Edward, king of Wessex (899–924), she was also responsible for the construction of a series of defences against the Danes, which included fortresses at Runcorn, Stafford, Tamworth and Warwick.

Aethelred II the Unready (Unraed) King of England 978–1016 (b. 968–69) Son of King Edgar by his second wife, Aethelfryth. His reign was disrupted by a series of Danish and Norwegian raids. His reputation has been blackened by the hostile account given in the Anglo-Saxon Chronicle, but recent scholarship has emphasized some of the positive attributes of the reign, such as the flourishing of vernacular literature and the efficiency of both secretarial and financial aspects of government. Even the payment of Danegeld was not all loss, in that it encouraged the development of a good coinage and taxation system. Incidents such as the massacre of the Danes in 1002, tales of treachery, and failure to find an able military commander tell nevertheless of a grave weakening of morale, and explain ultimate Danish success. In 1013 the Danish King Sweyn received the submission of northern England and London. Aethelred escaped with his family to Normandy, but in 1014 was recalled upon his promise to rule better in the future. After his death the kingdom was at first divided between his own son, Edmund Ironside, and Sweyn's son, Cnut. When Edmund died (1016), Cnut succeeded to the whole kingdom and married Aethelred's widow, Emma, daughter of the Norman duke, Richard II.

□ S. Keynes *The Diplomas of King Aethelred 'The Unready'* (1980)

Aethelwold, St (*c.*912–84) Bishop of Winchester, Benedictine monk and reformer. Born at Winchester, Aethelwold spent his early life at the court of King Athelstan (924–39) before joining St Dunstan at the monastery of Glastonbury. Dissatisfied with the monastic observances there, he requested permission to go abroad to study the reform movement on the Continent. When permission was refused he settled instead at Abingdon, where he began to re-establish the monastic life on the Benedictine pattern.

After St Dunstan's exile in 956, Aethelwold became

leader of the monastic reform movement and also served as tutor to the future King Edgar, who became the monks' greatest friend and patron. In 963 Aethelwold became bishop of Winchester and in 964 ousted the cathedral canons in favour of monks. As bishop he was responsible for the refoundation of the monastic life at Milton (Dorset) in 964, and at the New Minster and Nunnaminster in Winchester in 965, and for the establishment of monasteries at Peterborough (966), Ely (970) and Thorney (972). Aethelwold was also the chief figure at the Synod of Winchester (c.970) at which the *Regularis Concordia* was issued, and he is generally accepted as the scholar responsible for the changes to the Benedictine Rule embodied in that document.

□ *Regularis Concordia* ed. D.T. Symons (1959); *Tenth-Century Studies* ed. D. Parsons (1975)

15th-c. miniature from the *St Albans Chronicle* showing the battle of **Agincourt.**

Aetius Flavius (c.396–454) Roman general. Born on the Lower Danube, he was the son of a Roman general and an Italian noblewoman, but spent much of his youth as a hostage, first of the Goths and later of the Huns. In 435 he made use of Hunnish auxiliaries in his subjugation of the Burgundians, but when the Huns became a real threat to the Roman empire under the leadership of Attila, Aetius was forced to attack them. In May 451 he halted their progress at Orleans but failed to gain a resounding victory, and Attila was able to turn to fresh conquests in Italy. Aetius was murdered in 454 by Emperor Valentinian III, who feared that the continued success of Aetius as commander of the Roman military forces would eventually lead to his own deposition in Aetius' favour.

Africa The whole of North Africa was an integral part of the classical and early medieval world, but it was only slowly that knowledge of the rest of the continent came to Western minds. In 429, in the course of the 'folk-wandering' of the German peoples, the Vandals crossed from Spain to North Africa and set up a kingdom that contained much of modern Algeria and Tunisia with its centre at Carthage. The province was recaptured by the Byzantine empire 533–48, but the Muslim invasions of the 7th c. brought about a radical and permanent alteration in the political structures of the Mediterranean world. By 700 all North Africa was in Muslim hands, and 20 years later, most of Spain as well. Muslim traders opened up routes across the Sahara as early as the 8th c., and their political hold on Egypt and the Nile valley ensured continuous contact with, and knowledge of, the Sudan and Ethiopia.

Direct Western involvement came to some extent with the crusaders, but it was not until the late Middle Ages and the Portuguese ventures encour-

aged by Prince Henry the Navigator that serious European exploration began. After the capture of Ceuta (1415), the Portuguese pioneered a series of voyages down the West African coast – initially in an attempt to outflank the Moors in Morocco. The commercial success of these voyages, through the import of spices into Europe, accelerated their progress; they hoped to reach the better quality spices of the Indies and to encourage profitable Arab trade.

By 1482 the whole of the Guinea coast was known, and in 1487 Diaz rounded the Cape of Good Hope. A decade later Vasco da Gama undertook his epoch-making voyage to the Indies, ushering in an era of European overseas expansion.

□ *The Pelican History of Africa* (1968)

Agincourt, battle of (25 October 1415) Fought on St Crispin's Day between the forces of Henry V of England and the French army led by d'Albret, constable of France. The French were attempting to bar the way to Calais against the English, who had been campaigning on the Somme, but were completely routed. Their heavily armed knights were helpless against the more versatile English forces, whose particular strength lay in their crossbowmen. Five thousand French soldiers are said to have been killed and another thousand taken prisoner, whilst the English sustained losses of only very few men-at-arms and footsoldiers. *See* HUNDRED YEARS' WAR

□ A.H. Burne *The Agincourt War* (1956)

Agnes, Empress (1024–77) Wife of Henry III. A descendant of the kings of Burgundy and daughter of William the Pious, duke of Aquitaine, Agnes married Henry III on 1 November 1043, thus cementing the relationship between Germany and its western neighbours. After the death of her husband in 1056 Agnes served as regent during the minority of her son Henry IV. In 1062, however, she was ousted from her position by Archbishop Anno of Cologne and spent the remainder of her life in a convent, dying in Rome in 1077.

Agobard of Lyons (769–840) Archbishop of Lyons. Born in Spain, he first went to Lyons as the companion of Charlemagne's envoy, Leidradis. Ordained priest in 804 he succeeded Leidradis as archbishop of Lyons in 816. Following his support of Lothar I against Emperor Louis the Pious, he was deposed and banished at the Council of Théonville in 834, but was reconciled with Louis and reinstated in 838, dying at Saintonge in 840. His main writings were directed against the Adoptionist Felix of Urgella, and he also condemned superstition and the practice of trial by ordeal.
□ A. Cabaniss *Agobard of Lyons* (1953)

Agriculture Generalizations about European agriculture in the Middle Ages must be qualified by emphasis on vast regional differences and also a great diversity within regions. The basic technical knowledge needed for successful cultivation of cereal crops had been available to all European communities since Neolithic days, but its application and organization were quite another matter, dependent on the nature of the soil, the balance of pastoral and agrarian, the climate, the proximity of the sea and a dozen or more similar major variables. Social habit and terrenial custom were also closely interwoven with agrarian practice.

The Byzantine empire preserved the basic classical structures in the early Middle Ages, with a persistent strong commercial and monetary element in the economy. From the 8th c. onwards there are clear Byzantine parallels to Western developments in estate management, and the exaction and nature of labour services. Influential classes of free peasants appear in Anatolia and parts of the Balkans. Within the Western world, the Carolingian empire and its successors, including Britain and later extensions to the Scandinavian and Slavonic communities, agriculture became of paramount economic importance for most of the Middle Ages. The period was not sterile in technical advance, particularly in areas which, for reasons of soil fertility and climate, constituted the heartland of the medieval agrarian economy: France north of the Loire, Lorraine and the Franconian lands, southern and eastern England.

A fully fledged manorial economy, which was never completely closed in on itself, but which tended to aim more at self-sufficiency than at a market, emerged in 8th-c. and 9th-c. Carolingian Europe. Extensive use of watermills, improved methods of harnessing plough-beasts and greater efficiency in manuring the soil and in crop rotation, slowly made an impact on the human stock. Where peace could be maintained (and protection from barbarian invasion was substantially achieved by the 11th c.), a manorial economy proved capable of sustaining a steady increase in population. Its classic farming methods were based on the three-field system: each year in rotation wheat was grown in one field, oats and barley, beans and pulses in another, while a third lay fallow; in some areas a two-field system – one cultivated and one fallow – was more common. To each village would be attached a meadow or pasture from which animal fodder would be obtained. But the plough was king, and the division of fields into strips, some of which belonged to the

Agriculture: ploughing scene in January, from an early 11th-c. astronomical treatise.

lord and others to the men, combined protection with a harnessing of corporate effort, enabling communities to flourish.

The superstructure of the medieval civilization of the 12th c. and 13th c. was based upon this successful manorial economy, but by the end of the 13th c., inadequacies in its basic organization were already apparent. The famines and pestilences of the 14th c. are, it has been suggested, symptoms of an economy that had passed its point of saturation. Commutation of labour services into money payments to the lord of the manor had been widespread, and attempts to reimpose feudal service contributed to the peasant unrest and revolts of the later Middle Ages. Peasant status varied greatly and legal distinctions did not always match economic and social reality. Classical slavery had diminished by Carolingian times, though elements of it can still be found in the central Middle Ages. The tendency was for a uniform serfdom to take its place, but on most manors, freemen (who owed little more than judicial service to their lords), cottagers and prosperous craftsmen lived side by side with peasants bound to work three days a week and more, directly on their lord's lands.

Variation also existed in basic techniques. Open fields were common where soil conditions were right, but elsewhere smaller rectangular enclosures were used. In some areas the light plough, inherited from Roman times, persisted; in others the heavy plough came to dominate, while in remote areas, such as the Scottish Isles, primitive scratch-ploughs continued to be used. Colonization brought its own techniques, as in the Black Forest in the 12th c. or in the German advance to the Baltic lands of Pomerania and East Prussia in the 12th c. and 13th c.; a freer status was the normal reward for the enterprising colonizer. The introduction of the windmill from the East in the 12th c. contributed to general efficiency, particularly in big estates. The writing of books on husbandry, and improved dissemination of marling and liming techniques again testify to the efficiency of the great royal, baronial and ecclesiastical estates. The achievement of medieval agriculture in sustaining population in perilous times should not be underestimated, but by 1300 new techniques and a new attitude to the land were needed to achieve further advances. *See* CLIMATE; FAMINE; MILLS; WINE [*12, 67, 228*]   AD
□ B.H. Slicher van Bath *The Agrarian History of Western Europe* (1963); G. Duby *Rural Economy and Country Life in the Medieval West* (1968); R.-H. Bautier *The Economic Development of Medieval Europe* (1971)

Aidan (*c*.600–51) Bishop of Lindisfarne and British saint. Initially a monk of Iona, he later settled on the island of Lindisfarne and became its first bishop in 635. He was extremely influential in the reconversion of the Northumbrian people to Christianity, a task undertaken at the request of King Oswald (634–42). After Oswald's death at the battle of Oswestry, Aidan continued and intensified his efforts under the new King Oswy (642–70), until his death at Bamburgh on 31 August 651.
□ *Bede's Ecclesiastical History of the English People* ed. B. Colgrave and R.A.B. Mynors (1969)

Ailly, Pierre d' (1350–1420) Bishop of Cambrai. A leading theologian and later chancellor of the university of Paris, d'Ailly is chiefly remembered for the part he played in healing the Great Schism in the papacy. He initially accepted the idea of a general council as the best means of resolving the schism, but later supported the claims to the papacy of Benedict XIII before returning once again to his Conciliarist position. It was from Benedict XIII that he received first the bishopric of Le Puy (1395) and then that of Cambrai (1397). As bishop of Cambrai he played a prominent part in the Council of Pisa (1409) and above all as one of the principal French spokesmen at the great Council of Constance (1414–18). In 1411 d'Ailly was created a cardinal by Pope John XXIII and later served as a papal legate under Martin V. He is also noted for his suggestions concerning calendar reform, which were eventually put into effect by Gregory XII, and for his writings, which include the *Image of the World*, a work in which he supports the idea that the world is round and that the East Indies could thus be reached from Europe by sailing westwards as well as eastwards.
See CONCILIAR MOVEMENT
□ E.F. Jacob *Essays in Conciliar Thought* (1953)

Aistulf King of the Lombards 749–56 He was elected after the deposition from the throne of his brother Rachis. Aistulf's chief aim was to unite Italy under Lombard control. In 751 he took control of the exarchate of Ravenna, thus threatening many of the former Byzantine territories in Italy which were being claimed by the papacy. In 756 the progress of the Lombards was halted through the invasion of Italy by the Merovingian King Pepin III. The Lombards were defeated, and much of their former territory was ceded to the Franks by the papacy. It was during these campaigns that Aistulf died as the result of an accident.
□ O. Bertolini *Roma e i Langobardi* (1972); C. Wickham *Early Medieval Italy* (1981)

Aix-la-Chapelle (Aachen) Originally a Roman settlement. In 765 a palace was built there by King Pepin which was subsequently rebuilt by Charle-

The royal and imperial throne in the cathedral at **Aix-la-Chapelle.**

magne, the city thus becoming the centre of the Carolingian empire. Synods were held there, and from the coronation of Louis the Pious in 813 until that of Ferdinand I in 1531, German kings continued to be crowned there. The city was also known as a place of pilgrimage where the relics gathered by the Carolingians were on display; an additional cult also grew up in the 12th c. around the tomb of Charlemagne. In 1172 Aix-la-Chapelle was fortified by walls which were extended by William of Holland in 1250. In the later Middle Ages the city was strategically important in keeping the peace in the region between the Meuse and the Rhine. *See* ALCUIN

Alan of Lille (1128–*c*.1203) One of the leading masters of the schools at Paris. Known as *doctor universalis*, he was famous for his contributions to theology and philosophy, incorporating strong mystical and Neoplatonic elements into a philosophy which argued that the inner truths of religion were discoverable by the exercise of unaided reason. He symbolizes part of the paradox of the 12th-c. renaissance, being active in the schools yet attracted to the Cistercians. The central core of his teaching consisted in his definition of nature as an effective intermediary between God and matter, and he emphasized the analogy, and also the distinction,

between natural birth, which depended on the laws of nature, and the birth of the spirit attendant upon baptism and sacramental regeneration.
□ E. Gilson *Philosophy of the Middle Ages* (1952)

Alans A nomadic pastoral people first occupying the steppe region north-east of the Black Sea. They are described in Roman literature of the 1st c. as a warlike people specialized in horse breeding. During the following centuries they frequently raided the Caucasian provinces of the Roman empire. The Alans were overwhelmed by the Huns and in the early 5th c. moved westwards into Gaul. Some settled near Orleans, but the majority accompanied the Vandals to Spain and North Africa.
□ B. S. Bachrach *The Alans* (1969)

Alaric I King of the Visigoths 395–410 Remembered for the sack of Rome in 410, Alaric was a more complicated figure than the savage, ruthless plunderer of historical legend. He had served as a prominent commander of the federate Goths under Emperor Theodosius, and it was only on the death of the emperor (395) that he set up his Visigothic kingdom on the Adriatic. In the first decade of the 5th c. he continued to play a prominent part in imperial politics, and even after the sack of Rome moved towards an accord with imperial authorities. It was the symbolic shock as much as the reality of the capture of Rome that caused both contemporaries and later historians to regard 410 as the end of the Roman empire.
□ T. Hodgkin *Italy and her Invaders* vol. 1 (1916)

Albert I of Habsburg Holy Roman Emperor 1298–1308 (b.1250) Eldest son of Rudolf I. In 1282 he was entrusted by his father with the government of the duchies of Austria and Styria. Rudolf, however, was unable to secure the succession to the throne for his son and upon his death in 1291, the princes chose Adolf of Nassau as king. In 1298 Albert defeated Adolf at the battle of Göllheim and was then able to obtain his own election to the German crown. During his reign Albert played an active part in European politics. He maintained his position by playing upon the rivalry between Philip IV of France and Pope Boniface VIII, renewed German claims to Thuringia, successfully interfered in a dispute for the Hungarian throne and managed to secure the Bohemian crown for his son Rudolf. His defeat during his attack on Thuringia in 1307, and the death of his son in the same year seriously weakened Albert's position in Eastern Europe. His government was also threatened by the revolt of the Rhenish archbishops and the count palatinate of the Rhine, who greatly resented

Albert I of Habsburg

Albert's abolition of all the tolls introduced on the Rhine since 1250. Although this revolt was suppressed with the help of the towns, further unrest grew in Swabia, and it was whilst marching to deal with this problem that Albert was murdered by his nephew John, on 1 May 1308.
□ F.R.H. du Boulay *Germany in the Late Middle Ages* (1983)

Albert V (II) of Habsburg Holy Roman Emperor 1438–39 (b.1397) Succeeding to Austria in 1404, Albert ruled actively as duke from 1411. He assisted Sigismund, king of the Romans and of Bohemia and Hungary, against the Hussites, and in return received the hand in marriage of Sigismund's daughter and heiress Elizabeth (1422). After Sigismund's death in 1437, Albert succeeded to the kingdom of Hungary, but although he was crowned king of Bohemia in 1438, he failed to gain control of that region. The same year also saw his election as king of the Romans (under the title of Albert II) by the German princes gathered at Frankfurt, an honour which he does not appear to have actively sought. His reign, however, was short-lived; in 1439 he died on campaign at Langendorf whilst defending the Hungarians against Turkish incursions.

Albert of Cologne (Albertus Magnus), St (*c.*1190–1280) Medieval philosopher. Born in Swabia, he studied at Padua before joining the Dominican Order. In 1245 he went to Paris where he lectured successfully for several years. It was here that he first met Thomas Aquinas, upon whom he was to have a considerable influence. In 1254 he was appointed head of the Dominican Order within Germany before being elected to the bishopric of Regensburg in 1260; it was during this period that he condemned the writings of the Arab philosopher Averroes. In 1262 he retired to Cologne, where he remained until his death, apart from a short period in 1270 when he went to Austria to preach the Eighth Crusade. Known as *doctor universalis*, he made permanent contributions to philosophy, theology and the history of science. His work was one of the principal instruments for the transmission to Western Europe of Aristotelian knowledge of the natural world.
□ S.M. Albert *Albert the Great* (1948)

Alberti, Leon Battista (1404–72) Architect and Renaissance humanist, born at Venice and educated at Padua and Bologna. During his lifetime Alberti's fame rested upon his book *Della Famiglia*. In this work, guided by the Aristotelian principle, revived by St Thomas Aquinas, that art imitates nature, Alberti postulated that each child should be brought up according to his own nature. As an architect he

restored the papal palace in Rome for Nicholas V (1447–55), built the Palazzo Rucellai (1446) and the façade of S. Maria Novella (1456) in Florence, and designed the churches of S. Sebastiano (1460) and S. Andrea (1470) in Mantua and of S. Francesco in Rimini. He also wrote *De Pictura* (1435), a theoretical exposition of Italian art, and *De Re Aedificatoria* (1452), which had an important influence upon Renaissance building.
□ F. Borsi *Leon Battista Alberti: the Complete Work* (1977)

Albigenses Heretical sect based on Cathar beliefs. Beginning *c.*1144 around the town of Albi in southern France, it owed its success to the support of the nobility and to the ascetic life lived by the *perfecti*, which was in sharp contrast to the worldliness of the local clergy. The sect was powerful enough by 1167 to hold its own council at Saint-Félix-de-Caraman, near Toulouse.

Initially the church attempted to combat the spread of the sophisticated Cathar heresy by persuasion. St Bernard failed to reconvert them in 1147, and Innocent III sent envoys on preaching tours to the Languedoc in 1198 and 1203, but without success.

In 1208, the papal legate Peter of Castelnau was assassinated, and the pope launched the Albigensian Crusade. The papal strategy was to transfer land ownership from Cathar sympathizers to orthodox lords, who would assist with the removal of heresy. Although Count Raymond of Toulouse, the major Cathar patron, recanted quickly, the land-hungry crusaders led by Simon de Montfort the Elder pressed on with massacres and mass burnings. Their actions put an end to papal hopes of making the Cathars recant and accept Catholicism.

The Crusaders' decisive victory at Muret (1213) broke noble support for the Cathars, and by 1226 the region was under the effective control of the French crown, though it was not until the horrific massacre at Montségur (1244) that the sect was substantially stamped out and driven underground. Traces of the heresy continued to reappear sporadically throughout the later Middle Ages, in spite of the repressive instruments of the Inquisition. *See* CATHARS; HERESY
□ P. Belperron *La Croisade contre les Albigeois* (1945); B. Hamilton *The Albigensian Crusade* (1974); J. Sumption *The Albigensian Crusade* (1978)

Alboin King of the Lombards 565–*c.*72 Succeeding to the kingship of the Lombards during their occupation of the territory west of the Danube known as Pannonia, Alboin defeated the Gepidae on his eastern frontier, slew their King Cunimund, and abducted and married Cunimund's daughter Rosamund. In 568 he invaded Italy on the invitation of the Byzantine

general Narses, who had fallen foul of the Emperor Justin II. He overran Lombardy, and conquered Piedmont and Tuscany together with much of Benevento and Spoleto. His progress was, however, halted at Pavia which held out for three years against his forces. In *c.*572 Alboin met his death by assassination, reputedly at the instigation of his wife, whom he had insulted by making her drink from a cup fashioned out of her father's skull.
□ T. Hodgkin *Italy and her Invaders* vol. 5 (1916); L. Schmidt *Die Ostgermanen* (1969)

Albornoz, Gil (1310–67) Born at Cuenca in Spain, educated at Saragossa and Toulouse, he became archdeacon of Calatrava and an adviser of Alfonso XI (1312–50), king of Castile. In 1337 he became archbishop of Toledo and in 1350, cardinal. Active against the Muslims, he took part in the battle of Tarifa (1340) and the taking of Algeçiras (1344). Following the death of Alfonso XI and the succession of Peter the Cruel, Albornoz left Spain. He was appointed cardinal–legate in Italy and did much to restore papal authority there. By 1362 he had paved the way for the return of Urban V to Rome and died whilst escorting him there. He is also known for his work on the constitution of the church of Rome and for the foundation of the College of St Clement for Spanish students at Bologna.
□ E. Emerton *Humanism and Tyranny* (1925)

Alcantara, Order of A document which is almost certainly spurious places the foundation of the order in 1156, earlier than that of Calatrava, but the earliest reliable evidence points to 1176 as the date of foundation. Originally known as the Order of S. Julian de Pereiro, it followed the Cistercian Rule, and it was to some extent dependent upon Calatrava, though it gradually established its autonomy. In 1494 the Catholic Monarchs annexed the mastership of Alcantara to the crown, not long after that of Calatrava (1482), and for the same reasons.
□ J.F. O'Callaghan, 'The Foundation of the Order of Alcantara, 1176–1218', *The Catholic Historical Review* 47 (1962)

Alchemy The alchemy practised in Europe in the later Middle Ages was at once a science, with its own precise laws, and a secret and mystical art, revolving around the transmutation of base metals into silver and gold by freeing them from their impurities. It had possessed both a scientific and a mystical side ever since it had first emerged and developed in Alexandria in the first four centuries AD. From Aristotle the first astrologers drew the theory that the basis of all substances was *prima materia*. The four elements (fire, air, earth and water) all arose from

A master and his two apprentices engaged in the 'subtile werk' of **alchemy** (15th-c.).

this, and in different combinations they formed all matter; hence precious metals could be created from other substances. From the Mesopotamian astrologers came the idea that the most propitious time to attempt a transmutation could be divined by astrological means. Each metal was seen to be linked with a planet, and mystical symbols and codes were devised for other substances and for chemical processes.

Alchemy continued to flourish in the Byzantine empire, and in the 8th c. and 9th c. was discovered and adopted by the invading Muslims. Arab alchemists of this period, notably Jabir ibn Hayyan (Geber) and his followers, built upon earlier Hellenistic ideas and produced many influential tracts. They drew from the Chinese the concept of 'medicine', an agent which could transform other metals into gold and which, if eaten, could confer immortality. This became known as the 'Philosopher's stone' and was the later alchemists' first goal on the way to achieving their ultimate purpose. Other Arabic alchemists modified Aristotle's theory of the elements by suggesting that all metals were formed by the combination of two substances: sulphur, which represented the properties of fire, and mercury, which represented those of water. Correct mixture of the two would produce gold or silver. The mystical ideas embodied in the *Corpus Hermeticum*, a compilation made between the 1st c. and 3rd c. AD and containing the occult revelations of the Egyptian god Thoth or Hermes Trismegistos, were also taken up. A more practical experimental approach was adopted by, amongst others, the noted physician Avicenna.

Alchemy was little known in the early medieval West. Isolated treatises touching on it were produced, however, examples of which are the 10th-c. *Compositiones ad Tingenda*, which gives practical advice on using metals in artwork, and the more mystical *Mappe Clavicula*. After the crusaders reached the Holy Land, and southern Italy and Sicily fell to the Normans, the distinctive alchemical ideas of the Arabs began to appear in Western writings. Probably the first translation of an Arabic text on alchemy was that made by Robert of Chester in the *Book of Morienus* (1144), the justification for which was the ignorance in the West of 'what alchemy is, and what its composition'. In the 13th c., scholars such as Arnold of Villanova, Albertus Magnus and Roger Bacon made huge encyclopaedic compilations, in which the alchemical explanation of the nature of matter played an important part. In the last years of the century the circulation of other major treatises focusing upon alchemy (the *Turba Philosophorum* and the works of the Spanish alchemist Jabir, self-styled Geber after the Arabic master), resulted in an outburst of experimentation and the production of further alchemical writings in the 14th c. The more symbolic and occult side of alchemy was stimulated in the process and began to flourish again, despite papal attempts to outlaw it as a branch of sorcery. An indication of the growing secrecy of the alchemists' lore is that in the 15th c., when many works of science were printed, alchemical treatises continued to circulate in manuscript. The criticisms of Renaissance humanists and of disputators such as Pico della Mirandola failed to suppress the alchemists, and some of their ideas retained acceptance for many centuries.

Despite this secrecy and the relatively few practitioners of the art, medieval literature is full of tales about the successes and failures of alchemists. Aspirants must have derived inspiration from the story of Nicholas Flamel (1330–1418), a Parisian scrivener whose wealth was said to have been founded on his discovery, in 1382, of a way of making silver and gold from mercury. His fortune was spent on works of piety and charity, and his story became widely known. By contrast, Chaucer, in the *Canon's Yeoman's Tale*, demonstrates the fear and suspicion with which many alchemists were regarded, and tells of the penury and despair to which an obsession with alchemy could lead. Vasari provides a yet sadder story, of the early 16th-c. Italian artist Parmigianino, whose alchemical experiments drove him

Illumination from a mid-9th-c. copy of **Alcuin's** revised text of the Bible.

to insanity, imprisonment and, eventually to an early death. EMH
□ L. Thorndike *A History of Magic and Experimental Science* (1923–58); G. Sarton *Introduction to the History of Science* (1927–47)

Alcuin (735–804) Born in Northumbria, Alcuin became librarian of the cathedral church of York before going to the court of Charlemagne in Frankia in 782. There he played a prominent part in the Carolingian renaissance and founded the palace school at Aix-la-Chapelle, where the seven liberal arts were taught according to the educational system of Cassiodorus. His own writings included works on rhetoric, logic and dialectic, a revision of the Gregorian sacramentary, an edition of the lectionary and contributions to the *Libri Carolini*, a treatise written on the orders of Charlemagne against the Iconodules, who had been restored to a position of importance in Byzantium in 787. His most important scholarly contributions are his revision of the Vulgate and his voluminous letters, which were collated in the 9th c. to serve as a model of Latin composition. He was also active in the condemnation of Archbishop Elipandus of Toledo and the Adoptionist heresy. He founded an important library and school at the abbey of Saint-Martin-de-Tours where he was abbot for the last years of his life (796–804).
□ E.S. Duckett *Alcuin, a Friend of Charlemagne* (1956); L. Wallach *Alcuin and Charlemagne* (1959); S. Allott *Alcuin of York, c. 732–804* (1974)

Aldhelm, St (639–709) A relative of King Ine of Wessex, he was educated at Malmesbury and later studied at Canterbury under St Adrian. He became master of the school at Malmesbury and abbot there in 675. Upon the division of Wessex into two dioceses he was appointed to the westernmost see with its seat at Sherborne. A great builder, he constructed the minster at Sherborne and churches at Frome, Bradford-on-Avon, Corfe, Langton

Maltravers and Wareham. His most influential works were his letter to the British King Geraint on the dating of Easter, and a treatise on virginity dedicated to the nuns of Barking, which continued to be copied throughout the Anglo-Saxon period. His Latin style was elaborate, owing something to Celtic influences, but was also much in line with contemporary Continental Latin and with the teaching of the Canterbury School; he lacked the very unusual simplicity and directness of his contemporary Bede. We are told that his Anglo-Saxon religious verses (which have not survived) did much to help the spread of Christianity throughout Wessex. On his death he was buried at Malmesbury.

☐ M. Winterbottom, 'Aldhelm's Prose-Style and its Origin', *Anglo-Saxon England* 6 (1977); *Aldhelm, the Prose Works* trans. M. Lapidge and M. Herren (1979)

Alemanni Confederacy of German tribes who began to pressurize the borders of the Roman empire in the 3rd c., and in the 5th c. expanded into Alsace and Switzerland. In 496 the Alemanni were conquered by the Frankish King Clovis who incorporated them into his dominions. A loose-knit confederation, the Alemanni placed their military forces under the joint leadership of two commanders during campaigns, but, for the most part, found it difficult to unite and possessed no common core of centralized government.

Alexander III Pope 1159–81 (b. 1105) Born Rolando Bandinelli at Siena, he became professor of law at Bologna and then a cardinal, before being elected pope in 1159. As a canon lawyer, Alexander settled many disputes on church discipline and practice which culminated in the Third Lateran Council (1179). Alexander was opposed for much of his pontificate by the German Emperor Frederick Barbarossa, who refused to sanction his election as pope, but instead supported the rival candidature of Cardinal Octavian as Pope Victor IV. Alexander was forced to flee to France in 1162 and 1166, but following the Emperor's defeat by the Lombard League in 1176, he was able to force Frederick to make peace in Venice in 1177. Alexander also gave some support to Thomas Becket and was instrumental in trying to bring about a reconciliation between Becket and the English King Henry II.

☐ M. Pacaut *Alexandre III* (1956); *Boso's Life of Alexander III* ed. P. Murray (1973)

Alexander IV Pope 1254–61 (b. 1199) Born at Anagni, he was appointed cardinal-deacon by his uncle Gregory IX in 1227, and cardinal-bishop of Ostia in 1231 before becoming pope in 1254. He continued the papal war upon the Hohenstaufen of Sicily by excommunicating Manfred, the bastard

St Alexander Nevsky: detail from a mural in the Arkhangelsky cathedral, Moscow.

son of Frederick II, and granting Sicily as a papal fief to Edmund, the younger son of Henry III of England. In Europe he enforced religious conformity by increasing the powers of the Inquisition within France, and also did much to increase the efficiency of papal administration. In the East he tried to bring about a union with Byzantium and attempted to organize a crusade against the Tartars. He died at Viterbo.

☐ S. Sibilia *Alessandro IV* (1961); W. Ullmann *The Papacy and Political Ideas in the Middle Ages* (1976)

Alexander VI Pope 1492–1503 (b. c.1431) Born Rodrigo de Borgia at Jativa, Spain, he studied law at Bologna before becoming a cardinal in 1456 and pope in 1492. A Renaissance prince rather than a holy pontiff, he subordinated the interests of the church to his political ambitions and to the furtherance of the fortunes of his family. Although in principle encouraging a war against the Ottoman Turks, Alexander was not averse to making a treaty with them in 1494 against Charles VIII of France, who was claiming the kingdom of Naples and Sicily. During his pontificate Alexander reorganized the papal finances, restored the Castel S. Angelo and persuaded Michelangelo to draw up plans for the rebuilding of St Peter's in Rome, although these were in fact never executed.

☐ *The Borgia Pope, Alexander the Sixth* trans. F. J. Sheed (1942)

Alexander Nevsky, St (c.1220–63) In 1236, Alexander was made prince of Novgorod by his father, Grand Duke Yaroslav II. As the south and

the east of Russia fell more and more firmly under Mongol control, Alexander's northern principality grew in importance. He checked Swedish ambitions decisively by defeating them at the battle of the river Neva (July 1240) and in 1242 he crushed the Teutonic knights in a great battle fought on the ice of the frozen lake Paipus. He accepted Mongol lordship in Russia, even making a personal visit to the great khan. As a result of his cooperation, in 1252 the Mongols recognized Alexander as chief prince in Russia by appointing him grand duke of Vladimir and Kiev in place of his deposed brother Andrew. His victories, particularly the battle on the ice, became legendary and ensured his position as national hero of medieval Russia; the part he played in resisting the advance of Catholicism prompted the Orthodox church to recognize him as a saint.
□ G. Vernadsky *The Mongols and Russia* (1953)

Alexandria Provincial capital of Egypt during Roman times, which declined in importance after the fall of the empire. In 616 it was captured by the Persians and in 642 by the Arabs, who established a new capital at Fustat (Cairo). Alexandria was henceforward reduced to a commercial and naval base. The city grew once again in importance, however, during the Crusades of the 12th c. and the Mamlūk campaigns of the 13th c. It also became an important centre for the spice trade between East and West until the discovery of the sea route to India in 1498.

Alexius I Comnenus Eastern emperor 1081–1118 (b. 1048) Third son of John Comnenus and nephew of Isaac I (emperor 1057–59), Alexius seized the throne from Nicephoras III in 1081. He restored the flagging military power of Byzantium by driving the Normans back into western Greece in 1081 and by defeating the Pechenegs ten years later. He also managed to halt further Seljuk incursions into Anatolia. His achievements were marred by his unwillingness to limit the power of the magnates in Byzantium and by the First Crusade, which disturbed Alexius' agreement with the Muslims and led to the alienation of many former Greek territories into Western hands.
□ *The Alexiad of Anna Comnena* trans. E.R.A. Sewter (1969)

Alfonso V the Magnanimous King of Aragon 1416–58 (b. 1395) Grandson of John I of Castile and son of Ferdinand of Antequera, he was brought up at the Castilian court until his father was made king of Aragon in 1412. He succeeded his father as king in 1416 and during his reign in Aragon he was faced with numerous problems: the aristocracy were

jealous of his Castilian counsellors, whilst the Catalonian peasantry were constantly attempting to assert their independence from the crown.

He was successful, however, in continuing Aragonese expansion overseas. He pacified Sardinia and Sicily in 1420 and after numerous difficulties succeeded in capturing Naples in 1442. He subsequently transferred his court there and never returned to Spain. On his death in 1458 Alfonso was succeeded in Naples by his illegitimate son Ferrante, and in Aragon by his brother John. Alfonso's title, 'the Magnanimous', was earned through his generous patronage of a number of Renaissance humanist scholars.

Alfonso I King of Asturias 739–57 Son-in-law of Pelayo (leader of Asturian resistance to the Arab invasion), and probably a descendant of Visigothic kings, Alfonso was chosen to rule Asturias when his brother-in-law Fafila was killed by a bear. Within a year, the revolt of the Berber garrisons throughout Spain and the ensuing civil war gave Alfonso the opportunity to break out of his small mountainous territory and conquer lands as far south as the river Duero; Galicia, Cantabria, La Rioja, and much of Leon fell to him. The southern areas were laid waste and evacuated, leaving a wide no-man's-land, and the northern regions were demographically and militarily strengthened. By the time of Alfonso's death, the kingdom of Asturias was securely established and stretched from the Atlantic coast of Galicia to the eastern border of La Rioja; in the following century, it became the kingdom of Leon.
□ C. Sánchez-Albornoz *Orígenes de la nación española: el reino de Asturias* vol. 1 (1972)

Alfonso VIII the Noble King of Castile 1158–1214 Son of King Sancho III. Alfonso's minority was troubled by internal strife and the intervention of the neighbouring kingdom of Navarre in Castilian affairs. This interference culminated in 1195 in a joint attack by Navarre and Leon upon Castile which Alfonso was fortunately able to divert. His relations with Aragon were always good, and in 1179 the two states signed the Pact of Cazorla, which settled the demarcation of the future boundary between Castile and Aragon, and which would come into effect once Spain had been reconquered from the Moors. It was this war with the Moors which absorbed Alfonso's energies from 1172 to 1212. Although he was defeated by the Moors in 1195 he was able, with the help of Peter II of Aragon, to gain a great victory over them at the battle of Las Navas de Tolosa (1212), and thus did much to destroy the power of the Almohads in Spain. He married a daughter of Henry II of England and founded Spain's first university.

Alfonso VIII and Queen Eleanor with the grand master of Santiago (13th-c. Spanish manuscript).

Alfonso VI King of Leon and Castile 1065–1109 Second son of King Fernando I, and grandson of Sancho III of Navarre, Alfonso was 25 when he inherited the kingdom of Leon from his father. Six years of struggle with his brothers, who had inherited other parts of Fernando's realm, culminated in Alfonso's defeat at the battle of Golpejera (January 1072). He was exiled in the Muslim city of Toledo, but within nine months another turn of Fortune's wheel – the assassination of Sancho II of Castile – brought the exiled king back to rule over Leon, Castile and Galicia.

Despite sinister rumours of complicity in Sancho's murder, and even of incest with his sister, Alfonso proved an energetic and successful ruler, militarily, politically and culturally. He worked for the reconciliation of the three parts of his kingdom and established his ascendancy over the *taifa* kingdoms of the Muslim south, conquering Toledo in 1085. Influenced by his French wives, and continuing the Europeanizing policy of Sancho III, Alfonso strengthened the Cluniac hold on Spanish monasteries, appointed French bishops to his sees, encouraged the pilgrimage to Santiago de Compostela (French quarters grew up in the cities along the pilgrim road), replaced the Mozarabic (or Visigothic) liturgy with the Roman liturgy of the rest of Western Europe, despite popular resistance, and similarly replaced the old Visigothic script with the Carolingian; the spread of Romanesque architecture in Spain also dates from Alfonso's time.

Alfonso's relentless insistence on exacting tribute from the *taifa* kingdoms – described by a recent historian as a protection racket – proved self-defeating in the year after his triumph at Toledo; in desperation, the Muslim kings turned to the Almoravids, who defeated Alfonso's armies at Sagrajas (1086). Alfonso's policy towards the indigenous Muslim rulers became more conciliatory; he had already seen the importance of religious toleration, calling himself 'Emperor of the two religions' after the fall of Toledo. But it was too late: the Almoravids had come to stay, and a series of defeats followed, mitigated only by the successful defence of Toledo in 1090 and the victories of Alfonso's disgraced and exiled general Rodrigo Díaz, el Cid, who took Valencia in 1094. Valencia was abandoned in 1102, and Alfonso's only son was killed in the crushing defeat at Uclés (1108). The king died in 1109, and the lack of a male heir plunged his beleaguered kingdom into civil war, leaving his son-in-law Alfonso I of Aragon as the dominant figure in Christian Spain.   ADD
□ R. Menéndez Pidal *The Cid and his Spain* (1934)

Alfonso X the Learned King of Leon and Castile 1252–84 (b. 1221) Eldest child of Fernando III and Beatrice of Swabia. As heir apparent he took part in his father's later campaigns, including the siege of Seville, and showed an early interest in developing Castilian as a literary and technical language: he commissioned a translation from Arabic in 1251. Historians see Alfonso as a failure, because of his ruinously expensive and ultimately humiliating campaign for election as Holy Roman Emperor, and because of the rivalry over the succession which led to revolt and deposition. Cultural historians, on the other hand, see him as a success: he was patron of a brilliant court of poets, scholars, artists and musicians; he was a great supporter of the vernacular, leaving Castilian at the end his reign as the natural vehicle for all kinds of prose. Although the work had begun under Fernando III, Alfonso made an incomparably greater contribution, creating Castilian prose, as Alfred the Great had created Anglo-Saxon prose. Yet the two sides of Alfonso are interdependent, and the same pattern can often be observed in his political and his cultural life.

Alfonso, who had married Violante, daughter of James I of Aragon, succeeded to the throne of Castile and Leon in 1252. It was no easy task to be the heir to Fernando III's triumphs, and a wish to assert himself as a worthy successor led the new king to invade the Algarve (leading to a compromise that favoured Portugal), to try to annex Navarre (he had to be content with nominal suzerainty), and to lay claim to Gascony on the grounds that his grandmother was the daughter of Henry II of England. The claim was abandoned in a treaty of 1254, and Alfonso's sister married Edward I; their third son and for ten years the heir to the throne of England was named Alfonso. A far more protracted foreign adventure (1256–75) was the pursuit of the Holy Roman Empire. Alfonso, who claimed rights through his mother, spent vast sums to influence the electors – much more than Castile could afford – so that domestic discontent grew; a recent historian has entitled an essay on Alfonso's financial and economic policies

From the *Cantigas* **Alfonso X**: the king depicted as a poet and musician above one of his own songs.

'Paths to Ruin'. He secured election in 1257, but a papal veto undid his work, and he never came as close to success again. Nevertheless, he persisted for 18 more years, and only a revolt of the Castilian nobles made him renounce his claims.

Two of Alfonso's brothers rose against him (1255 and 1269), and he had a third summarily executed (1277), but the worst dissensions within his family followed the death of his eldest son Fernando in 1275, during a Moroccan invasion that lasted until 1279. Fernando's elder son should have become heir to the throne, but Alfonso's second son Sancho secured a change in the law, and when Alfonso tried to reverse this, Sancho rebelled with the support of the nobles, and an assembly stripped the king of his powers. He sought Muslim help, but to no avail, and died without regaining full control.

Alfonso's cultural achievements stand in contrast to this record of political failure: encyclopaedic vernacular legal codes, an extensive collection of translations and adaptations of Arabic scientific works (including the Alfonsine Tables, used by astronomers throughout Europe for nearly three centuries), the largest and best collection of Marian poetry in any vernacular (unlike his other works, the poems are not in Castilian, but in the conventional lyric language of most of the peninsula, Galician-Portuguese), and two historical works: a universal history and a history of Spain. Yet just as there are solid achievements amid the political failures (some progress in the Reconquest, and more importantly, the creation of the Castilian navy), so the cultural work of the king and his collaborators shows signs of overreaching ambition, and some grand designs miscarry: the main law code, *Las siete partidas*, was never promulgated in Alfonso's lifetime, and the two histories, both ideologically linked with Alfonso's imperial ambitions, remained unfinished.   ADD

□ E. S Procter *Alfonso X of Castile, Patron of Literature and Learning* (1951); *The Worlds of Alfonso the Learned and James the Conqueror* ed. R. I. Burns (1985); J. R. Craddock *The Legislative Works of Alfonso X, el Sabio*, Research Bibliographies and Checklists 45 (1986)

Alfred the Great King of Wessex 871–99 (b. 849) Youngest son of King Aethelwulf of Wessex. His father may have destined him for the church since he visited Rome in 853 and was ritually received by the pope. On Aethelwulf's death (858), his four sons succeeded in turn. Only during Aethelred's reign (866–71) did Alfred begin to play a leading role; although Aethelred had young sons, Alfred had probably been designated heir.

In 866 the Vikings attacked England in strength, dominating first Northumbria and then East Anglia. In 868 Alfred married a kinswoman of the Mercian king as part of a Mercian–West Saxon defensive alliance. This probably held until 877, but Mercia too was Viking-dominated from 874, and Viking attacks on Wessex became increasingly severe from 871, the year Alfred became king. His victory at Edington (878) eased the pressure, and in the 880s Viking settlement in East Anglia and the departure of a large Viking force to northern Frankia allowed

Anglo-Saxon penny of the mid-880s showing **Alfred the Great.**

The **Alhambra**, royal palace of the Muslim kings of Granada: a supreme architectural achievement.

Alfred to undertake an ambitious defensive strategy requiring unprecedented mobilization of men and resources, based on fortified and permanently garrisoned *burhs*. He annexed part of Mercia, including London, leaving the Mercian leader Ethelred under his authority, bound to him by marriage with his daughter Aethelflaed. The southern Welsh princes also acknowledged Alfred's overlordship. Renewed Viking attacks (892–96) were successfully fought off and Alfred died on 26 October 899, leaving Wessex more unified and with a stronger kingship.

The union of Wessex with Mercia proved permanent. Alfred had sought closer contacts with Continental Europe, especially with Frankia, whose kingship and culture inspired him. Developing native vernacular traditions, Alfred sponsored the translation into Old English of works such as Gregory the Great's *Pastoral Care*, and the production of the vernacular Anglo-Saxon Chronicle, in which Alfred's papal reception of 853 was presented as a royal consecration. By circulating these and promoting vernacular literacy among the aristocracy, Alfred consciously diffused royal ideology along with Christian culture. Though his later reputation is partly mythical, Alfred's unique achievements warrant his title, 'the Great'. *See* ASSER JLN
□ P. Wormald in *The Anglo-Saxons* ed. J. Campbell (1982); *Alfred the Great: Asser's Life of King Alfred and other contemporary sources* trans. S. Keynes and M. Lapidge (1983)

Alhambra A castle was built in the hills outside Granada in the mid-9th c., and lasted until 1162.

In 1238, the new Nasrid ruler of Granada, Muhammad I, who had driven out the Almohads, began the construction of a palace on the site. Each of his successors added towers, villas, gates, and courtyards, until by the time of Muhammad V (1362–91), the Alhambra was virtually complete. With wide courtyards and gardens plentifully supplied with water, and lavishly decorated in a distinctive blend of Islamic and Western styles, it justly became the most famous building of Muslim Spain, and perhaps the most famous of the entire peninsula. Kings of Spain added buildings after the Reconquest of Granada, and some damage was done over the centuries, but after restorations the surviving complex is largely the Alhambra of the late 14th c.

Alī (600–61) Cousin and son-in-law of Muhammad. Taken into Muhammad's house at an early age, Alī married his daughter Fātima and took part in the migration from Mecca to Medina in 622. Upon Muhammad's death in 632, Alī's claims to the caliphate were passed over in favour, first, of those of Abū Bakr, and then of 'Umar and 'Uthmān. Upon the murder of 'Uthmān in 656 Alī was acclaimed caliph but was accused of participating in the murder of his predecessor; some of his followers joined 'Uthmān's avenger Mu'āwiya, governor of Syria, and Alī himself was assassinated in 661. The quarrel over the caliphate split Islam permanently into two camps: on the one hand, the traditionalist Sunnite majority who opposed Alī, and on the other, the Shi'ites, who maintained that Alī and his successors had been divinely appointed.

Interior of a monk's cell at the convent of S. Marco in Florence, showing a fresco of the Baptism by Fra **Angelico.**

Almohads (From *al-Muwahhidūn*: believers in the oneness of God) A Muslim religious movement founded (*c.* 1120) in the Atlas mountains as a reaction against the sterile legalism of the Almoravids, whose original puritanism had by that time been corrupted. The Almohads preached a return to strict morality and to the text of the scriptures. They invaded Spain in 1146, and by 1172 had conquered all Muslim areas except for the Balearic Islands. The centralized Almohad state, ruled from Marrakesh by the amir, was even less tolerant of other religions than the Almoravids had been (in marked contrast to the tolerant policies of the Cordoba caliphate and the successor *taifa* kingdoms); the emigration of Christian Mozarabs and of Jews to the north weakened Muslim Spain both culturally and economically. The Almohads won a major battle at Alarcos (1195), and seemed about to overrun the Christian kingdoms, but their power was broken in 1212 at Las Navas de Tolosa and within a few decades their successors were confined to the kingdom of Granada, an anachronism within a vigorous, though still divided, Christian Spain.

Almoravids (From *al-murābit*: dweller in a religious frontier commune) A fundamentalist Muslim tribe from the southern Sahara, which conquered North Africa and crossed into Spain in 1086 at the request of the Muslim kings, who hoped for protection against the exactions of Alfonso VI of Leon and Castile. The Almoravid ruler Yūsuf ibn Tāshufīn defeated Alfonso's forces at Sagrajas (1086) and at other battles, and turned his power against the Hispano-Muslim *taifa* kingdoms, which he regarded as decadent; the 'Abbādid kingdom of Seville was overthrown in 1091. The military success of the Almoravids was due in part to their puritanical fanaticism, in part to their tactical innovations, including the use of three ranks of bowmen and of drums which terrified their enemies. Gradually, however, the Almoravids softened in contact with the civilization of Muslim Spain, and in the 1140s their empire collapsed under the double blow of revolts in Spain and attacks in North Africa by the new power of the Almohads. The Balearic Islands remained in Almoravid hands until 1203, when they fell to the Almohads.

Alp Arslan Seljuk sultan 1063–72 (b. 1029) Succeeding his father as ruler of Khurāsān in 1059 and his uncle Tughril Beg as sultan in 1063, he conquered Armenia and Sebastea before invading the Byzantine empire in 1064. Although he was defeated in 1070 he won a resounding victory over the Byzantine emperor Romanus IV at Manzikert on 19 August 1071, a blow from which the Byzantine empire never fully recovered. Alp Arslan was assassinated in 1072 whilst attempting to conquer Turkestan.

Ambrose, St (339–97) Son of the pretorian prefect of Gaul, Ambrose was appointed governor of Aemilia and Liguria at Milan in 370. Following the death of Auxentius, the Arian bishop of Milan in 374, Ambrose was elected as his successor despite the fact that he was not even baptized as a Christian; within a week he had been instructed in the Christian faith, baptized and consecrated bishop. Ambrose then began to study the scriptures and the writings of Christian thinkers such as Origen and St Basil, and quickly became an influential theologian. Since Milan was the administrative capital of the Western empire in the 4th c., Ambrose also played an important part in politics, advising the young Emperor Gratian and reproving his successor Theodosius. He also vigorously attacked Arianism and played an important part in reducing its influence in the West. Ambrose is remembered as one of the four learned doctors of the early church and for the stand he took on spiritual values over and against the power of the state.
□ F.H. Dudden *The Life and Times of St Ambrose* (1935)

Anagni, Humiliation of (September 1303) Scene of the imprisonment of Pope Boniface VIII by Guillaume de Nogaret, which marks the culmination of the struggle between the pope and the French King Philip IV. Supported by the Colonna family, de Nogaret entered Anagni on 7 September and seized Boniface, imprisoning him in the Gaetani palace. The local populace, however, rose in defence of the pope and released him three days later, at the same time driving de Nogaret and his men from the city. On 12 September Boniface was taken back to Rome, but he never fully recovered from his humiliation and died a month later at the Vatican palace. The seizure of a pope by the officials of a secular monarch sent shock waves throughout Christendom and yet Philip's power remained unchanged.

Andreas Capellanus Late 12th-c. writer in Latin who was active at the courts of the count of Champagne from *c.*1170. Andreas wrote what rapidly became recognized as a standard treatise on Courtly Love, *De Arte Honeste Amandi*. He based some of his ideas on Ovid's *Ars Amatoria* but was also strongly influenced by poetic notions transmitted through Muslim Spain.
□ *The Art of Courtly Love* trans. J. J. Parry (1959)

Angelico, Fra Giovanni de Fiesole (1378–1455) Italian fresco painter and Dominican friar. Born Guido di Pietro, he took the name of Fra Giovanni

upon entering the Dominican convent of S. Domenico at Fiesole (*c.*1418–21), but was known as Fra Angelico for the sweetness of his spirit and his art. His early works were much influenced by the style known as International Gothic with its use of gold backgrounds, elegant, delicate figures and rich, swinging drapery. The frescoes at S. Marco in Florence are considered by critics to be the best example of the spiritual purity of his style. In 1445 he began work on the frescoes in the Chapel of the Sacrament in the Vatican, subsequently destroyed, and these were followed by his Last Judgement scenes in Orvieto cathedral. In 1447 he returned to the Vatican at the request of Pope Nicholas V to paint scenes from the lives of SS Stephen and Lawrence in the newly constructed Nicholas Chapel. His painting career was interrupted for a short time between 1449 and 1452 when he was prior of Fiesole, but he subsequently returned to Rome where he died in 1455 and was buried in the church of S. Maria sopra Minerva.
□ J. Pope-Hennessy *Fra Angelico* (1974)

Anglo-Norman French The French imported into Britain by the Norman conquerors remained the spoken vernacular of the higher aristocracy until at least the end of the 13th c., albeit as an acquired rather than as a mother tongue. In its written form, Insular French served as the language of administrative record, sometimes supplanting Latin. Law French persisted anachronistically until the end of the 17th c. It was also the medium for an extensive body of predominantly didactic literature, from Philippe de Thaon in 1120 until Gower *c.*1400. The enrichment of the English vocabulary by lexical symbiosis is the most enduring and tangible contribution of Anglo-Norman French to British culture.
See LANGUAGE AND DIALECT

Anglo-Saxon Chronicle Surviving in several manuscripts, three of which take the story of England up to and beyond the crisis of the Norman Conquest, the Chronicle is a historical source of maximum importance, especially remarkable for its precocious use of the vernacular. Traditions of constructing tables of events and a record of major happenings were given a new twist during the reign of King Alfred, when a decision was made, probably through direct royal inspiration, to write a continuous chronicle on an annual basis. Great variety exists in the scope and intensity of the record; it is very full, for example, for the last campaigns of Alfred's reign (891–96) and again for the Danish wars of Aethelred's time (991–1016). The Chronicle continued to be kept up to date at the abbey of Peterborough until the mid-1150s, providing a vivid account of the troubles of Stephen's reign in a language which is visibly devel-

oping from Anglo-Saxon into early Middle English.
□ *The Anglo-Saxon Chronicle* ed. D. Whitelock (1961); *The Anglo-Saxon Chronicle MS A* ed. J. Bately (1986)

Anglo-Saxons Term used to denote the tribes of West Germanic origin who settled in the eastern part of Britain in the 5th c. and who came to exercise rule over England, and also over parts of the lowlands of Scotland in the course of the succeeding centuries. The term was first used by 8th-c. writers to distinguish between the Angles, Saxons and Jutes who had settled in 'England', and those of the same race who had remained on the Continent. They were conscious of their Continental heritage and were little affected by the culture of the native Britons. Some of the Latin inheritance, it is true, came back to them with their conversion to Christianity, which occurred substantially in the course of the 7th c. Awareness of diverse tribal origins persisted, and their kings were known from time to time and from place to place as kings of the South Saxons or West Saxons, of the East Angles, Mercians or Northumbrians. As the kingdom was unified, the title 'king of

Passage from annal 871 of the **Anglo-Saxon Chronicle** describing the 'year of battles'.

the English' or *rex Anglorum* became the favoured designation, but Anglo-Saxon remains a convenient term for the composite Germanic peoples and their language up to the time of the Norman Conquest.
□ P. Hunter Blair *An Introduction to Anglo-Saxon England* (1978); F.M. Stenton *Anglo-Saxon England* (1971)

Anjou An area of west-central France, Anjou became a county in Carolingian times and in the 10th c. and 11th c. was expanded by counts Fulk III Nerra and Geoffrey Martel. The Angevin ruling house reached its apogee under Geoffrey Plantagenet, count 1131–51, and his wife Matilda, widow of Emperor Henry V and daughter of King Henry I of England. After Henry I's death Geoffrey was able to capture Normandy from his successor Stephen of Blois in 1144, whilst by 1153 Geoffrey's son and successor, Henry II, was recognized as heir to Stephen in England, becoming king in the following year. The Plantagenets now held England, Normandy and Anjou in one great accumulation of territory, together with Aquitaine, which Henry had added to his dominions upon his marriage to the heiress Eleanor in 1152.

Although jealousy between Henry's sons was to cause severe family strife, the 'empire' remained intact until 1204 when Normandy and Anjou were confiscated from King John by Philip II of France. Between 1245 and 1285 Anjou was held as an appanage of the French crown by Charles, the brother of Louis IX. It was Charles (I) who founded the new house of Anjou which gave kings to Naples, Hungary and Poland. The county was incorporated into the lands of the French crown in 1480. *See* FULK IV; FULK V
□ L. Halphen *Le Comté d'Anjou au XIᵉ siècle* (1906); R. Southern *The Making of the Middle Ages* (1953); O. Guillot *Le Comté d'Anjou et son Entourage au XIᵉ siècle* (1972)

Anna Comnena (1083–1148) Byzantine princess and daughter of Alexius I Comnenus, she is chiefly known for her biography of her father, the *Alexiad*. In 1091 she was betrothed to Constantine Ducas with whom Alexius shared the throne. In the same year Alexius deposed Constantine and raised his own son John to the status of co-emperor. Anna never forgave her brother; and on Alexius' death in 1118 Anna and her mother Irene attempted to overthrow John in favour of Nicephoras Bryennius Caesar, Anna's husband. Their attempts were foiled, and John placed both Irene and Anna in a convent. Here the latter began to write the *Alexiad*, which, although it suffers in places from confused chronology and omission, is the best source for Alexius' reign.
□ *The Alexiad of Anna Comnena* trans. E.R.A. Sewter (1969)

Annals Together with saints' Lives and chronicles, annals were a major form of historical writing in the early Middle Ages. They consist of brief chronological listings of events which were important in the history of a kingdom, bishopric or monastery. The earliest surviving set of annals is the *Annales S. Amandi* (708–810), whilst other famous Continental annals include the *Annales Laurissenses Maiores*, the Royal Annals and the *Annales Bertiniani*, which between them cover the whole history of Carolingian Frankia 741–882; the Hildesheim Annals (818–1137), the Quedlinburg Annals (913–1025) and the *Annales Flodoard* (919–68). In Britain the most effective and useful sets of annals are those incorporated in the Anglo-Saxon Chronicle, assembled in 891 through the inspiration of King Alfred and carried on in one surviving version (the Peterborough Chronicle) to 1155; and on the Celtic side, the *Annales Cambriae* which, assembled in 954, are carried down to the late 13th c.

Anselm, St (1033–1109) Archbishop of Canterbury. Born at Aosta in Lombardy, Anselm became a monk at the abbey of Bec in Normandy where he studied theology under Lanfranc. In 1078 he became abbot of Bec in succession to its founder Herluin, and in 1093 was appointed archbishop of Canterbury. From then until 1106 he was involved in a series of disputes, first with William Rufus and then with Henry I, concerning the question of papal supremacy and the relationship between church and state in England. The struggles, which came to focus on the question of the investiture of prelates with their symbols of office, ended in 1107 with a compromise: the formalities of investiture passed to the archbishop and the ecclesiastical hierarchy, while the king was left with the means of influencing election and of safeguarding his feudal interests in the great ecclesiastical estates.

In the course of this conflict Anselm was forced to spend two long periods in exile. During the first of these (1097–1100) he wrote his most influential theological work, *Cur Deus Homo*, in which he laid down in a sophisticated manner Orthodox doctrine concerning the Incarnation. Certainly the ablest theologian ever to be archbishop of Canterbury, Anselm proved one of the most creative minds behind 12th-c. Scholasticism. His basic tenet *credo ut intelligam* (I believe in order that I may understand) became matter for some of the most fruitful and constructive discussion of the age.

After Anselm's death the monk Eadmer of Canterbury wrote an account of the saint which broke fresh ground in the sphere of biography.
□ R. Southern *St Anselm and his biographer* (1963)

Anselm of Laon (*c*.1050–1117) After studying under his namesake St Anselm at the monastic school of Bec, Anselm taught at Paris, where his ideas on realism were supported by his pupil William of Champeaux. In 1100 he returned to his native town of Laon, and it is there that Peter Abelard became one of his pupils. In his writings on theology Anselm was greatly influenced by Platonic and Neoplatonic ideas transmitted to the medieval world through the writings of St Augustine of Hippo. He was best known for his *Interlinear Glosses*, a complete commentary on the Latin Vulgate Bible, though only a small portion of his voluminous writings has survived.
□ G. Lefebvre *De Anselmo Laudunensi scholastico, 1050–1117* (1895)

Anskar, St (801–65) Missionary to Scandinavia. Educated at Corbie in Picardy where he became a monk, he later moved to Corvey in Westphalia, where he was appointed bishop of Hamburg, and later, after the Danes had sacked Hamburg with great ferocity in 845, archbishop of the joint see of Bremen and Hamburg. From his north German centres he encouraged missionary expeditions to Denmark and Sweden. His success varied according to the support given by the kings and to pagan reactions, but at worst he and his pupils exposed some of Scandinavia to the Christian message and set up churches, notably in the merchant settlements of Birka in Sweden and Hedeby and Ribe in Denmark.
□ C. H. Robinson *Anskar, Apostle of the North* (1921)

Antioch Syrian city and seat of one of the patriarchs of the early church which in the 3rd c. became the home of a school of theology that stressed a literal interpretation of the Bible, in opposition to the more allegorical interpretation put forward by the Alexandrian theologians. In 341 Antioch was the venue for an ecclesiastical council attended by the Eastern Emperor Constantius II and one hundred bishops which, on the question of Christ's substance, adopted a view close to that of Arianism and rejected the teaching of the Nicene Creed. It declined in importance in the early Middle Ages, partly for natural reasons (a series of earthquakes in the 6th c.), but mostly because of the political confusion caused by Muslim success in overrunning the greater part of Syria. Its long-drawn-out siege during the First Crusade was a critical event and after its capture in 1098, Antioch became the centre of the 'Norman' principalities in the Holy Land. Under its first two princes Bohemund of Taranto (1098–1111) and Roger (1112–19) the state of Antioch came to occupy the whole of the region between Cilicia in the north and central Syria in the south. When Jerusalem fell to Saladin in 1187, Antioch survived as a Latin stronghold and remained so until it was captured and brutally sacked by the army of Baybars I in 1268.

Aquinas, St Thomas (1225–74) Christian scholar and theologian. Born at Rocca Secca near Aquino in southern Italy, Thomas was educated first at Monte Cassino and then at the university of Naples before joining the Dominican Order in 1244. The Domini-

Siege of **Antioch**: from a late 13th-c. French continuation of William of Tyre's *History*.

cans sent him to Paris where he studied under Albertus Magnus, who had a profound influence on his later work. Aquinas spent the remainder of his life as a teacher both in Paris (1252–59, 1269–72) and in Italy (1259–69, 1272–74), where he was responsible for devising a programme of study to be followed in the Dominican Schools.

Although he wrote a handbook for the duchess of Brabant on how to treat her Jewish subjects and a treatise on the model ruler entitled *De Regimine Principum*, Aquinas was not primarily a political thinker, but a theologian. Above all he was convinced that it was possible to reconcile the writings of Aristotle with the tenets of Christian theology. In his *Summa contra Gentiles* (1259–64), for example, he defends the Christian doctrine from the attacks of Islam and Judaism, not by arguing from a position of faith but instead from pure reason drawn from the writings of Aristotle. A similar scholastic method was used in his greatest, but unfinished work, the *Summa Theologica* (begun 1266), which consists of a statement of Aquinas' beliefs on all Christian mysteries, again argued from a position of logic as well as from one of revelation. His views were rejected by some schoolmen led by John Duns Scotus, and the universities tended to divide into two camps of Thomists and Scotists. The force and elegance of Aquinas' thought ensured, however, that much of his teaching became central to the beliefs of the church. The Thomist aphorism, for example, that 'Reason does not destroy faith but perfects it', and his analysis of the theological basis for a just war, had a vastly influential impact.
□ F.C. Copleston *Aquinas* (1955); J. Maritain *St Thomas Aquinas* trans. J.W. Evans and P. O'Kelly (1958); J.A. Weisheipl *Friar Thomas d'Aquino: His Life, Thought and Works* (1975); A. Kenny *Aquinas* (1980)

Arabs Name applied to the Semitic peoples of the Arabian peninsula who in the 7th c. were the first converts of Islam and who dominated that religion during the period of the Umayyad amirate. With the 'Abbāsid takeover in 750, however, the Arabs lost their hegemony over Islam. The capital of the empire was now transferred to Baghdad where Persian rather than Arabic interests were paramount. *See* SARACENS; SPAIN
□ N. Daniel *The Arabs and Medieval Europe* (1979)

Aragon Medieval kingdom of north-eastern Spain, which (like Castile) began its rise in the 11th c. when it was left by Sancho III of Navarre in his will to his third son Romaro I. By 1100 Aragon had doubled in size and in the 12th c. expanded even further when it was united through marriage with Catalonia. Having

Drawing of an **Arabian** horseman, from a 10th-c. papyrus.

expelled the Moors from their domains, the kings of Aragon looked overseas. In 1282 they established themselves in Sicily, in 1320 in Sardinia and in 1442 in Naples. The long absences of their monarchs tended to make the Aragonese noblemen more independent than their Castilian counterparts. Aragon therefore continued to follow a rather independent policy even after the union of the two crowns in 1475. *See* ALFONSO V; PETER III
□ J.N. Hillgarth *The Spanish Kingdoms 1250–1516* (1976–78)

Arbroath, Declaration of (1320) Document in which, following their victories at Bannockburn (1314) and elsewhere, Robert I Bruce and other Scottish magnates pledged themselves to the cause of Scottish independence. As a result in 1322 Edward II signed a truce with the Scots which was later formalized in the Peace of Northampton (1328). By the terms of this treaty England relinquished her claim to suzerainty over Scotland, and Bruce's dreams of Scottish independence were thus formally fulfilled.

Architecture Much of our knowledge of medieval architecture is inevitably based on ecclesiastical examples. Christianity took many of its architectural forms from pagan Roman buildings, modifying them to suit its liturgical needs, and the basilican and centrally planned churches of the early Christian period have continued to be used until our own times.

With the conquest of Western Europe by the Germanic peoples, architectural developments in the West and East parted company. In Byzantium, the dome became a striking feature, Hagia Sophia in Constantinople (consecrated 537) being the most daring. Byzantine churches often combined the Greek-cross and octagon-dome types (Hosios Lukas, 1011) and their exteriors became rich through the use of contrasting materials and sculptural decoration. Brought to an end in 1453 by the fall of Constantinople to the Turks, Byzantine artistic traditions lingered on in the Balkan countries and in Russia.

Although some buildings of merit were being erected in Italy, Spain (before the Arab invasion of 711), Gaul and Anglo-Saxon England, it was only in the wake of the Carolingian revival that more ambitious and original structures were undertaken. Charlemagne sought to re-create the glory of Rome, not of pagan Rome but of the Christian Rome of Constantine the Great; thus, for instance, the gateway at Lorsch is a 9th-c. version, however distant, of the Arch of Constantine in Rome. The imperial palatine chapel at Aix-la-Chapelle, however, is modelled on the domed octagon of S. Vitale in Ravenna built by Justinian (consecrated 548). The development of monasticism encouraged a new type of building, needed for the worship and work undertaken by large communities. The celebrated plan preserved at St Gallen is an ideal layout for a Carolingian abbey – a model to be followed. The view of Centula abbey (Saint-Riquier, consecrated 799), now destroyed, is known from an engraving which shows to what extent a medieval church differed from an early Christian one, giving an equal emphasis to the east and west ends of the basilica and employing crossing towers. The western towers which have remained popular in Christian architecture were initiated in this period, although precedent existed in the 5th-c. and 6th-c. churches of Syria.

The disintegration of the Carolingian empire resulted in a decline in building activity almost everywhere in Europe. The revival was in large measure due to the reform of religious life inspired by the Order of Cluny, and by the emergence of a strong Germany under the Ottonian dynasty, heir to the Carolingian empire. Ottonian architecture continued the innovations of the 9th c., adding new elements, such as the alternation of piers and columns in the nave arcades (Gernrode, 960 and St Michael, Hildesheim, 1010–33), and these features were passed on to Romanesque buildings.

The Romanesque style in architecture evolved during the 11th c. and blossomed in the next, although some experiments, especially with stone vaulting, were initiated in the late 10th c. in the monastic churches of the Mediterranean coast. These early Romanesque buildings spread from Lombardy westwards to Catalonia, eastwards to Dalmatia and northwards to Burgundy. The blending of the technical achievements of these buildings with the monumental Ottonian style produced some of the most impressive Romanesque churches.

Apart from vaulting large spans and thus making a building safer – for timber was always prone to ignite in candle-lit buildings – Romanesque masons introduced a great innovation: the choir with an ambulatory and radiating chapels enclosing the eastern apse. This was ideal for the display of shrines with relics, and for the easy circulation of large crowds of pilgrims, as the pilgrimage had become a universally popular movement. The great abbey of Cluny and the pilgrimage churches of Saint-Martin-de-Tours, Saint-Sermin at Toulouse and Santiago de Compostela all had such choirs. The interiors of Romanesque buildings are divided into units of bays through the use of shafts, semi-columns and other devices.

Lombard and Anglo-Norman Romanesque architecture both contributed to the evolution of rib-vaulting which became an essential feature of the last medieval style in architecture: the Gothic. The expanding Cistercian Order helped to spread early Gothic forms throughout Europe, from the Atlantic to the Vistula. The first Gothic structure was the choir of Saint-Denis, the royal abbey near Paris (1140–44). Romanesque churches had to have thick walls in order to carry the weight of stone vaulting; the ingenious designer of Saint-Denis reduced the weight of the vaults by employing pointed rather than semicircular arches and ribs, which enabled him to span bays of various shapes. The cells between the weight-carrying ribs were filled with light masonry and the ribs were supported not by heavy walls, but by slender piers or columns. Furthermore, the wall space could now be reduced by the introduction of enormous windows filled with stained glass. Future developments were towards greater height, as at Chartres, Rheims, Amiens and Beauvais cathedrals. Flying buttresses in these and many other buildings linking the ribs of vaulting with the buttresses on the aisle walls, were given slender, graceful forms which added to the beauty of the exteriors.

For a time, Romanesque and Gothic forms continued side by side, but by the second quarter of the 13th c. the victory of the new French style was complete. Paris, capital of a now powerful France under St Louis (1226–70), became a cultural and artistic centre which inspired the whole Christian

The nave of Saint-Denis, looking east: the birth of Gothic **architecture** can be seen in the pointed arches, rib-vault and the greater height and lightness of the structure.

world. The Sainte-Chapelle in Paris (1243–48), built to house the relics of Christ's crown of thorns, is 'a space enclosed by stained glass', with intricate window traceries repeated in relief on the walls. This so-called Rayonnant Gothic replaced the High Gothic of the first half of the 13th c. Cologne and Strasbourg cathedrals are celebrated German versions of this style while in England, Henry III's patronage (e.g., Westminster Abbey) was in clear emulation of his French cousin.

England was to play an important role in the development of Late Gothic architecture. The style known as the Decorated (1280–1375) with its ever-increasing emphasis on decoration of every kind – rich, intricate mouldings, surface patterning and vaulting within a network of *liernes* – anticipates the last phase of Gothic architecture: the Perpendicular style in England, and the Flamboyant in France. Both are expressions of an art in which technical virtuosity and decorative richness became an end in themselves.

Of the secular buildings during the Middle Ages, the most impressive are castles and fortifications, but there are also, especially in Italy, important civic buildings. Most ordinary people lived in timber dwellings, and of these little is known. It is the houses of the wealthy, built in stone, that have survived in fairly large numbers.

The medieval architect acquired his knowledge not through theoretical training but by practical work, in the course of which he would gain some knowledge of mathematics and geometry and would be able to make plans and drawings. He would leave many of the details to be worked out while a building was being constructed, and not infrequently, when a design proved too ambitious or too costly, it had to be modified while work was in progress. The architect would organize the supply of building materials and machinery for hoisting loads, and would personally supervise every stage of the work from the foundations to the roofing. He also designed the templates (patterns) which the masons and carpenters needed to make mouldings, ribs, capitals, bases and other decorative features. A gifted architect had every chance of becoming a prosperous and even famous man. *See* GLASS, STAINED; GOTHIC; ROMANESQUE; SCULPTURE; STAVE CHURCHES   GZ

□ K. J. Conant *Carolingian and Romanesque Architecture* (1959); P. Frankl *Gothic Architecture* (1962); J. Harvey *The Master Builders. Architecture in the Middle Ages* (1971)

Archpoet (d. *c*.1165) Anonymous Latin poet, probably from the Rhineland, who sought the patronage of Rainald of Dassel, archbishop of Cologne and chancellor of Frederick Barbarossa. His most famous work, the *Confessio*, expresses brilliantly the torments and paradoxes of the 12th-c.

The building of St Albans Abbey, showing use of a windlass, a ladder and a plumb-level.

renaissance, heavily constrained by the church and yet rejoicing in its new-found vitality and confidence in reason and nature. *See* GOLIARDIC POETS
□ H. Waddell *The Wandering Scholars* (1935)

Arianism Heretical belief which arose in the early church from the teachings of the Alexandrian priest Arius (256–336). Facing the theological difficulty of combining the divinity of Christ with the unity of God in the Trinity, Arius advanced the view that the Son was not co-eternal with the Father. At the Council of Nicaea (325) the debate raged around the question of whether the Son was 'of the same substance' as the Father. Athanasius led the party supporting the view that became orthodox, that Father and Son were indeed 'of the same substance', and Arianism was condemned. Arius was banished to Illyria and died on the eve of his reconciliation with the church. His teachings remained very influential almost, so it seems, by historical accident. Many of the Germanic tribes beyond the frontier of the Roman empire were converted by missionaries led by Wulfila, an Arian bishop, and so Arian Christianity became the distinguishing characteristic of a number of the Ostrogoths in Italy (until the mid-6th c.), the Visigoths in Spain (until the late 6th c.), and the Vandals in North Africa.

Aristotle (384–322 BC) Greek philosopher and pupil of Plato in Athens, *c.* 343 he became tutor to Alexander, son of Philip of Macedon. On Philip's death in 335 Aristotle returned to Athens where he set up the peripatetic school outside the city. Here scientific research was undertaken into such subjects as music, physics, metaphysics, mathematics and astronomy in an attempt to increase man's understanding of the natural world. This scientific interest led Aristotle in his *Politics* and *Ethics* to regard man as no more than a superior kind of social and political animal. Although the writings of Aristotle were known to the Romans, the study of his works declined and almost totally disappeared after the fall of the Roman empire. Knowledge of his works was confined to the study of translations of two of his minor works, and a number of commentaries made by Boethius. In the 12th c. and 13th c., however, the *Politics* and *Ethics* began to be rediscovered, together with the writings of other Greek authors such as Plato, Galen and Hippocrates, especially through translations from Muslim sources by Jewish scholars in Spain. Aristotle's writings on man as a political and social animal appeared to conflict with the generally accepted Augustinian theology, which agreed that man was naturally social but that his political existence was un-natural and only necessary because of sin. Many schoolmen, including Aquinas, began the task of

Aristotle, holding an astrolabe, teaching students, from his *Guide to the Perplexed* (mid-14th c.).

reconciling Aristotelian and Augustinian philosophy, and the ensuing debate continued for more than a hundred years. *See* AQUINAS, THOMAS; DUNS SCOTUS, JOHN
□ F. van Steenberghen *Aristotle in the West* (1955)

Armenia Ancient kingdom situated between the rivers Aras and Jura, including the upper waters of the Euphrates. In *c.* 390 Armenia was divided into two parts under the jurisdiction of the Byzantines and Persians respectively. Although Byzantine Armenia was quickly assimilated into the empire, there was much resistance in Persian Armenia to the attempts to convert the local Christian population to Zoroastrianism. After 653 Armenia was at least nominally under the suzerainty of the Arabs, but remained virtually independent under the Christian rulers. In the 11th c. the country was devastated by the Seljuk sultans Tughril Beg and Alp Arslan. Many Armenians emigrated to Little Armenia in the western part of modern Kurdistan. This new kingdom had close links with the West; at the time of the First Crusade it was the Armenians who helped Baldwin du Bourg to establish the county of Edessa whilst

Armenia

Leo II (1187–1219) swore fealty to the Western emperor, Henry VI, and reformed the Armenian administration on Western models. In the 14th c. the murder of two of its kings, Guy de Lusignan in 1344 and Constantine I in 1374, caused civil strife in Armenia and left the kingdom unable to resist the Mamlūk advance. In 1375 the capital city of Sis was captured and the last king deposed.

□ T.S.R. Boase *The Cilician Kingdom of Armenia* (1978)

Armour There were three types of medieval armour: (1) soft armour–quilted fabric and leather (2) mail – interlinked metal rings (3) plate–metal, *cuir-bouilli* (leather soaked in heated wax), whalebone or horn; plate can mean large plates, smaller plates riveted or sewn to fabric (coat-of-plates construction), or small plates laced together (lamellar construction).

These were ancient techniques, but following the demise of the empire, full plate, except helmets, virtually disappeared from Western Europe. Lamellar armour was worn by the Vandals, the Franks under Charlemagne, the Vikings and in Eastern Europe. Coat-of-plates persisted, but until *c.* 1250 soft armour and plate were predominant. The Middle Ages witnessed the development from mail to full plate. Mail was followed, *c.* 1250, by a transitional period when plate reappeared. By *c.* 1330 plate defences existed for much of the body. By the early 15th c. this early plate had evolved into fully developed *alwite* (white) armour.

At the time of the Norman Conquest of England, defensive equipment consisted of a body garment (hauberk or *byrnie*), helmet and shield. Hauberks were often hooded (*coif*) and of mail, and were worn over padding for body (*aketon*) and head (arming-cap). Helmets were usually conical with nasal. Segmented *spangenhelms* and one piece helmet-skulls were also known. Shields were wooden with leather cladding and metal reinforcements. They were long and kite-shaped or, occasionally, circular and convex. Subsequent introductions included the surcoat, perhaps as protection from heat or rain, or for heraldic purposes. Between *c.* 1150 and the early 13th c., helmets developed through round and cylindrical forms to the 'great' helm (crested for identification). The ancient kettle hat (*chapel-de-fer*), resembling the modern tin hat, also reappeared, and *c.* 1220 the skull-cap (*bascinet* or *cervellière*) became popular, worn beneath helm or with visor.

Initial plate reintroduction is obscure. Body reinforcements occurred from the early 13th c., with real plate from *c.* 1250. The commonest 14th-c. body defence was a garment with metal plate lining (coat-of-plates, later *brigandine*). These forms developed and by *c.* 1330 full equipment incorporated

English miniature of *c.*1480: a man being helped into his **armour**, 'when he schal fighte on foote'.

aketon, arming-cap, hauberk, coat-of-plates, *gambeson (surcoat), vambraces* (arm guards), *chausses* (mail leggings), *gamboised cuisses* (thigh guards), *poleyns* (knee guards), *schynbalds* or *greaves* (shin guards), *sabatons* (foot guards), spurs, waistbelt, swordbelt, gauntlets, shield, *aventail* (*coif* replacement), and *bascinet*, supplemented, if visorless, by helm.

By *c.* 1410 this early plate had evolved into a more extensive covering. The breast plate achieved independence and, with back plate, hooped *fauld* (skirt) and, later, *gorget* (collar), formed the basic defence. Articulated tubular forms developed for the limbs. These solid forms required only the removal of their frequent fabric coverings to become true *alwite* armour.

With the early 15th-c. adoption of *alwite*, regional styles emerged, northern Italy (Milan and Brescia) and southern Germany (Nuremberg, Landshut and Augsburg) being the chief production centres. *Bascinet* variants were popular (*armet* in Italy, *sallet* and kettlehat in Germany). Shields were now largely redundant. From *c.* 1460 the German High Gothic style flourished, favouring slender forms with fluting to deflect blows.

It should be remembered that most developments only applied to the armour of the nobility. Gentry forms varied, whilst the common soldiery relied upon soft armour, with some mail, skull-caps or kettle-hats and bucklers to parry blows. There was also a distinction between plain field and decorative parade armour. For tournaments, reinforced armour supplemented field armour, special tilting pieces arose and heavier defensive suits were soon provided. A horse or sumpter carried the armour, and from the 12th c. the charger was often covered by a *trapper* of mail, coat-of-plates or cloth. *See* HERALDRY; KNIGHTHOOD; WAR   MB

□ F. M. Kelly and R. Schwabe *A Short History of*

Costume and Armour vol. 1 (1931); C. Blair *European Armour* (1958); J. Mann *European Arms and Armour* vol. 1 (1962)

Arnold-Amalric Abbot of Cîteaux 1192–1209 and archbishop of Narbonne 1209–25. Sent as a legate by Innocent III to preach against the Albigensians, Amalric assumed spiritual leadership of the crusade against them after the death of Peter of Castelnau in 1207. At the fearsome massacre at Béziers, he was credited with the appalling exhortation to the crusaders, all too readily followed: 'Kill them all. God will choose who is innocent.'
□ B. Hamilton *The Albigensian Crusade* (1974)

Arnold of Brescia (1100–55) Radical religious reformer. After studying in Paris under Abelard he joined the Augustinians and became prior of Brescia. He emphasized the absolute necessity of clerical poverty and of the abandonment of temporal power by the church. Condemned for his views in 1139, he was banished from Italy and took refuge in France, teaching at the school of Mont-Sainte-Geneviève in Paris. He was reconciled with the church for a short time under Eugenius III, but after he had allied himself with a rebel political party in Rome which attempted to abolish the temporal power of the papacy, he was excommunicated in 1148. He was expelled from Rome in 1155, captured by the Emperor Frederick I and handed over to the prefect of Rome who sentenced him to death. His followers, the Arnoldists, were condemned at the Council of Verona in 1184.
□ G. W. Greenaway *Arnold of Brescia* (1931)

Arnulf, St (*c*.580–*c*.640) Bishop of Metz. Appointed to his see in 614, Arnulf was a prominent counsellor of the Merovingian King Dagobert I (628–39), before resigning his bishopric in favour of a life of solitude. He became first a hermit in the Vosges mountains and then a monk in the monastery of Remiremont on the river Mosel.

Arpad (*c*. 850–905) Chief of the Magyars who *c*. 895 led his people from the banks of the Dnieper into the half-vacant territory around the Middle Danube. He established himself as duke and began the Arpad dynasty, which remained in control of Hungary until 1301. From 899 the Magyars continued their expansion westwards into Italy and Germany, and it was only after their defeat by Otto the Great at the battle of the Lechfeld (955) that they were finally confined to Hungary itself. Under St Stephen I (d. 1038), who was crowned king in 1000, the dynasty accepted Christianity from Western sources, dependent on the pope.

Art *See* **Architecture; Fresco; Glass, stained; Manuscript illumination; Mosaic; Painting and the minor arts; Sculpture**

Artevelde, Jacques van (d. 1345) In the opening stages of the Hundred Years' War, Van Artevelde, a prosperous merchant of Ghent, took control of the city as an ally of Edward III of England. Bruges and Ypres joined him in a federation of Flemish towns, but his murder in July 1345 led to the return of the count. Nearly 40 years later (1381), at a time of great social unrest, the townsmen of Ghent again looked for leadership to a representative of the family: Jacques's son Philip (1340–82). After initial successes which again brought Bruges into conjunction with Ghent, he was killed in battle against the comital power supported by France. Nevertheless, the name of Van Artevelde lived on as a symbol of Flemish urban independence.
□ H. van Werveke *Jacques van Artevelde* (1948)

Arthur Legendary British king who appears in a cycle of medieval romances as the sovereign of the knights of the Round Table. The basic story found fame in the *Historia Regum Britanniae* of Geoffrey of Monmouth (1136–38), but was expanded by Chrétien de Troyes and Robert de Boron, who between them added some of the more romantic elements to the saga, such as the sword in the stone, the finding of the Holy Grail, and the love affair of Lancelot and Guinevere. The historical truth about Arthur is more difficult to determine. Both Nennius in the 9th c. and the *Annales Cambriae* in the 10th c. talk of Arthur as heading Welsh resistance to the Saxon advance which culminated in Arthur's victory at the battle of

Arthur and his knights at the Round Table, from *La Queste del Saint Graal* (15th c.).

Mons Badonicus (Mount Badon); this story receives no confirmation from the 6th-c. writings of Gildas, however. The most that can safely be said is that Arthur seems to have been a British chieftain who commanded a military force along Roman lines on behalf of the British kings, and who may have been instrumental in winning an important battle at Mount Badon in the early years of the 6th c.

□ L. Alcock *Arthur's Britain* (1970); S. Knight *Arthurian Literature and Society* (1983)

Asia Minor Area of land bordered by the Black Sea in the north, the Mediterranean in the south, the Aegean in the west and Armenia in the east. Initially part of the Byzantine empire in the 11th c., it was conquered by the Seljuk Turks led by Sulaymān ibn Qutalmish, who fixed his capital at Nicaea and founded the sultanate of Rum. Following the First Crusade, the western part of Asia Minor returned to Byzantine control, Nicaea being handed back to the empire by the Latins whilst the Emperor Alexius I Comnenus recaptured much of the coastal territory between Nicodemia and Attalia. After the fall of Constantinople to the Latins in 1204, Nicaea became the headquarters of the Byzantine counter-attack which was finally successful in 1261. After 1265 however the Byzantines failed to protect Asia Minor against the growing encroachments of first the Mongols and then the Turks, who under their leader Osman won a decisive victory near Nicaea in 1301.

Assassins Religious sect of Muslim Shi'ites founded in *c.*1090 by the Persian Hasan ibn Sabbah, which terrorized Persia and Syria for two centuries. It was a secret order ruled over by a grand master, known as the 'Old Man of the Mountain'. The Assassins were divided into seven classes according to the extent of their initiation into the secrets of the order. The *fedayeen* or 'devoted ones', who carried out the actual assassinations under the rules of implicit obedience, belonged to the fifth group. They are supposed to have had ecstatic visions under the influence of hashish, thus giving rise to the name of the order: *hashishin* (which in time became corrupted to Assassin).

□ M.G.S. Hodgson *The Order of the Assassins* (1955); B. Lewis *The Assassins* (1967)

Asser (d. *c.* 909) Bishop of Sherborne. The author of a Life of King Alfred, which adds much information about the king that is not available in the Anglo-Saxon Chronicle or other sources. Asser also includes in his work much autobiographical material. He was born in Wales, became a monk at St David's in Dyfed and then in the 880s one of the chief advisers to Alfred, helping him with an educational programme and initially dividing his time between St David's and the West Saxon court. He was well rewarded for his services, receiving control of the religious houses of Congresbury and Banwell in Somerset, and becoming bishop with extensive jurisdiction in the West Country including Cornwall. He was finally appointed to the important see of Sherborne at some time between 892 and 901.

□ *Asser's Life of King Alfred* ed. D. Whitelock (1959); *Alfred the Great: Asser's Life of King Alfred and other contemporary sources* trans. S. Keynes and M. Lapidge (1983)

Assizes of the kingdom of Jerusalem Law code based on the customs and practices which developed in the Latin kingdom of Jerusalem during the 12th c. The basis of this code was laid down by the first king of Jerusalem, Godfrey de Bouillon (d. 1100), who ordered an enquiry to be made amongst the crusaders concerning the laws and customs to which they had been subject in the West. The resulting law code, the *Lettres du Sépulchre* was essentially French in character and contained details of the duties of royal officials, the granting of fiefs, the administration of justice and the regulation of trade. After the capture of Jerusalem by Saladin in 1187, the original code seems to have disappeared, but a similar code was drawn up in Cyprus in the 13th c., where it was used as the basis for the government of the remnants of the Latin community in the East for another 300 years.

Astrology The art of foretelling events on earth by observing the movements of the sun, moon and heavenly bodies, which permeated the outlook of the later Middle Ages. Astrologers gave advice to emperors and kings (e.g., Guido Bonatti at the court of Emperor Frederick II), and there were chairs of astrology in many universities. Great scholars, such as Albertus Magnus, were deeply influenced by astrological ideas, and leading physicians like John Fusoris perfected astrological instruments to aid them in healing their patients. Writings of the period clearly reflect this pervasive influence: in the *Knight's Tale*, for example, Chaucer portrays Saturn as a highly powerful, influential and individualistic deity. Yet it was not until the 12th c. that astrology had begun to gain such a powerful hold. It was then that the rediscovery and translation of many scientific and philosophical texts from the Greek and Arabic into Latin brought Western European scholars into contact with the powerful ideas of the earlier great astrological traditions.

Astrology appears to have originated in Mesopotamia, where in the first millennium BC there had

Astrology: Euclid observing the moon and stars with a *dioptra*, and Hermannus holding an astrolabe.

developed both the astronomical science of plotting the movements of the sun, moon and stars, and the astrological art of divination based upon these observations. The two branches, astronomy and astrology, were to remain virtually indistinguishable for many centuries; the Greeks, who built upon existing Mesopotamian and Egyptian astrological lore, on the one hand used their new understanding of geometrical principles to describe the orbiting planets, and on the other equated the heavenly bodies with their own pantheon of gods. They also fully developed the idea of the 12 constellations of the zodiacal belt. In the 2nd c. BC personal horoscopes began to be cast on the basis of the configuration of celestial bodies at the moment of birth. Thus, the position and relationship of the sun, moon, planets and constellations were worked out, as was the influence exercised by the 12 houses of the planets, sun and moon, which were part of the firmament and which governed matters such as wealth, marriage and death. Despite opposition from the Epicurean philosophers, astrology was accepted by the Stoics and rapidly influenced all scientific observation. In medicine, for example, various functions and organs of the body were associated with different combinations of planets and constellations.

The Romans, who had their own methods of divination, did not at first welcome Greek astrology. The Emperor Augustus, however, cultivated it as a royal art and tried in vain to prevent the popular astrologers from inflaming the populace. The early Christian church drew a distinction between astronomy and astrology, rejecting the latter as a pagan superstition; it was regularly condemned by church councils. St Augustine summed up the patristic criticisms of astrology in his *City of God*: the world is governed not by chance or fate, but by divine providence, and astrologers who predict a man's character from the stars do the work of demons by enslaving mankind's free will. Some of his contemporaries took a more tolerant view; Firmicus, for example, believed that astrologers could be put to the test and found accurate, and that their teachings could show the sinful the right way to live. The practice of astrology apparently continued in Gaul until the collapse of the Western empire.

After several centuries of decline, astrological ideas began to revive in the West at the time of the Carolingians. In the 11th c. Raoul Glaber wrote of portents and prodigies, and there were signs of Arabic astrological influence in the works of several of his contemporaries. It was not until the 12th c. that the Arabic astrological texts were translated into Latin on a large scale; then the ideas of Muslim writers such as Alkindli, who suggested that stars could radiate occult influences, and explained magic by astrology, re-entered the mainstream of European intellectual thought together with the corpus of Greek astrological ideas. Some translators, such as John of Spain, went on to write their own astrological treatises, and Bernard Silvester combined an interest in astrology and geomancy. Some of the leading men of learning in the 13th c., such as Albertus Magnus and Roger Bacon, accepted the influence of the stars on events on earth, although others, including Thomas Aquinas, who considered that many events were accidental rather than pre-ordained, took a more sceptical view. All were, however, influenced to a greater or lesser degree by astrological concepts.

In the later Middle Ages astrology was used on a wide scale to predict events: in 1337, for example, Geoffrey of Meaux foresaw famine and disorder following the appearance of a comet, and, like many others, was to attribute the Black Death to a malign planetary conjunction. The Hundred Years' War also provided astrologers with a golden opportunity for foretelling events, and Charles V of France had several in his service. The use of astrological forecasting in medicine was also widespread and had a bearing on matters such as diagnosis and cure for disease, and the most propitious date for carrying out surgery. Yet critics like Aquinas had their successors. In the early 14th c. the papacy condemned some astrological notions as part of its attack on magic and sorcery, and some 50 years later, Nicolas Oresme denied much of the influence of the occult and criticized contemporary astrology as pernicious and misleading. The early 15th-c. theologian John Gerson stressed the unreliability of the art, but perhaps the most scathing onslaught, by Pico della Mirandola, came in the 1490s; in the same decade, the astrological works of Simon de Phares were condemned by the *Parlement de Paris* and the Sorbonne. Renaissance humanism and the rise of new astrono-

A 9th-c. astrolabe from Iraq used to decipher the celestial mechanism that was said to govern life on earth.

mical methods did much to undermine the credibility of astrology at the highest intellectual levels, but its popular influence was to endure through the centuries. EMH

□ L. Thorndike *A History of Magic and Experimental Science* (1923–58); G. Sarton *Introduction to the History of Science* (1927–47); J. Tester *A History of Western Astrology* (1987)

Astronomy From its earliest beginnings astronomy was closely bound up with astrology, and like it, although to a lesser extent, underwent an eclipse in the earlier Middle Ages and a revival in the 12th c. The Mesopotamians, Egyptians and Greeks all made their own contributions to the astronomy of classical times which dominated astronomical thought until the 16th c. The Mesopotamians, for example, apparently first identified and named the 12 constellations of the zodiac and plotted their course around the heavens, while the Egyptians discovered that the length of the year approximates most closely to 365 days. Greek astronomy built on these foundations, but also became linked with philosophical speculation. To Aristotle, the cosmos was spherical, with the fixed earth at its centre and the moon, stars and planets rotating in their own orbits around it. Observation of the variation in light from the planets suggested that this notion had its flaws, and Eudoxus tried to explain the movement of the planets in terms of concentric spheres rotating around their axes. The erratic behaviour of some celestial bodies had also to be explained; in his *Almagest* (c. AD 150) the great astronomer and astrologer Ptolemy attributed this to the influence of epicycles, deferents and equants, permitting loops of retrogression. A number of Arab astronomers, such as Al-Bitruji, were to return to the ideas of Eudoxus.

The early Christian church condemned astrological practices, and much of this learning was lost, but a distinction was drawn in patristic works between astrology and astronomy, the latter meeting with less criticism. St Augustine admitted that there was nothing superstitious about plotting the course of the stars, and that knowledge of the moon's path was useful for predicting the date of Easter. He warned against a preoccupation with astronomy, however, because of its close relationship with the pernicious astrological art. In the early Middle Ages almost no speculative work in astronomy was carried out in the West, but its continuing practical value was recognized. Astronomical skills were required for the accurate calculation of the dates of church festivals, and in c. 525 Dionysius Exiguus invented a method of computing years by the Christian era, which was gradually adopted in Western Europe. Bede, among others, showed in his work a consider-

able interest in chronology. With the revival of classical learning from the reign of Charlemagne onwards, astronomy again had its accepted place among the four more advanced arts of the Quadrivium. Every theologian and philosopher needed some understanding of it, and it was to become a widely popular subject in the later Middle Ages.

The 12th c. and 13th c. saw the translation into Latin of many of the most celebrated Greek and Arabic works on astronomy. Of vital importance was Gerard of Cremona's translation of the *Almagest* in 1175, but the ideas of Eudoxus and his Arab followers also reached the West at about the same time, and in the 13th c. the two separate views fuelled major intellectual controversies in the universities. On the one side stood those who supported Ptolemy's epicentric system, on the other, followers of Al-Bitruji's homocentric system; and among the disputants was Roger Bacon, who found himself unable fully to accept either explanation. Astronomy was meanwhile caught up in the growing enthusiasm for astrology, and much work on it was carried out for astrological ends. Thus in the early 13th c. William the Englishman, a physician and astrologer practising at Marseilles, strongly emphasized the importance of correct astronomical tables to enable accurate predictions to be made. A preoccupation with such means of computation was widespread; among the most important were the Alphonsine Tables drawn up for Alphonso the Learned, king of Castile and Leon in the late 13th c. Another continuing astronomical interest was the calendar. By the 13th c. it was clear that the Julian year was too long, and Roger Bacon and Robert Grosseteste, followed in the 14th c. by John de Meurs, were among those who tried unsuccessfully to reform it. The adjustment was eventually made in most of the West in 1582, but even then some states, such as England, stuck resolutely for many years to the more ancient reckoning, by which there was ever less correspondence between the seasons and the calendar dates.

The growing precision and complexity of astronomy and astrology in the later Middle Ages depended on accurate astronomical instruments. The most important basic piece of equipment was the astrolabe, probably invented by Hellenistic astronomers, but widely used and understood in the medieval west. Chaucer's treatise on it shows that it was as much an aid to the calculation of latitudes and declinations, as a means of observing the heavens. More complicated versions were also built, many by physician-astrologers. In the early 15th c., for example, John Fusoris produced a sophisticated mechanical equatory for computing horoscopes. Richard of Wallingford, astronomer-abbot of St Albans, invented several instruments, including the *rectangulus*, used for making observations, and a remarkable, expensive and elaborate astronomical clock constructed for his abbey *c.* 1320.

Leading critics of astrology, such as Nicolas Oresme in the 13th c. and John Gerson in the 14th c., had considerable astronomical knowledge. Oresme, for example, even discussed the possibility of the diurnal rotation of the earth, although without breaking away from the Platonic idea of an earth-centred universe. It was not until 1543 that Nicholas Copernicus first published his heliocentric (i.e., sun-centred) theory, thereby revolutionizing astronomical thought. *See* COMETS; ECLIPSES   EMH
□ R.R. Newton *Medieval Chronicles and the Rotation of the Earth* (1972); O. Pedersen *Early Physics and Astronomy* (1974)

Athanasius, St (*c.* 296–373) Bishop of Alexandria. Born of Christian parents, Athanasius was trained in the catechetical school of Alexandria before becoming a deacon and secretary to the bishop. In 325 he attended the Council of Nicaea, which condemned the Arian heresy, and after his election as bishop of Alexandria in 328, vigorously defended the findings of that council despite persecution. Athanasius also gave practical help to the early groups of monks in Egypt and wrote a Life of St Anthony of Egypt. His writings include a famous treatise on the Incarnation, but he is chiefly remembered for the Athanasian Creed, composed for the Council of Nicaea, in which he affirms that Christ is of one substance with the Father, a creed that remains to this day the fundamental statement of belief in most Christian Trinitarian churches, Eastern Orthodox as well as Western.

Athens, Latin duchy of One of the principalities which was set up by the crusaders after the conquest of Constantinople in 1204. Although Constantinople itself was reconquered by the Greeks in 1261, Athens remained in the hands of the Latins for another 200 years. Ruled first by the Villehardouin family and then by Walter of Brienne, in 1311 the duchy was captured and taken over by the Catalan Grand Company. In 1381 however the duchy voluntarily submitted to Peter IV of Aragon before falling to the Ottoman Turks in the 15th c.

Attila King of the Huns 434–53 Originally co-ruler of the Huns with his brother Bleta, he reigned alone after killing his brother (445). In *c.*441 he devastated much of the Balkans and in 447 advanced across the Danube and swept through Germany and France. In 451 his progress was checked at Orleans by an alliance of imperial and Visigothic forces, and he soon suffered further defeat in a battle on the Catalaunian plains of Champagne. In 452 he entered Italy, destroyed Aquileia and plundered Milan and Pavia. He was prevented from entering Rome, however, by the entreaties of St Leo and the promise of tribute from the Emperor Valentinian III.
□ E.A. Thompson *A History of Attila and the Huns* (1948)

Gold **augustale** of the Emperor Frederick II demonstrating a strong classical influence.

Augustale (*agostaro*) Gold coin of classical design introduced by the Emperor Frederick II in the kingdom of Sicily in 1231, and continued with a different type by Charles of Anjou until 1278. It weighed 5.25 g, but was only 20½ carats fine, thus containing 4.48 g of pure gold.

Augustine, St (354–430) Bishop of Hippo. One of the four great fathers of the Latin church. Born at Tagaste of a pagan father and Christian mother, Augustine was raised as a Christian but not baptized. Studying rhetoric at Carthage university and then teaching rhetoric in Italy, Augustine totally abandoned his Christian upbringing, contemplating first Neo-platonist and then Manichaean beliefs. In 385, however, he was converted to Christianity by St Ambrose and baptized the following year. Returning to North Africa he was ordained priest and finally bishop of Hippo in 395.

He was active in his pastoral role and did much to refute the doctrines of various groups of heretics, such as the Manichaeans and the Donatists. He is best known as a Christian philosopher and theologian. His writings include the *Confessions*, in which he gives an account of his own conversion, various sermons on the Gospels, and the *City of God* (413–26). In this work he attempted to answer the criticisms of those whose rejected Christianity on the grounds that God had allowed Rome to fall, by attempting to show them the huge scale of the universe and God's plan for man, within which the fall of Rome was as a drop in the ocean. He saw all men as belonging to one of two cities; the city of God made up of the faithful, and the city of unbelievers. He was the first Christian theologian to express the doctrine of man's salvation by divine grace.

He also wrote a number of guidelines for clerical living for a number of local monasteries, and it was these which in the 11th c. were used as the basis of the so-called Rule of St Augustine. His general attitude to political government, which was to attribute it to the sinful nature of man and yet to see it as an effective means of canalizing the evil consequences of sin, proved immensely influential in medieval ecclesiastical thought. AD

☐ P. R. L. Brown *Augustine of Hippo* (1967), *Religion and Society in the Age of Augustine* (1972)

Augustine, St (d. 604) Archbishop of Canterbury. An Italian by birth, Augustine became a monk and later prior of the abbey of St Andrew on the Coelian hill at Rome before being chosen by Pope Gregory I to lead a mission of conversion to England in 596. Landing in Kent in 597, Augustine and his companions were well received by King Aethelbert of Kent, whose wife Bertha was already a Christian. Aethelbert gave Augustine a house in Canterbury and permission to preach to his people. Wisely Augustine did not try to abolish paganism in Kent at one blow, but sought instead to phase it out gradually whilst at the same time incorporating into the liturgy of the church many pagan customs and using the old pagan temples, where convenient, for Christian purposes. His methods were successful, and by 601 King Aethelbert and many of his people had accepted Christianity. In Canterbury itself Augustine established his metropolitan see staffed by secular priests, and also founded a monastery dedicated to SS Peter and Paul (later St Augustine's). Augustine also founded bishoprics at London and Rochester.

☐ H. Mayr-Harting. *The Coming of Christianity to Anglo-Saxon England* (1972)

Augustinian canons A religious order of priests, originating in the 11th c., which followed a Rule based on the monastic writings of St Augustine of Hippo. They arose out of the reform movement of the church which called upon secular clergy to adopt a common and regular life. They were especially popular in Rome, southern Germany and Lorraine, where they often controlled groups of churches or formed the staff of a cathedral. In England only one cathedral, namely that of Carlisle (1133), was served by Augustinian canons and only a few Augustinian houses, such as Barnwell in Cambridgeshire, were founded in order to perform parochial duties in the locality. The majority of Augustinian houses in England tended instead to serve the needs of pilgrims (as at Walsingham) or the sick (as at St Bartholomew, Smithfield, London). Although a few houses were established in England during the 11th c., the period of greater growth was in the 12th

c. during the reigns of Henry I and Stephen. Houses of Augustinian canons were small by monastic standards, usually consisting of no more than 12 canons and a prior.

☐ J.C. Dickinson *Origins of the Austin Canons* (1950); L. Verheijen *La règle de St Augustin* (1967)

Aurora borealis (Northern Lights) Visions of strange phenomena in the sky, recorded in medieval chronicles and described, for example, as 'holy lights', can often be explained as manifestations of the aurora. In 793 the 'fiery flying dragons' associated with Viking onslaughts on Northumbria were described as 'a rain of blood' by Alcuin who watched the aurora from a rooftop in York. On 10 September 1173 Gervase in Canterbury gave a reliable description of an aurora with redness in the northern regions and 'white rays like spears . . . traversing the redness'. Many accounts of active displays describe them in terms of celestial battles between the East and the West. Displays of Northern Lights reach a peak about every 11 years, and appear over extensive regions. Some celestial visions seen by crusaders in the Middle East were recorded on the same nights that the aurora was reported in Normandy and in Iraq, and indeed coincide with accounts of displays which were seen about the same time in the Far East. The peaks often occur in conjunction with the peaks of the sunspot cycle, and – to take an example from the well-recorded early 12th c. in Western Europe – it has been possible to deduce that sunspot maxima occurred in 1111, 1119, 1128 and 1137. In general terms, too, cumulative evidence suggests that the sun was very active in the

Augustine of Hippo receives visions that inspire his writing of the *City of God* (15th c.).

6th c. and late 14th c., while in the 7th c., mid-11th c. and 15th c. sunspots and aurorae were much less frequent. *See* ASTRONOMY; COMETS

□ D. J. Schove *Sunspot Cycles* (1983)

Austin friars Religious order drawn from several different groups of Italian hermits, including the Orthodox Waldensians, who in 1256 were organized into a mendicant order by Pope Alexander IV. Leaving their former apostolic life, the Austin friars joined the other mendicant orders in living a useful apostolic life in the towns.

□ R. Brooke *The Coming of the Friars* (1975)

Austria Originally march territory (the Ostmark or East Mark) in south-east Germany, founded by the Carolingians and Ottonians as a military buffer zone against barbarian invasion along the Danube. It became a margravate in the 10th c. and a duchy within the empire when in 1156 Henry II (Jasomirgott) of Babenburg was granted the office of duke, with extensive powers, in compensation for the loss of his duchy of Bavaria. The Babenburgs held the duchy for the succeeding century until the line died out in 1246. After a power struggle in which Bohemian interests were intimately concerned, the Habsburgs emerged as the dominant family and ruled the duchy from 1282 to the 20th c. In the later Middle Ages the addition of territory in Carinthia (1335), the Tyrol (1363) and Trieste (1382) raised Austria to the level of a powerful principality; it was increasingly regarded in the 15th c. as the natural centre of the empire, with Vienna as the chief imperial city.

□ A.W.A. Leeper *A History of Medieval Austria* ed. R.W. Seton-Watson and C.A. Macartney (1941)

Avars Nomadic Mongol tribe originating in central Asia who in the mid-6th c. swept across southern Russia, the Balkans and Bohemia under their khan, Baian. In 561 their westward expansion was halted in Thuringia by the Merovingian king Sigebert of Austrasia and they concentrated with Lombard help upon the capture of the Hungarian plain from the Gepidae. After the Lombard departure for Italy in 568, the Avars settled in Hungary, using it as a base for the domination of the Slavs and for an attack upon the Byzantine empire. Although they reached the gates of Constantinople in 617, further progress was checked by the successful revolt of the southern and western Slavs (622–26) which effectively limited the power of the Avars once again to the borders of Hungary.

Their power in the West, however, was not broken until Charlemagne undertook a series of successful campaigns against them (791–97). In the early 9th c., the Avars began to lose their individual identity.

After 805 many of them were converted to Christianity and absorbed by the Bulgars, Slavs, and ultimately by the Magyars.

□ J.B. Bury *The Invasion of Europe by the Barbarians* (1928)

Averroes (1126–98) Islamic philosopher. Ibn Rushd, Abū al-Walīd Muhammad was born at Cordoba in Spain, studied jurisprudence, theology, mathematics, medicine and philosophy in his youth, and later obtained important administrative positions under the Islamic rulers of Spain, Ya'qub Yūsuf and Yūsuf Ya'qub al-Nansur, as well as serving as a court physician. In 1196 he was banished together with other philosophers, but was restored to favour before his death in 1198. He wrote a number of works on medicine and philosophy, but he achieved greatest fame through his commentaries on such works as Aristotle's *De Anima* and *Metaphysics*, which were translated into Latin and used extensively in the 13th-c. universities of Christian Europe, especially in Paris where Siger of Brabant was the most prominent follower of Averroes. The great emphasis placed by Averroes on the work of Aristotle, and his opposition to the influence of religion on philosophy led to distrust on the part of the orthodox. Both Albert the Great and Thomas Aquinas attacked the Averroists, and in 1270 their errors were formally condemned by the church.

□ J.H. Randall Jr *The School of Padua and the Emergence of Modern Science* (1961); Ibn Rushd *The Encyclopaedia of Islam* vol. 3 (1971).

Avicenna (*c.* 980–1037) Arab physician, scholar and philosopher. Mastering logic, geometry and astronomy at an early age, Ibn Sīnā, Abū 'Alī al-Husayn went on to become an expert in both philosophy and medicine. Rising to a position of importance after healing the sultan of Bokhara, he spent most of his active life in the courts of various Muslim dignitaries in Persia. He was deeply influenced by Greek thinkers, both Aristotle and the Neoplatonists, and created an elaborate philosophical system which involved the natural world and the position of man in nature and society. His work was translated into Latin and became a significant element in the development of medieval scholasticism. The emphasis he placed on the religious approach to philosophy appealed to the orthodox, and Thomas Aquinas himself was endebted to Avicenna for elements in the structuring of the *Summa*.

Avicenna's medical work was even more influential, and his *Canon of Medicine*, translated by Gerard of Cremona, was a standard authority until as late as the 17th c.

□ S.M. Afnan *Avicenna, his life and works* (1958)

Avignon City in Provence, famous in the Middle Ages as the home of the papacy in exile during the 14th c. and still encircled by the ramparts which were built at that time. Its early history was fairly stormy, and it was severely harassed by both the barbarians and Saracens before becoming attached successively to the kingdoms of Burgundy and of Arles and to the domains of the counts of Provence, Toulouse and Forcalquier. Although the city obtained republican status at the end of the 12th c., it was dismantled in 1226 by Louis VIII for its support of the Albigensians and was also forced to submit to the counts of Toulouse and Provence in 1251. In 1309 Pope Clement V chose Avignon as his residence, and in 1348 the city was sold to Clement VI by Joanna, countess of Provence, the curia then remaining in Avignon until Gregory XI returned to Rome in 1377. Two anti-popes also resided at Avignon, Clement VII and Benedict XIII, the latter until his expulsion in 1408. The period 1309–77 is referred to at times as the Babylonish captivity or exile. Avignon remained in papal possession after the return to Rome and was not annexed to the kingdom of France until 1791.
□ G. Mollat *The Popes at Avignon 1305–78* (1963)

Azo the Glossator (*c.* 1150–1230) Born at Bologna, he was later appointed professor of civil law at the university there and also took an active part in municipal life. He is chiefly known for his readings on the *Code* which were gathered together by his pupil Alessandro de Sant' Aegidio. In these Azo developed a methodical exposition of Roman law which was of considerable use to contemporary jurists.
□ *Select Passages from the Works of Bracton and Azo* ed. F.W. Maitland, Selden Society VII (1895)

B

Bacon, Roger (1214–92) English philosopher and scientist. Born at Ilchester in Somerset, he studied at Oxford and was befriended by Robert Grosseteste, bishop of Lincoln, before withdrawing from current scholasticism in order to devote himself to the study of language and experimental science. In 1250 he returned to Oxford and entered the Franciscan Order, but doubts were soon raised concerning his orthodoxy, and in 1257 he was forbidden to lecture and sent to the Order's convent in Paris. Through the intervention of Pope Clement IV, Bacon was allowed to return to Oxford in 1265, where he continued to experiment and to write. Following Clement's

death, however, Bacon was again condemned by his Order and was even imprisoned. His chief works include the *Opus Majus*, a scientific treatise written for his patron Clement IV, and the *Compendium Studii Philosophiae*, an incomplete compendium of existing knowledge in the 13th c., in which he attacked the educational system of the Middle Ages. Bacon's practical grasp of the natural sciences, chemistry and physics was in advance of his age. He earned the title *doctor admirabilis* by his vast learning, but was also suspected, partly from jealousy, partly from sheer incomprehension, of sorcery and indulgence in the black arts.
□ D.C. Lindberg *Roger Bacon's Philosophy of Nature* (1983)

Diagram of the eye from Roger **Bacon's** *Optics* (late 13th c.).

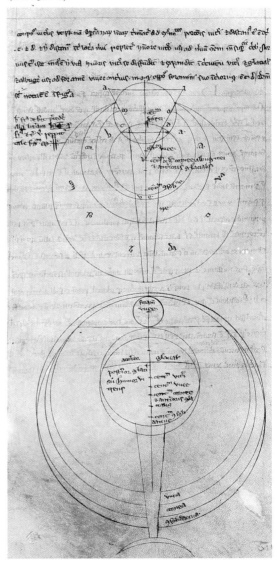

Baldus de Ubaldis, Peter (1320–1400) Italian canonist and civil lawyer. Graduating from the university of Perugia in 1344, Baldus taught in Bologna until 1351, when he returned to Perugia, his native city. He remained there until 1390, when he took up a teaching post at Pavia, staying there until his death. In addition to producing scholastic writings on Roman and canon law, which included commentaries on the work of Justinian and on the *Decretals*, Baldus was a practical lawyer of considerable repute. In 1380, for example, he was summoned to Rome by Pope Urban VI to aid him in his struggle against Clement VII. Baldus is perhaps most famous, however, for his contribution to the study of feudal law in the commentary on the *Usus Feudorum*.
□ J.A. Wahl *Baldus de Ubaldis: a study in reluctant Conciliarism* (1974)

Baldwin I King of Jerusalem 1100–18 On the death of his brother Godfrey de Bouillon, 'Advocate of the Holy Sepulchre', Baldwin, who had been count of Edessa since 1098, was elected as the first king of the newly created crusading kingdom of Jerusalem. In spite of the grave military, political and economic problems facing him, he proved an able and successful ruler. He beat back the Egyptian forces and with Genoese help took the important ports of Acre, Caesarea and Sidon. By skilful use of his authority as a feudal overlord, sensible encouragement of colonizers and Italian traders, and with support from the church, Baldwin succeeded in stabilizing the foundations of his new kingdom.

Baldwin IV the Leper King of Jerusalem 1173–85 (b. 1160) At the age of 12, Baldwin, son of Amalric I and Agnes of Courtenay, succeeded to his father's throne although already afflicted by the leprosy that was to make his life a torment. He faced two great problems that were, within two years of his death, to prove fatal to his kingdom: factions among the nobility, intensified by the marriage of his sister and heiress Sybil with Guy de Lusignan, and the rising power of Saladin, ruler of Syria and governor of Egypt. His personal courage and wisdom were beyond question and he even inflicted military defeat on Saladin at Montgisard (1177). He arranged for the succession, under a moderate regency, of his young nephew, Baldwin V (1185–86), but the death of the boy at Acre left the way open for the succession of Guy de Lusignan and the loss of Jerusalem to Saladin in 1187.
□ S. Runciman *A History of the Crusades* vol. 2 (1952)

Ball, John (d. 1381) Priest and English social reformer. A spokesman for the equality of all men, he played an important part in stirring up peasant unrest through

A 15th-c. illustration of the battle of **Bannockburn** from John Fordun's *Scotichronicon*.

his preaching. Imprisoned for his outspokenness, he was freed by the rebels led by Wat Tyler during their march on London. He was later recaptured by the authorities and hanged at St Albans on 15 July 1381. *See* PEASANTS' REVOLT

Bannockburn, battle of (24 June 1314) Battle at which Robert Bruce defeated English attempts to relieve their garrison at Stirling. The governor of Stirling had promised to surrender the city to the Scots if he had not received military support from England by a certain date. In order to meet the deadline an English force set out for Scotland and was met by the Scots just south of Stirling on rising ground flanked by a little brook, the Bannock burn, which gave its name to the battle. Bruce's skill as a general, his disposition of infantry, and the success of the Scottish pikemen in checking the cavalry defeated the formidable feudal army under Edward II, the remnant of which fled first to Dunbar, then south of the border. The victory of the Scots and the subsequent surrender of Stirling broke the English hegemony over Scotland which had been achieved by Edward I. In the history of war, Bannockburn illustrates the re-emergence of a well-deployed infantry supported by archers, as against the pre-eminence of the mounted knight. *See* DECLARATION OF ARBROATH
□ G.W.S. Barrow *Robert Bruce* (1976)

Barbour, John (1316–95) Scottish poet and ecclesiastic. Archdeacon of Aberdeen, he later became a high-ranking official in the Scottish exchequer. He is often considered the father of Scottish literature, his most famous work being *The Bruce*, a heroic poem on the life and adventures of Robert Bruce and his lieutenant Sir James Douglas.
□ L.A. Ebin, 'John Barbour's *Bruce*', *Studies in Scottish Literature* 9 (1972)

Barcelona Spanish Mediterranean port which owed its importance in the Middle Ages to its strategic position. The Visigothic kings Ataulf and Amalric made it their capital 414–18 and 531 respectively. It was conquered by the Muslims in 713 and reconquered by the Franks in 801. After the unification of Aragon and Catalonia, Barcelona grew into an important commercial centre, by 1258 possessing its own code of maritime law and trading with the Baltic, the North Sea and Alexandria. It was the centre of the Grand Catalan Company, which controlled and dominated the duchy of Athens for the greater part of the 14th c. In 1430 the magistracy of the city established a university there. Barcelona's importance declined in the 15th c. after the unification of Aragon and Castile.

Bartolus of Sassoferrato (1313–57) Italian jurist. After studying first at Perugia and then at Bologna, where he received his doctorate in 1334, Bartolus was appointed professor of law at Pisa (1339). In 1343 he returned to Perugia where he remained until his death. He is most famous for his commentary on the *Code* of Justinian, and for his application of Roman law to contemporary problems through the use of scholastic method. His special concern was to reconcile the universal teachings (as he saw them) of Roman law with local customs, and in his attempts to do so, he was led to argue that local custom depended on the sovereign will of the prince, a conclusion that contributed greatly to 14th-c. attitudes towards the nature of sovereignty.
□ C.N.S. Woolf *Bartolus of Sassoferrato* (1913); M.H. Keen, 'The Political Thought of the Fourteenth-Century Civilians' in *Trends in Medieval Political Thought* ed. B. Smalley (1965)

Basil I Emperor of Byzantium 867–86 (b.812) Son of a poor Armenian family, he won the favour of the Emperor Michael III and was made co-emperor in 866. In 867 he murdered his benefactor Michael and established the Macedonian dynasty (867–1056). In an attempt to placate Rome, he removed the patriarch Photius and restored his rival Ignatius to the patriarchate, although Photius found favour again after Ignatius' death. Basil won back Bari and parts of Calabria from the Saracens and defeated the Arabs who were besieging Dubrovnik. He reorganized the Byzantine navy and in 872 launched an attack on the Paulicians in Asia Minor. Through his initiative a revision of Justinian's *Code* was begun. He compiled a manual of law called the *Prochiron* and began the *Basilica*, a new collection of law.

Basil II the Bulgar Slayer Emperor of Byzantium 963–1025 (b.958) Acceding to the throne as a minor, he acquired power after the overthrow of his uncle Basil the Eunuch in 983. Between 987 and 989 he overcame the revolt of Bardas Phocas with the help of Vladimir, prince of Kiev, whom he rewarded with the hand of his sister Anna Porphyrogenita. In 991 he attacked Bulgaria and in 1014 he is said to have captured and blinded 14,000 Bulgars, sparing only one eye of every hundredth man so that he could lead his countrymen home. By 1018 he had annexed the whole of Bulgaria, although he left the church independent. In order to preserve the traditional Byzantine system of peasant soldier-farmers, he ruthlessly suppressed the aristocracy. During his reign the patriarch of Constantinople omitted the name of Pope Sergius IV (909–12) from the liturgy, thus beginning the formal schism between Rome and the Orthodox church.
□ S. Runciman *A History of the First Bulgarian Empire* (1930).

Basle, Council of (1431) General Council of the church called to bring about ecclesiastical reform, to deal with the growing threat of the Hussites and to reach an agreement with the Greek church. The Council was poorly attended and proved a disaster from the Conciliar point of view, although it managed to bring many Hussites back into the church. In an attempt to control the Council's activities more fully, Pope Eugenius IV dissolved it in 1437 and transferred its business to a new Council at Ferrara, then to Florence to make an agreement with the Greeks. Some of the delegates at Basle, however, refused to sanction the move to Ferrara, and in 1439 they elected the duke of Savoy as the anti-pope Felix V. The disarray caused by the simultaneous existence of two General Councils enabled the secular princes of Europe to strengthen their control over their national churches, and also confirmed the constitutional authority of the papacy.
□ M.D. Crowder *Unity, Heresy and Reform 1378–1460* (1977)

Bavaria Area of Germany situated between the Alps and Bohemia which, in the Middle Ages, formed one of the constituent duchies of the Holy Roman Empire. A semi-independent region under

Detail from the **Bayeux tapestry**: Harold performs brave deeds with William's army in Brittany.

its duke, Tassilo, Bavaria was forced to accept the sovereignty of Charlemagne in 787 and became part of the Frankish kingdom. Following the break-up of the Carolingian empire the duchy regained much of its former independence, and in the early 10th c. Duke Arnulf the Bad of Bavaria carried out his own independent foreign policy with his Slav neighbours and also possessed the right to appoint bishops and mint coins. The Saxon dynasty asserted its rights of appointment to the duchy, and Otto I's brother Henry became duke in 947, augmenting its boundaries after the victory at the river Lech in 955, and establishing the Ostmark, the foundation for the later Austria. His grandson Henry II (St Henry) became emperor (1002–24). In 1070 the duchy passed into the hands of the Guelph (Welf) family, but after the overthrow of Henry the Lion in 1180, Otto of Wittelsbach became duke. The Wittelsbach family, with variable fortunes, continued to rule the Bavarian principality, which emerged into the modern world as one of the more stable elements in the German polity under the guidance of Albert the Wise (1460–1508).

Bayeux tapestry Famous 11th-c. embroidery, 231 ft long by 20 inches wide, now housed at Bayeux and executed in coloured wools on linen. The work depicts the story of the Norman Conquest of England from Earl Harold's visit to Normandy until his death in battle. A short section, now missing, probably took the story through to William the Conqueror's coronation as king of England in December 1066. It constitutes an intelligent state-ment of the Norman case, portraying Harold as a brave warrior who betrayed his oath of loyalty to Duke William and succeeded to the throne of England as an oath-breaker and usurper. The success of Duke William at the battle of Hastings is interpreted as just retribution and the triumph of a rightful cause. It is

likely that the tapestry was made at Canterbury to the master design of an artist associated with St Augustine's abbey, and was commissioned by Odo, bishop of Bayeux and earl of Kent, probably on the occasion of the dedication of the cathedral at Bayeux in 1077.
□ *The Bayeux Tapestry* ed. F. Stenton (1958); *The Bayeux Tapestry* ed. D. Wilson (1985)

Beatrice (d. 1290) Noble Florentine lady to whom Dante dedicated most of his poetry. Usually identi-fied as Beatrice Portinari, she was the wife of Simone de'Bardi and died at the age of only 24 years. In 1293 Dante described his spiritual love for Beatrice in *La Vita Nuova* but his chief glorification of her came in the *Divine Comedy* (1308–20) in which Beatrice is Dante's intercessor in the Inferno, his goal whilst travelling through Purgatory and finally his guide in Paradise.

Beaufort family Family descended from the union of John of Gaunt, duke of Lancaster, with Catherine Swynford. Their children were legitimized by Richard II in 1397, and from them are descended the dukes of Somerset and earls and marquesses of Dorset of the 15th c. Henry Tudor (Henry VII) was descended on the maternal side from John Beaufort (1373–1410), eldest son of John of Gaunt and Catherine, who as earl of Somerset and marquess of Dorset was a prominent supporter of Richard II against the Lords Appellant.

The most interesting and important of John of Gaunt's Beaufort sons was Henry (1377–1447), royal servant, bishop and cardinal. He was made bishop of Lincoln in 1398 and translated to Winchester in November 1404. As royal chancellor in 1403 and again 1413–17 and 1424–26, he was a leading admin-istrator and political figure in the English kingdom. He also exercised his considerable talents on a wider stage, playing an active part in support of Martin V at the Council of Constance and, after appointment as cardinal in 1425, acting as papal legate in a complex and ultimately unsuccessful effort to launch a crusade against the Hussites in Hungary and Bohemia. He crowned the young Henry VI as king of France in Paris (1431), but emerged as a prominent seeker after peace with the revived French forces. In his later years he concentrated on domestic affairs at Winchester, and is chiefly remembered for his refoundation and endorsement of the Hospital of St Cross at Winchester.

The third brother, Thomas Beaufort, was a loyal servant of both Henry IV and Henry V. He was appointed chancellor in 1410 and also held offices in Aquitaine and Normandy. He was made earl of Dorset in 1412 and duke of Exeter in 1416. He gained a good reputation as a soldier and was an executor of Henry V's will. The family survived the Wars of the Roses in spite of a series of political disasters, in the course of which three successive earls and dukes of Somerset were killed or beheaded. The present dukes of Beaufort are descended from Henry, third duke of Somerset (a Lancastrian and firm supporter of Henry VI), who was executed after the battle of Hexham in 1464.

□ R.L. Storey *The End of the House of Lancaster* (1966)

Becket, St Thomas (1117–70) Educated at Merton Priory, Surrey, and at the university of Paris, he became a merchant's clerk in London before entering the service of Archbishop Theobald of Canterbury. In 1154, upon the recommendation of the archbishop, Becket was appointed royal chancellor by Henry II and proved an efficient and loyal servant. In 1162 he was appointed archbishop of Canterbury.

After his election he changed his policy and began vigorously to resist royal encroachments upon ecclesiastical liberties. Matters came to a head over

A 15th-c. copy of the *Divine Comedy*: Dante and **Beatrice** in the Earthly Paradise.

Enamel reliquary from Limoges depicting the martyrdom of **Thomas Becket**.

the question of criminous clerks, Becket maintaining that they should not be punished by the secular courts. He refused to accept the Constitutions of Clarendon (1164) and fled to France, appealing to the pope, Alexander III. Negotiations were long-drawn-out and bitter, and a fresh crisis occurred when Henry II had his heir crowned by the archbishop of York in 1170. A reconciliation was effected, but this proved only temporary.

Becket failed to come to terms with the bishops who had supported the coronation of the young king, and Henry in his wrath uttered words at his court in Normandy that prompted four of his knights to cross the Channel and to murder Becket in his own cathedral on 29 December 1170. The murder shocked opinion throughout Christendom. Henry was forced to do public penance and Canterbury became a great place of pilgrimage. Becket was quickly canonized (1173). *See* FOLIOT, GILBERT
□ D. Knowles, 'Archbishop Thomas Becket', *Proceedings of the British Academy* (1949); F. Barlow *Thomas Becket* (1986)

Bede, the Venerable (672–735) Monk, theologian and historian. Born in Northumbria, he was sent at an early age to the monastery of SS Peter and Paul at Wearmouth and Jarrow, where he became first a deacon and later a priest. His writings are very diverse; he wrote on grammar and chronology, composed many valuable commentaries on the scriptures, and compiled a history of the Lives of the abbots of Wearmouth and Jarrow and a metrical Life of St Cuthbert; he also popularized the dating of events from the birth of Christ. His most important work in modern eyes is his *Ecclesiastical History of the English People*, a masterpiece both in style and in the use of scholarly historical method, which relates the story of the conversion of England to Christianity and the history of the English church until the time of his writing in 731. Bede was the outstanding product of the Northumbrian renaissance, and his work remained powerfully influential throughout the Middle Ages.

□ *Bede's Ecclesiastical History of the English People* ed. B. Colgrave and R.A.B. Mynors (1969); P.H. Blair *The World of Bede* (1970)

Bedford, John, duke of (1389–1435) The elder of the surviving brothers of King Henry V (d.1422). Already well experienced in English administration, John became virtually regent in France on behalf of his infant nephew Henry VI. After initial successes which depended greatly on the Burgundian alliance, Bedford met severe reverses at the hands of Joan of Arc. The part he played in the trial and execution of Joan blackened his reputation. He died at Rouen at a time when the breaking down of the Burgundian alliance signified the end of English domination and the beginning of the final stages of the Hundred Years' War.

Beguines (Beghards) A powerful force within the Western church from the early 13th c., the Beguines were communities of women, in the first instance often from wealthy or comparatively wealthy urban backgrounds, who devoted their lives, sometimes in great austerity, to philanthropic ends: the care of lepers, the sick and the poor. Their focal point of origin was Liège in the first decade of the 13th c., and their name seems to have been given in contempt by the orthodox, who associated them with the Albigensian heretics. They spread along the trade routes of north-west Europe and were exceptionally powerful at Cologne, where Beguine communities existed as late as the 18th c. They became closely connected with the Franciscans, but were never accepted as an order. Their male equivalents were known as Beghards (from Robert le Bègue, the 'stammerer', a Liège preacher). Dedication to God, celibacy and employment in good works were their outstanding characteristics. Relations with the institutional church were uneasy throughout the Middle Ages, and the suspicion of heresy was never far distant. By the 15th c. many Beguine communities had developed virtually into charitable institutions.

□ R.W. Southern *Western Society and the Church in the Middle Ages* (1970)

Belisarius (*c.*505–65) Byzantine general. Serving first in the bodyguard of Justinian, he was appointed commander of the army. In 530 he successfully campaigned against the Persians and crushed the Nika riots in Constantinople in 532. He was given command of the expedition to Vandal Africa (533), taking Carthage and capturing the Vandal king. On Justinian's behalf he invaded Sicily and Italy (535), waged war against the Ostrogoths there and captured their capital at Ravenna in 540. During the 560s he fell into disfavour and was implicated in a plot against the emperor, although he was restored to full possession of his honours before his death.

□ L.M. Chassin *Bélisaire* (1957); R. Graves *Count Belisarius* (1938)

Benedict of Aniane, St (d. 822) A Spaniard by birth, Benedict began in 780 to promote the strict observance of the Rule of his 6th-c. namesake, St Benedict of Nursia, in his monastic foundation at Aniane. His fame soon grew and he was appointed by Louis the Pious to superintend the reform of the Frankish monasteries, imposing upon them a strict version of the Rule of St Benedict in 817. The movement did not long survive Benedict of Aniane's death, since many religious houses, including Saint-Denis at Paris, were loath to abandon their own long-standing customs, but his revised Rule became generally accepted as the orthodox statement of Benedictine observance.

□ W. Williams, 'St Benedict of Aniane', *Downside Review* 54 (1936); C.H. Lawrence *Medieval Monasticism* (1984)

Benedict of Nursia, St (*c.*480–*c.*550) The 'patriarch of Western monks' was a rather obscure Italian abbot in his day. All that is known of his life is derived from the second book of the *Dialogues* of Pope Gregory the Great, written *c.*593–94. Born in the region of Nursia, now Norcia – the traditional date of 480 is pure surmise – he was sent to the schools at Rome, but, disgusted by the debauched life of the capital, he fled to Afide without completing his education, and thence to the solitude of Subiaco, where he embraced the ascetical life, living for three years in a cave. He attracted disciples, whom he organized into small communities of 12. Finally, he migrated to Monte Cassino, where he built a monastery on the summit of the hill, and this he directed until his death. In 577 Cassino was sacked by the Lombards and left deserted and ruinous for 140 years. It was apparently during this period that a party of monks from Gaul came to Cassino, disinterred St Benedict's body and transferred it to their abbey of Fleury Saint-Benoît on the Loire. The monks of Cassino later denied this translation, and both monasteries claimed to possess the saint's body.

The Rule of St Benedict contains a prologue and

St Benedict, founder of Monte Cassino, with Abbot Desiderius (11th-c. Italian manuscript).

73 chapters, setting out a detailed and coherent plan for the internal organization and daily life of a monastic community. Internal evidence indicates that it was compiled and amplified over a period of some time, perhaps c.535–45. Recent textual scholarship has shown that it is not as original as was once believed, and that Benedict drew heavily upon the Rule of the Master, an anonymous work composed in Italy some 40 years earlier. Both Rules owe much to the Eastern monastic tradition, especially to the writings of John Cassian.

Although St Benedict recognizes the vocation of the hermit, he envisages a monastery as a completely cenobitical community living together in one house – a kind of villa monastery – and directed by a spiritual father, the abbot, who is elected by the brethren. In common with other early monastic legislators, he assumes that the majority of the monks, including the abbot, will be laymen, a few only being ordained to celebrate the weekly Eucharist. He provides for parents to donate children to the monastery to be brought up as monks, a practice that became an important source of recruitment in the Middle Ages. The Rule requires the adult postulant to undergo a year of probation as a novice before taking his vows, which include a promise of stability – to remain in the same community until death. Benedict regards personal poverty and obedience as central to the monk's profession. The Rule requires the recruit to renounce personal ownership completely: everything is to be the common property of the community. Benedict assumes that a monastery will be supported by endowments in the form of land, which in many cases will be cultivated by tenants, but he does not seem to have envisaged the

great territorial wealth that accrued to many abbeys in the following centuries. Like other ascetical writers, he makes total obedience to the will of the superior, the cardinal principle of the monastic life.

The monastery is to be 'a school of the Lord's service', designed to train the recruit in the spiritual life. To this end the Rule fills the monk's day with a carefully ordered routine of communal prayer, reading and manual work. The framework of the day is determined by the hours of worship, which Benedict calls the *opus dei*: the eight daily services sung in the monastic oratory (the night office of Vigils or Matins, sung in the early hours, Lauds, Prime, Terce, Sext, None, Vespers and Compline). The monk is enjoined to avoid contact with the outside world and to keep within the enclosure as far as practicable; but the Rule makes hospitality a solemn obligation – the guest is to be received as though he were Christ himself.

Although the Rule includes a penitential (a list of punishments for breaches of monastic discipline), Benedict's ascesis is not harsh. He allows eight hours of sleep in winter and six hours with an afternoon siesta in summer. His allowance of food, if not lavish, is adequate; meat is forbidden except to the sick, but meals can include a measure of wine. The moderation of Benedict's Rule and its completeness commended it to monastic founders, but it was some time before it established its position as the standard code of observance. No Roman monastery appears to have adopted it before the 10th c. In 7th-c. Gaul it is referred to (first at Solignac c.629) in conjunction with the Celtic Rule of St Columbanus, as a guide to the cenobitical life. This 'mixed Rule' persisted in the Frankish abbeys until the Synods of Aix-la-Chapelle, held in 816 and 817 under the auspices of Emperor Louis the Pious, prescribed the Benedictine Rule as the exclusive model of monastic observance in the Carolingian empire. The emperor's agent in promoting it was a monk drawn from the Gothic aristocracy of southern Gaul who was also called Benedict: St Benedict of Aniane. *See* FONTEVRAULT; GERARD OF BROGNE   CHL

□ C. Butler *Benedictine Monachism* (1961); D. Knowles *The Monastic Order in England* (1963); C.H. Lawrence *Medieval Monasticism* (1984)

Beowulf Epic poem of some 3000 lines, often dated to the 8th c., though surviving in a single manuscript of c.1000 now in the Cottonian collection of the British Library. It is a highly sophisticated poem in strict alliterative metre and is an invaluable source, handled critically, for Anglo-Saxon society, especially with regard to ideals of kingship, loyalty, service and kindred ties. The poet was a Christian and had some knowledge of Virgil and classical

Beowulf

traditions, though the substance of his story was heavily Germanic, dealing with the exploits of his eponymous hero in Denmark and south Sweden.

Beowulf's three great battles against the monster Grendel, against the even more monstrous mother of Grendel and against the dragon guarding the treasure hoard, rank among the most brilliant passages in early Germanic literature and have been subject to much analysis as allegories of the conflict of good and evil. There is a strong school of modern criticism that would take the construction of the poem forward to a date nearer that of the manuscript (which some consider the poet's holograph) in the late 10th c. or early 11th c.
□ J.R.R. Tolkein, 'Beowulf: the monsters and the critics', *Proceedings of the British Academy* 22 (1936); D. Whitelock *The Audience of Beowulf* (1951); *The Dating of Beowulf* ed. C. Chase (1981); *Beowulf* ed. M. Magnusson, S. Mackie and J. Glover (1987)

Berbers The native inhabitants of North Africa who successfully resisted the domination first of the Romans and then of the Arabs. Voluntarily accepting Islam by 711, the Berbers assisted the Arabs in the conquest of Visigothic Spain. Under the Almoravids, the Berbers ruled both Spain and North Africa until the 12th c.

Berengar of Tours (*c.*1000–*c.*88) Theologian and author of the Eucharistic heresy. Educated at Chartres he became superintendent of the School of Tours in 1031, and in 1041 was appointed archdeacon of Angers. In the 9th c. he followed and built upon the teaching of Ratramnus, who denied the existence of the real presence in the Eucharist. Berengar held that at the consecration, transubstantiation did not occur in the elements themselves but only in the sentiments of the believers. His doctrines were condemned in 1050, and his views encouraged church theologians such as Lanfranc and Guitmund of Aversa to tighten up the church's teaching on the Eucharist.
□ A.J. Macdonald *Berengar and the reform of Sacramental Doctrine* (1930)

Bernard, St (1090–1154) Abbot of Clairvaux. Born at Fontaine in Burgundy, Bernard joined the Cistercian Order in 1112 before being sent to found Cîteaux's third daughter house at Clairvaux in 1115. By Bernard's death, Clairvaux numbered some 700 monks whilst its own daughter houses included Rievaulx in Yorkshire (1132), and Whitland (1140) and Margam (1147) in Wales.

Bernard also had great influence in the church as a whole; in 1146 he was appointed by Pope Eugenius III to preach the Second Crusade and he took a leading part in the condemnation of the writings of

12th-c. sculpture of a Cistercian abbot, probably **Bernard of Clairvaux** (Holland).

Peter Abelard. His own writings include a number of sermons and a theological treatise on the love of God, but his most famous work is perhaps the series of letters addressed to Peter the Venerable, abbot of Cluny, in which he condemns the ceremonial character and sumptuousness of the Cluniac liturgy. For the last decade and more of his life he was the champion of Orthodox thought in the West and greatly influential in its political as well as in its spiritual life.
□ J. Leclercq *Etudes sur S. Bernard et le texte de ses écrits* (1953); *Bernard of Clairvaux: Studies presented to Dom J. Leclercq* (1973)

Bernard Gui (1261–1331) Inquisitor. A Dominican who acted as inquisitor at Toulouse from 1307 to the early 1320s, Bernard produced a formidable tract *c.*1325, known as the *Practica Inquisitionis Heretice Pravitatis* ('Practice of the Inquisition into Heretical Perversity'). It is the most important of his many written works, setting out the procedures of the Inquisition, their justification, and also incidentally shedding much light on the beliefs of the Walden-

sians, Cathars, Beguines, and the Jews. The tract is not completely original, drawing much from earlier writers on the theme, but the practical experience of the author adds a chilling element to the account of an arbitrary and much feared institution.
□ G.G. Coulton *Inquisition and Liberty* (1938)

Bernard of Chartres (d.*c.*1130) One of the great teachers of the early 12th c. and leading scholar at the School of Chartres up to 1124, he is now chiefly remembered for the remark attributed to him by John of Salisbury, that the moderns should be compared to the ancients as dwarfs standing on the shoulders of giants; they can see more and farther, not for any intrinsic virtue of their own, but because they are lifted up by the greatness of the giants. Steeped in the study of grammar and logiç, Bernard did much to strengthen knowledge of Platonism in the West, but it seems clear that his pre-eminence was personal, and that to attribute continued dominance to the School at Chartres after his retirement in 1124 is to distort the true picture. It is Paris, not Chartres, that emerges as the principal centre for scholastic and humanistic inquiry in the second quarter of the 12th c. *See* TWELFTH-CENTURY RENAISSANCE
□ *Renaissance and Renewal in the Twelfth Century* ed. R.L. Benson and G. Constable (1982)

Bernardino of Siena, St (1380–1444) Born at Massa di Carrera, Bernardino entered the Franciscan Order in 1402 and joined the Observants in the following year, settling first at Colombaio near Siena and later at Fiesole near Florence. In 1417 he began a career as a popular preacher and attracted large crowds all over Italy. In 1437 he became vicar-general of the Observant Franciscans, and through his influence the number of their houses increased from about 20 to more than 200. He guided the movement away from the eremitical life and encouraged them to take a more active part in the church as preachers and teachers, establishing schools of theology at Perugia and Monteripido for their instruction. In 1443 Bernardino resigned his office and started preaching once again, but his health began to fail and he died the following year at Aquila.
□ J. Origo *The World of San Bernardino* (1963)

Berno (850–927) First abbot of Cluny. Entering the Benedictine Order at the abbey of Saint-Martin at Autun, he reformed the monastery of Baume-les-Messieurs, and in 890 founded the abbey at Gigny, before being asked by William the Pious, duke of Aquitaine, to found a new abbey at Cluny in 909. His new foundation, which was placed under the direct authority of the holy see, was extremely popular, and several other houses, including the abbey of Souvigny, were also commended to Berno's care. Before his death Berno nominated St Odo to succeed him as abbot of Cluny.

Beyazet I (Bayazet) Ottoman sultan *c.*1389–1402 He consolidated Turkish rule in Asia Minor by suppressing Bulgaria (which had already been conquered by his father, Murād I), by invading Wallachia in 1394 and defeating the crusading army led by John the Fearless, heir of Burgundy, at the battle of Nicopolis in 1396. Although he subdued all the lesser Turkish dynasties of Asia Minor, bringing them under his rule 1390–93, he failed to take Constantinople, was defeated by Tamberlaine in 1402, and died in captivity.

Bezant Name given in Western Europe to the standard Byzantine gold coin (*solidus* or *nomisma*), which up to the 1030s was of virtually pure gold and weighed 4.55 g. After a period of debasement, it was re-established in 1092 under the name of *hyperpyron* (Italian *perpero*), but was only 20½ carats fine instead of 24. This in turn was progressively debased in the 13th c. and 14th c., until in the 1350s it ceased to be struck, though the term *hyperpyron* was retained as a money of account.

Biondo, Flavio (1392–1463) Humanist, historian of Roman antiquity and secretary to the papal curia. Entering papal service in 1433 he became scriptor of the apostolic letters and except for a short period (1449–53) he remained in this office until his death. His works include the *Decades*, a general history covering the period 410–1410 and published in Venice in 1483; *Roma Instaurata*, a descriptive catalogue of the monuments and ruins of Rome completed in 1446 and published in 1471; and *Italia Illustrata*, an archaeological and historical account of Italy which gives valuable information concerning the monuments extant in 15th-c. Italy.
□ D. Hay 'The *Decades* of Flavio Biondo', *Proceedings of the British Academy* (1959)

Black Death *see* **Plague**

Blondel Troubadour at the court of Richard Lionheart. Blondel was reputed, according to 13th-c. accounts of the captivity of his royal master, to have identified Richard in his fortress prison after hearing the king sing one of their favourite songs, thereby making it possible for negotiations to be opened for his ransom.

Boccaccio, Giovanni (1313–75) Born in Certaldo or Florence, he was early sent into the Bardi bank and studied law before turning to literature. Much of his youth was spent in Naples, but after 1340 he returned to Florence where he lived an active life in embassies to the Romagna, Milan, Naples and Avignon (1365), and as one of the Florentine magistrates for a two-year period late in his life. He is chiefly remembered for his tremendous contribution to vernacular literature, above all for the *Decameron* (*c*.1350), a human comedy based on the extent of good and evil in late medieval society. The plot concerns ten young aristocrats who retire to a Fiesolan hillside during the plague, set up a court of pleasure and relate tales to one another on various themes, many explicitly sexual. Their realism, secular tone and lustful probing of human nature, its greed and sexuality, quickly proved influential on a European scale, even though Boccaccio regretted the work's lack of *gravitas* in his later days.

His later writings in Latin, produced under the influence of Petrarch, react heavily against the spirit of the *Decameron*, which nevertheless remained one of the most important works of European literature, admired and copied by scholars and poets from Chaucer to leading Italian literary men of the 16th c.
□ C. Muscetta *Boccaccio* (1972); V. Branca *Boccaccio: the man and his works* (1976)

Boccaccio with Petrarch; from a Flemish copy of *Des cas des nobles hommes et femmes malheureux*.

Boethius at work with his writing tablets, from a 12th-c. manuscript of his *Consolatio Philosophiae*.

Boethius (480–524) Educated in Athens and Alexandria, Boethius had an important effect upon the development of medieval thought. In 510 he held the consulship of Rome under the Ostrogothic King Theodoric the Great, but was later accused of treason and put to death. Whilst in prison he wrote the *Consolatio Philosophiae* ('Consolation of Philosophy') in which he described the pursuit of wisdom and the love of God as the true sources of human happiness. Although he intended to translate the whole corpus of the work of Plato and Aristotle into Latin, this project was never completed. His use of Aristotelian method proved immensely influential in the early Middle Ages. Christian thinkers accepted Boethius as one of their own great teachers, and his work was widely known. Alfred the Great translated the *Consolation* into Anglo-Saxon. It was largely through the influence of Boethius that the Roman scheme of dividing education into the seven liberal arts was adopted as the basis of the medieval system of learning. [*234*]
□ *Boethius: His Life, Thought and Influence* ed. M. Gibson (1981); H. Chadwick *Boethius* (1981)

Bogomils Adherents of a heretical sect which first appeared in Bulgaria in the mid-10th c. and which spread in the 11th c. to Asia Minor and Provence. Owing their origins to Manichaeanism, the Bogomils were dualists who believed in the existence of both a good God, creator of the spirit, and an evil God, creator of the material world. In Bulgaria itself the Bogomils were crushed in 1211, but they survived in Bosnia for almost two centuries after the Tartar invasions. It was only in 1340 that Franciscan missionaries began to preach Catholicism to the Bosnians, and it was not until 1450 that King Thomas required his subjects to accept Orthodox Christianity. The remaining Bogomil adherents then fled to Herzegovina, where many of them became Muslims. *See* ALBIGENSES
□ D. Obolensky *The Bogomils* (1948)

Bohemia Territory which by the early Middle Ages was predominantly populated by a Slavonic people known as Czechs. They were ruled by the Premyslid dynasty *c.*870–1306 who accepted Christianity in the Western form in the 9th c. Relations with neighbouring Slavonic peoples (Moravians and Poles), with Magyars and above all with Germans were uneasy and often turbulent, though by the 13th c. German influence was strong and the Bohemians were accepted as an important political unit within the framework of the Holy Roman Empire. After 1306, on the death of the last ruler of the ancient dynasty, John of Luxembourg, son of the Emperor Henry VII, was chosen as king. The Bohemian kingdom reached its political height under his son Charles IV, Holy Roman Emperor 1346–78, who founded the great university of Prague in 1348 and framed an imperial consitution (the Golden Bull of 1356), which confirmed the king of Bohemia as one of the seven electors. Later medieval Bohemian history is dominated by religious struggles in which national Czech aspirations were intertwined with deep religious passions directed against the wealth and doctrines of the church. The burning of John Hus at the Council of Constance (1415) precipitated a bitter struggle, in the course of which the military genius of the Hussite general Ziska won substantial independence, confirmed by compromise between the moderate Hussites and the Catholics in 1433. *See* WENCESLAS
□ F. Dvornik *The Making of Central Europe* (1949); R. Betts *Essays in Czech History* (1969); J.F.N. Bradley *Czechoslovakia* (1970)

Bohemund I (1052–1111) Prince of Antioch. Eldest son of Robert Guiscard, Norman duke of Apulia and Calabria. Bohemund fought with his father against the Byzantine empire 1081–85. Although

The last Premyslid kings of **Bohemia**; Wenceslas III has the three crowns of Bohemia, Poland and Hungary.

Detail from the 12th-c. bronze doors of Gniezno cathedral showing **Boleslav the Great**.

disinherited on his father's death (1085), Bohemund raised a force and joined the First Crusade in 1096. On 3 June 1098 he was primarily responsible for the capture of Antioch, becoming its first Latin prince. In 1100 he was imprisoned by the amir of Cappadocia and on his release was attacked in 1104 by the Byzantine emperor Alexius Comnenus, who claimed Antioch as a fief of the empire; the Byzantine fleet devastated many of Bohemund's properties in Cilicia. Returning to the West, Bohemund retaliated by attacking the Byzantines in Dalmatia, but was defeated and forced to agree to terms by which he accepted Byzantine overlordship of Antioch.

Boileau, Etienne de (*c.*1205–*c.*70) His family ties were with Orleans where he held the office of provost, but he made his reputation as a lawyer and administrator in the service of St Louis, whom he accompanied on the ill-fated crusade of 1250. It is a measure of his importance that a ransom of 2000 gold *livres* was paid to redeem him from captivity. On his return to France he received royal preferment to the office of provost of Paris, and it was the experience gained in that office which enabled him to write his *Livre des Métiers* ('Book of Crafts'), a source of first importance for the history of 13th-c. industry and its organization, and indeed, for medieval urban development and the craft guilds.
□ R. de Lespinasse and F. Bonnardot *Les Métiers et Corporation de la Ville de Paris* (1879); E. Farel *La Vie quotidienne au temps de St Louis* (1938)

Boleslav I the Great King of Poland 992–1025 Son of Mieszko I, the first Christian prince of Poland, Boleslav succeeded his father in 992. In 996 he conquered

The mission of **St Boniface** to the Frisians and his martyrdom, from the 10th-c. Fulda Sacramentary.

Pomerania and subsequently occupied the Czech city of Cracow. He further increased his influence by his championship of the fugitive Adalbert of Prague (who was later martyred) and by his coronation in the year 1000 at the hands of Emperor Otto III. After Otto's death, Boleslav took further opportunities for the expansion of Poland. He penetrated to the Elbe and occupied much of Bohemia before gaining advantageous peace terms at Bautzen in 1018. Before his death he had also attacked Yaroslav, grand duke of Kiev, whom he routed on the banks of the river Bug, which at that time formed the boundary between Russia and Poland.

Bologna, university of Founded in the 11th c. as the result of a revival of interest in the study of law, the fame of Bologna was so great by the mid-12th c. that the Emperor Frederick I called its doctors of law to Roncaglia to adjudicate in his struggle with the Lombard communes. Like Paris, Bologna was organized into nations, and by 1265 these included students from as far afield as England, Hungary and Poland. Bologna's reputation rested mainly on the work of two men: Irnerius, who in c.1080 divided the study of law from the other arts, and Gratian, who in 1140 unified canon law in his *Decretum* and distinguished it from theology. Honorius III granted the university a measure of self-government in 1218, and later in the century it began the development of a distinguished school of medicine.
□ C.M. Ady *The Bentivoglio of Bologna* (1969)

Bonaventura, St (1221–74) Born at Bagnoreggio near Orvieto, Bonaventura became a Franciscan in 1243, studied under Alexander of Hales at Paris and in 1253 became master of the Franciscan School there. In 1257 he was elected minister-general of the Order. Although Bonaventura upheld many of St Francis' original ideals he rejected the extreme position of the Spirituals who condemned learning in their search for absolute poverty. Between 1266 and 1268 he wrote an exposition of the Rule of St Francis which helped to remould the Order as a whole, but also succeeded in further alienating the Spirituals. Bonaventura played an influential part in the church as a whole. In 1273 he was appointed cardinal-bishop of Albano, whilst in 1274 he also played a leading part in the Council of Lyons which temporarily ended the schism between East and West. A mystical theologian, Bonaventura advocated an emotional approach to the divine mysteries rather than the purely rational method employed by his contemporary Thomas Aquinas. His chief writings include the *Breviloquium*, the *Itinerarium Mentis ad Deum* and a commentary on the Sentences of Peter Lombard.
□ *S. Bonaventura 1274–1974* ed. J.G. Bougerol (1973–74)

Boniface, St (c.675–754) Apostle of the Germans. Born Winfrith of Crediton in Devon, Boniface was educated in Exeter and at Nursling in Hampshire. His first missionary expedition to Frisia in 716 was a failure, but in 719 he received a papal commission to undertake evangelical work east of the Rhine. He was consecrated bishop to the Germans in 722, archbishop in 732 and eventually established a permanent centre to his see at Mainz in 747. Throughout his career he remained in active touch with his homeland which provided him with many missionaries and much material support. In return, Boniface proved a great source of spiritual strength to the English church, encouraging, instructing and admonishing both laity and the spiritual order.

In Germany itself he founded many bishoprics, including sees at Salzburg, Regensburg and Passau in the south, and at Würzburg, Erfurt and Büraburg in the north. Late in life he set up the abbey at Fulda of which he himself became abbot. The Franks supported his missions with military power, and Boniface became a key figure in events which led to ecclesiastical reform inside Frankia in the 740s under Pepin the Short. He supported the deposition of the last Merovingian king and in 751 consecrated Pepin as king of the Franks; indeed, Boniface's role in the mission field, as an active reformer, helped to bring Rome and the new Christian monarchy in Frankia into fruitful partnership. In 754 Boniface set out in a last attempt to convert the Frisians, but on 5 June was martyred at Dokkum with some 50 companions. □ W. Levison *England and the Continent in the Eighth Century* (1946)

Boniface VIII Pope 1294–1303 (b. *c.*1233) Born Benedict Gaetani at Anagni in Italy, he studied law at Bologna before becoming cardinal-deacon in 1281, cardinal-bishop in 1291 and finally pope in 1294. He made substantial contributions to canon law in the *Liber Sextus*, an analysis of the principal ecclesiastical legal developments from 1234 to his own time. He quarrelled with the kings of France and of England over the question of taxation of the clergy, and in his bull *Clericis Laicos* (1296) asserted the principle that such taxation demanded papal assent if it were to be legal. In Rome, and in Italy generally, he became increasingly powerful, defeating his arch-rivals, the Colonna family, in 1298 and proclaiming successfully the first Holy Year in 1300 (commemorated by Giotto's fresco in the church of St John Lateran at Rome). Relations with the French King Philip IV grew increasingly stormy, particularly after the imprisonment of Boniface's friend, Bernard Saisset, bishop of Poitiers, in 1301. Overconfidence led the pope to issue the bull *Unam Sanctam* in 1302, and it is one of the ironies of medieval history that this extreme statement of the case for papal theocratic supremacy in both spiritual and lay matters should be issued at a time when the monarchies of England and France were building strong state systems which involved close control of the temporalities of their respective churches. French reaction was quick and brutal: the pope was captured, roughly handled at Anagni, and died in 1303, largely from the harsh treatment he had received. [*88*] □ T.S.R. Boase *Boniface VIII* (1933)

Books in manuscript Several aspects of manuscripts can be used as evidence for their dates and origins. The most conspicuous of these is the development of handwriting, or palaeography, while archaeological study of the materials, techniques and personnel involved in the production of a manuscript, from quire-formation to decoration, illustration and binding (codicology), is no less valuable, not only for dating and localization, but as a source of insight into the character of particular manuscripts, every one of which is the product of a unique set of circumstances.

In the 5th and 6th c. book production in the West was notable for high standards and high output; and by *c.* 600 the skills with which the lay workshops of *c.* 400 had copied pagan texts for senatorial patrons had been passed on to ecclesiastical scriptoria attached to monasteries or basilicas. Most books were in formal script, usually uncial, but scholars copied texts for themselves in literary cursive. All documents were still on papyrus, but most books were on parchment. The codex, which had been the original form of all Christian books and which had replaced the roll by *c.*400, typically consisted of parchment sheets folded to form quires of eight leaves, in which facing pages matched each other in

Frontispiece to St Ambrose's *Opera Varia*, illustrating how **books** were made, from sharpening the pens to binding the quires.

Books in manuscript: detail from an altarpiece by
Rogier van der Weyden (c.1399-1464), *Magdalene reading*.

appearance and lines were ruled with a hard point.
Text was normally in one or two columns, the
format was often roughly square, and quires were
numbered on the last page. Scribes might begin
paragraphs or pages with an enlarged letter, write
opening lines in red ink and decorate titles with
simple penwork flourishes; drawn and painted
initials originated in 6th-c. Italy. Greek and Latin
illustrated manuscripts of pagan authors (Homer,
Virgil, Terence) and of the Bible (Genesis, Kings,
the Gospels) were produced.

In 7th-c. and 8th-c. scriptoria on the Continent,
standards were often lower, and the old model of
the quire was not consistently followed. Books
became more colourful, if less elegant, due to the
development of the painted initial and titles in painted
capitals. In 7th-c. Insular books, parchment of distinctive preparation was arranged in ten-leaf quires
of primitive execution. Irish scribes never completely
abandoned simple forms of layout and titling, but
their innovative initials, decorated with motifs of
Celtic origin and followed by several letters of
diminishing size, were to influence all Europe until
the 13th c. By c.700 Northumbrian scribes had
developed these initials and display letters to fill

whole pages, adding Germanic animal ornament to
abstract Celtic designs. In the major Anglo-Saxon
scriptoria (e.g., at Canterbury, Wearmouth-Jarrow
and Lindisfarne), where early Italian models were
available, layout, script and titling were also further
developed, and successful copies of late antique
illustration were painted.

During the Carolingian renaissance (c.775–c.850)
books in Caroline minuscule achieved an impressive
synthesis between layout, titling and naturalistic
illustration based on late antique models, and major
initials of Insular (Anglo-Saxon) inspiration. The
magnificence of the liturgical manuscripts made for
Charlemagne (c.800) and Charles the Bald (d.874)
was never surpassed. A revised version of the late
antique quire was introduced at Tours c.830 and was
practically universal until c.1150, although catch-
words replaced quire numbers (c.1000 onwards)
and lead-point replaced hard-point ruling (c.1075
onwards). Books in proto-Gothic minuscule (late
11th to late 12th c. – the last flowering of the
monastic scriptoria) were usually taller than before
and were conspicuous for their excellent polychrome
initials and display script. Historiated major initials
often replaced miniatures as the vehicle for illustration.

After c.1200 books were produced almost entirely
in workshops associated either with universities
(Paris, Bologna, Oxford) or with centres of royal or
mercantile patronage (Paris, London, Bruges,
Cologne, Milan). Materials, textual exemplars and
writing were the province of stationers, decoration
and illustration, of illuminators; the work was sub-
divided between specialists in writing, gilding,
painting and binding. Since every stage was carefully priced, quality and elaboration varied widely
between illuminated books for royal patrons, who
sometimes paid retainers to the best artists, and
textbooks for university students or popular texts
in the vernaculars copied locally by a chaplain or
notary. After c.1175 leaves were ruled on
both sides in lead point and later in ink, and the
sheets in a quire began to be numbered c.1275.
Paper, a Chinese invention which reached the Arabs
during the 8th c., was used by the Greeks as early as
the 9th c. and began to be manufactured in Italy
c.1230. In the West, it was originally used only for
letters, notarial registers and account books, but
cheaper books on paper, especially in the vernaculars,
were common enough throughout the 15th c.

In Italy, specifically humanistic book production
began c.1350 with scholars like Petrarch copying
texts for their own use, and many 15th-c. humanists
followed his example. But after c.1440 the writing
and illumination of the luxurious volumes required
by rulers and churchmen for their libraries of classical
and humanistic texts were organized either by

stationers, like Vespasiano da Bisticci in Florence, or by librarians, as in Rome and Naples. Poggio Bracciolini (*c.*1400) copied from 12th-c. Italian models not only *litera antiqua*, but hard-point ruling and white vine decoration, all of which spread from Florence to other centres in Italy. Most humanistic illumination, and especially the originally Paduan style which dominated in Rome, differed considerably from the late Gothic decoration of contemporary liturgical books. After *c.*1480, when the classical market had been swamped by printed editions, the remaining humanistic scribes had to rely on rare special commissions or on posts as writing masters. *See* HANDWRITING; LIBRARIES; MANUSCRIPT ILLUMINATION; MANUSCRIPT STUDIES   TJB
□ *Codicologica* ed. A. Gruys and J.P. Gumbert (1976–80); S. Hindman and J.D. Farquhar *Pen to press* (1977); B. Bischoff *Paläographie des Römischen Altertums und des Abendländischen Mittelalters* (1979)

Books of Hours In many ways the most impressive written documents of the later Middle Ages, Books of Hours were essentially personal prayer-books commissioned by, and produced for the aristocratic laity by the leading calligraphers and book illuminators of the age. They were popular and often very beautiful, with illustrations that provide much information, not only of the religious, but also of the social life of the day. Their basic function was to give a series of prayers suitable for the canonical hours into which the day was divided. They invariably started with a calendar and normally included extracts from the divine offices, popular prayers to the Virgin, the Hours of the Virgin, penitential psalms and the office for the dead. The French and Burgundian courts were particularly noted for their patronage of artists engaged in this special type of book production.
□ J. Harthan *Books of Hours and their Owners* (1977)

Borgia family Family of Spanish origin who played an important part in the politics of Italy. In 1455 Alfonso Borgia, bishop of Valencia, became Pope Calixtus III, and the family moved to Rome. He greatly favoured his relatives, especially his nephew Rodrigo Borgia whom he created a cardinal. In 1492 Rodrigo himself was elected as Pope Alexander VI, and spent much of his pontificate consolidating the power of his own family. In 1496 he made his son Giovanni (d. 1497) duke of Benevento; he created his second son Cesare (b. 1476) a cardinal in 1493. In 1498 Cesare was released from his vows, married a French princess and then proceeded to conquer the Romagna and Umbria. He was totally unscrupulous; in order to protect his northern frontiers, he murdered the husband of his sister Lucrezia and married her to the future duke of Ferrara. He also disposed of

Books of Hours: January, from the *Très Riches Heures* of the Duc de Berry, seen here seated at table.

Cardinal Paolo Orsini and the duke of Gravina who were resisting his rule in Urbino. After his father's death in 1503 Cesare was banished from Rome by Pope Julius II and imprisoned in Spain, but he escaped and died fighting in Castile (1507).
□ M. Mallett *The Borgias* (1969)

Boron (Borron), Robert de Writer who inspired a vast Grail-Lancelot cycle of Arthurian romance and completed its Christianization by associating it with biblical history. It is not known whether he completed his intended *Grant Estoire dou Graal*; only two fragments survive, his *Verse Joseph* and *Merlin*. Prose versions of these, the *Didot-Perceval*, the *Mort Artu*, the Vulgate or Walter Map cycle and the Pseudo-Robert cycle have been attributed to him, but are most likely by later redactors drawing upon his work. He was probably from Boron (Burgundy) and of clerical background. He mentions reading his work to Gautier de Montbéliard who left on crusade (1202), and his works were probably produced at Montbéliard (Burgundy) *c.* 1200. *See* HOLY GRAIL
□ W.A. Nitze, 'Messire Robert de Boron: Enquiry and Summary', *Speculum* 28 (1953); L. Charvet *Des Vaus d'Avalon à la Queste du Graal* (1967)

Bosnia

Bosnia Originally part of Serbia, Bosnia became an independent political entity in 960. In the 12th c. Bosnia was overrun by the Hungarians and became officially converted to Latin Christianity under its bans Kulin Col (*c.* 1204) and Ninoslav (d.1250). Bogomil heretics, however, continued to be numerous in Bosnia until the 15th c., when many of them were converted to Islam after the country came under the control of the Turks. It was not until 1463 that Bosnia officially became a Turkish province.
□ S. Seton-Watson *A Short History of the Yugo-Slavs* (1938)

Botticelli, Sandro (1445–1510) Florentine painter. Son of a leather tanner, he was first apprenticed to a goldsmith before studying art under Fra Filippo Lippi. In 1470 he began to work independently, participating in the decoration of the Palazzo dell'Arte in the Mercanzia and executing several frescoes in the Sistine Chapel (1481). His major work was in Florence, where he was patronized by the Medici family; it was for them that he executed his two most famous works: the *Primavera* and the *Birth of Venus*. In the 1490s he became a follower of Savonarola, and henceforward his paintings were largely austere and religious in their subject matter.
□ R. Lightbown *Sandro Botticelli* (1978)

Bouvines, battle of (27 July 1214) Battle in which Philip II of France won a decisive victory against a coalition of the forces of John of England and the Holy Roman Emperor Otto IV. The imperial plan of campaign failed when King John, who was supposed to stir up revolt against Philip in western France while Otto and his allies attacked from the north, was defeated at La Roche-aux-Moines near Angers on 2 July 1214. Using this victory, Philip turned the whole might of his army against Otto and won a decisive victory at Bouvines in Flanders. The victory greatly strengthened Philip II, whilst both John of England and Otto IV faced severe internal troubles at home as a result of their defeat. Bouvines is taken as a symbol of the emergence of France as the dominant power in 13th-c. Europe.
□ G. Duby *Le Dimanche de Bouvines* (1973)

Bracciolini, Poggio (1380–1459) Renaissance humanist and calligrapher. Although he served as secretary to the papal curia in 1415 and again in 1423, Bracciolini spent many of his formative years visiting monastic libraries all over Europe in search of the lost works of ancient Roman authors. It was through the study of these works, many of which had survived until Bracciolini's day in 9th-c. copies, that he was led to invent the humanistic style of writing, based upon Carolingian script.

Bracciolini's most important works, which include *De Avaritia* (1428–29), *De Varietate Fortunae* (1431–

Detail of a **bracteate** of silver gilt from Gotland (7th to 9th c.).

48) and *De Nobilitate* (1440), stand out from other moralistic writings of the day because of the author's gift for accurate presentation of human character and conversation. During the later years of his life Bracciolini was less able to devote time to intellectual pursuits because of his involvement in administrative affairs as chancellor of the city of Florence (from 1453).
□ E. Walser *Poggius Florentinus* (1914)

Bracteate (Latin *bractea*, 'leaf') Name given by scholars since the 17th c. to the thin, uniface pennies struck in many parts of northern Germany and some neighbouring lands (Scandinavia, much of Central and Eastern Europe) from the mid-12th c. to the end of the 13th c. Later uniface pennies of the same regions, which are smaller in diameter and of high relief, are termed *Hohlpfennige* ('hollow pennies').

Bracton, Henry of (d. 1268) A royal judge from 1245, Bracton had an active career as a busy practical lawyer, serving on the King's Bench, working as a justice in the south-western shires, and in the last years of his life acting as one of a commission empowered to hear the complaints of the disinherited after the de Montfort rebellion. He also proved to be one of the outstanding legal thinkers of his age, and his treatise *De Legibus et Consuetudinibus Angliae*, written in the 1250s, became a standard and author-

itative work for lawyers of the later Middle Ages. His method of classification and analysis was undoubtedly influenced by Roman law, but the substance of his treatise, with emphasis on case law and precedent, embodied the essence of English common law. At the higher constitutional level, he did not follow the arbitrary principles found in Justinian's *Code* by, for example, his contemporary French colleagues, but rather held – as he stated in a famous dictum – that the king was under law: 'The king himself ought not to be under man but under God and the law, because the law made the king.'
□ *Bracton on the Laws and Customs of England* trans. S.E. Thorne (1977)

Brethren of the Common Life Religious society founded by Gerhard Groote (1340–84) which was first established at Deventer in the Netherlands. Although the Brethren lived a common life dedicated to God, they had no Rule and did not take vows. Since such religious freedom was regarded with suspicion and hostility by the clergy, Groote's followers later also founded houses of Augustinian canons, beginning with the priory of Windesheim in 1387, where the brothers lived according to a Rule of preaching and poverty. Although they occasionally founded schools, as at Utrecht and Liège, the Brethren were primarily engaged in pastoral work and in the copying of manuscripts for sale. The order was never particularly popular, however, and never spread outside the Netherlands and the area of northern Germany around Cologne. The strong mystical element attracted some of the best minds of the period, such as Thomas à Kempis and Nicholas of Cusa, and they successfully sustained the orthodoxy of their position at the Council of Constance in spite of strong opposition. Sometimes known as the Brethren of Modern Devotion, they survived as a limited but effective group well into the 16th c.
□ A. Hyma *The Christian Renaissance: A History of the Devotio Moderna* (1965)

Brethren of the Free Spirit Sect of mystical thinkers who first appeared in Swabia, the Rhineland and the Netherlands in the 13th c. Their beliefs were, at least in part, the result of an attempt to reconcile the works of Aristotle with Christian theology, which led them to stress the superiority of the human will above all else and to live in accordance with what they termed the 'free spirit' of piety. They were continually pursued by the Inquisition, but continued to exist until the 16th c.
□ R.E. Lerner *The Heresy of the Free Spirit* (1972)

Brétigny, Treaty of (1360) France suffered greatly in the early stages of the Hundred Years' War from disastrous military defeats at the hands of the English (Crécy 1346, Poitiers 1356), compounded by the ravages of the Black Death, constitutional turbulence and the pillaging of the Free Companies. King John II the Good had been captured at Poitiers, but peace was not finally settled until a treaty was negotiated at Brétigny near Chartres in May 1360 and sealed at Calais on 24 October. King John was freed from his English captivity, arrangements were made for a ransom of three million gold crowns to be paid in instalments, and a much enlarged duchy of Aquitaine was ceded to Edward III in full sovereignty, together with Calais and Ponthieu. In return Edward abandoned his claim to the French throne. The treaty marked a high point in English fortunes in the Hundred Years' War, though legal loopholes still remained which precluded a settlement of basic constitutional issues over sovereignty. King John chivalrously returned to England when the terms of his release were not fulfilled, dying in captivity in 1364.
□ E. Perroy *The Hundred Years' War* (1959)

Brian Borumha King of Ireland c.1005–14 (b.941) In 976 he became king of Thomond in place of his murdered brother Mahon, and in 978 king of Munster with his principal seats at Tara and Cashel. During the next 20 years he forced the tribes of Munster and Cashel to submit to him and defeated the Danes in Co. Dublin. So great was his success, that c.1005 he forced Malachy, chief king of Ireland, to recognize his sovereignty. In 1014 he again took arms against the Danes, but was killed at the battle of Clontarf on 23 April.

Bridget (Brigit), St (d. c.525) Born of humble parents at Vinmeras near Kildare, she was baptized by St Patrick and became a nun at an early age. Later, she is said to have founded the monastery of Kildare and thus to have contributed substantially to the spread of Christianity in Ireland. Little else is known of her life which is shrouded in legend, but her cult was certainly popular, being second only to that of St Patrick himself. Her Life was translated into Old French, Middle English and German, and in England and Wales many churches, including St Bride's, Fleet Street (London), were dedicated in her honour. *See* CELTIC CHURCHES
□ K. Hughes *Early Christian Ireland* (1972)

Brittany Until the 6th c. Brittany was known as Armorica, but on account of migration from Britain during the preceding two centuries, it became known as *Britannia Minor* or Little Britain. Its population in the early Middle Ages was almost entirely Celtic, speaking a language closely related to Cornish and Welsh; by the 9th c. the language boundary ran

through the east of the peninsula (excluding Rennes and Nantes). The Frankish kings appeared to control much of east Brittany during the 6th, 7th and early 8th c. The Carolingians made a concerted effort to conquer Brittany completely, mounting many expeditions between 753 and 824. Reaction led by the Breton Nominoe (who defeated Charles the Bald in 845) and his successors was further complicated by Viking attacks in the 860s, and resulted in the development of a distinct political identity in Brittany, in the course of which its rulers temporarily adopted royal titles. A separate archbishopric for Brittany was set up at Dol. From the mid-10th c. a single duchy was effectively established with a continuous history throughout the Middle Ages, and its fortunes were closely intermeshed with Normandy and with its ultimate overlords, the Capetian kings.
□ L. Fleuriot *Les Origines de la Brétagne* (1980)

Brunelleschi, Filippo (1377–1446) Florentine artist and outstandingly able architect. His early training as a metal-worker led him in 1401 to enter a competition to design the Baptistery doors in Florence (won by Lorenzo Ghiberti), but his career thereafter turned solidly to architecture, where his sense of proportion, concern with space and perspective, and grasp of mathematical and scientific laws of construction enabled him to create, adorn or initiate the buildings which still contribute so much to the grace and dignity of his native city: the Innocenti Hospital, the Old Sacristy at S. Lorenzo, the basilican churches of S. Lorenzo and S. Spirito, and above all the magnificent cupola of the cathedral. The influence of Rome (which he is said by his biographer Manetti to have visited in company with Donatello) was great, but attention has been drawn more recently to the equal, or even more potent influence of Ravenna and Byzantium.
□ E. Battisti *Brunelleschi* (1981)

Bruno, St (d. 965) Archbishop of Cologne from 953. Youngest son of Henry the Fowler (919–36), brother of Otto the Great and also brother-in-law to both the Carolingian king Lothar I, king of France 954–86, and the powerful ancestor of the Capetians, Hugh the Great, duke of the Franks 923–56. Bruno played a dominant part in European politics, as royal arch-chancellor from 950, as duke of Lorraine from 955 and as supporter of the move towards the imperial coronation of his brother Otto at Rome in 962. He left a reputation as a powerful spiritual and intellectual leader; he did much to create the so-called Ottonian renaissance and was a prominent church reformer, notably of the monastic observance at Lorsch and Corvey. In French politics he also played a stabilizing role, and his government of the duchy of Lorraine helped to ensure its continued role as an integral part of the German kingdom, while its future administration was foreshadowed by Bruno's delegation of authority to two princes, Godfrey in Lower Lorraine and Frederick in Upper Lorraine.

Bruno, St (*c*. 1030–1101) Founder of the Carthusian Order. Educated at Rheims and Cologne, he became a canon of the cathedral in Cologne before being appointed lecturer in theology and grammar at Rheims in 1052. He later became chancellor of the diocese of Rheims, but relinquished his authority in order to live an eremitical life. He originally joined the followers of Robert of Molesme, but subsequently moved to the diocese of Grenoble where Bishop Hugh gave them the forested, mountainous land of La Chartreuse. In 1084, Bruno and his companions here built their cells and an oratory in which to live a life of solitude, poverty and austerity. In 1090 he was summoned to Rome by his former pupil, Urban II, to advise him in matters of ecclesiastical reform. Refusing the archbishopric of Reggio, he died at La Torre, which he had founded in Calabria along similar lines to the Grande Chartreuse after his departure from Rome.
□ A. Ravier *Saint Bruno* (1967)

Bulgaria In origin the Bulgarians were a non-Slavonic people of Asiatic stock who did not acquire full political organization until the 9th c., although by that time they were so heavily mixed with Slavs and other inhabitants that they constituted a virtually new ethnic grouping with predominantly Slav language and customs. Their migration from the Volga to the Balkans had started as early as the 5th c., reaching a peak in the 7th c. In 864, under their leader or khan Boris I (852–89), they were converted to Eastern Orthodox Christianity. There followed a period of expansion and further assimilation under Simeon I (893–927) when, with the title of tsar (Caesar), he ruled his 'empire of the Greeks and Bulgarians' which stretched from the Adriatic to the Aegean and the Black Sea. Politically the Bulgarians remained a severe threat to the Byzantine empire until their savage defeat at the hands of the Emperor Basil the Bulgar Slayer in 1014. A second powerful Bulgarian empire came into being in the late 12th c. but, weakened by pressures from all sides and the assertion of independence by lesser princes, the Bulgarians were forced into subordination by the Tartars, the Serbs and finally, in the last decade of the 14th c., by the Ottoman Turks. *See* SAMUEL
□ S. Runciman *The First Bulgarian Empire* (1930); D.M. Lang *The Bulgarians* (1976); J.V. Fine Jr. *The Early Medieval Balkans* (1983)

The arms of the last dukes of **Burgundy** in the 15th-c. Flemish Tapestry of a Thousand Flowers.

Burchard Bishop of Worms 1000–25 Ecclesiastical reformer who in 1012 published the *Decretum*, which contained excerpts from canon law classified by subject matter. This was a great improvement upon earlier collections of canon law which had adopted a chronological approach. His work on ecclesiastical jurisdiction was regarded as authoritative in the West for the best part of a century and was only slowly replaced with the revival of Roman law and the writings of men such as Ivo of Chartres and, ultimately, of Gratian.
□ A.M. Koeniger *Burchard von Worms und die deutsche Kirche seiner Zeit 1000–1025* (1905)

Burgundy The first kingdom of Burgundy was created in the 5th c. in the valleys of the Saône and the Rhone by the Burgundii, a Germanic people whose traditional homeland lay on the Baltic shores and the island of Bornholm. Legends of their movements and of their conflict with the Huns in the chaotic years of the mid-5th c. form the basis of the greatest German epic poem of the central Middle Ages, the *Nibelungenlied*. Historically they passed under the control of the Franks in the early 6th c., though preserving a measure of legal and ethnic identity.

From the disruption of the Carolingian empire in the 9th c., two political units emerged: the kingdom of Burgundy, which passed after 1032 into imperial hands, and the duchy of Burgundy which became part of the kingdom of France and was ruled by a cadet branch of the Capetians (1031–1361). The kingdom formed a buffer between France and Italy, and consisted essentially of the lower Rhone valley and territories to the east, including Lyons, Vienne, Arles and the county of Provence to the Mediterranean. The duchy lay to the east of the Saône with important centres at Dijon and Autun, and made greatest impact on medieval civilization through its monastic life in the 11th c. and 12th c.; heavily influenced by Cluny, it was the home of Vézelay and Cîteaux.

The territorial position was further complicated in the 12th c. by the emergence into virtual independence (after 1127) of Cisjurane Burgundy, initially under the counts of Mâcon, the so-called Franche-Comté, Besançon and the rich lands between the northern course of the Saône and the Doubs. In the 14th c. the duchy and the county became united (1384) when Philip the Bold, duke of Burgundy, married Margaret of Flanders, heiress to the Franche-Comté, thereby initiating a century of Burgundian greatness. The dukes sought English allies in their efforts to avoid French control, and under Philip the Good (1419–67) and Charles the Bold (1467–77) created a powerful political unit along the so-called fault line of Western Europe dividing the French and the Germans. A colourful revival of learning, art and civilization took place within this greater Burgundy of the 15th c. *See* MARY OF BURGUNDY
□ J. Calmette *The Golden Age of Burgundy* (1962); R. Vaughan *Valois Burgundy* (1975)

Burial customs During the Middle Ages various methods of disposing of the dead were used at different times and in different places. The Persians, for example, exposed the corpses of their dead in the open air to be devoured by birds of prey, but in Europe the dead were cremated or buried. In the pre-Christian era cremation was much favoured, especially among the Angles, Saxons and Scandinavians, although the Jutes followed the Roman example of burying their dead. Once Christianity had taken root, however, cremation was abandoned in favour of burial, so that the dead might have bodies to which they could return on the Day of Judgement. Another change brought about by the advent of Christianity was that the dead were no longer buried with grave goods such as weaponry, jewellery and coinage for use in the after-life. In the central Middle Ages stone coffins, often with elaborately carved lids, were used at least for the burial of the rich, but by the end of the Middle Ages wooden coffins had become the rule. Occasionally the heart or intestines of important people were buried separately from the rest of their bodies.

Flemish miniature from the Hours of Philippe le Bon (mid-15th c.): a corpse is prepared for **burial**.

The most elaborate of known medieval burial customs were associated with ship burials, such as the 7th-c. example of the great mound in the cemetery at Sutton Hoo – with its brilliant array of precious grave-goods in gold, silver and garnet – or the superb 9th-c. Norwegian interments at Gokstad and Oseberg.
□ A. Meaney *Early Anglo-Saxon Burial Sites* (1964); T.S.R. Boase *Death in the Middle Ages* (1972)

Buridan, John (*c.*1297-after 1358) A pupil of William of Ockham at Paris, he became rector of the university there in 1327 and was still active as a philosopher and teacher in 1358. He represented an extreme nominalist position in the philosophical world, and his commentaries on logic and on Aristotelian thought in general, remained influential throughout the late medieval and early modern period. He is best remembered for his independent and sceptical treatment of the question of free will, which led logically to the limitation of such freedom to a mere power to suspend the deliberative process. The simile attributed to him likened free will to an ass, unable to act and dying of hunger because placed between two equidistant pastures or bundles of hay. This image (Buridan's ass) is not found in his surviving written work and is assumed to be either a favourite oral teaching device on his part, or a parody of his style put about by his philosophic opponents.
□ G. Leff *Paris and Oxford Universities in the Thirteenth and Fourteenth Centuries* (1968)

Byzantium Ancient Greek city on the Bosphorus, transformed into the city of Constantinople by Constantine the Great in 330. It became the New Rome, second capital of the Roman empire, the centre and propagator of what is known as Byzantine civilization. Its culture was an amalgam of Greek, Roman and Christian; its official language was Greek, though its citizens called themselves Romans. Their law was Roman law, periodically revised and adapted, and their lives were permeated by the Christian faith in its Orthodox form.

The conversion of Constantine to Christianity, and his foundation of Constantinople determined the future of the eastern part of the Roman empire. When the western part was overrun by barbarians in the 5th c., the New Rome gained still greater importance as seat of the emperor and of its bishop, the patriarch of Constantinople. It was from there in the 6th c. that Justinian directed the reconquest of North Africa, Italy and Spain, with some limited success. But in the 7th c. the Mediterranean world was permanently affected by the arrival of the Arabs and the Slavs. The Arabs captured the richest provinces of Byzantium in the East; the Slavs settled in the Balkans and in Greece, driving a wedge down the middle of the ancient Roman world. Constantinople and its remaining territories were impoverished and cut off from the West; their survival depended on defence.

The emperors of the 7th c. and 8th c., notably Heraclius and Leo III, divided the provinces into 'themes' or military zones, each under its own commander. The local peasant farmers provided and equipped the soldiers in return for an inalienable right to their land. The earlier social and economic patterns were thus radically changed. It was the armies of the themes that ensured survival, driving back the Slavs in Europe and the Arabs in Asia Minor.

Missionaries went out among the Slavs and Russians to spread the gospel of Orthodox Christianity – and with it, Byzantine culture, art and literacy. A new puritanism was reflected in the Iconoclast movement initiated by Leo III, who decreed that true religion had no need of visual aids. His policy provoked bitter conflict, but when the battle for survival had been won, tradition reasserted itself. Iconoclasm also deepened the rift between eastern and western Christians, for the pope declared it to be heretical. In 800 he crowned an emperor of his own in the person of Charlemagne.

The golden age of Byzantium lasted from about 850 to 1050. The empire once again extended from south Italy to Syria and Armenia. It had a powerful army and navy, and a buoyant monetary economy based on its gold coinage. The victorious dynasty of the 'Macedonian' emperors, beginning with Basil I in 867, reinforced the myth of its divinely ordained superiority and permanence. They commissioned

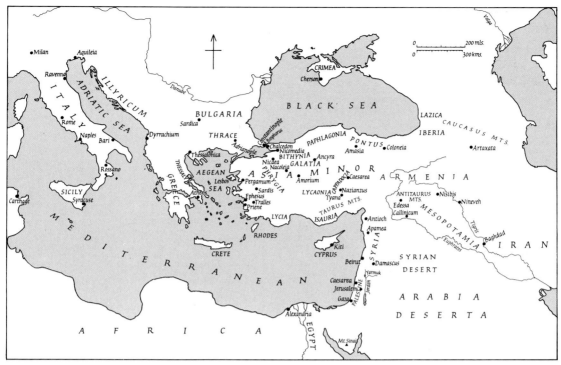

Chief cities and provinces of the eastern Mediterranean during the early **Byzantium** period.

Byzantium: plan of Constantinople from an Italian manuscript of 1422. S. Sophia is clearly visible.

some of the finest products of Byzantine art and architecture; learning and literature flourished under the patronage of such men as the Patriarch Photius and the Emperor Constantine VII Porphyrogenitus. The soldier-emperors, Nicephoras II Phocas and John I Tzimisces, carried the frontiers further east than ever before. Basil II settled the long-standing problem of his northern neighbours by ruthlessly annexing Bulgaria. But decline set in shortly after his death in 1025; the theme system was undermined by the growth of a new class of hereditary land-owning aristocrats able to buy out the free peasant farmers, and centralized authority began to break down. In 1071 the Seljuk Turks defeated the Byzantine army at Manzikert in Armenia and advanced into Asia Minor. In the same year the Normans conquered the last Byzantine possession in south Italy.

The decline of Byzantium coincided with the revival of Western Europe. Westerners came to the East first as pilgrims to the Holy Land, and then as crusaders. Their presence and actions strengthened Byzantine prejudice against them. The schism between the churches of Rome and Constantinople, dramatically announced in 1054, was a symptom of a much deeper ideological divergence. Venetian merchants who followed the crusaders acquired an appetite for the wealth of Byzantium. In 1204 they satisfied it through the Fourth Crusade, which found (or lost) its way to Constantinople.

For a while the New Rome and much of its

territory were under alien, Latin management. Byzantium never fully recovered from the shock of the Fourth Crusade. The Latins were expelled from Constantinople in 1261, and a fragmented empire lived on for almost 200 years. In the 14th c. it produced a remarkable renaissance of art, scholarship and the monastic life. But its structure, economy and defences had been shattered; it found no strength to resist the new and vigorous force of the Ottoman Turks when they broke into Asia Minor. Appeals for help from the West evoked little response; the popes would not come to the rescue of Christians who were in schism from Rome. In 1439, at the Council of Florence, the emperor sank his pride, and a union of the Greek and Roman churches was proclaimed. Most of his subjects denounced it as a betrayal of their Orthodox faith, however, and it came too late, for the Turks had already conquered most of Eastern Europe. Constantinople was isolated. On 29 May 1453, after a long and heroic resistance, the walls of the city which had for a thousand years defended the eastern flank of Christendom were broken by the new technology of heavy artillery. Byzantine Constantinople became Turkish Istanbul, capital of the Ottoman empire. *See* CHURCH, EASTERN ORTHODOX; DUCAS DYNASTY; ISAURIAN DYNASTY; NICAEA, EMPIRE OF; PALAEOLOGI; TREBIZOND, EMPIRE OF   DN

□ A.A. Vasiliev *History of the Byzantine Empire* (1952); G. Ostrogorsky *History of the Byzantine State* (1968) D.M. Nicol *The Last Centuries of Byzantium 1261–1453* (1972); D. Obolensky *The Byzantine Commonwealth* (1974); R. Browning *The Byzantine Empire* (1980); C. Mango *Byzantium, the Empire of New Rome* (1980); M. Angold *The Byzantine Empire 1025–1204* (1984)

C

Cade, Jack (d. 1450) Of Irish birth, Cade settled in Kent after serving as a soldier in France in the later stages of the Hundred Years' War. He emerged as the head of a rebellion in the summer of 1450, and led the rebels into London on 4 July, securing the execution of James Fiennes, Baron Saye and Sele and the sheriff of Kent, William Crowmer. Cade then withdrew to Southwark, and on 6 July was prevented from re-entering London by the citizens. Peace was arranged by the archbishop of York and the bishop of Winchester, and Cade was pardoned, but continued to lead the rebels. They broke open Southwark jail and attempted to capture Queenborough Castle. Cade was wounded and captured

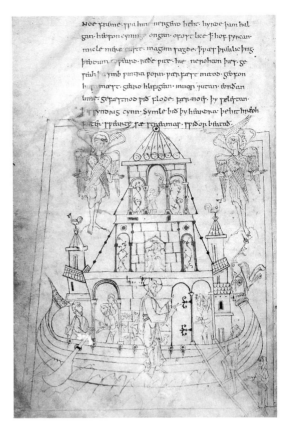

A drawing of Noah's Ark from the so-called **Caedmon** manuscript.

on 12 July, but died before standing trial. His rebellion had little lasting effect, but it kept alive the tradition of agrarian discontent and helped to focus attention on elements of misgovernment at the royal court.

□ R.A. Griffiths *The Reign of Henry VI* (1981)

Caedmon (d. *c*.680) Bede, in his *Ecclesiastical History of the English People*, gives a moving account of Caedmon, the first English poet known to us by name. He tells how Caedmon, a humble servant on the estates of the abbess of Whitby, was so ashamed of his lack of ability in verse and music that he would steal away from company when the harp was passed around, until one night, by the intercession of a divine vision which came to him when he was asleep in the stables, the gift of poetry was passed on to him, and he found himself able to transmit passages from scripture and religious writings into melodious verse. Abbess Hild received him as a brother in the monastery, and Bede preserves a fragment of the poem that came to him in his vision, which is enough to suggest the existence of a sophisticated tradition of alliterative poetry.

□ M. Alexander *The Earliest English Poems* (1977)

Caesaropapism Theory of government by which the exercise of royal and sacerdotal powers are combined in a single lay ruler. The idea grew from the concept of the classical Roman emperor as head of both church and state, since he was worshipped as a deity. The first Christian emperor, Constantine (306–37), attempted to control the church by laying down the tenets of religion to be observed by his subjects, and by personally appointing and dismissing church officials. Despite the promulgations of the Council of Chalcedon (451), this policy was continued by the emperors Zeno (474–91) and Justinian. Although during the Middle Ages papal authority was largely accepted in the West, the Byzantine emperors continued to exercise a dual role as head of church and state, and it was this which was partly responsible for the breach with the Roman church.

Calatrava, Order of Oldest of the military orders of medieval Spain, Calatrava combined the monastic and chivalric ideals on the pattern established in the 12th c. by the Templars and Hospitallers. The Order was founded in 1158 by Abbot Raymond of Fitero, whose monks undertook the defence of the town of Calatrava against the Almohads. In 1164 the Order was recognized by the pope and formally affiliated to the Cistercian Order, whose Rule it

Tree-pruning scene: **calendar** entry for part of March and April in a breviary of Queen Isabella of Spain.

adopted. When Alcantara and other military orders were founded, the masters of Calatrava were given rights as their visitors. In the 14th c. the seat of the Order was established at Almagro, and at its peak, the Order owned some 350 towns and villages with 200,000 inhabitants. By the 15th c. its functions and membership had greatly changed; it was an association of nobles, involved in politics, and in 1489, therefore, the Catholic Monarchs annexed the mastership to the crown.

□ J.F. O'Callaghan *The Spanish Military Order of Calatrava and its Affiliates: Collected Studies* (1975)

Calendars The numerous medieval methods of calculating dates rendered calendars particularly important. Many liturgical manuscripts were prefixed by a calendar, often following the usage of a particular centre, and the inclusion within these of specific local saints' days often assists in localizing such works. Calendars also occurred within official documents (as in the English Black Book of the Exchequer); in private, devotional works; and in products for university use. Much of the community therefore possessed the means of chronological assessment, although practices varied.

The Middle Ages inherited the Roman Julian (Old Style) calendar, used until the introduction of the Gregorian (New Style) calendar by Pope Gregory XIII in 1582, and for even longer in some areas. The Julian calendar, introduced by Julius Caesar in 45 BC, contained a 365-day year, with an extra day every fourth year to rectify the discrepancy between the calendar year and the solar year (calculated as 365¼ days), 24 February being doubled in an *annus bissextilis* every fourth year from AD 4. The year was divided into 12 months, each containing periods of Kalends, Nones and Ides (the days after the Ides being reckoned backwards from the next Kalends); the actual days of the Kalends, Nones and Ides were sometimes excluded from calculations. *Dies Aegyptiacae* also occurred, representing unlucky days. These Roman days were commonly used, but were in competition from an early date with the modern system of reckoning days of the month, and with dating by reference to church feasts and the ecclesiastical division of the year into weeks. Dating from saints' days and feasts was obviously popular within the church and was frequently used by chroniclers, but only from the 13th c. was this usual in letters and documents. They also specified fairs, rent days and similar occasions. Another method of counting days was the 'custom of Bologna' (*consuetudo Boloniensis*), a largely notarial system indicating the day by its position in the first 16 (15 in 30-day months) or last 15 days of the month.

The historical year begins on 1 January, as did the

Roman civil year which was used until the 7th c., but its pagan associations led to the formulation of a Christian year (*annus gratis* or *annus domini*). This year arose from the Dionysian Easter Table, compiled *c.*525, which calculated from the Incarnation, AD 1. This was used by Bede and was soon adopted by every Western European Christian country except Spain. Either Christmas, the Annunciation or Easter was used to determine at what point of the calendar year the year of grace began. Christmas was used theoretically by Bede and became popular, being used in the Empire until the second quarter of the 13th c., by the papacy (962–1098), by the English royalty until the Plantagenets, in ordinary letters (pre-12th c.) and by the Benedictines. The Annunciation (Lady Day, 25 March, calculated from the preceding 25 March) was adopted in late 9th-c. Arles, spreading to Burgundy and northern Italy, and used by the papal chancery until *c.*1145. It survived in Pisa until 1750, termed *calculus Pisanus*. The use of 25 March, calculated from Christmas, as the starting point was possibly due ultimately to Cluniac influence, and was adopted by the Cistercians. Rivalry with Pisa led to its adoption by Florence (*calculus Florentinus*). It spread to France and the papal chancery (after 1098) and persisted in England from the late 12th c. until 1752 (termed *secundum consuetudinem* or *secundum cursum et computationem ecclesiae Anglicanae*). Reckoning from Easter (*mos Gallicanus*) was introduced by Philip Augustus, but was never popular. Germany sporadically restored the 1 January reckoning.

Other types of year were often used with, or instead of, the year of grace. One method was the Indiction, originally a civil reckoning, which computed from AD 312 in 15-year cycles. There were three opening dates: (1) the Greek or Constantinopolitan Indiction, beginning 1 September and used by the papacy until 1087; (2) the Bedan, Caesarean or Imperial Indiction (Indiction of Constantine), beginning 24 September, usual in England and adopted by the papacy under Alexander III; (3) the Roman or Pontifical Indiction, beginning 25 December, or occasionally 1 January, sporadically used by the papacy and elsewhere. Indictions simply showed the year's place in an unspecified 15-year cycle; they were used for formal privileges and legal documents until relegated to notarial use in the late 13th c. (To find the year's Indiction number subtract 312 from the year of grace and divide by 15.) The commencement of the Indiction was occasionally used to begin the year of grace (e.g., Bede's *Ecclesiastical History*). Pontifical and regnal years appeared in official documents and related to the person within whose jurisdiction they were issued. Other years occurred, such as the English Exchequer's financial year (Michaelmas, 29 September, to Michaelmas). Spain, Portugal and south-west Gaul retained their own Spanish Era, which began on 1 January 38 BC, used in some areas until the 15th c. (To find the equivalent year of grace subtract 38.)

The importance of calculating moveable feasts occasioned several devices within the calendar, rendering it 'perpetual' (continually functional). The Golden Number (*numerus aureus, cyclus decemnovennalis*) calculated the date of the Paschal moon. It employed cycles of 19 years from 1 January 1 BC, the number for each year (1–19) being the Golden Number. (To find this, add 1 to the year of grace, divide by 19 and the remainder will equal the Golden Number, unless it equals 0, when it will be 19.) The Epact (*epacta lunaris*) established the relationship between the solar year and the phase of the moon on 22 March, the earliest Easter date. (To find the Epact number divide the year of grace by 19, multiply by 11 and divide by 30.) The Dominical letter (*littera dominicalis*) determined Easter by establishing the sequence of weekdays following the Paschal full moon. The letters A–G indicated a seven-day cycle from 1 January; the year's Dominical letter was that of its first Sunday (if Sunday fell on 4 January the letter was D.) Leap years had two letters, one before and one after 28 February. Concurrents (*concurrentes septimanae*) represented the number of days between the last Sunday in the preceding year and 1 January. They served the same purpose as Dominical letters and therefore correspond.

Calendars were often illustrated, the most popular schemes, both of classical origin, being the labours of the months (occupational calendars) and the zodiacal signs. Specialist schemes included astronomical and medical calendars. Calendar iconography also occurred in other media, such as stone and stained glass. *See* EASTER, DATE OF [*94*]   MB
□ *Handbook of Dates* ed. C.R. Cheney (1970); F.P. Pickering *The Calendar Pages of Medieval Service Books* (1981)

Calmar, Union of (1397) Assembly of Scandinavian nobles which united the kingdoms of Norway, Denmark and Sweden under one crown. A common rule of succession was prescribed, although each state retained its own laws. The first king of this united province was Eric of Pomerania, grandson of the Swedish king, Albert, though the union was never fully ratified because of the refusal of the Norwegian prelates to take any part in the proceedings. The moving spirit behind the whole enterprise was Margaret, daughter of Waldemar of Denmark, wife of Haakon VI of Norway, and great-aunt of Eric in whose name she ruled as regent. Tensions between the Scandinavian communities themselves

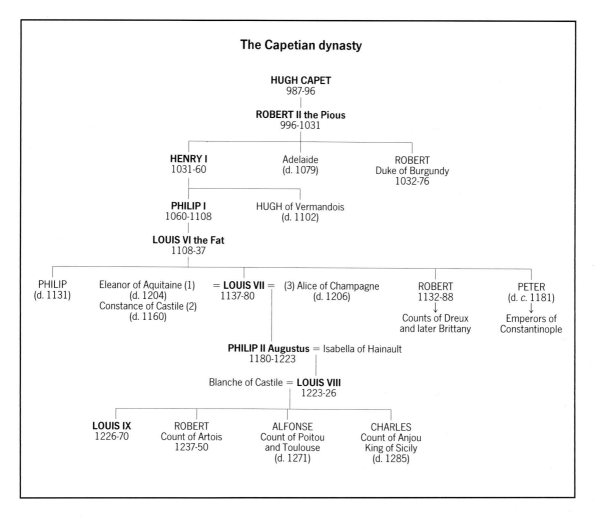

The Capetian dynasty

HUGH CAPET
987-96

ROBERT II the Pious
996-1031

HENRY I　　　Adelaide　　　ROBERT
1031-60　　　(d. 1079)　　　Duke of Burgundy
　　　　　　　　　　　　　　　1032-76

PHILIP I　　　HUGH of Vermandois
1060-1108　　　(d. 1102)

LOUIS VI the Fat
1108-37

PHILIP　　Eleanor of Aquitaine (1)　**= LOUIS VII =**　(3) Alice of Champagne　ROBERT　　PETER
(d. 1131)　　(d. 1204)　　　1137-80　　(d. 1206)　　1132-88　　(d. c. 1181)
　　　Constance of Castile (2)
　　　　(d. 1160)　　　　　　　　　　　　　　Counts of Dreux　Emperors of
　　　　　　　　　　　　　　　　　　　　　and later Brittany　Constantinople

PHILIP II Augustus = Isabella of Hainault
1180-1223

Blanche of Castile = **LOUIS VIII**
　　　　　　　　　　1223-26

LOUIS IX　　ROBERT　　ALFONSE　　CHARLES
1226-70　　Count of Artois　Count of Poitou　Count of Anjou
　　　　　1237-50　　and Toulouse　King of Sicily
　　　　　　　　　　(d. 1271)　　(d. 1285)

and the intrusive presence of the Hanseatic League diminished the force of the Union after Margaret's death in 1412, but it nevertheless remained in being until 1523.

Canute *See* **Cnut**

Capetian dynasty Kings of France continuously from the accession of Hugh Capet until 1328. In 987 the dynasty took its name from Hugh's by-name, which referred to his distinctive cloak. Hugh was descended from Robert the Strong, marquess of Neustria (d. 866), whose descendants ranked among the strongest men in West Frankia in the succeeding century; three of them (Odo 887–98, Robert 922–23, and Raoul 923–36) held the royal title.

The early Capetians could do little more than cling to their power base around Paris, but under Philip I (1060–1108), and more so under Louis VI the Fat (1108–37), the royal demesne was slowly consolidated around Paris and Orleans with important

extensions north to the Channel. Abbot Suger, who acted virtually as chief minister of the kings in the reign of Louis VI and the early years of Louis VII (1137–80), did much to foster the cult of kingship, and the poets and lawyers of the second half of the 12th c. built up the prestige of French kingship as directly descended from Carolingian, and indeed Merovingian roots. Owing to the strength of the Angevin Henry II of England, little of this potential could be realized until the defeat of John in 1204 and the consequent acquisition of Normandy, Anjou and much of the Plantagenet empire by Philip II Augustus; the moral and religious prestige of his grandson Louis IX (1226–70) brought the reputation of the dynasty to its highest point. *See* PHILIP IV THE FAIR

□ E.M. Hallam *Capetian France 987–1328* (1980)

Carat (also, as a weight, *siliqua*) Initially a weight (0.189 g) derived from that of the bean of the carob tree (*ceratonia siliqua*), but more widely used in the

Middle Ages as a term for expressing fineness of gold (1/24th), since the Constantinian *solidus*, of pure gold, weighed 24 carats.

Carmelites (White Friars) Mendicant order founded in the mid-12th c. by hermits on Mount Carmel. In the Rule of the Order (1206–14) an eremitical life was enjoined, although the Carmelites possessed a common oratory; abstinence, fasting and silence were also practised. In 1238 they were driven out of Palestine by the Muslims and established their main base in Cyprus. Under Pope Innocent IV in the late 1240s their constitution was brought into line with the Dominicans, and Carmelite houses were permitted within towns. By the end of the 13th c. there were more than 150 houses within Europe, and their popularity persisted to some extent throughout the later Middle Ages. An order of Carmelite nuns was set up in the 15th c.
□ D. Knowles *The Religious Orders in England* (1948)

Carmina Burana Collection of Latin songs, attributed to students and wandering scholars of the 12th c. and 13th c., that contain elements of deep satire at the existing order as well as rejoicing in love poetry, and express acceptance of and delight in nature, youth and student life. The work of the Archpoet is transmitted through this collection, which was put together by an anonymous editor in the second quarter of the 13th c., possibly at the abbey of Benedictbeuern in Bavaria. *See* GOLIARDIC POETS; VAGANTES
□ J. Lindsay *Medieval Latin Poets* (1934); *Carmina Burana* ed. A. Hilke, O. Schumann and B. Bischoff (1970)

Carolingian dynasty The history of the Carolingian family began in the 7th c., when the Merovingian King Chlotar II appointed Pepin of Landen (d.640) as mayor of the palace of Austrasia. Pepin was eventually succeeded in this office by his nephew Pepin of Herstal (d.680) and by Pepin's son Charles Martel, who gave his name to the dynasty.

The first member of the family to hold the royal title, however, was Pepin the Short, who in 750 deposed the last of the Merovingian kings, Childeric III, and established himself as king of Frankia (751) with papal approval. The family reached its zenith under Pepin's son Charlemagne, who by vigorous personal monarchy held together the far-flung dominions of his empire and in 800 received the imperial title from the pope. On his death in 814, Charlemagne was succeeded in all his dominions by his only son Louis the Pious, but on Louis's death in 840 the empire was divided up in the traditional

Fresco by Fra Lippo Lippi showing **Carmelite** monks, in the cloister of S. Maria del Carmine, Florence.

manner between his three sons. By the terms of the Treaty of Verdun (843), Lothar, the eldest (d. 855), was granted the Middle Kingdom, which included parts of Italy, Lotharingia and Provence; Louis the German (d.876) was granted eastern Frankia, whilst Charles II the Bald (d.877) received the western part of his father's kingdom. These territories were again divided between their sons and grandsons, so that within 60 years of Charlemagne's death the unity of his empire had completely disappeared.

Members of the respective branches of the family, however, continued to rule their much smaller patrimonies until well into the 10th c.: in eastern Frankia until the death of Louis the German's grandson, Louis the Child (911), and in western Frankia until the death of the last of Charles the Bald's descendants, the childless Louis V (987).
□ H. Fichtenau *The Carolingian Empire* (1957); E. James *The Origins of France: from Clovis to the Capetians 500–1000* (1982); R. McKitterick *The Frankish Kingdoms under the Carolingians* (1983)

Carolingian renaissance Name given to the flourishing of art, architecture and learning which took place at the court of Charlemagne and his

Drinking song from the Benediktheurer manuscript of the **Carmina Burana**, c. 1225.

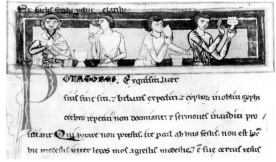

successors. Centred around the palace school of Aix-la-Chapelle, this renaissance had as its main aim the gathering together of all surviving remnants of the classical past. This involved both the copying of classical manuscripts and the use of classical models in architecture (as at the palace church at Aix-la-Chapelle which, although very Northern European in execution, was inspired by Justinian's church of S. Vitale at Ravenna and enriched with columns from Theodoric's palace). The latter also led to the development of a new type of very clear script known as Caroline minuscule, which was highly influential in the history of medieval handwriting and substantially the model for so-called Roman type when printing was invented in the 15th c.

The most prominent scholars included Alcuin (d.804), a Northumbrian scholar, excellent teacher and letter-writer, who helped to create a better version of the Vulgate; the historian and grammarian, Paul the Deacon, from Lombardy; the Visigothic poet Theodulf, bishop of Orleans (d.821); and, of a slightly younger generation, Einhard (d.840), who wrote a superbly effective biography of Charlemagne. The characteristic emphasis on Latinity and the Roman heritage continued throughout the 9th c. in the works of scholars of the calibre of Hrabanus Maurus, Walafrid Strabo, John Eriugena the Scot, and several unnamed church-builders and artists, many operating from cathedral schools and monasteries such as Corbie, Saint-Martin-de-Tours (where Alcuin was abbot), Reichenau and St Gallen. □ D.A. Bullough *The Age of Charlemagne* (1965); W. Ullmann *The Carolingian Renaissance and the Idea of Kingship* (1969)

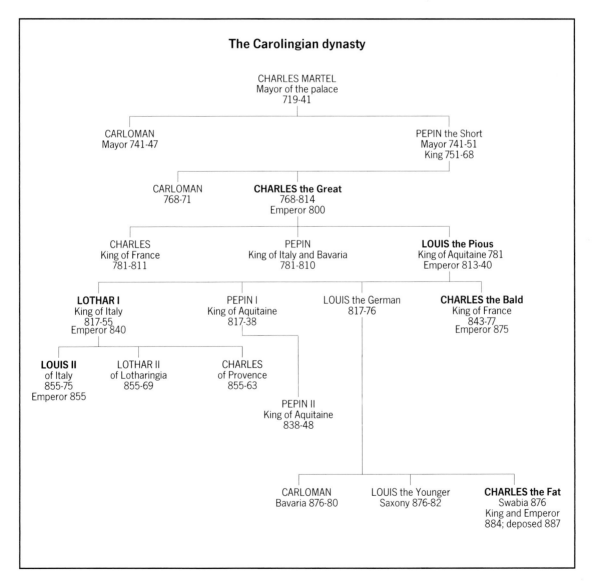

The Carolingian dynasty

CHARLES MARTEL
Mayor of the palace
719-41

CARLOMAN
Mayor 741-47

PEPIN the Short
Mayor 741-51
King 751-68

CARLOMAN
768-71

CHARLES the Great
768-814
Emperor 800

CHARLES
King of France
781-811

PEPIN
King of Italy and Bavaria
781-810

LOUIS the Pious
King of Aquitaine 781
Emperor 813-40

LOTHAR I
King of Italy
817-55
Emperor 840

PEPIN I
King of Aquitaine
817-38

LOUIS the German
817-76

CHARLES the Bald
King of France
843-77
Emperor 875

LOUIS II
of Italy
855-75
Emperor 855

LOTHAR II
of Lotharingia
855-69

CHARLES
of Provence
855-63

PEPIN II
King of Aquitaine
838-48

CARLOMAN
Bavaria 876-80

LOUIS the Younger
Saxony 876-82

CHARLES the Fat
Swabia 876
King and Emperor
884; deposed 887

Carrara family Dominant 14th-c. family in Paduan history. The Carrara family, notably Francesco il Vecchio (1350–88), asserted the independence of the city against the ambitions of both Milan and Venice – ultimately unsuccessfully. Francesco was a patron of the arts, especially interested in frescoes and coins, and Petrarch bequeathed most of his books to him.

Carthusian Order Monastic order founded in 1084 by St Bruno of Cologne in the valley of La Chartreuse, north of Grenoble. The Carthusian way of life provided the opportunity to live as a hermit within a religious community. Each monk had his own cell where he prayed, ate, studied and slept, but each day he would also meet with his fellow monks in the church for the night office, morning mass and Vespers. Each Carthusian monastery also had a number of lay brothers who lived a communal life and provided the necessary labour for the smooth running of the house.

The Order was never very popular, possibly because of the austerity of its way of life, and by 1521 there were only 195 Carthusian monasteries in existence. In England the number of Carthusian houses was always very small; with the exception of Witham in Somerset, founded in the 12th c. by King Henry II in part reparation for the death of St Thomas Becket, there were no Carthusian priories in England until the 14th c., when several houses were founded, including the Charterhouse in London and Mount Grace Priory in Yorkshire. A Rule was drawn up by the fifth prior, Guigis of Chatel, in 1127, and with modifications served as a basis of Carthusian observance with its combination of the cenobitic and eremitic elements within the community for the succeeding centuries, so leading to the proud Carthusian boast that it was never reformed, because never deformed.
□ E.M. Thompson *The Carthusian Order in England* (1930); D. Knowles *The Monastic Order in England* (1963)

Cashel, Synod of (1172) Meeting of the Irish church called by the papal legate (who was also the bishop of Lismore), which passed reforming decrees for the Irish church and acknowledged Henry II of England as king of Ireland. [*181*]

Casimir III the Great King of Poland 1333–70 (b.1310) At the time of Casimir's succession to the throne, Poland was in difficulties. Although his father Vladislav I had succeeded in uniting Great and Little Poland under one crown, there were still numerous regional differences between the two territories which were a potential source of conflict.

In addition, Casimir faced war on two fronts, with John of Luxembourg, king of Bohemia, who wanted Poland for himself, and with the Teutonic knights, who disputed Poland's rights to eastern Pomerania. By 1349, however, Casimir had made peace with both groups and had enlarged his kingdom by the annexation of Red Russia and Masovia; he further strengthened his borders by marrying two of his daughters to Poland's most important neighbours, the first to Louis of Brandenburg in 1345 and the second to Wenzel, son of the Holy Roman Emperor Charles IV, in 1369.

Within Poland itself, Casimir initiated the work of uniting the various provinces of the kingdom under one administration. Although Red Russia and Masovia retained their own customary laws, the written laws of Great and Little Poland were codified while a special court of arbitration was established at Cracow. Casimir also increased the economic potential of Poland by founding several royal towns with wide trading privileges, whilst his establishment of a university at Cracow in 1364 secured for the country a place in the intellectual world of medieval Europe.

Cassiodorus, Flavius Magnus Aurelius (*c*.490–580) Born at Sylacium in Italy, Cassiodorus spent much of his early life as an administrator in the service of the Ostrogothic kings of Italy. From 507 to 511 he served as quaestor, in 514 was appointed consul and in 526 became chief of the civil service. In 540 he gave up his political career and returned to his family estates at Vivarium where he founded a monastery. Here he collected together much pagan and Christian literature which was copied by his monks, and was thus responsible for the survival of a substantial quantity of ancient classical learning which might otherwise have been lost. The most important of Cassiodorus' own writings are his *Institutes*, written for the monks at Vivarium, which not only discuss the study of scripture, but also give a brief exposition of learning, based on the seven liberal arts as they had survived in his own day.
□ J.J. O'Donnell *Cassiodorus* (1979)

Castile Name first used in the 9th c. to refer to a small, politically fragmented district in the Calabrian mountains north of Burgos. The importance of Castile only emerged in the 10th c. when Fernando Gonzalez (d. 970) made himself count of all Castile and established his capital at Burgos. During the 11th c., the county lost its independence when it passed into the hands, firstly of Sancho III of Navarre, and then of his son Ferdinand I of Leon. In the 12th c., however, it was Castile which took the leading part in the reconquest of Spain from the Moors and

Castles: aerial view of the Tower of London. The 11th-c. White Tower dominates the complex.

soon surpassed Leon in importance. By the 13th c. Castile controlled the whole of the Iberian peninsula with the exception of the kingdoms of Portugal and Aragon, and the area around Granada, which was still controlled by the Moors. Although Castilian attempts to conquer Portugal were defeated in 1385, Aragon and Castile became at least nominally united with the marriage between Ferdinand of Aragon and Isabella of Castile in 1469; thus the foundations of modern Spain were laid. *See* ALFONSO VI; ALFONSO VIII; ALFONSO X

Castles The castle is perhaps the best known and least understood of medieval monuments. It was both the fortified residence and the residential fortress of a lord; this duality of function is peculiar to it in the history of fortification and points to its feudality. All buildings reflect the society which produces them, and castles are the characteristic product of a feudal society, dominated by a military aristocracy for which they are the appropriate setting. While unfortified palaces and houses also existed, as well as the comparatively lightly fortified dwellings, known to the English as fortified manors and to the French as *maisons fortes*, castles were among the most

prestigious of stately homes in the feudal period and became the symbols as well as the substance of feudal lordship. For the castle was the fortified residence not only of the king or prince, but of any lord; and while it thus stands for that fragmentation or delegation of civil and military power which is essentially feudal, so also it is private as opposed to communal, the seat and centre of one man's lordship, his household and retainers: a very different concept from the fortified town.

Apart from linear defences, fortifications of the pre-feudal period were communal and public, as, for example, the Iron Age camps, Roman camps and walled cities, their Merovingian and Carolingian successors, Anglo-Saxon burghs, or such great Viking camps as Trelleborg. On the other hand, apart from linear defences and fortified towns, modern fortifications, beginning in England with Henry VIII's coastal forts, are, unlike the castle, purely military, and again are public, pertaining to the state.

It is essential to emphasize that the residential role of the castle was at least as important as the military. It is this, as much as any tactical or strategic consideration, which may account for the siting of a

A scene from the Bayeux tapestry: building the motte at Hastings.

castle; for the sumptuous accommodation within – halls, chambers, chapels, etc.; and (combined with the castle's strength as a secure place) for both such subsidiary uses as treasury, armoury and prison; and for its general function, whether royal or seigneurial, as the centre of local government. It is significant that in France, the cradle of feudalism, the word *château* has been retained for the great house, albeit no longer fortified. In England, Windsor remains a principal residence of the Queen, and Arundel, that of the premier duke of Norfolk. The state apartments in both are obviously not barracks, nor is the soaring majesty of St George's Chapel in the former a garrison chapel.

It is equally important to emphasize that the military role of the castle was not only defensive. Defence determined its design and most prominent architectural features. A great keep or *donjon* (Latin *dominium*, 'lordship') dominated the whole as the ultimate refuge, but also contained the best residential accommodation. Strong walls with a wall-walk and crenellation surrounded the castle, studded with projecting towers as strong-points able to put flanking fire on the exposed outer face; the gatehouse was defended and eked out by posterns and sally-ports in case attack revealed itself as the best form of defence; walls, towers and gates were often further protected by projecting galleries of timber (hoarding) or stone (machicolation). Great sieges, like those of Rochester (1215), Bedford (1224) or Kenilworth (1266) in English history, are the best known occasions in the history of castles. But the reason why castles had to be attacked and taken by an opposing army was that they controlled the surrounding land by means of the mounted force within them. The range of the castle was the range of the horse and armoured rider, not the limited field of the defensive weaponry based within it and which,

with its design, made it a near impregnable base. In the military analysis, the offensive role of the castle is primary, the defensive secondary, though the two things go together in the arbitrement of war.

The origin of the castle is found in northern France, possibly in the 9th c., though certainly the 10th c. along with the origins of feudal society itself. The earliest known castles still remaining are those of Doué-la-Fontaine (*c.* 950) and Langeais (*c.* 994), both of which are in the Loire region. Both pertain to great lords, emergent feudal princes (respectively Theobald, count of Blois, and Fulk the Black, count of Anjou), who were at that time founding their feudal principalities. In England castles arrived *c.* 1066 with the Normans, who imposed feudal lordship upon an ancient kingdom; they subsequently took castles with them into Wales, Scotland and Ireland. As castles were so closely bound up with feudalism, the decline of the castle is symptomatic of the slow waning of feudal society; gunpowder had very little to do with it. *See* FEUDALISM; WAR   RAB
□ W. Anderson and W. Swann *Castles of Europe* (1970); R.A. Brown *English Castles* (1976), *The Architecture of Castles* (1984)

Catalan, Grand Company of Spanish mercenary force led by the German, Roger de Flor, who in 1303 was hired by the Byzantine emperor Andronicus II to fight the Turks. The Company defeated the Ottomans, but when their pay was not forthcoming, they turned upon their former employers and ravaged the Byzantine state. After Flor's murder in 1306, the Company turned its attention to Europe. In 1308 they allied themselves with the Anatolian Turks in their attacks upon Thrace and Macedonia. Finally, in 1311 they overthrew Walter of Brienne, duke of Athens, at the battle of Cephisus, and established themselves in the duchy for the greater part of the 14th c. (until 1388), introducing Catalan customs and language, and recognizing the overlordship of the Aragonese rulers of Sicily.
□ *A History of the Crusades* vol.3, ed. H.W. Hazard (1975); J.N. Hillgarth *The Spanish Kingdoms 1250–1516* vol.1 (1976)

Cathars Group of heretics who seriously challenged the major tenets of orthodox Christianity. Their beliefs were derived from the teachings of a 3rd-c. religious teacher in Mesopotamia named Mani, who attempted to reconcile Christianity with age-old Persian ideas, interpreting the world as a battleground between the two powerful sources of good and evil, the life of the spirit and the life of the flesh. The resulting attitudes, loosely called Manichaean, led to a rejection of basic Christian theology concerning God's role in creation, Christ's humanity at the

Incarnation and the resurrection of the body. The Cathars' deep distrust of material things, regarded as the province of the devil, involved the most committed among them to renounce sexual activity, especially where there was a question of begetting children, to practise an austere form of vegetarianism and to refuse to comply with secular duties such as those which demanded the swearing of oaths.

Cathars were introduced into Western Europe in the early 11th c. from Bulgaria, and several were put to death for their heretical beliefs at Orleans in 1022. The most famous group flourished in southern France in the later 12th c. and were called Albigenses from their chief centre at Albi in Languedoc. Followers were divided into two categories: the *perfecti*, or 'perfected ones', and the *credentes*, or 'believers', who lived a normal life but who were expected to receive the absolution or *consolamentum* at some stage before their death. After absolution they too were expected to conform to the intense austerity of the *perfecti*. *See* ROBERT LE BOUGRE; WALDENSIANS
□ S. Runciman *The Medieval Manichee* (1947)

Cathedrals The principal church of a diocese, so called because it contained the seat or *cathedra* of a bishop or archbishop. In the early church these buildings were often unpretentious, but as the political and administrative duties of the bishops increased the need was felt for an impressive physical focus for the diocese, especially in the great cities such as Constantinople, Rome and Ravenna. From the days of the Carolingian empire in the West impressive Romanesque and, later, Gothic edifices came to symbolize the majesty and power of the faith and of its servants.

Organization of cathedrals was often complex. The bishop remained a key figure throughout the Middle Ages, but other ecclesiastical dignitaries, not always in full accord with the bishop, tended to grow and flourish around the cathedrals. In England, for example, from the 10th c. monks served cathedrals, including Canterbury, Winchester and Worcester, with the bishop exercising the function of an abbot presiding over a monastic chapter. After the Norman Conquest the system was extended, and monastic chapters were set up at Durham, Norwich, Ely and Bath. Elsewhere cathedrals were more commonly entrusted to a community of clerics, called canons, formed into chapters, most of which gained the right to elect their own deans.

The very existence of great buildings, which often took a century or more to construct and which demanded constant care and attention to maintain, led to the growth of a strong corporate sense among the cathedral clergy in most dioceses. The great architectural achievements of the cathedral builders of the Middle Ages may still be enjoyed throughout Europe from Trondheim to Palermo; England and northern France are especially rich in surviving great churches, such as those at Durham or Canterbury, Amiens or Chartres. *See* ARCHITECTURE

Catherine of Siena, St (1347–80) Daughter of a Sienese dyer, Giacomo Benincasa, Catherine rejected marriage at an early age, devoting herself to a life of prayer, penance and good works. After joining the Dominican Order as a tertiary she gathered a number of followers around her, and together they travelled around Italy preaching repentance and the reform of the church. She was particularly anxious to see the papacy restored to Rome and went to Avignon to exhort Pope Gregory XI to return there. After Gregory's death in 1378 Catherine supported Urban VI against his Avignonese rival and died in Urban's service at Rome in 1380. Her literary compositions, which were dictated because of her illiteracy, include the *Book of Divine Doctrine*, which came to be regarded as one of the most important mystical works of the 14th c. She greatly influenced her confessor and biographer Raymond of Capua, who in 1380 became minister-general of the Dominicans and initiated the foundation of Observant convents.
□ *Life of Catherine of Siena* ed. C. Kearns (1980)

Caxton, William (1422–91) English printer. Born in Kent, Caxton was apprenticed to an influential London mercer, Robert Large, in 1439. On Large's

Caxton presents his *Recuyel of the Histories of Troye* to Margaret of York (*c.*1475).

death in 1441, he went to Bruges to complete his training, and by 1464 had reached the influential position of acting governor of the Merchant Adventurers in the Low Countries. During a visit to Cologne in 1471 he learned the art of printing. Returning to England, he was responsible for the first English printed book, the *Recuyel of the Histories of Troye* (1474). In 1476 he set up a press at Westminster where he printed 96 books, including Chaucer's *Canterbury Tales* and Malory's *Morte d'Arthur*. He was succeeded in the business by his assistant Wynkyn de Worde. *See* PRINTING

□ N.F. Blake *Caxton: England's First Publisher* (1976); G.D. Painter *William Caxton* (1976)

Celestine V Pope 1294 (1209–96) Born Pietro de Merone, he became first a Benedictine monk and then a hermit in the Abruzzi mountains, where he founded the Celestine Order for his followers. When elected pope he was already 85 years old. Lacking administrative ability, he became dependent upon Charles II of Naples and filled the curia with his supporters; Celestine was also unsuccessful in his attempts to bring peace between Aragon on the one hand, and France and England on the other. During his pontificate he showed favour towards the Franciscan Spirituals, whom he allowed to secede from the Order. After a pontificate of only five months, Celestine resigned and Benedict Gaetani was elected as Pope Boniface VIII in his stead. Since some regarded Celestine's abdication as unlawful he was not allowed to return to the eremitical life, but was kept in strict confinement until his death.

Celtic churches Christianity reached the Celtic communities in Britain in the later phases of Roman rule and was extended beyond the old imperial frontier to Ireland and Scotland in the 5th c. and 6th c. Celtic Christians made a special contribution to the European scene in two respects: by the inspiration and reputation of their saints, and by their direct missionary activity on the Continent.

Celtic saints Tradition says that during the 6th c. very large numbers of people became ascetic saints in the Celtic areas of Britain, often retreating to islands, and that large numbers of these saints set off for unfamiliar parts, influencing local populations and founding monasteries as they went. Such tradition exaggerates both the numbers involved and the asceticism, and unduly concentrates the activity in the 6th c. However, good evidence exists for some 6th-c. saints, and there was undoubtedly a movement of monastic foundation during the later 6th c. and 7th c. in western Britain and Ireland; these foundations were characteristically made in central, not isolated, places. Best evidence is available for

movements of Welsh, journeying from Wales to Ireland in the 5th c. and 6th c., and to Cornwall and Brittany in the 6th c. and 7th c.

Since the same saints were venerated in Wales, Cornwall and Brittany, medieval and later writers wrongly supposed that the only possible explanation for widespread cult was common origins. Yet it does not follow that there was a single Celtic church with a unitary organization and practice common to all Celtic areas. Practice and institutions were extremely diverse in the different regions; Celtic clerics never met as a group and recognized no presiding figure. They shared one common characteristic however; the veneration of minor local saints, such as Cadog or Mochutu, with no pan-European cult, appears to have been far more common and sustained for far longer, in Celtic, than in other parts.

The Celtic mission to the Continent The monastic movement of the 6th c. and 7th c. encouraged some individuals to seek spiritual fulfilment by making a journey (*peregrinatio*) away from home and country, cutting off all contact with known sources of support, the struggle of spiritual warfare leading to the overcoming of the self. In the course of such journeys preaching was undertaken and new monastic foundations made as a source of continuing spiritual support for the population, whether pagan or already Christian.

The Celtic mission to the Continent was dominated by Irishmen, although it included some British too. The most famous of these early *peregrini* was St Columba, who left northern Ireland about 565 and founded the monastery of Iona off the west coast of Scotland. Though Iona was of considerable importance in missions to the Picts and pagan English, Columba retained an interest in Irish politics and often returned to Ireland.

A more typical *peregrinus* was St Columbanus. Trained at Bangor, he set out *c.* 590 for Continental Europe, heading for the Merovingian rulers of the Franks; with their patronage he made foundations at Annegray, Luxeuil and Fontaines. Subsequently he came into conflict with the rulers, and at one stage was forced to leave the country. Later he travelled through eastern Frankia to Italy, encouraging foundations at St Gallen and finally Bobbio, where he died in 615. Others followed, some stopping, like Fursa *c.*630, in pagan East Anglia before passing on to the Continent; some, like Tomianus, bishop of Angoulême, holding office within the Frankish church; others, like Cillian of Würzburg (martyred 689), travelling further east to pagan parts.

The example of the Irish led others to establish monasteries in Frankia – Richarius, a noble from Picardy who founded Saint-Riquier, and Wandregisl who founded Saint-Wandrille, for example. The monastic movement continued during the 7th c. and early 8th c., but was overtaken in the mid-8th c. by the English mission to pagan Germany. However, a sphere of Irish influence had been established in Switzerland, Austria and southern Germany, and this was a source of long-lasting traditions. By the 12th c. monasteries would claim Irish foundation in that area, even if it were untrue, and it remains very difficult to distinguish intrinsically Irish characteristics within early medieval Continental monasticism.

The centres established by the Irish, or through Irish influence, were not merely important for spiritual reasons, but contributed to learning and education; places like Luxeuil, its daughter house Corbie, and Bobbio were of special significance in the production and copying of manuscripts – classical, patristic and legal works. The main monastic movement may have terminated by the late 8th c., but the movement of Irish individuals did not, and Frankish courts continued to attract Irish scholars in the later 8th c. and 9th c. The poet and thinker Sedulius and the theologian and philosopher John Eriugena were prominent among the many foreigners who made invaluable contributions to the Carolingian intellectual renaissance, and the tradition that associated Ireland with learning remained a powerful force in European development. *See* AIDAN, ST   WD
□ G.H. Doble *The Saints of Cornwall* (1960–70); L. Bieler *Ireland: Harbinger of the Middle Ages* (1963); E.G. Bowen *Saints, Seaways and Settlements in the Celtic Lands* (1969)

Chalcedon, Council of (451) The fourth ecumenical council of the church, convoked by the emperor Marcian in 451 and attended by 600 representatives of the church. It approved the Creeds of Nicaea (325) and Constantinople (381) and accepted Leo I's *Tome* as the basis for further doctrinal reform. More importantly it condemned Monophysitism and affirmed the basic orthodox belief that Christ, though one person, possessed two natures. Finally, the Council decreed that henceforth the patriarchate of Constantinople should be regarded as the second most important see in the whole empire, subordinate only to the see of Rome.

Champagne, fairs of At the crossing of the roads from Flanders, Germany, Italy and Provence, they became Europe's international marketplace in the 12th c. and 13th c. English wool, Mediterranean spices and dyes, German furs and linens, and leather goods from Spain were the staple commodities of exchange. The great fairs lasted forty-nine days each, and were six in number: one at Lagny and at

Bar-sur-Aube, two at both Provins and Troyes. The first week was spent in receiving merchandise and the last in settling accounts. Thus the fairs became regular and important banking centres. The end of the 13th c. saw the decline of the fairs, with the increasing use of water communications between Northern Europe and the Mediterranean, and the spread of disruptive warfare in France. *See* COMMERCE

Chanson de geste Generic name for the 80 to 100 medieval epic poems in Old French, usually anonymous, which form the bulk of the Charlemagne legends. This literature, dominated by feudal and aristocratic preoccupations, narrates the warring deeds of the great Merovingian and Carolingian barons. The poems form two overlapping groups. The first deals with the struggle between Christian France, headed by Charlemagne, and Islam; Roland and its related poems belong to this group. The second series includes the poems of the barons, such as Girart de Roussillon, Doon de Mayence, Ogier the Dane and Raoul de Cambrai. The poems present the new ideal of a hero who dedicates himself to warring against the enemies of God. The characters reflect the values of the audience, sharing the poets' love of intricate, stylized description. By combining local oral tradition and conventional themes, a literature of complex vitality was produced.
□ M.D. Legge *Anglo-Norman Literature and its Background* (1963); R.S. Loomis *The Development of the Arthurian Romance* (1963)

Chanson de Roland The most celebrated and best of the medieval French epics, the 'Song of Roland' survives in its earliest form in an Anglo-Norman manuscript comprising 3998 assonating decasyllables. This version, apparently of Norman provenance, probably dates from the very end of the 11th c. The narrative gives, in a highly formulaic style, a skilfully structured account of the heroic defeat of the Franks in the Pyrenees (778), of the death of Roland, impulsive yet totally committed, the vengeance wrought by the Christians with God's help on the Saracen enemy, and the punishment of Ganelon, whose personal vendetta against Roland led him treacherously to disregard his feudal obligations to his overlord Charlemagne.
□ D.D.R. Owen *The Legend of Roland* (1973)

Charlemagne (Charles the Great) King of the Franks 768–814 and Emperor 800–814 (b.742) A great figure in legend as in history, Charles sometimes appears almost larger than life. Contemporaries emphasized his physical size, his strength, his restless energy (hunting and swimming as well as governing and soldiering), his simplicity and his intellectual

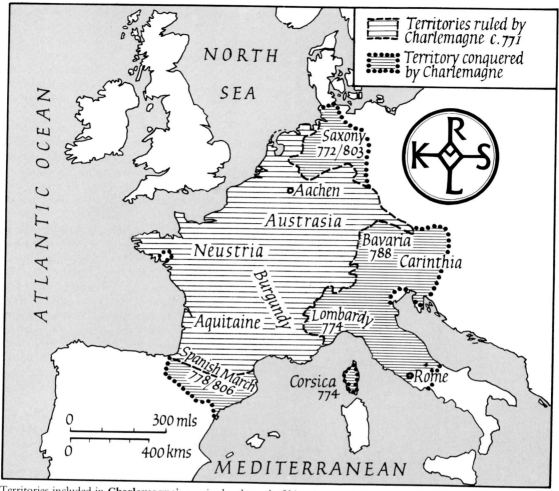

Territories included in **Charlemagne**'s empire by the end of his reign, with his monogram: Karolus.

curiosity and ability. If he failed to learn to write (this was a skilled occupation in the 8th c. and he was a late starter), he was splendidly competent in other cultural fields, such as reading and disputing; he was an able linguist, as fluent in Latin as in his native German Austrasian tongue, and deeply interested in mathematics, astronomy and especially astrology. His palace school at Aix-la-Chapelle masterminded by the English scholar Alcuin, became a power-house of intellectual life for the Western world.

It is sometimes hard to realize how new to royal dignities Charles' family was. The royal title was granted to his father Pepin in 751 when Charles was nine years old. As if to emphasize the new Christian nature of the Frankish kingship and the transmission of royal power from the Merovingians to a new dynasty, the two young princes, Charles and his brother Carloman, received consecration in 753. On Pepin's death (768) the Frankish kingdom was divided between the two brothers, an unhappy arrangement that nearly led to civil war. Carloman's

death in 771 left the way clear for Charles to succeed to the whole inheritance, and for the succeeding 40 years and more the Frankish king dominated and reshaped the political life of the West.

His achievements can be summed up simply: he consolidated and refined the Christian kingship of the Franks inherited from his father; he extended the authority implicit in that kingship over all other existing Christian communities on the continent of Western Europe up to the boundary with the Byzantine empire in southern Italy; he further extended that authority by a policy of encouragement to missionary efforts and military strength over all Continental Germanic peoples, establishing a firm military frontier of marchlands with the Danes and the Slavonic peoples, and routing the Avars, forcing them to recoil to their lands in the middle Danube. At a great ceremony in Rome on Christmas Day 800, Pope Leo III crowned Charles as Emperor and Augustus, Emperor of the Romans. This must have seemed a fitting consummation to the work of a

Statue of **Charlemagne** now dated to the late 12th c.

neighbours to the favoured royal centres in Lorraine, especially at Aix-la-Chapelle. Early campaigns up to 780 were little more than punitive raids, but for the following 20 years, conquest was the objective. The massacre of prisoners in 782, the open use of the church in the interests of the Frankish army and rulers, the heroic resistance of the pagan Saxon leader Widukind, and measures such as the forced transplantation of peasant populations have darkened the reputation of Charles and the Franks; but the result was undoubtedly successful. Forcible conversion brought Saxons and Frisians into the new empire; and by paradox, it was from Saxony in the 10th c. that the Carolingian empire was in turn revived.

Government of such a vast and complex empire (for its age) proved cumbersome and only partly effective, yet there were elements of strength within it, and Carolingian precedent served as a model for much in the successor Christian kingdoms of the West. Charles issued capitularies, general statements of law, that were intended to be of general application, particularly in the years following his imperial coronation. He relied heavily on the counts, who were in charge of local districts, and on the church, bishops and abbots. From his royal centre he sent out commissioners (*Missi Dominici*) empowered to supervise the workings of local government. The interpenetration of ecclesiastical and secular spheres gave a theocratic flavour to the kingship and to the empire. The empire itself was too large for the ruralized and manorialized economic base available to support it, and the 9th c. saw it divided along what became the familiar medieval pattern into the kingdom of France, a Middle Kingdom (Lorraine, Burgundy and Lombardy) and a kingdom of Germany (eventually closely linked with the Middle Kingdom).

Charles' force and dynamic personality were needed to create the empire, and without him, disintegrating elements quickly gained the ascendancy. It is a tribute to his personality, as well as to his military and political skill, that so much survived. His work stands at the end of one age, the sub-Roman period, and at the beginning of the new, the Holy Roman Empire, from which were to emerge the familiar feudal monarchies of the central medieval world. *See* LIBRI CAROLINI [*17*]   HRL

□ H. Fichtenau *The Carolingian Empire* (1957); D.A. Bullough *The Age of Charlemagne* (1965); J. Boussard *The Civilization of Charlemagne* (1968); F.L. Ganshof *Frankish Institutions under Charlemagne* (1968), *The Carolingians and the Frankish Monarchy* (1971); H.R. Loyn and J. Percival *The Reign of Charlemagne* (1975); L. Halphen *Charlemagne and the Carolingian Empire* (1977)

military leader who had brought under military and political control the Christian or newly Christianized Romanic and Germanic peoples of Western Europe.

The process of consolidation of the Christian communities had started early in Charles' reign. In 773 he invaded the Lombard kingdom of northern Italy, partly to defend papal interest, and defeated the Lombard king (who retired to a monastery), assuming the iron crown of Lombardy. In southern Germany the Bavarians had been converted to Christianity, and Charles, by heavy political pressure as well as military force, was able to compel their duke Tassilo to accept Charles as his feudal lord. In Spain, in spite of a disaster at Roncesvalles (778) in which Count Roland perished, Charles enforced authority on the northern fringe, founding the Spanish March. Extension of Christian kingship depended essentially on what proved to be the most immediate political problem of Charles' reign, the conquest and conversion of the Saxons and Frisians,

Charles the Bald in majesty, from the 9th-c. *Codex Monacensis.*

Charles I the Bald King of France 840–77 (b. 823) Youngest son of Louis the Pious and his only son by Empress Judith. Charles' reign saw the formation of a West Frankish kingdom that later became France, and marked, largely thanks to his patronage of art and scholarship, the heyday of the Carolingian renaissance. It also offers an exceptionally well-documented case of the early medieval pattern of politics, dominated by rivalries within the royal family and by associated aristocratic factionalism. Louis the Pious' succession plans involved disinheriting his grandson Pepin II of Aquitaine in favour of Charles. On Louis's death (840) his eldest son, the Emperor Lothar, in alliance with Pepin, tried to exclude Charles. In counter-alliance with his other half-brother Louis the German, Charles defeated Lothar and Pepin at Fonteney (June 841) and at Verdun (August 843), thus securing a division of the Frankish heartlands between himself, Lothar and Louis. Charles gained the territory west of the Scheldt, plus Aquitaine; the West Frankish lands, which formed his power base, gave their name to his kingship.

In the first half of his reign, Charles faced recurrent factional revolt in Aquitaine, partly linked with support for Pepin, and in Neustria, associated with Breton separatism; these problems were compounded by Viking attacks which peaked c.845–65. Carolingian rivalries continued: 858 Louis the German exploited dissidence to spread east of the Seine and invade Charles' kingdom. Supported by leading nobles and churchmen, Charles quickly regained control. The second half of the reign saw successes in innovative defence against the Vikings, in firmer maintenance of aristocratic support, some centralization of government in the north-east and the acquisition of territory through successive Carolingian repartitions. Finally Charles gained the imperial crown

(875) as Emperor Charles II, but died on 6 October 877.

□ *Charles the Bald: Court and Kingdom* ed. M. Gibson and J. Nelson (1981); R. McKitterick *The Frankish Kingdoms under the Carolingians* (1983)

Charles V the Wise King of France 1364–80 (b.1338) Although he did not succeed to the throne until 1364, Charles' political career began as early as 1356 when he entered into negotiations with the Engish for the release of his father John II the Good, who had been captured at the battle of Poitiers. Charles was forced by the treaties of Brétigny and Calais to attempt to pay a ransom of three million gold crowns to the English, as well as ceding to them much of south-western France. Upon his father's death in 1364, however, Charles began to reverse his earlier capitulation. With the help and guidance of the great soldier Bertrand DuGuesclin – for he was no military man himself – he restored order in the French territories, reorganized the army and established a navy; by 1375 he had won back many of the territories formerly ceded to England. In order to strengthen his position, he sought to defeat the over-mighty house of Brittany and succeeded in depriving the king of Navarre of most of his French lands. Charles was also a patron of the arts: he built the Hôtel de Saint-Pol and redecorated the Louvre as a fitting home for his magnificent library.
□ J. Calmette *Charles V* (1945)

Charles VI the Well-beloved King of France 1380–1422 (b.1369) Crowned at Rheims, Charles spent his minority largely under the control of his uncle Philip the Bold, duke of Burgundy. In 1388 he began to rule alone, and with the advice of his father's former counsellors initiated a programme of governmental reform. By 1392, however, Charles was suffering from periodic fits of madness, and political control passed into the hands of the various rival factions of his family, chief of whom were Charles' wife Isabella of Bavaria and his brother the duke of Orleans. In 1418 Charles' son, the dauphin Charles, declared himself regent, but in 1420 Henry V of England was proclaimed regent and became heir to the French throne upon his marriage to the royal princess Catherine of Valois.

Charles VII 'le bien servi' King of France 1422–61 (b.1403) After his father's death in 1422 Charles was faced with a serious situation. His rule was only recognized in the south of France, since the north had accepted as king Henry V of England, whom Charles VI had designated as his heir, and there also existed a powerful Anglo-Burgundian alliance. In

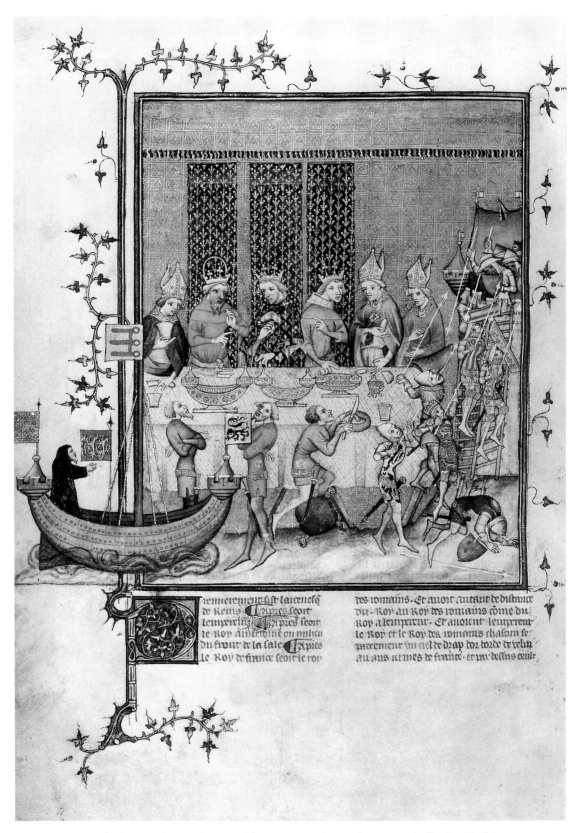

Emperor **Charles IV** of Luxembourg and his son Wenceslas at a banquet with **Charles V** of France.

1429 however Charles' luck began to change, chiefly through the influence of the Maid of Orleans, Joan of Arc. She restored the confidence of Charles' army, liberated Orleans and brought about Charles' coronation as king at Rheims.

After Joan's capture and execution (1431), Charles continued to follow up his advantage; in 1435 he made peace with Burgundy and in 1436 captured Paris, whilst by 1453 he had even conquered Guyenne, thus bringing the Hundred Years' War to an end. Under the influence of his counsellors, who included Pierre de Brézé and Jacques Coeur, Charles reorganized the administration and overcame his financial difficulties by obtaining the permanent right to levy taxes without the permission of the Estates General. He also strengthened royal authority over the French church in the so-called Pragmatic Sanction of Bourges in 1438. His favouring of counsellors drawn from the bourgeoisie inspired rebellion on the part of the nobility throughout his reign, the most famous example being the revolt of the Praguérie in 1440, led by Charles' son, the dauphin Louis XI.
□ M.G.A. Vale *Charles VII* (1974)

Charles I of Anjou King of Sicily and Naples 1266–85 (b. 1226) Count of Anjou and Provence. The younger brother of King Louis IX of France, whom he accompanied on a crusade of Egypt 1248–50, Charles was granted the counties of Anjou and Provence as appanages of the French crown in 1246. During the 1260s he aided the papacy in its war against the Hohenstaufen, defeating Frederick II's illegitimate son Manfred at the battle of Benevento (1266) and capturing and executing Conradin, last surviving member of the dynasty, in 1268. Charles at this stage held the kingdom of Sicily as a papal fief. His rule, however, was far from popular; his transference of the capital from Palermo to Naples and his use of French officials sparked off the rebellion commonly known as the Sicilian Vespers (1282). Charles was expelled from the kingdom in 1284 and it was whilst planning a counter-offensive that he died.

Charles IV of Luxembourg Holy Roman Emperor 1355–78 (b. 1316) Grandson of the Emperor Henry VII, Charles succeeded his father John as king of Bohemia in 1346, when the latter was killed at the battle of Crécy, an engagement in which Charles himself also fought. In the same year he was elected to the German throne in place of the deposed Louis of Bavaria and in 1355 he became Emperor. As king of Bohemia, Charles centred his administration in that country rather than in Germany itself, and during his reign Bohemia enjoyed a period of great

Portrait of **Charles VII** – 'le bien servi' – by Jean Fouquet (*c.* 1415-85).

prosperity. In Prague he constructed a bridge over the river Ultava and founded the university in 1348. The Upper Palatinate was annexed to Bohemia in 1355, as were the principalities of Jaue and Schweidnitz in Silesia, which formed part of the dowry of his third wife, the Polish princess Anne (d. 1362). Charles was an ally of the Avignon popes, and this enabled him to gain control of Burgundy (1365). In 1376, shortly before his death, Charles also managed to secure the German throne for his eldest son Wenceslas, an action unparalleled during the previous century. He is perhaps best known as the author of the Golden Bull of 1356, which laid down procedures for imperial elections. [*145*]
□ J. Speracek *Karl IV* (1978); F.R.H. du Boulay *Germany in the Later Middle Ages* (1983)

Charles Martel (688–741) Mayor of the palace of Austrasia from 719. Illegitimate son of Pepin of Herstal, Charles continued the consolidation of Frankish political power characteristic of his father's work, extending his authority over Austrasia, Neustria and Burgundy and winning recognition of overlordship from Aquitaine. Although officially only mayor of the palace, he granted ecclesiastical and secular offices at will and ruled effectively for some years without the need to establish a puppet Merovingian king. He drew on the finances of the church to equip his army, an act which gave him a mixed reputation among ecclesiastical writers. The germs of rudimentary feudal institutions are to be found in his military arrangements. He is chiefly remembered for his great victory over a massive Muslim raid into his territory at Poitiers in 732, now recognized as a symbol of Christian resistance and resurgence, as well as a great military success. The Muslim leader, 'Abd ar-Rahmān, was killed and Muslim casualties were heavy; Frankia was safeguarded, while the Muslims were ravaged by civil wars. It was from this victory that Charles gained his by-name Martel, 'the hammer'.

Charles the Bold (1433–77) Duke of Burgundy. Son of Philip the Good, Charles took over the government of Burgundy during his father's last illness and immediately came into conflict with the French king, Louis XI. Becoming duke in his own right in 1467 he proceeded to extend his rule as far as the Rhine, but this entailed confrontation with the German Emperor Frederick III and the Swiss, who were afraid that an expansion of Burgundy's territories would upset the balance of power in Europe. It was during this struggle that Charles was killed in a battle with the Swiss outside Nancy in 1477. With his death ended the most ambitious of the Burgundian political schemes.
□ R. Vaughan *Charles the Bold* (1973)

Chaucer, Geoffrey (*c.*1340–1400) One of the greatest English poets, Chaucer was also a man of business and a Londoner active about the court, principally under the patronage of John of Gaunt, duke of Lancaster. He travelled widely, especially in Italy in the 1370s, and his offices included control of important aspects of the customs services in London, and a period as clerk of works at the palace of Westminster, at the Tower of London and at St George's Chapel, Windsor. His published work began to appear in the late 1360s, but it is by the productions of his high maturity, notably *Troilus and Creseide* (*c.*1382) and, supremely, the *Canterbury Tales* (after 1386) that he is chiefly remembered.

He chose English as the principal medium of his work at a time when the triumph of the native language over French was by no means assured, and he introduced French and Italian styles of prosody which came to oust the traditional attachment of the English to alliterative verse. His superb blend of realism and imaginative insight, his humanity and sense of comedy mark him out as one of the finest creative minds of the age. The structure of the *Canterbury Tales* (told by a party of pilgrims, a cross-section of contemporary society, on the journey from Southwark to the shrine of Thomas Becket at Canterbury) owed much to Boccaccio's *Decameron*, but the treatment is English, original, and especially valuable to all historians interested in the thought and social attitudes of the late 14th c.
□ D. Brewer *Chaucer, the Critical Heritage 1385–1933* (1978)

Children's Crusade (1212) A curious by-product of the religious enthusiasm of the early 13th c., the so-called Children's Crusade originated in France and the Low Countries when a great crowd of children with a mixture of adults – some supportive, others bent on exploitation – set out for the Holy Land to free Jerusalem from the Infidel. The movement ended in fiasco and tragedy. Many of the children were brought home, but some perished in the Mediterranean and others were shipped from ports in the south of France to slavery in the Muslim-controlled territories of North Africa.

China The Mongol conquest of China began *c.*1206 when Jenghiz Khan rose to a position of supremacy amongst the Mongol peoples of the Steppes and initiated a period of expansion. Allying himself with the Tangut state in north-eastern Tibet in 1209, Jenghiz Khan then proceeded to attack the Chin

Chaucer depicted in the early 15th-c. Ellesmere manuscript of his *Canterbury Tales*.

Chivalry: a victorious knight is rewarded with a garland by his lady during a tournament (14th c.).

dynasty, who ruled the northern Chinese state of Juchen. By 1215 he had captured their capital at Ta-tu (Peking) and had reduced the Chin territory to a small area of Central China. In 1250 the Mongols resumed their attacks, this time against the Sung dynasty of southern China. Under the leadership of the grandsons of Jenghiz Khan, Grand Khan Mangu and his brother Khublai Khan, the Mongols overran the Sung state and by 1276 also controlled the capital city of Lin-an (Hangchow), where they established the Yuan dynasty (1279–1368). In the governmental sphere, the Mongols brought few changes either to northern or southern China, since they allowed to remain all that seemed best in the existing administration and religion of contemporary China. The impact of Chinese civilization on the Western world was minimal, though travellers to 'Cathay', notably Marco Polo, brought back stories from the 13th c. onwards which helped to enrich the Western imagination.
□ *China among equals* ed. M. Rossabi (1983)

Chivalry Accurately described as 'the secular code of honour of a martially oriented aristocracy', chivalry flourished in its Western European context between the mid-12th c. and 16th c. There are many strands in the evolution of what became a complex set of rules and conventions that applied primarily to the aristocratic fighting men, but which also had strong effect deep in the workings of medieval society.

Initially the impact of the church was great, and the notion of chivalric behaviour can properly be attributed to a softening of the epic virtues of bravery in battle and courage in adversity, to a more gentle attitude invoking a degree of respect for human life and dignity, even where mortal enemies were concerned. The blessing of banners, the inclusion in liturgical prayers of special intercession for warriors defending the Christians against the pagans, and growing interest in the warrior-saints St Michael and St George, anteceded the Crusades but coincided with the rise of the armed mounted warrior in Carolingian and Ottonian Europe.

The evolution of feudal society in the central Middle Ages, at home in Western Europe as well as on crusade, brought into being conditions especially favourable to the growth of chivalric ideals with their twin, but not always inseparable elements of Christianity and bellicosity. Associated etymologically (*chevalier*, 'knight') with the mounted elite of a feudal society, chivalry developed its characteristic institutions, rules and conventions in the course of the 12th c. and 13th c. at the hands of poets, as much as at the hands of legislators. Ceremonies of dubbing to knighthood, the giving of arms, the adoption of distinguishing emblems and blazons, emphasized the secular attributes of the ruling military aristocracy. The formation of military orders for the Crusades again brought in a strong religious element.

The tournament became the characteristic institution of the chivalric world, disapproved of by the church but flourishing, notably in the second half of the 12th c. and 13th c. Heralds became important and influential figures, partly because of the part they played in regulating tournaments. For all the dangers of tournaments – and casualties were often very heavy – the secular feudal world adopted them as profitable training grounds for young warriors and as great spectacles at which military valour could be colourfully displayed.

Another element entered strongly into the chivalric story: women were present as spectators at tournaments, and ideas of service to ladies and Courtly Love became entangled with the notion of the ideal warrior. A 13th-c. poem laid four obligations on the knight: to eschew false judgment and treason, to honour women, to attend mass every day and to fast on Friday. Poets generally, dealing with the matter of Rome, the matter of Charlemagne and his paladins, or the matter of Arthur, Britain and the Holy Grail, helped to implant notions of chivalric behaviour firmly into Western consciousness.

These ideas outlasted the loss of the Holy Land and were indeed strengthened in the later Middle

Ages, notably by the patronage of great kings and dukes and by the formation of chivalric orders such as the Order of the Garter in England or the Order of the Golden Fleece in Burgundy. Knights errant, embodying both the spirit of adventure and the religious quest, the search for the Grail or for union with God, became a significant part of the poetic consciousness of the West. Heraldry and interest in genealogy ensured that traditions of descent and good family remained a strong feature of the ruling group, but increasing attention was given to the notion that honour and nobility of manners would signify more than nobility of race.

Chivalry slowly but surely civilized a military society that, starting from rude and violent roots in the epic world of the early 11th c., blossomed through the romance, secular and religious, of the 12th and 13th c. into the formal regulated world of the later medieval period when knights, in theory at least, were also gentlemen. *See* COURTLY LOVE; KNIGHTHOOD HRL
□ G. Duby *The Chivalrous Society* (1977); M. Keen *Chivalry* (1984); B.B. Broughton *Dictionary of Medieval Knighthood and Chivalry* (1986); J. Barker *The Tournament in England 1100–1400* (1987)

Chrétien de Troyes (c.1135–83) Writing for a cultivated audience in the aristocratic courts of northern France between 1165 and 1180 (Marie, countess of Champagne, and Philip, count of Flanders, were among his patrons), Chrétien stands out as the most innovative and influential figure of 12th-c. vernacular literature. The founding father of the romance genre, his works were translated and imitated throughout Europe. Drawing inspiration both from a corpus of ultimately Celtic Arthurian legend, and from contemporary culture and courtly society, his best-known works include five long narrative poems: *Erec, Cligés, Yvain ou le Chevalier au lion, Lancelot ou le Chevalier à la charrette* and *Perceval ou le Conte du Graal.*

His principal concern seems to have been the chivalric ethos of his day and its moral implications. The action of his romances focuses on the knight errant in search of adventure who, confronted with various problems and crises, usually precipitated by love, grows in stature as he acquires an identity and new values, which enable him better to realize his individual potential and to fulfil his role in society. With his last, unfinished romance, *Perceval*, a religious dimension is introduced where previously love for a woman was presented as the main civilizing and ennobling influence on man. Some critics are content to interpret Chrétien's works as illustrating the reconciliation of man's dual need for love within marriage, and adventure. Others prefer to read between the lines, seeing him as a provocative, even subversive poser of difficult questions.

Chrétien's modern readers are likely to be struck by his constantly changing tone, and in particular by his juxtaposition of ostensible realism and obvious fantasy. In addition to his versatile handling of the octosyllable, his dramatic exploitation of dialogue and rhetoric, and his skill in structuring the narrative, Chrétien's unobtrusive learning, his gift for psychological observation and analysis (particularly of love), his humour and pervasive use of irony combine to give a sense of easy elegance and sophistication to his work. *See* ROMANS D'AVENTUR IS
□ J. Frappier *Chrétien de Troyes* (1957); L. Topsfield *Chrétien de Troyes: a Study of the Arthurian Romances* (1981)

Christianity According to the definition of the Council of Nicaea (325), the belief in one God manifested in three persons – Father, Son and Holy Spirit – and in the redemption of the world by the Incarnation, Passion and Resurrection of Jesus Christ. Subsequent Councils at Ephesus (431) and Chalcedon (451) added further definitions in the field of Christology, declaring that the Son, who is the Divine Word, became truly incarnate by the Holy Spirit in the flesh of the Virgin Mary, and that he combines within himself, without distinction of persons, the perfect and complete natures of God and man. The code of behaviour which should bind all believers had been laid down by Christ himself in the Golden Rule (*Matthew* 22, v.37–40).

During the first three centuries AD the full implications of this faith had developed slowly, in a society which treated its adherents at best with indifference, and at worst with active persecution. The rulers of the Roman empire regarded Christians as the tiresome, slightly mad members of a potentially dangerous secret society. It was not until the Emperor Constantine issued his edict of toleration (312) that Christianity was accepted as a respectable religion, and the assembling of the Council of Nicaea was a testimony to the fact that the church had emerged from the state of a proscribed sect into that of a fashionable religion. It was not, however, until 395 that the Emperor Theodosius officially suppressed the public worship of pagan gods. Between 325 and 451, by the decrees of ecumenical councils, orthodox Christianity was disentangled from several major heresies (Gnosticism, Arianism, Nestorianism and Apollinarianism) which had grown up since the end of the Apostolic period.

From c.400 to c.1500 Christianity was accepted as the spiritual aspect of civilized society, at first in those parts of Europe, Asia and North Africa which had formed part of the Roman empire. Gradually, by missionaries, it was spread over the barbarian kingdoms of Northern and Eastern Europe, while at the same time the advance of the Muslims reduced the position of the Christians in Asia, Africa and the Spanish peninsula to that of dependent, though not usually persecuted, minorities.

Within the Christian lands it was normally assumed that all people would, at the earliest possible opportunity, be brought into the church by the sacrament of baptism, and that they would remain in it, periodically refreshed by the sacrament of the Eucharist, until the time of their death. The Fourth Lateran Council (1215) laid down the rule that Communion, preceded by the confession of sins, was to be received at least once a year. Besides baptism and the Eucharist, the church recognized five other sacraments: confirmation, penance, extreme unction, holy orders and marriage. Since most lay people were unable to read or write (the word *clericus* means both a man in orders and one who is literate), education – from the simplest teaching by the parish priest to the advanced speculations of the higher schools of learning – was the responsibility of the church, and theology was accepted as the supreme branch of knowledge. Although most people failed to live up to the moral standards imposed by the Christian faith, there is little evidence (after the initial troubles of conversion) of resistance to the faith itself. Attacks upon the clergy nearly always arose from social and political, rather than doctrinal or moral disputes, and attacks upon outsiders, Jews, Muslims, heretics and infidels, were more often the result of popular intolerance than of official disapproval.

The orthodox teaching of the church was guaranteed by the doctrine of the Apostolic Succession. Authority to teach had been given by Christ to St Peter (*Matthew* 16, v.18–19) and confirmed to the Apostles at Pentecost. The Apostles had passed on their doctrine to the bishops, the correctness of the tradition being guaranteed by the fact that the bishops and all their successors had to receive consecration in the presence of at least three existing bishops of accepted orthodoxy. Priests and those in lower orders (door-keeper, reader, exorcist, acolyte, sub-deacon and deacon) in turn received ordination from their local bishop. Bishops were traditionally under the authority of five patriarchs (of Rome, Constantinople, Jerusalem, Antioch and Alexandria), but from the 7th c. onwards the last three of these cities were in Muslim hands, and the supremacy of Rome and Constantinople, the two ruling cities of the empire, had been firmly established by the time of the Council of Chalcedon (451). The Council had declared the primacy of Rome, which was the city honoured by the double tradition of St Peter and

St Paul, but from the 6th c. onwards Rome and Constantinople increasingly went their separate ways, and their deepening political divisions were complicated by a doctrinal dispute (over the procession of the Holy Spirit) which led to a schism, still unhealed, in 1054.

The coercive authority of the church was embodied in canon law, defined as the branch of law dealing with five main subjects: *jus*, *judicium*, *clerus*, *connubia* and *crimen*. It covered all cases of sin (as opposed to crime, cognizable by the lay courts), and all cases concerning churches, the persons of the clergy and their property (except when this was held in lay fee), marriage, legitimacy and inheritance; it also extended special protection to *miserabiles personae* such as widows, orphans and refugees. It was based upon the scriptures, the teachings of the fathers of the church, and the decrees of general and regional ecclesiastical councils. These were supplemented in the Western church (the patriarchate of Rome) by the decrees of successive popes and, before the end of the 11th c., by some rulings made by accredited lay rulers upon subjects such as marriage and the suppression of idolatry. It was generally accepted that the teachings of scripture and the decrees of the first four ecumenical councils – Nicaea (325), Constantinople I (381), Ephesus (431) and Chalcedon (451) – were inviolable, but that other decrees could be modified later by the pope in council, when the church had received further light upon the subject.

From the 12th c. onwards the canon law of the Western church was brought together in five great official collections – the *Decretum* of Gratian, the *Gregorian Decretals*, the *Sext*, the *Clementines* and the *Extravagantes* – which together make up that section of canon law which is called *Jus Novum*. It was held to be binding upon all baptized persons, and was enforced by ecclesiastical courts in every part of Western Christendom. Final authority rested with the pope, as the successor of St Peter, to whom Christ had given the power to bind and loose. To him, as the universal ordinary, belonged the power to grant dispensation, alleviating the rigour of the law, provided he did not reverse its fundamental principles.

In the Eastern empire (the patriarchate of Constantinople), which remained faithful to Roman law, the scriptural, patristic and conciliar basis of canon law was accepted, but otherwise imperial legislation covered the law of the church. Christian emperors such as Justinian made considerable modifications to Roman law for the benefit of the Christian religion, but the power of legislation remained with them alone. The emperor, as viceroy of God, was the supreme ruler in church and state; 'I am he', in the words of Leo the Isaurian, 'whom God has ordered to feed his flock, like Peter, Prince of the Apostles'. The only surviving compilation of canon law, the *Exegesis Canonum* of Balsamon of Antioch, dates from about 1175.

Throughout the Middle Ages the basic doctrines of Christianity were extensively studied, but they were never seriously questioned in Europe except by a relatively small number of heretics. Strife between the leaders of church and state was common and frequently bitter, but it turned upon political and economic rivalries, rather than upon fundamental questions of belief. However deplorably Christians failed in practice, they were united in theory by the conviction that 'the true end of man is to glorify God and to enjoy him for ever'. *See* CHURCH, CATHOLIC; CHURCH, EASTERN ORTHODOX; CRUSADES; MONASTI-CISM; PAPACY RH
□ R.H. Bainton *The Penguin History of Christianity* (1967); *Oxford History of the Christian Church* (1967–)

Christine of Pisa (1364–*c.*1430) A leading French poet of her generation, Christine was Italian by birth, the daughter of a scholar and statesman active in Bologna and Venice, who became astrologer to King Charles V of France. Christine married the king's notary and secretary, Etienne du Castel, and after his death (1389) concentrated on literary work under the patronage of the French kings and dukes of Burgundy. Initially she wrote many love poems after the fashion of the age, but turned to more didactic and historical themes. Her most important

Title page for an English translation (*c.*1521) of the *City of Ladies*, showing **Christine of Pisa**.

work was produced in the first decade of the 15th c. and included a history of Charles V, tracts in favour of the honour of women and opposed to the satirical flourishes of the ever-popular *Roman de la Rose*, and suggestions for the literary education of women. In the last years of her life she wrote a poem in praise of Joan of Arc. Her work contains much of prime value for the history of court life and for an understanding of contemporary attitudes to women.
□ J.M. Pinet *Christine de Pisan* (1927); *Christine de Pisan: The Treasure of the City of Ladies* trans. S. Lawson (1985)

Chrodegang, St (d. 766) Bishop of Metz. Born near Liège and educated at the abbey of Saint-Trond, Chrodegang became successively secretary, chancellor and chief minister of Charles Martel. After Charles' death (741), Chrodegang continued to serve his son Pepin the Short. Appointed bishop of Metz in 742, he was largely responsible for the negotiations between Pepin and the papacy, which resulted in the recognition of Pepin as king of the Franks by Pope Stephen III in 754; he also did much to help establish Frankish rule in Italy after the overthrow of the Lombards. He is perhaps most famous for his Rule for canons, which in time became very influential in regulating the life of many cathedral chapters in both Germany and England.
□ *The Old English version of the Enlarged Rule of Chrodegang* ed. A.S. Napier (1916)

Chronicles Like annals, these played an important part in the development of historical writing in the Middle Ages. They too describe events, but usually in more detail than annals, sometimes to the point where the chronicler produces acceptable history even if his work is generally bound to a strict chronological sequence. The first chronicles were the so-called world or universal chronicles which dealt with history from the date of the Creation until the writer's own times. The earliest of these was the chronicle of Eusebius of Caesarea written in the 3rd c., and this was followed by the world chronicle of Sulpericus Severus in the 4th c.

Although world chronicles continued to be written until the 11th c., when Marianus Scotus (1028–83) wrote his *Universal History*, from the 9th c. onwards more localized chronicles describing the history of a particular kingdom or abbey became more popular. Examples of the former include the Anglo-Saxon Chronicle in its different versions (assembled initially into chronicle form during the reign of Alfred, *c.*891), the *History of the Kings of Saxony* by Thietmar of Marseburg in the 10th c., the *Gesta Regum* of William of Malmesbury in the 12th c. and the *Polychronicon* of Ranulf Higden in the 13th c.,

Catholic church: the College of Cardinals, from an early 14th-c. manuscript of the Decretals of Boniface VIII.

whilst famous monastic chronicles include the *Battle Abbey Chronicle* in England and the *History of the Abbey St Evroul* by Ordericus Vitalis in France, both belonging to the 12th c. Late in the Middle Ages, chroniclers still prided themselves, notably and self-consciously in Italy, on their skill in setting down purely factual material, no more and no less, in proper chronological order, even when they were in fact moving towards a new conception of history.
□ L. Green *Chronicle into History* (1972)

Chrysoloras, Manuel (1350–1415) Byzantine nobleman and founder of Greek studies in Renaissance Italy. He first came to Italy in 1394 on a mission for the Emperor Manuel II, and in 1396 he was made professor of Greek at the School of Florence. After 1400 he resided permanently in Europe, teaching at Venice, Milan, Pavia and Rome. Pope Gregory XII sent him on several missions, and he died whilst attending the Council of Constance (1414–18). His translations into Latin of Homer and Plato, and his Greek grammar did much to revive the study of Greek in the West. His pupils included both Leonardo Bruni and Guarino of Verona.
□ G. Cammeli *I dotti Bizantini e le origini dell'humanesimo: I Manuele Crisolora* (1941)

Chrysostom, St John (347–407) Bishop of Constantinople. Born at Antioch, in 373 John became a monk in an austere mountain community. In 381, however, he returned to Antioch where he was ordained priest and subsequently became the bishop's chief assistant. In 397 he was appointed patriarch of Constantinople and quickly began to attack the immorality which he found there amongst the clergy and laity alike. This earned him the hostility of the Empress Eudoxia who, together with Theophilus, patriarch of Alexandria, worked to bring about John's disgrace. They were largely successful: John was exiled on two separate occa-sions, the second time in 404, and continued to be hounded around the empire until his death at Pontus in 407. He is best known for his treatise on the priesthood and for his biblical commentaries on the Epistles and Gospels, in which he insisted upon a literal interpretation of the scriptures and attempted to apply their teaching in a practical sense to the problems of his time.
□ R. Janin *Constantinople byzantine* (1964)

Church, Catholic Christian church which accepts the doctrine laid down in the Nicene and Athanasian Creeds, as opposed to heretical congregations such as Nestorians or Arians. It was the undivided orthodox church before the schism of 1054, and the orthodox church of Western Christendom throughout the Middle Ages. Catholics accepted the pope, bishop of Rome and lawful successor of St Peter, as vicegerent of Christ and universal ordinary (bishop whose authority extended throughout the whole church). This doctrine of papal supremacy grew up gradually at Rome during the first six centuries AD, and was spread north of the Alps by the fact that (except in the territory which became modern France) conversion to Christianity was carried out by missionaries sent from, or indirectly dependent on, the church of Rome. The plenitude of papal authority was not finally or universally claimed until the time of Gregory VII (1073–85). Thereafter it was made binding in canon law, and elaborated in a series of general councils from the First Lateran (1123) to the Council of Basle (1431). Decretals and letters issued by the pope in solemn conclave were binding upon the whole church, and his curia was the final court of appeal in all cases of canon law. Any deviation from the basic doctrines of the church was heresy, and as such punishable by penance, imprisonment or, in extreme cases, death, although this penalty had to be inflicted by the secular authority. Papal power was exercised through legates, either sent directly from the curia or permanently resident in each country (*legati nati*), nuncios (generally concerned with financial affairs) and judges delegate, appointed to deal with particular cases in ecclesiastical courts.

The church was organized in provinces (each ruled by an archbishop) and dioceses (each ruled by a bishop). By the 12th c., dioceses were sub-divided for administrative purposes into archdeaconries and rural deaneries, although the bishop always retained overriding authority and he alone could administer the sacraments of confirmation and ordination. Church discipline was organized through a series of ecclesiastical courts, ranging from the court of the archdeacon to that of the senior archbishop of the country (in England known as the Court of Arches).

The lowest unit of organization was the individual parish; here, responsibility for the cure of souls lay with the rector, or in the case of an appropriated church or a dispensed non-resident, with the vicar, sometimes assisted by a stipendiary chaplain. Rectors and vicars were instituted by the bishop of the diocese, after presentation by the patron of the living, and normally held secure tenure until death or resignation. They could be removed for misconduct, but this rarely happened.

This 'regular', as opposed to 'secular', clergy included monks, nuns, canons regular, friars and members of military orders such as the Templars. They lived by Rules imposed by the heads of their own orders, under the final authority of the pope. Many, though not all, were exempt from diocesan jurisdiction. They could hold (or in the case of the Franciscans, have the use of) corporate property, although individual members were vowed to poverty. Members of such orders could become bishops, but not archdeacons or parish priests. Hermits and anchorites existed, and some became famous, but generally their influence was much less than in the Eastern church. All members of religious orders and all secular clergy above and including the state of subdeacon were vowed to celibacy, although before the end of the 11th c. this rule was not always enforced. All clergy were under the protection of the canon law. *See* GREAT SCHISM; HERESY; INVESTITURE CONTEST; NICAEA, COUNCIL OF; PAPACY   RH
□ R.H. Bainton *The Medieval Church* (1962); R.W. Southern *Western Society and the Church in the Middle Ages* (1970); J. Gaudemet *La société ecclésiastique dans l'Occident mediéval* (1980)

Church, Eastern Orthodox The term 'orthodox' should correctly be applied to the Catholic church in contradistinction to heretical sects, but it is generally used to describe the Eastern church, consisting after the Islamic invasions of the patriarchate of Constantinople, together with those churches in Slavonic-speaking lands which owed their conversion to it. This church accepted the authority of the scriptures and of the seven ecumenical councils: Nicaea I (325), Constantinople I (381), Ephesus (431), Chalcedon (451), Constantinople II (553), which condemned the Nestorian Three Chapters, Constantinople III (680), which condemned the Monothelites, and Nicaea II (787), which condemned the Iconoclasts. It repudiated the primacy of the pope, and regarded the emperor as its divinely authorized head, although (since his office was in theory elective) he ruled as representative of the whole body of the faithful. It was he who appointed the patriarch of Constantinople, and who, after the Muslim overrunning of the patriarchates of Jerusalem, Antioch and Alexandria, was accepted as the senior spiritual authority in the East. The church of Constantinople was instrumental in converting the Serbians, Bulgarians, Rumanians, Moravians and Russians.

In 867 and in 1054 quarrels broke out between the Orthodox and Catholic clergy, which led to breaches of unity. The cause of these disputes was basically political (the claim of Rome to represent St Peter and the ultimate authority of Christ) rather than doctrinal (the nature of the procession of the Holy Spirit), so it is doubtful whether the generally used description of schisms (defined as a 'formal and wilful separation from the unity of the church') is not too strong a term to be correct. Communion between the two churches was restored after 867, but not after 1054; an attempt at reunion was made at the Council of Ferrara (1438), but the Orthodox church never accepted it. This was not entirely surprising, as political relations between East and West had grown steadily worse since the 10th c., and in 1204 the city of Constantinople and the metropolitan church of S. Sophia had been brutally sacked by the Catholic Franks.

In the Orthodox church, bishops and all higher clergy were traditionally drawn from monasteries and were celibate. Parish priests were chosen locally by their congregations and presented to the bishop for ordination; they were required to marry. The authority of the priesthood was rather less than in the West; correspondingly, the influence of lay theologians who were monks or hermits was much greater. The basic Rule of Eastern monasticism was that of St Basil. Doctrinally, the church was marked by an unchanging liturgy and a particularly deep devotion to the Resurrection. The Blessed Virgin, the 'All-Holy', was acclaimed as patroness of the church and city of Constantinople.

During the 8th c. the Orthodox church was involved in a serious controversy over the veneration of images. A dynasty of 'Iconoclast' emperors from the Asiatic provinces (possibly influenced by the strict prohibition of images in Islam) tried to abolish the use of images and icons on the grounds that it led to idolatry. Their teaching was unpopular and was formally condemned in 787; since then, icons have played a major part in Orthodox worship. In the 14th c. a dispute arose over the teaching of Hesychasm, a system of mystical contemplation leading to illumination by the divine light of God, practised among the monks of Mount Athos. Since the opponents of Hesychasm were generally identified with Western influence, it became after 1351 an accepted teaching of the church, although its influence declined after the 16th c. *See* ICONOCLASTIC CONTROVERSY; NESTORIUS   RH
□ H.W. Haussig *A History of Byzantine Civilization*

Eastern Orthodox church: the magnificent cathedral of S. Sophia in Constantinople, built by Justinian.

(1971); S. Runciman *The Byzantine Theocracy* (1977); J.M. Hussey *The Orthodox Church in the Byzantine Empire* (1986)

Cid, el (Rodrigo Diaz) (*c.*1043–99) Born in the village of Bivar, near Burgos. His family were *infanzones*, the lowest rank of the Castilian nobility (roughly equivalent to baronets). Knighted by Sancho II of Castile, Rodrigo became his *alférez* (standard-bearer; in effect, commander-in-chief), and defeated Alfonso VI of Leon at Golpejera (1072). A few months later Sancho's assassination and Alfonso's return to the thrones of Leon and Castile removed Rodrigo from the centre of power. Although Alfonso arranged a marriage (1074) with Jimena Díaz, of royal Leonese blood, as a measure of reconciliation, distrust remained. (Rodrigo and Jimena were not related: Díaz is not a surname, but a patronymic, 'child of Diego'.) Jealous courtiers from the higher nobility intrigued against Rodrigo, whom they saw as a threat, both for his personal qualities and as a member of a vigorous new class.

Their chance came in 1081, when Rodrigo raided the Muslim kingdom of Toledo. He was banished, and took service with the amir of Saragossa, whose army he commanded for several years with great success – there was nothing unusual in such alliances until the invasion of the Almoravids. There he acquired the Arabic title *sayyid* ('lord'), hispanicized as *Cid*. A reconciliation with King Alfonso (1087) lasted only two years, and, banished again, Rodrigo moved south-east, using his military and political skills and his intimate knowledge of the Spanish Muslims to make the kingdom of Valencia his sphere of influence. He kept the Almoravids at bay (his were the only victories won against them by any Christian general at this time), and when his protégé the king of Valencia was murdered in a pro-Almoravid coup (1092), he besieged the city, which surrendered after two years. From 1094 Rodrigo ruled Valencia, nominally for Alfonso, in practice as sovereign (e.g., appointing a French Cluniac as bishop). He defeated an Almoravid offensive, and, reconciled again with Alfonso, held the city until his death.

The only son of Rodrigo and Jimena died in battle (1097) without issue. One of their daughters married a Navarrese prince, and the other married the count of Barcelona. Their descendant became king of Castile and Leon in the 12th c., and their blood entered the English royal line in the mid-13th c. through Eleanor of Castile. Rodrigo is depicted by Arabic historians as a cruel oppressor, but by the 12th-c. *Historia Roderici* and the legends of the monastery of S. Pedro de Cardeña (where he and Jimena are buried) as a lay saint. The real man may emerge most clearly in the *Poem of the Cid* (*c.*1207), though much of its plot is fiction: he is presented as brave, loyal, a wise and realistic ruler – perhaps the only epic hero ever to have worried about his ability to pay his soldiers. Later ballads, from which Corneille's *Le Cid* indirectly descends, give a more fanciful picture. ADD
□ R. Menéndez Pidal *The Cid and his Spain* (1934); S. Clissold *In Search of the Cid* (1965); *The Poem of the Cid* ed. I. Michael, trans R. Hamilton and J. Perry (1975)

Ciompi, revolt of the (1378) An uprising of the artisan classes in Florence which was directed against the degree of control exercised by the major guilds in city affairs. The rebels, who demanded higher wages and a share in town government for the minor guilds, took over control of the municipality on 22 July and thus brought into being one of the most democratic governments in the history of Florence. One small group, the Ciompi, or wage-earning woodworkers, were dissatisfied with the new regime, however, and in August rebelled against it; the major and minor guilds united with one supreme effort to defeat them. Although after the suppression of the Ciompi the minor guilds remained nominally in control, the major guilds again began to take the initiative, and within four years had regained power. *See* LANDO, MICHELE DI
□ F. Schevill *Medieval and Renaissance Florence* (1961)

Cisneros, Francesco (Ximenes) (1436–1517) Archbishop of Toledo. Spanish cardinal who, following the capitulation of the Moors of Granada (1492), refused to sanction the promised religious toleration. His actions resulted in a long and bitter insurrection on the part of the Muslims, which was only ended by a decree (1502) granting them the choice of either banishment or conversion. Many Moors therefore became nominal Christians or Moriscos, but their religious convictions remained questionable.
□ J. Garcia Oro *Cisneros y la reforma del clero español en tiempo de los Reyes Catolicos* (1970)

Cistercian Order One of the new religious orders which grew up during the early 12th c. in response to the call for greater asceticism. Founded in 1098 by Robert, abbot of Molesme, who had left his own abbey because of the laxity of its religious observance, it took its name from the location of its first house at Cîteaux in France. The aim of the Cistercian Order was to live the Rule of St Benedict, literally interpreted. Although Robert himself was forced to return to Molesme in 1099, his work was continued by the next two abbots of Cîteaux, Alberic (1099–1109), who obtained formal recognition of the Order from the papacy, and Stephen Harding (d. 1134), who was responsible for the compilation of much of the first legislative document of the Order, the *Carta Caritatis* ('Charter of Divine Love').

The greatest expansion of the Order, however, took place under St Bernard, abbot of Clairvaux, a leading figure both in the Order itself and in Christendom as a whole. The growth of the Order was rapid: by 1132 there were Cistercian houses in France, Italy, Germany, England and Spain, whilst the Order later spread as far afield as Norway, Sicily and Rumania. By 1200 there were over 500 Cistercian houses, and the number had increased to an estimated 742 by the early 16th c.

The Cistercians provided for two separate classes of monks: the choir monks, many of whom were priests and therefore well educated, and the lay brothers who tilled the fields or pursued their trade within the monastery. The Cistercians therefore provided a much needed opportunity for ordinary men from a non-aristocratic background who wished to lead the monastic life. As a result of their strict interpretation of the Rule of St Benedict, the liturgy of the Cistercians was much simpler than that of contemporary Benedictines. Their monastic buildings too were plain, with little or no decorative

The abbey of Rievaulx in North Yorkshire, one of the many **Cistercian** houses founded during the 12th c.

detail, and in the 12th c. at least, most of their churches had plain, square east ends. In order to resist wordly temptations the Cistercians chose secluded sites for their abbeys; Fountains and Rievaulx, for example, were established on the Yorkshire moors, whilst some 15 houses were situated in the uncultivated wastelands east of the river Elbe in Germany.

Economically, therefore, the Cistercians became very important, since they were responsible for reclaiming much marginal territory in the interests of agriculture. They aimed at self-sufficiency, growing their own corn and rearing their own sheep in order to provide wool for their habits. Unlike the Benedictines, the Cistercians did not rent out their landholdings to lay tenants, but instead farmed them directly through a series of granges or farmsteads administered by the lay brothers. Another striking feature of the Cistercian Order was the close watch kept by the abbey of Cîteaux upon the other Cistercian houses. Each year, every Cistercian abbot was expected to journey to Cîteaux for a general chapter of the Order, although exceptions were made because of the distances involved. At this general chapter regulations concerning the whole Order were made, and individual abbots were reprimanded or commended. In addition, the abbot of each mother house was responsible for the visitation of all its daughter houses. The usefulness of this constitutional framework was soon recognized by the whole church, and at the Fourth Lateran Council (1215) the duty of holding regular general chapters was imposed upon all religious orders.   AD

□ *Statuta Capitulorum Generalium Ordinis Cisterciensis* ed. J.M. Canivez vol. 1 (1933); C.N.L. Brooke *The Monastic World* (1974)

Clara of Assisi, St (1194–1253) Born at Assisi into the Offreduccio family, Clara was so inspired by the life of St Francis that in 1214 she renounced all her possessions and joined him at the Portiuncula. Unwilling to allow women to participate in his wandering life of begging and preaching, Francis established Clara and her companions in a house adjacent to the church of S. Damiano in 1215, thus founding the Order of Poor Clares. Although they were an enclosed order, owing much to the traditions of the Rule of St Benedict, the Poor Clares lived a life of great poverty and austerity and soon became extremely popular. By the end of the 13th c. there were 47 houses in Spain alone, whilst convents of Poor Clares were also established in England, France and Bohemia.

□ J. Moorman *A History of the Franciscan Order* (1968); R.B. and C.N.L. Brooke, 'St Clare', *Medieval Women* ed. D. Baker (1978)

St Clara laments the death of St Francis as the cortège halts before her convent in Assisi.

Clarendon, Constitutions of (1164) Decrees by Henry II of England which attempted to establish a formal relationship between church and state. In the Constitutions, appeals to Rome were forbidden without royal permission; all litigation between clerks concerning benefices was to be heard in the royal court; royal permission was required for clergy to leave the realm and also for tenants-in-chief to be excommunicated. Great opposition was shown to the decree, which stated that criminous clerks were to be tried first in the secular court and only then sent to the ecclesiastical court, the secular court also reserving the right of punishment. Although purporting to declare usages common in the reign of Henry I, the Constitutions were not accepted by Thomas Becket and the English clergy; the customs prejudicial to the church were renounced by Henry at Avranches (1172) after Becket's murder.
□ C. Duggan, 'The Becket Dispute and the Criminous Clerks', *Bulletin of the Institute for Historical Research* (1962); W.L. Warren *The Governance of Norman and Angevin England 1086–1272* (1987)

Clement V Pope 1305–14 After studying canon law at Orleans and Bologna, he became bishop of Commignes in 1295 and archbishop of Bordeaux in 1299. A Gascon by birth, he was crowned pope at Lyons and never in fact entered Italy. In 1309 he transferred the curia to Avignon and appointed nine new French cardinals. For the most part he failed to exert substantial influence on the French King Philip

IV. He exonerated Philip in the question of the trial of Pope Boniface VIII, whom Philip had indicted and imprisoned, and at the king's request abolished the Templars at the Council of Vienne in 1312. Clement did much, however, to centralize papal government and also founded the university of Perugia in 1307
□ G. Mollat *The Popes at Avignon* (1952)

Clermont, Council of (1095) It was here that, following a request for military aid against the Muslims by the Emperor Alexius I Comnenus, Urban II launched the First Crusade. Urban's intention was not only to aid the Byzantines, but also to recapture Jerusalem for Christianity, whilst at the same time channelling the troublesome and war-like knightly classes into a useful campaign outside Europe. His preaching was greeted with an outstanding degree of enthusiasm by those present at the Council, many of whom rushed to take up their crusading vows with cries of *Deus volt* ('God wills it'), the phrase which became the battle-cry of the campaign.
□ H.E.J. Cowdrey, 'Pope Urban II's preaching of the First Crusade', *History* (1970)

Climate The climate of Europe in the Middle Ages was usually warmer than in the Little Ice Age that followed (1590–1850), the warmest centuries being comparable to the 20th c., and the coldest to the 19th c. Evidence for the early Middle Ages comes especially from tree-rings that reflect summer temperature fluctuations; in the later Middle Ages chroniclers provide information about ice and snow, and it is thereby possible to determine the temperature of every decade. Rainfall fluctuations are difficult to assess in the early Middle Ages, although changes in the density of peat verify the hypothesis that at the time of the 5th-c. migrations, the North European plain was especially dry.

The main sequence of climate change was thus as follows: in *c.*400 the weather was both dry and warm, and until 800 it was mainly warm, although cooler summers had occurred in the mid-6th c. and late 7th c. The period 800–950 was particularly cold, but this was followed by a very warm phase (950–1100), the period in which Greenland was colonized. Summers were cold again in the first half of the 12th c., but very hot in the second half. Minor fluctuations then occurred, but another cold phase in the mid-15th c. was followed by a long warm period beginning in 1470 and lasting until 1560. During the warm periods of the Middle Ages wine was made in many parts of northern France and, as Domesday Book confirms, grapes were grown successfully in parts of England.

Climate

In the period 1000–1500 documentary evidence makes it possible to determine more precisely the characteristics of almost every decade. Some, such as the 1090s (the time of the First Crusade), 1190s, 1310s (when demographic expansion ended), 1340s and 1360s, were very wet in north-west Europe; others, such as the 1130s, 1200s, 1300s and 1470s, were very dry.

Crop failures, demographic crises and famine often reflect a series of wet years in Europe, which led to typhus in winter, ergotism in rye localities, and sheep-rot, with all its disastrous consequences for the economy. In north-west Europe the years 1125, 1151, 1174, 1193, 1195, 1224, 1233, 1256, 1257, 1258, 1271, 1294, 1315, 1316, 1330 were excessively wet. In Europe 1257–58 excessive rains (possibly associated with the volcanic eruptions of that period), led to such a famine that the poor devoured horse flesh, the bark of trees and things still worse. In 1315 and 1316 the rains were worse still, and the St Swithin's flood of 17 July 1316 partly explains the legend.

There is good evidence for decades of warm winters in north-west Europe centred c.1187, c.1197, c.1240, c.1292, c.1387 and c.1475. Decades of cold winters are c.1128, c.1206, c.1218, c.1305, c.1376, c.1398, c.1403, c.1422, c.1436 and c.1455. Long cold winters were experienced in 671, 764, 860, 913, 1074, 1150, 1205, 1225, 1282, 1306, 1264, 1299, 1408, 1423, 1435, 1443, 1458, 1460, 1465, 1481 and 1491.

English evidence is scattered but comparatively rich; it is known, for example, that the winter of 764 was exceptionally severe, the snow and ice lasting into the spring, and that the year 871, when there was a great mortality of birds, also experienced a very severe winter. A full picture on a European scale will only be possible when all the evidence is brought together from the south as well as the north of Europe, with details relating to both drought and cold, to widespread summer fires (as in 764 and 1087 in England) and to complaints of excessive rain, flooding and other such disasters. *See* DENDROCHRONOLOGY   DJS

□ H.H. Lamb *Climate: present, past and future* (1972)

Clocks In the early Middle Ages time was kept by means of sun-dials, waterclocks, sand-glasses and candle-clocks, all of which had existed in the ancient world. The first weight-driven mechanical clocks date from the 14th c.; some, like those at Milan (1335), Salisbury (1386) and Rouen (1389), had a chiming device, although others simply activated an alarm system which alerted a keeper who then rang a bell. These early clocks were very large and had no hands or dials, although a smaller domestic version was soon invented. The first portable timepieces were invented c.1500 by Peter Henlein of Nuremberg and were driven by a spring. These had an hour hand, but no minute hand, the latter first appearing in 1672.

□ D.S. Landes *Revolution in Time: Clocks and the Making of the Modern World* (1984)

Clovis King of the Franks 480–511 (b.465) Son of Childeric I, he became king of the Salian Franks at Tournai in 480. He increased his power by brute force, disposing of his enemies, such as King Cloderic of Cologne. In 486 he defeated Syagrius, an independent Roman governor at Soissons and in the course of the succeeding 20 years won decisive victories over the Alemanni and the Visigoths, gaining control of most of Gaul except for the Mediterranean littoral. In 508 the Emperor Anastasius recognized him as a consul and patrician. His power was greatly enhanced by his conversion to Catholic Christianity at a time when most of the barbarian tribes embraced Arianism. In his law code, the *Lex Salica* (508), Clovis combined elements of both the Germanic and Roman traditions. He is generally recognized as the founder of the historic French monarchy.

□ E. James *The Origins of France from Clovis to the Capetians* (1982)

Possible evidence for changes in **climate**: an English calendar for February shows men pruning vines.

Types of **clock**, from a Flemish manuscript, *c*.1450, of *L'Horloge de Sapience*.

Cluny, abbey of Founded in 910 by Duke William the Pious of Aquitaine and placed under the strict protection of the papacy, the abbey reached its greatest peak under the abbots Odilo (994–1048) and Hugh the Great (1049–1109). During this period Cluny numbered more than 300 monks and possessed over 200 dependencies. To cope with this expansion, the abbey church was rebuilt twice in just over a century, Cluny II being dedicated in 981, and Cluny III in the early 12th c. The period of Cluny's greatness, however, came to an end with the disastrous abbacy of Pons (1109–22). Although this was partially remedied by the wise abbacy of Peter the Venerable (1122–57), he was unable to counteract the growing tendencies in the church as a whole towards asceticism and a simplification of the liturgy. *See* BERNO, ST; ODO [*324*]

□ J. Evans *The Romanesque Architecture of the Order of Cluny* (1938); K.J. Conant *Cluny, les églises et la maison du chef d'ordre* (1968)

Cluny, Order of Order of reformed Benedictines which received its name from the abbey of Cluny in French Burgundy. Although nominally following the Rule of St Benedict, the Cluniacs placed great stress upon the liturgical element of monastic life, thus having little time for manual labour, which was carried out by lay servants. Although initially those houses which were reformed by Cluny remained constitutionally independent, during the 11th c. the abbey began to gather a large number of dependencies over which it maintained strict control. All Cluniac monks owed direct obedience to the abbot of Cluny, whilst all Cluniac priors were expected to attend a general chapter at the mother house once a year. Since Cluny had been founded in direct dependence on the papacy, the Order was able, in time, to free itself from episcopal jurisdiction, and thereafter appointed its own visitors. Extremely

Reconstruction of the abbey of **Cluny** in *c*. 1157, viewed from the east (Kenneth Conant).

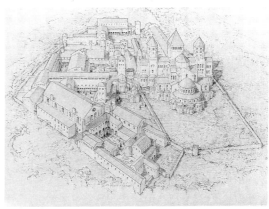

Stained-glass window from the house of **Jacques Coeur** in Bourges, showing a merchant's ship.

influential in providing the background for moral reform, the Cluniacs are now recognized as an element of indirect, rather than direct importance in the ferment of opinion that led to the assertion of papal monarchy by Gregory VII and to the Investiture Contest.
□ L.M. Smith *Cluny in the Eleventh and Twelfth Centuries* (1930); J. Evans *Monastic Life at Cluny 910–1157* (1931); G. Constable *Cluniac Studies* (1980)

Cnut King of Denmark 1019–35 and England 1016–35 (b. *c.*995) Cnut's first journey to England came in 1013 when, with his father Sweyn Forkbeard, he invaded England and took part in the defeat of Aethelred the Unready. Following Aethelred's death (1016), Cnut overcame the resistance of Edmund Ironside to become king of England. At first he was actively hostile towards the native English and generously rewarded his own followers, but after his marriage (1017) to Aethelred's widow, Emma of Normandy, Cnut showed himself much more willing to use native talent in his government.

In 1019 Cnut also became king of Denmark. Here his position was constantly threatened by the danger of attack from Norway and Sweden, although in 1026 the balance was at least partially redressed by the part he played in the overthrow of the Norwegian King Olaf II Haraldsson (St Olaf). Cnut was also known as a sponsor of trade and a patron of the church, founding monasteries and even making a pilgrimage to Rome (1027). He was succeeded by his illegitimate son Harold Harefoot (d. 1040) and then by his legitimate son Harthecnut (d. 1042).
□ L.M. Larson *Canute the Great* (1912)

Code of Justinian (*Codex Justinianus*) Collection of the laws and legal writings of ancient Rome, which were gathered together by order of the Emperor Justinian I. The *Code* consisted of four parts: the *Codex Constitutionum* (527–34), a collection of ancient Roman laws gathered together in ten books; the *Digest* (530–33), consisting of 50 books of quotations from Roman lawyers; the *Institutes* (533), an elementary textbook of legal institutions for those studying law; and the *Novels* or *Novellae* (534–65), a collection of all the laws issued by Justinian himself. With the exception of the *Novels*, which were written partly in Greek, the *Code* was written in Latin, and became the standard reference work on Roman law for much of the Middle Ages. *See* LAW; TRIBONIAN
□ P. Collinet *La genèse du Digeste, du Code et des Instituts de Justinien* (1952); J.A.C. Thomas *The Institutes of Justinian* (1975)

Coeur, Jacques (1395–1456) Son of a rich merchant of Bourges, Coeur was trading with the Levant by 1432, competing with the Italians for its custom. In 1436 he was made master of the Mint in Paris and in 1438, steward of the royal expenditure, for which he was ennobled. In 1444 he presided over the new *Parlement* of Languedoc; in 1445 his agents negotiated a treaty with the sultan of Egypt and in 1448, with the knights of Rhodes. In 1451 he was accused of poisoning Agnes, former mistress of the French king Charles VII; his property was confiscated and he was imprisoned. He escaped in 1455, was welcomed by Pope Nicholas V and became captain of the naval forces of the papacy in the attempt to recapture Rhodes. He died on this expedition at Chios on 25 November 1456.
□ A.B. Kerr *Jacques Coeur* (1927); P. Clément *Jacques Coeur et Charles VII* (1966)

Coimbra, university of Founded by King Dinis in 1290, Coimbra was the first university in Portugal and the only one to be established there in the Middle Ages. The university consisted of the four faculties of medicine, civil law, canon law and the arts. In the 14th c. it was chiefly noted for the study of astronomy, and did much to prepare the way for the Portuguese explorers. By the 15th c., the university was deeply committed to the study of mathematics.

Coinage and currency Medieval coins were very thin and light by modern standards (*c.*1g–*c.*4g), since the purchasing power of the precious metals was high, and were mostly made of silver or billon (silver less than 50 per cent pure). These were preceded in the 6th c. and 7th c. by a coinage of gold, and coins of this metal came back into general use between the mid-13th c. and the mid-14th c. In most of Europe copper was not minted at all, though the low quality billon widely used in the 14th c. and 15th c. was almost indistinguishable from copper; both this metal and lead were used for the unofficial tokens which supplemented regular coinage in these centuries. The basic unit, from the late 7th c. onwards, was the silver penny or denier. Generalizations about its history are difficult; although the same evolutionary pattern is found almost everywhere, the timetable varies from country to country.

Coinage and currency: gold tremissis minted at Dorestad by the moneyer Madelinus (mid-7th c.).

The Germanic states set up within the former Roman frontiers mainly had coinages of imitation gold tremisses (one-third *solidi*), distinguishable from their imperial prototypes only by their blundered inscriptions and distorted types. Imitations of *solidi* were minted only rarely – after 550 virtually only at Marseilles – and fractional coins of silver and copper were limited to Ostrogothic Italy, Vandal Africa and the Rhone valley down to *c.*550. Eventually the pseudo-imperial tremisses were replaced by national gold coinages varying in type and organization from one people to another. Frankish coinage, the most disorganized, was essentially private in character, the coins normally bearing the name of the mint where they were struck and the moneyer responsible, with no reference to a ruler. The change-over, which in the Merovingian kingdom occurred *c.*580, was accompanied by a reduction in the weight of the coins from 1.5 g to 1.3 g and involved a change in the weight system, 1.5 g representing eight Roman *siliquae* and 1.3 g being the equivalent of 20 (Troy) grains, or the Germanic shilling. This weight was also adopted for Anglo-Saxon gold coins in the 7th c., the coins traditionally called thrymsas by numismatists, being in reality shillings of 20 *sceattas* (grains).

The gold shilling, by that time somewhat debased, began to be replaced in the Frankish kingdom *c.*670 by a silver *denarius* (denier) of the same weight

and consequently worth its 1/12th, since the gold: silver ratio at the time was 1:12. A similar change occurred in England, probably at the same time and certainly before *c.*690, since the new coins appear in the Laws of Ine with the name of pennies. Under Pepin the Short and Charlemagne the designs of the Frankish coins were made uniform and their issue brought under royal control, the process ending

Denier of Charlemagne minted at Bourges (768–814). The silver denier replaced the gold shilling from *c.*670.

with the creation of Charlemagne's *novus denarius* in *c.*793. Again, corresponding developments took place in England under Offa of Mercia, though the eventual weights of the two coins differed, the new Frankish denier apparently weighing in principle 1.75 g (32 wheatgrains) and the English penny 1.56 g (24 barleycorns).

The coinage thus created dominated Latin Christendom for the next five centuries. Silver deniers modelled on those of France spread to north and central Italy (781), northern Spain (early 9th c.), Germany (10th c.), Bohemia (930s), Poland (980s) and Hungary (*c.*1000), passing to the eastern Mediterranean with the crusaders, and to southern Italy and Sicily with the Hohenstaufen. From England, the penny passed to Ireland and Scandinavia in the 11th c., and to Scotland in the 12th c. In some parts of Europe halfpennies and farthings were also struck (French *oboles* or *mailles*, *pites*), but fractions were more usually made by cutting the thin pennies into halves and quarters. No multiples were minted, and gold coins were struck only occasionally for ceremonial purposes. Exceptions to this rule were Christian Spain, southern Italy and Sicily, and the crusader states, for these were familiar with Muslim gold dinars and minted imitations of these (*besanti sarracenati*) or of their fractions (*taris*).

The number of mints in feudal Europe was very large. Minting was normally carried out locally, even in states where royal control of the coinage remained unimpaired. There were at one time over 70 mints in England, though all were striking coins of a uniform type and weight. In France and the Empire the *jus monetae* passed (by concession or successful usurpation) to a multitude of feudatories, and in Italy to many of the communes. Designs were extremely varied, and from the mid-11th c. there was in most places a considerable falling away from Carolingian standards of both weight and fineness. Most coins were struck to weights of between 0.7 g and 1.4 g, and were between 50 per cent and 90 per cent fine. But debasement was sometimes carried very far. In the late 12th c. the Venetian *denaro*, one of the worst in Europe, weighed about 0.36 g and was only about 25 per cent fine, so that its silver content was under 0.1 g, as against the 1.7 g of Carolingian days.

In the 13th c. silver multiples of virtually pure metal began to be struck under the generic names of groats (French *gros*, German *Groschen*, Italian *grosso*, i.e., *grossus denarius*), in contrast to the ordinary 'small' pennies (French *petits deniers*, Italian *piccoli*, *parvuli*). They generally weighed 2-4 g, and their values depended on how far the local penny had been debased. Venetian *grossi* weighed 2.1 g, and at the time of their creation (?1201) were worth 24 *denari*; the French *gros tournois* (1266) weighed 4.22 g

Silver *gros tournois* (1226–70) of Louis IX of France that weighed 4.22g.

and was worth a *sou* (12d); while the English groat (1351), though it weighed 4.67 g, was worth only four pennies (sterlings), since the English penny, in comparison with its Continental counterparts, had been only slightly reduced in weight and not at all in fineness. Gold coins also began to be struck on a regular basis, beginning with the Emperor Frederick II's *augustale* (1231) and continuing with the far more influential Florentine florin (1252), the Genoese *genovino d'oro* (1252), and the Venetian ducat (1284). The minting of gold spread more slowly north of the Alps: the first successful French gold coin, the *masse d'or* of Philip the Fair, and the English noble of Edward III date from 1295 and 1344 respectively. In the intervening period use of the gold florin was spread by the great Florentine merchants and bankers, while the Venetian ducat dominated the currency of the Near East.

The introduction of gold and silver multiples made life easier for merchants, for the new coins of good metals were acceptable internationally in a way that no earlier Western coin save the English sterling had been. Their disadvantages were the emergence of extremely complicated denominational patterns and constant fluctuations in value, for the system was virtually trimetallic, involving gold, silver and billon. Exchange rates fluctuated partly because of changes in the market ratios of gold and silver, partly because of the occasional overproduction of billon coins, and partly because governments were constantly altering the weight and fineness of the coins. This was usually in the hope of keeping coin values stable in terms of the traditional £sd system, but sometimes derived simply from a wish to increase their own profits. From the late 13th c. merchants found it necessary to compile increasingly complicated lists of coins and their values, of which the most famous is in the Florentine merchant Pegolotti's *La Pratica della Mercatura* (c.1340), and governments had to issue tables of exchange rates. The abundance of available silver in the late 13th c. and early 14th c. from Bohemian and Serbian mines was followed before the end of the 14th c. by a serious dearth, only partly balanced by the large output of the Hungarian gold mines in modern Slovakia. Not until the second half of the 15th c. was there an improvement, when increased supplies of European silver, and direct access to African gold as a result of the Portuguese exploration of the West African coast, formed a prelude to the arrival in the 16th c. of vast new supplies of precious metals, after the European discovery of America. *See* AUGUSTALE; BEZANT; BRACTEATE; CARAT; DUCAT; ECU; FLORIN; GULDEN; MARK; NOBLE; POUND; RENOVATIO MONETAE; SHILLING; SOLIDUS; STERLING; TARI [*9, 13, 24, 184, 291*] PG

□ P.Grierson *Monnaies du Moyen Age* (1976); P. Grierson and M. Blackburn *Medieval European Coinage* vol.1 (1986); P. Spufford *Money and its Role in Medieval Europe* (1988)

Colleoni, Bartolomeo (c.1400-75) Italian soldier of fortune. Initially serving in the forces of other mercenaries such as Braccio de Montone, Colleoni entered the service of the Venetian republic in 1432. Under Francesco Maria Gonzaga he won many victories for Venice, including the battles of Brescia and Verona. When Venice made peace with Milan in 1441 he changed sides, but in 1455 upon the offer of increased inducements from that republic, he returned to Venice with the rank of captain-general for life. When not at war he occupied his time in improving the agricultural yield of his estates.

□ B. Belotti *La Vita di Bartolomeo Colleoni* (1971)

Colonna family Powerful Roman family whose support for the imperial party and struggles with both the papacy and the Orsini family played an important part in medieval Italian politics. Members of the Colonna family supported the Emperors

Frederick I and Frederick II in their quarrels with the papacy, whilst Sciarra de Colonna aided the Frenchman Guillaume de Nogaret in his attack on, and imprisonment of Pope Boniface VIII in 1303. Although the secular members of the family were thus often at loggerheads with the papacy, the Colonna also boasted seven cardinals amongst its members: Giovanni (appointed 1212), who served as a legate to the Holy Land in the Fifth Crusade; Giacomo (appointed 1278); Pietro (appointed 1288); Giovanni (appointed 1327), who was responsible for the construction of the first steps up the Capitoline hill in 1348; Stefano (d. 1379); Agapito (d. 1380), who had previously served as nuncio to Emperor Charles IV and as peace envoy to Castile and Portugal; and Oddone, who in 1417 became Pope Martin V.

The secular Colonna were often renowned as great generals: Prospero and Fabrizio Colonna, for example, became so important in this role that when Charles VIII of France visited Rome in 1495 they formed part of the cavalcade which rode out to meet him. They drew their strength initially from their large estates around Rome and enjoyed a period of exceptional authority in Rome and the papal states when the papacy withdrew to Avignon (1309-77). □ J. Hook, 'Clement VII, the Colonna and Charles V', *European Studies Review* (1972).

Columba, St (521-97) Born at Gartran in Donegal, Columba trained as a monk under both Finnian of Moville and Finnian of Clonard before founding his own monasteries at Derry in 546 and at Durrow ten years later. In 563 he left Ireland and established a monastery on Iona. Although Iona was later to become an influential centre for the dissemination of Celtic monasticism throughout Scotland and northern England, Columba's own missionary work was largely confined to making conversions to Christianity in those parts of Scotland where Irish influence was particularly strong, and more especially in the Western Isles. He was also the scribe of the later 6th-c. psalter, the *Cathach of Columba*, the earliest surviving example of Irish majuscule script. □ A.D. and M.O. Anderson *Adomnan's Life of Columba* (1961); A.P. Smyth *Warlords and Holy Men* (1984).

Columbanus, St (543-615) Born at Leinster in Ireland, Columbanus became a disciple of Comgall of Bangor, with whom he remained until leaving for Gaul in 590. Establishing his first monastery at Annegray on a site given to him by King Childebert II of Austrasia, Columbanus soon attracted wider support and founded a further house at Luxeuil, where his monks lived according to the Irish tradition. After the death of Childebert, Columbanus

Halley's **comet** was seen as a portent of disaster in the year of the Norman conquest

increasingly came under attack both for his failure to accept the Roman date of Easter and for his refusal to bless the illegitimate sons of Theodoric II. Driven out of Frankia, he settled instead at Bobbio in Italy (613), where he founded a monastery which was subsequently to become famous for its fine library. Columbanus' writings include both a Penitential and a Rule, but the latter was never as popular as the much less strict Rule of St Benedict. □ K. Hughes *The Church in Early Irish Society* (1966); *Columbanus and Merovingian Monasticism* ed. H.B. Clarke and M. Brennan (1981)

Comets Like eclipses, these are useful for the accurate dating of chronicles, although historians do not always know their correct dates. Bede's comet of 678 actually occurred in 676, and his 'two' comets of 729 may subconsciously have been misplaced one year early to precede two deaths. Certainly, in the Anglo-Saxon Chronicle one copyist transferred the comet of 989 to 995, so that it would precede the death rather than the accession of Archbishop Sigeric. The correct date of comets can be more safely determined from the objective reports of the Far East than from the Christian chroniclers.

Halley's comet, which returns every three-quarters of a century, was particularly striking in the Middle Ages, appearing in 451, 530 607, 684, 760, 837, 912, 989, 1066, 1145, 1222, 1301, 1373 and 1456. It is depicted on the Bayeux tapestry as a portent of the Norman Conquest of England. In Russia (Muscovy) it was likewise regarded as a military portent. The Lavrentievsky Chronicle states: 'About this time there was a sign in the West. A very great star with blood rays was rising in the evening after sunset and it remained there for seven days. This appearance was not for good. After it

there was much civil strife and an invasion of the Russian land by infidels. It all happened because the star was a bloody one and foretold bloodshed.' In Constantinople Halley's comet of 530 was blamed for the drought, famine and mortality that followed in 536. In 1456 Toscanelli reported: 'Its head was round and as large as the eye of an ox, and from it issued a tail, fan-shaped like that of a peacock. Its tail was prodigious, for it trailed through a third of the firmament.' Other important comets were seen in 539, 565, 770, 773, 838, 975, 1006 (Supernova), 1106, 1264, 1337, 1366, 1402, 1468 and 1472. *See* ASTRONOMY DJS
□ D.J.Schove *Chronology of Eclipses and Comets, AD 1 – 1000* (1985)

Commentators School of Italian jurists led by Bartolus of Sassoferrato (1314-57), which aimed not merely to discover the meaning of Roman civil law by objective study, as the Glossators had done, but also to apply that law to contemporary society by fusing it with elements from canon law, municipal law and feudal law. Although the Commentators were extremely influential in both France and Germany, their methodology, which often involved hair-splitting logic, tended to confuse rather than to clarify the law; for this reason they were much criticized by the Italian humanists in the 15th c. *See* LUCAS DE PENNA
□ W. Ullmann *Law and Politics in the Middle Ages* (1975)

Commerce Trading and commercial activity played an important part in the economic life of the Middle Ages. Firstly there were the local markets, established for the exchange of surplus foodstuffs and other necessary commodities. Since they were so profitable, the right of granting these markets was jealously guarded by the monarchs of Europe; Charlemagne, for example, ordered the compilation of a complete list of the markets within his empire.

Yet commerce also involved long-distance trade in luxury goods. In the early Middle Ages, the Byzantine empire carried on the ancient Roman trade in silks, spices and dyestuffs with the East, whilst by the 9th c. she was also trading with the Scandinavian colony at Kiev. The greatest period of mercantile expansion for the West came about in the 12th c. The growth of agriculture in Western Europe resulted in increasing profit margins, and therefore higher living standards, whilst the discovery of the Freiburg silver mines meant that there was an increase in the amount of currency available, always an impetus to trade. As a result, new towns were set up all over Europe and those already in existence grew in power and independence. Thus the Lombard towns of Italy and the towns of the French Midi, for example, were involved in a trade which exported wood, iron and furs from Europe, importing in their stead cottons, silks and spices to be distributed in the fairs of Europe.

In the 13th c. another vigorous line of trade grew up between the wool-producing towns of England and the cloth-manufacturing towns of the Netherlands. One of the most famous trading alliances of the Middle Ages is the Hanseatic League, which provided much economic support for the towns of the Baltic seaboard and reached a highpoint in the mid-14th c. It is Italy, however, in the later Middle Ages, which provides evidence for the most intense commercial activity, with the evolution of banking and credit-raising facilities on a truly international scale. *See* FAIRS; SAN GIORGIO, BANK OF; WINE; WOOL
□ *The Cambridge Economic History of Europe* vol. 2, ed. M. Postan and E.E. Rich (1952); E. Carus-Wilson *Medieval Merchant Venturers* (1955); J. LeGoff *Marchands et Banquiers au Moyen-Age* (1956); M.M. Postan *Medieval Trade and Finance* (1973); E. Ashtorn *East-West Trade in the Medieval Mediterranean* (1986); R.S. Lopez *The Shape of Medieval Monetary History* (1986)

Communes Towns in medieval Western Europe which acquired self-governing municipal institutions by rebellion or force; the term is often also used to describe towns which obtained similar rights by charter. The characteristic privileges so obtained included personal liberty for the townsmen, freedom of tenure, the authority to regulate local trade, to levy tolls and to control the judicial procedures of the towns. Communes were particularly numerous in areas where political authority was weak, such as in northern Italy and Flanders. Eventually, however, civil strife in northern Italy led to the breakdown of communal organization, and the towns fell into the hands of *signori* such as the Medici in Florence. *See* TOWNS
□ H. Pirenne *Les villes du Moyen-Age* (1927); S. Reynolds *An Introduction to the History of English Medieval Towns* (1977); C. Petit-Dutaillis *The French Communes in the Middle Ages* (1978)

Communications During the Middle Ages transport, and therefore communication, was by means of road, sea and river. Few new roads were built, and the road network remained largely that laid down by the Romans. In England the Norman kings issued frequent laws for the protection of travellers and the clearance of vegetation from the roadsides. Although road travel by foot, horse or mule was necessarily slow and expensive, the distances travelled were often greater than might be

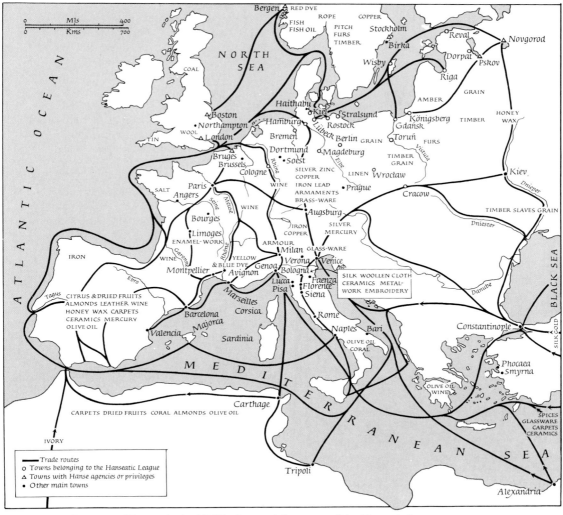

The major trade routes of Europe in the Middle Ages and the towns of the Hanseatic League.

Commerce: merchants from Bologna bargain over the sale of animal hides (1339).

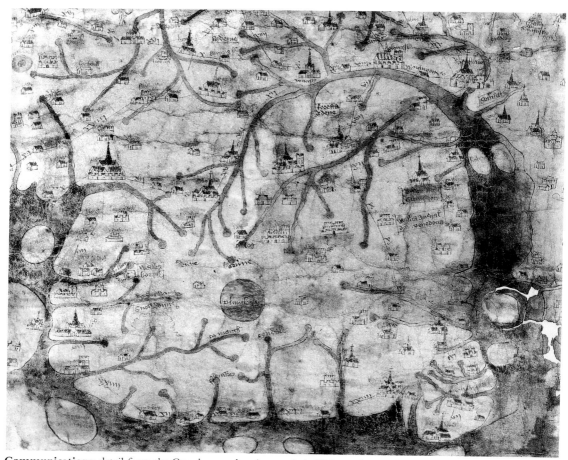

Communications: detail from the Gough map showing roads in Wales and around the Severn estuary, *c.*1360.

expected. The roads to Rome were always busy, and there were frequent pilgrimages to Jerusalem and Santiago de Compostela.

The greatest masters of water transport were the Scandinavians whose journeys of settlement led them as far afield as Iceland and Greenland, whilst their trading exploits took them to Constantinople. Journeys would often combine travel by road and river; a medieval traveller from Lincoln to York, for example, would travel by road to Burton Stather on the Trent, then by boat up the Trent and Yorkshire Ouse to Howden, and finally along 18 miles of level road to York. Medieval society was by no means necessarily static. *See* ROADS, ROMAN; SHIPS AND SHIPPING [*125, 300*]

Commynes, Philippe de (*c.* 1447-1511) Statesman and biographer whose memoirs of the life of Louis XI of France established him as one of the greatest contemporary historians of the Middle Ages. Godson of Philip the Good, duke of Burgundy, Commynes was brought up at the Burgundian court and in 1464 became squire to the heir apparent Charles the Bold.

When Charles became duke of Burgundy, he appointed Commynes as one of his chief advisers. He was present at the famous meeting between Charles the Bold and Louis XI at Péronne in 1468 and also served as ambassador to England, Brittany and Spain. In 1472 he deserted Charles for the court of Louis XI, where he proved extremely useful to his new employer. Although after Louis's death he was imprisoned for some months because of his alleged part in a conspiracy against the regent, Anne of Beaujeu, he was later again employed in foreign affairs as an ambassador to Venice 1494-98 and as one of the chief formulators of the Italian policy of Louis XII. He regarded Venice as 'the most triumphant city'.
□ *Memoirs: the Reign of Louis XI* trans. M. Jones (1972)

Conciliar movement Theory which claimed that a general council of the church had greater authority than the pope and might, if necessary, depose him. It originated in the writings of 12th-c. and 13th-c. canonists who were attempting to impose juridical limitations upon the power of the papacy. The most radical exponents of Conciliarism were Marsilius of Padua, who rejected the divine origin of the papacy, and William of Ockham, who taught that only the church as a whole was preserved from error in faith. In the 15th c. there was a serious attempt to employ the general council in healing the Great Schism and reforming the church. Although in 1417 the Council of Constance (1414–18) declared that general councils should meet periodically, the determination of the papacy to reassert its independence and the continuous quarrels which arose between the delegates, meant that no further councils were called after the dissolution of the Council of Basle in 1449. *See* AILLY, PIERRE D'; MARTIN V; ZABARELLA, FRANCESCO; *see also individual Councils*

□ E.F. Jacob *Essays in the Conciliar Epoch* (1953); B. Tierney *Foundations of Conciliar Theory* (1955)

Conrad V (Conradin) Nominal king of Germany and Sicily 1254-68 (b.1252) Son of Conrad IV and grandson of Frederick II. On his father's death in 1254 he was brought up by his uncle the duke of Bavaria. He was early opposed by the papacy who wished to break Hohenstaufen power, Pope Alexander IV offering the Hohenstaufen lands to Alfonso X of Castile and forbidding Conradin's election as king of the Romans. In 1262 Conradin became duke of Swabia and in 1266 entered Sicily. At first he was victorious against Charles of Anjou, who had taken control there, but was defeated at the battle of Tagliacozzo (1268) and handed over to Charles. He was beheaded on 29 October 1268, and with his death the Hohenstaufen line came to an end.

Conrad of Marburg (1180-1233) German inquisitor. Educated at Bologna, in 1214 he was commissioned by Pope Innocent III to preach a proposed crusade. By 1226 he had become the confessor of St Elizabeth of Hungary and in 1227 was employed by Gregory IX to stamp out heresy and ecclesiastical abuse in Germany, where he was particularly active and ruthless in Hesse and Thuringia. In 1233 he accused Henry, count of Sayn, of heresy. Henry was exculpated by the German princes and bishops at Mainz, and Conrad was murdered shortly afterwards on his way to Marburg.

Conrad of Montferrat (1146-92) Italian adventurer and crusader who successfully defended the city of Tyre against the Saracens after the fall of Jerusalem to Saladin. In 1191 he was made nominal king of Jerusalem in place of the deposed Guy of Lusignan, who was given Cyprus in compensation. Conrad's reign, however, was very short, since in 1192 he was murdered by the Muslim sect, the Assassins.

Pope John XXIII offers a golden rose to Emperor Sigismund at the **Council of Constance**.

Conrad of Zähringen (d. 1152) A 12th-c. German duke who was granted the rectorate of Burgundy by the Emperor Lothar III (1125-37). Here he built up a strong power base and extended his lands towards the east. He also supported Henry the Lion, duke of Saxony, in his struggles with Lothar's successor, Conrad III (1138-52).

Constance (1154-98) Daughter of Roger II of Sicily. In 1186 Constance married the future Holy Roman Emperor Henry VI, son of Frederick Barbarossa, and was crowned empress in Rome in 1191. As early as 1189 Constance had contested the claims of her natural nephew Tancred of Lecce to the kingdom of Sicily, but it was only on Tancred's death in 1194 that she was able to consolidate her own claim to the throne. When Henry VI died in 1197, Constance managed to maintain her position in Sicily largely through the aid of Pope Innocent III. Shortly before her death, she was able to obtain the coronation of her son Frederick as king of Sicily, a position which he continued to hold even after he had been elected Holy Roman Emperor in 1212.

Constance, Council of (1414-18) The sixteenth ecumenical council of the church which was called in an attempt to heal the Great Schism. It deposed the rival popes Gregory XII, Benedict XIII and John

Coronation of the young **Constantine VII Porphyrogenitus**, from the Chronicle of John Skylitzes (*c*.1300).

XXIII and elected Oddone Colonna in their place as Pope Martin V. The delegates at Constance, who included both lay and clerical representatives from all over Europe, also issued the decree *Sacrosancta*, which stated that the general council of the church was superior to the pope and made provision for further general councils to be held at regular intervals. In addition the Council condemned a number of the beliefs of both Wycliffe and Hus. Although Hus possessed a promise of safe conduct, he was nevertheless handed over to the secular authorities and burned as a heretic, a disastrous move which strengthened rather than weakened his followers in their resolve. The Council was prevented from taking any further reforming actions because of the deep-seated national differences which existed between the delegates, but it had succeeded substantially in ending the Schism. *See* CONCILIAR MOVEMENT

□ J. Gill *Constance et Bâle-Florence* (1965)

Constantine VII Porphyrogenitus Eastern emperor 908–59 (b. 905) Crowned as a child, Constantine did not gain power until the deposition of the usurper Romanus I Lecaperus in 944. In Byzantium he was very successful and managed to preserve the property and status of the peasant soldiers upon whom his army depended. He also led a cultural revival, gathering around him scholars who published exerpts from the ancient classics, whilst he himself wrote a paraphrase on the characteristics and tactics of various nations. In his foreign policy he was less successful, achieving only moderate success against the Arabs in Syria towards the end of his reign. In southern Italy and Sicily he had to pay a humiliating tribute. He established peace along the northern borders of the empire, and during his reign Olga, the first Christian princess of the Ukraine, was baptized. He was murdered in 959 by his son Romanus II.

□ A.A. Vasiliev *A History of the Byzantine Empire* (1952)

Constantinople, Councils of Four councils of the church which dealt with a number of important doctrinal issues. The First Council of Constantinople (381) defined the church's position on the doctrine of the Holy Trinity and established the Nicene Creed as the basis of Christian belief; the Second (553) defined the unity of the person of Christ as consisting of two distinct natures, human and divine, thus rejecting the position of the Nestorians; the Third (680–81) condemned the Monothelites by asserting that Christ had two wills and two operations corresponding to his two natures; whilst the Fourth (869–70) excommunicated Photius, the patriarch of Constantinople, and prohibited lay interference in episcopal elections. Although the Catholic church regarded all four Councils as ecumenical, the Greek Orthodox church only recognizes the first three.

Contarini Doge of Venice 1368–82 Member of a distinguished Venetian family which had already provided the republic with several doges, Andrea Contarini was elected doge in 1368. Under his rule the Venetians were successful in the war against the Genoese, who had taken the port of Chioggia and were besieging Venice herself. Contarini melted down his plate and mortgaged his property to raise funds, and then, with the aid of the admiral Victor Pisani, attacked and drove out the Genoese besiegers in midwinter 1379–80.

□ A. da Mosto *I Dogi di Venetia nella vita pubblica e privata* (1977)

Conventuals The majority of the Franciscan Order who soon after St Francis' death deviated from the original observance of the Rule and came to own property against the express wishes of the saint. They were opposed by the much smaller number of Spiritual Franciscans who interpreted St Francis' teachings on poverty more literally. The Spirituals were persecuted by Pope John XXII and were forced to go underground when in 1322 he declared their doctrine of the absolute poverty of Christ and the Apostles to be heretical. The Conventuals became increasingly lax, until in the late 14th c. there was a revival of the Order under the Friars of Strict Observance led by St Bernardino of Siena.

□ C.N.L. Brooke *The Monastic World 1000–1300* (1974)

Cornwall In the very early Middle Ages Cornwall joined Devon and west Somerset in forming a relatively large British kingdom – the kingdom of Dumnonia – whose kings are evidenced from the early 6th c. Many traditions with a wide currency in the central Middle Ages, like that of Tristan and Isolde, located their heroes of the past in this area. Irish settlement had probably already taken place in the far west by *c.* 500, as the movement has left traces of Irish words in place names, and of Irish script on early tombstones. Pressure from the east was more consistent, however, and the English had conquered Somerset and Devon by the 8th c., reaching the river Tamar by 710, penetrating into east Cornwall by 722, and thereby confining the kingdom of Dumnonia to the area now known as Cornwall; the term 'Cornwall' originates from this time. The reduced kingdom of Dumnonia survived for nearly two more centuries, the death of the last king to be noted occurring in 875, although the English had been ranging over Cornwall throughout the 9th c. Independent Cornwall thereafter disappeared.

The English settled in many parts of the southwest, but not in sufficient numbers to wipe out the characteristic form of British speech in the peninsula, known as Primitive Cornish, and the ancestor of the modern Cornish language. Though there was some settlement of English on the richer lands in the east of the county, Cornwall retained its Celtic character and sustained contacts with its Celtic neighbours to the north and south, in Wales and Brittany, sharing the cults of Celtic saints found in those areas. Despite its small size and the constant attacks, its religious institutions (like that at Bodmin) and its centres of learning seem to have thrived. During the 10th c. the English drew upon its scholars and manuscripts in the revival of written culture associated with 10th-c. religious reform. WD
□ G. H. Doble *The Saints of Cornwall* (1960–70); S. Pearce *The Kingdom of Dumnonia* (1978)

Cortes Parliament of the medieval Spanish kingdoms which developed when, because of the crowns' need for financial aid, elected representatives of the free municipalities began in the 13th c. to be admitted to meetings of the royal court in order to debate certain matters of government. The *Cortes* of Leon and Castile, which comprised the nobility, clergy and town representatives (*procuradores*), tended to be very much an instrument of royal government; but the *Cortes* of Aragon and its dependencies of Catalonia and Valencia exercised a much more independent policy which was frequently in direct opposition to royal interests. *See* ESTATES
□ G. Jackson *The Making of Medieval Spain* (1972); A. R. Myers *Parliaments and Estates in Europe* (1975)

Courtly Love (*amour courtois, höfische Minne*)
First introduced as a term by Gaston Paris in 1883, Courtly Love received its finest expression in the songs of the 12th-c. troubadours in Languedoc. The actual nature of this highly ritualized code of love remains debatable; several sources have been suggested – Ovid's *Ars Amatoria*, Hispano-Arabic poetry and Platonic thought, among others – but the language and imagery of Courtly Love reflect above all the feudal, courtly environment in which the concept evolved.

The protagonists assumed distinct roles: the lover submitted to his lady as a knight to his lord, swearing loyal and enduring service. Drawing attention to his *pretz* ('worth') and *valor* ('courage') – further increased by his pure and noble love – he would request *merce* ('pity') and some reward. Although the lady might seem the dominant partner in this private drama, she was bound by convention to comply with the knight's reasonable demands, much as a lord was bound to reward his faithful retainers; if she failed to offer some favour or hope she was branded cruel and heartless. The adulterous nature of Courtly Love has been much debated and often exaggerated; there are very few cases in which the lady is explicitly a married woman. Nevertheless, she was almost always unattainable, by virtue

The **Cortes**, or parliament, of the Spanish kingdom of Catalonia, presided over by James I the Conqueror.

An idyllic scene of **Courtly Love** in a walled garden, from a late 15th-c. copy of the *Roman de la Rose*.

of her high rank or physical distance, and by fear of social censure; it was, paradoxically, her very distance that lent value to the lover's patient suffering. The lady's worth could be increased by dispensing *merce* to a worthy and deserving suitor, yet the lady who submitted too soon was to be condemned.

The lover's inner struggle between his desire for immediate fulfilment and his awareness of the moral value implicit in striving for the unattainable; between individual ambitions and outward social constraints; between the self-imposed state of submission and the overwhelming need to express pain and resentment: it is these antitheses that lend the poetry of Courtly Love its dramatic tension and emotional richness.

True love, or *Fin'amors*, was contrasted with the *Fals'amors* of the majority, characterized by inconstancy, insincerity and petty jealousy, and which excluded them from the loving elite. *Fin'amors* became increasingly 'Christianized' in the later 12th c., as the image of the aspiring lover was assimilated into a code of religious striving toward God, in which Christian virtues were acquired through service to the Lady Mary.

The tradition spread from the Languedoc to Italy, influencing the *dolce stil nuovo* (Dante's *La Vita Nuova*), and northwards, where it fused with the French allegorical tradition to produce such works as Chrétien de Troyes's *Lancelot* and the *Roman de la Rose* of Guillaume de Lorris. Other responses include Wolfram von Eschenbach's *Parzival* in Germany, and in England, Chaucer's *Troilus* and Gower's *Confessio Amantis*. *See* ANDREAS CAPELLANUS; CHIVALRY; LITERATURE[285]

□ C. S. Lewis *The Allegory of Love* (1936); M. Lazar *Amour Courtois et 'Fin'Amors'* (1964); *The Meaning of Courtly Love* ed. F. X. Newman (1968)

Courtrai, battle of (11 July 1302) The French army led by the count of Artois was heavily defeated on this occasion by the citizens of Bruges, Ypres and Courtrai, who thereby proved their growing independence from French tutelage. Flanders looked increasingly to England for support in trade and politics, and the resulting tensions contributed to the outbreak of the Hundred Years' War.
□ H. Pirenne *Histoire de Belgique* vol. 1 (1929)

Crécy, battle of (26 August 1346) Edward III of England here defeated the French king Philip VI. Although the English forces were vastly outnumbered, they were aided both by the disarray of the French troops and by the skill of their own longbowmen, who could fire both faster and further than the French crossbowmen. The French suffered heavy losses, and the consequent capture of Calais by the English opened the way for continued and continuous pressure on the French realm. John, the blind king of Bohemia, was killed at Crécy, and his motto *Ich dien* ('I serve') and emblem (the three feathers) were adopted by the Black Prince and subsequent princes of Wales.
□ A. Burne *The Crécy War* (1976)

Crusades War proclaimed by the pope on Christ's behalf and fought as Christ's own enterprise for the recovery of Christian property, or in defence of Christendom against external or internal foes.

The crusading movement, which was in one sense an extension of the warfare being waged against Muslims in Spain and Sicily, was greatly influenced by St Augustine of Hippo's concept of divinely authorized violence, which was revived by the papal reformers during the Investiture Contest. The First Crusade, preached by Pope Urban II at the Council of Clermont in 1095, took Antioch in 1098 and Jerusalem in 1099, establishing the principality of Antioch, the counties of Edessa and Tripoli, and the Latin kingdom of Jerusalem, which survived until 1291. It was justified on two fronts: the recovery of Christ's inheritance (Jerusalem with the Holy Land around it) and the defence of fellow Christians in the East against the advancing Muslims. This twin causation was peculiar to crusades to the East, and from the first gave them the character of pilgrimages. The First Crusade was succeeded by a series of great expeditions, of which the most important were the Second Crusade (1146–48); the Third Crusade (1188–92), in the course of which Cyprus came under Latin rule, to be governed by Western Europeans until 1571; the Fourth Crusade (1202–04), which went off course, took Constantinople and established Latin rule in Greece, which survived vestigially into modern times; the Fifth Crusade

(1217–21) and the First Crusade of Louis IX of France. There were also many smaller enterprises, and these became the most popular form of crusading 1254–91. There were crusades, and plans for crusades, in the 14th c. and 15th c.; there were crusaders in the Eastern Mediterranean in the 16th c.; and the Order of St John, one of the military orders which grew out of the movement, was still engaged in desultory warfare against the Turks in the 18th c.

Crusading was extended to Spain by Pope Urban II almost as soon as he had preached the First Crusade: he had already been pressing for a more active policy on the frontier south of Barcelona and did not want knights diverted from it. Crusades were preached periodically in Spain until the 16th c. Crusading against political opponents of the papacy appears to have been introduced by Pope Innocent II in 1135, when he granted an indulgence to those who fought the Normans and the anti-pope Anacletus; it was to be used extensively by the popes in 13th-c. and 14th-c. Italy against the Hohenstaufen and the Ghibellines. Crusading along the Baltic was authorized by Pope Eugenius II in 1147 and continued until the 15th c. A feature of the German crusades was that they were also wars of conversion, and missions operated in conjunction with them. The first crusade against heretics was launched by Pope Innocent III in 1208 when he despaired of the ability and willingness of the secular powers to crush the Cathars in Languedoc. It was to be followed by crusades against the Staedinger peasants in Germany and against Cathars in Lombardy in the 13th c., against the followers of Fra Dolcino in Piedmont in the 14th c., and against the Hussites in Bohemia in the 1420s and 1430s.

From the point of view of most contemporaries these crusades were all equally valid, although a

Christ leading knights on a **crusade** to the Holy Land, from a 14th-c. English *Apocalypse*.

crusade in defence of the Holy Land or for the recovery of Jerusalem had more prestige and was the measure against which others were judged. At times in the 13th c. popes would discourage crusading in one direction in favour of more effort and resources in another. They came to be actively involved in strategic decisions of this kind partly because, after the institution in 1199 of the mandatory taxation of clerical incomes in favour of crusading, there were in theory large sums of money with which expeditions could be endowed. There was occasional criticism of crusading – some of it extreme – partly engendered by resentment over this taxation; but on the whole it seems to have been unrepresentative of public opinion.

From 1095 until at least 1400 crusading was a genuinely popular devotional activity, the period of its greatest popularity being from 1187 to 1250. Attracting laymen from all classes, it was accompanied by the formal penitential and liturgical exercises that were the features of contemporary popular worship. Some of the participants took vows based on those of pilgrims, and enjoyed privileges similar to those given to pilgrims; they were also given indulgences. The early indulgences were authoritative pronouncements to the effect that the crusade was so severe a penitential exercise that it made adequate satisfaction for all previous sin. The more advanced idea, propounded in the 1140s, held that satisfaction could never be adequate, and that, consequently, the indulgence was a free and generous remission of the punishment due to sin. This view was not definitely adopted for crusaders until the pontificate of Innocent III.

Although every crusade must have had its adventurers, and many benefited materially by settling in Palestine, Syria, Greece, Spain and along the Baltic shore, there is little evidence for most gaining or intending to gain anything other than merit and honour. Indeed, according to contemporary opinion, it was miserly to refrain from crusading rather than avaricious to crusade. *See* ALBIGENSES; CHILDREN'S CRUSADE; PEASANTS' CRUSADE; WENDS   JR-S

□ S. Runciman *A History of the Crusades* (1951–54); R. C. Smail *Crusading Warfare 1097–1193* (1956); H. E. Mayer *The Crusades* (1972); E. Christiansen *The Northern Crusades* (1980); P. M. Holt *The Age of the Crusades* (1986); J. Riley-Smith *The First Crusade and the Idea of Crusading* (1986), *The Crusades* (1987)

Cumans Nomadic Turkish people who in the 12th c. acted as mercenary troops in the pay of the Russian princes. The failure of the Cumans to organize any effective Russian resistance to the Mongol onslaught, however, forced them in 1237 to seek refuge in the territories of Béla IV, king of Hungary.

Sea-creatures dry **St Cuthbert's** feet after he has prayed in the sea; from Bede's Life of St Cuthbert (12th c.).

Béla's son Stephen V married a Cuman princess, and under their son Vladislav II Cuman influence in Hungarian affairs grew considerably. Although the Cumans had been converted to Christianity before their arrival in Hungary, they found it difficult to assimilate and were not fully absorbed into Hungarian society for centuries.

Customs (*Consuetudines*) In its more general sense the term refers to all imposts or customary dues, but in time it became increasingly technical. From the middle of the 12th c. it was used in England in the modern sense of a customs duty paid on imported wine, and a system of national customs at ports gradually arose after King John issued at Winchester in 1204 an Assize of Customs, which imposed a duty of one fifteenth on all imports of seaborne trade, except for coastal traffic. This did not prove permanently successful, but by the end of the 13th c. customs duties, notably on wine and wool, constituted a most important element in royal finance, and remained so throughout the Middle Ages.
□ N.S.B. Gras *The Early English Customs System* (1918); E.B. Fryde *Studies in Medieval Trade and Finance* (1983)

Cuthbert, St (634–87) Bishop of Lindisfarne. Monk of the Celtic observance at Melrose from 651, Cuthbert became prior there in 661 before accepting Roman customs at the Synod of Whitby in 664. He was nominated prior of Lindisfarne, but in 676 relinquished that office and withdrew to Inner Farne in order to become a hermit. In 685 he was chosen by Ecgfrith, king of Northumbria, and Archbishop Theodore as bishop of Hexham, but exchanged that see soon afterwards with Bishop Eata for that of Lindisfarne. Upon his death, Cuthbert was buried at Lindisfarne, but following the sack of Lindisfarne

by the Danes in 875 his body was exhumed and carried around the north until it reached Durham in 995. During the 11th c. the site of Cuthbert's tomb grew in importance. A Benedictine monastery was founded to serve it by Bishop William of St Carilef in 1083, and a new cathedral was built to which Cuthbert's relics were translated in 1104. His cult was popular throughout the Middle Ages, some 83 churches being dedicated to him from Scotland to Cornwall. [*244*]
□ B. Colgrave *Two Lives of St Cuthbert* (1940)

Cyprus Passing into Greek hands after the collapse of the Roman empire in the West, Cyprus was captured by the Arabs in 644. For the next few centuries the political history of the island was turbulent. It was recovered by the Greeks, reconquered by the Arabs under Hārūn ar-Rashīd and finally restored to Byzantine influence by the Emperor Nicephoras Phocas (963–69). In 1191, in retaliation for the treatment of his crusading forces by the Emperor Isaac Comnenus, Richard I of England conquered the island and sold it to the Knights Templar, who presently resold it to the king of Jerusalem, Guy de Lusignan. Under Guy, his brother Amaury and their successors, the government of the island resembled that of feudal Europe. During the 14th c. and 15th c., Italian influence became more important; between 1376 and 1464 the mercantile city of Famagusta was in the hands of the Genoese, whilst in 1489, following the death of King James III, the whole island passed into the sphere of the Venetian empire, where it remained until captured by the Turks in 1571.
□ G. Hill *A History of Cyprus* (1948–52)

Cyril, St (826–69) Apostle of the Slavs. A Thessalonican by birth, Cyril became librarian of S. Sophia in Constantinople and an influential figure at court. In 868, following a request from Roteslav, prince of the West Slavs, Cyril and his brother Methodius were sent as Christian missionaries to Moravia by the Emperor Michael III. They converted many to Christianity and translated the liturgy and some of the scriptures into Slavonic, for which purpose Cyril invented a new alphabet. They encountered problems with the German missionaries who had preceded them, and were forced to leave. Cyril died in Rome in 869, but Methodius later returned to Moravia and became archbishop of the West Slavs. In Moravia itself, German influence and the Latin liturgy persisted and came to dominate after an accord in 872, but elsewhere among the Slavonic peoples, to the east in modern Russia and to the south in modern Yugoslavia, Cyril's contribution proved permanent; cyrillic script, based on his adaptation of the Greek alphabet to Slavonic sound systems, became the normal instrument for liturgy and liturgical work.

□ S. Runciman *A History of the First Bulgarian Empire* (1930)

D

Damascus Muslim holy city situated between desert and mountains. Well watered and fertile, Damascus developed early into a great marketplace and caravanserai. Muslim conquest (636) confirmed Islam's control of Syria, ending a thousand years of Western domination. After centuries of anarchy Damascus reached its greatest heights during the 12th c. and 13th c., under Nūr ad-Dīn and Saladin, as a centre for the Holy War against the crusaders. The Mamlūks made Damascus a political dependency of Egypt after 1260.

□ H.A.R. Gibb *The Damascus Chronicle of the Crusades* (1932)

Dance of Death (*danse macabre*) A common motif in the art of the later Middle Ages, reflecting some of the manifestations of extreme religious hysteria connected with penitential processions. It was associated in origin with morality plays and poems treating of the inevitability of death and the call to penitence. This theme is also depicted in wall paintings where three young men confront three skeletons, with variations on the caption: 'As I am so shalt thou be'. The image of a long file of human beings twisting and turning their way to the inevitable grave developed artistically in the later Middle Ages to the point where, at its most complex, it involved the whole of living society, from pope and emperor to the humblest peasant. [*275*]

□ J. M. Clark *The Dance of Death in the Middle Ages and the Renaissance* (1950); *Encyclopaedia of World Art* vol. 4 (1971)

Dandolo, Enrico (*c.*1107–1205) Doge of Venice from 1192, he began a period of vigorous rule by swearing the 'ducal promise', which outlined the nature of his office. He went on to revise the penal code, publish the first civil statute collection and reform the coinage. Dandolo played a decisive role in the events of the Fourth Crusade: he provided sea transport to Egypt for the crusaders; in payment for this service he accepted help in the capture of Zara, a Dalmatian town under Hungarian control; and he encouraged the diversion of the Crusade to Constantinople. After the capture of the city Dandolo died there, having made valuable acquisitions for Venice in Greece and the Aegean.

□ D. E. Queller *The Fourth Crusade: the Conquest of Constantinople* (1978)

Dance of death: a vivid representation of the three living and the three dead kings (early 14th c.).

Danegeld

Danegeld Term used to describe formal payments made by Christian kingdoms in the Viking Age to buy off the Dane. Such payments were made by Frankish and English rulers in the 9th c., but the whole process was put on a more systematic basis in England after the defeat at Maldon in Essex in 991. Huge sums were raised and paid to the Danes during the latter half of the reign of King Aethelred, and the system of levying and exacting such *geld* or tax was refined and made efficient under pressure of the need to meet Danish demands. The use of *geld* to provide fleets and a skilled element in the army (*heregeld*) led to complexities in terminology, but the term 'Danegeld' persisted in general use until 1162.

Dante Alighieri (1265–1321) One of the greatest poets of the Middle Ages, Dante spent his early years transplanting Occitan romances into a more acceptable medium for the rising bourgeois audience of Florence, paring down their romantic elements to stress the bare essence of love. This complemented his own love for Beatrice, the childhood sweetheart who inspired his poems. Her death in 1290 was a great blow to Dante, who produced *La Vita Nuova*, a hagiographical work of adoration, in her memory. During his friendship with the influential Cavalcanti, Dante had been introduced to the Neoplatonism of Boethius and the Aristotelian philosophy of the Schools. He became passionately involved in the politics of Florence, supporting the Guelph party, which was divided into bitter factions. He was elected one of the *priori* (the highest office in the commune) and in this role visited the papal court of Boniface VIII. When he was away, a coup d'état took place and Dante was banished from Florence on pain of death.

In his wanderings he continued to work on Aristotle, producing the *Convivio* based on the Greek's *Ethics*. It aimed to give the layman a glimpse of the philosophical vitality in the works of contemporary university philosophers. About 1309, he began work on the *Monarchia*, the master statement of his political ideas, which extended the theories to be found in the *Convivio*, in particular those concerning world monarchy. He used Aristotelian and Neoplatonic ideas of perfection to fashion an elaborate defence of the Holy Roman Empire; his work at this point echoed that of Franciscans who sought the removal of the temporal power of the church. Thus Dante supported the Emperor Henry VII when he invaded Italy in 1310, but by 1313 this venture had failed.

It was against this background that the *Divine Comedy* took shape over a period of about 15 years. It consists of three main sections: *Inferno, Purgatorio* and *Paradiso*. The work is a scholarly puzzle, com-

Dante and Virgil cross the Styx, from a 15th-c. copy of the *Divine Comedy*.

bining a pervasive allegory, which teases the reader, with a gritty realism, involving Florentine characters and historical figures now forgotten. These elements are bonded together by the intricate symmetry of the poem. It is a coherent narrative of the ascent of man from darkness to God. A recent commentator pinpoints Dante as a 'genius isolated by his originality', but it was a genius admired by future generations in its highest form in the *Divine Comedy*.
□ E. Gilson *Dante and Philosophy* (1963); G. Holmes *Dante* (1980)

David, St The patron saint of Wales whose day is celebrated on 1 March, St David was a prominent ascetic missionary of the 6th c. associated with the founding of monasteries and the work of two reforming synods. A mass of legendary material grew up around his name and was put into literary form in the 11th c. and 12th c. with the object of asserting the independence of the see of St David's against Canterbury. The cognomen *aquaticus* probably signified no more than his ascetic qualities, though attempts have been made to connect the David legends with primitive Celtic worship of river and water deities. In art he is often portrayed with a dove on his shoulder.
□ *Rhigyfarch's Life of St David* ed. J. W. James (1967); W. Davies *Wales in the Early Middle Ages* (1982)

Della Scala family (Scaligeri) Under the domination of the della Scala family the city of Verona rose to powerful heights in northern Italy, at one point even threatening the commercial supremacy of Venice. After the death of the despotic Ezzelino da Romano, the commune of Verona chose Mastino della Scala as *podestà* (1260). Before his assassination in 1277, he was able to extend control over some of the neighbouring countryside. His brother and successor Alberto consolidated the position of authority held by the della Scala. The ablest member of the family was Cangrande della Scala (1311–29), who made his court an asylum for exiled Ghibellines and a haven for poets and scholars, as well as bringing many northern Italian cities under his control.
□ J. Larner *Italy in the Age of Dante and Petrarch* (1980)

Della Torre family (Torriani) Aristocratic Milanese family who, after gaining leadership of the *Credenza di Sant'Ambrogio* (an organization of small masters) in the mid-13th c., established themselves as rulers of Milan. In 1263 Martino della Torre became perpetual lord and was succeeded by Napoleone della Torre (1265–77). Hopes of consolidating the family power further were frustrated by the appointment of a member of the rival Visconti family as archbishop of Milan in 1262, and, although the Torriani were able to prevent his taking possession of the see for 15 years, they were eventually defeated in battle by the Visconti, at Desio in 1277 and again in 1281 near Vaprio. After a brief exile, the Torriani returned to Milan (1302), and by 1308 had re-established themselves, with Cassone della Torre as archbishop and Guido della Torre as perpetual lord. However, their rule did not long survive the arrival in Italy of the Emperor Henry VII. After the abortive Torriani revolt of 1311, which was suppressed by both the Emperor and the Visconti, Matteo Visconti was appointed imperial vicar in Milan, and the Torriani never returned to the city.
□ J. K. Hyde *Society and Politics in Medieval Italy* (1973); M. Mallett *Mercenaries and their Masters* (1974)

Dendrochronology Tree-ring dating, based on the characteristic patterns of different centuries, can be very successful in elucidating the chronology of a building, as for example in the case of Trier cathedral, where the age of the various parts of the building can be determined by matching the ring patterns of the component timbers. At Trier one corner of the square-cut wood was rounded, and contained the sapwood rings nearest the bark, so the years when the oaks were felled could be precisely specified. In many cases the sapwood is missing and the date of the latest visible ring may be a decade or so earlier than the date of the building. A large number of rings are necessary for unambiguous dating, so watermills (as in AD Ireland) or tables (e.g., King Arthur's Winchester Round Table, *c.* 1200) are more easily dated than small objects. Underwater archaeologists can date old ships and even locate the source of some of the timbers, but wet timber must not be allowed to dry quickly if dendrochronological dating is needed. Dendrochronology is proving a useful dating method, and one that is more exact for the medieval period than radiocarbon-dating; it has resulted in the accurate dating of many medieval structures: from cottages to panel-paintings.

Tree-ring dating of oak and elm is very successful in regions such as the Welsh or German mountains, where in years of drought the ring is narrow. In the high Scandinavian and Alpine mountains summer warmth is needed for a wide ring to develop, and the density of the latewood (measured by X-rays) reliably reflects the temperature of the late summer. In general, climatic relationships are complex, and progress in dating was slow in Europe until computer programs were developed.

Where trees are sensitive to rainfall, as in southern Germany, we can check the years of drought from the characteristic narrow rings of years such as AD 67–69, 591–92, the 680s and 850s, 931–50, and 977–98. A narrow tree ring in English trees in 1137, for example, confirms the chronicler's report that 'the streams and wells, and very many rivers . . . dried up'. DJS
□ M. G. L. Baillie *Tree-ring Dating and Archaeology* (1982); D. J. Schove *Chronology of Eclipses and Comets, AD 1–1000* (1984)

Denmark The southernmost of the Scandinavian kingdoms, Denmark takes its name from its position on the border (a *mark*) with the Carolingian and German empires. It consisted of the Jutland peninsula, a number of islands, notably Funen and Zeeland, and parts of what is now considered southern Sweden. It came into prominence in the early Viking period when Danish rulers effectively resisted Charlemagne and his successors, initiating the building of a massive earthwork (the Danewerk or *Danevirke*) set up with the primary purpose of protecting the port of Hedeby (Schleswig). The Danes proved active seamen, traders, and colonizers in the Viking Age, notably in England and Normandy.

Politically they reached the height of their power under Cnut, king of England 1016–35 and king of Denmark 1019–35. At this time they completed their conversion to Christianity (initiated effectively in mid-10th c.) and Danish scholars and ecclesiastics came to play a significant part in the 12th-c. renaissance.

Denmark

Under Waldemar II (1202–41) they extended both their commercial and religious interests east to the Baltic, working sometimes in cooperation with, but often in opposition to, German merchants. In the 13th c. and 14th c. the formation of the Hanseatic League reinforced internal weaknesses in the Danish polity. By the Treaty of Stralsund (1370), for example, Waldemar IV, who had attempted to curb the activities of the German merchants, was forced after military defeat to recognize their virtual domination of the Baltic and even to allow them a say in the selection of a Danish king. By the Union of Calmar (1397) Denmark became part of a loose federation of Scandinavian kingdoms until the dissolution of the Union in 1523. *See* GORM THE OLD; WALDEMAR I
□ J. H. Birch *Denmark in History* (1938); L. Musset *Les peuples scandinaves au Moyen-Age* (1951); A. E. Christensen, 'Denmark between the Viking Age and the time of the Valdemars', *Medieval Scandinavia* I (1968)

Despensers English family whose members became notorious in the service of Edward II. In 1308, Hugh the Elder supported the king and his favourite, Piers Gaveston, against baronial opposition, and as a result held the office of chief adviser to the crown 1312–15. Hugh the Younger became chamberlain in 1318. His attempts to gain sole control of the vast Clare inheritance through his wife's rights as co-heiress provoked baronial censure, and banishment for himself and his father. However, they returned to power in 1322 and continued to exploit their position for personal gain, securing, for example, the earldom of Winchester for Hugh the Elder. The rebellion of Queen Isabella and Roger Mortimer in 1326 resulted in their downfall and execution.
□ G. A. Holmes *The Estates of the Higher Nobility in Fourteenth-Century England* (1957); N. Fryde *The Tyranny and Fall of Edward II* (1979)

Diaz, Bartholomew (d. 1500) Left Portugal with a fleet of three ships in 1487, under orders from John II to find the southernmost point of the west coast of Africa. His mission was successful, and his discovery was dubbed the Cape of Good Hope as it opened up the possibility of sea travel to Asia.

Dictatus Papae Important list or memorandum consisting of 27 short statements relating to the theocratic aims and policies of the papacy under Gregory VII (1073–85). Its exact purpose and standing are uncertain, but it was probably a form of index to documents and arguments useful to the papal curia in its struggle with the Emperor, commonly known as the Investiture Contest. The statements are diverse in character, ranging from positive and absolute statements of papal supremacy to points of detail. Two arguments dominate the collection: firstly, that the pope was superior to the Emperor, even having the right to depose him; and secondly, that the pope was superior to all other metropolitans and bishops in the ecclesiastical hierarchy.
□ E. Caspar *Das Register Gregors VII* (1920); W. Ullmann *The Church and the Law in the Earlier Middle Ages* (1975)

Dictum of Kenilworth (1266) Negotiated between Henry III and the English barons, this was an important constitutional agreement which ended the baronial attempt at governmental reform begun in 1258. It gave the rebels an opportunity of recovering their lands, in return for their acceptance of the restoration of the monarchy.
□ F. M. Powicke *King Henry III and the Lord Edward* (1947)

Dietrich of Bern *See* **Theodoric the Great**

Dimitri of the Don (Donskoi) (1350–89) Grand duke of Moscow and Vladimir from 1359, Dimitri built up the fortunes of his principality at Moscow so that it became the most influential of the more or less independent Russian constitutional units. He fortified Moscow, establishing the Kremlin as a formidable citadel, and won a great victory over the Tartars at the battle of Kulikovo (1380). Tartar domination was quickly re-established, but the example and legend of the victory remained a powerful element in Russian national sentiment.

Domesday Book The product of an ambitious and successful survey of the kingdom of England initiated by William I at a great Christmas council in 1085. Domesday Book consists of two massive volumes, the first and more polished of which deals with most of England, while the second more detailed and less compressed volume covers the eastern counties of Essex, Suffolk and Norfolk. Together they provide a mass of evidence relating to royal lands, the lands of the great tenants-in-chief (ecclesiastic and lay), the wealth and taxable capacity of the land, the nature of landowners and peasantry, and the natural resources of the community: forests, mills, fisheries and many other miscellaneous items.

It is unique among medieval European records in its completeness and is a product of the extraordinary circumstances attending the Norman Conquest of England. It was used as an authoritative statement of the tenurial position, and received the name Domesday (i.e., Day of Judgement) Book in the 12th c., because there could be no appeal against its findings.

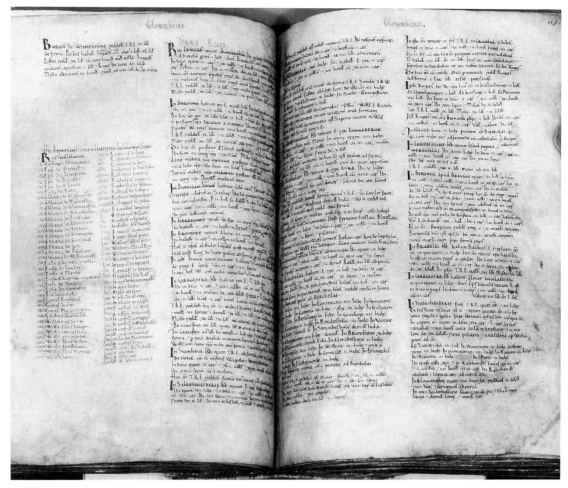

The Gloucester folios in **Domesday Book**, 1086: a list of tenants-in-chief and entries for the royal lands.

Its legal and financial importance ensured its survival as a prestigious Treasury, and then Exchequer document. Abstracts were made, and most great landowners had access to information relating to the state of their lands at the time of Domesday Book. Appeals were made to its contents well into the later Middle Ages, especially in connection with the status of land of ancient demesne and with urban rights. □ V. H. Galbraith *The Making of Domesday Book* (1961); E. M. Hallam *Domesday Book through Nine Centuries* (1986); *Domesday Studies* ed. J. C. Holt (1987)

Dominic (Guzman), St (*c.* 1170–1221) Founder of the Dominican Order, he began his career as a Castilian nobleman and priest. A canon (*c.* 1196) and sub-prior (1201) of Osma, he was involved in royal embassies to Languedoc where he encountered the Albigenses; he determined to reconcile them to the church, joining the Cistercian mission (1206) and remaining in Languedoc until 1217. The commencement of the Albigensian Crusade (1208) ran counter to Dominic's work, which employed logic, theology and the example of personal poverty, rather than force to counter Catharism. Accordingly he founded an order characterized by mendicant poverty, learning and preaching, confirmed by Pope Honorius III (1216). Unlike the members of earlier orders, the Dominican friars (Blackfriars, Order of Preachers) were not permitted corporate property and had to beg food. They followed the Augustinian Rule and received rigorous theological training, aiming to produce an informed laity impervious to heretical errors.

The Order spread rapidly throughout Western Europe (divided into provinces under the master general and exempt from episcopal jurisdiction), focusing particularly upon the university towns (Paris 1217, Bologna 1218, Oxford 1221), producing scholars such as Albertus Magnus and Thomas Aquinas (whose ideas it championed). Here the Dominican Order differed most substantially from the other major order of friars, the Franciscans, who did not consider scholarship to be a part of their vocation.

The Order was suited for combatting heresy, but conversion gave way to suppression, the medieval Inquisition often being described as the Dominican Inquisition (although only a minority was involved, and Franciscans also participated). The pastoral role of the Dominicans made an equally significant contribution to the fight against heresy. From the 14th c. onwards, despite missions in Africa, India and China, the Order declined in importance. *See* CARMELITES   MB
□ M. H. Vicaire *St Dominic and his Times* (1964); W. A. Hinnebusch *A History of the Dominican Order* (1965); B. Hamilton *The Medieval Inquisition* (1981)

Donatello di Niccolò (1386–1466) One of the greatest sculptors of his age, Donatello is chiefly remembered for his superb work in bronze, notably his life-size nude *David*, made for his Medici patrons in Florence. A Florentine by birth, he worked on the Baptistery in his early years and established a reputation in marble as well as in bronze. Florence, Siena and Padua (from 1443) were his principal fields of operation, the equestrian monument to Gattamelata and the relief tableaux *The Miracles of St Anthony* constituting the principal memorials of his Paduan period.
□ H. W. Janson *The Sculpture of Donatello* (1957)

Donati family Prominent in Florentine politics of the 13th c. as chief representatives of the old elite. The family, led by the 'baron', Corso Donati, headed the extreme Guelph faction, the Blacks, chiefly remembered for their coup (1301) under Valois protection, which resulted, among other things, in the exile of Dante. Corso was killed in 1307, one of the last significant representatives of the group of active warrior magnates who had threatened the stability of the Florentine constitution.

Donation of Constantine This purported to be a grant in which the Emperor Constantine (306–37) conceded supreme authority in the church and unrivalled control over Italy to Pope Sylvester I (314–35). It was a papal forgery of the 8th c., first appearing in 755 when Pepin, king of the Franks, concluded a military campaign to defend papal territory from Lombard encroachment by confirming the document. It continued to be cited in support of papal claims to temporal authority in Italy until it was shown to be spurious by Lorenzo Valla in 1440. *See* VALLA, LORENZO
□ W. Ullmann *The Growth of Papal Government in the Middle Ages* (1955)

Altarpiece by the Master of Terenzano: Christ and the Virgin with Dominican saints, including St Dominic.

Donatist schism Intended to protect the North African church from the taint of contact with *traditores*, who had abandoned Christianity during the persecutions of Diocletian 303–05. It began in 311, after the consecration of Caecilian by the alleged *traditor* Felix of Aptunga, and took its name from Donatus, the second bishop to be elected in opposton to Caecilian. As Donatism derived great strength from African regionalism, it resisted both imperial repression and ecclesiastical censure, notably by Augustine, surviving until the African church disintegrated in the wake of Islamic expansion during the 7th c. and 8th c.

□ W. H. C. Frend *The Donatist Church* (1952)

Donatus Grammarian of the mid-4th c., whose *Ars Minor* was much in use in the Middle Ages as a standard teaching instrument. Even in the 15th c. it was one of the commonest texts to be found in the new grammar schools.

Dubois, Pierre (*c*.1250–*c*.1320) French lawyer and political writer. He studied at Paris and Orleans before returning to his native Normandy *c*.1295 to take up a career in law at Coutances. He appears as king's advocate in the surrounding *balliage* by *c*.1300, and represented the city in the Estates General of 1302 and 1308. His ambition to secure political office at Paris, which remained unfulfilled, contributed to his emergence as a prominent political pamphleteer. His most famous treatise was the *De Recuperatione Terre Sancte* (*c*.1306). Under the guise of advising on crusading methods, this work expresses the convictions which characterize all of Dubois's work: that the French crown should increase its administrative powers in the interests of internal peace, and assume the leadership of Europe in the interests of external peace.

□ W. I. Brandt *The Recovery of the Holy Land* (1956)

Ducas dynasty Byzantine imperial family prominent during the second half of the 11th c., and eclipsed by the accession of Alexius I Comnenus in 1081. Constantine X Ducas (1059–67) owed his elevation to the Civil party in Constantinople, reacting against the policies of the military emperor, Isaac I Comnenus. The times were inauspicious for the installation of a civilian emperor, and Constantine X and his son Michael VII (1071–78) presided over the collapse of Byzantine power in Asia Minor caused by Turkish incursions. The problems of the civil aristocracy, headed by the Ducas family, paved the way for the rise of the military aristocracy after 1081.

□ D. I. Polemis *The Doukai* (1968)

Ducat (from *ducatus*, the 'duchy' of Venice) Venetian gold coin weighing 3.56 g, first struck in 1284 and continuing unchanged in weight, fineness and design to the end of the Venetian Republic in 1797. It was the dominant gold coin of the eastern Mediterranean area in the later Middle Ages, and the name was widely applied elsewhere in Europe to coins of the same weight and fineness.

Gold **ducat** issued by the Doge Giovanni Soranzo (1312-28).

DuGuesclin, Bertrand (*c*.1320–80) A brave and capable military commander who provided the soldiering skills that enabled Charles V to restore the fortunes of France after the disastrous opening stages of the Hundred Years' War. A Breton in origin, DuGuesclin won his reputation through campaigns in Normandy and later in Spain, suppressing the Free Companies which ravaged the countryside, and ultimately succeeding in setting up the French ally, Henry of Trastamara, as king of Castile (1369). As constable he played the main part in reorganizing the armies, and supported the cautious, sensible policy that resulted in the virtual rejection of English rule. By the Treaty of Bruges (1375) the English were left with no more than Calais and a coastal strip in Gascony.

□ M. Dulud *DuGuesclin* (1958); P. Contamine *Guerre, état et société à la fin du Moyen-Age* (1972)

Duns Scotus, John (*c*.1265–1308) *Doctor subtilis*, he was a philosopher and theologian of the foremost importance. Of Scottish birth, he entered the Franciscan Order *c*.1280, spending 13 years at Oxford studying theology (1288–1301), and seeking ordination in 1291. He died in possession of a chair in theology at Cologne, having lectured at Oxford, Cambridge and Paris. The thought of the Scotist school, which was profound and conservative rather than innovative and exciting, was established as an influential force, especially in Franciscan circles, by the mid-14th c.

□ *John Duns Scotus: 'God and Creatures'* ed. F. Alluntis and A. B. Wolter (1975)

Dunstan, St (*c*.909–88) Abbot of Glastonbury and archbishop of Canterbury. He was educated at Glastonbury abbey before entering the household of his uncle Athelm, archbishop of Canterbury. He later joined the court of King Athelstan, to whom he was also related, but his enemies secured his expulsion by claiming that he was involved with the black arts. Under the influence of Aelfheah, bishop of Winchester, he became both monk and priest, and retired to live as a hermit at Glastonbury.

St Dunstan at the feet of Christ. The drawing and inscription of *c*.960 could be by Dunstan's own hand.

In 939 he was recalled by Athelstan's successor, Edmund. Opponents engineered a second expulsion from court, but Edmund restored Dunstan to favour and made him abbot of Glastonbury after a miraculous escape from death whilst hunting near Cheddar Gorge *c*.943. Dunstan served as counsellor and treasurer to Eadred, but was exiled to Flanders on the accession of Eadwig in 955. He stayed at the monastery of Mount Blandin in Ghent, where he experienced at first hand the Continental monastic reform movement, until Edgar seized power in 957 and recalled him.

He was appointed bishop of Worcester immediately, becoming bishop of London in 959 and archbishop of Canterbury in 960. With Edgar, he masterminded a reformation of church and state, which was rooted in a revival of Benedictine monasticism. In Wessex he encouraged the spread of the Benedictine values he had promoted at Glastonbury, whilst restoring the monastery after the Danish invasions. He also supported the work of Aethelwold, bishop of Winchester, and Oswald, bishop of Worcester, in similar projects based on the houses of Abingdon and Westbury-on-Trym, respectively. Moreover, *c*.970 he attempted to co-ordinate these independent efforts by calling a synod which agreed on the common monastic observance known as the *Regularis Concordia*. Dunstan remained influential during the reign of Edward the Martyr (975–78), but fell into political eclipse on the accession of Aethelred, becoming increasingly concerned with diocesan affairs. JH

□ E.S. Duckett *Saint Dunstan of Canterbury* (1955); *Tenth-Century Studies* ed. D. Parsons (1975)

Durandus of Saint-Pourcain (*c*.1275–1334) Chiefly remembered as one of the principal theological opponents of Thomas Aquinas, Durandus was a nominalist and something of a forerunner of William of Ockham. Whereas Aquinas endeavoured to reconcile reason and faith, Durandus maintained that there was so sharp a contrast between them that it was not possible to move to a rational defence of the inner mysteries. He was also profoundly sceptical of the reality of abstract universal ideas, holding to the view that reality consisted only in the specific and individual. His commentaries on the Sentences of Peter Lombard and his tract on the beatific vision of the just souls were greatly valued in the later Middle Ages. Because of the power of his personality as a teacher and in debate, he was known as *doctor resolutissimus*.

□ E. Gilson *A History of Christian Philosophy in the Middle Ages* (1955)

Durandus the Elder, William (*c*.1230–96) A leading interpreter of canon law, Durandus – known as the 'Speculator' from the title of his best-known work, the *Speculum Judiciale* – was active as an administrator in the papal states and contributed greatly to study of the liturgy. His revision of the *Pontificale Romanum* and his *Rationale Divinorum Officiorum* rapidly became standard authorities. He was elected bishop of Mende in Languedoc in 1285, an office in which he was succeeded by his nephew William Durandus the Younger (*c*.1271–1330).

□ A.C. Flick *The Decline of the Medieval Church* (1930); L. Falletti, 'Guillaume Durand', *Dictionnaire de droit canonique* vol.5 (1953)

E

Easter, date of The Council of Nicaea (325) fixed Easter on the Sunday following the first full moon after the spring equinox, and approved the Alexandrian method for calculating when it should fall. The Alexandrians reckoned 21 March as the spring equinox, and used a 19–year 'Paschal cycle' to deal with the fact that the solar year was known to consist of 365 days and an indeterminate fraction. From the 5th c. onwards this system was adopted increasingly in the West, replacing those favoured by the Roman, Frankish and Celtic churches.

□ M. O'Connell and A. Adam *The Liturgical Year* (1981)

Eckhart, Master (1260–1327) Dominican mystic. An aristocratic German scholar trained at Paris, he proved a master preacher and teacher both in Latin and in the German vernacular. His chief centre was Cologne, and it was there that the mysticism in his teaching, which came near to expressing a pantheistic interpretation of the Trinity, brought about charges of heresy. He was convicted in 1326 at Cologne, appealed to the pope at Avignon, but died before the papal decision (condemning some of his work) was made known. His reputation and influence remained formidable, helping to create a background of theological uncertainty and unrest in later medieval Germany.

□ J. M. Clark *The Great German Mystics* (1949)

Eclipses Astronomical knowledge of the causes of eclipses was transmitted to the Middle Ages by scholars interested in the calendar and chronology for religious and liturgical purposes. Dungal from Ireland, for example, is said to have explained them to Charlemagne, and there is even evidence for the successful prediction of eclipses. In the Muslim world Greek knowledge was better preserved, and eclipses were studied scientifically in Baghdad in the 9th c. and at Cairo in the later 10th c.

Medieval chroniclers and historians in the West, however, were more inclined to treat eclipses as portents, sometimes dating historic events inaccurately in consequence: for example, saga writers associated the death of St Olaf at the battle of Stiklestad near Trondheim on 29 July 1030 with an eclipse which could not have taken place until 31 August. At other times chroniclers borrowed notices of eclipses from fellow chroniclers or historians in distant parts, even though the phenomenon itself could not have been seen in the area where the writer was operating. Nevertheless, if handled critically, references often serve as an accurate indication of the chronological framework for events, and comparative studies on a world-wide basis have demonstrated an equivalence in observation of eclipses between Europe, China, and even the Mayan civilization of pre-Columban America.

□ R. R. Newton *Medieval Chronicles and the Rotation of the Earth* (1972); D. J. Schove *Chronology of Eclipses and Comets, AD 1–1000* (1986)

Ecu ('shield') Name given to a French gold coin struck by St Louis in 1266, having a shield as its type, and subsequently applied to many coins (especially

Ecu à la chaise of Philip VI of France (1328–50) showing the king seated on his throne.

French), weighing between 4 and 5 g and of thin, broad fabric. The coins were usually identified with some descriptive epithet, e.g. *écu à la chaise*, with the king seated, or *écu à la couronne*, with a crowned shield. Since the latter was the commonest type from 1380 onwards, the coin was known in England as a 'crown'.

Edda, the Elder and the Younger The two principal Icelandic sources for Scandinavian mythology. The Elder Edda contains 33 poems, some of which date from as early as the 9th c., though the compilation was made in the 13th c. The Younger Edda was arranged, also in the 13th c., by Snorri Sturluson, but is generally thought to be of mid-12th c. date. It contains the *Gylfaginning*, the 'delusion of Gylfi', which gives a synoptic account in prose of Northern mythology, and is the basis for the later popular *Tales from Asgarth*.

□ U. Dronke *The Poetic Edda* (1969); C. Clover *The Medieval Saga* (1982)

Edgar the Peaceable King of England 959–75 (b. 943) One of the ablest of the West Saxon dynasty, Edgar is usually held to be the first ruler of a united English monarchy, though his uncle Athelstan (924–39) has some claim to that position. Edgar had the good fortune to live in a period of comparative lull in Scandinavian attacks and took the opportunity to build on his predecessors' successes. He is remembered for his law codes, his vigorous support of the reformed Bendictine monastic movement and for his solemn coronation at Bath in 973, when the full panoply of ecclesiastical ritual and pomp was exploited by Archbishop Dunstan to lend extra strength to the Christian kingship of a united England.

Edmund, St King of East Anglia *c.* 855–69 (b. 841) Defeated by the Danes at or near Hoxne in Suffolk, Edmund was captured and martyred on 20 November 869. Details of his death were preserved vividly in legend: he is said to have been tortured, shot to death with arrows and afterwards beheaded. Some accounts say that he was buried first in a wooden church at Hellesdon in Norfolk and then reinterred at *Beadoricesworth*, later Bury St Edmunds. Certainly the solid evidence of the issue of a substantial coinage in the saint's name by the end of the 9th c. indicates the quick and, indeed, dramatic growth of a cult around the person of the dead king. His death was attributed to a steadfast refusal to renounce his Christian faith, and it is as a Christian martyr that he was remembered both in England and the Scandinavian North. Bury St Edmunds subsequently became an important centre

St Edmund feeding the hungry, in an early 12th-c. English Life of the king.

of popular pilgrimage in the central Middle Ages. □ D. Whitelock, 'Fact and Fiction in the legend of St Edmund', *Proceedings of the Suffolk Institute of Architecture* (1969)

Education In comparison with even the early modern period, education in the Middle Ages was a luxury always confined to the minority; it was principally organized for the benefit of males, and, to the extent that it was available to the layman, it was likely to be demanded most by those needing to acquire the skills of government, administration or commerce, and those who were in a position to afford it (in terms of time as well as material resources). In practice, for most of the Middle Ages this meant aristocratic or urban demand.

Even where efforts were made to keep the costs of study down or to subsidize access for the poor, an individual's chances of acquiring formal education would depend on his ease of access to its supply. For much of the Middle Ages the chief supplier was the church. The monasteries, which had carried the torch of learning and scholarship through the Dark Ages, the cathedrals and, gradually, the parish schools, formed a network which the authorities had attempted to maintain for centuries with very limited success. In the high Middle ages this system blossomed, taking its cue from the spectacular growth of the cathedral schools of northern France, academically the home of the 12th-c. Renaissance. The growth of the 11th c. and 12th c. was lasting, receiving fresh stimulus with the formal and autonomous development of universities in the late 12th c. and 13th c.; with the rise of the mendicant orders with their particular emphasis on learning and teaching; and finally with the proliferation, in the later Middle Ages, of chantry and other endowed schools.

It would, however, be wrong to suppose that the church had a monopoly on education. By the 13th c. many towns, particularly in Italy, were taking the initiative in hiring schoolmasters to teach at various levels; and there is evidence for a surprising extent of literacy in some of these towns. To these must be added court and household schools (Charlemagne's palace school being a celebrated early example), which might well feature churchmen as teachers, but which were independently initiated and run. Schooling was in any case only one aspect of education, which might also take the form of training and apprenticeship (a vital role was played by the guilds in imparting a wide range of artisanal and professional skills), or of informal, private teaching and, indeed, self-teaching.

There was a great divergence between theory and practice in the structure of formal education. The disciplines were divided notionally into the seven liberal arts, comprising grammar, rhetoric and dialectic (the *Trivium*), arithmetic, geometry, astronomy and music (the *Quadrivium*), and the higher subjects of theology, law and medicine. But while the division of the higher subjects was closely reflected in university organization at least until the end of the Middle Ages, at the lower level it was not really a syllabus so much as a loose conceptual framework within which there was plenty of scope for shifts of emphasis and for development. Teachers felt free to select, to emphasize their own interests, or to discuss those topics and texts they felt to be

Education: a teacher and his pupils, in a manuscript possibly made for David II of Scotland, *c.*1340.

Cino de Pistoia lecturing to his pupils, in a 14th-c. marble relief by a Sienese master, after 1337.

most relevant to the times. Eventually some, like Hugh of Saint-Victor, proposed alternative classifications, although these too remained models of pedagogical theory, rather than causing a revolution in what was actually taught. In practice, the pattern of the medieval 'syllabus' shows great consistency, at least as regards basic education. At the elementary level children were taught to read, and then to write, to sing and to carry out some basic *computus* (essential for the calculation of the Christian calendar). From an early stage the psalter featured prominently; psalms could be learnt by heart without much grasp of the Latin language.

The next level centred on Latin, passport to the serious cultural world, to all the professions and to a fuller understanding of the Bible and the church's rites and doctrine. To the basic texts bequeathed by late antiquity, such as Donatus' *Ars Minor* (a short treatise describing the eight parts of speech), the Grammar of Priscian, Aesop's *Fables* and Cato's *Distichs* (a collection of aphorisms), were gradually added medieval masters' reworking or reinterpretation of the same material, sometimes more teaching aids than new texts: Aelfric's Grammar (10th c.), Alexander of Villedieu's *Doctrinale* (*c.* 1200), Evrard of Béthune's *Graecismus* (13th c.). Grammar schools, as their name implies, taught more than a second, international language; they trained students in the analysis and use of language (grammar, rhetoric, dialectic, or logic), and this training in turn shaded into those branches of philosophy which ultimately prepared the student for the higher, university subjects. The elements of the *Quadrivium*, while they would certainly be taught in 'grammar' schools as well, often became the focus of a different type of school, known in its humblest form as an 'abacus' school, often approaching a business school in the range of skills taught there (e.g., notarial skills and *dictamen*, the art of letter-writing).

However varied in type and syllabus, the medieval schools had some essential features in common. In most of Europe, scholars had clerical status (although by the end of the period this had ceased to mean very much); they thus came under ecclesiastical jurisdiction and were targets for the ideals and moral strictures of the church. Schoolroom life was severe; corporal punishment was an integral part of education, and the school day was a long and demanding one, although relaxation was supplied partly by the religious calendar and undoubtedly by the inclinations of the scholars themselves.

Perhaps the most fundamental contrast with modern educational systems relates to the method of learning. In class, texts were used above all by the teachers; the rarity and cost of books put them beyond the reach of most pupils, many of whom would have been lucky to possess a psalter, traditionally the first book given to a child. The medieval classroom reflected the overwhelmingly oral nature of medieval culture, with the teacher reading and explicating the text, and the student absorbing it and committing it to memory; the capacity of medieval memories was highly developed. This emphasis on oral transmission permeated all levels of education and affected the method of study and exercise (e.g., disputation and dialogue), the structure of texts and even the attitudes to the *auctores* thus digested. *See* LIBERAL ARTS; UNIVERSITIES   PD

□ N. Orme *English Schools in the Middle Ages* (1973); J. Bowen *A History of Western Education* vol. 2 (1975); P. Riché *Education and Culture in the Barbarian West* (1978); A. Piltz *The World of Learning* (1981)

Edward I King of England 1272–1307 (b. 1239) One of the most powerful English kings of the Middle Ages, Edward made permanent achievements in both the political and constitutional fields. His conquest of Wales was stabilized by the imposition of the Statute of Rhuddlan (1284) and made secure physically by the construction of a network of great castles (notably Caernarvon, Harlech, Conway and Beaumaris), from which royal officers maintained peace throughout Gwynedd, the heartland of native Welsh independence. Attempts to impose similar authority over Scotland seemed in the 1290s to be near success, but ultimately failed in the face of revolts by William Wallace and Robert Bruce. Internally, Edward served a hard apprenticeship as a young man, the Lord Edward, in the Barons' War, emerging finally as successful leader in the fight against Simon de Montfort. He was away from England on crusade when his father, Henry III, died, but Edward's reputation was so high that there was no opposition to his succession.

For his work in reorganizing his feudal state at both central and local levels he is sometimes referred to as the English Justinian. Most important among the legislative enactments of his reign are the Statutes of Westminster (1275 and 1285), the Statute of Gloucester (1278) and the Statutes *Quo Warranto* and *Quia Emptores* (both of 1290). Building on precedents, notably those of de Montfort in 1264 and 1265, Edward consistently summoned representatives of local communities, knights of the shire and burgesses of towns, to central assemblies, and so fostered the notion of a more sophisticated community of the realm. For example, in November 1295, on the grounds that what affected all should justly be approved by all, he ordered to attend what later historians sometimes described as a 'model' parliament, his earls, barons, prelates, and also select knights of the shire, burgesses, and representatives of the lower clergy.

On the death of his wife, Eleanor of Castile, in 1290, Edward had constructed the great Eleanor crosses, some of which still survive, to mark the passage of her body from Harby in Lincolnshire to

King **Edward III** in the robes of the Order of the Garter, which he instituted (15th-c. illumination).

Westminster Abbey. In spite of his great achievements, and in some measure because of the expenditure they entailed, he suffered periodic financial crises. He left a difficult heritage to his son, Edward II, whose disastrous reign (1307–27) experienced military defeat in Scotland (Bannockburn, 1314) as well as bitter and ultimately fatal constitutional conflicts.
□ F. M. Powicke *King Henry III and the Lord Edward* (1947), *The Thirteenth Century 1216–1307* (1953); M. C. Prestwich *War, Politics and Finance under Edward I* (1972)

Edward III King of England 1327–77 (b. 1312) Son of Edward II and Isabella (daughter of King Philip IV of France, and the so-called 'she-wolf' of France). In 1328 Edward married Philippa, daughter of the count of Hainault, and had 12 children by her, including Edward (the Black Prince), John of Gaunt, duke of Lancaster, and Edmund of Langley, duke of York. Edward III brought England to a high peak of success in the Hundred Years' War with France, though his later years were clouded by French recovery and by his own ill-health. A naval victory at Sluys (1340), left him in a position to dictate terms. The Black Prince led the army at Poitiers, taking the French King John II captive.

Socially Edward's reign was conspicuous for the growth of chivalric ideals; the Order of the Garter was instituted in 1348, resulting in the refinement of concepts of knightly behaviour, and of the science of heraldry. Financial troubles accumulated in the last decades of his life, brought about in part by the social and economic dislocation caused by the Black Death and recurring plagues, and in part by the expense of the French wars, renewed to French advantage under the leadership of Charles V (1365–80) and DuGuesclin. Parliament became more highly developed and powerful; the division into Lords and Commons grew more clear-cut as the financial needs of the king increased. The death of the old king so soon after that of his eldest son, the Black Prince, led to general lament at the loss of 'such two lords of high parage'; and an uneasy heritage passed to his young grandson, Richard II.
□ M. C. Prestwich *The Three Edwards* (1980)

Edward the Confessor, St King of England 1042–66 (b. 1003) Son of King Aethelred II and his Norman wife Emma, daughter of Duke Richard II of Normandy, Edward spent his youth in exile in Normandy, but was recalled to England in 1041, and succeeded his half-brother Harthecnut to the throne in the following year. In a period of great political turbulence, Edward kept his kingdom in relative peace, though he had to rely to a large extent on the

military capacity of Earl Godwin of Wessex (d. 1053) and his sons, notably Harold, who succeeded to the throne in January 1066. Edward had brought some Normans back to England with him and remained in touch with the duchy; Norman apologists claimed that he had designated Duke William as his successor as early as 1051. Edward's piety was great and some of his best energy was devoted to the building of Westminster Abbey. He was canonized in 1161. [341]
□ F. Barlow *Edward the Confessor* (1966)

Egypt At the beginning of the Middle Ages, Egypt was a prosperous province of the Byzantine empire with its chief city at Alexandria – the home of a patriarch and one of the leading cultural centres of the Hellenic world. Increasing political and religious dissatisfaction with Constantinople on the part of the Egyptians, among whom the Monophysite heresy was popular, facilitated the Muslim conquest in the 630s, and for the rest of the period Egypt was an integral part of the Muslim world, at times subject to the authority of Baghdad or Damascus, but more often virtually, or completely, independent.

In the early centuries, thanks to Alexandria, Egypt became one of the principal areas through which Greek learning, philosophy and science were transmitted (by translation) to the Arab world. The political successes of the Fātimids in the second half of the 10th c. and the foundation of a new city at Cairo, brought Egypt into a central position in the Muslim Shi'ite world.

Turkish successes, followed by the establishment of crusading principalities in Palestine, led to decline, and it was not until the successes of Saladin, who united Syria and Egypt in 1174, that its importance revived. In the 13th c. crusading efforts were directed, on the whole unsuccessfully, against Egypt, at Damietta in 1219 and again under St Louis in 1250. Internally, the overriding military needs of Egypt resulted in the emergence of the Mamlūks, hired military elements who preserved political control until the 16th c.
□ S. Lane-Poole *A History of Egypt in the Middle Ages* (1901); P. Hitti *History of the Arabs* (1951)

Einhard (*c*.770–840) Frankish scholar and court official, best known for his biography of his friend and master, Charlemagne. He was educated at the School of Fulda, joining the royal court *c*. 793 and rising to an important position in the palace school at Aix-la-Chapelle. He became a close and trusted associate of both Charlemagne and his successor Louis I, and continued in public service until *c*. 830, when he retired to the estates which Louis had given to him at Michelstadt and Mühlheim (Seligenstadt).

Stained-glass window (1325-33) from Wells cathedral showing **Edward the Confessor**.

□ *Eginhard, La Vie de Charlemagne* ed. L. Halphen (1923); A. Kleinclausz *Eginhard* (1942)

Ekkehard (910–73) A monk of St Gallen and one of the most skilful Latin poets of his age, Ekkehard is chiefly remembered for his part in transmitting the epic story of *Waltharius* to the mainstream of Western tradition. Germanic poetic legends relating to 5th-c. Aquitaine, Burgundy and the court of King Attila had been welded into an epic poem which Ekkehard translated (from the German) into Latin hexameters, after the style of Virgil.
□ *Waltharius* ed. K. Strecker (1907)

Eleanor of Aquitaine (*c*. 1122–1204) Daughter of Duke William X (d. 1137), she succeeded to the duchy and married the dauphin Louis (later Louis VII), to whom she bore two daughters. She accompanied her husband on crusade 1147–49, where they became estranged; Louis had their marriage annulled in 1152.

Two months later, Eleanor married Henry, duke of Normandy, later Henry II of England. She provided him with eight children, but his flagrant adultery alienated her into supporting the rebellion of their sons against Henry, in 1173–74. She was imprisoned by Henry 1174–83, but when released, shared in the government of Aquitaine with her son Richard Lionheart. After Henry's death in 1189, her political influence continued to be great. Her support for Richard was vital, especially after his capture by the Emperor, and as late as 1202 she was active in military and political support of King John, her youngest son.

As patron of troubadours and courtly literature, great legends grew up around her, including accusations of witchcraft. By her marriage to Henry II she brought Aquitaine firmly into the Plantagenet orbit, and it was her ancestral lands which remained loyal to the English crown after the loss of Normandy (1204), thus providing the English king with a foothold on French soil for the next two centuries.
□ A. Kelly *Eleanor of Aquitaine and the Four Kings* (1950); *Eleanor of Aquitaine: Patron and Politician* ed. W. W. Kibler (1976); J. Markale *Alienor d'Aquitaine* (1979)

Emma, lady of Winchester (d. 1051) Wife of King Aethelred and then of Cnut, Emma was an influential figure in English politics throughout her life. She was daughter of the Norman duke Richard II, and so accustomed the English court to Norman ways. After a period of exile under Cnut's sons she returned with her own son, Edward the Confessor, but amassed so much wealth and power during his early years that he was forced to move against her, to seize the treasury, and more or less confine her to Winchester, where she died.

Empire, Holy Roman The concept of an empire was transmitted in Christian times from Rome to Constantinople, restored to the West (from Greeks back to Latins) by Charlemagne in 800, and carried forward from 962 by German rulers through several

The tomb of **Eleanor of Aquitaine** and Henry II in the abbey church of Fontevrault.

dynasties to the Habsburgs of the 15th c. and 16th c. It had much force in the Middle Ages, and indeed among historians interpreting the medieval experience deep into modern times. The term 'Holy Roman Empire' is something of an approximation to reality, and clearly it meant different things at different times to different people.

To Charlemagne and the scholars grouped around him at Aix-la-Chapelle, there was something in the notion of an *imperium christianum*, the imperial title carrying an echo of the right to rule people other than one's own, after the Roman model. Otto the Great revived the empire with his coronation at Rome by the pope in 962, but to him and his successors it meant essentially political domination of Germany and the Middle Kingdom, especially Italy. Saxons, Salians and above all the Hohenstaufen (1138–1254) refined the imperial idea: under Frederick Barbarossa the epithet *sacrum* (sacred) came to be used officially, apparently as a reaction against papal claims and pretensions resulting from Greogry VII's successes in the Investiture Contest. The revival of Roman law also prompted the creation of conscious links with the Roman empire of classical days.

After the great Interregnum (1254–73) there was little chance of a powerful, unified and unifying empire capable of governing the greater part of the West. Indeed, effective hope of controlling the old heartlands of Germany and Italy diminished, and both leading dynasties of the later Middle Ages drew much of their strength from non-German sources: the house of Luxembourg from Bohemia, and the Habsburgs from their Danubian possessions. Yet it was then that the word *sanctum* (holy) came to be used of the empire; it was able political thinkers, notably Dante and Marsilius of Padua, who put forward the most advanced theories of imperial authority based on ancient classical and Christian models. Lord Bryce's great *mot* that the Holy Roman Empire was 'neither Holy, nor Roman, nor an Empire' has substantial elements of truth in it, and yet the importance of imperial theory as a moulding force, notably in German history, cannot be denied. HRL

□ G. Barraclough *The Medieval Empire: Idea and Reality* (1950); F. Heer *The Holy Roman Empire* (1968); R. Folz *The Concept of Empire in Western Europe from the Fifth to the Fourteenth Century* (1969)

England Heathen Germanic peoples, commonly known as Saxons, who had long raided the shores of Roman Britain, were first permitted to settle in the eastern part of the island in the 4th c., in return for their services as fighting men. In the middle of the next century, however, they quarrelled with the

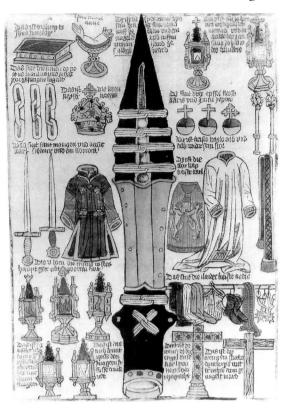

Relics and insignia of the **Holy Roman Empire**.

British chieftains who had taken control after the collapse of Roman rule, and, aided by new waves of settlers, began the conquest of eastern Britain. Though their advance was briefly halted *c.* 500, the subjugation of the area which became known as England had been largely completed by the end of the 7th c.

By this time the original warbands had coalesced into a number of small kingdoms, each dominated by a warrior aristocracy headed by a king, who ruled by virtue of his military power. The native British were reduced to a servile status and gradually adopted the language and customs of their conquerors. In so doing, most lost their Christianity, though it continued to flourish in the British kingdoms remaining in the north and western parts of the island.

The conversion of the Anglo-Saxons was initiated by the Roman church at the end of the 6th c. Nearly a century elapsed before all the kings and their immediate followers were converted, still longer before Christianity was accepted in the countryside. Yet by virtue of its diocesan organization, underpinned by a parish system still far from complete by the Norman Conquest, the church became the only authority to override the boundaries of the various kingdoms.

England

The relations of the Anglo-Saxon kingdoms were those of ceaseless warfare, in the course of which kings of Northumbria (in the 7th c.), Mercia (in the 8th c.) and Wessex (in the early 9th c.), secured in turn the *bretwalda* (British ruler) or overlordship of the others. Especially important was the rule of Offa of Mercia, who constructed the great dyke to define the boundary between his subjects and the Welsh in the 8th c. His use of titles such as *rex Anglorum* betokens the belief that the English were a single people who could be subject to one ruler. Nevertheless, the turning-point in the emergence of a united English monarchy came in the 9th c. with the Viking invasions, ending two centuries in which England had been free of external attack. By destroying all the other Anglo-Saxon kingdoms, they left Wessex, in the south-west, the unchallenged leader of the English community.

Under Alfred and his successors, the territory settled by the Danes – the Danelaw – was systematically reconquered and eventually shired on the pattern of Wessex. By the third quarter of the 10th c. they had created a loosely knit, but durable, united English kingdom with a unified taxation and coinage system. Despite a period of Danish rule (1016-42), royal administration developed steadily, and by the end of the Anglo-Saxon period the secretariat was relatively advanced, issuing sealed writs in English from the royal court to royal officers and thegns of the shire.

The Norman Conquest, the last occasion when England was successfully invaded and settled by people from overseas, turned its development in new directions: the Anglo-Saxon upper class was replaced by a carefully structured feudal society with distinctive social arrangements and customs; the strong links between the English church and the papacy were reinforced, and bishoprics and abbeys converted into feudal baronies. But though the French-speaking Normans abandoned the use of English in favour of Latin as the language of government, they took over and developed the Anglo-Saxon administrative system. This made possible the compilation of Domesday Book, the most impressive record of royal government of its time. The Conquest also brought England into the mainstream of European affairs, binding the fortunes of England and France closer together. For a century and a half the kings of England were also the rulers of large dominions in France, and under the Angevins in the late 12th c., their interests centred on their French possessions. This period only ended with the loss of all these territories, with the exception of Gascony, in the early 13th c.

The Norman–Angevin royal household gave birth to the principal organs of a more elaborately organized central administration which maintained itself by taxing the wealth of landowners and the trade of merchants. Improved financial resources made possible the conquest of Wales in the late 13th c., and prolonged wars with Scotland, whose border with England was fixed in 1237. They also enabled kings of England to lay claim to the French throne, and for two periods – the 1350s and 1410s – to conquer much of France.

Despite their growing power, English kings could not rule effectively without the co-operation of the great landowners. At first, royal concessions took the form of the issue and re-issue of Magna Carta. Later, co-operation was secured by 'parleyings' or parliaments between king, lords and, eventually, representatives of the commons as well. Even so, by the end of the Middle Ages, English kings had become free of the need systematically to consult the wishes of their subjects.

Meanwhile, there had been profound changes in the structure and character of English society. The Black Death (1349) and later plagues caused a catastrophic fall in population which helped to change the relationship between lords and peasants. Despite the failure of the Peasants' Revolt (1381), lords abandoned the direct cultivation of their estates, and unfree or villein tenure gradually died out. Finally, the identity of the English as a distinct people was shown to have survived the Conquest. The English language had continued to be used, in speech if not in writing, and from the 14th c. onwards, as it became socially acceptable, its increasing use in literary works reflected a growing measure of national self-awareness. *See* DANEGELD; EXCHEQUER; FRANKPLEDGE; HUNDRED ROLLS; PARLIAMENT; PLANTAGENET; WILLS; WRITS; *see also individual kings*   CHK
□ *Oxford History of England*, especially F. M. Stenton *Anglo-Saxon England* (1970) and M. McKisack *The Fourteenth Century* (1959); *Pelican History of England*: D. Whitelock *The Beginnings of English Society* (1952), D. M. Stenton *English Society in the Early Middle Ages* (1952) and A. R. Myers *England in the Late Middle Ages* (1956); B. Lyon *A Constitutional and Legal History of Medieval England* (1960)

Ephesus, Council of (431) Third ecumenical council of the church, dismissed by the great historian Gibbon as 'a tumult of bishops'. It was summoned to decide the orthodox view of matters concerning the person and nature of Christ. The influential priest and theologian Nestorius preached ideas which seemed to conclude that Christ possessed not one, but two persons. In 431 Cyril of Alexandria, the papal legate, imprudently began the Council in the absence of clergy from the eastern part of the empire, and his forum condemned Nestorius. When the easterners arrived they set up a shadow council

England: a map of Britain by Matthew Paris, *c.* 1250, showing the major waterways and defences.

under John of Antioch. Mutual recriminations, condemnations and excommunications followed, before Emperor Theodosius intervened and sent the prelates home.

In 433 John of Antioch and Cyril of Alexandria reached an agreement on the central issue: Christ was held to have two distinguishing natures, united and assigned to one person. Pope Sixtus III confirmed the ordinances of Cyril's council, which had promulgated a decree forbidding any formula of faith other than that of the Nicene Creed. This formulation was to have considerable consequences for later conciliar activity, reinforced by the survival of the *conciliar Acta* from Ephesus.
□ P. T. Camelot *Histoire des Conciles Oecuméniques* vol. 2 (1962)

Estates The basic idea of 'estates of the realm' was foreshadowed in the work of 9th- and 10th-c. scholars who divided society into three groups: those who prayed, those who fought, and those who worked. This raw division was complicated in the vigorous 12th c. by the emergence of active groups of townsmen, ranging from wealthy merchants to poor artisans, masters, journeymen, craftsmen and unskilled workers. When political expression came to be given to the notion of a community of the realm, and representative institutions developed in consequence, the idea of division into estates (normally three) persisted.

The English Parliament provides a conspicuous example. From the later 13th c. it became customary for burgesses of the towns and knights of the shire to be summoned to a central assembly: these groups eventually, and somewhat untypically of Europe as a whole, coalesced into a House of Commons, exercising significant power over the levying and collection of taxes. In turn, the barons and upper clergy grew into a House of Lords, though the church through convocation attracted the lower clergy into its own institutions.

The French experience was somewhat different, partly because of the strength of the monarchy, but also because of the continued existence of provincial assemblies. In the opening years of the 14th c. Philip IV summoned representatives of towns, together with feudal vassals, to an Estates General. The lesser nobility and the burgesses did not work together as in England, and the estates remained more disparate.

Elsewhere in Europe, the *Cortes* in Spain, assemblies in the German principalities, Scandinavia and the Slavonic communities (notably Poland), exhibited similar characteristics, though only rarely were such assemblies summoned on a regular basis. By the end of the Middle Ages, with the growth of a more dynamic money economy, the notion of rigid and

The Anglo-Irish court of the **Exchequer**, showing the chequered pattern of the table-cloth.

separate estates was growing inadequate over large tracts of Europe, though socially it retained force well into the modern period, certainly up to the time of the French Revolution.   HRL
□ A.R. Myers *Parliament and Estates in Europe to 1789* (1975)

Estates General The first meeting of the French Estates General (*états généraux*) was held in 1302 at the request of Philip the Fair. Anxious to forestall the ecclesiastical council proposed by Pope Boniface, he summoned the three estates of his realm – nobles, clergy and commons – to meet in Paris. As a result of this assembly all three groups wrote separately to Rome in defence of the king and his temporal power. From that time onward, the Estates General was assembled only in emergencies (i.e., usually for the purpose of supporting the monarchy in times of crisis), and the meetings (1302, 1308, 1314, etc.) were carefully controlled by the lawyers who served the king as a *conseil d'état*. This representative assembly continued to meet sporadically over the succeeding centuries, but it was not the beginning of an effective governmental institution; the concept of government by consent of the realm was still in the early stages of development.
□ J. P. Strayer *Medieval Statecraft and the Perspectives of History* (1971)

Exchequer (of England) As a consequence of the Norman Conquest, England's financial administration was tightened and made more efficient. In the early years of the reign of Henry I (1100–35) new institutional form was given to the central financial offices, which resulted in the creation of the Exchequer, so called because of the chequer-board pattern of the cloth used to cover the table on which accounts were rendered. In essence, the novelty of the Exchequer, as opposed to the Treasury, consisted in its efficiency as an accounting agency, its authority as a court, and its record-keeping capacity. Rolls of the Exchequer survive for 1129–30 and are continuous from 1156. An elaborate and detailed record of procedures, Richard FitzNigel's *Dialogue of the Exchequer*, was written in the 1170s, by which time it held its permanent home at Westminster with only occasional sessions elsewhere.

The prime purpose of the Exchequer was to examine twice a year the debts and dues owed to the king and to audit the sheriff's accounts. It developed into the most efficient financial office in Europe and had great influence on organization in Normandy. There were also strong contacts with Norman Sicily, where Thomas Brown acted as judge and financial officer (1143–58), before returning to England to become a key figure at the Exchequer in the 1160s and 1170s.

The Exchequer underwent a series of reforms 1236–42; a new tally system was introduced to simplify the shrieval accounts, and specialization occurred with the use of new accounting procedures for escheators and foreign accounts. These measures reduced the sheriff's workload. Statutes in 1270 and

1284 (Rhuddlan) elaborated these processes, and the reforms 1323–26 instituted by Bishop Stapledon refined them further, simultaneously simplifying debt collection. Few substantial changes occurred before the Reformation. The Exchequer provided the bureaucratic model for other departments; a shadow Exchequer existed for Normandy by 1130, and these departments in time followed the Exchequer out of the peripatetic household to a fixed location.
See PIPE ROLLS; ROGER OF SALISBURY

□ R. L. Poole *The Exchequer in the Twelfth Century* (1912); C. Johnson *Dialogus de Scaccario* (1950); G. L. Harriss *King, Parliament and Public Finance in Medieval England* (1975)

Ezzelino III da Romano (1194–1259) Ghibelline lord. A cruel and ruthless tyrant, Ezzelino was active for nearly 40 years in the wars of northern Italy. With the help of the Emperor Frederick II, he was able in only a few years to establish control over Verona, Vicenza and Padua. He was excommunicated in 1254 by Pope Alexander IV, and died four years later from a wound received in battle at Cassano, refusing both medical aid and peace with the church.

F

Peasants trading in cattle and pigs at the Hamburg **fair**, 1497.

Fairs Originating for the most part in meetings of traders on church festivals and holidays (*feriae*), the fairs blossomed in the central Middle Ages in Europe into great regional, national or even international events where merchants, money-changers and men operating banking skills assembled. Special privileges and powers of jurisdiction were normally conceded at these fairs, many of which became noted for special products: wine, leather, textiles, metalwork, agricultural products, or horses. Fairs often lasted several days, sometimes weeks, and retained vestiges of their religious origins in taking the names of saints, such as St Bartholomew in London or St Giles in Oxford and Winchester. Their importance was great in the cultural and intellectual, as well as in the commercial life of Europe, in that they served as regular meeting places at a fixed time and fixed place where men from widespread communities could exchange news and ideas along with goods and chattels. *See* CHAMPAGNE, FAIRS OF; COMMERCE

□ C. Verlinden, 'Markets and Fairs', *Cambridge Economic History of Europe* vol. 3 (1963)

Famine It is important to define famine in medieval Europe in such a way as to distinguish 'true' famine

Dying of the **famine**; from the *Chronique d'Angleterre* of Jean de Warrin, *c.*1470-80.

from the sporadic great hungers which were inevitable in an age when the basic agrarian economy depended to a large extent on the vagaries of weather and harvest. Generally, the techniques of food production and distribution were sufficient to sustain population, provided that – and this is an important proviso – there was freedom from warfare, banditry, piracy and the general savagery associated with such violence, notably in times of barbarian invasion. Given relative peace, the medieval manor and agrarian and pastoral practices both within and without a manorial economy were efficient enough to preclude famine. But enormous variation occurred from region to region and from district to district; and every community in Europe in the early Middle Ages suffered occasional, localized famine.

In the central Middle Ages the situation improved, and during the period of climatic optimum from the mid-11th c. to the end of the 13th c. most of Western Europe was well fed, though continued political disasters, culminating in the Mongol invasions, brought great affliction and regular famine conditions to large tracts in the east of the Continent. Curiously, it is not until after 1300 that records become clear of serious and protracted famine in the West, in towns as well as the countryside. Two general reasons have been suggested for the phenomenon: a climatic decline, and an exhaustion of the economy which had reached its point of saturation – that is to say, the point at which existing techniques

of agrarian exploitation and urban organization could no longer support the high level of population which had resulted from the preceding period of growth; in other words, Malthusian checks began to operate.

Certainly the opening decades of the 14th c. were harsh, and the famines of 1315-17 exceptionally severe. The Black Death in mid-century and subsequent outbreaks of plague further exacerbated affairs, and the fall in rural population in the West proved longlasting, with no significant sign of recovery until the late 14th c. Vivid artistic representation of apocalyptic disasters in the later Middle Ages – famine, pestilence, war and death – serve to remind us of the 'true' famines caused by the economic dislocations of the age. *See* AGRICULTURE HRL
□ H.S. Lucas *The Great European Famines of 1315, 1316 and 1317 (1930)*; G. Duby *Rural Economy and Country Life in the Medieval West* (1968); E. LeRoy Ladurie *Times of Feast, Times of Famine* (1971); R. Tannahill *Food in History* (1973)

Fātimid dynasty 909–1171 Shi'ite caliphate ruling North Africa and Egypt, named after Fātima, daughter of Muhammad. Their claim to universal sovereignty by virtue of divine decree was contested by the 'Abbāsids. The Fātimids' primary objective was the construction of an eastern policy which would allow them to wrest control from the 'Abbāsids. To that end a Mediterranean fleet and Fātimid control of Egypt (973) became necessary, bringing them within the political and military spheres of, first, Byzantium, and then the crusaders. The periodic expeditions against the Christians were costly diversions from their constant attempts to control Damascus, and as much energy was poured into diplomacy as war. The caliphate reached the height of its powers in the 11th c., but the unsettled conditions of the 12th c., coupled with internal anarchy, economic crises and devastating famines sped the decline of the Fātimids. Saladin abolished the dynasty in 1171.

□ B. Lewis *The Arabs in History* (1950); P. Hitti *History of the Arabs* (1951)

Feltre, Vittorino da (1378–1446) Educationist and humanist, this Mantuan scholar established a school, the *Casa Giocosa,* which concentrated on educating the young in Latin and Greek, without neglecting physical education and moral instruction. Some poor boys, and even some girls, were included in his groups, although fundamental support for his venture came from the aristocratic and wealthy. His achievements signify, among other things, a reaction against concentration on the vernacular, and a conscious reversion on the part of the scholarly to the Latinate universality of the central Middle Ages, which many in the 15th c. considered to have been lost.

□ W.H. Woodward *Vittorino da Feltre and other Humanist Educators* (1963)

Ferdinand II King of Aragon 1479–1516 (b. 1452) Son of John II of Aragon, he married Isabella of Castile in 1469, bringing their two kingdoms into a form of dyarchy when he succeeded his father in 1479. The two monarchs proceeded to complete the Reconquest with the capture of Granada in 1492. After Isabella's death in 1504 he gave only limited support to Cardinal Cisneros' attempts to extend the Reconquest to Africa (1505–10). He conquered Naples in 1503 and Navarre in 1512, the former victory drawing him deeper into the European political arena. He attempted to bolster his dynasty by a series of carefully arranged marriages, which were spoilt by unexpected deaths. His shrewd introduction of ambassadors and astute, wily diplomacy gained the respect, if not the admiration, of his contemporaries, including Machiavelli.

□ J.H. Elliott *Imperial Spain 1479–1716* (1963)

Ferdinand III, St King of Castile and Leon 1217/30–52 (b. *c.* 1201) Son of Alfonso IX of Leon and Berenguela, heir to the throne of Castile through her father Alfonso VIII. When his parents' marriage was annulled, he lived in Leon, but on the sudden death

of Henry I of Castile (1217) Berenguela renounced her rights to the throne, brought her son to Castile and proclaimed him king, overcoming simultaneously rebellions by Castilian nobles and a Leonese invasion that almost reached Burgos. Other rebellions followed, but none came so close to dethroning the young king. Ferdinand married Beatrice of Swabia, grand-daughter of Frederick Barbarossa, in 1219. Five years later he launched his campaigns against the Almohads, who had been decisively weakened at Las Navas de Tolosa, and as the Almohad strongholds fell to Muslim rivals, he fought against the successor states.

He was now king of Leon also: Alfonso IX died in 1230 leaving his kingdom to his two daughters, but with Berenguela's help Ferdinand persuaded them to yield the crown to him. From this time on, Leon and Castile were definitively united, with Castile as the senior partner. Moreover, the economy expanded and Ferdinand developed the universities. What had been a war of raids and unsuccessful sieges (e.g., Jaén 1225 and 1230) became one of permanent conquest: Cordoba fell in 1235, Jaén in 1245 and Seville in 1248 after a two-year siege; the kingdom of Murcia had surrendered peacefully in 1243. Ferdinand had not only made the first major advance in the Reconquest for 150 years; at his accession he found Muslim Spain occupying nearly half the peninsula, and when he died, planning the invasion of Africa, Muslim rule was confined to the kingdom of Granada. This and his personal piety led to his canonization in 1671.

Feudalism 'Feudal' and 'feudalism' are terms much abused; in popular speech they are ignorantly intended as insults even more derogatory than 'medieval'. Even historians seldom agree on a date for the beginning or the end of feudalism, or on what precisely it was. One reason for what is, at best, the loose usage of these words is that they are modern terms coined to describe a society which was passing or already past; the root word 'feudal' (Latin *feudum,* 'fief') first appears in 1614 (OED), while 'feudalism' was not invented until the 19th c.

Granted continuous development, and therefore a gradual start and finish, the origins of feudal society are best placed in northern France in the 9th c. and 10th c. with the decline of Carolingian monarchy (in England, more dramatically, in 1066 with the Norman Conquest), and its waning, in the 16th c.

M. Bloch defined it thus: 'A subject peasantry; widespread use of the service tenement (i.e., the fief) instead of a salary . . . ; the supremacy of a class of specialized warriors; ties of obedience and protection which bind man to man and, within the warrior class, assume the distinctive form called vassalage; fragmentation of authority – leading inevitably to disorder; and, in the midst of all this, the survival of other forms of association, family and state. . . .'

However, it is misleading to put first 'A subject peasantry', which is neither an outstanding nor a unique feature. Better by far to begin with 'the supremacy of a class of specialized warriors', and call them knights, for they were the dominant class. Indeed, in the classic view, the origins of feudalism lie in a military revolution whereby the Franks, who had hitherto fought on foot, increasingly adopted heavy cavalry from the mid-8th c. Mounted warfare being expensive, specialized and exclusive, the military elite became a social elite and the ancestors of a new, feudal nobility. Not until the 10th c., or even later, did the knights achieve military and therefore social dominance, and the modern trend is to emphasize the survival of a Carolingian aristocracy into the early feudal period; but there is no doubt of the importance of these military developments, which will also give rise to chivalry (one cannot be chivalrous without a horse), and to armorial bearings which distinguished the armoured knight in action.

The same military developments also account for the fief, which is the tenurial essence of feudalism and rivets feudal lordship and relationships to the land. The fief was land held of a lord by his vassal in return for honourable services, including military service, aid and counsel. While in the earlier period especially, landless knights abounded – young men and younger sons serving directly in the lord's household – the fief, bestowed by investiture, was the most desired form of maintenance, and quite early became hereditary. Logically, however, in an analysis of the fundamental features of feudalism we might put vassalage before the fief, for this was a society based upon lordship, in a hierarchy of vassals and lords culminating in the king or prince. The relationship was created by a developed and elevated form of ancient Germanic commendation, whereby one freeman submitted to another by the act of homage (joined hands placed between those of the lord), confirmed by a sacred oath of fealty and usually accompanied by investiture with the fief. The ceremony and the tie were solemn, for they were the bonds of society at its upper and politically conscious levels.

Monarchy itself became feudalized, and was strengthened thereby, the king deriving more real power from his feudal rights as suzerain, the lord of lords, than from time-honoured regality. It is therefore regrettable that Bloch, by his reference to 'fragmentation of authority – leading inevitably to disorder', subscribes to the seemingly ineradicable

Feudalism: William gives arms to Harold, creating a feudal bond between them.

heresy that feudalism is a negative, rather than a positive political force. Feudal monarchy in fact has been called the New Leviathan (R.H.C. Davis) and feudalism is one of the foundations of the modern Western state. It prohibited absolutism, for the lord had obligations (not least of doing justice) as well as rights, and the vassal's obligation to give counsel blended into the right to be consulted, and ultimately to give consent. The great councils of kings and their tenants-in-chief are thus the direct ancestors of modern parliaments.

To Bloch's definition should also be added the castle (the earliest surviving example dating from the mid-10th c.); this was the unique architectural manifestation of feudal society. As the fortified residence of a lord, it was the symbol and the substance of feudal lordship, which it imposed upon the land by means of the mounted men based within it. To those 'other forms of association' surviving in the feudal period should certainly be added the church, which was feudalized also; prelates became vassals, and monks were thought of as 'knights of Christ', holding fiefs in return for the service of prayer. When we pray with joined hands we are rendering homage to God – one example of the potent influence of feudal concepts, which include the fundamentality of personal relations, reciprocal obligations and discipline, institutionalized loyalty, and honourable service tempering the reality of hierarchy. *See* CASTLES; KNIGHTHOOD   RAB

□ P. Guilhiermoz *Essai sur l'origine de la noblesse en France* (1902); F.L. Ganshof *Feudalism* (1952); M. Bloch *Feudal Society* (1961); F.M. Stenton *The First Century of English Feudalism 1066–1166* (1961)

Fibonacci, Leonardo (*c.*1180–*c.*1240) Known also as Leonardo de Pisa from the place of his birth, he is chiefly remembered for his remarkable exposition of the properties of certain numbers in sequence, the Fibonacci numbers, which have application not only in the field of pure mathematics, but also in the biological sciences and in art. When expressed fractionally the numbers (1, 1, 2, 3, 5, 8, 13, 21, 34, etc.) have a direct relationship to the spiral growth of leaves and the stems of plants ($\frac{1}{2}$: $\frac{2}{3}$: $\frac{3}{5}$: $\frac{5}{8}$ $\frac{8}{13}$), and to the so-called 'Golden Section' in art ($\frac{3}{5}$: $\frac{5}{8}$: $\frac{8}{13}$ etc., converging in decimal terms towards 0.618). His career was much bound up with the cultural developments at the court of Emperor Frederick II, and he wrote treatises on the abacus and on practical geometry and trigonometry which were influential in introducing the use of Arabic numerals to medieval Europe.
□ D.J. Struik *A Concise History of Mathematics* (1948)

Finland The Finns were an Asiatic people whose language, distantly allied to Hungarian, is of the non-Indo-European group commonly designated Finno-Ugrian. Settled substantially in their modern homeland by the 8th c., they were not converted to Christianity until the 12th c., largely under Swedish pressure. Their patron saint is an Englishman, Henry, who became bishop of Uppsala *c.*1152 and was martyred on a missionary expedition to Finland *c.*1160. Politically their fortunes were bound closely to the ebb and flow of Swedish strength, and by the end of the Middle Ages Finland was no more than a dependent duchy within Sweden, just as, in the same period, Novgorod was falling under Muscovite control. The Finns, however, retained elements of self-government and a strong social and linguistic identity.
□ E. Jutikkala and K. Pirinen *A History of Finland* (1962); E. Kivikoski *Finland* (1967)

Flanders From the 9th c. an increasingly autonomous county evolved out of the disintegration of Carolingian Europe. Several capable rulers (Baldwin IV 988–1035; Baldwin V 1035–67 and Robert the Frisian 1071–93) welded together these heterogeneous, but dynastically connected principalities, which reached the height of their prestige under Thierry of Alsace (1128–68) and his son Philip (1168–91). The unity and prosperity of Flanders was achieved as the old feudal structures were replaced by an administration and fiscal organization employing salaried officials, and complemented by a centralized judicial system. The region's wealth was fostered by comital overlordship which allowed the towns to expand economically.

French advances and machinations to incorporate the principality had been weathered during the 12th c. However, the growth of internal divisions between the aristocratic factions and social groups within the towns permitted the French to gain considerable control in 1300 before being heavily defeated at Courtrai in 1302. The Treaty of Athis-sur-Orge (1305) recognized Flemish independence but imposed substantial financial burdens on the county and the loss of Lille, Douai and Orchies.

In the 14th c. the towns, especially Ghent, tried to establish communal autonomy from the count, a conflict aggravated by the demands of the Hundred Years' War. The count sided with his French suzerain; the towns, dependent on English wool and cloth, favoured the English. Louis de Mâle (1346–84) reconciled these discordant demands in a more flexible policy. Upon his death Flanders passed to the dukes of Burgundy who were usually allies of the English kings in the French dynastic struggles. Charles the Bold tried to develop a Netherlandic-Burgundian state, but on his death in 1477 the territories passed to his daughter Mary. Her subsequent marriage to Maximilian of Austria saw Flanders united to the Habsburg domain. Wealth, complex urban developments and political divisions, mirrored partly by language divisions between French and Flemish, provide the main themes of Flemish history in the Middle Ages. *See* NETHERLANDS
□ H. Pirenne *Histoire de Belgique* vol. 1 (1929)

Florence Of relatively minor importance in the early Middle Ages in spite of her role as seat of a Langobard duchy and, later, as occasional residence of the margrave of Tuscany, Florence rose to prominence in Tuscany and to a leading position in the European economy after the 12th c. Her great wealth, chiefly derived from industry (especially in textiles), combined with commerce and banking, encouraged immigration, which led to a rapid growth of her population, but also contributed to internal divisions.

From the early 13th c. the nobility and great merchants, followed by lower social groups, were divided into two parties: the Ghibellines, who supported the imperial cause in the struggle between Empire and papacy from about 1230, and the Guelphs, who favoured the papal cause, although either parties' interests and loyalties were predominantly local. Civil conflict demanded new devices to maintain order, and at the end of the 12th c. the consular government that had ruled the independent commune of Florence since soon after the

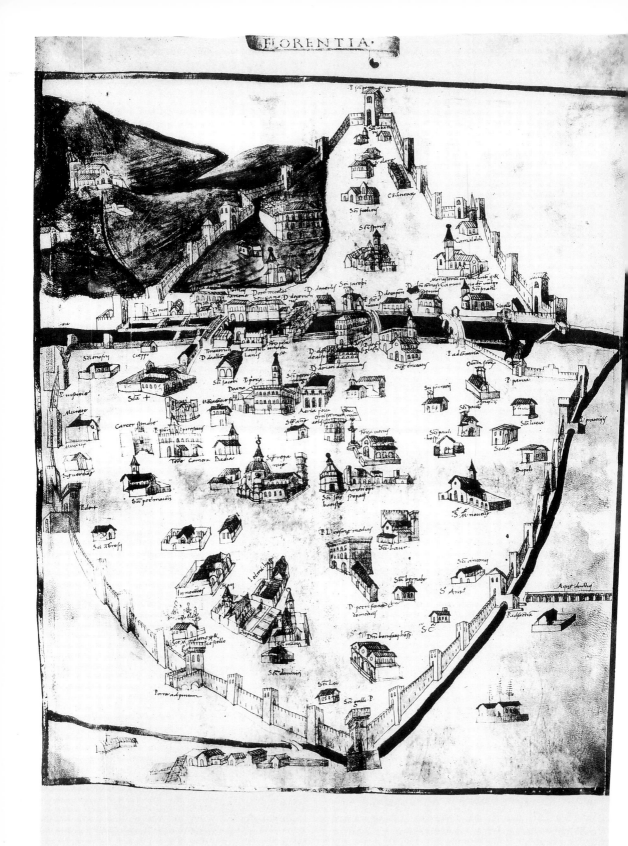

View of **Florence** (1472): miniature from a codex of Ptolemy's *Geografia*.

death of Matilda of Tuscany (1115) was replaced as supreme magistracy by the office of *podestà*. To secure impartiality, the *podestà* was recruited, from the early 13th c., from outside the city.

In the course of the 13th c., political power came to rest increasingly with the merchants organized in the greater guilds, thanks to the international success of Florentine commerce and banking, which was confirmed by the issue, from 1252, of the gold florin. Two years earlier, the non-noble population had set up its own organization – a kind of state within the state – duplicating communal institutions in its own magistracies and councils. This lasted until the Ghibelline victory over Guelph Florence in 1260, and was revived on a guild basis, now permanently, in 1282. In 1293 the victory of the new regime of the *popolo* culminated in the exclusion from government of noble families, defined as magnates, and their subjection to harsh punishments for offences against *popolani*. The six, later eight, priors and the gonfalonier of justice remained until the 16th c. the government of the city, the *podestà* being reduced to his judicial functions. The building, begun at the end of the century, of the new cathedral and of the Palazzo Vecchio indicates the prosperity of Florence and the citizens' pride in her achievements; it also reflects, the spectacular growth in her population, which by 1338 probably amounted to over 100,000.

The popular regime adopted Guelphism as the city's allegiance, but the division of the Guelph party at the turn of the century foreshadowed the factionalism from which Florence continued to suffer during the 14th century, and which was intensified after the Black Death. Other sources of internal conflict were the antagonism, sharpened by the Ordinances of Justice of 1293, between the magnate nobility and sections of the *popolo*, and, increasingly, social contrasts between the artisans of the lesser, and the patricians of the greater guilds. After the short-lived despotic rule (1342-43) of Walter of Brienne, duke of Athens, the 'new men', organized in the craft guilds, succeeded in substantially increasing their share in government; but patrician recovery was followed by an attempt of the oligarchical leadership of the Guelph party to establish virtual control of the state. In the wake of reaction against this policy, discontent among the workers subject to the wool and silk guilds erupted in 1378 in the revolt of the Ciompi. The Black Death of 1348 had dramatically reduced, possibly more than halved, the population of Florence, but its economic effects were only indirectly related to this social upheaval. The democratic guild regime set up after its suppression was the last and most radical manifestation of corporate organization in the city's government.

The regime which replaced it in 1382 was no longer dominated by the guilds or the Guelph party. Corporate institutions and values remained important elements in Florentine politics, but ceased to have the influence they had previously enjoyed. The new regime was aristocratic, in that the patriciate held a predominant position within a ruling class defined by eligibility to high offices; but the craft guilds were not entirely excluded from it. The authority of the government was reasserted, although major decisions remained subject to the consent of the legislative councils. One of the outstanding achievements of the regime was the expansion of the Florentine dominions by the acquisition of Arezzo, Pisa and Cortona with their territories, and their gradual transformation into a territorial state. Tuscan opposition to Florentine expansionism helped the lord of Milan, Giangaleazzo Visconti, in his advance into that region. In their wars with him from 1390 the Florentines proclaimed themselves defenders of liberty against tyranny; his death in 1402 and the conquest of Pisa in 1406 secured not only the city's independence, but also her hegemony in Tuscany.

The aristocratic regime enjoyed a remarkable measure of cohesion until the 1420s, when, against the background of fiscal crisis and renewed war with Milan, the city once more divided into two factions. Neither the introduction in 1427 of a progressive tax based on property, the *catasto*, nor peace with Milan in 1428 softened that division, which in 1433 culminated in the victory of the Albizzi over the Medici, and in the exile of Cosimo de' Medici. His return in 1434 marked the defeat of the Albizzi, followed by their exile and that of many of their supporters. Through reforms, especially of the method of electing the Signoria, Cosimo gradually established his own and his party's ascendancy by achieving control over government and legislation. But these reforms met with repeated resistance and suffered their most serious setback in 1456-66. Although short-lived, the success of that opposition to Medicean controls demonstrated the strength of republican traditions.

In 1478 hostility of the Pazzi supported from Rome brought about an attempt on Lorenzo de'Medici's life, to which his brother Giuliano fell victim. The Pazzi conspiracy led to war with the pope and the king of Naples; on the conclusion of peace, Lorenzo's position as virtual ruler of the republic was decisively stabilized and strengthened, but also the role of the political elite of the regime was enhanced, by the creation of a supreme Council of Seventy, who were to control legislation, as well as foreign and domestic policy; established for five years, its term of office was periodically renewed until the fall of the regime. After Lorenzo's death in 1492, Piero failed to preserve the delicate balance between divergent interests that his father had achieved in Florence, and had made the keystone of his foreign policy. Failing to prevent Charles VIII's invasion of Tuscany, Piero fled the city amid a popular rising (1494). All Medicean institutions were abolished, but the patricians, who had played a leading role in the demise of the Medici regime and who had belonged to its most prestigious group, did not succeed in restoring the aristocratic regime of the early 15th c. The creation, largely due to Savonarola's preaching, of a Great Council of over 3,000 citizens, who – in imitation of the Venetian *maggior consiglio* – were solely responsible for legislation and elections to office, was a radical constitutional reform which, while substantially widening the citizens' active participation in politics, made it possible for a political elite to maintain a major role in the government of Florence. Even so, patrician discontent with the increasing democratic tendencies in the Great Council led in 1502 to the transformation of the gonfalonierate of justice into an office for life. Nevertheless, it was not domestic opposition, but military pressure in the wake of the battle of Ravenna that was the chief cause of the fall of the republican regime and the restoration of the Medici in 1512. NR

□ F. Schevill *History of Florence* (1936); G. A. Brucker *Florentine Politics and Society, 1343-1378* (1962), *Renaissance Florence* (1969; new ed. with biblio. suppl. 1982); N. Rubinstein *The Government of Florence under the Medici, 1434 to 1494* (1966)

Florence, Council of (1438) With its clear recognition of papal authority and its attempts, both successful and unsuccessful, to achieve Christian unity, the Council of Florence reveals elements of weakness and of strength in the 15th-c. Conciliar movement. In 1437 Pope Eugenius IV transferred the noisome Council of Basle to Ferrara, and in 1438, to Florence. A rump remained at Basle in defiance of the pope. A powerful Greek delegation visited the Council, led by the Byzantine Emperor John VIII, seeking military aid for Constantinople and offering religious union in exchange; and compromise formulas were reached on outstanding theological differences concerning the *Filioque* clause and the type of bread used for the Eucharist. In return, a papally sponsored crusade was initiated, but this was crushed at Varna in 1444. The fall of Constantinople within the decade ended hopes of union.

Other religious unions established at Florence were more permanent: the Latins were united to the Coptic church of Egypt (1440), the Armenians (1439), the Chaldeans and Maronites (1445). The Council also dealt a significant blow to anti-papal elements in the movement. Serious deliberations

with the Greeks took place at Florence, not at Basle; authority was seen to rest with the pope, rather than with the Council *per se*. After the death of Eugenius IV (1447), Nicholas V achieved reconciliation with the recalcitrant cardinals who remained at Basle.
□ J. Gill *The Council of Florence* (1959)

Florin (Latin *florenus,* Italian *fiorino*) Florentine gold coin weighing 3.54g and struck continuously, unchanged in weight, fineness and design, from 1252 to 1533. Its initial value was £1 in local money of account, but the inflation of silver and billon coinage greatly increased its value; in 1450 it was worth £4 16s. In the late 13th c. and throughout the 14th c. it was the most generally accepted international means of exchange in Western Europe, and in the 14th c. was widely imitated, especially in the kingdoms of Arles and Aragon.

Florin (1331): the first regular gold currency, and symbol of the growing power of Florence.

Foliot, Gilbert (d. 1188) Bishop of London. Of aristocratic Norman parentage, Foliot was trained at Cluny and played a prominent part in English ecclesiastical history, representing a strong element of deep opposition to Thomas Becket. He was abbot of Gloucester in 1138 and bishop of Hereford from 1148, remaining close to the Angevin cause throughout his career. He was clearly disappointed when Becket was appointed to Canterbury in 1162, though his own translation to London in the following year came to provide something of a counterpoise to Becket; Foliot acted as Henry II's agent in negotiations with the papacy, played a part in the coronation of the young King Henry in 1170, and was in Normandy at the time of Becket's martyrdom. Excommunicated for his part in those turbulent events, he was absolved in 1172 and continued to play an active part in English ecclesiastical life.
□ D. Knowles *The Episcopal Colleagues of Archbishop Thomas Becket* (1951)

Fontenoy, battle of (841) A decisive event in the history of the Carolingian empire, the battle demolished the hopes of Charlemagne's grandson Lothar of establishing an effective unitary lordship over his brothers Louis the German and Charles the Bald of France. Defeated by their coalition, he was forced to agree to the terms of the Treaty of Verdun (843) by which the empire was effectively partitioned into three units ripe to develop into the historic moulds of France, Germany and the Middle Kingdom, held directly by Lothar, which included Lorraine, Burgundy and Lombardy as well as much of Italy.

Fontevrault Abbey founded *c.* 1100 by the Breton hermit and preacher, Robert of Arbrissel. It was a double monastery for monks and nuns. The Order was inspired by the Benedictine Rule, but the abbess was in complete authority over both houses. More than a hundred houses of the Order were set up in France, several in Spain and three in England. Its clientele mainly comprised daughters of the aristocracy. At Fontevrault itself, there are eight English Plantagenet royal tombs, including those of Henry II, Eleanor of Aquitaine, Richard I and Isabella of Angoulême, wife of King John.
□ D. Knowles *The Monastic Order in England* (1963)

Forest law Hunting rights and the setting aside of tracts of land, wood or pasture for the use of a lord's hunting were commonplace throughout feudal Europe, but it was in Norman England that the development of a law of the forest, which lay outside the normal law of the land, became most pronounced. William I's creation of the New Forest, and the savage penalties (including mutilation) imposed to safeguard the game are notorious, but forest laws, with their elaborate apparatus of courts, officers, verderers and agisters, were the product of the legalistic 12th c., notably of Henry II and his lawyers. The Assizes of Woodstock (1184) forced compulsory attendance at forest courts, and by 1215 the forests were so much a symbol of royal tyranny that Magna Carta contained special clauses forbidding the worst abuses. Separate Forest Charters were introduced in the minority of Henry III, closely associated with the re-issues of Magna Carta, and in the later Middle Ages forest law began to fall into disuse. Best known among the English forests were the New Forest itself, the Forest of Dean, Windsor Forest and Sherwood Forest, but forest land was to be found sporadically in many shires; at one stage nearly all of Essex was declared under forest law. The legends of Robin Hood encapsulate the poetic truth that in the common mind forests and forest law were synonymous with the worst aspects of arbitrary royal rule.
□ C. Petit-Dutaillis *Studies Supplementary to Stubbs' Constitutional History* vol. 2 (1935); C.R. Young *The Royal Forests of Medieval England* (1979)

Forged Decretals The canon law of the papacy came to rely on collections purporting to embody decretal legislation of the early papacy. Much of this was the work of 9th-c. scholars, notably those operating around Rheims. The Pseudo-Isidorian Decretals were of special importance, and were put together *c.*847–52 as a response to vigorous secular intervention into ecclesiastical affairs under Louis the Pious and his successors, when several bishops were deposed or exiled (Paris in 829 and 845–46).

The forgeries sketched a golden age with a plethora of intricate regulations on the liturgy, the sacraments and jurisdictional matters; the power of the papacy was stressed, but in such a way that it favoured episcopal rights against the authority of the archbishops, the laity and the bishops' own clergy. The forgeries had reached Rome by 865, but the reform popes cited them sparingly until Urban II (1088–99). Their chief channel of influence was not the papacy, but the collections of canons, notably the *Collectio Anselmo Dedicata* (*c.*890), and those of Burchard of Worms, Ivo of Chartres and Gratian. Hincmar of Rheims had rejected some of their material in the 9th c. as spurious, and later scholars, including Marsilius of Padua, doubted their authenticity. Yet the texts continued to be cited as authorities until the 17th c. They incorporated some genuine material, and their emphasis on papal primacy and opposition to lay control within the church ensured their survival and political force. *See* ISIDORUS MERCATOR
□ W. Ullmann *Law and Politics in the Middle Ages* (1975)

Fortunatus, Venantius (*c.*530–600) Poet and Christian apologist. He was influential in transmitting evidence for the spread of the Christian message in the early church through his Lives of saints, and poems. He was patronized by the Merovingian ruling house, notably by King Sigebert and his family (*c.*565–87). Encouraged by Gregory of Tours, he was accepted into the priesthood and eventually became bishop of Poitiers shortly before his death.
□ F.J. Raby *A History of Secular Latin Poetry in the Middle Ages* vol. 1 (1957)

Foscari, Francesco (1373–1457) Elected doge of Venice in 1423. His policies were those of the War party, which advocated territorial expansion in mainland Italy; in 1425 he began a recurrent war with Milan which was only brought to an end by the Peace of Lodi in 1454. Foscari's Italian preoccupations left Venetian interests in the East open to Turkish attack, and this contributed to the loss of Constantinople (1453), after which Foscari had to accept a disadvantageous treaty in order to retain

access to oriental trading routes. He faced increasing opposition in Venice, and was finally discredited by the series of convictions brought against his son Jacopo. He was forced to resign in October 1457.
□ W.C. Hazlitt *The Venetian Republic* vol. 1 (1915)

France Neither a homogeneous political community, nor a well-defined geographical area during the period from the dissolution of the Carolingian empire to the later 15th c. That a 13th-c. charter could suggest that the bishopric of Le Mans was capable of passing outside the kingdom of France indicates that the territorial boundaries of the French monarchy's power rarely coincided with the indeterminate frontiers of 'France'. Indeed, for much of its medieval history the kingdom of France seems little more than a convenient geographical expression within which to locate many of the more important formative developments of the medieval period, such as the Norman expansion, the beginnings of Cistercian monasticism and the Crusades, the 12th-c. revival of theological studies, or the Avignon papacy.

For a long time political fragmentation and regional diversity are the dominant themes. From the 9th c. until the early 13th c. the monarchy was weak and lacking in influence. The conquest of the Angevin empire by Philip Augustus 1203–04 was a major turning-point; yet throughout the 13th c. and 14th c. efforts to centralize royal jurisdiction and to levy extraordinary taxes through representative institutions, along the same lines as the English and Spanish monarchies, were only partially successful. What ultimately transformed monarchy and kingdom in the 15th c. was the Valois triumph in the Hundred Years' War, which paved the way for 16th-c. absolutism.

During the 10th c. and 11th c. the dominant form of political organization was the territorial principality. Such local concentrations of power, recognizing little or no external authority, emerged during the highly disturbed conditions of the 10th c. in, among numerous cases, Flanders, Normandy, Anjou and Aquitaine. Everywhere there occurred social changes centred on the construction of technically rudimentary castles, which became the focus of a type of power termed 'banal lordship' by modern authorities. Such lordship was identified with a total domination of the local peasantry through force and the exercise of what had once been royal rights. Associated with it was a complex and fundamental social transformation: the depression of peasants of free status and the replacement of slavery by serfdom as the most common method of exploitation. The pace of change varied from region to region, but its manifestations were clear in most places by

the early 11th c. One consequence was that by 987 when Hugh Capet (the first of the Capetian dynasty) became king, effective royal authority was confined to the area around Paris and Orleans where the family had its lands. Little remained to the early Capetians beyond a unique and never challenged right to be called king, and the largely nominal rights of lordship over the territorial princes. More generally, the changes even threatened to dismember several of the principalities, the royal one included. Princely authority was at its strongest in Normandy and Flanders; in some southern regions, it collapsed completely.

The territorial balance between monarchy and individual principalities was drastically altered by Philip Augustus' conquests. His achievements did, however, draw on the efforts of his predecessors and on the economic developments of the 12th c., which tended to favour those who already possessed wealth. The uniqueness of the royal title was a major factor in lending legality to Philip Augustus' destruction of the Angevin empire. In the 13th c. great superiority of resources relative to the remaining princes underpinned the prestige of a ruler such as St Louis, who could pose as the ideal medieval ruler, guaranteeing all men's rights and leading crusades. But the legacy of the long period of localization was a regional particularism which obstructed the far more intense efforts to centralize authority under Philip the Fair. Throughout the 13th c. and 14th c. the administrations of the remaining territorial principalities of Flanders, Brittany, Burgundy and Aquitaine – the latter under the rule of the English king – had developed along parallel lines to the royal administration. Increasingly frequent clashes, such as the war with Flanders under Philip the Fair and

France depicted as a courtly lady, with her 'people', represented by the knight, the clerk and the labourer.

the provincial leagues of nobles 1314–15, merged after 1328 with the Valois-Plantagenet succession dispute to bring about the Hundred Years' War. Although ultimately the solvent of much local political autonomy, this series of conflicts took the Valois monarchy to the brink of disaster after Henry V's victory at Agincourt (1415).

The medieval history of the French kingdom must in many respects be seen in terms of the sum of its constituent parts. For this reason a great deal of regional history has been written. Yet the monarchy can never be completely ignored, because in conformity with accepted medieval attitudes, no one ever thought of abolishing it. As a result, even the greatest principalities never developed political authority which was truly independent of the monarchy, while the kings could regularly claim powers which they did not actually possess, although in doing so, they sometimes appeared foolish. It cannot be overlooked that in 1202 Philip Augustus was able to proceed judicially against King John as the ultimate feudal lord of France, or that it was to the battered court of Charles VII that Joan of Arc's voices directed her. With the emergence of French patriotism during the Hundred Years' War, the monarchy became a positive force for unity. At the same time, despite the presence of formidable local Estates in Normandy and Brittany, for instance, the absence of genuine national consultative institutions enabled the kings and their advisers to tax without seeking consent, and to formulate arbitrary rules of judicial procedure. *See* ESTATES GENERAL; FRANKS; *see also individual kings*   DB
□ R. Fawtier *Les sources de l'histoire de France des origines à la fin du XVe siècle* (1971); E.M. Hallam *Capetian France* (1980)

Francis of Assisi, St (*c*.1181–1226) Son of a well-to-do merchant of Assisi, Francis was brought up to know the difference between wealth and poverty, and between the standards of chivalry and those of the counting house. He first showed his independence by tasting the knightly life, and then – after a long period of indecision and searching – he surrendered all the material comforts of his home to become a beggar: he chose the harsh life of poverty, eased by a chivalrous devotion to the Lady Poverty, but more truly inspired by the literal interpretation of Jesus' charge to give up everything and follow him. In Francis' *Testament,* written at the end of his life, he described the stages by which he overcame his natural fastidiousness and pride: by ministering to lepers, who had until then filled him with revulsion; by showing love and honour even to the humblest of parish priests; and by reverence for, and literal interpretation of God's word. 'After the Lord

Perhaps a true, near-contemporary portrait of **St Francis of Assisi**, *c.* 1220.

gave me brothers no one showed me what I ought to do, but the Most High himself revealed to me that I ought to live according to the pattern of the Holy Gospel.'

Following Francis' conversion in 1206, he became a wanderer and a beggar in and around Assisi, repairing S. Damiano and other churches, serving the lepers and the clergy of the region. In 1209 disciples began to gather round him, and by 1210 the Primitive Rule was written and taken to the pope. Francis' message was intensely personal, in his own view God-given, spontaneous, inspired by the words of the Gospel. This is not the whole truth, however, for there can be little doubt that he was inspired by two other influences, one obscure, the other tolerably clear.

In the valley of Spoleto, around Assisi, was a substantial community of Cathar heretics, with a bishop of their own. In Francis' writings and the early Lives, they are virtually ignored. They believed the material world to be wholly evil; their view of human destiny was gloomy. Francis preached that the world was God's creation and good – he summoned the birds and, in the *Canticle of Brother Sun* of his last years, all creation, to join him in praising the Creator. When he preached to the birds he showed his deep sympathy with animals; he also taught those who were with him, with the inspired insight of a born teacher, to worship God through his creation. He thus contradicted the

Cathar doctrine in a very direct, positive way. How much of this was due to meditating on the Cathar message is far from clear.

More evident is the influence of groups and communities similar to his own which already existed. These had been inspired by the search for the Apostolic life, in imitation of the first disciples; by the sense that poverty was part of God's calling to the religious as well as part of the harsh face of the world; by the urge to form communities of evangelical preachers to do the pastoral work which many felt the parish clergy neglected. These ideas were part of the air a sensitive man of Francis' age must breathe. Nor was he the first to ask Pope Innocent III to give his approval. It is not easy to be precise as to where Francis' originality lay, yet there was the mark of a very individual personality and inspiration on all he did, and his success was spectacular. He carried the refusal of property to an extreme point and forbade his disciples even to handle coins; he trained preachers but expected most of his followers to be ordinary lay folk, teaching by example and earning respect and alms by hard work; he laid special emphasis on respect for the clergy; and he established a special relationship with the pope through chosen cardinals, particularly with Ugolino, the future Pope Gregory IX.

Meanwhile the Order grew. From a dozen in 1210 it grew into hundreds, perhaps thousands, and spread over the face of Christendom; Francis tried to carry it beyond, even to the court of the sultan of Egypt. By 1212 he had given the tonsure to St Clare, who became the foundress of the second order – the Poor Ladies or Poor Clares. In the late 1210s steps were taken to form missions and provinces in France, Germany and Spain, and in 1224 the Franciscans came to England.

Francis had little belief in, or capacity for organization. In some ways the Order was established in spite of him, and efforts to define hierarchy and status within it, to prescribe a ritual asceticism in place of his more individual practice, and to relax his extreme measures of poverty, caused him evident disquiet. Yet he had the firmest faith in the Rule and in a number of central principles which defined the life and nature of the 'friar'. The Primitive Rule had received verbal approval from Innocent III in 1210, but in 1215 the Fourth Lateran Council attempted, it seems, to check Pope Innocent's kindness to informal groups of religious (who had, in some parts of France and Italy particularly, proved the spearhead of non-conformity) by forbidding new Rules. Francis steadfastly maintained that his Rule should not be affected since it had been approved, even if only by word of mouth, and after a long pause and many revisions, its final form was enshrined in the papal bull of Pope Honorius III (1223), which can still be seen in the treasury of the basilica of S. Francesco at Assisi.

Francis' last years were clouded by illness, yet to them belong many of the most characteristic stories of his heroism and teaching, collected by Brother Leo and other faithful companions. On the night of 3 October 1226 he died, and with great rapidity his friend Pope Gregory IX canonized him (1228), while his disciple Brother Elias built the beautiful church which still houses his body. This monument may be viewed as a brilliant expression of the paradox of his life, the dedication of wealth and artistic creation to the apostle of poverty – or as a simple denial of his ideals. By the same token, the growth of his Order has been viewed as the apotheosis of his ideals and their abandonment; in his destiny, as in his life, he followed the pattern of his Maker. *See* BERNARDINO OF SIENA; CONVENTUALS; FRIARS OF THE STRICT OBSERVANCE; JOHN OF PARMA; MICHAEL OF CESENA; THIRD ORDER OF ST FRANCIS [*93*]   RB

Late 12th-c. gilded reliquary bearing the features of **Frederick Barbarossa**.

□ P. Sabatier *Vie de St François d'Assise* (1893–94); R.B. Brooke *Early Franciscan Government* (1959); M.D. Lambert *Franciscan Poverty* (1961); J. Moorman *A History of the Franciscan Order* (1968); R.B. Brooke *The Coming of the Friars* (1975)

Frankfurt, Synod of (794) Frankfurt-am-Main, site of one of the favoured palaces of Charlemagne, is important in the ecclesiastical history of Western Europe for a synod held under the direct supervision of the Frankish king, at which excessive Byzantine worship of images was condemned and decisions taken which accepted the view of Spanish theologians, that the *Filioque* clause should be accepted as part of the Creed (i.e., that the Spirit procedes from both the Father and the Son). It is a potent symbol of the way in which the king was prepared to interfere even in the innermost workings of the Christian church, a foretaste of the imperial theocracy shortly to come.
□ J.M. Wallace-Hadrill *The Frankish Church* (1983)

Frankpledge Anglo-Norman system, based on older practices, binding every freeman into a tithing, or association of ten men, who bore collective responsibility for the good behaviour of the group. The hundred court enforced participation in this system, and the sheriff held a biennial 'view of frankpledge' in each hundred of his county to check the efficiency of these courts.
□ W.A. Morris *The Frankpledge System* (1910); W.L. Warren *The Governance of Norman and Angevin England 1086–1272* (1987)

Franks One of the principal elements in the West Germanic peoples. At the time of the folk migrations of the 4th c. and 5th c., the Franks settled in two principal groups, the Salians to the north-west of the Rhine frontier including much of modern Belgium, and the Ripuarians around Cologne in the lands between the Moselle and the Rhine. Roman federate allies for much of the 5th c., they assumed political mastery of much of Gaul under the leadership of the Salian Clovis (481–511). Still pagan at this stage, with their rulers, the Merovingians, claiming descent from a sea-god, the Franks underwent what Gibbon called a 'seasonable conversion' to Roman Catholicism (496–506).

Their new identity of religion with the Romanic population of Gaul helped them politically, notably in their struggle with the Arian Visigoths, whom Clovis defeated in the battle of Vouillé (507). Retention of customs of divided inheritance made for great political disturbance in the course of the succeeding centuries, but their Catholicism, the developing establishment of mutual interest between bishops and kings, and the preservation of a reserve of agrarian and landed strength in the north-east of Gaul enabled the Franks to lay the foundations for what was to become the kingdom of France.
□ J.M. Wallace-Hadrill *The Long-Haired Kings* (1962); E. James *The Origins of France from Clovis to the Capetians* (1982)

Frederick I Barbarossa Holy Roman Emperor 1152(55)–90 (b. *c.* 1123) Son of Frederick II, duke of Swabia, and Judith, daughter of Henry the Proud, Frederick was elected German king and king of the Romans in 1152. It was hoped that he would put an end to the destructive fighting between the Guelphs and Ghibellines, being himself half-Guelph and half-Hohenstaufen by birth.

His one ambition was to restore the Empire to its former glory. Having first secured peace at home, he turned his attention to the Italian peninsula. Frederick set out for Rome in 1154, the first of six such expeditions, and was crowned Emperor by Adrian IV a year later. On his return to Germany, he restored law and order by granting Henry the Lion the duchy of Bavaria, and Henry Jasomirgott, the transformation of his margravate of Austria into a duchy.

In 1158 Frederick set out again for Italy, this time bent on the submission of the Lombard communes. He reasserted his control at the Diet of Roncaglia and also elected *podestàs* as his representatives in various cities. The 17-year schism of the papacy that broke out in 1159 with the death of Adrian isolated Barbarossa in Europe: he supported the claims of the anti-popes against Alexander III. His fifth expedition to Italy (1174) ended in disaster; defeated at Legnano (1176) by the forces of the Lombard League, Barbarossa was forced to sue for peace with Alexander. He did manage to win a secure foothold in Italy in 1186, with the marriage of his son Henry to Constance, heiress to the kingdom of Sicily. En route to the crusade against Saladin, he was drowned in the river Saleph. An earnest and commanding ruler, he was noted for his sagacity and enthusiasm for the restoration of the Empire. *See* RAINALD OF DASSEL
□ Otto of Freising *The Deeds of Frederick Barbarossa* trans. C.C. Mierow (1953); M. Pacaut *Frederick Barbarossa* (1967); P. Munz *Frederick Barbarossa* (1969)

Frederick II Holy Roman Emperor 1212(20)–50 (b. 1194) German king from 1212, king of Sicily from 1198 and king of Jerusalem from 1229. Son of the Emperor Henry VI and Constance of Sicily, and grandson of Barbarossa, in 1212 Frederick was offered the imperial crown by the princes of Germany who opposed the rule of Otto IV; by 1220, he had established his rule there and was crowned Emperor.

From 1220–25 he set out to consolidate his hold over Sicily. Despite his promises to set out on a crusade to the Holy Land in 1215 and 1220, he only began his preparations in 1227. Irritated by the constant delays, Pope Gregory IX finally excommunicated him. Nevertheless, Frederick still set out for the Holy Land and was able to secure Jerusalem and other important places through negotiations with the sultan. On his triumphant return to Italy, the ban was lifted according to the Treaty of S. Germano (1230).

The *Constitutions of Melfi* (1231), promulgated by the Emperor, represented a major statement about the legal foundations of his reign. His involvement in the affairs of the northern Italian communes in the 1230s brought about a breakdown in imperial-papal relations. Gregory IX waged a war of propaganda against him and, following the pope's death in 1241, his successor Innocent IV excommunicated and deposed Frederick at the Council of Lyons (1245).

A complex personality, the Emperor was described as *stupor mundi* (the amazement of the world) by Matthew Paris. His scientific and philosophical interests are represented by his book on falconry, *De Arte Venandi cum Avibus,* and he also wrote poetry in the Sicilian vernacular. *See* GIACOMO; LIBER AUGUSTALIS; YOLANDE OF BRIENNE

□ E. Kantorowicz *Frederick the Second* (1931); *Stupor Mundi* ed. G. Wolf (1966); D. Abulafia *Frederick the Second* (1988)

Fresco Fresco painting was immensely popular in the Middle Ages. By the 13th c., and especially in

Giotto's *Lamentation of Christ*; one of the Arena Chapel **frescoes** in Padua, *c.*1304-13.

Italian Gothic churches and cloisters, this art form had reached its most perfect expression. Frescoes provided a quicker and less expensive alternative to mosaics, another important form of mural decoration in medieval times.

There were a number of stages in fresco painting. First, the surface to be covered was coated with a layer of coarse plaster (*arriccio*). At this stage, the artist might sketch in the general outline of the composition with a reddish-brown substance known as *sinopia*. If the work was to be done in true or *buon* fresco, the artist, working from the top of the wall down, applied only enough plaster for one day's work; these small sections of fine plaster were known as *giornate*. The artist then applied his pigments, ground in pure water, to this small section of plaster; the pigments bound permanently with the wet lime plaster. A less durable form of fresco painting was *fresco al secco,* in which the pigments were applied to the wall once the plaster was dry. In many medieval frescoes where the *al secco* technique has been used, the colours have flaked away.
□ E. Borsook *The Mural Painters of Tuscany* (1960); U. Procacci *Sinopie e affreschi* (1961)

Friars Minor *See* **Francis, St**

Friars Preacher *See* **Dominic, St**

Friars of the Strict Observance Under the leadership of St Bernardino of Siena, a reforming group within the Franciscan movement attempted to revert to the primitive simplicity enjoined by their founder, notably in matters relating to poverty and the use of property. They became one of the strongest religious forces within Italy, but their relationship to the more lax generality of the Order, the Conventuals as they came to be known, was consistently difficult and at times stormy, until in 1517 Pope Leo X established them as an order in their own right.
□ D. Douie *The Nature and Effect of the Heresy of the Fraticelli* (1932); M.D. Lambert *Franciscan Poverty* (1961)

Frisians West Germanic people. The Frisians were the principal seafarers and traders in north-western Europe during the early Middle Ages. They were converted to Christianity in the 8th c. by the efforts of Anglo-Saxon and Frankish missionaries and also by Frankish military force. St Boniface, the greatest of the Anglo-Saxon missionaries, was martyred by them at Dokkum in 754. Military defeats at the hands of Charlemagne confirmed Frankish dominance, altered the balance of power and gave the Vikings their chance to dominate the North Sea,

Fulk V is killed in a hunting accident; from a 13th-c. manuscript of the School of Acre.

setting up a powerful pirate base at Walcheren. Frisia was brought back into the imperial fold by the Ottonians, but proved exceptionally resilient in preserving its old free institutions, resisting feudalization deep into the Middle Ages. Skill in all crafts connected with the sea, and in the arts of reclaiming land by the building of polders and setting up of dykes remained dominant social characteristics.

Froissart (*c*.1337–*c*.1410) Born at Valenciennes, in the period 1361–69 he enjoyed the patronage of Philippa of Hainault, wife of Edward III of England. His later benefactors were Wenceslas of Luxembourg, duke of Brabant, and Guy, count of Blois. During the years 1373–82, he was rector of Les Estinnes near Thun, and in 1383 he became a canon of Chimay. He is famed for his four-volume description of the major countries of Europe in the period 1325–1400. These chronicles, a notable literary achievement, are deeply concerned with the imaginative portrayal of aristocratic chivalry.
□ H. Wilmotte *Froissart* (1958); *Froissart* ed. J.J. Palmer (1987)

Fulbert (*c*.960–1028) Bishop of Chartres. Probably a native of northern France, he studied under Gerbert at Rheims and Chartres. He was appointed master of the School at Chartres and established its reputation as one of the foremost centres of learning in Europe. In 1007 he was elected to the see of Chartres, and began the rebuilding of the cathedral after the fire of 1020. He was an adviser of Robert II of France and held the post of treasurer of Saint-Hilaire-le-Grand at Poitiers from Duke William V of Aquitaine.
□ H. Johnstone *Fulbert of Chartres* (1926)

Fulk IV Rechin (1068–1109) Count of Anjou. Younger son of Count Geoffrey Martel, he succeeded to lands south of the Loire on his father's death in 1060, but moved back north, overthrowing his elder brother Geoffrey in 1067 and winning recognition as count of Anjou in the following year. Under his powerful military leadership Norman ambition was successfully resisted, and he consolidated his fief north of the Loire to the point where it became one of the most potent units in feudal France, famous for its castles and administrative skills.
□ O. Guillot *Le Comte d'Anjou et son entourage au XIe siècle* (1972)

Fulk V King of Jerusalem 1131–43 (b.1095) Count of Anjou 1109–28, Fulk V made significant contributions in two spheres important for the general development of 12th-c. Europe by helping to lay the foundations for the Angevin empire and by contributing greatly to the consolidation of the kingdom of Outremer. In both communities he showed the same characteristics: skill in the arts of government and administration, and superb strategic gifts in the setting up of castles and fortresses. Inheriting a powerful fief from his father Fulk IV, he also inherited intense rivalry and hostility to the Normans. In an extraordinary reversal of traditional policy he agreed to the marriage in 1128 of his son Geoffrey Martel (Plantagenet) to the only surviving legitimate child of King Henry I of England, Matilda, and abdicated in favour of his son, leaving his own homeland for the Crusading kingdom in the Holy Land. There he married Baldwin II's heiress Melisende, and was proclaimed king of Jerusalem in 1131. As a newcomer he had difficulty in asserting royal authority over the great regional vassals of Tripoli, Antioch and Edessa, but within the core principality of Jerusalem itself he proved a capable and effective king.
□ H.E. Mayer *Studies in the History of Queen Melisande* (1972)

G

Gaetani family According to a family tradition the Gaetani (Caetani) were descended from the consuls and dukes of Gaeta (10th c.). Records of their activities survive from at least the 12th c., and members of the family appear in Naples, Rome, Anagni and Pisa. The Gaetani of Anagni were raised to sudden prominence with the election of Benedetto Gaetani (Boniface VIII) to the papacy in 1294. Throughout his reign Boniface sought to diminish the power of the Colonna, who were the dominant feudal family in Rome at the time. By the 14th c. the Gaetani had assumed this position.

□ V. Novelli *I Colonna e i Caetani, storia del medio-evo di Roma* (1892–93)

Gaimar, Geffrei Author of *L'Estoire des Engleis,* a long romance history in Norman French verse written in England *c.*1140, Gaimar seems to have been a secular clerk writing under the patronage of Richard FitzGilbert. His history, based on a lost version of the Anglo-Saxon Chronicle, deals with English history from the time of the settlements in the 5th c. to the death of William Rufus in 1100. Filled out with legendary matter it is of chief interest in showing both the new 12th-c. romantic attitudes to historical material and the increased sensitivity of contemporary artists to the use of vernacular poetry. He was no great stylist, but the passages he devotes to Haveloc the Dane, Hereward the Wake and the death of William Rufus are lively and well written.

□ *Geffrei Gaimar, L'Estoire des Engleis* ed. A. Bell (1960)

Gaiseric King of the Vandals *c.*429–77 One of the outstanding leaders of the Germanic peoples. In the course of the 'folk-wandering', Gaiseric coordinated the Vandal peoples in their movement south (under Visigothic pressure) from Spain into the North African province. In the period 429–39 he brought virtually all the heavily Romanized province under control, and so organized his kingdom that for the best part of a century it dominated the Western Mediterranean. Alone of the Germanic peoples, the Vandals took effectively to the sea; in 455 they sacked Rome. An Arian Christian, given to occasional persecution of the Orthodox Catholic provincials, Gaiseric established a duality of function within his kingdom which left the Vandals in charge of the army and extensive revenues from the great estates (notably the imperial estates), while the Romans continued to enjoy their own law and magistracy in a position subordinate to the Vandals. He safeguarded the succession by a form of virtual primogeniture, but social and political tensions within the Vandal kingdom were exaggerated by the basic division between Arian and Orthodox.

Gall, St (*c.*550–645) An Irish monk, who went to Gaul with St Columbanus *c.*590 and began missionary work around Luxeuil in the Vosges. He accompanied St Columbanus to Bergenz in 610, but did not follow him to Italy in 612. Instead, he took up an eremitic life. He refused King Sigebert's offer of a bishopric and did not take up the abbatial office to which he was elected by the monks of Luxeuil.

Alan Sorrell's reconstruction of the monastery of **St Gall**, according to the early 9th-c. plan.

A century after his death the famous Benedictine monastery of St Gallen was erected on the site of one of his hermitages. Its scriptorium and manuscript collection were for a long time among the most famous in Europe. A 9th-c. architectural plan of St Gallen, one of the earliest architectural drawings of

From a 15th-c. depiction of the Seven Deadly Sins: **Genoese** bankers at work.

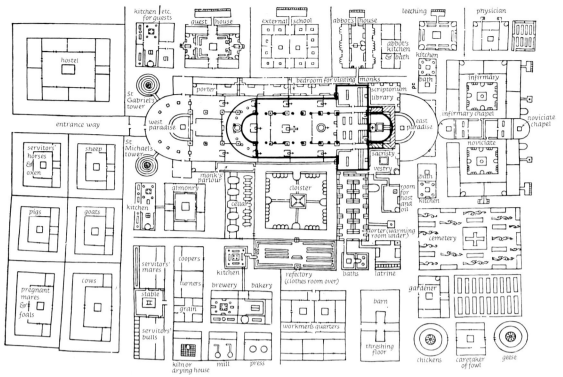

Plan of **St Gall**, based on the original of *c*.820 in the Stiftsbibliothek at St Gall.

the Middle Ages, shows the layout of an ideal Benedictine monastery with the buildings for living and work grouped around the church.
□ J.M. Clark *The Abbey of St Gall as a Centre of Literature and Art* (1926); W. Horn and E. Born *The Plan of St Gall* (1979)

Gelasian doctrine Propounded by Pope Gelasius I in a letter written to the Byzantine Emperor Anastasius I in 494, it attempted to define the relationship between the secular and spiritual powers in temporal government. Gelasius apparently advocated a system of joint and equal responsibility, but as his terminology allowed his statement to be interpreted in other ways, it became one of the fundamental ingredients of the later controversies over this matter, being cited in support of both papal superiority and royal autonomy.

Genoa The story of Genoa in the Middle Ages is primarily that of its commercial and mercantile successes and of its rivalries with other Italian cities, notably Pisa and Venice, for control of Mediterranean trade. Its fortunes were already in the ascendant before the Crusades, but its full opportunity came with the First Crusade, as a result of which it won special privileges in Acre. The city grew fast, in population (estimated at about 100,000) and in poli-

tical influence (most of Liguria, effective power in Corsica and Elba, privileges in Norman Sicily) in the course of the 12th c. With the set-back to the crusading cause and its ultimate defeat, Genoa sought compensation elsewhere. It consolidated its hold on Western Mediterranean trade and (in spite of severe losses to the Venetians) extended its activities in the revived Byzantine empire after 1261, setting up colonies and trading stations on the Black Sea at the mouth of the Danube and the Crimea, so opening the way for trade with the Mongols. The later Middle Ages saw gradual decline and occasional political domination by outside powers, though Corsica remained under its authority late in the 15th c.
□ D. Waley *The Italian City-Republics* (1969)

Geoffrey of Monmouth (*c*.1100–54) Bishop of St Asaph (1152) who was famed for his *Historia Regum Britanniae*, published *c*.1136–38. This chronicle purported to be the translation of an ancient Breton manuscript; in reality it was a work of fictional creativity which freely interwove material based on Welsh legend and on early British sources such as Gildas and Nennius. Despite its lack of historical accuracy, it enjoyed wide circulation during the Middle Ages, and as it provided the basis for the later popular tradition surrounding characters such as Arthur and Merlin, emerged as a work of seminal importance for the literary development of Western Europe.

□ *The History of the Kings of Britain* ed. L. Thorpe (1973)

Gerard of Brogne (d.959) Monastic reformer. The lord of Brogne, near Namur in Lower Lorraine, Gerard was one of the most influential among the group that helped to revitalize Benedictine monasticism in the mid-10th c. Like Gorze in Upper Lorraine, the abbey of Brogne became a centre for those who remained loyal to the principle of the autonomy of the individual house, and of maintaining close contact with the diocesan bishops.

□ J.M. de Smet and J. Wollasch in *Revue Bénédictine* 70 (1960)

Gerard of Cremona (*c*.1114–87) Though born in Cremona, he spent much of his life in Toledo, where he went to learn Arabic. He was the most prolific translator of scientific and philosophical works from Arabic in the Middle Ages; some 80 translations have been attributed to him or his school. The quality and scope of his work, which included texts on medicine, mathematics, astronomy, astrology and alchemy, made a decisive contribution to the progress of medieval Latin science.

□ C.H. Haskins *Studies in the History of Medieval Science* (1927)

Gerbert of Aurillac *See* **Sylvester II**

Germanus, St (*c*.378–448) He held civil office in Gaul before becoming bishop of Auxerre in 418. He paid two visits to Britain in order to oppose the spread of Pelagianism; in 429 he crushed the heresy at Verulamium and led a force of Britons to victory over the marauding Picts and Saxons, using 'Alleluia' as his war cry, according to tradition. In 443, or possibly even as late as 447, he again returned to Britain to combat heresy. He died at Ravenna whilst pleading the cause of some Armorican rebels to the Emperor Valentinian III.

□ *The Life of St Germanus by Constantinus* trans. F.R. Hoare (1954)

Germany The history of Germany in the Middle Ages is intimately bound up with the history of Italy and with the idea of 'empire' (Holy Roman Empire). It was not until the 9th c., with the disintegration of the Carolingian empire, that shape was given to the idea of Germany as a separate political unit. By the Treaty of Verdun (843) Louis the German, grandson of Charlemagne, succeeded to the East Frankish lands, essentially the territories of the Saxons, Swabians, Bavarians and Franks east of the Rhine.

The boundaries were far from stable and it is unwise to talk of a kingdom of Germany in the full sense of the word until the Ottonian dynasty imposed its will on the so-called stem duchies in the 10th c., basing its strength on the ancient heartlands of the Carolingians in Lorraine, in combination with the duchies of Franconia and Saxony.

The creation of a German kingdom, the first *Reich,* coincided with a revival of imperial ambitions, and Otto the Great was crowned Emperor at Rome in 962. Royal authority within Germany was drawn from four principal sources: military skill, a rigorous control of the church, insistence on the right of appointment to ducal office, and the wider attributes which came from involvement in Italy and the imperial title, a conscious echo of the Carolingian past. Otto I aimed to be the true heir of Charlemagne, though the range of his effective government was confined to Germany and the Middle Kingdom (Lorraine, Burgundy and Lombardy). The stabilization of the eastern frontier after the great victory over the Hungarians at the river Lech (955) and the establishment of an impressive line of march territories provided a springboard for later expansion and created the conditions under which institutional life could flourish.

Even so there remained fundamental weaknesses in the German constitution; monarchy had come relatively late on the scene and the independence of the nobility was firmly rooted. The crises of the Investiture Contest in the reign of Henry IV (1056–1106) gave opportunity to the disruptive forces. Anti-kings were elected, notably Rudolf of Swabia at Forchheim (March 1077), and the German nobility accustomed itself to acting corporately against the king, ultimately forcing Henry V to reach an accord with the church (1122). Civil wars weakened the monarchy at a critical time of expansion and colonization, when much new wealth was generated – mostly to the advantage of the nobility. Elective principles were commonplace in the medieval world and not necessarily harmful to monarchy, but in the early 12th c. they were asserted in conditions that encouraged dynastic instability.

The successes of the Hohenstaufen family, with its strength based on Swabia (1138–1254), and especially the election of Frederick Barbarossa, in 1152, brought revival, though attempts to reassert royal authority were made more difficult by the newly entrenched local independence of the German princelings. Intelligent use of feudal bonds is the key to his policy. He left his cousin, the Guelph Henry the Lion, with a free hand inside Germany as duke of Saxony and Bavaria for more than 20 years, and it was under his patronage that a surge forward was made in the process of German colonization to the

Emperor Charles IV and the Seven Electors of
Germany, *c.* 1370.

east along the Baltic. When Henry ultimately
proved disloyal, contributing to Barbarossa's defeat
at Legnano (1176) by failing to send reinforcements,
it was by feudal processes that the king brought him
to justice and declared the greater part of his land and
wealth forfeit.

The settlement reached after the fall of Henry at
Gelnhausen (1179–80) represents an attempt to
legalize a feudal monarchy, which in the event
failed. The Hohenstaufen lacked the strong territorial base essential for the success of such a project,
and the disputed succession (1197–1212) weakened
the Hohenstaufen principality, painfully built up as a
nucleus of royal power. Even so, for all his preoccupation with Italy, and especially Sicily, Frederick II
(1212–50) was far from negligible in Germany. His
privileges in favour of the church and princes were
not in themselves symptoms of weakness, but by
the end of his reign it was painfully obvious that of
the two strong constitutional forces involved in the
settlement of 1180 – the king and the great princes –
the future lay with the princes. The rejection of the
Hohenstaufen and the long Interregnum (1254–73)
exaggerated the process. In 1273 Rudolf of Habsburg
was elected, and for most of the rest of the Middle
Ages political power at the royal level rested with
two dynasties which drew their authority from
predominately non-German lands: the Habsburgs,
with their slow consolidation of authority over the
Middle Danube from their Austrian base, and the
house of Luxembourg, which built up an impressive
power base in Bohemia.

Under the strongest of the kings of the latter
house, Charles IV (1346–78), a formal constitution
safeguarding the processes of election to the monarchy
was embodied in the Golden Bull (1356). Seven
electors, drawn from the great princes, were to
assume responsibility for the election of the king-
emperors. The German princes themselves became
increasingly independent, many of them virtually
sovereign in their own territories. A growing urban
and mercantile element found some substitute for
royal authority and protection in the creation of
leagues of towns, such as the Hanseatic League and
leagues of south German towns. Kingship still
served as an occasional focal point for German
loyalties, but the centre of constitutional interest
passed in the 14th c. and 15th c. to the principalities
and to the towns. On the eastern frontier the
exploits of the Teutonic knights and the steady
pressures of colonization and mercantile enterprise
anticipated the military and political strength of
areas such as Brandenburg and Prussia. *See* BAVARIA;
HOHENZOLLERN DYNASTY; GHIBELLINES; RUPERT
OF WITTELSBACH   HRL
□ J. Fleckenstein *Early Medieval Germany* (1978); K.
Leyser *Medieval Germany and its Neighbours* (1982);
F.R.H. du Boulay *Germany in the Later Middle Ages*
(1983); H. Fuhrmann *Germany in the High Middle
Ages* (1986)

Gerson, Jean (1363–1429) A student of Pierre d'Ailly,
Gerson became a doctor of theology in 1394 and
chancellor of the cathedral of Notre-Dame and of
the university of Paris in the following years. One of
the leading theologians of the day, he worked
zealously for the healing of the Great Schism and
became one of the principal spokesmen of the Conciliar movement at the Council of Constance (1414–
18). Although unsuccessful in two of his principal
aims – the assertion of the superiority of a general
council over the pope, and his defence of the rights
of the Gallican church in matters of dogma – the
influence of his works and example was great in
15th-c. political and ecclesiastical thought.
□ J.L. Connolly *John Gerson, Reformer and Mystic*
(1928)

Ghibellines The two words 'Ghibelline' and
'Guelph' entered the vocabulary of Italian politics at
the time of Frederick II (1220–50). Derived from the
German 'Waiblingen' and 'Welf', they gradually
came to be adopted by rival Florentine factions in the
1240s who favoured either the Emperor or the pope
(Innocent IV). By 1256 the use of these terms had
extended to northern Italy, with the papal partisans
known as Guelphs, and their opponents as Ghibellines.

An important change occurred 1256–58 with
the defeat of the Hohenstaufen cause. After 1270
Guelphism came increasingly to be identified with
Angevin supporters; the Ghibellines were anti-
French. Their writers portrayed the Angevins as
usurpers of the Hohenstaufen, lacking any legitimate claim to rule. By 1300 the two terms for the
most part represented only local or family factions,
rather than papal or imperial persuasions.
□ P. Brezzi *I communi medioevali nella storia d'Italia*
(1959); D. Waley *The Italian City-Republics* (1969)

Ghiberti, Lorenzo (1378–1455) Florentine sculptor and writer. Ghiberti executed two pairs of bronze doors for the Florentine Baptistery, commissions which occupied him for most of his career. He made an extensive study of antique sculpture and was expert at modelling the human form. His Commentaries on art are of major importance for the study of Italian art.
□ R. Krautheimer *Lorenzo Ghiberti* (1971); *The Florence Baptistery Doors* intro. by K. Clark (1980)

Giacomo Archbishop of Capua. He took part in the compilation of the *Liber Augustalis (Constitutions of Melfi)* issued by Frederick II in 1231, and was probably responsible for the sections dealing with the church and the Sicilian clergy. Trained in law at the university of Bologna, he was regarded as one of the best legal minds of the time. He was also one of Frederick's most trusted courtiers, accompanying the Emperor on crusade in 1228.

Giano della Bella (d.1305) Florence in the 1290s was torn apart by feuds among the *magnati*, or noblemen, who dominated city politics. This Florentine nobleman decided to put an end to the fighting. He managed to win the support of the middle and lesser guildsmen of the town, and in January 1293 helped to draw up the Ordinances of Justice, which were intended to control the behaviour of the *magnati*. Although the Ordinances were retained in somewhat modified form, Giano himself fell from power in 1295 and spent the rest of his life exiled in France.
□ F. Schevill *Medieval and Renaissance Florence* (1961)

Gilbert de la Porée (1076–1154) One of the principal students of the theological school at Chartres, Gilbert became head of the cathedral school at Poitiers and, in 1142, bishop of the diocese. His teaching was considered to be an extreme statement of the theology of the universalist school and was roundly condemned as such by Bernard of Clairvaux, who failed, however, to have the doctrines declared heretical at the Council of Rheims (1148).
□ N.M. Haring *The Case of Gilbert de la Porée* (1951)

Gilbert of Sempringham, St (c.1089–1189) Founder of the Gilbertine Order. Gilbert was famous among contemporaries for his personal holiness, but his long-term reputation rests upon his foundation of the only purely English monastic order. He was born into a well-to-do family which held estates in Lincolnshire. Some physical disability seems to have overshadowed his youth, and instead of pursuing a secular career he followed a course of ecclesiastical study in France. After his return to England he lived for a while in the household of the bishop of Lincoln, where his ascetic way of life attracted notice and admiration. However, Gilbert only reluctantly became a priest and refused higher preferment within the church.

He chose, rather, to return to Sempringham and devote himself to serving the poor and ignorant whom he found on his father's estates. Fulfilling his pastoral vocation, he organized a school, hospitals and orphanages for them. In 1131 he founded a small community of nuns who followed a simplified form of the Benedictine Rule. Lay sisters and lay brothers were added to their number, and later, canons. This form of double religious house proved popular in the 12th c. and others were founded, mostly in Lincolnshire and Yorkshire. Pope Eugenius III conferred authority for the new order upon Gilbert in 1147. He accepted the responsibility unwillingly, but thereafter spent the rest of his long life closely supervising his religious communities, and in particular maintaining strict discipline. Gilbert's own holiness gave rise to stories of miracles, performed both during his lifetime and after his death. An account of these was sent to the pope, together with a biography and testimonials from many eminent men, and in 1202 Gilbert was canonized by Pope Innocent III.   GK
□ *The Book of St Gilbert* ed. R. Foreville and G. Keir (1986)

Gildas British cleric of the 6th c., whose tract *De Excidio et Conquestu Britanniae* is the earliest literary work to describe developments in Britain after the Roman withdrawal of 410. The tract provides a fundamentally credible outline of events, but as its historical content is incidental to its main purpose of exhorting repentance for the moral corruption which Gildas maintains characterized that period, it is problematic as a historical source. The traditional date for the writing of the tract is c. 540, but modern scholars are inclined to place it later in the century.
□ *Gildas: The 'Ruin of Britain' and other works* ed. M. Winterbottom (1978); *Gildas: New Approaches* ed. M. Lapidge and D. Dumville (1984)

Giotto di Bondone (1267 or 1277–1337) Tuscan painter and architect. Probably trained in the workshop of the great Florentine master Cimabue, Giotto was acknowledged by his contemporaries Dante, Petrarch and Boccaccio as the leading artist of his day. Uniting in his art the study of Italo-Byzantine painting and Tuscan Gothic sculpture, Giotto stands at the end of a long development in Italian Gothic painting; his art also points in many ways to new trends in the Renaissance. His work is noted for its simple, clear solutions to the problem of the representation of space and the human figure –

The *Ognissanti Madonna*: **Giotto's** most important panel painting.

he was also an unparalleled master of dramatic narrative. The tremendous solidity of his figures impressed even Michelangelo, who made a study of Giotto's frescoes in the Peruzzi Chapel which survives today.

A precise chronology of his development is elusive. The *Navicella* mosaic in Rome (*c.*1300), regarded by his contemporaries as his finest work, is now a shadow of its former self, having been so often reworked that Giotto's hand is no longer discernible. Although unsigned and undocumented, the cycle of frescoes at the Arena Chapel, Padua (*c.*1304–13), has always been attributed to his hand, as have the frescoes of the Bardi and Peruzzi Chapels in S. Croce, Florence, which belong to his mature period. The three signed altarpieces by Giotto – the Louvre *Stigmatization of St Francis,* the Baroncelli altarpiece and the Bologna *Madonna and Saints* polyptych – seem to be largely products of his workshop. His authorship of the fresco cycle on the *Life of St Francis* has long been a matter of dispute among scholars. English scholars in general reject the attribution to Giotto, although this does not hamper appreciation of the works as some of the finest in the period. One of Giotto's last commissions was for the campanile

of Florence cathedral (1334); only the first storey of the base was completed at his death.

Despite the fact that Giotto is usually presented as the harbinger of the Italian Renaissance, it is worthwhile noting that many 14th-c. Byzantine paintings in Serbia and Constantinople bear comparison with his work. This in no way detracts from his genius, but suggests a parallel development of artistic expression. [*140*]   CH
□ A. Martindale *The Complete Paintings of Giotto* (1969); A. Smart *The Assisi problem and the art of Giotto* (1971)

Glass, stained Throughout the Middle Ages painted glass was the principal form of church decoration, especially in Europe north of the alps, where the development of large traceried Gothic windows gave particular prominence to the medium.

Although the Romans had used glass as a window filler, it probably did not bear any painted decoration. In Gaul, this use of glass survived into the post-Roman period, for in 674 it was to Gaul that Abbot Benedict Biscop sent for craftsmen to glaze his churches at Monkwearmouth and Jarrow. Excavations at Jarrow have uncovered fragments of unpainted coloured glass made with the high soda content typical of Roman glass. The oldest surviving painted glass comes from Carolingian and Ottonian Germany – a roundel from Lorsch (Hessen) and a striking head of Christ from Wissembourg. The figures of prophets in Augsburg cathedral, dating from the early 12th c., display such technical assurance that it can be assumed that by this date glass-painting had a well-established craft tradition. Theophilus, writing at much the same time, certainly recognized French achievements in the field.

It was, however, in the great Gothic cathedrals of 13th-c. France that stained glass came into its own. It is particularly appropriate that at Chartres cathedral, in which the traceried window is of such architectural importance, there survives one of the most extensive series of windows of 13th-c. date. Unlike Canterbury cathedral choir (glazed *c.*1180–1220), where the funds from the pilgrim traffic were so great that the monks were able to glaze their church without recourse to external patrons, the windows of Chartres reflect the participation of a wide variety of secular patrons, including tradesmen like the furriers and butchers. The involvement of the lay community in the donation, and thus the composition of stained glass windows, increased in the 14th c. The development of the traceried window and the aesthetic requirement for lighter interiors led to the evolution of a new layout, in which figures and

Stained-glass window from Chartres donated by the cloth merchants' guild.

scenes were placed under canopies that imitated the architectural styles of the day. Horizontal panels of colour now alternated with panels of *grisaille,* white glass decorated with a foliage design – a marked departure from the deeply colour-saturated windows of the 12th c. and 13th c. The range of colours also changed, moving away from a predominance of red and blue in favour of earthy browns and greens. The most revolutionary development of all, however, was the discovery of yellow stain, a silver compound that when painted onto the glass and fired, produced a stain varying from deep orange to pale yellow. This simple discovery freed the glass-painter of the need to cut and lead in certain details such as hair, beards and decorative items that could now appear yellow on a single piece of white glass. The rather academic typological windows of the 13th c. were replaced in popularity by single figures of saints usually carrying an attribute associated with their martyrdom as a form of identification. This type of subject was favoured by the secular patron, who could chose his own name saint; the most popular source book for these figures was undoubtedly Jacobus de Voragine's *Golden Legend.* Another popular 14th-c. subject, especially in England, was the Tree of Jesse, presenting in pictorial form the genealogy of Christ, and giving especial honour to the Virgin Mary.

The figure-and-canopy window type persisted into the 15th c., but from *c.*1350 a major transformation of the glass-painter's palette can be discerned. One of the earliest examples can be seen in the east window of Gloucester cathedral: figures in white glass, heavily modelled to give an almost cadaverous appearance, are set off against red and blue backgrounds that, with the exception of the silvery yellow stain, provide almost the only colour. Nor was glass-painting to be unaffected by the values of

the International Gothic style. By 1400 a new 'soft style' of painting had replaced the linear, mannered elegance of the earlier century with a more painterly style, an interest in spatial effects and a high degree of facial characterization. In cities such as York, Coventry, Bourges, Strasbourg and Nuremberg, this new, more naturalistic style was favoured by the urban-based merchant classes who now provided so much of the patronage of stained glass. Thus in the 15th-c. Reiter window in St Lorenz in Nuremberg, the biblical characters strongly resemble wealthy German burghers. Even in a sumptuous courtly piece, such as Jacques Coeur's gift of the *Annunciation* in Bourges cathedral, observation of the real world is acute, reflected in the astounding realism of Gabriel's feathers.

In Quattrocento Italy, a medium of lesser importance took on new significance with the need to glaze structures such as Florence cathedral and the flamboyantly Gothic cathedral in Milan. Although in Milan Cristoforo de Mottis appears to have been a glass-painter by training, in Florence the challenge of the windows attracted artists better known in other media, such as Ghiberti, Donatello and Uccello, together with foreign glass-painters from north of the Alps. The startling spatial reality found in 15th-c. Italian glass had, by the end of the century, begun to be important in Northern European glass-painting. Just as the artists of the Low Countries had been such a catalyst in the development of International Gothic, so now they played an important role in the introduction of Renaissance ideas. Galyon Hone, a Fleming employed by Henry VII to glaze the windows of King's College Chapel, Cambridge, led a workshop well versed in the innovations of the Renaissance; in Rouen, Arnoult de Nimègue, a native of Tournai, was to revitalize glass-painting in his adopted home. Even in such remarkable work as the King's College glass, the adoption of Renaissance motifs was not total, for Renaissance architecture rubs shoulders with a traditional Gothic structure. Only in the Charles V window in Brussels cathedral by Bernard van Orley, for example, do we see a window entirely Renaissance in all its details.

Perhaps more damaging to the Gothic tradition in stained glass was the beginning of a new approach to the cutting and leading of glass. The use of large areas of white glass, heavily modelled in imitation of easel painting, led the glass-painters (at King's College, for example) to employ large rectangular panels that cut across the outlines of their design in a way that would have been anathema to their forbears. This, together with the introduction of enamel stains that did away with the need to cut and lead any pot-metal glasses at all, had already sown

the seeds of decay, long before Reformation and religious war in Europe destroyed the medieval glass-painters' traditional world for good. SB
□ L. Grodecki and C. Brisac *Gothic Stained Glass: 1200–1300* (1985); C. Brisac *A Thousand Years of Stained Glass* (1986); S. Crewe *Stained Glass in England 1180-1540* (1987)

Glastonbury Abbey With the conspicuous and dramatic mound of Glastonbury Tor near by, the abbey ruins at Glastonbury still carry a sentiment of mystery and antiquity. There was a Celtic monastery on the site, and the continuity appears to have been virtually unbroken through the Saxon period. Under St Dunstan in the mid-10th c. it was reconstituted and became one of the chief sources for the Benedictine revival in England. At the time of the Norman Conquest it was the wealthiest monastic house in the kingdom, with a rent roll of over £800. The 12th c. saw the flowering of the legends which made it famous on a European scale: the attribution of a visit by Joseph of Arimathea in the 1st c. AD and the growth of Arthurian legends culminating in the discovery of the purported graves of Arthur and Guinevere in the early 1190s. Glastonbury became a great centre for pilgrimage, and other legendary material developed, such as that associated with the Holy Grail and with the Glastonbury Thorn, which bloomed twice a year, in May and at Christmas.
□ R.F. Treharne *The Glastonbury Legends* (1967); J. Carley *Glastonbury* (1987)

Glossators Term commonly applied in the Middle Ages to scholars who wrote extensive commentaries on texts of civil and canon law, but which in a more general sense could also refer to those who wrote on biblical or rabbinical texts. Of outstanding reputation was the work of Irnerius in the late 11th c. and early 12th c., and of Accursius in the 13th c., whose glosses were widely accepted as authoritative statements of Roman law, based as they were on Justinian's *Code*. Similar systematic intellectual glosses were also made to the great collections of canon law associated with the work of Gratian in the 12th c. and his successors. *See* VACARIUS
□ H. Kantorowicz *Studies in the Glossators of the Roman Law* (1969)

Glyndwr, Owain (Owen Glendower) (*c.*1365–*c.*1417) A landowner and descendant of Welsh princes, Glyndwr became the leader of rebellion against Henry IV of England, operating successfully inside Wales, in uneasy alliance with the Percys and with Mortimer. He claimed a princely title, established diplomatic relations with the Scots and French, and at the height of his power in 1405 was widely recognized as a virtually independent ruler throughout Wales. The failure of his allies led to defeat, but the legend of his bravery, faithfully preserved by court bards, and memories of his councils, including the summons of the first Welsh parliament, served as an inspiration to later generations. Glyndwr was never captured and is believed to have died early in the reign of Henry V.
□ R.R. Davies *Conquest, Coexistence and Change: Wales 1063–1415* (1987)

Godfrey de Bouillon (*c.*1060–1100) Ruler of Jerusalem. Son of Count Eustace II of Boulogne and nephew of Duke Godfrey of Lower Lotharingia, he succeeded to his uncle's duchy in 1082. He joined the First Crusade in 1096, and replaced Raymond of Toulouse as its popular leader in 1099. Jerusalem was captured in that year and Godfrey was chosen as its ruler, taking the title of Defender of the Holy Sepulchre. He apparently considered entrusting Jerusalem to theocratic government, but he died before the matter could be settled, and his brother and successor Baldwin I took the title of king.

Gokstad ship Excavated in the Oslofjord in 1881, it is a fine Viking vessel of the mid-9th c. which was used as the burial ship for a Viking chieftain some 50 years later. About 23 metres long, it is built almost completely of oak with mast, decking, and 16 pairs of oars in pine. The ship possessed both strength and flexibility in heavy seas thanks to its clinker construction about a keel, stern and stern-post; its shallow draught of little more than a metre, made it manoeuvrable in shallow estuaries and easy to beach. *See* SHIPS AND SHIPPING
□ P.H. Sawyer *The Age of the Vikings* (1971)

Golden Bull (1356) Agreed between Charles IV and the German princes, this was an important constitutional document, recognizing and codifying the federal framework for government which had developed in Germany. It prescribed the procedure for the election and coronation of the Emperor and emphasized the pre-eminence of the seven electors, besides according implicit acceptance to princely autonomy.
□ B. Jarrett *The Emperor Charles IV* (1935)

Golden Horde Name for the khanate of western Kipchak. It arises from the Russian name for the golden tent (*Zolotaya Orda*) that its first ruler, Batu (d. 1256), pitched at Sarai on the Volga, which was his power centre from 1243. Batu was the grandson of Jenghiz Khan; the lands he inherited consisted of the western half of his grandfather's dominions, which included most of European Russia. Batu extended and consolidated the area he commanded 1236–41, eventually subjugating most of the territories between the Urals and the Carpathians. Batu's brother and successor Berke (1257–67) became a Muslim, and over the next 50 years Islam became a dominant force in the Golden Horde, encouraging independence from the overlordship of the great khan of the Mongol empire. The death of Berdibeg (1359) was followed by a series of destructive dynastic disputes.

There was a period of resurgence under Tokhtamish (1381–95), who united the Golden Horde with the White Horde of eastern Kipchak, but this ended with his decisive defeat at the hands of Tamberlaine in 1395. After the reign of Edigü (1399–1419) the Golden Horde was considerably weakened by the emergence within its boundaries of the independent khanates of Astrakhan, Kazan and the Crimea.
□ G. Vernadsky *The Mongols and Russia* (1953)

Goliardic poets Student songs, outrageous critical and satiric verses, delicate poems extolling human love and nature, tend to be ascribed (not always justly) to the legendary poet Golias and his followers. They constitute a direct product of the 12th-c. renaissance, symptomatic of the vigour of the urban communities and of the groups of students and scholars gathered together around the schools and new universities of Western Europe.

They composed in Latin, and at their best achieved fine works of art, disguised rather than enhanced by their fondness for easily memorable jingles, but mercifully revealed in the best of modern translations. The work of the Archpoet, notably his *Confession,* ranks among the best-known and the best of their achievements.
□ H. Waddell *The Wandering Scholars* (1935)

Gorm the Old King of Denmark *c.*936–*c.*50 The founder of a powerful dynasty of Danish rulers whose centre of authority lay in Jutland, especially at Jelling, where two great mounds or barrows are still associated with the names of Gorm and his son, Harold Bluetooth. He raised a memorial stone to his wife Thyri, and his son Harold further raised a magnificent memorial stone, one of the outstanding monuments of the Viking Age, to commemorate his parents – and to claim that he, Harold, had won for himself all Denmark and Norway, and made the Danes Christian. Gorm himself was a heathen and owed his strength to a successful rallying of Danish chieftains against heavy pressure from the south, by the revived Christian kingship of Henry the Fowler and Otto the Great in Germany.
□ G. Jones *A History of the Vikings* (1968)

A fine example of **Gothic** carving, from Tilman Riemenschneider's Heiligblutaltar (1518).

Gothic Term first used by Vasari (1511–74) to describe all art between the fall of the Roman empire and the emergence of the Renaissance. He made no distinction between pre-Romanesque, Romanesque and Gothic, and considered them all barbaric. His contempt, based on ignorance, did not last long, but the name, although absurd, survives.

Gothic was essentially an urban art, centred on the big cathedrals, and relied not on monastic patronage – as was the case with Romanesque art – but on the courts and city guilds. This style, born in the mid-12th c. in the Ile-de-France, lasted north of the Alps, until the first half of the 16th c., thus spanning nearly 400 years. There were, consequently, considerable changes in style during this long period. The courtly Gothic art of the mid-13th c. has, for instance, little in common with the tormented and mystical art which followed the Black Death. The International Gothic style of *c.*1400 again becomes courtly, almost sentimental, and provides a contrast to the last dramatic and realistic stage of this style, best illustrated by German art of the late 15th c.

Throughout the period the French royal domain, with Paris at its centre, was the most inventive and influential in every field of artistic creativity; not surprisingly, the Gothic style became known in Europe as the *opus francigenum.* This does not mean, however, that other countries slavishly followed the French. England's contribution, in particular, was outstanding, whether in ecclesiastical architecture,

The Wilton diptych (*c.* 1400) epitomizes **Gothic** painting in its rich detail and flowing lines.

Kingdoms of the **Ostrogoths** and **Visigoths** at the death of Theodoric in 526.

castle-building, book illumination, stone sculpture or embroidery, for which the English were renowned. During the second half of the 14th c. Bohemia became an important artistic centre, owing to the patronage of the Emperor Charles IV, who made Prague his capital.

In Italy, where the traditions of antique art were ever present, the influence of French art was on the whole superficial, and buildings as thoroughly Gothic as Milan cathedral are rare. The great Italian Gothic sculptors Nicola Pisano and his son Giovanni both show a knowledge of Gothic forms, but they are indebted above all to antique sculpture. Many other Italian artists borrowed Gothic decorative details, but their aims were, on the whole, different. Their pre-occupation with the relationship of figures, the logical use of light and shade, the expressive qualities of the human figure and other concerns which led to the emergence of the Renaissance style, set Italian art apart. *See* ARCHITECTURE; SCULPTURE [*222-3*]   GZ

□ A. Martindale *Gothic Art* (1967); J. Pope-Hennessy *Italian Gothic Sculpture* (1970); G. Zarnecki *Art of the Medieval World* (1975)

Goths Although the term came to be applied indiscriminately to many of the Germanic peoples who invaded the Roman empire, historically it refers to a specific branch of the East Germans whose native home may well have been southern Scandinavia and the island of Gotland. They migrated to the east and south, and in the 4th c. formed a loose, straggling federation of tribes settled along the waterways of Russia, the Ostrogoths for the most part in the lands between the Don and the Dneister, and the Visigoths between the Dneister and the Danube. Thanks to the labours of Wulfila (Ulphilas) *c.*311-85, many of them were converted to Christianity, though of the Arian persuasion, and the Gospels were translated into the Gothic tongue, a new Gothic alphabet – a compound of Greek and Latin elements – being created for the purpose. The Goths crossed the Danube frontier in 376 under heavy pressure from the Huns, and in consequence of the tangled and dramatic politics of the following generation fell permanently into their two historic divisions: the Visigoths, who played a prominent part in the overthrow of Roman political mastery of the West in the first half of the 5th c., and the Ostrogoths,

who under the leadership of Theodoric brought temporary equilibrium to Italy and much of the Western Mediterranean at the end of the 5th c. and beginning of the 6th c.
□ E.A. Thompson *The Early Germans* (1965)

Gottfried von Strassburg One of the leading medieval German poets, Gottfried wrote much in the full Courtly Love tradition of the 12th c. and early 13th c. His greatest contribution to European literature came in his romance of *Tristan and Isolde*. Written in the first decade of the 13th c. and based on French Arthurian legends, it contributed much, in its great length and poetic skill, to universal recognition of the German vernacular as a proper vehicle for high poetic achievement.
□ J. Ferrante *The Conflict of Love and Honour: the Medieval Tristan Legend in France, Germany and Italy* (1973)

Gratian (d. *c.*1179) One of the greatest lawyers of the Middle Ages he, trained in the schools of Bologna, applied both the new learning based on Roman law and the advanced dialectic methods of his age to create a textbook of permanent value to the law of the church, known as the *Decretum* (1139–40). His own title for the work was the *Concordantia Discordantium Canonum* ('Concordance of Discordant Canons'); it drew heavily on the authority of the early fathers, on the Councils and on the decrees of emperors and popes. It provided a systematic and up-to-date arrangement of canon law and quickly became an essential stand-by for the training of canon lawyers. As such it was seized upon avidly by the popes and, indeed, reflects the legal aspirations of the reformed papacy of the 12th c. Gratian, a monk of the Camaldunensian persuasion, was created cardinal by Pope Alexander III. [*320*]
□ *Corpus Juris Canonici* ed. E. Friedberg (1879–81); S. Kuttner *Gratian and the Schools of Law 1140–1234* (1983)

Great Schism (1378–1417) The return of the papacy from Avignon to Rome (1378) was followed by a long period of division and dissent. A majority of cardinals, under pressure, elected the Italian archbishop of Bari as Pope Urban VI at Rome in the April, but support quickly fell away from him, partly because of his cruelty and autocratic nature. In the following year, on the grounds that Urban's election was invalid, the cardinal Robert of Geneva, strongly supported by the powerful French cardinalate, was elected as Clement VII and set up his pontifical see, again at Avignon. Europe was divided in allegiance essentially on political grounds: support for Avignon came from France, Scotland, Castile, Aragon and some German princes; the Emperor, England, Scandinavia and most Italians supported Rome.

The existence of two popes, each with substantial backing, caused great scandal and financial hardship throughout the West. Scholars at Paris, forming a group known as the Conciliar thinkers, attempted to find a solution to the problem in the summons of a general council. Such a council was held at Pisa (1409); it declared the existing popes deposed and proceeded to elect the cardinal-archbishop of Milan as Pope Alexander V. There was not enough political will and muscle to make the depositions effective, however, and the immediate result was that Europe was left with three popes in place of two.

The situation was finally resolved at the Council of Constance with the election of the powerful Colonna Pope Martin V, in November 1417. Elected before an effective programme of reform could be drafted, Martin was able effectively to reassert papal headship of the church. Nevertheless, in spite of his efforts, elements of schism continued with some Spanish support until deep into the 1420s.
□ G. Mollat *The Popes at Avignon* (1963); Y. Renouard *The Avignon Papacy 1305–1403* (1970); W. Ullmann *The Origins of the Great Schism* (1972)

A caricature of the **Great Schism** showing Pope Nicholas V, from the prophecies of Joachim of Fiore.

Greece A great deal of interest has been shown in the reclamation of Greek culture, often from Muslim sources, which was so much a feature of the intellectual life of Europe in the central Middle Ages. But the political history of the Greek-speaking lands, including the area now thought of as mainland Greece and its dependent islands, is a matter of complexity, and has been treated by Western historians as incidental to other themes, such as the history of the Byzantine empire, the Crusades, or the rise of the Ottomans.

Generally speaking, Byzantium or the Eastern empire, based in Constantinople, was regarded as the empire of the Greeks until its overthrow by the Fourth Crusade (1204). From then until its final conquest by the Ottoman Turks in 1460, the history of 'Greece' was chequered and fragmentary. Under Byzantine rule there was some Slavonic immigration, but reasonable identity was maintained through the predominance of the Greek language and Greek Orthodox religion. Muslim pressure was at times intense, and Crete was ruled by Muslims 823–961. In the 11th c. and 12th c. Norman intervention from southern Italy proved a constant irritant.

After the fall of Constantinople (1204) the Greek lands attracted the political ambitions of a variety of Western peoples: 'Frankish' feudal nobles, Burgundians, Angevins, Italians and the commercial and feudal interests associated with the Grand Catalan Company and the great Italian towns, notably Venice. The restoration of the Byzantine empire in 1261 made little impact on Greek politics until the early 15th c., by which time Ottoman Turkish expansionist ambitions were becoming overwhelming, resulting in the conquest of Greece and the capture of Constantinople itself in 1453.
□ D.M. Nicol *The Last Centuries of Byzantium, 1261–1453* (1972)

Greek fire Byzantine naval weapon invented by Callimachus, a Syrian engineer, and first used at the siege of Constantinople (674–78). It was a highly combustible compound, based on a mixture of petroleum, sulphur, saltpetre and unburnt quicklime, which ignited on impact and burnt in water. It was used ballistically in the form of a hand grenade or in conjunction with a copper 'siphon' or catapult. *See* WAR

Greenland Island settled in the late 10th c. by Scandinavians, mostly Icelanders, under the leadership of Eric the Red. They set up two chief settlements: the eastern settlement (ultimately the home of the cathedral at Gardar, an Augustinian monastery, a Benedictine nunnery and 12 parish churches) and a western settlement (around modern Godthaab).

Christianity was accepted at an early stage and the Greenlanders flourished, extending knowledge of navigation further west into Vinland and keeping firm and continuous contact with Iceland and Norway. In 1261 they accepted Norwegian sovereignty.

Deteriorating climatic conditions drew the Eskimos south, and made the existence of the Scandinavian communities increasingly precarious. By the mid-14th c. the western settlement had collapsed and communication with Norway became increasingly spasmodic. It seems likely that some lingering survivors lived on deep into the 15th c., possibly even into the early 16th c.; but Greenland demanded recolonization in the early modern period. A combination of increasing cold, Eskimo attack and Norwegian indifference brought an end to one of the bravest and most impressive colonizing efforts of the Middle Ages.
□ G. Jones *The Norse Atlantic Saga* (1964)

Gregory I the Great, St Pope 590–604 (b. *c.*540) Born into a wealthy Roman family, Gregory was involved in the secular administration of Rome by 573, possibly as prefect. He relinquished his post to become a monk, and having inherited the family estates, established seven monasteries, one of which, S. Andrea, formerly the family home on the Coelian hill, he entered himself. Following a papal summons, he left S. Andrea to be ordained as a deacon. In 579 the Lombards besieged Rome, and it was perhaps then that, as papal ambassador, Gregory was sent to Constantinople to seek assistance from the emperor. He returned to his deaconate at the Lateran *c.*586. On the death of Pope Pelagius II (590), Gregory was unanimously elected to succeed him.

Notwithstanding his chronic ill health – attributed by Gregory of Tours to excessive fasting – he dedicated himself unstintingly to his papal responsibilities, as his 854 surviving letters testify. It fell to the church to feed Rome's sizeable indigent population, and Gregory was the first to systematize such charitable activities, referring to himself as 'steward of the property of the poor'. Building on the work of his predecessor Gelasius I (d.496) Gregory instituted important reforms in the administration of the papal estates to safeguard the church's interests. He was inevitably drawn into the political arena, where the incursions of the Lombards posed the major problem. Gregory negotiated with their leaders, intervening whenever the operations of the Byzantine exarch proved inadequate. Unlike many of his successors, Gregory was not concerned to curtail imperial authority, acknowledging the emperor as temporal lord and protector of the church. He recognized the seniority in the East of the patriarch

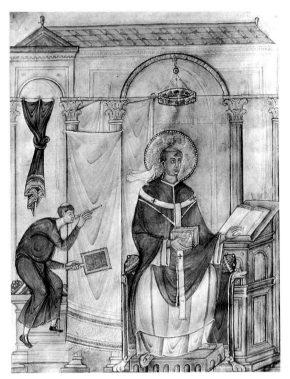

Monk painting a portrait of **Pope Gregory the Great** in his study. From a copy of his *Registrum, c.*983.

of Constantinople, but zealously defended papal primacy within Christendom. He attempted to resolve doctrinal disputes, notably with the Three Chapters schismatics in Istria, as well as among those Lombards who had accepted Catholicism.

Gregory placed great importance on missionary activity, directing Augustine, prior of S. Andrea, to embark on the conversion of the English in 596. Gregory's famous exchange with the young Angles in Rome may, however, simply be legend; the incident is first reported by his earliest biographer, the Anonymous of Whitby (704–14) and by Bede. It is unlikely that the formulation of Gregorian Chant owed anything to Gregory I, and only a fraction of the Gregorian sacramentary is attributable to him. He criticized the condemnation of religious paintings, considering these to be 'the books of the unlearned'. His own writing style was often deliberately anecdotal rather than esoteric. The basis for accepting Benedict of Nursia as a historical personage is Gregory's account of Benedict's life and miracles in his *Dialogues* (593). Gregory's other principal works are: the *Regula Pastoralis,* a handbook for bishops; the *Homilies,* discourses on Ezekiel and the Gospels, delivered 591–93; and an exegesis on Job, the *Magna Moralia* (595).

The first pope with a monastic background, Gregory was an ardent promoter of monasticism.

He is acknowledged as the last of the four major Latin church fathers.

JF

□ J. Richards *Consul of God: The Life and Times of Gregory the Great* (1980)

Gregory VII (Hildebrand) Pope 1073–85 Rightly regarded as leader and representative figure in the great ecclesiastical reform movement of the second half of the 11th c., Pope Gregory VII has left a reputation for tenacity of purpose and imaginative vision of how the Western church should be governed. He first came to prominence in the service of Pope Gregory VI (1045–46), and the rest of his life was spent being active in papal politics and administration. His career was fostered by the reforming Pope Leo IX (1049–54) and for more than 20 years he was busy in the papal curia, acting as emissary to France and Germany, and prominent in the vigorous group which slowly developed the idea of centralized reform that would cut across the political boundaries and transcend the peculiarities of the separate ecclesiastical communities of the West.

Concern for moral reform lay at the heart of all his political activity. In the late 1050s the alliance of the papacy with the Normans of southern Italy and assertion of the principle of free election to papal office strengthened the position of the Roman church, although in a sense these moves may be read as merely a means to an end. Anxiety over the moral state of the church provided the motive force for political action. Special concern was expressed over simony (the sale of clerical office), over lack of celibacy (clerical marriage was common, especially in Germany), and over lay appointment to the highest offices in the church; this was symbolized in the act of investiture, by which a king would hand over the trappings of office to a prelate, instructing him to 'receive this church'. Principles of lay control at the lower level also caused intense anxiety on the part of the reformers; landlords would appoint their own nominees to benefices (sometimes – again notably in German lands – their own serfs). Attack on these principles, however, had of necessity to be conducted more circumspectly. Hierarchical control of the church's own higher offices became a main plank in the so-called Gregorian reform movement; transmission of authority passed in a clear line from the pope (successor of St Peter), through the cardinals and metropolitans, to freely elected bishops.

Such ideas were contrary to the practice of much of Europe, where the emperors and kings were accustomed to choosing their own bishops, who were more often than not great landowners and key men in government and administration by virtue of their office. Nevertheless, on his election to the papacy, Gregory determined to give reality to his vision of a free and effective reformed church; 'I am not custom, but truth' became one of his favourite texts, often quoted in the voluminous body of letters that have survived from his pontificate. The result was the precipitation of one of the greatest conflicts between empire and papacy known to medieval history. The name often given to it, the 'Investiture Contest', is somewhat misleading: the question of the rights and wrongs of lay investiture were only incidental; the true issues concerned the supremacy of the pope within the church. It was indeed, as many historians have suggested, a struggle comparable to the 16th-c. Reformation, a struggle for 'right order' in the Western world.

Gregory's own view of the position is well stated in the *Dictatus Papae,* a memorandum surviving from the early days of his pontificate in which are set out the arguments concerning the nature of the papacy. At first sight there are some incongruities in the document – the apparently important is jumbled with the apparently unimportant – but there is a hard logic running through the whole set of 27 propositions. It is a clear assertion of the infallibility of the Roman church and the supremacy of the papacy. The pope alone had the right to the imperial insignia and the right to depose bishops; no person could judge the pope; he had the right to depose unworthy emperors. The theory of a centralized and centralizing papacy emerges fully grown in the *Dictatus,* and it was quickly tested in practice.

Quarrels with the young German King Henry IV over the royal reception of excommunicated bishops, over failure to implement moral reform, and over principles of election to the key archbishopric of Milan erupted into dramatic confrontation and violence between December 1075 and March 1077. The initiative lay in the first place with the king, who in January 1076 at a great assembly of German notables, strongly supported by his bishops, declared Gregory deposed. The pope's response was swift and effective: at the Lenten synod in Rome, he in turn deposed the king, excommunicating him and freeing his Christian subjects from their oaths of allegiance. Support rapidly fell away from Henry, and dissident elements within the kingdom, both lay and ecclesiastical, took their opportunity. In the autumn, at a confrontation that nearly came to open war, they threatened their excommunicated king at Tribur and Oppenheim. By a political manoeuvre of some dexterity Henry avoided capture and moved south over the Alps in mid-winter to confront the pope, at the castle of Canossa, in one of the most dramatic scenes of medieval history. The chronicles and later historians make the most of this story, describing the young king, barefoot and clad in woollens, waiting as a penitent for absolution from Pope Gregory. The pope could do no other, as a priest, than absolve him, but the king's political opponents inside Germany carried on with their schemes, deposing Henry and electing Rudolf of Swabia as anti-king in March 1077.

Gregory seems to have attempted to hold a balance, concentrating on moral reform, extending his range of influence and attempting to implement the principles of papal monarchy throughout Europe. His energy was phenomenal, and active papal interference was experienced far beyond the bounds of the empire, in Hungary, Poland, Scandinavia, England and Spain. Gregory was forced to turn back to the German scene, and here, from 1080 his political judgment appears to have deserted him. He moved in favour of Rudolf, who was killed in a skirmish. His second deposition of Henry proved ineffective; the German king now gained strength, moved into Italy, appointed a respectable anti-pope in the person of Clement III, archbishop of Ravenna, and had himself crowned Emperor. Gregory was forced to call in his turbulent Norman allies, but by 1084 ravages in Rome were so great that Gregory had to withdraw with the Normans when they moved south.

He died in exile at Salerno, and his bitter last comment, 'I have loved *justitia* ['righteousness'], therefore I die in exile', was long remembered. As a man he roused high passion, and descriptive epithets range from 'ill-favoured Tuscan monk' to 'Holy Satan'. For all the apparent failure and tragedy of his last years, his achievements were phenomenal. No emperor after Canossa, not even the strongest of the Hohenstaufens, attempted to reassert the theocracy of the Carolingians, the Ottonians or Henry III. The strong papacy of the central Middle Ages, confident in its supremacy over spiritual things and of its superiority to the temporal, was brought firmly into being.   HRL

□ A.J. Macdonald *Hildebrand: a Life of Gregory VII* (1932); J.P. Whitney *Hildebrandine Essays* (1932); G. Tellenbach *Church, State and Christian Society at the time of the Investiture Contest* (1940)

Gregory IX Pope 1227–41 (b. *c.*1148) Cardinal-bishop of Ostia, on his election excommunicated Frederick II for non-fulfilment of a crusading vow. After unsuccessfully attempting to invade Sicily, an imperial power base, Gregory accepted Frederick's reconciliation with the church under the terms of the Treaty of San Germano (1230). Frederick's anti-papal activities in Lombardy and Sicily caused a renewal of the ban in 1239, and in 1241 Gregory tried to convoke a general council at Rome to judge the emperor. Gregory promulgated the *Liber Extra,* an important collection of papal law in 1234. He was a fervent supporter of the Franciscan and Dominican friars.

□ *Régistres de Grégoire IX* ed. L. Auvray (1896–1910)

Gregory of Tours, St (*c*.540–94) Born of a Gallo-Roman senatorial family, he succeeded a cousin as metropolitan bishop of Tours in 573. During his episcopate he dealt with three Merovingian rulers: Sigibert, who was assassinated in 575; the despotic Chilperic, whom Gregory vigorously opposed for ten years; and the young Childebert II, for whom Guntram acted as regent. Gregory's writings are mostly hagiographical in character, but his chief work is the *Historia Francorum,* a chronicle which runs from the Creation to 591, but is particularly concerned with 6th-c. affairs.

□ *The History of the Franks* ed. L. Thorpe (1974)

Groote, Gerhard (1340–84) Founder of the Brethren of the Common Life. Of wealthy Dutch stock, he gave up a successful academic career to enter the Carthusian monastery of Munnikhausen *c*.1375. Leaving the cloister three years later, he sought ordination and took up missionary preaching in the diocese of Utrecht. He made a fundamental contribution to the spirituality of the contemporary religious revival known as the *devotio moderna,* but the criticism he levelled at corruption in the church led to the withdrawal of his license to preach in 1383.

The community he founded in his native Deventer formed the nucleus of the religious group called the Brethren of the Common Life; his ideals also had a formative influence on the regular canonical congregation of Windesheim.

Grosseteste, Robert (b. *c*.1175) Bishop of Lincoln 1235–53, and statesman-bishop of great energy and enduring influence, he applied himself vigorously to church reform. In his Statutes (1240–43) he laid down guidelines for the administration of a diocese and for the imposition of a moral order on the clergy which were to be extensively copied and used as a model throughout the Middle Ages in England. He was also a moving force in the rising fortunes and standards of Oxford university, and stood in the forefront of language studies – he was a good Hebraist as well as a Greek scholar – and of 13th-c. scientific thought and theology. His commentaries on Aristotle's work on physics and his compendium of scientific knowledge were quickly recognized as authoritative in their generation, and he anticipated Roger Bacon in his emphasis on experiment and rudimentary scientific method.

□ J. McEvoy *The Philosophy of Robert Grosseteste* (1982); R.W. Southern *Robert Grosseteste* (1986)

Stone relief in Florence showing the device of the **Guelph** party.

Guelph (Welf) Family descended from the early 9th-c. Bavarian Count Welf I, who came into bitter rivalry with the Hohenstaufen for hegemony in Germany between the early 12th c. and early 13th c. In 1070 Welf IV had become duke of Bavaria, to which his son Henry the Black (d. 1126) added substantial estates, and his grandson Henry the Proud (d. 1139) the lands of Emperor Lothar II, both by marriage. Henry the Proud appeared to be a leading contender for the imperial crown, but one of his rivals, Lothar III, a Hohenstaufen, was successful, and went on to deprive Henry's heir, Henry the Lion, of some of his lands. Henry the Proud's brother, Welf VI (d. 1191), the heir to Bavaria, made a marriage alliance with the Hohenstaufen and was endowed with Tuscany, Spoleto and other Italian lands by his Hohenstaufen nephew, Emperor Frederick I Barbarossa. In 1156 Bavaria was granted to Henry the Lion, who was already duke of Saxony and now became virtual ruler of northern Germany. In 1176, however, Henry refused aid to the Emperor of Italy. In 1180 he was formally deprived of his fiefs and driven out of them by force, leaving him with

A **guild** treasurer and his secretary, 1388; from the state archive at Siena.

only the family's allodial estates around Brunswick.

The family of Welf came back into political prominence when in 1201 Henry's second son, Otto of Brunswick, claimant to the Italian lands of Welf VI, was elected Emperor Otto IV with the support of Pope Innocent III. By 1209 he had consolidated his hold on Germany and moved into Italy to reclaim his lands and capture those of the Hohenstaufen. An alarmed papacy now turned to Frederick II of Sicily, who gradually took back Germany from Otto, and whose ally, Philip II of France, decisively defeated Otto and his English allies in 1214.

The Welfs were again confined to their Brunswick allods, but their fortunes revived when in 1235 Otto the Child did homage for them to Frederick II, who granted him Lüneburg and in addition erected the lands into an imperial principality. In Italy, however, conflict continued between the two parties, called from about the 1240s Guelphs (from Welf) and Ghibellines (from Waiblingen, the castle and battle cry of the Hohenstaufen). The Guelphs at first supported the church, their opponents, the Emperors, but all sight was soon lost of the origins of the disputes, and the names were simply attached to rival factions in the Italian communes.

□ K. Hampe *Germany under the Salian and Hohenstaufen Emperors* (1973)

Guilds A guild is a sworn association, a group of people who gather for some common purpose, establish fraternity by an oath, and express the connection between them by ritual eating and drinking. Similar institutions appear in many cultures. The word is cognate with Old English *geld,* a payment, and whilst the payment of membership fees and dues is a constant feature of guilds, an older association of payment and sacrifice lies behind them. The earliest guilds were probably pagan sacrificial feasts of a lurid kind, and the substitution of beer, a sacred drink to the Germans, for the flesh and blood of a victim did little to make them more acceptable to the Christian church. The earliest references to be found to them in the West are as pagan rituals which should be firmly suppressed by the clergy.

The guild was, however, a deeply-rooted institution which proved easier to assimilate than to abolish, and throughout the Middle Ages its only rivals as a form of social organization were the household and the court. Guilds of clergy appear early, and in the 10th c. London had a guild for keeping the peace, which numbered the bishop among its members. The most important role of the guild in the church was probably the building of churches and, in some sort, the definition of the parish as a community of worshippers. The upkeep of a parish church, except for the chancel itself, was the responsibility of the parishioners, and the business of building and maintaining the fabric required a co-operative effort which the guild was well able to promote. Parish guilds, and social guilds which undertook the addition and maintenance of chapels and altars in parish churches, provided stipends for priests and paid for lamps and particular services, continued the close association of guild and parish life to the end of the Middle Ages.

Two applications of the guild have served to distort its history. One was the guild merchant, which emerges into view as the documentation of town life intensifies from the 11th c. onwards, and which maintained a central role in the affairs of some towns for centuries. Its nature and function have been largely misunderstood, because historians have tried to classify guilds as entities, rather than as means adaptable to a variety of ends. When townsmen sought privileges from the king or another lord, it was natural for them to use the guild as a symbol and a reinforcement of their common purpose: it was also natural for merchants to protect their interests at home and abroad in the same way. From the 12th c. English boroughs frequently, though not invariably, sought the right to establish a guild merchant amongst the privileges of the town, and in some places, as at Ipswich in 1200, membership of the guild was equated with the freedom of the borough.

There are many towns, however, in which there is no trace of a guild merchant; those in England in which it played a leading and enduring part in civic affairs are either of minor consequence, such as Calne in Wiltshire, or, like Leicester, had lords who were not disposed to allow the burgesses control of their own courts. The presiding officer of a guild was called an alderman, and municipal aldermen may have had their origins in guilds. The chief magistrate of Grantham was known by that title until the 19th c. In most boroughs, however, the guild merchant soon lost whatever commanding significance it may have had to the borough court, which became an administrative as well as a judicial body. Even so, the building in which the court assembled was often known as the Guildhall, as happened in London, where no guild merchant is known to have existed.

The other prominent urban use of the guild was as a means of organizing and controlling crafts. Guilds would almost certainly have been used in some early attempts by artisans to assert a collective independence of merchant masters, but in the time of their fullest documentation, in the later Middle Ages, the craft-guilds regulated quality, production and recruitment to the crafts in the interests of the employer and the established skilled man. Once again it was the purpose of the organization, not its form, which distinguished it from other guilds, and it was the social context of the day, not some ideology peculiar to the guild, that determined this purpose. In the 14th c. and 15th c. however, in a society deeply permeated by religious forms, all guilds had religious and social purposes that were as prominent as any other ends that they avowed. The maintenance of chaplains, of prayers for the dead, of provision for sick and indigent brethren and their dependants, were regular features of craft-guilds, just as they were the only avowed aims of numerous other fraternities.

It was usual also, by that time, for guilds to profess the cult of a particular saint or saints, a convention which both reflected and promoted the association of saints with individual crafts and occupations. The Blessed Virgin was a widespread object of devotion, but of all the later cults that of Corpus Christi was probably the most influential. From the early 14th c. ritual enactments of the Passion of Christ at Easter developed into elaborate dramatic displays in churches and pageants on the streets; it was in these that the secular drama eventually found its beginnings. In the 16th c. the Reformation swept away the guilds and many of their works, but the social forms of the new age owed their origins to the medieval world, in which the sworn brotherhood of the guild had been not only a stabilizing force, but a powerful engine of change. *See* TOWNS   GM

□ C. Gross *The gild merchant* (1890); G. Unwin *The gilds and companies of London* (1908); S. Reynolds *Kingdoms and communities in Western Europe* (1984)

Gulden (Goldgulden) Gold coin. Name given in the 14th c. and 15th c. to derivatives of the florin in Germany, especially those struck by the Rhineland electors and by such imperial cities as Frankfurt-am-Main, Lüneburg and Basle, in the names of the Emperors from Sigismund (d. 1437) onwards. The coins were about the same weight as the florin (3.5g) but inferior in fineness, usually *c.* 19 carats.

Gulden of John II of Nassau, archbishop of Mainz (1397-1419).

Gutenberg, Johann (*c*.1396–1468) A trained gold-smith, he left his native Mainz for Strasbourg *c*.1430. In the interval before his return in *c*.1449 he seems to have perfected the technique of printing from moveable type, inventing and developing a typecasting machine and type cast in individual copper letters. Financed by Johann Fust, a banker, he produced the partly printed *Letters of Indulgence* and the fully printed 42-line Gutenberg bible (1453–55). After the dissolution of the partnership, Gutenberg continued alone, printing the 36-line bible, for example. The archbishop of Mainz gave him a pension in 1465. *See* PRINTING

□ V. Scholderer *Johann Gutenberg: the inventor of printing* (1970)

Guy de Lusignan (1129–94) Poitevin adventurer. He married Sybil, sister of King Baldwin IV of Jerusalem, in 1179 and was elected king himself in 1186 after the death of the child king, Baldwin V. He was defeated and captured at the battle of Hattin by Saladin in 1187, but on his release attempted to retain his royal title until forced to renounce it by Richard I of England. In compensation he became ruler of Cyprus (1192) and founder of the Lusignan dynasty, which maintained its rule in the island until the 15th c.

A page from the fully printed 42-line bible produced at Mainz by **Johann Gutenberg** and decorated by hand (1452–55)

Gwynedd The kingdom of Gwynedd lay in the north-west corner of Wales and included the island of Anglesey, always its lowland focus and contrast to the mountain heights of Snowdonia. There is evidence for kings from the early 6th c. and even at that date they are mentioned in terms which suggest a pre-eminence among the kings of Wales. Gwynedd kings, unlike other Welsh kings, ranged widely over English Britain in the 7th c., and the (tomb)stone from Llangadwaladr on Anglesey commemorating King Cadfan in the mid-7th c. calls him the 'wisest and most renowned king of all'. Later Gwynedd kings, especially Rhodri Mawr in the 9th c., absorbed the Welsh kingdoms of Powys and Ceredigion, and in the 10th c. the dynasty took over Dyfed in the south-west, although the kingdoms continued to remain separate.

Despite a period of southern dominance Gwynedd survived to become the focus of Welsh resistance to the English and Normans. The Norman Conquest of England had immediate repercussions for Wales. Initially, the Normans were highly successful in Gwynedd, but after the death of Earl Hugh of Shrewsbury in Anglesey in 1098, their hold slackened. Thereafter, the border country and much of the south were governed by Marcher lords, but the princes of Gwynedd, especially Owain Gwynedd (1137–70), preserved substantial independence.

In the early 13th c. Llywelyn ab Iorwerth – Llywelyn the Great (1200–40) – built up his authority as prince in North Wales (and, indeed, more widely throughout Wales), subject to the homage he paid to the English king. After his death, further advance was made by his grandson Llywelyn ap Gruffydd (1255–82), whose position as prince of Wales with feudal control over 'all the Welsh barons of Wales' was accepted by the English at the Treaty of Montgomery (1267).

Edward I's succession to the kingdom of England brought defeat, however, and in the second phase of the Welsh wars of independence Llywelyn ap Gruffydd was killed (December 1282), and resistance was finally abandoned in June 1283. The work that they had done in building up a territorial principality was turned to good advantage by Edward I and his successors.

Though never again as near to independence, Welsh princes, such as Owain Glyndwr (*c*.1365–*c*.1417), continued to revolt against English rule until the accession to the kingdom of England of Henry VII Tudor, of Anglesey stock, after the battle of Bosworth in 1485.

□ J.E. Lloyd *History of Wales from the Earliest Times to the Edwardian Conquest* (1911); A.D. Carr *Medieval Anglesey* (1982); D. Stephenson *The Governance of Gwynedd* (1984)

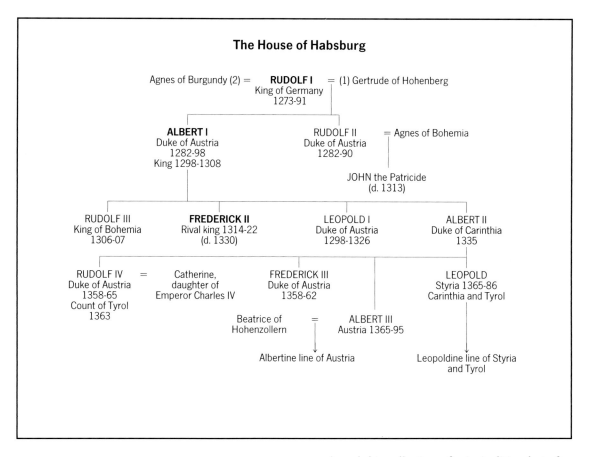

The House of Habsburg

Agnes of Burgundy (2) = **RUDOLF I** = (1) Gertrude of Hohenberg
King of Germany
1273-91

ALBERT I
Duke of Austria
1282-98
King 1298-1308

RUDOLF II = Agnes of Bohemia
Duke of Austria
1282-90

JOHN the Patricide
(d. 1313)

RUDOLF III
King of Bohemia
1306-07

FREDERICK II
Rival king 1314-22
(d. 1330)

LEOPOLD I
Duke of Austria
1298-1326

ALBERT II
Duke of Carinthia
1335

RUDOLF IV = Catherine,
Duke of Austria daughter of
1358-65 Emperor Charles IV
Count of Tyrol
1363

FREDERICK III
Duke of Austria
1358-62

LEOPOLD
Styria 1365-86
Carinthia and Tyrol

Beatrice of = ALBERT III
Hohenzollern Austria 1365-95

Albertine line of Austria

Leopoldine line of Styria
and Tyrol

Habsburg dynasty Swabian family, originating in the north of modern Switzerland. The Habsburgs (Hapsburgs) ranked among the lesser nobility of Germany until, by service to the Hohenstaufen, they became powerful and wealthy in Alsace, Zürich and ultimately, in the early 13th c., over much of south-west Germany. During the great Interregnum (1254–73) many of the Hohenstaufen supporters looked to Rudolf, count of Habsburg, and in 1273 he was elected Emperor, forcing his unsuccessful rival, the king of Bohemia, to yield the duchies of Austria and Styria (1278). From that point the Habsburg interest became identified with the Middle Danube, and their centre shifted to Vienna. In spite of the loss of their Swiss homelands and failure to maintain their hold over the imperial title, the Habsburgs extended their territorial influence in the 14th c., acquiring Carinthia and Carniola (1335), the Tyrol (1363), and finally Trieste with access to the Adriatic (1382). Division of inheritance weakened this collection of principalities, but after the death of the Emperor Sigismund in December 1437 the German princes elected his successor and son-in-law Albert, duke of Austria, as the senior representative of the Habsburg house. From then on the Habsburgs provided the natural choice for the imperial title. *See* ALBERT I; MAXIMILIAN I
□ R. A. Kann *The Habsburg Empire* (1957); A. Wandruszka *The House of Habsburg* (1964)

Hakīm Caliph 996–1021 (b. 985) Sixth Fātimid caliph, famous for his persecution of Christians and Jews, though he was born of a Christian mother. His reign coincided with the Byzantine offensives in Syria and Palestine (974–75; 995). In 1001 a ten-year truce with the Byzantines was struck, but peace was disturbed by Hakīm's destruction of the Church of the Holy Sepulchre in Jerusalem (1009), leading to a break in relations.

His cruelties were manifold, and his assumption of divinity, coupled with his general instability, has been read as a sign of madness. He disappeared suddenly and mysteriously in 1021, most probably victim of an assassination.
□ S. de Sacy *Exposé de la religion des Druzes* (1838)

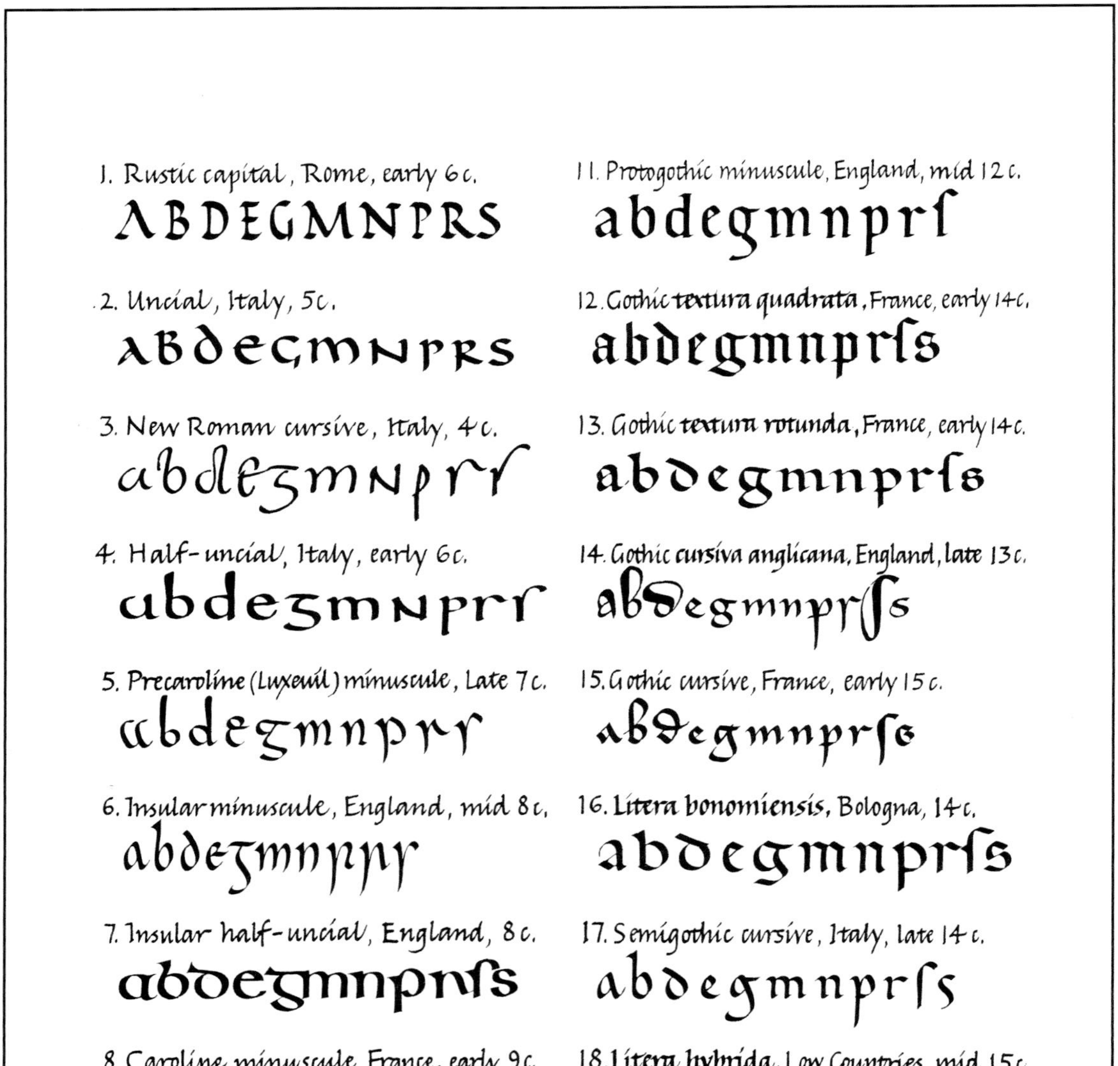

1. Rustic capital, Rome, early 6c.

ABDEGMNPRS

2. Uncial, Italy, 5c.

ABDEGMNPRS

3. New Roman cursive, Italy, 4c.

abdegmnprr

4. Half-uncial, Italy, early 6c.

abdegmnprr

5. Precaroline (Luxeuil) minuscule, Late 7c.

abdegmnprr

6. Insular minuscule, England, mid 8c.

abdegmnppr

7. Insular half-uncial, England, 8c.

abdegmnprs

8. Caroline minuscule, France, early 9c.

abdegmnpr

9. Caroline minuscule, Italy, mid 12c.

abdegmnpr

10. English Caroline minuscule, mid 11c.

abdegmnpr

11. Protogothic minuscule, England, mid 12c.

abdegmnpr

12. Gothic textura quadrata, France, early 14c.

abdegmnprs

13. Gothic textura rotunda, France, early 14c.

abdegmnprs

14. Gothic cursiva anglicana, England, late 13c.

abdegmnprs

15. Gothic cursive, France, early 15c.

abdegmnprs

16. Littera bononiensis, Bologna, 14c.

abdegmnprs

17. Semigothic cursive, Italy, late 14c.

abdegmnprs

18. Littera hybrida, Low Countries, mid 15c.

abdegmnprs

19. Littera antiqua, Italy, mid 15c.

abdegmnpr

20. Humanistic cursive, Italy, late 15c.

abdegmnprs

The development of medieval **handwriting** from Roman capitals to Renaissance cursive.

Handwriting Most surviving examples of late antique and medieval handwriting were written by expert scribes trained to write either books or documents, and sometimes both. In the set scripts used in books each separate letter was formed from several distinct strokes of the pen, while letters in the cursive documentary scripts were formed by fewer strokes and could be joined to each other in various ways. The former were designed primarily for legibility, the latter for speed as well as legibility. Different grades of both literary and documentary handwriting were used in all periods: a psalter would be more formally written than scholia in the margins of a classical text, a papal bull or royal letters patent more decoratively than a notarial register or private letter. Examples of writing by inexpert writers, some of whom were authors, are rare before the 15th c., when the ability to write was beginning to be taken for granted. Besides one or more grades and even styles of writing, a scribe's training included systems of punctuation and abbreviation, both of which, like scripts themselves, varied considerably between periods and areas.

The overall development of handwriting in Western Europe was largely determined by four factors. Set scripts could evolve into cursive scripts through changes in the ductus of letters (i.e., in the number, order and direction of their constituent strokes); hence the gradual evolution in the Roman period of set, majuscule AEBDGP into cursive, minuscule *aebdgp*. In reverse, the rapid ductus of a cursive, documentary script could be elaborated to create a new set script suitable for books. Once a new script had achieved a canonical style, further gradual and unnecessary development almost always compromised its quality, and sometimes even its legibility. Finally, a superannuated script could be deliberately replaced by a more or less revised version of some more suitable and attractive earlier script. One or more of these factors were at work in each of the six main phases of the development of handwriting in Western Europe after *c.* 400.

In the late antique phase (5th – 6th c.) major classical texts such as Virgil could still be written in rustic capital (1), the original Roman book script; but most pagan and Christian texts were in uncial (2), a simpler but still formal script derived from early Roman cursive. Half-uncial (4), a new script based on contemporary cursive, rivalled uncial in the 6th c.; scholarly marginalia in professionally written books are in an unpretentious literary cursive. The later Roman cursive (3) of official and notarial documents, a somewhat decorative script, had reached maturity by *c.* 350. Standards were high and the script system was diverse enough to meet all the needs of a highly literate society. The half-uncial and cursive alphabets are easily recognizable as the ancestors of all subsequent European scripts. In the East, texts of Roman law were written in regional versions of uncial and half-uncial.

During the Precaroline phase (7th – 8th c.), uncial was still widely used for biblical and liturgical texts, and the elaborate Roman variety was skilfully imitated in several Anglo-Saxon centres; but other texts were mostly in various Precaroline minuscules, based on regional types of documentary script descended from later Roman cursive. These included Visigothic minuscule in Spain and Beneventan minuscule in southern Italy, which survived into the 12th c. and 13th c. respectively. In France local types evolved in monastic or cathedral scriptoria such as Luxeuil (5), Corbie and Laon. The Insular scripts, which the Irish taught to the Anglo-Saxons (7th c.) and which spread to certain Continental scriptoria (especially those of the Anglo-Saxon and Irish missions in Germany), seem to have descended from handwriting in sub-Roman Britain (5th c.). The system, which included several grades of minuscule (6) and a half-uncial (7), owed nothing to contemporary Continental script; but the Anglo-Saxons elaborated it under the influence of late antique book script, which they knew from older books imported from Italy. For vernacular texts, Irish minuscule lasted into the 9th c. and Anglo-Saxon minuscule into the 12th c.

The crucial Caroline phase (late 8th–12th c.) began with new, experimental book scripts in several scriptoria influenced by Charlemagne's cultural *renovatio*: some were straightforward simplifications of Precaroline minuscule, while others depended heavily on Roman half-uncial. Canonical Caroline minuscule (8), which emerged *c.* 800 in Charlemagne's palace scriptorium and at Saint-Martin-de-Tours, owed something to both tendencies. The new script became almost universal on the Continent by *c.* 850 and dominated south Germany and central Italy (9) until the late 12th c.

The Protogothic phase (late 11th – late 12th c.) originated in England and in parts of northern France influenced by the version of Caroline minuscule, incorporating features of contemporary Anglo-Saxon minuscule, that had been adopted in English scriptoria *c.* 950 for texts in Latin (10). Protogothic minuscule (11) soon replaced Caroline as the book script of the Low Countries, north Germany, Scandinavia and Spain. Between *c.* 875 and *c.* 1125 Precaroline documentary script had been replaced in most areas by Caroline or Protogothic documentary scripts, which, however, often retained the decorative quality of their predecessors.

During the Gothic phase (late 11th – early 16th c.) several types of heavier, more compressed minuscule (*textura*) were used for all literary purposes, from liturgical (12) to university (13) and vernacular texts; after the 14th c., the higher grades survived only for biblical and liturgical texts, while the lower were replaced by grades of Gothic cursive book hand. Some English royal writs were already in semi-cursive script by *c.* 1150, and by *c.* 1230 fully developed Gothic *cursiva anglicana* (14) was the norm for all public and private documents and records in England. Similar documentary cursive was in use throughout Europe by *c.* 1250, and most of its earlier, regional types were abandoned, *c.* 1375–1425, in favour of an elegant type which had been perfected in the French royal chancery by *c.* 1350 (15); the English 16th-c. secretary and court hands descended from this and from *anglicana* respectively.

In Italy, with Protogothic script confined to zones of French influence in the extreme north and south, Caroline minuscule gave way *c.* 1200 to Gothic book hands, including the *litera rotunda* typical of liturgical books and the *litera bonomiensis* (16) of legal text-books, both introduced by university scribes at Bologna. Also of Bolognese origin was the Gothic notarial cursive, while the Gothic mercantile cursive was of Tuscan origin. Petrarch (d. 1374) wrote a group of Semigothic scripts which set a fashion and included grades of cursive widely used by notaries and some humanists (17) in the 15th c. The *litera hybrida* (18), written after *c.* 1425 in the Low Countries and north Germany, was based on the Semigothic script of papal briefs.

The final, humanistic phase began in Florence (*c.* 1400) when Poggio Bracciolini launched *litera antiqua* (19), a revised version of the Caroline minuscule of 12th-c. Tuscany. Niccolò Niccoli crossed it with his own mercantile cursive (*c.* 1420) to produce the quicker, more economical humanistic cursive which is the direct ancestor of all modern European handwriting. Both scripts were designed for the transmission of classical texts, but by *c.* 1460 the cursive (20) had been adopted for papal briefs and for diplomatic correspondence. Roman and Italic type were based on *antiqua* (*c.* 1460) and the cursive (*c.* 1500) respectively. In Italy *c.* 1500 liturgical books and business correspondence were still in Gothic scripts, and notarial documents largely in Semigothic, but the triumph of the humanistic scripts and type faces was assured. Elsewhere in Europe Gothic script survived into the 18th c., and in Germany until 1945. See MANUSCRIPT STUDIES TJB

□ E. M. Thompson *An Introduction to Greek and Latin Paleography* (1912); E. A. Lowe *Codices Latini Antiquiores* (1934–71); B. Bischoff, G. I. Lieftinck and G. Battelli *Nomenclature des écritures livresques* (1954); B. Bischoff *Paläographie des Römischen Altertums und des Abendländischen Mittelalters* (1979)

Hanseatic merchants, probably in the harbour at Lübeck, *c.*1497.

Hanseatic League Federation of north German towns formed to protect mutual trading interests. German coastal expansion eastwards in the 12th c. and 13th c. enabled German merchants to establish a monopoly over Baltic trade, centred on the island of Gotland, which dealt in fur, wax and luxury goods from the Orient. This helped to stimulate older trading links with England and Flanders. Cologne also became an important trading centre. Towns negotiated small-scale agreements, such as the 1241 alliance between Hamburg and Lübeck or the Wendish League of 1264, which coalesced into a more powerful union in 1356, when the towns of the Hanse met together to resolve common trading difficulties in Flanders. The Hanse reached its peak in the late 14th c., with 70–80 members and a lucrative network of trading routes hingeing on the *Kontors* (counting houses) in London, Novgorod, Bergen and Bruges. It consolidated its dominant position in the Baltic by emerging victorious from nine years of conflict with Waldemar IV of Denmark in 1370. Lübeck took the lead in Hanseatic affairs, generally summoning the *Hansetag* or diet, and using its seal on behalf of the Hanse. The Hanseatic League began to decline during the 15th c., challenged in the Baltic by the increased activity of non-Hanseatic merchants and threatened by the growing power of territorial rulers. [*101*]

□ P. Dollinger *The German Hanse* (1970)

Harald I Fairhair King of Norway *c.* 870–945 (b. *c.*860) A figure as great in legend as in history, Harald is rightly seen as the true founder of the Yngling dynasty. He drew the greater part of Norway under his control and all of it under his influence. The decisive battle was fought at Hafrsfjord, dated no later than 900, and probably not before 885. It was a sea battle and Harald's authority in his prime was essentially that of a sea king, imposing discipline on Viking crews and sea routes. He was active also in Orkney and Shetland, and later Scandinavian opinion ascribed much of the Viking turbulence of the late 9th c. to the dissatisfaction of a young aristocracy of sea-captains, against the centralizing and authoritarian rule of King Harald.

He had a long life and many sons, among whom Haakon the Good, foster-son of King Athelstan, and Eric Bloodaxe (d. 954) were prominent in British affairs.

Harald III Hardrada King of Norway 1047–66 (b. 1015) One of the most glamorous of 11th-c. figures, taken by many to be the last of the true Viking chieftains. Harald was wounded at the battle of Stiklestad (1030) in which his half-brother St Olaf was killed. He escaped into Russian territory, served in the Varangian guard at Constantinople, and returned to contend successfully for the Norwegian throne, where his strong rule earned him the sobriquet *Hardrada*, or 'hard counsel'. He made his bid for the kingdom of England in 1066, won initial victories against the English earls and captured York; but was taken by surprise, routed and killed by Harold II Godwinson at the battle of Stamford Bridge, not far from York, on 25 September 1066.

Harding, St Stephen (d. 1134) Abbot of Cîteaux. A student, and perhaps also a monk, at Sherborne, he left the abbey to travel to France and Italy, eventually joining the Benedictine monastery of Molesme. In 1098 he supported St Robert of Molesme in founding an ascetic community at Cîteaux, where he became the third abbot in 1109. Harding was a major influence in the development of Cistercian ideals and organization; indeed, it is probable that he wrote the first draft of the Cistercian Rule, the *Carta Caritatis*, which sought to safeguard ascetic standards by the provision of a juridical framework.

Harold II Godwinson King of England 1066 (b. *c.* 1022) Earl of Wessex (1053–66) under Edward the Confessor and the strongest man in the country, Harold was elected king in the first week of January 1066 on Edward's death. He was a man of considerable talent and sophistication, and the little available

evidence suggests that he won general acceptance within the kingdom and had the makings of a good ruler. Harold won a great victory against the Norwegian king, Harald Hardrada, at Stamford Bridge on 25 September 1066, but was defeated and killed by William, duke of Normandy, at Battle, near Hastings, on 14 October 1066. Legends concerning his survival testify to his popularity.
□ H. R. Loyn *Harold Godwinson* (1966)

Hārūn ar-Rashīd Caliph 786–809 (b. 766) Fifth 'Abbāsid caliph. His reign marked the turning point in the fortunes of the 'Abbāsids as they wound towards decline and political disintegration. Hārūn nominally led two expeditions against the Byzantines 779–80 and 781–82; the latter brought the 'Abbāsid army to the shores of the Bosphorus for the first and last time, and won Hārūn high office and nomination to the throne. Although the *Arabian Nights* portrays his reign as a 'golden age', Hārūn faced a long series of political upsets in both East and West. His sponsorship of *Jihād* (holy war against the infidel), coupled with the destruction of churches along the Muslim–Byzantine frontier and his tough approach to the status of the subject peoples, probably reflect his need to please public opinion. However, despite constant campaigning and the construction of a Mediterranean fleet which attacked Cyprus in 805 and Rhodes in 807, the frontiers were practically unchanged at the end of Hārūn's reign. An exchange of embassies between Hārūn and Charlemagne allegedly took place, giving Charlemagne rights of protection over Jerusalem, but no mention of this has been found in Arabic sources. At his death Hārūn left conflicting historical reports of his reign and character.

The death of King **Harold** at the battle of **Hastings**, from the Bayeux tapestry.

Hasan ibn Sabbah (d. 1124) Leader of the Nizārīs, a heterodox Islamic sect, Hasan was an ascetic puritan: both his sons died by his hand, one for an alleged murder, the other for dissolute behaviour. He has been credited with the organization and training of the Assassins. In 1090 he captured the fortress of Alamut aided by converts within. This was the start of a general rising against Seljuk power, marked by the assassination of key opponents and seizure of fortresses. The last major Seljuk attack on Alamut was in 1118. The remaining years of Hasan's life were spent in relative peace, consolidating Nizārī gains.
□ M. G. S. Hodgson *The Order of Assassins* (1955)

Hastings, battle of (14 October 1066) Decisive battle which resulted in the conquest of England by Duke William of Normandy, who claimed, by right of designation, to be the lawful successor to King Edward the Confessor (1042–66). The engagement was fought at a site henceforward known as Battle, some seven miles from Hastings, and is well recorded visually in the Bayeux tapestry. Harold II of England, fresh from his victory at Stamford Bridge, fought valiantly, and was well supported by seasoned troops equipped for the familiar infantry tactics of the North, armed with swords and battle-axes and drawn up in an impressive shield-wall. William opposed him with forces relying heavily on cavalry, and it was the strength of the cavalry arm, helped by the archers, that clearly won the day for the Normans, giving them extra mobility and flexibility in tactics. It has been estimated that 6000–7000 troops took part on either side.
□ R. A. Brown, 'The Battle of Hastings', *Proceedings of the Battle Conference 1980* (1981)

Hawkwood, Sir John (*c.* 1320–94) One of the great foreign *condottieri* who played an important role in the military life of the Italian peninsula in the late Middle Ages. The son of an Essex tanner, Hawkwood began his military career in France as leader of a group of mercenaries called the White Company (1359); this restless and ambitious group of soldiers gradually moved southward to Piedmont, and then Italy. In 1364 the Pisans chose him as commander-in-chief in the war against Florence. He worked in the service of the papacy and later for the Visconti family until 1377, when he agreed to fight for the Florentines, who granted him citizenship and tax exemption for life. At his death he was given a magnificent state funeral in Florence cathedral.
□ G. Tease *The Condottieri: Soldiers of Fortune* (1970)

Henry III King of Germany and Holy Roman Emperor 1039–56 (b. 1017) One of the strongest German rulers of the Middle Ages, Henry imposed internal peace and strengthened his position on the eastern frontier by defeating the Hungarians and subordinating the Bohemian duchy in the early years of his reign. He was a zealous supporter of church reform and used clerical orders, notably the Cluniacs, intensively in government and administration. In 1046 he intervened in the affairs of Rome to settle the scandalous situation which had arisen, whereby three men claimed to be pope. At the Synod of Sutri, held under his patronage, followed by a further Synod at Rome, the existing claimants were declared deposed and a German bishop elected as Clement II, who then crowned Henry Emperor on Christmas Day 1046. There followed a succession of German popes, culminating in the election of Henry's own cousin as the strong reformer, Leo IX (1049–54). In the light of the Investiture Contest which was to follow, it is often held as something of a paradox that German and imperial enterprise could have been so prominent in the creation of the reformed papacy, which was to prove its bitterest enemy in the succeeding generation. Henry's early death at the age of 39 and the succession of his young son Henry (aged only six or seven) left the German kingship weakened at a critical moment. *See* AGNES

Henry II Plantagenet King of England 1154–89 (b. 1133) Creator of the Angevin empire, son of Geoffrey Plantagenet, count of Anjou, and Matilda, daughter of Henry I and grand-daughter of the Conqueror. Henry II was of equal importance in the history of France as in the history of England. Recognized as duke of Normandy by 1150 (at the age of 17), and count of Anjou on the death of his father in the following year, he married Eleanor of Aquitaine in 1152, thus acquiring control of extensive territories in south-west France. King Stephen of England was forced to accept him as heir, and Henry succeeded to the English throne in 1154.

For the following 35 years this hot-tempered, able and energetic Angevin played a prominent and, at times, dominant part in European politics. The skill of the French kings, notably of Philip II Augustus after 1180, and the disloyalty and turbulence of Henry's sons ('From the devil they came, to the devil they will go') caused failure in the most ambitious of his Continental schemes; but even so he left a formidable inheritance to Richard Lionheart, and ultimately to his youngest and favourite son, John. In England he achieved great and permanent advance in the fields of finance, justice and administration. The country needed a period of peace and reconstruction after the disruption of King Stephen's days and Henry was the man to provide such a period.

His most enduring work was performed in the

legal sphere: royal courts became more efficient, new writs dealing with the possessory assizes helped to stabilize the landed position, and regular eyres on the part of royal justices in the shire courts made real the power of the common law of England. In financial affairs the continuous records of the Exchequer from 1155 testify to the sophisticated nature of English financial techniques. Henry had mixed success with the church. The translation of his able chancellor Thomas Becket to the archbishopric of Canterbury proved a personal disaster. Becket resisted Henry's reforms, was forced into exile, and on his return after partial reconciliation in late 1170, was martyred in his cathedral at Canterbury.

Henry also proved immensely important in wider British fields. Wales was kept relatively quiet and the Marcher lords, notably Richard Strongbow in Pembroke, busy and loyal. The capture of the king of Scotland during the unsuccessful rebellion of Henry's sons enabled him to assert English overlordship in the northern kingdom. Most significant of all, taking advantage of Strongbow's military successes in Ireland, Henry intervened personally, and ultimately established his son John as lord of Ireland. In the range of activities and degree of permanent success, Henry Plantagenet ranks high among all medieval European rulers. [122]   HRL
□ W. L. Warren *Henry II* (1973)

Henry V King of England 1413–22 (b. 1387) Taken by later generations as the archetypal medieval hero-king, Henry V is greater in legend than in history, although his achievements were considerable. Succeeding his father Henry IV (1400–13), he showed a combination of tolerance and ruthlessness that spoke well of his innate capacity as a medieval ruler. He was savage in suppressing Lollardy and rebellion, but did much to reconcile the factions that had

Stone effigies of **Henry the Lion** and his wife Matilda, from Brunswick cathedral, *c.*1240.

formed following the deposition of Richard II and the rebellion of the Percy family, with Welsh help, in the reign of his father. He is chiefly remembered, however, for his extraordinary success in inaugurating what was virtually a new phase in the Hundred Years' War. His spectacular triumph at Agincourt (1415) brought about near collapse of French resistance. Combining genuine piety with statesmanship, Henry made an accord with the Emperor Sigismund (1416), by which he nullified Genoese support for the French and helped to end the papal schism, through the election of Martin V in 1417. Through siege warfare Henry achieved a virtually complete conquest of Normandy by 1419, and an alliance with the Burgundians forced French agreement to the Treaty of Troyes (1420), whereby Henry was recognized as heir to the French throne, and married Catherine, daughter of the French king Charles VI. Henry died on campaign in France in August 1422, less than two months before the death of the French king. His early death, in his mid-thirties, condemned England to a long and difficult minority.
□ E. F. Jacob *Henry V and the Invasion of France* (1947)

Henry the Lion (1129–95) Duke of Saxony from 1142 and of Bavaria (1156–80), he was the outstanding representative of the great Guelph dynasty. Henry supported his cousin Frederick Barbarossa in his campaigns in Italy and against the Poles, but his failure to send reinforcements in 1176 led to imperial defeat at Legnano at the hands of the Lombard League. Henry's seizure of church lands gave Emperor Frederick opportunity for revenge, which he took, depriving Henry of both his duchies by judicial means in 1180. Having spent his exile in England at the court of his father-in-law Henry II, he made a turbulent return to Germany after 1190, but failed to restore his fortunes.

His principal contribution consisted in his initiation of a steady process of colonization to the east from his Saxon base, and also in the maintenance of internal peace in Germany when Barbarossa was busy with his imperial and Italian schemes. His overthrow in 1180 indicates the importance of the tie of feudal dependence on the king, and the division of his vast complex of lands foreshadows the emergence of a new class of imperial princes who were to be the ultimate beneficiaries of the failure of kings and emperors to impose unitary sovereign control on Germany in the later Middle Ages.
□ K. Jordan *Henry the Lion* (1986)

Henry the Navigator (1394-1460) Third son of John I of Portugal and Philippa, daughter of John of Gaunt. Henry accompanied his father in the capture

Heraldic devices are clearly displayed on these knights in combat from *Sir Thomas Holme's Book*, *c.*1443.

of the African city of Ceuta in 1415. This had been organized as part of the Reconquest of the Iberian peninsula. Henry continued this programme by sponsoring a series of voyages along the African coast to outflank the Moors and disrupt or seize the Arab gold trade. Progress was slow until Cape Bojador was passed in 1434. The Madeiras and Cape Verde Islands were populated, and sugar introduced into Europe in substantial quantities, as well as coarse peppers, with their preservative values. More important was Henry's settlement at Sagres, to which he attracted mathematicians, chartmakers, shipmasters and translators. This school utilized classical and Arabic learning and synthesized this knowledge with practical experience to produce the caravel type of vessel, particularly suited to long voyages, and astronomical and navigational instruments which were used with the first set of latitudinal tables. The spirit of achievement and competence fostered the self-confidence which provided the springboard for later European expansion.
□ C. R. Boxer *The Portuguese Seaborne Empire* (1969); J. Ure *Prince Henry the Navigator* (1977)

Henry of Langenstein (d. 1397) Theologian. An important apologist for the Conciliar movement whose *Concilium Pacis* (1381) proved influential at a critical time. It owed its influence in part to the relative simplicity of its argument, which stated that a general council was superior to the pope, that it was infallible and could be summoned by a secular ruler.

Henry of Susa (d. 1271) Cardinal of Ostia and canonist. Trained in Roman and canon law at Bologna, he also taught there, and later taught canon law at Paris. Innocent IV promoted him to the see of Sisteron (1244), to the archdiocese of Embrun (1250), and in the same year made him cardinal of Ostia and Velletri. His reputation as a canonist was well established even in his lifetime. His *Summa Aurea*, a collection of glosses and expositions on law composed 1250–61, earned him the title 'Lord of the law and most luminous interpreter of the Decretals'.
□ C. Lefebvre, 'Hostiensis', *Dictionnaire de droit canonique V* (1953)

Heraclius I Byzantine emperor 610–41 (b. *c.* 575) Son of Heraclius, exarch of Africa, in 610 he sailed to Constantinople, seized and executed the unpopular Emperor Phocas, and was proclaimed emperor himself. His reign was dominated by military conflict. In a series of four campaigns (622–28) he broke Persian power in Anatolia and Armenia, and precipitated the collapse of the Persian empire. He held at bay the Slavonic advances in the Balkans, but was powerless to halt the Arabs as they swept through Syria, Palestine and Egypt. Heraclius attempted to resolve the theological disputes within his empire by a series of compromises, but open condemnation of his policies by the papacy resulted in failure.

Heraldry In the sense of a science of armorial bearings, heraldry originated in Western Europe in the 12th c. and developed into a sophisticated intellectual and artistic discipline in the course of the two succeeding centuries. The placing of distinguishing marks on a warrior's shield or helmet was a custom of immemorial antiquity, but the growth of a systematic method of identifying noble kindreds in war or in peace was a characteristic of fully formed feudal society in the West, with its emphasis on hereditary right and hereditary succession to lands and authority. The cosmopolitan nature of the military aristocracy was emphasized by the general mobility characteristic of 12th-c. Europe, notably as a result of the crusading movement. The granting of arms, initially a matter for the feudal lord, rapidly became a royal prerogative, and to wear or use another's arms became tantamount to forgery. Heraldry applied to the church as well as to the lay nobility, and heraldic devices also came to be used by guilds and corporations in towns.

Variety was permissible in the early days, but by the 14th c. strict rules concerning usage became the custom throughout the Western world, enforceable through royal courts such as the Heralds' College in England, incorporated in 1483 by King Richard III. The language of heraldry was, and is basically French – an indication of the central position occupied by France and the Angevin empire in feudal society. The most elaborate vocabulary concerned the blazoning of the shield, its colours (tinctures), divisions (ordinaries), common charges (beasts, trees, plants, often with a punning reference to a family name – ferns for Verney, for example), and the way in which it is 'differenced' in favour of younger sons or collateral branches. Similar complicated rules and terms apply to helmets and to 'supporters', that is, symbols of men or creatures used in cases of high honour, to stand in support of the shield (e.g., the lion and the unicorn).

Heraldry and the role of the herald were closely associated with concepts of nobility, gentility and chivalry, which reached their point of clearest expression in 13th-c. and 14th-c. Europe by the creation of institutions such as the Order of the Garter by Edward III of England (1348). HRL
□ A. R. Wagner *Heralds and Heraldry in the Middle Ages* (1956); *Boutell's 'Manual of Heraldry'* ed. J. P. Brooke-Little (1973); A. R. Wagner *Heralds and Ancestors* (1978)

Herbals Some of the most beautiful manuscripts to survive from the Middle Ages are illustrated herbals that treat the properties of herbs (i.e., useful plants, largely used for medicinal purposes). Information, and also much legendary material about plants such as the mandrake, is derived from classical sources, especially from the work in the first century AD of Pliny and his contemporary Dioscorides, and from the 4th-c. writer Apuleius Platonicus. Great claims were made for even the humblest of plants.
□ W. Blunt and S. Raphael *The Illustrated Herbal* (1979)

Heresy Attitudes to heresy, as indeed to the strict interpretation of orthodoxy, varied from age to age within the Christian church. In the early centuries theological disputes, which sometimes marked profound racial and social differences, mostly centred around the nature of the Trinity, and more specifically, around the nature of the second person of the Trinity. These disputations continued to vex the Eastern Orthodox church, but the Western church on the whole accepted the orthodox Nicene Creed and was largely free from major splits on heresy from the Council of Chalcedon (451) up until the 12th c.

The first heretics to be burned in the medieval West were some fifteen clerks and nuns caught in a palace intrigue at Orleans in 1022, and the members of a religious community found near Turin in 1028,

Herbals often provided precise botanical detail; this Byzantine example depicts agrimony (6th c.).

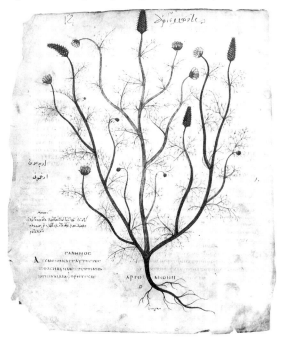

Ty connence le trere suue du toy phe stau bome
De serese des amortes qui su estampte z punme.
ntellui temps flouissort a
parte philosophie z toute
dergue z y estort lestud des
sept ars siouant z enssi qui
autoute que on ne tirroue
pas qui seust onerques st

Burning **heretics** during the reign of Philip Augustus; from a miniature by Jean Fouquet.

whose devotion to the Holy Spirit led them to maintain a constant chain of prayer, and not to eat meat or to sleep with their wives. The rapid spread of anti-clerical preaching during the 12th c. was accompanied by a sharpening of the definition of orthodox belief, and a hardening of attitudes towards the unorthodox. In 1184 the bull *Ab Abolendam* was issued in an attempt to impose uniformity and orthodoxy; it required bishops to make an annual search (*inquisitio*) of their diocese and to excommunicate both heretics and officials who failed to act against them. After the Fourth Lateran Council such measures were incorporated into secular law, including that of the Empire (1220), Aragon (1223) and France (1226). From 1231 inquisitors acting directly under papal authority were active in the Languedoc and Italian cities; they were authorized to use torture in 1252, and extended their activity through most of Continental Europe in the following centuries.

Warned by St Paul that 'in the last times some shall depart from the faith . . . forbidding to marry, and the eating of meat', bishops were quick to interpret manifestations of lay spiritual enthusiasm as revivals of the ancient heresies of Mani and Arius, and to associate them, with or without evidence, with the denial of the sacraments and the orgiastic behaviour regularly attributed to heretics (from the clerks of Orleans to the largely mythical Brethren of the Free Spirit of the 14th c.). This helped to create a

stereotype for the later witch craze. At Cologne in 1143 two sects were discovered in public dispute. They shared an ascetic spirituality and hostility to the ecclesiastical hierarchy, but members of one claimed Apostolic authority for their own hierarchy. They turned out to be converts of the Bulgarian Bogomils, whose influence spread in the next four decades through the Low Countries and the Languedoc to Lombardy, creating the Cathar churches whose distinctive dualist theology (i.e., one founded on the conviction of the essential evil of all created things) was reinforced by direct contact with the Bogomil churches of the Byzantine world.

The sophisticated teachings, ritual and organization of the Cathars, and the influence which humility and personal austerity brought their male and female missionaries, made them the principal object of the Albigensian Crusade and of subsequent persecution. But the native tradition was more ancient and more enduring. The call to Apostolic poverty and the simplicity of the primitive church was no less potent in the mouths of heretical preachers like Tanchelm in Flanders or Peter of Bruys in Provence (early 12th c.), than they had been in those of the prophets of monastic and papal reform in the 11th c. Henry of Lausanne (*fl. c.* 1116–45) could fashion resistance to the expanding mediatory role of the clergy, especially in baptism, marriage, confession and death, into a coherent creed which commanded widespread and, for a time, tenacious support in the Languedoc. Whether less fundamentally anti-sacerdotal enthusiasm led to heresy was largely a matter of chance and of the sensitivity of authority. The Waldensians, founded *c.* 1176 by a Lyonnais merchant to resist the spread of Catharism, were driven into heresy by insistence on episcopal control of their preaching, and under the force of persecution became increasingly radical and bitterly anti-papal in their doctrines; the Lombard Humiliati, very similar in their beliefs and demeanour, were anathematized with them and others in 1184, but reinstated as a religious order by Innocent III, gaining many converts in the very cities where the Cathars were most active.

Popular heresy did not owe its currency to external contamination from antiquity or the Orient, nor to its appeal to the interests of any particular social class. Doctrinally, its most consistent tendency, most completely expressed by John Wycliffe, was to resist the elaboration of teaching and ritual, the elevation of priesthood over laity, and the secular power of the church. Socially, too, heresy and orthodoxy were inseparable; each defined the other. As a strong tendency to insist on spiritual and economic brotherhood implies, heresy was often embraced by those who suffered from social change. Cloth-workers in 11th-c. Arras or nobles in 13th-c.

Florence might both see worldly corruption made manifest in the growing power of merchants, who were themselves more likely to advertise their rising status by conspicuous piety than to jeopardize it by dabbling in heresy. Conversely, accusations of heresy were less likely to be effective in checking the progress of such groups – though it was tried, notoriously against the Maurand family of Toulouse – than in warding off the resentment of their rivals and victims.

The most stubborn heresies often defended tradition, against the sacralization of marriage in the 12th c. or the institutionalization of the spirit of St Francis in the 13th c. But however conservative their inspiration, by the very act of expressing it heretical preachers made a bid for popular endorsement against the established order, and by the austerity of their lives as well as the eloquence of their words, offered their followers an alternative focus of loyalty and solidarity. None challenged that order more radically than Arnold of Brescia, whose followers seized control of Rome from the pope in the 1140s, or John Hus, who gave his name to the bloodiest wars of the later Middle Ages. Neither was guilty of doctrinal error. [*332*] RIM

□ G. Leff *Heresy in the Later Middle Ages* (1967); M. D. Lambert *Medieval Heresy* (1977); R. I. Moore *The Origins of European Dissent* (1977); E. Peters *Heresy and Authority in Medieval Europe* (1980)

Herman Billung (d. 973) An active military commander of the Saxons in their campaigns against the Slavs, Billung proved himself a loyal servant of King Otto I when the king was busy in wider German and Italian (ultimately imperial) schemes. Within Saxony he had exercised many of the ducal functions from early in the reign, and the gradual recognition of his position as duke within Saxony marks an important phase in the royal attitude towards the subordination of the ducal office. Billung's mastery of the military situation on the eastern border, and the part he played in stabilizing the pattern of March lands against the Slavs, ensured the perpetuation of his kindred as defenders of the German frontier.

□ K. Leyser *Rule and Conflict in an Early Medieval Society* (1979)

Herman of Salza (d. 1239) Virtual creator of the effective and formidable German crusading order, the Teutonic Order, Herman was active in two principal spheres. As a traditional crusader with the Emperor Frederick II, he took part in the negotiated recovery of Jerusalem in 1228, and began the building of the great castle of Montfort. He was also responsible from 1211 onwards for a policy of forced conversion to Christianity on the eastern frontier of Germany, ultimately canalizing efforts, in collaboration with the Poles, against the still pagan Prussians. Intense German colonization, which accompanied his conquests, resulted in the foundation of the historic German-dominated Prussian principality.

□ E. Christiansen *The Northern Crusades* (1980)

Hildebrand *See* **Gregory VII**

Hildegard of Bingen, St (1098–1179) Abbess of the Benedictine house of Rupertsberg near Bingen from 1136, Hildegard proved highly influential at a personal level with some of the leading figures of the age, notably St Bernard of Clairvaux and Frederick Barbarossa. She was learned in the medical arts, but was also a powerful visionary (suffering apparently from some form of epilepsy), and her tract, the *Scivias*, written in the 1140s, contains much that is apocalyptic in its denunciation of vice. The work of her old age, the *Liber de Operatione Dei*, attempts a subtle and ingenious resolution of the spiritual and the physiological, in order to explain the inner motives of men, the drive to the sexual and sensuous, and the associated periods of repentance.

□ B. Newman *Sister of Wisdom* (1987)

St Hildegard, 'Sybil of the Rhine', dictates her prophecies to Volmer, her secretary (*c.*1141-51).

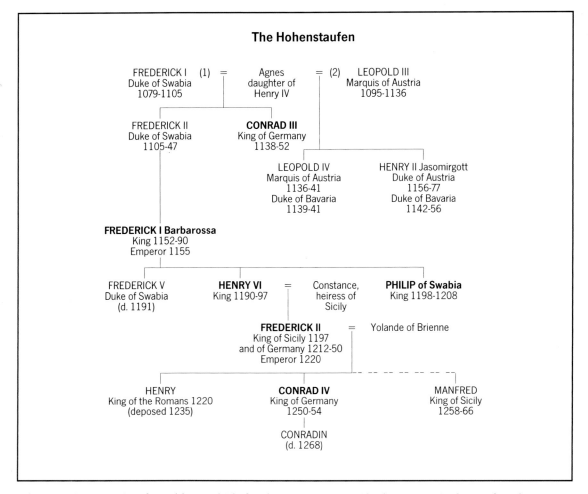

The Hohenstaufen

FREDERICK I (1) = Agnes = (2) LEOPOLD III
Duke of Swabia daughter of Marquis of Austria
1079-1105 Henry IV 1095-1136

FREDERICK II **CONRAD III**
Duke of Swabia King of Germany
1105-47 1138-52

LEOPOLD IV HENRY II Jasomirgott
Marquis of Austria Duke of Austria
1136-41 1156-77
Duke of Bavaria Duke of Bavaria
1139-41 1142-56

FREDERICK I Barbarossa
King 1152-90
Emperor 1155

FREDERICK V **HENRY VI** = Constance, **PHILIP of Swabia**
Duke of Swabia King 1190-97 heiress of King 1198-1208
(d. 1191) Sicily

FREDERICK II = Yolande of Brienne
King of Sicily 1197
and of Germany 1212-50
Emperor 1220

HENRY **CONRAD IV** MANFRED
King of the Romans 1220 King of Germany King of Sicily
(deposed 1235) 1250-54 1258-66

CONRADIN
(d. 1268)

Hincmar (*c.* 805–82) Of a noble Frankish family, Hincmar was a child-oblate to Saint-Denis. Well educated under Abbot Hilduin, Hincmar joined Louis the Pious' palace clergy. After Louis's death (840), he entered the service of Charles the Bald, and in 845 was appointed archbishop of Rheims, the most important metropolitan see in the West Frankish kingdom. His priority was the resumption of Rheims' lands lost during a preceding ten-year vacancy, and the assertion of metropolitan authority. His wider aim was the maintenance of social order through the church's pastoral functions and the preaching of individual moral responsibility against advocates of predestination. The help of a strong kingship was necessary to realise Hincmar's aims; he consistently supported Charles by the military service of his church vassals and money raised from church lands. In the first half of Charles' reign he was often a favoured counsellor, managing assemblies and recording their proceedings. He produced appropriate canonical arguments when Charles wished to block his nephew Lothar II's divorce.

Later Charles increasingly preferred younger counsellors. With Charles' successors after 877, Hincmar partially recovered his influence, but their weakness undermined his political strategy. In ecclesiastical politics too, Hincmar needed royal help to succeed. One suffragan deposed by Hincmar was reinstated by Pope Nicholas I with Charles' connivance; another appealed to Rome in vain because Charles also sought his downfall. Hincmar wrote in many genres: a polyptych, a Life of St Remigius and episcopal statutes, reflecting his care for Rheims' property and its clergy's conduct; numerous theological works and contributions to the theory of Christian marriage; several treatises on kingship and royal consecration rites. His many letters, and his continuation of the *Annals of St Bertin* (covering 861–82), are invaluable historical documents. He died while fleeing from a Viking attack on Rheims.

□ J. Devisse *Hincmar, Archevêque de Reims 845–882* (1975–76); *Charles the Bald: Court and Kingdom* ed. M. Gibson and J. Nelson (1981)

Hohenstaufen dynasty The greatest of the German ruling families of the Middle Ages, the Hohenstaufen originated in Swabia, where they at one stage held the rank of counts of Waiblingen (Italian form, 'Ghibelline'). They came to prominence in the late 11th c. as the leading lay supporters of King Henry IV, and the head of the family, Frederick I, married the king's daughter Agnes (1079) and ultimately succeeded to the duchy of Swabia. In 1138 Conrad of Hohenstaufen was elected as Emperor Conrad III (1138–52). From 1138 to 1254 the Hohenstaufen played an important and often dominant role in European politics. In succession the imperial title passed to Conrad's nephew Frederick Barbarossa (1152–89), and then to Frederick's direct male descendants, his son Henry VI the Severe (1190–97), his grandson Frederick II (1212–50) and great-grandson Conrad IV (1250–54). The great poetic works elaborated by German poets of the early 13th c. at the court of Philip of Swabia (younger brother of Henry VI), helped to keep the Hohenstaufen legends alive. The death of Manfred, illegitimate son of Frederick II, in 1266, and the tragic murder of Conradin, son of Conrad and last of the line, by Charles of Anjou in 1268, perpetuated these legends.

Crusaders and powerful rulers, they failed for a variety of complex reasons to build permanent institutions of government in Germany and in Italy, but left behind the flavour of failure in great though perhaps impossible causes that was to haunt German historiography for many generations.
□ K. Hampe *Germany under the Salian and Hohenstaufen Emperors* (1973)

Hohenzollern dynasty Although known as a noble family from the 10th c., and prominent from time to time in the affairs of their native Swabia and Franconia, and (from the late 12th c.) in Nuremberg, the Hohenzollern did not emerge into the top rank of German princely families until the later Middle Ages. In 1415 Frederick, burgrave of Nuremberg, became margrave of Brandenburg and an elector of the Empire. Their movements thereafter were closely linked with affairs in Prussia and with maintenance of the general German position in north-east Germany and the Baltic lands.
□ R. Schneider *Die Hohenzollern* (1953)

Holy Grail One of the most potent symbols of medieval legend, the Grail makes its first appearance in Chrétien de Troyes's *Perceval* (c. 1180), where it is described as a jewel-encrusted serving dish. It has been linked with the *dysgyl* or 'dish of plenty' of Welsh legend. It rapidly came to be identified with the chalice of the Last Supper which had passed into the possession of Joseph of Arimathea. The quest for

15th-c. French manuscript showing Perceval, Galahad and Bors achieving the **Holy Grail**.

the Grail in medieval literature becomes synonymous with the knight's search for perfection, and its development through Robert de Boron's *Estoire dou Graal* (c. 1200), and eventually to Malory's *Morte Darthur* (1469–70), shows the progressive spiritualization of secular romance. Knights who strove for perfection – Percival, Galahad, Lancelot – were associated with the search for the Grail, which, in the hands of the poets, became the symbol for inner soul-searching. [37]
□ *La Queste del Saint Graal* ed. A. Pauphilet (1949); J. Marx *La Légende Arthurienne et le Graal* (1952)

Hrabanus Maurus (c. 780–856) *Preceptor Germaniae*, he was educated at Fulda and later studied at Tours

Hrabanus Maurus kneels before his patron; from a 9th-c. Carolingian manuscript.

under Alcuin. He returned to Fulda and became master of the school there, building it into one of the most influential centres of learning in Europe. He served as abbot of Fulda for 20 years, resigning in 842, and then became archbishop of Mainz in 847. His scholarly works, such as the *De Clericorum Institutione*, do not show philosophical or theological originality, but their depth of learning earned their author widespread respect.

□ E. F. Duckett *Carolingian Portraits* (1964)

Hugh the Great, St (1023–1109) Abbot of Cluny from 1049. A noble of Semur-en-Brionnais, he was renowned for his exemplary life. Gifted as a statesman and close to the French king, emperor and pope, Hugh did much to promote and enrich the Cluniac Order, elevating the position of Cluny's abbot and extending its power over satellite houses. Under Hugh a new principle of monasticism emerged – an independent Order under a monarchical head. He extended the Order to Italy, England and Spain, as well as encompassing France; he was a patron of the arts and a great builder (Vézelay, Moissac and the outstanding basilica of Cluny itself, begun in 1088). Participating in the ideals of Gregorian reform, Cluny grew and became a valuable instrument of the papacy; in 1088 it was placed under sole papal jurisdiction by Urban II, increasing abbatial autonomy. Hugh's Cluny was in many respects the spiritual centre of Europe, but his protracted personal dominance entailed problems. The vast and unwieldy Order lacked constitutional structure, depending entirely upon the abbot. By Hugh's death the dangers of such a situation were apparent, and had begun plaguing the abbacies of his less competent successors.

□ N. Hunt *Cluny under St Hugh* (1967); H. E. J. Cowdrey *The Cluniacs and the Gregorian Reform* (1970)

Hugh Capet King of France 987–96 (b. 941) His sobriquet (Latin *capa*, cape or cope) gave the title to the dynasty which he founded. Son of Hugh the Great, he succeeded his father as duke of the Franks in 956. Initially loyal to the Carolingian king Lothar (d. 986), against Otto II (978–80), he distanced himself from the monarch under the influence of Archbishop Adalberon of Rheims. On the death of Lothar's successor Louis V (987) he claimed the throne by election with the support of the archbishop, while the claims of the hereditary heir, Charles of Lower Lorraine, were by-passed. By crowning his son during his own lifetime Hugh eased his future passage to the throne. *See* CAPETIAN DYNASTY

Hugh of Orleans (Hugh Primas) (1093–1160) Satirist who criticized the church and existing institutions in Latin verse of a high order. Hugh also showed a more positive side to his poetic nature in his work on love, wine and the pleasures of the flesh. He was steeped in classical learning and yet achieved an originality that gained him the title of *primas* ('the first') among contemporaries. His main field of operation was the north of France: Paris, where he studied, Orleans, where he lived for substantial periods, and also Amiens and Rheims. He had great impact on succeeding generations, notably on the Goliardic poets.

□ F. J. E. Raby *A History of Secular Latin Poetry in the Middle Ages* (1967)

Hugh of Saint-Victor (*c*.1096–1141) French scholar and mystical theologian. With Richard of Saint-Victor (d. 1173), the most prominent of the Victorines. Under Canon Hugh the abbey of Saint-Victor, Paris (founded 1108), rose to prominence, becoming one of France's most important intellec-

Hugh of Saint-Victor lecturing to fellow Victorines; from an early 13th-c. English manuscript.

tual centres. During the 12th c. the School of Saint-Victor and the Cistercian abbeys became the major centres of mysticism, in response to the growth of reason and dialectics, which did not preclude reason but attempted to harness it for the purposes of faith, incorporating reason into a process which transcended it.

Hugh fashioned a rationale of mysticism in which personal experience was considered the highest form of knowledge, and all that was open to experience was germane to the knowledge of God through contemplation. His works include the *Didascalion* (a guide to knowledge which provided the essentials for a liberal education, the seven liberal arts and theology), the *Summa Sententiarum* and the *De Sacramentis* (which provided an impetus towards systematization, built upon in the 13th c.).
□ G. Leff *Medieval Thought* (1958); F. Copleston *A History of Philosophy* (1963)

Humbert of Silva Candida (*c.*1000–61) Born in Lorraine, he achieved great influence as papal secretary and was made cardinal of Silva-Candida by Pope Leo IX. A friend and adviser of Leo IX, Stephen IX and Hildebrand (the future Gregory VII), Humbert was the most extreme exponent of papal reform and of the supremacy of Rome. An abrasive character, he fostered the vituperative tone of papal attacks on abuse (aimed at the Western empire and Eastern church). He particularly condemned simony (buying and selling of ecclesiastical offices and spiritual benefits), viewing it as heresy in his *Adversus Simoniacos*. As legate to Constantinople (1054), sent to uphold Roman supremacy and to correct Greek usages, he seriously mishandled the situation, excommunicating the Patriarch Cerularius and being anathematized in return. The year 1054 is often taken to mark the final breach between Rome and the East, but the incident would not have compromised the papacy had Humbert not retained influence and inflated the matter. Gradually, recognition of a state of schism grew, and by the 14th c. the Greeks saw 1054 as the decisive year of origin for the break.
□ J. B. Russel *Dissent and Reform in the Early Middle Ages* (1965); J. C. S. Runciman *The Eastern Schism* (1971)

Humiliati A product of the vigorous 12th-c. religious ferment, the Humiliati began in Lombardy, drawing on a strong noble and patrician constituency. They lived as devout laymen and women or in double convents, and were distinguished by their penitential austerity, communal poverty and work amongst the sick, lepers and indigent poor. Although orthodox in intention, they were forbidden

to preach by the Third Lateran Council (1179) and even excommunicated by the indiscriminate decree, *Ad Abolendam*, of Lucius III (1184). Their similarities to the heretical Patarines and Cathars were overcome by Innocent III's enlightened policy of distinguishing between dissenting movements and heretical sects. He reorganized the Humiliati into a three-order institute, with canons and sisters in double monasteries, celibate laity and finally, married laity as secular tertiaries. (This last tier withdrew in 1272.) The order of seculars received the remarkable privilege of being permitted to preach, provided they confined their sermons to exhortations to the Christian life, eschewing theology. The contemporary prelate and bishop Jacques de Vitry was a great admirer of the Humiliati, stating that they alone were keeping heresy at bay in Milan. In the 15th c. their numbers declined, and in 1571 Pius V suppressed the male branch.
□ B. Bolton *The Medieval Reformation* (1983)

Humphrey, duke of Gloucester (1390–1447) The younger of the surviving uncles of the infant Henry VI, Humphrey acted as defender and protector of his nephew in England during the absence overseas of the elder uncle John, duke of Bedford. Relations with the king's council were often difficult and his own position called into account, particularly after the coronation of Henry (just under the age of eight) in 1429. Gloucester's ambitions in the Low Countries led to tensions with Burgundy, and many contemporaries blamed him for the declining fortunes of England in the 1430s and -40s. He ended his days in political disgrace, dying immediately after his arrest at Bury St Edmunds in 1447. He was a great patron of the arts and learning, especially connected with the abbey of St Albans and with Oxford, to which he bequeathed a fine collection of books which ultimately formed part of the Bodleian Library.
□ R. Griffiths *Henry VI* (1981)

Hundred Rolls A product of an extensive survey ordered by Edward I (1272–1307) in 1274. The inquiry investigated primarily encroachments on royal rights, but also extended to cover the activities of local officials from sheriffs to castle constables. Information was collected by questioning local juries on oath; their replies constitute the Hundred Rolls. The survey uncovered widespread mismanagement and corruption, and in response, Edward introduced the first Statute of Westminster in 1275 to remedy the abuses. It was the first in a series of legal reforms which he carried out.
□ H. M. Cam *The Hundred and the Hundred Rolls* (1930)

The battle of Poitiers during the **Hundred Years' War**, portrayed in the St *Albans Chronicle* (15th c.).

Hundred Years' War Name given to a series of wars waged between England and France in the later Middle Ages, substantially 1337–1453. For most of the period the initiative lay with the English, and the main fighting and resulting devastation took place exclusively in France. The active warfare fell into four clearly marked phases: (1) 1337–60, a period of sensational English success (Crécy, 1346; Poitiers, 1356) leading to the Treaty of Brétigny (1360), which left England in control of nearly all the coastline of northern and western France; (2) 1360–80, characterized by French recovery under Charles V and DuGuesclin; (3) 1380–1420, a time of cumulative French disaster, faced with the madness of King Charles VI, the rise of Burgundian power and the sweeping successes of King Henry V (Agincourt, 1415); by the Treaty of Troyes (1420) virtually all France north of the Loire fell under the control of the English, and Henry V was recognized as heir to the French throne; (4) 1420–53, the slow recovery of France marked by the inspiration of Joan of Arc (relief of Orleans in 1429 and the coronation of Charles VII at Rheims), the accord with the Burgundians (1435), and general improvement of morale and efficiency in the French cavalry and artillery.

The causes of the wars were complex, including specific matters (such as piracy in the Channel, territorial disputes in Gascony, commercial rivalries, and dynastic claims based partly on the immediate family connections of the Capetians and Plantagenets), and partly on historical awareness of the territorial strength of the former Norman and Angevin rulers of England within France. Most modern analysts lay heavy emphasis on the impossible terms of the out-of-date constitutional arrangements, by which the English kings held their French possessions from the kings of France under full feudal obligation. At a time when the structures of government were developing fast in both communities, the king of England could not exercise the same authority in his French lands that he was able to exercise and exploit in England. In other words, the wars are interpreted as a vital part of the crisis in Western Europe that led to the creation of relatively efficient national states in England and France.

Certainly there was a stiffening of national consciousness on both sides of the Channel. French had ceased to be the official court language of England by *c.* 1380 and there was a fine flowering of the English language in the last decades of the 14th c., notably in the work of Chaucer. Materially, England suffered less than France, which was ravaged by peasant uprisings (the Jacquérie) and by the Free Companies of the 15th c. Precocious importance was given to the Estates General in France (1356), and the English Parliament increased its influence in financial affairs; but the ultimate result in both communities was to strengthen the monarchy.
□ E. Perroy *The Hundred Years' War* (1951); *The Hundred Years' War* ed. K. Fowler (1971)

Hungary The land on the Middle Danube was subject to a constant, restless movement of peoples in the early Middle Ages. The Huns, who have given their name to modern Hungary, were a nomadic Asiatic people of legendary ferocity whose initial moves in the 4th c. served to trigger the migratory folk-wandering of the Germans. After the defeat of Attila, their greatest leader, at Châlons in 451, his confederation broke up, and the Hungarian lands were subject to numerous invasions until the Avars temporarily stabilized conditions in the 8th c. They were in turn routed by Charlemagne in 791, and permanent settlement was not brought to the area until, in the late 9th c., a further Asiatic people, the Magyars, ravaged westwards across the Carpathians and made Hungary their permanent base.

For two generations they terrorized much of the West, but after their decisive defeat at the hands of King Otto I at the battle of the Lech (955) they slowly settled down to agriculture; towards the end of the century they accepted Christianity under the rule of St Stephen (997–1038), founder of the Arpad dynasty. Uncertainties over succession contributed to relatively slow institutional growth, and the Golden Bull (1222), conceded to the magnates by King Andrew II, suggests some basic weaknesses in the monarchy. The church on the other hand was strengthened, partly as a mark of national identity, Roman as opposed to the Greek Orthodox faith of Byzantium and the Southern Slavs.

Hungary was completely overrun by the Mongols 1241–43, but recovered and became a significant centre of European culture under an Angevin dynasty linked with Naples (1308–82). For the rest of the Middle Ages Hungary played a special part in resisting Turkish pressures, even as the Byzantine empire was overcome. Under John Hunyadi, and more so under his son Matthias Corvinus (1458–90), the Turks were repulsed and the Muslim–Turkish advance into Europe brought to a temporary halt. *See* MATTHIAS I HUNYADI

□ C. A. Macartney *Hungary, a short history* (1962); *A History of Hungary* ed. E. Pamlényi (1975)

Hunyadi, John (Janos) (*c.*1387–1456) Hungarian soldier-hero under Emperor Sigismund, he drove the Turks from Semendria and was rewarded with a place on the royal council. In 1443 he captured Nish and Sofia, breaking the sultan's power in the Balkans. Further Christian advances were halted by the Turkish victory at Varna (1444). In 1446 Hunyadi was elected governor of Hungary on behalf of Ladislas V. Two years later he led the Hungarian counter-offensive which was halted at Kosovo. Turkish pressure increased, and in 1456 Hunyadi, supported by the Franciscan friar St John of Capistrano, raised a large peasant host which destroyed the Turkish armada, and a week later routed Muhammad II's forces before Belgrade. The independence of Hungary was thus assured for another 70 years. Hunyadi died of plague in his camp in late 1456.

□ P. Engel, 'Janos Hunyadi: the Decisive Years' in *From Hunyadi to Rakoczi* ed. J. M. Bak and B. K. Kivaly (1981)

Hus (Huss), John (*c.* 1369–1415) Czech religious reformer born in Husinec, Bohemia, and educated at the university of Prague. Ordained in 1400 and appointed rector of the university in (1409), he was an academic theologian who preached in Czech and promoted anti-German feeling in Prague university. This nationalistic policy was politically advantageous to the Bohemian monarchy and culminated in a German exodus from the university (1409). Hus fell under suspicion of heresy and was excommunicated (1410) following his protest at the burning of the English reformer Wycliffe's books by the archbishop of Prague. Hus remained popular and continued preaching (causing Prague to be placed under interdict, 1411). In 1412 he was compelled to leave Prague and composed his greatest work *De Ecclesia* – his works comprise the dogmatical, polemical, homiletical, exegetical and epistolary. Hus borrowed from the work of other reformers, notably Wycliffe, but did not adopt their systems. He was concerned with the moral reform of the church and a return to purity, but did not envisage a break with Rome. He attacked the sale of papal indulgences and challenged papal claims to head the church (1412). In 1414 he was summoned to the Council of Constance to defend his beliefs, where, despite safe conduct from King Sigismund, he was arrested, condemned for heresy and burned (6 July 1415). Hus had attracted a number of followers, the Hussites (Calixtines or Utraquists, who insisted, unlike Hus, on restoring communion in both bread and wine) and his death subsequently provoked the Hussite wars.

□ M. Spinka *John Hus: a Biography* (1968); F. M. Bartos *The Hussite Revolution 1424–1437* (1986)

Iceland Although known to Celtic hermits and monks, Iceland was not settled permanently until the period 860–930 when, as part of the Viking expansion, Scandinavians, mostly Norwegians, set up farmsteads in those parts of Iceland capable of supporting agriculture and pastoral farming. They were converted to Christianity *c.* 1000, though some pagan practices persisted. Learning and literature flourished in the 12th c. and 13th c., and the finest vernacular prose of the Middle Ages was produced in Iceland by saga-writers such as Snorri Sturluson (d. 1241), writing in Old Norse. Institutionally, the evolution of a formal deliberative assembly, the *Althing*, in the 10th c. and 11th c. provides an early example of relatively sophisticated development, with overtones of freedom and independence. From the 13th c., however, Iceland was brought into increasing dependence on the Norwegians and then, on the Dano-Norwegian monarchy.

□ F.G. Foote and D.M. Wilson *The Viking Achievement* (1970)

Iconoclastic controversy (726–843) This resulted from sharp disagreement about the veneration of icons in the Byzantine church. In 726 Emperor Leo III the Isaurian, with strong army support, ordered the destruction of all images used as idols and began to persecute defenders of the icons, especially the monks. Pope Gregory III signified the disapproval of the papacy by condemning the Iconoclasts in two synods at Rome (731). Leo's son Constantine V Copronymus continued his father's policy, calling the Iconoclastic Synod of Heiria (753). It was not until the regency of the Empress Irene (780–90) that this trend was reversed; Irene convoked the Second Council of Nicaea (787) which defended icons, and decreed their restoration. However, the controversy

Iconoclast white-washing an image; scene from the 9th-c. Chludov psalter from Byzantium.

flared up again in 814, at the instigation of Leo V the Armenian, a general elected emperor by the army. It did not finally subside until 843, when Theodora, widow of the Emperor Theophilus, called a synod to confirm the pronouncements made at Nicaea; a procession on the first Sunday in Lent marked the return of orthodoxy. *See* CHURCH, EASTERN ORTHODOX

□ E.J. Martin *A History of the Iconoclastic Controversy* (1930)

Idrisi (*c*.1100–*c*.65) Muslim geographer, author of the *Book of Roger*, produced by order of Roger II the Great, king of Sicily. The book was completed in 1154, the only certain date for Idrisi's biography. Little is known of him, as Muslim biographers judged him a renegade for residing at a Christian court and for praising Roger II in his works. Western sources claim that he was born in Ceuta and studied at Cordoba. Idrisi himself states that he travelled much in Spain and North Africa, but does not explain why he settled in the Norman court of Roger II.

□ M. Amari *Storia dei Musulmani di Sicilia* vol. 3 (1854–72)

Indulgences In theological terms an indulgence was technically the remission of the temporal punishment due to sin, the guilt of which had already been forgiven, by the application of Christ's merits. Originating in the commutation of physical penitential punishments, indulgences gained influence through the deep-rooted Christian concept of the solidarity of the whole fellowship and communion of saints.

From the 11th c. they were used to channel penitential activities towards particular ends, a notable example being Urban II's plenary indulgence to support the First Crusade (1095). Later crusades were likewise supported by indulgences, but the growth in the commutation of the crusader's vow for a monetary payment debased the spiritual force of the indulgence. More widespread was the use of indulgences to raise funds for necessary public works, including church-building, the care of the sick and poor, road maintenance, bridge-building and education. William of Auvergne, bishop of Paris (1228–49) and a leading theologian, justified these diverse penances as the manifestation of neighbourly Christian love.

The scope for abuse was rife, and reformers from John of Salisbury onwards warned of the dangers. Under increasing financial pressure, various ecclesiastical authorities, including the papacy, resorted to dubious practices, especially in the employment of professional pardoners, thus realising the reformers' worst fears.

□ P. Paulus *Indulgences as a social factor in the Middle Ages* (1922)

Innocent III Pope 1198–1216 (b.1161) One of the strongest and most effective of all medieval popes, Innocent III was active in two main interlocking spheres of activity. During his pontificate, principles of papal monarchy were at their height. He was a zealous church reformer in the traditional sense, anxious that the Christian church throughout Christendom should put its own moral house in order. As a papal monarch he is chiefly remembered for his actions towards the Empire and the German monarchy, and it was customary for German nationalist historians to attribute much of the blame for Germany's failure to emerge united from the Middle Ages to the malevolence of the relatively young and very able pope.

Elected to the holy see at the age at 37, Innocent made it one of the principal diplomatic aims of his career to separate Germany from Italy, to keep northern and southern Italy (including Sicily) apart, and to safeguard the political integrity of Rome and the papal states. In order to do so he showed himself willing to switch support from the Guelph candidate for the imperial throne, Otto IV of Brunswick, to the Hohenstaufen house, and ultimately to his ward the young Frederick, king of Sicily from infancy and Emperor 1212(20)–50. By one of the deep ironies of history, Frederick became an arch-enemy of the papacy; but there was a cold logic behind Innocent's policy, in his attempt to win pledges that Rome should be free.

Elsewhere in Europe his interventions were consistent, coupling moral questions with an assertion of papal supremacy. His most spectacular success came in England, when after a bitter struggle over appointment to the see of Canterbury, he laid King John's kingdom under an interdict which was raised only after John had capitulated and pledged his kingdom as a fief, to be held on feudal terms from the papacy. In France, after a protracted struggle, he succeeded in reconciling the French king Philip Augustus with his Danish wife Ingeborg, but made little headway on the key question of ecclesiastical rights in feudal courts. In the more peripheral communities of Spain, Hungary and Poland, he and his legates achieved greater success in imposing papal ideas of ecclesiastical order; the same was true of Scandinavia, apart from Norway where King Sverre resisted papal demands.

Innocent's attitude towards crusading was also much bound up with his ideas of papal monarchy, though there again, some ironies appear. He supported the Fourth Crusade, despite initial misgivings over the diversion of effort against Christian states, and attempted to impose Roman authority in the Balkans in the wake of the crusaders' capture of Constantinople in 1204. Deep anxiety over heresy in the south of France prompted him to preach the Albigensian Crusade, to the ultimate political advantage of the French king and northern French nobility.

Trained in theology and law, he preserved an abiding concern for the moral and institutional health of the church, and in two respects his achievements proved permanent. Despite superficial resemblances between the teaching of St Francis and some heretical movements, Innocent recognized the value of the friars, and his support for the Franciscans and Dominicans (used extensively as preachers and inquisitors) added a new, intense dimension to the spiritual life of the West. Increasing emphasis on definition and legality reached its climax towards the end of his pontificate at the Fourth Lateran Council, held at Rome in 1215. Its decrees, described as 'a blue-print for reform', bring together all the ingredients for a reformed church with moral initiative stemming from the centre. Lack of administrative material and local support made much of the effect stronger in theory than in practice, but the Council marked a high point in papal prestige in the Middle Ages.   HRL
□ A. Luchaire *Innocent III* (1904–08); L. Elliot-Binns *Innocent III* (1931); H. Tillmann *Pope Innocent III* (1980)

Inquisition The foundation of the papal Inquisition can be attributed directly to Pope Gregory IX who, in his bull *Excommunicamus*, laid down procedures by which professional inquisitors were to be sent out to trace heretics and persuade them to recant. The bull was published in 1231, and in the succeeding

years the business of questioning those accused of heresy was entrusted to the mendicant orders, above all to the Dominicans.

Gregory's actions came at the end of a long period of struggle against heresy on the part of the established church. Various papal and conciliar decrees (1139, 1179, 1184 and 1199) attempted to regulate the detection of heresy and to prevent its growth through the institution of episcopal inquisitions. Pope Lucius III in 1184 enlisted the help of the Emperor Frederick Barbarossa to set up such regular episcopal inquisitions, and it must be remembered that the alternative was often the blatant savagery of mob violence and lynch law. The situation in Western Europe was further complicated by the popularity of the heretical Waldensians and Cathars in the south of France and the resulting Albigensian Crusade. Pope Innocent III was especially concerned to combat heresy by persuasion and preaching, and it is one of the paradoxes of his exceptionally rich and complex pontificate that some of the worst atrocities of the movement against the Albigenses came in his time.

Gregory IX attempted to bring a degree of Roman legal rationality into proceedings: tribunals were to be set up under two local judges appointed by the pope; the proceedings required evidence from two witnesses who remained anonymous and could not be directly challenged; the suspect gave his testimony on oath. In 1252 Innocent IV permitted the use of torture to obtain a confession. If a confession were made, the individual could recant and be given a canonical penance; if he remained obdurate he was handed over to the secular power which customarily executed heretics by burning at the stake.

Opportunity for abuse was only too evident. With the decline of the Cathars its influence waned, but its arbitrary power and judicial flexibility encouraged its use against groups hostile to the interests of the papacy, and its reputation suffered from, for example, the squalid actions undertaken

'A violent manner of search for truth where other proofs fail': the **Inquisition** at work.

against the Knights Templar in France in the early 14th c., and against the Spiritual Franciscans. It proved impotent against the later reforming movements of the 14th c. and 15th c., but was reactivated in Spain under Isabella and Ferdinand, who used it more or less as a centralized arm of the state. *See* BERNARD GUI; CISNEROS, FRANCESCO; CONRAD OF MARBURG; ROBERT LE BOUGRE

□ H.C. Lea *History of the Inquisition in the Middle Ages* (1888); B. Hamilton *The Medieval Inquisition* (1981)

Investiture Contest (or more strictly, Investiture Disputes) Term given to the great crisis that ravaged relations between Empire and papacy, and indeed between church and state generally, between 1075 and 1122 in Western Europe. It marked the end of the period of so-called 'Carolingian compromise' when the church was subordinate to the kings, and when the kings, above all the emperors, claimed virtual theocratic powers. It also marks the beginning of the period when the potential power of the medieval papacy was realised not only in the spiritual field, but also in the secular and political; a period of 'papal monarchy', as it is sometimes called.

Investiture – the physical act of investing a cleric with the insignia of his office – was no more than one of the outward symbols of the struggle. Deeper issues concerned the nature of the church; the special position of the pope as successor to St Peter; fears concerning the increasing secularization of the church, and specific matters connected with the freedom of election to bishoprics and abbacies; the rejection of simony; the upholding of the celibacy of the clergy; and the freedom of the church to insist on its own pattern of moral reform. Nevertheless, it was the issue of a papal decree (1075) forbidding lay investiture that helped to spark off the struggle, and – after the dramatic traumas of imperial humiliation at Canossa, imperial recovery and the death of Gregory VII in exile (1085), and the assertion of leadership of Christendom by Urban II at the preaching of the First Crusade (1095) – it was precisely the issue of investiture which proved capable of a compromise solution.

The struggle was not limited to the Empire, and in 1106 and 1107 compromises were reached in both France and England which left the ecclesiastical hierarchy in control of the processes of investiture, while safeguarding royal interest in the appointment of bishops, who were also great feudal lords, royal administrators and servants. The German and imperial position proved more difficult. At one stage in 1111 Pope Paschal II offered to renounce ownership of great feudal fiefs in return for freedom to elect and invest, a solution as deeply disturbing

and unacceptable to the bishops as to the secular powers. Compromise was ultimately reached in both Germany and the Empire by the Concordat of Worms in 1122. The Emperor renounced the use of the staff and ring in granting an investiture, but received homage within Germany from the bishops elect for their temporalities before they were consecrated; elsewhere in the Empire he was permitted to receive homage after the consecration. The ecclesiastical hierarchy had asserted its right to maintain symbolic and spiritual control, but the secular rulers still exercised extensive practical power over appointments and control of temporalities. *See* DICTATUS PAPAE; MATILDA; TRIBUR, DIET OF   HRL

□ Z.N. Brooke, 'Lay investiture and its relation to the conflict of empire and papacy', *Proceedings of the British Academy* 25 (1939); G. Tellenbach *Church, State and Christian Society at the time of the Investiture Contest* (1940); C.N.L. Brooke *The Investiture Disputes* (1969); *The Investiture Controversy* ed. K.F. Morrison (1971); I.S. Robinson *Authority and Resistance in the Investiture Contest* (1978)

Iona Hebridean island which became the focal point of Celtic Christianity and an important centre of learning after St Columba founded a monastery there in 563. Many missions were sent to the mainland, the most famous being Columba's mission to the Pictish King Brude in 574 and Aidan's mission to the Northumbrian King Oswald in 635. Despite frequent Viking raids on Iona, Columba's relics attracted pilgrims to the island, until they were taken to Dunkeld in the 9th c., and many Scottish kings were buried there. The bishopric of the Western Isles, set up on Iona in 838, was combined with that of Sodor in 1098. The monastery became a Benedictine house *c.*1203.

□ D.A. Bullough, 'Columba, Adomnan and the Achievement of Iona', *Scottish Historical Review* 43–44 (1964–65)

Ireland The political history of Ireland in the early Middle Ages was unique, not only because there were a large number of kings (perhaps as many as a hundred) exercising lordship over small units of people and their territories (called *tuaths*), but because there were many grades of kings and over-kings, with elaborate rules and customs concerning succession.

By the 8th c. four provinces had emerged, effectively defined by the attempts of the leading families to exert a consistent and dominant overkingship: the Uí Cheinnselaig in the south-east (Leinster), until replaced by the Uí Dúnlainge from *c.*738; the Eógannachta in the south-west (Munster), especially the Cashel branch of the family; the Uí Briúin in the north-west (Connaught) from the mid-8th c.; and the Uí Néill (O'Neill) in the north-east (Ulster) from the early 7th c. The O'Neills developed a pattern of alternating kingship between the northern and southern branches of the family, associated with the kingship of Tara, a symbolic focus similar to that of the Eógannachta's Rock of Cashel in the south. Conflict between the overkings became common, though at this stage the substructure of minor king and *tuath* remained substantially intact.

From 795 a new element was introduced into Irish politics by the Vikings, who ravaged (often severely) and then set up permanent bases, the first at Dublin in 841. Their arrival did not involve a total change in Irish politics as they tended to fit into existing patterns, allying with overkings and being used as mercenaries by them. Competition for overkingship continued, with the Uí Néill most successful in their attempts to extend their range outside their own quarter; from the mid-10th c. they assumed titles suggesting predominance over the whole island. However, their pretensions were undermined by the eastward penetration into the midlands of the Uí Briúin, although they were in turn overtaken by a new family, the Dál Cais from Munster, who seized Cashel in 964. From 976 their

most famous member, Brian Borumha campaigned until he achieved the submission of the south and midlands in 1002 and of the rest of the north 1005–11. Brian's success was short-lived; a revolt in Leinster in 1012 led to his death at Clontarf two years later. Nevertheless, the fact that all overkings submitted to him marks an important change in Irish politics, which henceforth became increasingly closely connected with the thriving town of Dublin.

Change also became apparent as power was territorialized: minor kings lost their independence and the size of the fundamental units of kingship increased. During the 11th c. and 12th c. a series of unrelated kings from various families established a wide hegemony. Just as earlier kings had used Viking military capacity for their own purposes, so the rival overkings sought help from outside, and in a decisive move in 1167 a Leinster ruler turned to Henry II of England. Henry may already have received acknowledgment of his lordship of Ireland from the English pope Adrian IV in 1156, and his response proved quick and devastating. With the intrusion into the political framework of an Anglo-Norman aristocracy, the end of the old order was sealed. Richard de Clare (Strongbow), earl of Pembroke, led an armed force to Ireland. Dublin fell

An aerial view of the Rock of Cashel, stronghold of the kings of Munster in south-west **Ireland**.

in 1170, and in 1171 Henry II himself crossed to Waterford and made what was virtually a triumphal progress through the island.

The Norman Conquest of Ireland was very different from that of England. It was never complete, and though by 1300 most of the island was nominally under the control of the English king or his representatives at Dublin in the Pale, in reality the situation was exceedingly complex, a honeycomb of lordships with much survival of Gaelic chieftains ruling their communities according to the ancient laws and customs of the Celtic world. Some benefited greatly from the new feudal order, and great fiefs were carved out, notably by the Fitz Geralds, the de Lacys and the Butlers. Towns flourished; some of the Anglo-Norman newcomers were assimilated into Gaelic culture, becoming more Irish than the Irish.

The interest of the English monarchy was constant, but its involvement was spasmodic. Richard II at the end of the 14th c. and the Yorkists in the 15th c. attempted to impose peace and unity, but their success was ephemeral. Efforts to proscribe the use of the Irish language, laws and customs, such as those made by the Statutes of Kilkenny in 1366, proved failures. The later Middle Ages experienced a Gaelic resurgence outside the areas directly controlled by Dublin and other towns.   WD

□ J.C. Becket *A Short History of Ireland* (1966); *The Course of Irish History* ed. T.W. Moody and F.X. Martin (1967); D.O. Corráin *Ireland before the Normans* (1972); K. Hughes *Early Christian Ireland : an Introduction to the Sources* (1972)

Irene Empress and Byzantine ruler 797–802 (b. *c.*752) Irene was the first woman to exercise imperial power in her own right following the removal from power of her son Constantine VI. By all accounts a powerful and resolute woman, she acted as regent and co-emperor to her son from the death of her husband Leo IV (775–80) until well into Constantine VI's majority. Dissatisfied with Irene's refusal to relinquish power, Constantine allied himself with the Iconoclast opposition to her imperial policy of icon veneration. In 790, when Constantine VI was 20, Irene was forced to step down, but her son's weak and ineffective rule brought her back to power-sharing in 792. Increasingly irritated by his incompetence, Irene took matters into her own hands in 797, when she had Constantine blinded to render him unsuitable for rule. The novelty of Irene's position in the Byzantine polity is reflected in the way she styled herself *basileus* (emperor) rather than *basilissa* (empress). Her reign persisted until a palace revolution deposed and exiled her.

□ S. Runciman, 'The Empress Irene the Athenian', *Studies in Church History, Subsidia* 1 (1978)

Irish church Although tradition attributes the conversion of the Irish to St Patrick, it is clear that some missionaries were working before him and that his activities were confined to northern and midland Ireland. However, his importance is indisputable and two of his 5th-c. writings survive. The church buildings and priests that he established were under the jurisdiction of a few bishops, without the urban centres that characterized the Continental church.

During the course of the 6th c., the Irish church began to change with the foundation of many

Early monument of the **Irish church**: a 9th-c. cross of St Patrick and Columba at Kells.

monasteries, often under royal patronage. Communities at Bangor, Clonfert, Derry and Durrow, Iniscealtra and Terryglass, Lismore, Moville and Killeedy were in existence by the late 6th or early 7th c. Many of these foundations retained strong connections with the families of their founders, who exercised influence in the appointment of abbots and thereby in the administration of their properties. In the course of this movement some monks set out for foreign parts, establishing other monastic foundations and engaging in some mission work. By the 8th c. many monasteries in Ireland itself had become exceptionally wealthy, patronizing the production of artworks – elaborate service books and vessels – and playing a part in politics too. By the end of the century the abbots of the major monasteries were controlling smaller dependent monasteries, sometimes quite widely scattered, and were becoming more powerful than the bishops to whose jurisdiction they had originally been subject.

In the later 8th c. and 9th c. their involvement in politics was such that abbots took to war, while their connections with aristocratic families were so close that kings sometimes held clerical as well as secular office. This was most striking in the case of the kings of Munster, as, for example, Olchobar, abbot of Emly and king of Cashel in 848. By contrast some bishops strove to assert superiority over others, and the church of Armagh was notable in attempting to establish hegemony (rather like an overkingship) over the entire Irish church. Initially content to share such a hegemony with the church of Kildare, by the 8th c. Armagh was claiming appellate jurisdiction throughout Ireland and a position comparable to that of the bishops of Rome in Italy. These claims were not sustained in the long term, although Armagh remained a powerful church.

In the meantime some clerics and monks had become disillusioned with the worldliness of the church and campaigned for more ascetic practice. This movement, known as the Culdee movement, was in progress by 800, especially associated with Tallaght; it led to the foundation of more ascetic houses, sometimes in very isolated places, to the reform of practice at some existing houses, and to the production of eremitic works of devotion. Both the powerful and the ascetic strands continued to mark the Irish church until the 11th c. Some of the most elaborately carved standing crosses were the product of 10th-c. patronage and skill.

In the late 11th c. the Continental reform movement began to touch Ireland, but the great advance came in mid-12th c. with the work of St Malachy (d. 1148); his design for the Irish church came to fruition after his death, when at the Synod of Kells (1152) Ireland was divided into 4 archbishoprics and 36 bishoprics. The new monastic movements began to exert influence and the Anglo-Norman Conquest (1169–72) under Earl Strongbow and King Henry II brought much of Ireland even more directly into the mainstream of Western Christendom. Cathedrals were built in typical Norman style and powerful new monastic houses were founded, notably by Cistercians. In the 13th c. encouragement was given to the friars; and they (particularly the poorer and more ascetic element among them) retained their good reputation for the most part to the very end of the medieval period.

In the later Middle Ages the Irish church continued to mirror the social divisions of the island, notably along the linguistic lines of English- and Gaelic-speaking, but by and large it conformed more exactly to the usages of the Western church than had been the case in the early Middle Ages. *See* CASHEL, SYNOD OF

WD

□ J.F. Kenney *Sources for the Early History of Ireland: Ecclesiastical* (1929); K. Hughes *The Church in Early Irish Society* (1966)

Irnerius (d. *c.*1130) Possibly German by birth (Guarnerius). One of the founders and greatest teachers of the powerful school of law at Bologna in the later 11th c., Irnerius made permanent contribution to the method by which the newly introduced Roman law of Justinian was taught in the West. His surviving work consists essentially of glosses to texts written as the basis for oral exposition in lectures. The little known of his career indicates that he was a servant of the great papal supporter Matilda of Tuscany, and then of the emperors Henry V and Lothar, but his tremendous reputation, which persisted throughout the 12th c., was as virtual father figure to the revival of law and to the university of Bologna.

□ H. Kantorowicz *Studies in the Glossators of the Roman Law* (1969)

Isaac I Comnenus Byzantine emperor 1057–59 (b. *c.*1005–d. 1061) A representative of the military aristocracy of Asia Minor. Isaac, uncle of Alexius I Comnenus, usurped the throne after the forced abdication of the elderly Michael VI, head of the Civil party in Constantinople. Isaac was helped by the Constantinopolitan church and, in particular, by the Patriarch Michael Cerularius, who held the balance of power between civil and military factions in the capital. But Isaac soon alienated Cerularius by his confiscation of church property, a measure taken to pay for the strengthening of the empire's defences neglected by previous emperors, who had represented the interests of the civil aristocracy. After exiling the patriarch as a dangerous political opponent, Isaac

Gold coin of **Isaac I Comnenus** with drawn sword, from Byzantium.

found popular feeling rising against him. This, coupled with the enmity of a powerful civil aristocracy, prompted his abdication in 1059. The pressure of external events had not yet dictated the choice of a military emperor for the empire.
□ M. Angold *The Byzantine Empire* (1984)

Isabella of France (d.1357) Wife of Edward II of England and daughter of King Philip IV of France. Together with her adulterous lover Roger, earl of March, Isabella organized the revolt which overthrew her husband in 1327. By 1330 the new king, her son Edward III, was strong enough to take power into his own hands. Roger was executed and Isabella confined to her dower lands. Her ferocity became something of a legend, as indicated by her nickname, 'the she-wolf of France'.

Isaurian dynasty Warlike dynasty which governed the Byzantine empire 717–802 and whose strength was based on the military capacity of the Anatolian plateau. The founder of the dynasty in its imperial dimension was the Emperor Leo III, who was responsible for the effective defence of Constantinople against the Muslims. The Isaurians were generally associated with the puritan Iconoclastic movement of the 8th c.

Isidore, St (*c.*560–636) Bishop of Seville. He was born into a pious Catholic family of Byzantine or Hispano-Roman origin, which apparently moved from Cartagena in south-eastern Spain to Seville in the mid-6th c. As bishop of Seville, Isidore's brother Leander was instrumental in procuring the official renunciation of Arianism within the Visigothic realm,

proclaimed at the Third Council of Toledo (589). Isidore succeeded Leander as bishop *c.*600, and during his episcopate, Seville enjoyed pre-eminence as an intellectual centre, with the leading Spanish scholar of the day as its bishop.

Throughout his reign the Visigothic King Sisebut (612–21) was advised by Isidore on ecclesiastical and scholarly matters and, somewhat exceptionally, displayed a proclivity for learning. Isidore dedicated a treatise on natural phenomena to the king, *On the Nature of Things*, and was commissioned by him to compose the *Etymologies*, completed in the early 630s. In this compendium of information, covering subjects such as the liberal arts, medicine, law and the Bible, Isidore applied, with as much ingenuity as accuracy, a system of knowledge wherein the essential meaning of an object or phenomenon is disclosed by revealing the supposed origin of the word used to refer to it. The work was highly influential throughout the Middle Ages.

Isidore also contributed to the vitality of the 7th-c. Spanish church. He emphasized the need for an educated clergy and criticized the use of brutality to achieve conversion among Spain's Jewish population. He presided at the Second Council of Seville (619), where many theological issues were considered, and at the Fourth Council of Toledo (633), which insisted upon uniformity in the liturgy and promulgated excommunication for rebellion against the king.

Isidore's writings reveal his desire to see Spain flourish under Visigothic dominion and his hostility toward the Franks. His works were renowned among Irish scholars from the mid-7th c. and were influential during the 9th-c. intellectual revival of the Frankish church. Isidore wrote a Chronicle (*c.*615) and a *History of the Goths, Vandals and Sueves* (*c.*625) – the only record of Visigothic history during the period 589–625/6. His other works include: *On the Differences and the Meaning of Words*; *Lamentations of a Sinful Soul*; *On Famous Men* and *On the Christian Faith, against the Jews*. A few authentic letters also survive, among many forgeries.   JF
□ J. Fontaine *Isidore de Séville et la culture classique dans l'Espagne wisigothique* (1959); R. Collins *Early Medieval Spain 400–1000* (1983)

Isidorus Mercator Frankish scholar of the mid-9th c., responsible for a collection of papal decretals (the *Forged Decretals* or *Pseudo-Isidore*) which placed heavy emphasis on the absolute supremacy of the papal see. The collection consisted of a mixture of genuine and false decretals, ingeniously arranged, and attributed to the Isidorian statements on canon law which originated in Spain.
□ E. Davenport *The False Decretals* (1916)

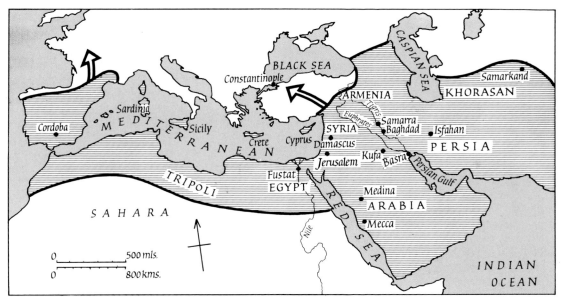

Map showing the extent of **Islam** in the 9th c. at the time of the 'Abbāsid caliphs.

Islam The youngest of the great world religions, dependent on the teachings of Muhammad, as formulated in the Koran. The root meaning of the word is 'surrender', and a Muslim is one who has surrendered to the will of God, as revealed by his true prophet.

In essence its teaching is a product of the religious experience of the Near East, and historians of religion tend to treat Judaism, Christianity and Islam not as separate faiths, but as three branches of the same faith. Islam was certainly as deeply rooted as Judaism and Christianity in its sense of history and concern with chronology – the working out of God's purpose in time. Islam is rigidly monotheistic, recognizing the validity of the Old Testament, the prophets and Jesus Christ; Abraham himself is considered in the Koran as the founder of the sanctuary at Mecca, with its sacred black stone (the Ka'ba), and is respected as the destroyer of idols.

The major point of divergence is that Islam believes Muhammad to be the latest and most perfect of the prophets, commanded to reveal the truth of God and his purpose for the world in the writings of the Koran. As the faith matured, Islamic teachers were prepared to recognize the force of Christ's ministry (and even to accept the Virgin birth), but not to accept the notion of Christ as God incarnate. They rejected the concept of the Trinity as an aberration which led men astray from the strict monotheistic path.

The new faith spread with extraordinary rapidity. Muhammad preached his monotheistic creed in Mecca, in the 610s, with only moderate success. In 622 – the date from which Muslims calculate their new era – he made his flight (the *hijra* or *hegira*) with his followers to Medina, a settlement with a substantial Jewish presence. It was here that the mission gained momentum. Muhammad's own close involvement in politics, warfare and social organization ensured a strong socio-political element in the new faith from the earliest days. A strong military vein entered Islam, directed against polytheistic and idol-worshipping tribes; and the concept of *jihād*, in the sense of a legal, as much as a holy war, can be traced back to the 620s.

Although Muhammad's followers were not uniformly successful in these military activities, a turning point came with his triumphal re-entry into Mecca (629–30). By the time of his death (632), the entire Arabian peninsula was brought into a novel state of political unity. Internecine tribal warfare had been the curse of the peninsula, but in binding new believers in a universal faith, Muhammad transcended local tribal ties; the use of Arabic as the dominant holy language further helped to hold Muslims together in spite of their vastly disparate traditions.

Through this newly forged unity, an immense reserve of latent military energy was released. Muhammad's successors, the caliphs, took full advantage of this, unleashing the new force against the decaying empires of Byzantium and Persia. In one short generation (632–56) the Muslims gained control of the heart of the Near East, Jerusalem, Damascus and Syria, Mesopotamia and the Persian empire, Alexandria and Eygpt. They extended their authority further under the Umayyad caliphate based on Damascus (660–750). By 720 the muezzin

Conversion of Abu Zayd in the **Islamic** mosque at Basra.

was calling the faithful to prayer from the foothills of northern Spain to the valley of the Indus. The whole of the southern half of the 'fertile crescent' was in Muslim hands. Under the 'Abbāsids (750–1258), the centre of power moved eastwards, from Damascus to Baghdad, and the universality of Islam was confirmed by an extra-Arabian preponderance.

Muslim attitudes to non-believers varied, but tended often to be tolerant, provided taxes were paid and the scriptures observed. They could be savage, however, against idol-worship and rejection of the unity of the godhead. Political unity was often illusory; an Umayyad dynasty persisted in Spain until the 11th c., while other dynasties sprang up along the length of the straggling Muslim complex: Fātimids in Egypt (909–1171); the Seljuk Turks in Syria and Anatolia (1077–1307); the Almoravids (1036–1147) and Almohads (1130–1269) in the Maghreb and Spain. The intrusion of the Mongols in the 13th c. led to the fall of the 'Abbāsid caliphate, by which time Iran, Iraq and Syria were in Mongol hands. The political turmoil caused by the creation of the Crusading kingdom (1100–1292) was further complicated by powerful Turkish moves; the later Middle Ages saw the emergence of the Ottoman Turks as the dominant Muslim power. Nevertheless, throughout the period Islam developed and flourished in considerable integrity.

To the Western European world Islam was from time to time the 'great menace', 'the religion from without' – clearly not pagan and more than a simple heresy. Conflict in Spain, Sicily and on the Crusades sharpened awareness, and often, fears. But there were also times of more peaceful contact, notably in the 12th c. and among Jewish scholars in Spain. Western Europe owed much in knowledge of mathematics, medicine and philosophy to Arab sources, where the inheritance of Greek culture had been better preserved by Muslim scholars.

Islam was embraced by peoples of diverse traditions: Latin, Greek, Persian, and at its widest extent, Central Asiatic, Indian and even Chinese. Variations therefore naturally grew up in forms of worship, though the central core remained firm: monotheism, reliance on the Koran and obedience to the sayings of Muhammad (the *hadīth*). All Muslims came to be expected to pray five times a day toward Mecca (initially Jersualem); to fast during the holy lunar month of Ramadan; to give alms to the poor, to observe the sabbath on a Friday; and to make at least once in their lifetime a pilgrimage to Mecca (the *hajj*) and other holy places associated with the life of the prophet.

The main division in Islam, between the Sunnites and the Shi'ites, still haunts the Muslim world today. The Sunnites are those who conform to the tradition (the Sunni) transmitted through the orthodox caliphs, while the Shi'ites look back to the figure of Alī, son-in-law of the prophet (600–61). The Shi'ites (men of the Party) were opposed to the official theologians' and legislators' tendency to rely only on a fundamental interpretation of the Koran. Some looked for a new or hidden leader, a *Mahdī*, and provided the basis for revolutionary movements throughout Islamic history. Generally speaking, they favoured charismatic leadership transmitted through the Imāms descended from Alī and Fatima. The Ismā'īlī and the Fātimids became the most important Shi'ite sects, and the Assassins (12th c.), the most notorious. A strong mystical strain was expressed through the Su–fīs, influential in Muslim cities of the 8th c. and 9th c. HRL
□ *The Cambridge History of Islam* ed. P.M. Holt, A.K.S. Lambton and B. Lewis (1970); *The World of Islam* ed. B. Lewis (1976); B. Lewis *The Muslim Discovery of Europe* (1982); D. Sourdel *Medieval Islam* (1983); O. Leaman *An Introduction to Medieval Islamic Philosophy* (1985)

Italian Renaissance The term 'Renaissance', used to describe the period *c.*1330–1530, was first coined by 14th-c. and 15th-c. Italian writers who perceived a fundamental change in their age. The humanists, the intellectual elite of the period, believed that classical studies, lost in an age of darkness after the

The cathedral, bapistery and tower at Pisa (13th c.), one of the flourishing city-states of **Italy**.

collapse of the Roman empire, were now awaiting rebirth at their hands. These men fostered an increasing concern with civic life, partly as a result of their new vision of man as a comprehensible being placed midway between God and the lower orders of nature. In their opinion, classical studies provided innumerable examples and methods that could prove useful for the needs of the society in which they lived; every area of life, from art to politics, eventually felt the impact of these studies.

□ P. Burke *Tradition and Innovation in Renaissance Italy* (1972); *A Concise Encyclopaedia of the Italian Renaissance* ed. J.R. Hale (1981)

Italy By the mid-4th c., Rome had been supplanted as the political capital of the empire by Milan in the West and Constantinople in the East. By 402 the Western capital had been transferred again, in the face of barbarian onslaught, to a more defensible position at Ravenna. Rome was invaded by the Visigoths (410) and the Vandals (455), and northern Italy by the Huns (452), none of whom settled. The overthrow of Romulus Augustulus, last Latin emperor in the West, by Odoacer in 476 marked no dramatic turning-point, for the Western empire, by now comprising only Italy, had experienced

government by barbarian military leaders intermittently since the 380s.

The first major and enduring barbarian invasion of the peninsula was that of the Ostrogoths (490–93) whose King Theodoric deposed Odoacer and installed himself at Ravenna. The Ostrogothic kingdom was finally eclipsed by the Byzantine reconquest of Italy under Justinian, after prolonged warfare (535–55). In 568 Italy was invaded by the Lombards, who established a kingdom in the north and duchies in Spoleto and Benevento, engulfing most of the peninsula in a further series of wars. Rome, still the spiritual centre of Christendom, resisted and was effectively under papal control by the late 6th c. The Byzantine exarchate of Ravenna fell in 751.

In compliance with papal requests, Charlemagne conquered the Lombard kingdom and duchy of Spoleto (773–74), which were thereby absorbed into the Frankish realm. In 800 his coronation as emperor was performed by the pope in Rome. Northern and central Italy were governed effectually by the Carolingians until the death of Louis II (875), and for almost 90 years thereafter by a succession of less competent rulers of Frankish origin. During this period the mainland was raided at intervals by the Magyars (899–950s) and the Saracens, established in

Sicily since 825. Under Basil I Byzantium expelled the Saracens from the southern mainland, and by 900 power in the region was divided between the Byzantines and the Lombards. Having annexed Italy to the ascendant German kingdom, Otto I secured his coronation as Emperor by the pope (962) and the imperial title was thereafter held by successive German kings until the mid-13th c. Relations with the papacy, almost invariably bad, were especially bitter during the Investiture Contest (1076–1122).

The 11th c. saw important political and economic developments within the peninsula. As the integrity of the state fragmented during the 10th c., authority became increasingly localized, reflected in the spread of fortified towns (castelli). By the late 11th c., the formation of the communes had begun, with Pisa and Genoa among the first. In the south, the Norman conquests of the 1070s, displacing the Lombards and Byzantines, terminated Byzantium's trading monopoly in the eastern Mediterranean, to the profit of Venice. With the onset of the Crusades, trade in the maritime cities of Pisa and Genoa also flourished. The growth of civic wealth and independence was rapid; by the mid-12th c., communes had been established in all the major cities of north and central Italy. Frederick Barbarossa's attempt to reassert imperial authority over the northern cities provoked the retaliatory confederation of the Lombard League (1167), but inter-city rivalry was the norm. In the decades following the death of Frederick II (1250) power within the communes came increasingly to be concentrated in the hands of urban autocrats (signori) in a period of continued economic buoyancy.

Frederick's death, which severed the direct connection with Germany, also marked the beginning of the gradual decline of effective imperial control within the peninsula, though not of external intervention; 1266–68 the Angevins superseded the Hohenstaufen as the major foreign dynasty on the mainland, vying with the Aragonese after 1282 for lasting control of Sicily and the kingdom of Naples. The papacy, whose temporal authority in central Italy had been considerably extended under Innocent III (1198–1216), became increasingly politicized, and the late 13th c. saw the rise of powerful papal families such as the Colonna and Gaetani, whose machinations led to the transfer of the papal residence to Avignon (1309–77).

From the early 14th c., the political arena in Italy was dominated by internal affairs, especially in the papal states, Tuscany and the north. Allegiance to the Guelph and Ghibelline parties, originally denoting support for the papacy and the Empire respectively, had come to signify political alignment within and between the cities. Warfare among the cities became particularly intense and economically damaging in the early 14th c. The collapse of the international banking houses of Peruzzi and Bardi in Florence (1340s) was followed by the ravages of the Black Death (1348), which swept away in some areas perhaps as much as half of a population already debilitated by economic distress. This was, nevertheless, the germinal period of the Renaissance. During the ensuing 150 years, the city-states experienced varying fortunes, usually under oligarchic or despotic government. Warfare continued between the most powerful of the states, notably Venice, Milan and Florence, until the Peace of Lodi (1454), and thereafter less frequently until the Wars of Italy began in 1494. During this period the peninsula witnessed foreign intervention on an unprecedented scale, instigated by Charles VIII of France.   JF
□ D.P. Waley *The Italian City Republics* (1969); J.K. Hyde *Society and Politics in Medieval Italy 1000–1350* (1973); D. Herlihy *The Social History of Italy and Western Europe 700–1500* (1978); L. Martines *Power and Imagination; City-states in Renaissance Italy* (1980)

Ivan III the Great (Vasilievich) (1440–1505) He succeeded his father Vasili II in 1462 as grand prince of Moscow and inaugurated a programme of expansion; Yaroslav (1463) and Rostov (1474) were annexed. In a series of campaigns (1471, 1477, 1478) Novgorod was subjugated and its colonies absorbed, and Tver followed suit in 1485. By skilful diplomacy, utilizing the internal divisions of the Kazan Horde, Ivan was able to nullify his nominal vassalage to the khan. His territories were moulded into a unified bloc by simultaneously reducing the authority and sequestrating the lands of the appanage princes, and from this stronger base, Ivan began a war of attrition against Poland-Lithuania, making large gains before a temporary truce in 1500. When this ruptured, more territory was seized before peace in 1503. Emphasis on his special position as defender of Greek Orthodox Christianity enabled him to consolidate his authority in spite of internal dynastic quarrels. With Constantinople in Muslim hands since 1453, Moscow was now set fair to lay claim to be the 'third Rome'.
□ J.L. Fennell *Ivan the Great of Moscow* (1961)

Ivo of Chartres, St (1040–1115) Bishop of Chartres from 1090 and the most important canon lawyer of his age, Ivo had been trained at Bec and Paris and had held office as prior at Beauvais. He was much influenced by the new systematic arrangement of law according to themes and subjects, characteristic of the more advanced legal thought of the late 11th c. His collection of decretals in 17 volumes became a standard work of reference and was not even completely displaced by the authoritative work of Gratian later in the century. His summary of canon law, the *Panormia*, remained in wide use in ecclesiastical courts. In the political field he was immensely influential, adopting a moderate Gregorian stance and helping to achieve the compromise solutions to the Investiture Contest brought about in France and England 1106–07.

□ R. Sprandel *Ivo von Chartres und seine Stellung in der Kirchengeschichte* (1962)

J

Jacopone da Todi (*c*.1230–1306) Franciscan poet. On the death of his wife in 1268, Jacopone da Todi underwent a religious conversion. Ten years later, he became a Franciscan lay brother, and in 1294 he and some of his brethren were granted permission by Pope Celestine V to live in a separate community of strict observance. He wrote many popular poems (*Laudes*) in Latin and the Umbrian dialect, among them, probably, the *Stabat Mater*.

□ L. Olschi *The Genius of Italy* (1949); G.T. Peck *The Fool of God: Jacopone da Todi* (1980)

Jacquérie Name given to the violent outbreaks of peasant revolt in the 1350s in France, attendant upon the dislocation caused by the plague and by the military and political disasters in the war with England. These reached a point of maximum intensity in the years following the French defeat at Poitiers (1356) and the ravaging that followed by the Free Companies. Atrocities were committed in the first stages of the rising, but even worse resulted when, after a failure to coordinate the peasant unrest with the urban movement in Paris, led by Etienne Marcel, the nobility and upper bourgeoisie regained control and crushed the risings with great ferocity. Memory of the savagery remained powerful, and fear of a recurrence persisted in the agrarian history of late medieval and early modern France.

□ M. Mollat and P. Wolff *The Popular Revolutions of the Late Middle Ages* (1973)

Jacques de Molai (d.1314) Grand master of the Order of the Templars, Jacques de Molai faced the full fury of the French King Philip IV, and his advisers, who brought charges against the Order in 1307, accusing them of heresy, homosexuality and a multiplicity of sins, including devil-worship. Under threat of torture de Molai initially confessed, but later, under temporary papal protection, retracted. After a long, bitter and particularly

Etienne Marcel, allied to elements in the **Jacquérie**, was killed by royal troops reacting against peasant revolt.

villainous diplomatic struggle, the Order was abolished as a matter of expediency, rather than of conviction, in 1312. De Molai remained in prison but finally, in a dramatic affirmation of his innocence, laid himself open to the charge of being a relapsed heretic and was burned alive. *See* KNIGHTS OF THE TEMPLE

James I the Conqueror King of Aragon 1213–76 (b.1208) A leading figure in the reconquest of Spain from the Muslims, James extended the authority of Aragon in three directions. Taking advantage of the weakness of Moorish political organization after their great defeat of 1212, and using the naval and commercial skills of the Catalans, he conquered Majorca and the Balearic Islands (1229–35). To the south he captured Valencia in 1238. By treaty with Louis IX of France he freed Catalonia from French suzerainty (1258), renouncing in return his claims to lordship in Languedoc. Under his guidance the familiar shape of the powerful Aragonese kingdom with its extensive political and commercial interests throughout the Mediterranean, began to take firmer shape. [*105*]

□ F. Soldevilla *Life of James I the Conqueror* (1968)

Jenghiz Khan (*c*.1154–1227) One of the most successful military conquerors of all time, he imposed a brutal Mongol despotism on the greater part of the steppe lands of Asia and China. Of Mongol stock himself, he ruled an empire built up

Contemporary portrait of **Jenghiz Khan**

increasingly by subordinated Turkish tribes. In his lifetime the effects of his conquests in Europe were indirect though potentially immense; some of this potential was realized within a generation of his death when Mongol or Tartar hosts penetrated deep into Europe along the Danube, ruling Hungary for a while and having permanent impact on the political shaping of historic Russia. [*231*]
□ H.D. Martin *The Rise of Chingis Khan* (1950)

Jerome, St (*c*.341–420) He became a Christian at Rome, where he had gone to study some time before 366. He travelled in Gaul and then returned to his native Dalmatia *c*.370 to become a monk at Aquileia. Further travel took him to Palestine and then on to Syria, where he spent five years as a hermit at Chalcis learning Hebrew, the original language of the Bible. He visited Constantinople before returning to Rome for three years, during which time he became spiritual adviser to St Paula's group of pious women. Finally, in 386 he settled to a life of monastic scholarship at Bethlehem. A prolific scholar, Jerome took part in many theological controversies and led the field in contemporary biblical studies; his most important works are his Letters, his biblical commentaries and his Latin version of the Bible, known as the Vulgate. [*330*]
□ J. Steinmann *Saint Jerome and his Times* (1959); J.N.D. Kelly *Jerome* (1975)

Jerome of Prague (*c*.1370–1416) Influenced by John Hus, he arrived at Oxford in 1398 and studied the theological works of Wycliffe. After visiting several other European universities he returned to Prague in 1407 and took an active part in the religious controversies of the day. When Hus was pronounced a heretic by the Council of Constance (1416) and then burnt at the stake by the secular authorities, Jerome's refusal to repudiate him and renounce the teachings of Wycliffe condemned him to share the same fate.
□ J.M. Klassen *The Nobility and the Making of the Hussite Revolution* (1978)

Jesse, Tree of One of the favourite and most impressive themes in medieval iconography, the Tree of Jesse (father of King David) illustrated the descent of Jesus from the royal line of Israel. It appears in illumination and especially in stained-glass windows in Western Europe from the mid-12th c. onwards. The superb Jesse window at Chartres is the most famous, and proved the most influential of the whole group, being much copied in the north of France.
□ G. Schiller *Iconography of Christian Art* vol. 1 (1971)

Jews The Middle Ages should properly be interpreted as a vital episode in the *Diaspora*, or dispersal, of the Jews, in the course of which they became a people predominantly European and urban. The story starts with the destruction of the Temple at Jerusalem by Vespasian in AD 70 and the subsequent savage acts of imperial Rome against the Jews and Jerusalem in the 2nd c. The loss of a Jewish kingdom meant that responsibility for the survival of Judaism and the awareness of a Jewish heritage rested with scattered groups loyal to the sense of Jewish history embodied in the Old Testament and the Hebrew language, and to Jewish ritual, notably male circumcision and the keeping of the Sabbath.

Jewish learning kept the groups together, flourishing in the early centuries among those who had emigrated east to Mesopotamia. There they established great schools at Sura (early 3rd c.), at Nehardea and Pumbeditha. Here the *Talmud* (or 'teaching') was slowly assembled and refined to constitute a body of law, custom and comment on history, which served as a spiritual and intellectual cohesive force throughout the long centuries of the *Diaspora*. The teachers came to be known as rabbis, and the spiritual leaders as the *geonim*.

Muslim conquests in the 7th c. helped rather than hindered Jewish development in Mesopotamia, where their political leaders, the Exilarchs, claiming descent from King David, together with the *geonim*, were universally recognized as the chief repositories of Jewish traditions until at least the first half of the 11th c.

Within the Mediterranean world of the Roman

empire Jewish communities survived, but with great difficulty. Acceptance of Christianity in the 4th c. and its development into the dominant orthodox religion brought great complications. Jews had status as representatives of the old law of the Old Testament, but also stood condemned for the greatest crime in history: the crucifixion of Christ. In the Eastern empire periods of acceptance were followed by times of active persecution. The Emperor Heraclius (610–41) even attempted to prohibit the exercise of Judaism in public. Some groups settled outside the bounds of the empire in the Crimea; in the early 8th c. the Khazars, an Asiatic people with a strong Mongolian strain, adopted Judaism as their official religion and for two centuries provided an important centre of Jewry to the north and east of Byzantium. For the West Pope Gregory the Great (590–604) set the example, encouraging conversion, though opposing persecution and forced baptism. Under the Carolingians there was a period of comparative toleration which permitted Jewish communities to thrive and to exercise their skills as traders deep into the northern part of Frankia.

The most significant developments, however, undoubtedly took place within the Muslim world, above all in Spain. After 750, with the fall of the Umayyad caliphate at Damascus, the main focus of Muslim political power moved east to the 'Abbāsids at Baghdad, leaving Spain in a somewhat isolated state as the last bastion of Umayyad influence. Virtual political autonomy was accompanied by a period of considerable prosperity through to the 11th c., and Jewish communities played a prominent part in the trading life of Muslim Spain, especially in the great cities of Cordoba and Seville.

The Christian reconquest in the high Middle Ages brought sporadic persecution, though up to the end of the 13th c. Spanish Jewry produced some of the strongest academic intellects of the age. Moses Maimonides (1135–1204), for example, born in Cordoba though active as a scholar for much of his life in Egypt, played a major part in transmitting the Graeco-Roman heritage back to the West, showing a grasp of much Aristotelean thought as well as a mastery of Arabic and Hebrew. The Jews of Spain and North Africa came to be known (from the Hebrew name for Spain) as Jews of the Sephardim, and their scholars were characterized by their grasp of Hebrew and of what to many of them appeared as the vernaculars of Latin, Arabic and Castilian. Under persecution in Spain later in the Middle Ages a strong mystical strain emerged based on the *Kabbalah*, traditional lore reinforced by the 13th-c. discovery in Spain of the *Zohar* or 'Book of Splendour', a mystical commentary in Aramaic on the Pentateuch. Pressure from Christian kings caused many Spanish Jews to accept conversion, often merely nominal (the Marranos), and in 1492 the Jews were expelled, some going to Turkey, where they were well received, and others to France, Italy and Holland.

In the meantime Jewish communities continued to exist elsewhere in Europe in towns scattered along the great trade routes. From the mid-11th c., as Western Europe entered a dynamic phase in its economic development, they grew more conspicuous. By 1100 they were to be found in substantial numbers in France and Germany, and communities were set up in England after the Norman Conquest. One of the first and ugliest manifestations of the First Crusade was a set of pogroms, especially violent in the Rhineland in the early summer of 1096 at Worms, Mainz, Cologne and Trier. From that point onwards sporadic outbursts occurred against the distinctive Jewish communities, fuelled by the crusading spirit. Stories connected with the supposed ritual murder of children (such as the legends surrounding the death of William of Norwich in 1144) or with alleged defilement of sacramental bread and wine helped to stir up the passion of the Christian mobs.

Deprived of a specific power base of their own, the Jews looked for support to existing authorities to whom they could give service, to landlords, counts, great ecclesiastical princes, kings or the Emperor himself. In Germany attempts were made somewhat clumsily to equate their status with that of a royal serf, a *servus camere*, and similar notions were common elsewhere. In Spain, for example, Jews were described as *servi regis*, and in England in the 13th c., they were subject to a series of heavy impositions of tallage, a mark of servile status. They were natural scapegoats in time of trouble, part of their unpopularity stemming from their exclusiveness,

Jewish priest wearing the tallith, reading from the Pentateuch (c.1395).

their obvious difference from the native communities, and their involvement in finance and the handling of debt. They were by and large excluded from the possession of land and from handicrafts. Christians were forbidden to indulge in usury, and the Jews, helped by the cosmopolitan nature of their religion, took on increasingly the function of moneylenders and providers of credit, acquiring a reputation for extortion in the process.

Papal legislation provides a useful index to Western European thought of the time (though it would be utterly false to consider that the decrees were universally obeyed). At the Third Lateran Council in 1179, where stringent decrees were issued against Christian participation in usury, Jews were forbidden to have Christians as servants, and Christians were forbidden to lodge with the infidel, so preparing the ground in parts of Europe for the setting up of special ghettoes for the Jews. Pope Innocent III at the Lateran Council of 1215 went further, freeing Christian debtors, notably crusaders, from their obligation to pay interest on their debts to the Jews, excluding Jews rigidly from positions of authority, and initiating the compulsory wearing of means of identification: a piece of cloth in yellow or crimson, a badge or even a hat of distinctive colour.

Heavy persecution accompanied this period of intense legislation, stimulated by the loss of Jerusalem to the Muslims (1187–1227), anxieties over the heresies in Languedoc and the Albigensian Crusade, and by the general turmoil of the Third and Fourth Crusades. At York in 1190, in an incident which touched even the case-hardened Christian chroniclers, the Jewish community led by their rabbi resorted to self-immolation in the castle, the heads of families killing their wives and children and finally themselves, rather than submit to the massacre planned for them by their besieging enemies. The besiegers, incidentally, were led by representatives of the lesser baronage heavily in debt to the Jews. Yet persecution helped in a curious way to consolidate Western Jewry. Their inner strength lay in their intellectual heritage. Traditional Talmudic and rabbinical learning from the east was transmitted through the work of scholars such as Gershom of Mainz (c.960–1028), the 'Light of Exile' and a great authority on the *Talmud*, to whose pen were ascribed many later commentaries on the law.

In the 13th c. the Jews were protected, used and abused by Western rulers. They were subject to special tallages in England, recorded in the exchequer of the Jews, and from the 1240s these impositions grew so heavy as to be self-defeating. Edward I attempted to regularize matters, but in 1290 resorted to his own version of a final solution and expelled the Jews. A similar rhythm of protection and exploitation took place in France. In 1306 Philip IV ordered their expulsion, and although some were later allowed back on excessively harsh terms, this proved the end of the long-lasting and significant presence of French Jewry. The term *Ashkenazi* came into common use to describe European Jews outside Spain and Italy (where they sporadically enjoyed papal protection). *Ashkenazi* was the Hebrew term for 'German', and the *Ashkenazis* spoke a western German dialect which came to be known as Yiddish.

In the later Middle Ages further persecutions, savage and cruel but more localized in Germany because of the fragmentation of effective German political power, led to emigration eastwards to Hungary and especially to Poland, where they enjoyed a degree of religious freedom and intermittent privilege under royal protection. Poland was attached in a straggling uncertain union to Lithuania in the 15th c. and exerted control over much of the south of historic Russia including Kiev, where strong Jewish elements were again introduced.

At the end of the Middle Ages the demographic pattern of European Jewry assumed a shape which determined the future, sometimes tragic fate of the Jewish people. Strongest in Poland and the surrounding territories, the *Ashkenazi* Jews, treasuring their ancient religious and social heritage and their German-based Yiddish tongue, provided the most numerous element. Spanish or Sephardic Jews, as they were known, were dispersed, some of them back into the Low Countries, but also throughout the Mediterranean world, in North Africa, Italy and the Ottoman empire. They preserved their tradition of respect for language and learning wherever they were given the chance to establish relatively stable communities. HRL

□ C. Roth *A Short History of the Jewish People* (1936); *The Standard Jewish Encyclopaedia* ed. C. Roth (1966); J. Parkes *The Jew in the Medieval Community* (1975); B.S. Bachrach *Early Medieval Jewish Policy in Western Europe* (1977); *Aspects of Jewish Culture in the Middle Ages* ed. P. Szarmach (1978–81); *The Cambridge History of Judaism* vol. 1, ed. W. Davies and L. Finkelstein (1984)

Joachim (c.1132–1202) Abbot of Fiore. Mystic and prophet, he proved more influential in his legendary afterlife and in the interpretations given to his writings than in his career and deeds. In 1177 he became abbot of the Cistercian house at Corazzo, but withdrew to live a hermit's life at Fiore in Calabria, attracting disciples and contemplating apocalyptic visions. He divided human history into three periods: the age of the Old Testament (the Father), that of the New Testament (the Son) and that of the world to come (dominated by a new spiritual order),

which he foresaw would begin in the 1260s. The millenary aspects of his work, coupled with the hope of realization within a finite time, seized the imagination of the immediately succeeding generations. Joachimism had profound effects on many social groups in the 13th c. and early 14th c., notably among the Spiritual Franciscans, spearheading some elements of resistance to, and protests against the established ecclesiastical order. [153]
□ M. Reeves *The Influence of Prophecy in the Later Middle Ages: A study in Joachimism* (1969)

Joan of Arc, St (1412–31) A woman of peasant stock from Domremy on the Lorraine border, she played a great part in rousing French patriotic feeling against the English and Burgundians, so ensuring French success in the Hundred Years' War. Her career, even when legend is disentangled from fact, tells a story of single-minded bravery and devotion on Joan's part, matched by a sad tale of indolence, treachery and sheer wickedness on the part of many of her friends as well as her enemies. In

French miniature of 1451 representing **Joan of Arc** wearing armour.

adolescence she claimed to receive mystical exhortations from the Archangel Michael, St Margaret and St Catherine, ordering her to rally French armies to rescue Orleans. Stories of her difficulties in persuading first the local military leaders and then both soldiers and theologians at the royal court of her mission ring true.

Dressed as a knight, she began her military successes with the relief of Orleans in 1429, and then faced successfully the more difficult task of forcing the Dauphin to see the importance of ensuring his coronation. Eventually she escorted him to Rheims and stood by his side during his coronation as Charles VII. The following year (1430) she was captured by the Burgundians near Compiègne and sold to the English, who brought her before the court of Pierre Cauchon, bishop of Beauvais, at Rouen to be tried for heresy and witchcraft. Full records of her trial survive and reveal both the simplicity and nobility of Joan, and the determination of the English and their French accomplices to find her guilty. She was burnt at the stake in Rouen on 30 May 1431, on a technically accurate charge, as a relapsed heretic. To the lasting shame of Charles VII he did nothing effective to help her. In 1456 a papal commission reversed the verdict of her trial and she was canonized.
□ F. Gies *Joan of Arc: the Legend and the Reality* (1981); M. Warner *Joan of Arc: the Image of Female Heroism* (1981)

John XXII Pope 1316–34 (b.1249) Born at Cahors and French in upbringing, he was elected to the papacy as a compromise candidate, in part because of his advanced age, and then proceeded to reign at Avignon for 18 years. He proved a gifted administrator, introducing a new system of papal finance, reorganizing the curia, centralizing ecclesiastical patronage and creating many new sees. In the dispute over the nature of poverty which split the Franciscan Order into Spiritual and Conventual factions, John condemned the extreme Spiritual stance and advised some of its supporters to ally with his enemy, the Emperor Louis IV of Bavaria. John excommunicated Louis for heresy in 1324 and four years later Louis, having been crowned at Rome, arranged the election of a Spiritual Franciscan as the anti-pope Nicholas V. John, however, prevailed over these adversities and spent the last years of his pontificate locked in a theological dispute over the nature of the Beatific Vision.
□ G. Mollat *The Popes at Avignon 1305–78* (1963)

John Balliol King of Scotland 1292–96 (d.1315) Out of the tangle of possible claimants to the Scottish throne in the early 1290s, three leading candidates emerged: John Balliol, Robert Bruce and John

John Balliol

Charter of privileges granted to London by **King John** shortly before the issue of Magna Carta.

Hastings. Asserting his own claim to overlordship, the powerful Edward I of England set up a commission which decided in favour of Balliol, a descendant through the maternal line of King David I. Edward recognized him as king and received from him homage and fealty for the fief of Scotland. Balliol, however, took advantage of Edward's other pre-occupations to reassert Scottish independence, but was defeated and captured by the English king in 1296. The fight for Scottish independence passed into the hands of William Wallace, and then of the descendants of Robert Bruce.
□ G.W.S. Barrow *Robert Bruce* (1965)

John Lackland King of England 1199–1216 (b.1167) He succeeded to the throne of England and to the extensive Angevin possessions in France on the death of his brother, Richard I Lionheart. The inheritance was not an easy one; failure to fulfil

feudal obligations to his nominal overlord Philip II of France, the murder of his nephew Arthur of Brittany, which alienated much opinion in the north of France, and financial difficulties in a period of severe inflation, led to the loss of Normandy and Anjou to the French crown in 1204.

In England itself, quarrels with the church over the appointment of an archbishop of Canterbury led to the imposition of an interdict and ultimate capitulation to Pope Innocent III, with John recognizing the pope as his feudal overlord. Quarrels with the barons led to the prolonged crisis of 1213–15 and the issue of Magna Carta. Innocent III, fearing that Magna Carta represented an anarchic renunciation of kingship and order, supported John at this stage, but the king died in 1216 faced with French invasion and a disrupted kingdom.

Chroniclers were quick to paint John as the archetypal tyrant, but modern scholars point out that great advances were made during his reign in royal administration and in the keeping and preservation of written records of royal government.
□ S. Painter *The Reign of King John* (1949); F.M. Powicke *The Loss of Normandy 1189–1204* (1961); J. Holt *King John* (1961)

John of Gaunt (1340–99) Third son of Edward III of England. John, who became duke of Lancaster in 1362, was the wealthiest and most powerful man in the realm for long periods during the reign of his nephew Richard II (1377–99). Largely responsible for crushing the Peasants' Revolt in 1381, he remained deeply unpopular with sections of the community but acted substantially as a stabilizing element in the constitutional struggles involving the king, barons and Parliament. He also had personal and dynastic interests in the throne of Castile, which took up much of his time, and from which he gained only limited success. The rash acts of King Richard against John's heir, Henry Bolingbroke (later Henry IV), helped to precipitate the deposition of Richard and the Lancastrian succession to the throne of England.
□ S. Armitage-Smith *John of Gaunt* (1904); R. Somerville *History of the Duchy of Lancaster* I (1953)

John of Jandun (1286–1328) One of the leading philosophers at the university of Paris, he is remembered as a teacher of Aristotle both in the field of natural history (to which he made some original contributions) and of political ideas. He was a friend and supporter of Marsilius of Padua and defended the imperial position in the struggle between the Avignonese papacy and Louis of Bavaria.
□ G. Leff *Paris and Oxford Universities in the Thirteenth and Fourteenth Centuries* (1968)

John (Quidort) of Paris (1225–1306) Perhaps the most powerful and influential of the immediate pupils of Thomas Aquinas. John Quidort, teacher at the university of Paris, wrote his tract *De Potestate Regia et Papali* in the opening years of the 14th c. at the height of the conflict between Pope Boniface VIII and the French king. His arguments, based on Thomist lines, recognized papal rights to deal with moral issues, but implied that a council was superior to a pope. In the secular field he favoured an elective kingship, whereby a king could be deposed by the people. His separation of the powers of church and state was suspect in his own age but highly influential in following centuries.
□ J. Leclercq *Jean de Paris et l'ecclésiologie du XIIᵉ siècle* (1942); *On Royal and Papal Power* trans. A.P. Moynahan (1974)

John of Parma (1204–84) Minister-general of the Franciscan Order. He was appointed minister-general of the Order in 1247. He instituted an energetic programme of spiritual revival amongst the Franciscans and travelled widely in order to supervise its implementation. He was also deeply interested in attempts to reunite the Eastern and Western churches. However, his sympathies with the doctrines of Joachim of Fiore laid him open to accusations of heresy and he was forced to resign office in 1251. He was absolved of the charges brought against him and allowed to retire to the hermitage of Greccio. After 32 years in retreat, he died on the way to Camerino whilst engaged on a mission for church unity.
□ R. Brooke *Early Franciscan Government* (1959)

John of Plano-Carpini (d. 1252) Franciscan friar who set out in 1237 on a mission to convert the Mongols to Christianity. He reached the court of the great khan at Karakorum, returning to Italy via Kiev in 1240. His book on his travels provides one of the first accounts of the Mongol empire.
□ J.J. Saunders, 'John of Plano-Carpini', *History Today* 22 (1972)

John of Pomuk (Nepomuk), St (*c*. 1340–93) A Bohemian, he studied at Padua and Prague, and by 1390 had risen to the office of vicar-general of the archdiocese of Prague. In 1393 John of Jensteyn, archbishop of Prague, opposed attempts by Wenceslas IV of Bohemia to encroach on his prerogatives. John's implication in the archbishop's resistance led to his arrest and torture, after which he was drowned in the Moldau river. The tradition that John died as the result of his refusal to reveal state-

Late 15th-c. Flemish miniature showing **John of Gaunt** dining with the king of Portugal

ments made by Wenceslas' wife in the confessional can be traced to the 15th-c. chronicler Thomas of Ebendorffer, who may have confused John with another of the king's victims.

John of Salisbury (*c*.1115–80) Bishop of Chartres. He studied in Paris and Chartres for 12 years, then spent short periods in clerical service at Celle and in the papal curia before entering the household of Theobald, archbishop of Canterbury, *c*.1148, where he specialized in papal affairs. He supported Theobald's successor Thomas Becket in his dispute with Henry II, and as a result spent the years 1163–70 in exile at Rheims. Although not an eye witness to the event, John was in Canterbury cathedral at the time of Becket's assassination (1170). Six years later he was elected bishop of Chartres under the patronage of Becket's protector Louis VII.

John wrote the *Historia Pontificalis* (*c*.1163), a lively account of his years at Rome, and produced a collection of Becket's correspondence after the saint's death. He was a notable contributor, in the philosophical field, to the 12th-c. renaissance, being the first major figure to write in the light of Aristotle's work on logic. The most famous examples of his scholarship, both written in 1159, were the *Policraticus*, a discussion of the state, and the *Metalogicon*, which advocated the study of logic and metaphysics. His letters, for example his correspondence with Peter

From **Joinville**'s *Histoire de Saint Louis*: the king participating in the siege of Damietta.

of Celle, reveal him as a leading proponent of 12th-c. humanism, and one of the most elegant Latinists of his day.
□ H. Liebeschütz *Medieval Humanism in the Life and Writings of John of Salisbury* (1950); R. and M. Rouse, 'John of Salisbury and the Doctrine of Tyrannicide', *Speculum* 42 (1967); *The World of John Salisbury* ed. M. Wilks (1984)

John Scot Eriugena (*c*.810–77) The most original of the scholars who flourished at the court of Charles the Bold in Frankia. John brought to his philosophy a rare knowledge of Greek and Neoplatonic thought. His influential *De Divisione Naturae* attempted a systematic four-fold division of all natural things, by which God appeared in, and yet transcended all his creatures. It owed something to the work of Dionysius the Areopagite, but many of the mystic elements were John's own contribution. An Irishman, he seems to have returned to Britain late in life, and some traditions associate him with the revival of learning at King Alfred's court.
□ E.K. Rand *John the Scot* (1906); *The Mind of Eriugena* ed. J.J. O'Meara and L. Bieler (1973)

Joinville, Jean de (*c*.1224–1319) A noble from Champagne, he went on crusade with Louis IX in 1248. Returning to France in 1254, he took up hereditary duties as seneschal of Champagne and applied himself to the management of his estates, refusing to accompany the king on another crusade in 1270. He gave evidence for Louis's canonization in 1282 and witnessed the exhumation of his body in 1297. At the command of Jeanne of Navarre, wife of Philip IV, he wrote the *Histoire de Saint Louis*, which incorporated autobiographical reminiscences of his experiences abroad. He finished his task in 1309.
□ H.F. Delaborde *Jean de Joinville et les seigneurs de Joinville* (1894); *The Life of St Louis* trans. R. Hugue (1955)

Jongleurs Name given to entertainers in the Romance-speaking communities of Western Europe, and then extended to cover men with a repertoire of song and verse who moved from court to court or town to town in the central Middle Ages. They were associated especially with the spread of courtly entertainment and the spirit of chivalry. *See* TROUBADOURS

Justinian I Emperor 527–65 (b. *c*.482) Often called 'the last Roman and the first Byzantine emperor', Justinian gained governmental experience as the power behind the throne of his uncle Justin I (518–27). Justinian was unique in his single-minded purpose to re-establish the undivided Roman

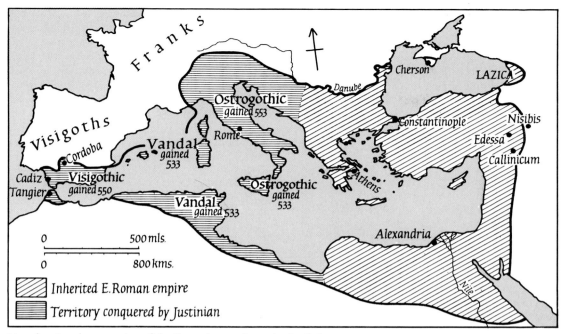

Map showing the expansion of the Byzantine empire under **Justinian**.

empire, whose Western provinces had long been controlled by Germanic kingdoms. To that end he subordinated all his imperial policies, administrative, fiscal, economic and religious, while the great codification of Roman law, the *Corpus Juris Civilis*, provided the unitary legal framework for the whole spectrum of imperial powers and prerogatives exercised by Justinian. He was lucky in the quality of his officials and generals, but the driving spirit was his alone, fuelled by his belief in one state, one law, and one church.

Justinian's principal military efforts were concentrated on recapturing the Western provinces, and there he deployed the bulk of the empire's wealth in manpower and money. This in turn deprived the northern and eastern frontiers of adequate resources for their defence. Justinian's answer was diplomacy – a supple pattern of shifting alliances aimed at maintaining a balance of power between the various barbarian tribes roaming the empire's borders – a policy which, coupled with tribute, was cheaper than warfare but which attracted criticism from contemporaries.

The cost of Justinian's ambition was huge, and within a decade of his death much of his work collapsed in reconquest. In 568 the Lombards entered Italy, the province for which Justinian had fought a 20-year-long series of campaigns, and in 572 the Visigoths recaptured Cordoba. The impracticability of Justinian's 'grand design' was an important factor in the development of the early

Byzantine phase of the empire. After 565 the concept of universality was little more than a splendid rhetorical flourish. Justinian, the heir of Augustus, had made it his goal. *See* THEODORA [*90, 232*]   SW
□ P.N. Ure *Justinian and his Age* (1951); J.W. Barker *Justinian and the Later Roman Empire* (1966); R. Browning *Justinian and Theodora* (1987)

K

Kenneth MacAlpin King of the Scots c.840–58 In 843 Kenneth was able by conquest to overcome the rulers of the Picts and to bring about a union that was to prove permanent. It seems likely that the weakening effects of Viking raids contributed to the defeat of the Picts. Linguistically, the Scottish variety of the Q-Celtic (Goidelic) tongue came quickly to predominate in the new, united kingdom of Alba (Albany) or Scotland.
□ A.A.M. Duncan *Scotland: The Making of the Kingdom* (1978)

Kiev Its position on the Dnieper river made Kiev an important trading centre from early times. Dominated first by the Goths and then by the Khazars, by the 9th c. Slavonic interest was great. Viking penetration of the Russian waterways further increased the importance of Kiev as a vital link in the

Virgin of Vladimir: 12th-c. icon commissioned in Byzantium for **Kiev**.

route from Scandinavia to Constantinople. The political shape of historic Russia began to emerge in the second half of the 9th c. with the establishment of the principality of Novgorod by Rurik in 862, and the conquest of Kiev and other towns by Oleg in 882. Under Oleg and his successors Kiev became the centre of the new polity, and its rulers took on the title of 'grand prince'.

Slavonic elements, resulting in a virtual assimilation of the Scandinavians, reached a high-point in the late 10th c. when the great Prince Vladimir was converted to Eastern Orthodox Christianity (988). Vladimir reunited the loose political organization of the Russian towns and brought them firmly into the orbit of the Eastern imperial world. Periods of prosperity and political success under Yaroslav the Wise (1019–54) and Vladimir Monomach (1113–25) could not disguise the basic defects in the loose, straggling grand principality, and in 1240 the city was conquered by the Mongols under Batu, leaving some churches and the great cathedral of St Sophia (founded 1037) as symbols of Kiev's prestigious past.
□ G. Vernadsky *The Origins of Russia* (1959); R.A. Rybakov *Early Centuries of Russian History* (1965)

Kingship Form of monarchy widespread in the medieval Latin West and replicated in Palestine after the First Crusade. Unlike Roman emperorship, it carried no implication of universality, and kingdoms were many and varied. Concepts of royal office and royal government (*regale ministerium, regimen*) were familiar to the Latin-educated throughout the period. Kingship was compounded of military, civil and religious authority, varying in proportion and strength according to the qualities and fortunes of individual kings. Usually qualified as a member of a royal kindred (*stirps regia*), the king ruled over a people or peoples conceived as a large-scale kin group (*gens*); these connotations are clear in the oldest Germanic 'king'-word, *kuning*, often associated with *thiudans* (people). Though rule over territory was increasingly stressed from the 10th c., the king's power was exercised – on the basic model of all medieval political relations – as a superior lordship over men bound to him by personal loyalty. The potentially arbitrary powers of kingship were restrained, in practice, by economic underdevelopment, which hampered institutionalization and enforced power-sharing with the aristocracy, and, in theory, by aristocratic and ecclesiastical ideologies which stressed royal accountability.

Kingship was formed in the successor states to the Roman empire in the West during the 5th c. and 6th c., partly in response to the need of barbarian immigrants for unified military commands and the allocation of scarce resourses, but especially through the self-interest of Roman provincial elites, who secured power by investing barbarian warlords like Clovis and Theodoric with territorial authority, a demesne and tax revenues. By calling them 'kings' (*rex, reges*), Sidonius, Cassiodorus, Gregory the Great and Isidore clothed the new rulers with a legitimacy based on Christian and Roman political ideas. Though God might permit bad rulers to punish sinful men, kingship itself, and especially Christian kingship, was modelled on God's cosmic kingdom, and therefore good. Scripture offered exemplars like David and Solomon, and indicated divine preference for hereditary succession. The image of the Christian Roman emperor as God's deputy in maintaining the social order through peace, law and justice was transferred to the king. Bede and the Carolingian scholars transmitted this ideology to the later Middle Ages; it was shared by Hincmar of Rheims, John of Salisbury and Thomas Aquinas. The church mediated it through liturgy to a wider audience; royal consecration rituals were elaborated from the 8th c. onwards, and in anointing kings, the church promoted both the sacral authority of kingship and the sacral identity of the Christian people.

Kingship was also seen as a conditional office, for although usually hereditary, kings had to be formally chosen by the leading men of the realm. A king had to subordinate his rulings to the law, or he lapsed into tyranny; he had to take counsel from his faithful men, insisted Hincmar; he had to respect their sense of fair dues and to legislate for the common good; otherwise fidelity could be justifiably withdrawn. The coronation oath highlighted the king's duties; in later medieval Aragon, the nobility offered their allegiance to the king only if he would observe their laws and privileges: 'and if not, not'.

The practice of kingship likewise shows continuity throughout the medieval period. The palace was the political heart of the kingdom: it was from here that the king distributed treasure; here that he entertained his noble companions and led them out on hunts that politically and economically sustained his regime; here were summoned the aristocratic assemblies where the king took counsel and secured collaboration. On such occasions the king's central role in rituals, whether tournaments, the dubbing of knights or liturgical processions, enhanced the prestige of kingship and gave a focus to the participant aristocratic group. Good communications and adroit patronage were indispensable to successful kingship. As judge, the king demonstrated and strengthened his power: losers could accept royal decisions without shame because of kingship's unique prestige, while winners were willing to pay for authoritative settlements. Control of aristocratic heiresses provided revenue, while reinforcing the king's role as protector of the weak.

Royal itineracy spread the power and aura of kingship. *Iter*, journey, also meant military campaign, and the 'war-machine' was the political motor of early medieval kingship; victorious kings replenished treasuries through plunder and tribute, and acquired territory to reward faithful followers. Expansive kingship was fissile, however, as partitioning between heirs produced separate kingdoms (as in 843, when the empire of Charles the Great was divided between his three grandsons). From the 11th c., with the increased practice of primogeniture and the crystallization of kingdoms as territorial units, partitions no longer caused a proliferation of kingship.

With the increasing monetization of society and escalating costs of warfare, kings turned to taxation, fostering later medieval representative institutions as tax-raising instruments, and employing familiar techniques of management, including ritual, to keep these assemblies crown-centred. Tax-farming offered new rewards, and the court increased its pull for aspiring bourgeois as well as nobles. Medieval kingship was never truly bureaucratized, though later medieval kings could recruit higher numbers of increasingly literate and numerate servants from universities under royal patronage.

Kingship's most enduring support was the church. In each kingdom the clergy were always prominent among the personnel of government. Contingents raised from holders of church lands were essential to early medieval royal armies, and later the church contributed taxes, while in return, kingship protected the church's wealth. Few churchmen criticized this mutually beneficial relationship, and kings appointed bishops after, just as before the Investiture Contest. The church also sustained kingship by forming lay opinion through sermons and ritual.

Kingship survived weak reigns. Princes, unanointed, claimed power from God via the king; the aristocratic community of the realm held its shape around the crown; peasant rebels attacked evil counsellors in the name of kingship; the 'royal touch', invented by palace clerks (which was supposed to cure disease), was sought by the humble. At the end of the Middle Ages, the emergent states of France, England and Spain drew strength from a pervasive ideology of kingship.   JLN

□ F. Kern *Kingship and Law* (1939); M.L. Wilks *The Problem of Sovereignty in the Later Middle Ages* (1963); W. Ullmann *A History of Political Thought: the Middle Ages* (1965); M. Bloch *The Royal Touch* (1973); S. Reynolds *Kingdoms and Communities in Western Europe 900–1300* (1984); J.L. Nelson *Politics and Ritual in Early Medieval Europe* (1987)

Knighthood The state of being a knight. With its trappings of chivalry and pageantry, knighthood was a characteristic element of European society and culture for much of the Middle Ages. In essence, the knight combined the functions of horseman and servant; the former is represented by the common Western European nomenclatures of *chevalier*, *cavaliere*, *caballero* and *Ritter*, and the latter by the Old English *cniht* and the German *Knecht*. Despite attempts to trace the development of knighthood back to Roman *equites* or mounted barbarian forces, this dual character of knighthood apparently emerged in the late Carolingian empire of the 9th c. and 10th c., when the early medieval practices of vassalage and commendation (the procurement by a freeman of a lord's protection and provision, in return for service in labour or goods) were extended to include military service and the donation by the lord of a grant of land (fief, fee, benefice). Contemporary innovations in cavalry equipment and armour (notably the stirrup and horse-shoeing) served to increase cavalry service, producing the specialist mounted warrior or knight.

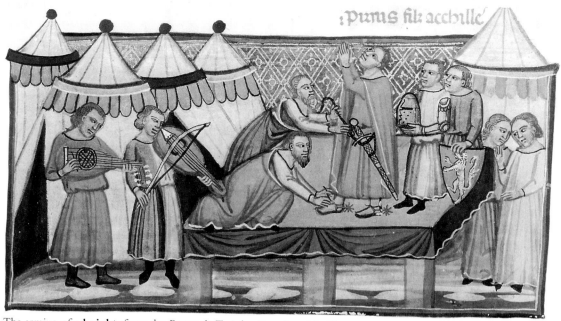

:punis fit acchille

The arming of a **knight**, from the *Roman de Troie* by Benedict of St Maur.

The utilitarian origins of knighthood were gradually obscured by the financial and political implications of knightly land tenure and the maintenance of arms, which increasingly led to the identification of knighthood with the upper classes, a process virtually complete by the late 12th c. The knight's image was greatly enhanced, on a moral and cultural plane, during the Crusades, when the church concerned itself with the ethics of knighthood, imbuing it with a quasi-religious nature as the secular arm of the church, responsible for the defence of the weak and the church itself. This was heightened by the institution of the religious orders of knighthood in the early 12th c.

The growth of courtly practice and chivalry during the 12th c. further crystallized the medieval concept of knighthood, which assumed mystical and romantic connotations, bolstered by the growth of a literature of chivalry embodied primarily in the *chansons de geste* and *romans d'aventur*. Requirements for training (apprenticeship as a page and squire) and arming, and elaborate rituals of investiture evolved; these included preparatory bathing, clothing, a nocturnal vigil and the utterance: 'Be thou a knight' accompanied by a light blow to the shoulder (the dubbing, *colée*, *paumée*). By the 13th c. knighthood was generally conferred by a ruling prince. Likewise, a humanizing code of knightly (chivalrous) behaviour emerged, entailing reverence for religion and noble ladies, and an etiquette of combat towards fellow knights. Further late 12th-c. developments include an increased pride in ancestry, which heightened patriarchal descent and inheritance by primogeniture and, coupled with the need for clear identification in combat, encouraged the growth of heraldry.

Such elaborations continued throughout the 14th c. and 15th c.; the knight declined as an important military force as his energies became increasingly channelled into tournaments and rich pageantry. Secular, largely honorary orders emerged (Spanish Order of the Sash, 1332; English Order of the Garter, 1348) and by the 16th c. the transformation from knight to gentleman was virtually complete. Another factor in this transformation was the political role of the knight, acquired in late 13th-c. England, where he sat in Parliament as a 'knight of the shire', contributing to the modern perpetuation of knighthood as a mark of favour. *See* ARMOUR; CHIVALRY; HERALDRY; WAR [*36*] MB

□ R. Barber *The Knight and Chivalry* (1974); R. Rudorff *Knights and the Age of Chivalry* (1974); B. Arnold *German Knighthood 1050–1300* (1985)

Knights of St John (Hospitallers) Knights of Jerusalem, Rhodes, Malta. This religious military order originated as a Benedictine hospital for pilgrims near the Holy Sepulchre, founded *c.* 1070 by merchants from Amalfi. This charitable foundation, dedicated to alms-giving, hospitality and care of the sick, flourished under the patronage of Godfrey de Bouillon (d. 1100) and, under Grand-Master Gerard, crystallized into an order (confirmed 1113). It established hospitals and commanderies in Europe and the East, and

Recumbent effigy of Bernat de Foixa, **knight of St John**, in his family chapel at the Castell de Foixa.

was fully transformed into a military order (with monastic vows on the lines of the Templars) for the defence of pilgrims. The Hospitallers and their rival Templars formed the finest fighting force in the Holy Land.

Following the fall of Acre (1291), signalling the loss of the Holy Land, the Hospitallers moved to Cyprus, where they set up the Grand Commandery at Kolossi, and, following their conquest of Rhodes (1307), Grand-Master Fulk de Villaret established their headquarters there (1310), effectively forming an independent sovereign state which benefited from Templar confiscations. The Hospitallers continued to fight the Muslims for control of the Eastern Mediterranean until compelled to surrender to Sulaymān the Magnificent (1522). The Order subsequently declined, transferring its principal seat to Malta (1530), whence it continued its anti-Muslim activities. Napoleon's conquest of Malta (1798) effectively brought an end to the Order, which was revived in Rome (1878) as a secular charitable organization.
□ *A History of the Order of the Hospital of St John of Jerusalem* ed. L. Butler (1967); *The Medieval Nobility* ed. T. Reuter (1978)

Knights of the Sword (Brethren of the Sword, *Fratres Militiae Christi*) A small German military order, founded *c.*1202 in the turbulent Baltic missionary field of Livonia (now Estonia, Latvia and Lithuania). Violent pagan opposition and the commercial rivalry of the bishops of Riga compelled them, by 1230, to negotiate a union with the Teutonic

Order, already interested in the area by its absorption of the minor Order of Dobrin. Little advance was made until much of the Brethren's force was annihilated at Saulen (1236), causing Gregory IX to enforce the union. Livonia continued to trouble the Teutonic knights, resisting conversion, rebelling and occasioning conflict with the Russian princes. Not until 1290 was the area decisively united with their Prussian territory, although activity persisted in Lithuania (with Polish intervention), and reached a climax in the Teutonic defeat at Grünwald (1410).
□ F. Benninghoven *Der Orden der Schwertbrüder* (1965)

Knights of the Temple (Templars) The first of the religious military orders, designed to supplement and protect the crusader states. The Templars originated *c.*1115 in the activities of Hugh de Payens (d.1136) and fellow French knights (the Poor Soldiers), dedicated to protecting pilgrims between Jaffa and Jerusalem. They gained the support of Baldwin of Jerusalem *c.*1118 and subsequently that of Bernard of Clairvaux who praised them in his pamphlet, *De Laude Novae Militiae*, and composed their monastic Rule, approved by the Council of Troyes (1128). Innocent II's bull (1139) established their sole papal allegiance and they evolved a constitution with an elected grand-master, provinces, districts and individual preceptories, adopted a white mantle with red cross, and constructed characteristic round churches of the type still to be seen today in Temple Church, London.

An early 14th-c. manuscript of the **Koran** in Muhaqqaq displaying elaborate calligraphy.

Unlike the Hospitallers, whom they influenced, the Templars engaged primarily in anti-Muslim military endeavours. Immensely popular and enriched by bequests during the Crusades, they grew powerful in Europe and the East and became bankers. The fall of Acre (1291) and their transfer to Cyprus left them purposeless and, with their banking, unpopular. They resisted mergers with rival Hospitallers and encroachments by Philip IV of France, prompting him and Pope Clement V to engineer their fall. Accusations of heresy led to the Order's suppression (Council of Vienne, 1312); Grand-Master Jacques de Molai and others were executed and the Order's property confiscated, passing to the Hospitallers and secular princes. The Order was refounded in Portugal as the Order of Christ.
□ E. Simon *The Piebald Standard: a Biography of the Knights Templar* (1959)

Koran (Qur'an) The Muslim holy book. It consists of *suras* or chapters, each containing one of the sayings which Muslims believe to be revelations from Allah, given through the Prophet Muhammad. Zayd ibn Thabit, under orders from the first caliph Abū Bakr, began the task of establishing a definitive text of the Koran after Muhammad's death (632), and completed this work in 651. *See* ISLAM
□ W. Montgomery Watt *Bell's Introduction to the Qur'an* (1970)

Kosovo, battles of (1389, 1448) *Kosovo polje*, the 'Field of the Blackbirds', in Serbia was the scene of two important clashes between Ottoman and Christian forces. In 1389 Sultan Murād I defeated Prince Lazar of Serbia in an action which led to the death of both leaders and crushed the last centre of effective resistance to Ottoman expansion in the Balkans. In 1448 Sultan Murād II put paid to the attempts of John Hunyadi, king of Hungary, to recoup Christian forces after the crusade of Varna in 1444.
□ H. Inalcik *The Ottoman Empire: the Classical Age 1300–1500* (1973)

Kublai Khan (1215–94) Grandson of Jenghiz Khan, he completed the Mongol conquest of China and set up his capital at Peking, where he was visited by Marco Polo. His legend had impact on the imagination of the West.
□ R. Sawma *The Monks of Kublai Khan, Emperor of China* (1928)

L

Lando, Michele di (1343–1401) Leader of the Ciompi in the revolts of 1378. Di Lando, a wool-carder by trade, set up a new constitution for Florence which gave rights to new employee-guilds and unskilled workers. Resolute against the mob and extremists, he took part in a coalition, democratic in character, which ruled the city for over three years. Failure to revive prosperity led to his overthrow and exile in 1382.
□ G. O. Corazzini *I Ciompi . . . con notizie intorno alla vita di Michele di Lando* (1887)

Lanfranc of Bec (*c.*1010–89) Archbishop of Canterbury 1070–89. Born in Pavia, Lanfranc was a dominant figure in the intellectual, monastic and political life of 11th-c. Western Europe. His education appears to have had a strong legal as well as theological content. He left Italy *c.* 1030, earned a reputation as a student and teacher in France and settled as a monk at the new reformed Norman monastery of Bec in 1042.

For nearly 20 years (*c.* 1045–63) he was prior of Bec, where he flourished as a teacher, applying his great skills in grammar, rhetoric and dialectic to the study of the scriptures, and also as a theologian, establishing an orthodox conservative position with regard to the Eucharist, in opposition to the advanced and ultimately unacceptable views of Berengar of Tours. Although his relationship with Duke William was sometimes stormy, his stature was such that he was chosen to be abbot of the duke's great new foundation of Saint-Etienne at Caen (1063–70) and then, in spite of protestations that seemed more than conventional humility, archbishop of Canterbury.

He proved one of the greatest archbishops, asserting the primacy of Canterbury against the claims of York, and holding a series of reforming councils that gave England the substance of up-to-date moral reform. He worked closely with the Conqueror, giving an at times curiously old-fashioned look to English ecclesiastical affairs, with the king and the archbishop cooperating fully in the interests of the moral state of the church. England was thus able to avoid the rigours of the Investiture Contest for a further generation. In the royal absence Lanfranc on occasion acted as regent, and on William I's death was instrumental in ensuring the succession of William Rufus to the English throne.

His work for the monks was naturally subordinate to his wider political interests in England, but he drew up the fresh constitutions for his cathedral at Canterbury, encouraged the spread of monastic chapters, and remained loyal, as his voluminous letters show, to the principles of reformed Benedictine monasticism which he had done so much to foster at Bec. He showed respect to the papacy, but supported the king in rejecting Hildebrand's claim to fealty, though agreeing to the active collection of papal dues in the form of 'Peter's Pence'.　　　HRL
□ M. Gibson *Lanfranc of Bec* (1978)

Langland, William (*c.* 1330–*c.* 1400) A native of the West Midlands, he spent much of his life in London. He took minor orders, but never entered the priesthood, and was a supporter of John Wycliffe. He is known for his alliterative poem *The Vision of Piers Plowman*, which deals with the theme of salvation and belongs to the popular medieval genre of allegorical dream literature. He wrote three separate versions of the work, which have been dated to *c.* 1362, 1377 and 1393–98.
□ *Piers the Ploughman* trans. J. F. Goodridge (1959)

Langton, Stephen (*c.*1150–1228) Archbishop of Canterbury. He became a noted theologian after studying at Paris. In 1206 Innocent III made Langton cardinal-priest of St Chrysogonus, and in the following year resolved the dispute between the monks of Canterbury and King John over election to the primacy of England, by securing his appointment to the position. However, John's opposition to the election caused a breach with the papacy and condemned the new archbishop to exile in Pontigny until a *rapprochement* was effected in 1213. Langton played a leading role in the baronial opposition to John, and it was at his suggestion that the demands included in Magna Carta were modelled on the charter of Henry I.

Langton's refusal to impose papal excommunication on the barons led to his suspension from office in 1215, but he was absolved in the following year and reinstated in 1218. Thereafter, he gave full support to the royalist party. He worked in close cooperation with the justiciar, Hubert de Burgh, and was responsible for the definitive re-issue of Magna Carta in 1225. He was also active in ecclesiastical affairs. In 1221 he furthered the archbishop of Canterbury's claim to be a *legatus natus* by securing the recall to Rome of the papal legate Pandulph, and obtaining a promise from Honorius III that no legate would be sent to England during his lifetime. Moreover, he formulated an important set of constitutions for the English church which were promulgated, with the decrees of the Fourth Lateran Council, at a provincial council in Oxford (1222).
□ F. M. Powicke *Stephen Langton* (1928)

Language and dialect Language problems in the Middle Ages are complex, presenting the historian with methodological difficulties of the first order if he attempts to draw racial and institutional conclusions from linguistic evidence. In Western Europe Latin was the universal language of the church and substantially, too, of written government and permanent administration; to be literate meant to be literate in Latin. The Latinity of the Middle Ages was modified and made more flexible in the course of the centuries, notably by the grammarians of the Carolingian period, although the essential classical structures were preserved. In the hands of the best stylists, such as John of Salisbury in the 12th c., it bears comparison with anything from the great prose writers of the ancient world. Greek, recognized from the later 6th c. as the official language of the empire, fulfilled a similar function in Byzantium.

Native vernaculars continued to flourish, especially in the dynamic 12th c. and 13th c. when troubadours, poets, preachers and teachers turned increasingly not only to composition, but to a written record of their works. 'What is French, but Latin badly spoken?', asked an Anglo-Saxon writer in the early 11th c.; but by 1200, from basic Latin stock, the standardized forms of the ancestors of the modern Romance languages were already complete: French, Occitan, Catalan, Spanish, the Italian dialects, notably Tuscan, and a host of others.

Similar developments took place in the Germanic-speaking world. England was unique in its elaborate use of the written vernacular in late Anglo-Saxon times, but in the Continental lands the full flowering of literature came at the turn of the 13th c., especially in the High German of southern Germany. Scandinavia experienced its finest literary flowering with the Icelandic sagas of the 13th c. These were to have great effect on the standardization of the vernaculars. The Celtic-speaking world experienced similar phenomena, and the Welsh lyric poets produced work of European standing. Among the Slavonic-speaking peoples there was heavy concentration on ecclesiastical liturgy in Old Slavonic, but the languages themselves underwent sharp differentiation that resulted in the creation of modern Russian, Polish, Czech and the southern Slavonic tongues. The familiar language map of modern Europe slowly took shape in the latter half of the Middle Ages, with some of the language boundaries proving astonishingly resilient and more or less permanent after the 12th c. Most of the language stock was Indo-European, but there were some survivals from a very remote age, as with the Basques and Albanians, and some intrusions, as with the Finno-Ugrian group which, from ultimate Asiatic origins, in time yielded to Europe the distantly connected languages of Finnish and Hungarian. In Rumania, the ancient Roman province of Dacia, a Latin-based language persisted, though heavily transformed by a mixture of Greek, Slavonic and Bulgarian elements.

This multiplicity of language growth and experience makes the continued strength of Latin and Greek appear all the more remarkable, though analogies can quickly be drawn with Arabic in the Muslim world of the Middle Ages, and beyond to English in the 20th c. *See* ANGLO-NORMAN FRENCH; STRASBOURG, OATHS OF   HRL

□ E. Auerbach *Literary Language and its Public in Late Latin Antiquity and in the Middle Ages* (1965); J. M. Williams *Origins of the English Language* (1975); *Latin and the Vernacular Languages in Early Medieval Britain* ed. N. Brooks (1982); B. Mitchell *Old English Syntax* (1985)

Lateran Councils From the earliest days of the Christian empire until the beginning of the 14th c., the Lateran in Rome was the principal residence of the pope, with its church on the site of the present St John Lateran. Religious councils were held there regularly, and during the period of strong papal monarchy in the 12th c. and 13th c., general ecumenical assemblies also took place there. Their general purpose was to effect a unifying reform of the church throughout the West. The first was held after the settlement of some of the issues involved in the Investiture Contest (1123); the second, to settle a schism and to condemn the heresy of Arnold of Brescia (1139); and the third, called by Alexander III, to confirm the settlement with Barbarossa and to initiate a wide-ranging reform (1179). The greatest and most important, however, was the Fourth Lateran Council, convened by Innocent III in 1216 as the climax of his energetic papacy; it dealt not only with moral reform, but with decrees that clarified doctrine and tackled the suppression of heresy.

□ C. J. von Hefele and H. Leclercq *Histoire des conciles* (1907–52); M. Gibbs and J. Lang *Bishops and Reform, 1215–72* (1934); P. Hughes *The Church in Crisis* (1964)

Marginal drawing of the Fourth **Lateran Council** in the *Chronica Maiora* of Matthew Paris.

Law students at Bologna. This 15th-c. manuscript assumes each student will possess a written text.

Law The rule of law is one of the most powerful concepts bequeathed by the medieval to the modern world, but its origins are complex, drawn from Germanic as well as Romanic roots. To Byzantium and the eastern parts of the Roman world, the legal heritage survived intact, though dramatically modified, first under the impact of the Muslim invasions, then by the Crusades, and ultimately by the Turkish conquests culminating in the capture of Constantinople (1453).

The greatest of the early Eastern emperors, Justinian, made it his business to codify Roman law (527–34) with the help of his legal expert Tribonian. The resulting publications, known to medieval scholars as the *Corpus Juris Civilis*, must rank among the most influential written works ever to be produced in Europe. There are two major constituents: the *Digest* and the *Code*. The *Digest* (or *Pandects*) stated basic principles and dealt mostly with private laws; it consisted of 50 books, divided into titles and *leges* (laws), drawing into a systematic unity material from the lawbooks of the empire. The emperor was recognized as the source of positive written law and was not held to be bound by the law. Historically, however, the *Digest* follows Ulpian in attributing the basis of imperial authority to a *lex regia*, by means of which the Roman people had transmitted power to the ruler in Republican days: this attribution proved of major significance to political thinkers in the later Middle Ages.

The *Code* published formal constitutions or rescripts, and replies from the emperor on controversial points. It consisted of 12 books and was heavily concerned with ecclesiastical affairs, applying to the Christianized empire notions derived from pagan days, when the emperor was *pontifex maximus*. The *Code* also contained matter connected with the judicial machinery and functions of public officers. Two other compilations associated with Justinian are also important for the transmission of Roman law. His later legal decisions, many of them connected with ecclesiastical affairs, and issued significantly in Greek rather than the Latin of the *Digest* and *Code*, were collected together (168 in all) as the *Novellae*, while his *Institutes* (in four books) presented an officially approved textbook, laying down general principles, but containing nothing that was not in the *Digest* or the *Code*.

For the eastern part of the empire the law of Rome, as presented by Justinian and his advisers, continued to be the basis of ordered social life. The West was different. The rudiments of Roman law survived in Italy and the south of France, and some of the barbarian law codes, notably that of the Visigoths, show strong Roman influence; notaries who appear in connection with grants of land and rights in Carolingian Italy are presumed to have had more than a smattering of Roman law.

It was above all the church that kept Roman ideas alive. The law of the Ripuarian Franks recognized in mid-8th c. that the church lived according to Roman law. In other more subtle ways the church also preserved the heritage of Roman law: its institutional structure was modelled on that of the Roman state and demanded a measure of universal territorial law; the Vulgate, the great Latin Bible, was impregnated with Latin legal vocabulary, carrying through to the medieval world intelligible notions of an ordered kingship and territorial state.

The rulers of the Western world were for many centuries Germanic barbarian kings and their followers, whose basic ideas of law were radically different from the Roman. The emphasis which appears in their law codes on status, on *wergeld* (blood-price), on the feud or fear of the feud, indicates a society in which to be law-worthy and oath-worthy depended upon belonging to a free kindred; the ultimate basis of Germanic law was membership of a free tribal group.

Notions of Christian kingship and of a just society helped to reintroduce vestiges of Romanism, but there was little specific knowledge of Roman law to fall back on. Not until the latter half of the 11th c., coincident with the outbreak of the Investiture Contest, was there a true revival of Roman law. The only surviving copy of the *Digest* was rediscovered *c.* 1070, probably at Monte Cassino, and systematic study of Roman law developed quickly in north Italy under the inspiration of great teachers: Irnerius at Bologna, to be followed by the Glossators in the 12th c. and then by the Commentators. Needs of both church and state prompted close examination of the Roman heritage, though in detail the differences in social organization between the Roman empire and 12th-c. Europe demanded the hard intellectual discipline of the law schools to make the rulings intelligible. Canon law developed along its own paths, and the genius of Gratian in the early 1140s set the law of the church on a new methodical basis. His *Concordance of Discordant Canons* owed an immense debt to the Bolognese School.

The secular world also benefited, and civil law took coherent shape. Peter Crassus, who wrote in defence of the Emperor Henry IV, seems to have been the first to realize the full potential of the Roman law in defence of lay power, but royal servants throughout the 12th c. and 13th c. drew heavily on the legal maxims of Rome to support their imperial and royal masters. Law, next to theology, became the most prestigious of academic disciplines, a training for the literate elite who rose through the ranks of government in the central Middle Ages. Conflicts naturally emerged between the new civil lawyers and those steeped in tradition, feudal law and custom. Lawyers under the Hohenstaufen Emperors accepted and exploited the universality explicit in Roman law, but the French and English monarchies were initially less welcoming, and there were occasions when its study was forbidden. The comforting doctrine that the king was emperor in his own kingdom helped to encourage its study, notably in France, but in England Roman law remained of less practical influence, and the fabric of common law emerged in the hands of writers such as Glanville and Bracton, not untouched by Roman law, but structurally more dependent on custom and the practice of royal law courts.

At the high theoretical level, theology and law were closely interwoven. In the 13th c. refinements were made – most subtly and effectively by St Thomas Aquinas – to the basic views of St Augustine concerning the relation of divine law (revealed by faith), natural law and positive law. Politics, political theory and the study of law were also close partners, and many of the great legal masters of the later Middle Ages involved themselves actively in the disputes over the ending of the Great Schism and the Conciliar movement. Concepts of sovereignty and of public *utilitas* were formulated by the Roman lawyers. The discipline of law persisted academically as one of the most rewarding, in both intellectual and practical senses of the word. Organized in universities, such as Bologna, or in the English Inns of Court, the study of law exerted a powerful and permanent effect on the intellectual life of Europe. *See* FOREST LAW; LIBER AUGUSTALIS; THEODOSIAN CODE   HRL
□ W. Ullmann *Law and Politics in the Middle Ages* (1975), *Jurisprudence in the Middle Ages* (1980); H. J. Berman *Law and Revolution: the Formation of the Western Legal Tradition* (1983)

Layamon (*fl. c.* 1200) Layamon's *Brut*, based on Wace's account of the establishment in Britain of the Trojan dynasty by Brutus of Troy, is of great interest to students of language as well as to those concerned with the Arthurian legends. Layamon was a parish priest in Worcester, writing in the West Midlands dialect, and his attempts to standardize orthography according to phonetic principles make his work a prime source for the study of pronunciation and the development of Middle English.

The links between the Trojan myth and the Arthurian legends were strengthened by his text, which formed the basis of much 13th-c. Arthurian writing. Indeed, the transmission of the 'matter of Britain' and of the part played by King Arthur, from Geoffrey of Monmouth in Latin, through Wace in Norman French, to Layamon in English provides a theme of major importance to both the social and the literary historian.
□ *Layamon's Brut* 2 vols. ed. G. L. Brook and R. F. Leslie (1963-78)

Lech, battle of the (955) Fought near Augsburg, it was a resounding victory for Otto I the Great, king of Germany, over the Magyars, who had been threatening the borders of his kingdom since the mid-9th c. By ending Magyar incursions into his territory, Otto contributed towards the establishment of a settled Hungarian kingdom, besides ensuring that his personal prestige was equal to the task of securing the imperial crown. After the battle his successful soldiers are said to have hailed him as *imperator*.
□ K. J. Leyser *Rule and Conflict in an Early Medieval Society* (1979)

Leo I the Great, St Pope 440-61 (b. *c.* 400) He strove to destroy heresy and unite the Western church under papal supremacy. In 449 he countered the Monophysite heresy of Eutyches with the *Tome*, an outline of Catholic Christology which was accepted as a pronouncement of orthodoxy by the Council of Chalcedon (451). He claimed jurisdiction in Africa, Spain and Gaul, and obtained a rescript accepting his authority in the West from Valentinian III. His letters and sermons provided theoretical justification for these claims, developing in particular the doctrine of the Petrine commission. His skilful handling of Attila the Hun (452) and Gaiseric the Vandal enhanced the temporal prestige of the papacy.
□ T. G. Jalland *The Life and Times of St Leo the Great* (1941)

Leo III, St Pope 795-816 (b. 750) He faced considerable opposition from the supporters of his predecessor, Adrian I. He crowned Charlemagne as the first

Pope Leo IX consecrating the new church built by Abbot Warino of St Arnulf.

emperor of Western Christendom on Christmas Day 800, thus formalizing the political secession of the West from the Byzantine empire. However, he upheld ecclesiastical unity between East and West. In 809 he refused Charlemagne's request for the *Filioque* clause to be included in the Creed, fearing that this would alienate the Greeks. His other interests included the English church where he acknowledged the promotion of the see of Lichfield to metropolitan status, albeit temporarily, and he intervened in several disputes between archbishops of Canterbury and English kings.

□ H. K. Mann *The Lives of the Popes in the Early Middle Ages* II (1925)

Leo IX, St Pope 1049–54 (b. 1002) He became a canon of Toul in 1017 and was appointed bishop there in 1026. He supported the work of the monastic reform centres of Gorze and Cluny, ensuring that monasteries in his diocese, such as Moyenmoutier and Remiremont, followed their example. Henry III appointed him pope at Worms in 1048, but Leo insisted on election by the people and clergy of Rome before he was enthroned at St Peter's in 1049. The contemporary impetus for ecclesiastical reform was brought under papal control during his pontificate and he gathered able and zealous men such as Hildebrand and Humbert of Silva Candida at Rome to act as his advisers.

Leo travelled extensively, holding 12 synods in places such as Rome, Mainz, Pavia and Rheims, which enforced clerical celibacy and censured simony. In 1050 he twice condemned the Eucharistic

teachings of Berengar of Tours. With Henry III, he planned a military campaign to deal with the Norman threat in southern Italy (1053), but found himself facing the enemy alone with an inadequate army at Civitate. After a devastating defeat, Leo was captured and kept in detention near Bari for nine months. His activities in southern Italy, where the Eastern church traditionally exercised widespread jurisdiction, combined with his assertion of papal primacy, brought him into conflict with Michael I Cerularius, patriarch of Constantinople. In 1054 Humbert of Silva Candida was sent to Byzantium on a mission of reconciliation, but negotiations exacerbated the situation, and the church drifted towards open schism soon after Leo's death that year.

□ A. Garreau *Saint Léon IX, pape alsacien* (1965)

Leo III the Isaurian Eastern emperor 717–40 (b. *c.* 680) Born at Germanicea in northern Syria, not strictly in Isauria. A successful military career under Anastasius II led to his appointment as *strategos* of the Anatolian theme, and in 717 he rebelled against the weak Theodosius III and seized the imperial dignity for himself. He immediately beat off a Saracen attack on Constantinople, thus foreshadowing his future clashes with Islam in Asia Minor. Leo implemented extensive administrative reforms: he subdivided the vast themes of Asia Minor and, in 726, introduced a new legal code, the *Ecloga*. In that same year his religious policy inaugurated the lengthy Iconoclastic controversy. His historical reputation depends, however, in the last resort on his successful defence of Constantinople (717), an event which marks the end of the first relentless advance of Muslim military power.

□ S. Gero *Byzantine Iconoclasm during the reign of Leo III* (1973); *Constantinople in the Early Eighth Century* ed. A. Cameron and J. Herrin (1984)

Liber Augustalis Law code issued in September 1231 by the Emperor Frederick II to apply to his kingdom of southern Italy, the *Regno*. His close legal adviser, Piero della Vigna, was chiefly responsible for the compilation, made in conscious imitation of Justinian and representing a high point in the theoretical claims of the Emperor to possess the authority associated with Roman law. It was issued in both Latin and Greek and, again in imitation of Justinian, was supplemented by a series of new laws, or *Novellae*.

Liberal arts Basic education for the learned elite in the Middle ages consisted in instruction in the liberal arts. The tradition was directly descended from classical times, through the writings of St Augustine, and was refined and transformed into a teaching framework by Cassiodorus and Boethius in the early 6th c. The formal division of the liberal arts into Trivium and Quadrivium probably dates from the Carolingian period, and remained the theoretical basis of medieval education until the 12th c.

The Trivium, or three-way course, consisted of grammar, dialectic and rhetoric. These three branches contained the essential disciplines necessary for service in the church, and gradually also in secular government: command of the structure of language, ability to present argument, and appreciation of the force of speech in prose and poetry. An uneasy balance was maintained initially between the use of classical and scriptural texts as examples in instruction, with the balance falling heavily, from Carolingian days, towards the scriptures. The second part of the syllabus was more scientific; the Quadrivium, or four-way course, included arithmetic, geometry, astronomy and music. *See* EDUCATION [*319*]
□ A. Murray *Reason and Society in the Middle Ages* (1978)

The south door at Chartres: the **Liberal arts** of music and grammar represented by Pythagoras and Donatus.

Libraries As they are now used and understood, libraries are a legacy of early Europe and of the manuscript era. Although both personal and institutional libraries were an important feature of Greco-Roman culture, none survived the dissolution of the Western Roman empire. Between the late 6th c. and mid-8th c. European churches, especially monastic communities, possessed small collections of basic books, as did a small number of individuals (mostly clergy, except on the Mediterranean seaboard); but there were no libraries in the full sense of the word.

True libraries – sizeable collections of books focused on a core of standard texts, stable, secure, accessible and properly maintained – appear quite suddenly within the Frankish empire under Charlemagne (768–814). They were begun in cathedrals and abbeys as part of the emperor's programme to revive Christian Latin learning within his dominions. By the late 9th c. some of these libraries contained 200–500 books and would never grow much larger. Between the collapse of the Carolingian empire and the 12th c., libraries spread across Europe in the wake of missionary enterprise and monastic reform.

Many generalizations that can be made about European libraries in the 9th c. remain valid until *c.* 1300. Within that period, with a few exceptions, libraries were found in religious institutions: cathedrals and the much more numerous Benedictine abbeys. Two to five hundred books constituted a large collection, such as might be found in a populous monastic house. The composition of such collections, and even the specific texts found in them, was at any given time similar across Europe. Libraries were catalogued, written lists surviving from the 9th c. onward. These collections were for the use of members of the communities housing them; only a particularly privileged outsider, such as a well-known scholar, might have access to them. Books were, however, commonly lent by one community to another, often for the purpose of recopying, which gives a clue to one of the principal methods by which libraries were built up; this copying might be done locally or where the exemplar was held, either by the clergy themselves, or by professional scribes. The other main method of acquisition was by donation, a virtuous act often performed by those who became monks or canons after pursuing a scholastic career. Sometimes library catalogues record the names of donors and the titles of their books, and these lists indicate that 6–24 books was the usual size of an individual's library, although some wealthy book-lovers – whose numbers increased from the 12th c. – might have many more. Until the 14th c., religious institutions did not keep their books in a special room, or even in a single place. Books were kept in chests or cupboards, the main one usually

Libraries: a clerk locking a book cupboard, in the university statute book of Freiburg-im-Breisgau.

near the entrance to the chapter-house, others perhaps within the church itself. Security and maintenance were the concern of the precentor. Institutions often wrote some form of identification into their books, an *ex libris* inscription, followed by a severe anathema against theft or damage. When library rooms were built, during the 14th c. and 15th c., they were fitted with specialized furniture – lecterns or carrels – and the books were chained into position.

Important intellectual and social changes affected the development of European libraries between the 13th c. and 15th c. The first of these was the rise of the universities. Initially, like the antecedent schools, they did not have their own libraries. This was a problem, for the growing number of new universities, of students and of prescribed texts created an unprecedented demand for books. This could partly be met by streamlining and cheapening book production, but books were still expensive. One solution was to make accessible the large number of institutional libraries already in existence. The English Franciscans, in the second half of the 13th c., created the first 'union catalogue', listing standard authors and their works, together with the monastic libraries in which they could be found, using a system of numbers and a key. But eventually universities had to found their own libraries; these were sited in the constituent colleges, the earliest at Paris (the Sorbonne) and Oxford (Merton College) late in the 13th c. The second important influence was the growing class of wealthy and literate noble or mercantile laymen, for whom the patronage of learning and possession of fine books was a manifestation of social status. Kings and princes had long had small collections of devotional books for their personal use or of de luxe copies of works dedicated and presented to them. Such books, often in the vernacular, continued to form the nucleus of their libraries north of the Alps – the most famous being those of the kings of France and dukes of Burgundy

and Berry. However, in those areas influenced by humanism, especially its heartland of northern Italy, mercantile princes with more learned tastes and aspirations owned sizeable libraries whose contents were freely lent out to their circle of scholarly acquaintances. The library of S. Marco convent, Florence, founded in 1444 by Niccolò Niccoli and Cosimo de' Medici, was the first public lending library in Europe. The books owned by all such people were professionally made and of a high degree of splendour.

Over the whole of this period, from the 9th c. to the 15th c., the basic constituents of the institutional libraries remained fairly constant: the works of the great Latin fathers and a selection of pagan classics. To these were added, in the progress of time, a small body of technical literature on such subjects as law and medicine, the writings of European theologians and biblical scholars, and items of local interest, such as domestic chronicles. The accession of new material grew to a flood in the 12th c. and 13th c., made up of texts used in the schools and universities: glossed biblical books and the works of Aristotle and his Arabic and Western commentators. The Italian humanists added more Latin classics, and for the first time, both pagan and Christian Greek writings. Throughout this period the reading public, especially those reading Latin, was a minute fraction of the population, and before *c.* 1300 it was limited to the clergy. Even so, because books were fearsomely expensive, reading a library book was a much more common experience for the literate than personal ownership of even a single volume. Thus, the role of institutional libraries in preserving and disseminating knowledge was vital, while the part played by privately owned books was negligible before the 14th c. *See* BOOKS IN MANUSCRIPT; HANDWRITING   RT

□ J. W. Clark *The Care of Books* (1902); *The Medieval Library* ed. J. W. Thompson (1939); F. Wormald and C. E. Wright *The English Library before 1700* (1958); *Medieval Scribes, Manuscripts and Libraries; Essays presented to N. R. Ker* ed. M. B. Parkes and A. G. Watson (1978)

Libri Carolini Theologians at the court of Charlemagne wrote the 'Caroline books' in direct response to the situation at Constantinople, where the church, under the Isaurian dynasty, seemed to Westerners to be lapsing into heresy. As a statement of Charles' defence of orthodoxy, they are a pointer to his theoretical views and an important stage in the events which led to his coronation as emperor in 800. *See* THEODULF

□ W. Ullmann *The Carolingian Renaissance and the Idea of Kingship* (1969)

Decorated initials from the opening of St Matthew in the **Lindisfarne Gospels** (*c.*700).

Lindisfarne Gospels These contain the most impressive surviving examples of early Hiberno–Saxon decorative art and a fine version of the Vulgate text. They were written and decorated in the monastery of Lindisfarne *c.* 696–98, and were dedicated to St Cuthbert. During the 10th c. an interlinear gloss in Anglo-Saxon was added and a colophon appended, attributing the production of the Gospels to Eadfrith, later bishop of Lindisfarne. *See* NORTHUMBRIAN RENAISSANCE

□ J. Backhouse *The Lindisfarne Gospels* (1981)

Literature Destined predominantly for collective public recitation rather than for individual private reading, medieval vernacular literature flourished under aristocratic patronage in secular courts. Given the vagaries of lay manuscript preservation, a surprisingly large volume of writing has survived, though this doubtless represents only a small proportion of what was actually produced, still less copied down. The vernaculars, long regarded as poor relations to Latin (the traditional international language of learning and culture), came nonetheless to be the vehicle for the greatest imaginative achievements of the Middle Ages. Secular literature in Latin is largely confined to subjects deriving directly or indirectly from classical models. Notable exceptions are the irreverent verse of the Archpoet

(*c.* 1160), the love poetry of the *Carmina Burana* (13th c.) and Geoffrey of Monmouth's highly popular pseudo *Historia Regum Britanniae* (1136), which launched the literary vogue of King Arthur.

Vernacular literature naturally drew on written sources, but at the same time combined disparate elements from popular culture, including myth, folklore and other oral traditions. Its free mixture of tones is characteristic: the blending of the popular and the learned, the entertaining and the didactic, the supernatural and the concrete, produced a richly diverse and innovative literature with broad appeal, affording different levels of appreciation and interpretation.

Throughout the Middle Ages, poetry rather than prose was the preferred medium of literary expression. A wide range of genres is represented, among which the narrative romance, forerunner of the modern novel, occupies a prominent position. Anonymity was the norm – at least in the early period – and writers would create variations on accepted conventions, rather than aiming at originality. Attention was often focused on an individual, who would function as the embodiment of a feudal or chivalric ethos, or as the agent of human conflict. Religion formed an ever-present background, with love – usually in a ritualized form – providing another major theme. Social realism was not a particular preoccupation in a literature which was above all celebratory and idealizing, but social and moral concerns, set within a highly symbolic framework, were among the more frequently recurring motifs. Characterization and psychological analysis were seldom explicit, and ambiguity and irony consistently exploited. The best of the named authors show an impressively wide range of learning and considerable artistic self-awareness.

France is generally regarded as the literary trendsetter of medieval Europe, but its pre-eminence does not antedate the 12th c. The Germanic world claims the earliest survivals: the Old English *Beowulf*, thought to date from the 8th c. , a powerful evocation of a lone warrior's struggles against the powers of evil, and the fragmentary Old High German *Hildebrandslied*. This epic tradition is continued into the Middle High German *Nibelungenlied* at the end of the 12th c., and the Old Norse *Eddas* and prose sagas from Iceland. The medieval French epic makes its appearance at the end of the 11th c. with its masterpiece, the *Chanson de Roland*, by far the best of the hundred or so French epic poems still extant, in terms of oral formulaic style, narrative structure and the portrayal of conflicting loyalties in a warrior society. By contrast, the Spanish *Cantar de Mio Cid*, from the start of the 13th c., seems less popular in inspiration, less heroic and uplifting in tone.

The Celtic *Tristan and Isolde* legend is represented in 12th-c. French only by fragmentary survivals, with the Anglo-Norman Thomas providing the source for Gottfried von Strassburg's brilliant reworking into German (*c.* 1210). The other master of Middle High German narrative, Wolfram von Eschenbach, also took inspiration for his *Parzival* (1200–16) from French models, more specifically from the pioneer and most accomplished exponent of medieval romance, Chrétien de Troyes. Chrétien's corpus of five octosyllabic romances composed 1165–90 (of which *Yvain* and the unfinished *Conte du Graal* are the best known) reflects social concerns, in its juxtaposition of contemporary realism and Arthurian legend, and questions the prevailing chivalric ethos. In the wake of Chrétien, the psychology of love is further explored in the allegory of Guillaume de Lorris' *Roman de la Rose* (*c.* 1225–30), the continuation of which, by Jean de Meung (1269–75), soars off into encyclopaedic exuberance. The Courtly Love tradition is continued through to Juan Ruiz's diverse and enigmatic *Libro de Buen Amor* (1330–43).

The cult of love originated in the technically elaborate, sometimes hermetic songs of the Occitan troubadours of the late 11th c. and 12th c. It was further fostered by the German *Minnesänger*, Walther von der Vogelweide (*c.* 1170–1230) being their outstanding representative, while the Galician–Portuguese *cantigas de amigo* reflect a more popular facet of the varied output of medieval lyric poetry.

Middle English literature, retarded in its development by the aftermath of the Norman Conquest, blossoms in the latter half of the 14th c. with Langland's learned social allegory *Piers Plowman*, with the *Gawain* poet, and particularly with Chaucer, who in his *Canterbury Tales* (*c.* 1387) presents a living portrait gallery of contemporary types in a sophisticated poetic style. Medieval drama is largely limited to Passion plays, of which the Middle English mystery cycles are perhaps the most enduring examples.

Pride of place among medieval writers is traditionally – and rightly – reserved for Dante (1265–1321), whose *Divine Comedy* allies loftiness of theme with poetic beauty, presenting a Christian world vision in a *dolce stil nuovo* which raises vernacular eloquence to new heights of expressivity. Boccaccio's *Decameron* (1348–53) marks the coming of age of prose as a literary medium, while Petrarch (1304–74), whose love sonnets were to be widely imitated, heralds humanism and the start of a new era. In the 1460s in France, Villon continued to use traditional modes of expression, superimposed with cogent social realism under an autobiographical veneer. *See* CHANSON DE GESTE; COURTLY LOVE; ROMANS D'AVENTUR; SAGAS, NORSE; TROUBADOURS IS

□ W. P. Ker *Epic and Romance* (1908); E.R. Curtius *European Literature and the Latin Middle Ages* (1953); F.J.E. Raby *A History of Secular Latin Poetry in the Middle Ages* (1957); M.D. Legge *Anglo-Norman Literature and its Background* (1963); *Medieval Secular Literature* ed. W. Matthews (1965); P. Dronke *The Medieval Lyric* (1968), *Poetic Individuality in the Middle Ages* (1970); A. D. Deyermond *History of Spanish Literature: the Middle Ages* (1971); F.B. Artz *The Mind of the Middle Ages* (1980); C. Clover *The Medieval Saga* (1982)

Lithuania A backward pagan people in the 13th c., speaking an Indo-European tongue distinct from Slavonic, the Lithuanians achieved political unity under pressure from the Teutonic Order and the Poles, and under the Jagiello dynasty, in conjunction with the Poles, came to rule large tracts of Eastern Europe and historic Russia. Their acceptance of Catholicism (though pagan elements survived into the 15th c.) and their part in the great defeat of the knights at Tannenburg in 1410, ensured a degree of political and social strength, but the alliance with the Poles was always uneasy, and pressure both from the Orthodox Russian side and from the Germans ultimately proved too much for the somewhat ramshackle empire.
□ M. Gimbutas *The Balts* (1963)

Liudprand of Cremona (*c.* 922–*c.* 72) Deacon of Pavia. He served as chancellor to Berengar of Italy until he was disgraced *c.* 956. He then left Italy for Germany and the court of Otto I. The Emperor appointed him to the see of Cremona in 961 and used him as an imperial ambassador. He is an important authority for contemporary affairs in Italy and Germany; his most famous work is the *Relatio de Legatione Constantinopolitana*, which gives an account of his embassy to Constantinople (968–69). □ *The Works of Liudprand of Cremona* trans. F. A. Wright (1930). M. Litzel *Studien über Liutprand von Cremona* (1933)

Llywelyn ab Iorwerth the Great Prince of North Wales *c.* 1190–1240 (b. 1173) Perhaps the ablest of all Welsh princes of the Middle Ages. Taking full advantage of weakness and uncertainty in the political life of England, Llywelyn consolidated his hold on his native principality of Gwynedd in the early days of the 13th c. and by skilful diplomacy, as well as by war, extended his authority over other Welsh princes. When he paid formal homage to the young King Henry III in 1218 he was in a dominant position throughout most of Wales, both south and north. The rest of his long reign was substantially successful, and by his death Llywelyn, prince of

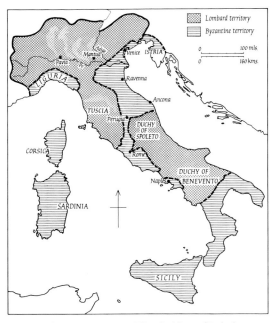

Lombard territory in 640. The division of Italy between Lombards and Byzantines was constantly fluctuating.

Aberffraw and lord of Snowdon, was well on his way to establishing a powerful feudal principality in which Welsh law, poetry and culture flourished, and in which positive advances were made in the field of government and in cooperation between the prince and the church.
□ R. R. Davies *Conquest, coexistence and change: Wales 1063–1415* (1987)

Llywelyn ap Gruffydd the Last Prince of Wales *c.*1246–82 The fortunes of the last of the virtually independent princes of medieval Wales fluctuated according to the strength of the English crown. By the Treaty of Montgomery (1267), in the aftermath of the Barons' War, Llywelyn won the right to bear the title of prince of Wales, confirmed to him and his heirs, and to exercise direct feudal overlordship over most other Welsh lands. His territorial gains were also great, and at this point it seemed as if he had consolidated and extended the position held by his grandfather, Llywelyn the Great. As the English kingship grew stronger under Edward I, and in the face of Welsh rivalries, his position crumbled, and by the Treaty of Conway (1277) he was confined to his heartlands in Gwynedd with only vestigial traces of his former authority. A revolt against the English in 1282 ended in tragedy when Llywelyn was killed in a skirmish near Builth. His constructive efforts to institute effective government in a curious fashion benefited the victor, Edward I, who by the Statute of Rhuddlan (1284) and by the initiation of a power-

ful policy of castle-building, ensured the destruction of Welsh hopes of an independent principality.

Lollards (from a Platt-Deutsch term meaning mutterer or mumbler) Name given to opponents of the established order within the English church at the end of the 14th c., who professed to be followers of Wycliffe. In the opening years of Henry IV's reign the government took savage action against them under the terms of the statute *De Heretico Comburendo* (1400). A rebellion led by Sir John Oldcastle after Henry V's accession in 1413 was cruelly suppressed, but Lollardy subsisted, to provide some element of independent religious experience in which emphasis was placed on studying scripture in the vernacular and on the rejection of priestly authority.
□ K. B. McFarlane *John Wycliffe and the Lollards* (1950); A. Hudson *Lollards and their Books* (1985)

Lombards The movement of the Lombards (Langobards), a small but well-organized Germanic people, into Italy in 568 is the last significant political act in the long-drawn-out process of Germanic settlement within the boundaries of the Roman empire. They were ruled by a king and dukes, and in the aftermath of Justinian's attempts to reconquer Italy, established a kingdom in the north, which still bears their name, and principalities elsewhere, two of which, the duchies of Spoleto and Benevento in the south, proved long-lasting. The Lombards were predominantly Arian, but as they settled Roman influences in both law and religion became strong. By the mid-8th c. they were universally recognized as a Catholic kingdom, and as such provided a serious political threat to the papacy, especially when in 751 they temporarily took over the exarchate, based at Ravenna. Frankish intervention saved the papacy from sinking to the status of a mere Lombard bishopric, and in 774, at the start of his victorious career, Charlemagne defeated the Lombard king and took over the Lombard kingship. *See* AISTULF; ALBOIN
□ T. Hodgkin *Italy and her Invaders* vols. 5 and 6 (1895); L. Musset *The Germanic Invasions* (1975); W. Goffart *Barbarians and Romans* (1980)

London Owing its position to the fact that it was the first point at which the Thames could be bridged, and described by Bede as an emporium to which people of many nations resorted, London remained an important centre of trade and communications throughout the Middle Ages. Development took place further west along the river in Saxon days, and under Edward the Confessor the building of the new Westminster Abbey established Westminster as one of the principal royal and eccle-

The manuscript text in the illumination reads:

es nouuelles Dalbion
Sil vous en plaist escouter
mon frere z mon compaignon
Lchiez qua mon retorner
Ly este sera sa mer

E ceu a ioyeuse chiere

A 15th-c. Flemish miniature of the Tower of **London** with the city in the background. Charles of Orleans appears three times in the picture, as he was imprisoned in the Tower after Agincourt.

siastical sites in the country; but the heart of London remained the old Roman *Londinium* and the bridge.

The Normans typically consolidated activity with the building of the Tower and other fortifications. A full description by Fitzstephen in the 1170s tells of a city 'blessed by a wholesome climate, in Christ's religion, in the strength of its fortifications, the nature of its site, the repute of its citizens, and the honour of its matrons: happy too in its sports, prolific in noble men'. Its citizens played a prominent part in politics and the choosing of kings, from the days of King Aethelred to the Peasants' Revolt of 1381, and its liberties were safeguarded by Magna Carta.

The complexity of its organization, its courts and hustings, the wealth of its citizens and of its churches from St Paul's to the multitude of small churches within and immediately without the walls, bear witness to London's standing. In its search for communal status and the institution of mayoral office, London showed its rank within the European community. In the central and later Middle Ages it became increasingly important as the financial centre of the kingdom. By 1300 and in many respects long before it had all the essential attributes of a capital city.
□ C.N.L. Brooke *London 800–1216: the Shaping of a City* (1975); G. Williams *Medieval London, from Commune to Capital* (1970)

Manuscript poem from Fulda with a portrait of **Louis the Pious** (9th c.).

Louis (Lewis) I the Pious Emperor 814–40 (b. 778) Charlemagne's son, he assumed full power in 814, having been king of Aquitaine from 781 and joint emperor from 813. He designated his eldest son Lothar as his successor in 817, reserving subordinate kingdoms for Lothar's brothers, Pepin and Louis. Remarrying in 818, he tried to alter this arrangement in favour of Charles, the child of his second union, thus causing the rebellion of his other sons. He was deposed in 833, but restored in 835, and maintained a precarious hold on the throne thereafter. He supported ecclesiastical reorganization in Germany, especially the monastic reforms of St Benedict of Aniane, and was a notable patron of scholarship.
□ R. McKitterick *The Frankish Kingdoms under the Carolingians* (1983)

Louis IX, St King of France 1226–70 (b. 1214) He married Margaret of Provence in 1234. His mother, Blanche of Castile, acted as regent during his minority, and seems to have retained a controlling hand in government until at least 1242. Louis acquired the Crown of Thorns from Constantinople in 1239, and built the Sainte-Chapelle in Paris as a repository for the relic 1245–48. He went on crusade to Egypt in 1249 and captured Damietta in the following year; but in 1250 he was captured after his defeat at Mansurah, and Damietta was surrendered as his ransom. He then spent four years fortifying Christian strongholds in Syria before returning to France, where he busied himself with the improvement of governmental administration, issuing, for example, ordinances dealing with the duties of provincial officials (1254 and 1256) and the circulation of currency (1263 and 1265). His work encouraged moves towards a differentiation of the judicial and financial functions of the *curia regis*, and this led to the beginnings of specialization amongst governmental personnel.

Louis's desire for peaceful unity between Christian princes in the face of the Islamic threat to the Holy Land led him to settle disputes over suzerainty with Aragon and England by the terms of the Treaties of Corbeil (1258) and Paris (1259) respectively. It also established him as an international arbitrator of high repute; amongst his most notable work in this field was his mediation between Henry III and his barons, which led to the Mise of Amiens (1264). Louis again departed on crusade in 1270 and died of dysentery at Tunis. *See* JEAN DE JOINVILLE; PEACE OF PARIS
□ W. C. Jordan *Louis IX and the Challenge of the Crusade* (1979); J. Richard *Saint Louis* (1983); M. Slattery *Myth, Man and Sovereign Saint* (1985)

Louis XI King of France 1461–83 (b. 1423) The 'spider-king', Louis earned a reputation for craft in diplomacy, unscrupulousness and treachery. Chronicles have little good to say of him, and yet his ability and intelligence clearly strengthened royal institutions, diminished the risk of feudal disorder and took full advantage of the political difficulties of his principal rivals, the kings of England and the dukes of Burgundy. At the end of his reign France was heavily taxed and increasingly under the control of royal bureaucrats, but at the same time clearly on the slow road to recovery from the ravages of the Hundred Years' War, and indeed, with its standing army and expensive government, well on the way to the royal absolutism of the early modern period.
□ P. S. Lewis *Later Medieval France: the Polity* (1968); P. M. Kendall *Louis XI* (1971)

Lucas de Penna (*c.*1320–90) One of the most important commentators on Roman law of the early 14th c. Lucas, a Neapolitan steeped in the practice of southern Italy and aware of the legal teachings of the Eastern empire, proved an inspiration and a source for many later medieval jurists. Through his work and his copious quotations from John of Salisbury, ideas concerning the sovereign power of the state and its right to confiscate property were transmitted to a ready audience, notably at the French royal court.
□ W. Ullmann *Medieval idea of law as represented by Lucas de Penna* (1946)

Ludwigslied Late 9th-c. poem which celebrates the victory of Louis III, king of the West Franks 879–92, over a Viking host on the Somme in 881. Written in a Rhenish Franconian dialect of Old High German, it celebrates the victory of the young 'French' King Louis and is a key text for the early history of the German language.
□ R. Harvey, 'The Provenance of the Old High German *Ludwigslied*', *Medium Aevum* 14 (1945)

Lull, Raymond (*c.* 1235–1315) He turned to the religious life *c.* 1263 and, influenced by the Moorish presence in his native Majorca, devoted himself to the conversion of Muslims. During his lifetime repeated efforts to gain European support for his work resulted only in the foundation (1276) by James II of Majorca, of a short-lived college at Miramar, where missionaries could study Arabic. This led him to set out on unaided missions to Asia and Africa; he was eventually stoned to death by Muslims at Bougie in North Africa. Almost 300 of Lull's written works survive to reveal his gifts as a mystic and poet, besides his accomplishment as a philosopher and theologian; the most famous is the *Ars Generalis sive Magnis*, which outlines a method for establishing ultimate truth. He pioneered the use of romance vernacular for theological and philosophical writings, thus inaugurating literary Catalan.
□ *Life of Ramon Lull* ed. E. Allison Peers (1927)

Lupus Servatus (*c.* 805–62) Abbot of Ferrières by 840, Lupus was an outstanding figure of the Carolingian renaissance, active unsuccessfully in the political field in his attempts to preserve the unity of the empire, but successful in his literary and academic efforts to make his monastery at Ferrières an acknowledged centre for classical culture. He represents one of the strong Romanizing intellectual elements that gave a degree of unity to the Carolingian ventures.
□ C. H. Beeson *Lupus of Ferrières* (1930)

Lyons, Council of (1274) General council summoned by Pope Gregory X with the object of ending the imperial Interregnum, of reuniting the Latin and Greek churches, and of dissuading Charles of Anjou from his ambitious schemes in the Byzantine empire. Although it was temporarily successful in establishing a political and ecclesiastical order congenial to the papal curia, its deeper aims could not be achieved, and it is remembered as a brilliant, but rather showy and impermanent demonstration of papal political leadership.
□ S. Kuttner, 'Conciliar Law in the Making: the Lyonese Constitutions of Gregory X', *Miscellanea Pio Paschini* 2 (1949); J. M. Powell, 'Frederick II and the Church: a Revisionist View', *Catholic Historical Review* 48 (1962–63)

M

Magna Carta Royal charter, sealed and issued by King John at Runnymede on the Thames near Windsor in June 1215. Magna Carta was the product of over two years of negotiations between the king and his barons, prominent among whom were Stephen Langton, archbishop of Canterbury, and William Marshall. In its initial form it consisted of 63 clauses, but the re-issues (1217, 1225 *et al.*) omitted certain clauses, notably the so-called sanction clause (61) which attempted to place institutional restraints on a headstrong king acting contrary to law (a council of 25 barons of whom four would act as an executive committee).

The charter is a rich source for the legal and social historian of the age, but also has a legacy of great symbolic importance. Throughout the 13th c. both

Magna Carta and the allied Forest charters were invoked by the barons when they opposed arbitrary government. It became recognized as first among the statutes of the realm and was reaffirmed at the opening of many medieval parliaments. In the 17th c. its significance as a bastion of English liberty was invoked, especially by lawyers in the struggle against Charles I and the resulting civil war. This tradition was carried through the English-speaking world; Magna Carta was given a special place of honour, for example, in the celebrations of the bicentenary of the foundation of the USA.

It is in one sense a feudal document, concerned with what the barons saw as abuse of feudal law on John's part, in matters of succession to feudal tenements, rights over marriage and wardships, and exaction of aids and reliefs. It is, indeed, something of a hotchpotch, including arrangements for peace with Scotland and Wales, an assertion of the freedom of the church, a defence of the liberties of London and other boroughs, regulations for taking counsel according to proper forms and with due notice given (barons summoned by special writ severally), and details over weights and measures, forest law and even fishing rights. Emphasis on baronial rights has led many to interpret it as a selfish document, though all recognize the attempt to extend its rulings deep into society, into the *communitas regni*. As a royal charter it could be (and was) revoked as legally as it was granted. Pope Innocent III was bitterly opposed to what he saw as its excessively anti-monarchical principles, though it did receive papal assent in re-issued form, in the minority of Henry III, with the more offensive passages removed.

For all its inadequacies and awkwardness in detail, it provided a dramatic statement of the rule of law which justified later instinctive support. The best of Henry II's legal reforms were affirmed and guaranteed, notably those relating to the holding of common pleas at a fixed place, and the safeguarding of landholding by means of the possessory assizes. General clauses (39 and 40) stated that action against freemen should be initiated only by the judgment of peers and/or the law of the land; and that justice would not be denied, sold or delayed. As a practical measure against tyranny and as a move towards rational government according to law, Magna Carta deserved its later fame.   HRL
□ W. S. McKechnie *Magna Carta* (1905); J. C. Holt *Magna Carta and Medieval Government* (1985)

Maimonides, Moses (1135–1204) One of the greatest Jewish philosophers, Maimonides was a close contemporary of Averroes. Born in Cordoba, Spain, he and his family were forced to leave, owing to persecution of the Jews, and finally settled in Fostat, a suburb of Cairo. He had a good reputation as a doctor and also became the official leader (*nagid*) of the Egyptian Jewry. Of his voluminous writings, his greatest rabbinic work, *Mishneh Torah* (1180), was a systematic statement of Jewish law and belief. His celebrated *Guide for the Perplexed* (1190) attempted to rationalize Jewish theology by applying Neoplatonic Aristotelianism, and the work played a valuable part in conveying more completely the philosophy of Aristotle to Europe.
□ A. Heschel *Maimonides* (1982); N. Roth *Maimonides* (1985)

Mamlūks Term (meaning slave) used from the 9th c. to describe soldiers of servile origin recruited into the bodyguards of Muslim rulers. In Egypt in the mid-13th c., it came to describe the mercenaries, largely of Turkish origin, gathered together by the sultan of Egypt to resist the crusade launched by St Louis. In 1254 they established their own dynasty in Egypt, expanded eastwards to defeat the Mongols at Ayn Jalud (1261), taking control of Syria and much of the Crusading kingdom. In 1291 the last of the crusading principalities at Acre was captured, and the Mamlūk dynasties, famous for courage and horsemanship, continued to exercise authority in the Near East for the rest of the Middle Ages.
□ W. Popper *Egypt and Syria under the Circassian Sultans* (1955–60); E. Atil *The Renaissance of Islam* (1981); R. Irwin *The Middle East in the Middle Ages* (1986)

Mandeville, Sir John (d. *c.*1370) A native of St Albans, in Hertfordshire, Mandeville travelled widely in Europe and the Middle East, and claimed to have penetrated deep into Asia, serving the sultan of Babylon and the great khan in China. Some of his stories were based on other men's work and some on pure hearsay, but his narrative skill and command of language (both English and French), ensured that his *Travels* became one of the most popular books of the later Middle Ages.
□ M. Letts *Sir John Mandeville: the Man and his Book* (1949); C. K. Zacker *Curiosity and Pilgrimage* (1976)

Manfred King of Sicily 1258–66 (b. 1232) Illegitimate son of Frederick II, Manfred, prince of Taranto, claimed the Sicilian throne on the death of Conrad IV. Defeating the armies of Pope Innocent IV and his successor Alexander IV in Apulia, Manfred was crowned king of Sicily at Palermo in 1258. A Ghibelline, he asserted his authority in Lombardy and Tuscany, winning a great victory against Florence at Montaperti (1260). Such domination persuaded Alexander's successor Urban IV to offer Sicily to

Charles of Anjou. In a battle near Benevento (February 1266), Manfred was defeated and killed by Charles, who then succeeded to the Sicilian kingdom.

Manicheanism Founder of a new religion, Mani (b. *c*.216) preached successfully in the Persian empire, but was killed by Zoroastrian priests *c*. 276. Manicheanism was a dualistic religion based on two conflicting principles: salvation lay in releasing goodness, or light, which was imprisoned in matter, or darkness. Partly monastic, Manicheanism was especially a missionary faith, spreading to China, India, North Africa and, in the 5th c., to Spain and southern Gaul. Although suppressed as a heresy, it influenced later sects (e.g., Bogomils, Cathars). In its most extreme form it led to excessive austerity in diet, abstinence from sex and from eating things sexually begotten; in other words, rejection of what Christian theologians came to term the 'creatureliness' of man.
□ S. Runciman *The Medieval Manichee* (1947)

Manuscript illumination Parchment or vellum (a material prepared from the skins of calves, sheep and other domestic animals) was the chief writing material used throughout Europe in the Middle Ages. Paper-making was known in Spain and Italy by the 12th c., but did not seriously rival parchment until the later 14th c.; indeed, the full triumph of paper as the normal base for book production coincided in some measure with the development of printing.

Parchment lent itself to ornamentation as well as to writing, and from the early Middle Ages to the superb Books of Hours of the 15th c., some of the finest artistic work of the medieval period is to be found in illuminated manuscripts, in the form of illustrations to devotional texts or in simple elaboration and colouring of title pages or individual letters.

Byzantine art, with its florid use of gold and vermilion, provided an early and continuous inspiration to the artists of medieval Europe. Special developments in Ireland and Northumbria produced schools capable of work that has seldom, if ever, been surpassed, demonstrating extraordinary skill in the art of interlacing and counterpointing of animal and geometric patterns, with subtle variations of delicate colour; the Lindisfarne Gospels and the Book of Kells remain the outstanding examples. The Carolingian world, benefiting from Byzantine and Celtic traditions, produced first-class work, initially with emphasis on purely ornamental motifs, especially in gold. Each of the Western communities made its own contribution in the succeeding centuries (late Anglo-Saxon England with the Winchester School and the tense vigour of

A classic example of **manuscript illumination**: the opening words of Genesis in the Winchester Bible.

the line drawings, for example), reaching a peak of creation in the Romanesque style of the 12th c.

From about 1200 to the end of the Middle Ages the art of the miniaturist was refined and extended, especially in the great Bibles. (The word miniature is derived not from a word meaning small, but from the verb *minire*, to colour with red lead.) In the later Middle Ages increasing use was made of enlarged initial letters as a means of inserting illustrations of events, foliage, human beings and realistic scenery. Calendars provided an opportunity for the portrayal of ordinary folk and the rhythm of the agrarian year, and conventions quickly hardened over the types of scenes and biblical stories that one would expect to find in psalters and service-books of all description. Increasing awareness of, and delight in the natural world is a characteristic of the illumination of the later Middle Ages. *See* WINCHESTER BIBLE
□ F. Henry *The Book of Kells* (1974); C. Nordenfalk *Celtic and Anglo-Saxon Painting* (1977); J. J. Alexander *Insular Manuscripts from the 6th to the 9th Century* (1978); R. G. Calkins *Illuminated Books of the Middle Ages* (1983); G. Henderson *From Durrow to Kells* (1987)

Manuscript studies A manuscript book was written to be read, and might be illustrated both to reinforce the message of the text and to make it more attractive to the eye. For textual criticism, and indeed for the whole history of literary culture in antiquity and the Middle Ages, manuscripts are our fundamental source of knowledge, and thanks to their numbers and excellent state of preservation, they are of comparable importance for the history of medieval art. The more specialized disciplines of palaeography and codicology are also concerned with aspects of manuscripts; the former deals with the reading, dating and localization of handwriting, in documents as well as in books; the latter, with the materials, techniques and personnel involved in book production. Closely associated with palaeography are the study of inscriptions (epigraphy) and the study of the form, contents and production of documents and records (diplomatic). Where decoration and illustration are concerned, codicology may in practice be indistinguishable from the history of art; indeed, palaeography, codicology, philology and the history of art form a close symbiotic relationship.

The late antique set of names for scripts included *literae virgilianae*, doubtless for rustic capital, and *literae africanae*, perhaps for half-uncial. In the early Middle Ages scripts not in current use might be named: *libri scotice scripti* for books in Irish script at St Gallen; *literae saxonicae* for Anglo-Saxon script in post-Conquest England; *in Romana scriptura* for an early manuscript in uncial at Canterbury (12th c.). Medieval scribes who replaced lost documents, sometimes with improved versions, generally imitated an earlier script, but never without some anachronism. From *c.* 1350 onwards better descriptions of books in library catalogues and a few advertisement sheets of writing masters testify to the existence of an elaborate set of names for both literary and documentary scripts which is, however, too inconsistent to be of much use to modern palaeographers. Italian humanists recognized late antique books as *codices vetustissimi* and Beneventan minuscule as *literae langobardicae*; their name for the new humanistic book script, *litera antiqua*, meant that it was of 12th-c. Caroline inspiration, not just another variety of contemporary Gothic writing.

Some 16th-c. writing manuals include examples of earlier, disused scripts, but systematic historical study began with *De Re Diplomatica Libri Sex* (1681), the work in which the French Benedictine historian Jean Mabillon successfully defended against Jesuit scepticism the authenticity of the diplomata by which Merovingian kings had conveyed estates to his order in the 7th c. and 8th c. As part of his systematic study of all aspects of medieval documents, Mabillon devoted his fifth book to a connected history of the scripts of Latin books and documents. In *Palaeographia Graeca* (1708) Bernard de Montfaucon did for Greek handwriting what his brother in religion, Mabillon, had done for Latin. Mabillon's fundamental misconception of the relationship between the formal Roman scripts and the Pre-

Caroline minuscules was corrected by Scipione Maffei, after his rediscovery of the ancient library of Verona cathedral in 1713; and the monumental *Nouveau traité de diplomatique* (1750–65) by two more French Benedictines, Tassin and Toustain, remained the authority on Latin palaeography for nearly a century. Thomas Astle published the first English handbook (1784), notable for its attention to Insular script; and Charles O'Conor's pioneering work on early Irish script appeared in 1814. These early treatises were all illustrated by hand-engraved facsimiles of respectable quality.

On the Continent, *c.*1775–*c.*1825, widespread suppression of decayed religious houses and the political and military consequences of the French Revolution led to the wholesale transfer of medieval books and documents, directly or via private collections, to public libraries and archives, in which they were readily accessible to the philologists and historians whose research was to inaugurate the 19th-c. flowering of classical and medieval studies. Their improved knowledge of Latin and Greek palaeography began to be available after *c.* 1870, thanks to photography, with facsimiles of complete manuscripts and sets of full-page reproductions from dated or localized manuscripts and documents; a new wave of well-illustrated handbooks were based on these in the generation before 1914. L. Traube (1861–1907), professor of medieval Latin philology at Munich, inaugurated a new era by his insistence on the value of soundly dated and localized manuscripts as evidence for movements in the history of thought. His exhaustive lists of early Latin books have been the ultimate foundation of much later work, including E. A. Lowe's *Codices Latini Antiquiores* (1934–71), on Latin manuscripts to *c.* 800, and B. Bischoff's catalogue of 9th-c. Continental manuscripts.

Since *c.* 1890, discoveries of papyrus in Egypt have carried Greek palaeography back to the 4th c. BC and Latin palaeography back to *c.* 31 BC from their previous starting point in the 4th c. AD. Research on illuminated manuscripts, which also began *c.* 1890, has developed since *c.* 1930 into an indispensable branch of late antique and medieval art history and archaeology. After 1945, particularly distinguished contributions to knowledge of the early Roman period were made by J. Mallon and E. G. Turner; systematic study of humanistic script was initiated by B. L. Ullmann and J. Wardrop. The international catalogue of dateable manuscripts, inaugurated in 1953 by the Institut de Recherche et d'Histoire des Textes, Paris, already comprises 24 volumes from eight countries; and essays in the associated *Nomenclature des écritures livresques* (1954) have greatly enhanced understanding of late medie-

val scripts. Concern with aspects of early manuscripts other than text, script and illustration, and notably with the formation of the quire in different periods and areas, began to be shown in the 1920s by Lowe and E. K. Rand; and since 1945 this codicological approach to 'the archaeology of the manuscript book', thanks originally to the advocacy of F. Masai and L. M. J. Delaissé, has had a profound influence on Greek and Latin palaeography in general. The study of later medieval illuminated manuscripts, in particular, has been inspired by Delaissé's use of codicology as evidence for the attribution of 15th-c. Flemish illuminated books to writing houses run by scholarly scribe-publishers, as well as to painters' workshops. Recent work on late medieval books includes quantitative studies of production and format. *See* BOOKS IN MANUSCRIPT; HANDWRITING   TJB
□ L. Traube, 'Geschichte der Paläographie' in *Vorlesungen und Abhandlungen* I (1909); T. J. Brown, 'Latin palaeography since Traube' in *Codicologica I* ed. A. Gruys and J. P. Gumbert (1976)

Manzikert, battle of In August 1071 the Seljuk army of Alp Arslan annihilated the numerically superior forces led by Romanus IV Diogenes at Manzikert, near Lake Van in Armenia. The Byzantine army had been formed from a heterogeneous and undisciplined collection of foreign mercenaries: Normans, Armenians, Patzinaks and Uzes. It was no match for the highly manoeuvrable, lightly armed Turks, and for the first time a Roman emperor was captured in battle. Alp Arslan, content with tribute and an alliance with the empire, soon released Romanus, but his absence gave the Civil party in Constantinople the chance to organize a bloodless coup d'état, returning the Ducas dynasty to power. The overthrow of Romanus IV led Alp Arslan to repudiate the treaties he had made, thus opening Asia Minor to Turkish attack. Byzantine political weakness and disunity, rather than defeat at Manzikert, was to cost the empire Asia Minor.
□ M. Angold *The Byzantine Empire* (1984)

Marco Polo (*c.* 1254–*c.* 1324) Of Venetian birth, Marco travelled overland to China with his father and uncle, and in 1271 entered the service of Kublai Khan. After nearly 20 years, having been employed on numerous official missions, Marco left China and returned to Venice. In 1298 he was captured by the Genoese and while in prison he dictated his famous *Description of the World* to a Pisan writer called Rusticiano. This account of his travels was one of the earliest detailed descriptions of the Far East, and of the routes to the Far East, and was translated into many languages.
□ H. Yule *The Book of Sir Marco Polo* (1903)

Margaret Queen of Norway, Denmark and Sweden *c.* 1388–1412 (b. 1353) Daughter of Waldemar IV of Denmark (d. 1375), by 1388 Margaret was queen of Denmark and Norway after the deaths of her husband, Haakon VI of Norway (1380) and their son Olaf (1387). At the battle of Aasle in 1389 she defeated and captured her long-standing rival, Albert of Mecklenburg, king of Sweden. In 1397 Margaret united the three kingdoms by the Union of Calmar and the coronation of her great-nephew Eric of Pomerania as king of Norway, Denmark and Sweden. Margaret remained effective ruler and recovered many alienated estates for the crown, besides acquiring Gotland and much of Schleswig.

Margaret, St (*c.* 1045–93) Wife of Malcolm III of Scotland and granddaughter of Edmund Ironside, king of England 1016–17. Margaret was born to the exiled Edward Aetheling, in Hungary. From 1057 she lived at the English court, but after 1066 fled with her brother Edgar Aetheling to Scotland, where she was married to Malcolm Canmore (*c.* 1070). Margaret is credited with anglicizing and refining the Scottish court. She was saintly and

Title page from the first German edition (1477) of **Marco Polo**'s *Travels.*

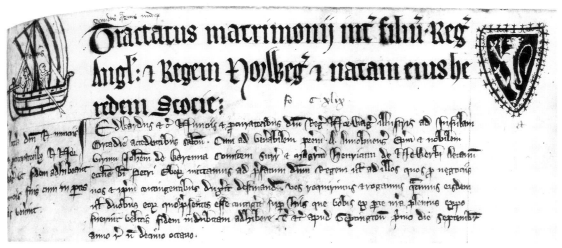

Projected marriage treaty between the son of Edward I of England and **Margaret**, heir to Scotland.

devout, according to her biographer Turgot; her church reforms were chiefly limited to points of observance. Her three sons, ruling in succession, brought the Scottish church more into line with Western Christendom. Margaret was canonized in 1249.

□ G. W. S. Barrow *The Kingdom of the Scots* (1973)

Margaret, Maid of Norway (1283–90) Only child of Eric II of Norway and Margaret (d. 1283), daughter of Alexander III of Scotland. On Alexander's sudden death in March 1286, the infant Margaret was proclaimed queen and her marriage was arranged to Edward, son of Edward I of England (July 1290). The last of the line of Canmore, she sailed from Norway, but died in Orkney (September 1290). The two main claimants to the disputed Scottish throne were Robert Bruce and John Balliol; in November 1292 Edward I named John as the next king of Scotland.

□ A. A. M. Duncan *Scotland, the Making of the Kingdom* (1975)

Mark Early Germanic unit of weight first mentioned in the treaty between Guthrum and King Alfred of 886–90. Its origins and original weight are unknown, but the weight was probably about 230 g as the main European marks gravitate around this figure: Cologne mark 229.46 g; Paris mark 227.54 g; Montpellier mark 235.19 g. Its wide adoption as a weight of 8 oz in the 11th c. was a consequence of the ambiguity of 'pound', which could stand both for a weight and a money of account of 240 pennies. 'Mark' in due course became a money of account also (e.g., in England as 13s 4d, or two-thirds of a pound, since this was its ratio to the Troy pound of 12 oz).

Marshall, William (1146–1219) Earl of Pembroke. A landless younger son and frequenter of tournaments, William was made tutor in chivalry to Henry II's eldest son. In 1189 William married Isabel, daughter and heiress to Richard de Clare, earl of Pembroke and lord of Striguil, and thereby inherited the enormous estates of the Clare family and lordship of Leinster in Ireland, besides buying half the lands of the earls of Giffard. One of the most powerful English barons, William helped John succeed to the throne, but in 1205 he apparently swore allegiance to Philip II of France, concerning his Norman estates. To escape John's persecution, William went to Ireland (1207–13) where, as one of the foremost figures, he brought a remarkable degree of peace and prosperity. A loyal royalist at the end of John's reign, he helped govern England in the king's absence (1214), was prominent in the negotiations that led to the issue of Magna Carta (June 1215), and supported John in the civil war. On John's death (October 1216), William became regent to the young Henry III and was instrumental in bringing peace to England in the course of the following year.

□ *L'histoire de Guillaume le Maréchal* ed. P. Meyer (1891); S. Painter *William Marshall* (1933); G. Duby *William Marshall: The Flower of Chivalry* (1986)

Marsilius of Padua (*c.*1280–*c.*1343) Marsilio Mainardini probably began his university education in Padua, and continued it in Paris, where he is recorded as rector of the university in 1313, and where he studied philosophy, medicine and later, theology. After a period in the service of Lombard Ghibelline lords, he returned to Paris, where he completed his major work, the *Defensor Pacis* (1324). When in 1326 his authorship became known, he fled together with the Parisian Averroist John of Jandun to the king of the Romans, Louis the Bavarian, who had been excommunicated by Pope John XXII; in 1327 their writings were condemned as heretical. In 1328 he accompanied Louis to Rome, and may have helped to draft the decree of deposition of John XXII. After his return to Germany, he appears to have spent most of his time at Louis's court, until his death before April 1343.

In the *Defensor Pacis* ('Defender of Peace'), Marsilius proposes to discover the chief cause of the strife which was destroying Italy, and finds it in the usurpation of secular authority by the papacy, and the consequent disturbance of the right order of church and state. The first of the two main parts, or Discourses, of the work enquires into that order in the state, the second, in the church; its aim is to demolish the hierocratic doctrine of the papacy. Marsilius' political theory, as expounded in Discourse I, is based on Aristotle, but differs from contemporary Aristotelianism in its radically naturalist conception of the state as solely designed to serve man in society. Law, like the state itself, is independent of higher law; its essence is its enforceability, its source, the people – the 'human legislator', or its 'weightier part' – which also elects the government. The ruler consequently derives his authority from the sovereign people, which may correct or even depose him. Marsilius' theory of the state applies to monarchies as well as republics; its republican aspects relate to institutions and problems of Italian city-republics in the early period of despotism. The priesthood forms part of the state and is, like the ruler, subject to the will of the people, and consequently to the ruler elected by it. Within the church, defined as consisting of both clergy and laity, the ultimate source of authority is, in its turn, the whole body of the faithful, represented by the general council, to which the pope is subject, and by which he may be deposed. Marsilius not only rejects the doctrine of papal plenitude of power; in denying the primacy of the papacy he subverts the entire hierocratic structure of the church, and reverses the established relationship between pope and council.

In Discourse II, the 'human legislator' becomes practically synonymous with the ruler, and accordingly endowed with absolute authority. It has been argued that the ultimate aim of the work was, from the beginning, to justify the supreme power of the Emperor. Later, in his *Defensor Minor*, Marsilius certainly used conclusions reached in his major work to provide theoretical foundations for imperial absolutism; but the republican structure of the state as expounded in Discourse I is too evident for this argument to be plausible, and it is preferable to explain this apparent inconsistency as a shift from republicanism to absolutism. This shift was completed in the *Defensor Minor*, where Marsilius explicitly states that the Roman people, by the *lex regia*, conferred its power on the Emperor.

After joining Louis, Marsilius' literary activity was dominated by the defence of the Empire. The *De Translatione Imperii*, while practically reproducing the text of a papalist treatise by Landolfo Colonna, confutes its argument that the Emperors owed their authority to the papacy as a result of the popes having transferred the Empire from the Greeks to the Franks and from the Franks to the Germans; for as Marsilius had already argued in the *Defensor Pacis*, such translations could legitimately be enacted only by the 'human legislator'.

In the *Defensor Minor*, composed probably in 1340, Marsilius subjects the papalist doctrine once more to a critique which, while summarizing arguments expounded in the *Defensor Pacis* (Discourse II), gives them a definitively absolutist slant. The second part of the treatise relates to the marriage affair of the countess of Tyrol. Marsilius supported, in a tract written for this purpose, the right of the Emperor to dissolve her previous marriage so that she could marry his son; in the *Defensor Minor* he argues that the papacy had usurped not only the temporal, but also the spiritual authority of the Emperor. NR

□ *The Defender of Peace* ed. A Gewirth (1951); *Oeuvres Mineures* ed. C. Jeudy and J. Quillet (1979)

Martin V Pope 1417–31 (b. 1368) In November 1417, at the Council of Constance, Cardinal Odonne Colonna was elected as Pope Martin V. His election marked the end of the Great Schism and the beginning of the 'Renaissance papacy'. The authority of Rome had been seriously damaged by the Schism, and Martin's greatest achievement was to restore control over the papal state by means of skilful diplomacy, warfare and nepotism. He was strongly opposed to the Conciliar movement, which aimed at the subjection of the papacy to the control of councils. By the prescription of the Council of Constance, he called the Council of Pavia-Siena (1423–24), which signally failed to further the cause of Conciliarism. Martin was also involved in the crusades against the Hussites. In 1431, after the failure of imperial forces in Bohemia, Martin was forced to convene a Council at Basle, but died before it opened.

□ P. Partner *The Papal State under Martin V* (1958)

Martin, St (c. 316–97) Bishop of Tours. The father of monasticism in Gaul, Martin was born of pagan parents in Pannonia, and served in the Roman army until his conversion to Christianity. After living as a recluse, he founded a community of hermits at Ligugé, near Poitiers, which became the first

Simone Martini's use of sinuous line and embossed gold are typical of Gothic art.

monastery in Gaul. He then founded Marmoutier, outside Tours, before reluctantly accepting the bishopric of Tours *c.* 372. His disciple, Sulpicius Severus, described Martin's missionary work and miracles in *De Vita Beati Martini* (*c.* 410). Martin died in November 397 at Caudes and was buried at Tours, where his church became a centre of pilgrimage.
□ A. Régnier *Saint Martin* (1925); C. Donaldson *Martin of Tours* (1980)

Martini, Simone (*c.* 1284–1344) One of the most influential Sienese painters, Martini was probably a pupil of Duccio, whom he excelled in his harmonies of line and colour and in his development of the Gothic style. Among his masterpieces are the *Maestà* fresco (1315) in Siena, the S. Caterina polyptych (1319), the frescoes of the chapel of St Martin in the church of S. Francesco, Assisi, and the famous *Annunciation* triptych (1333). Martini died at Avignon, where he had taken up residence under papal patronage from 1339.
□ M. C. Gozzoli *L'Opera Completa di Simone Martini* (1970)

Mary, St The cult of Mary, mother of Christ, was recognized in the early church and formally approved at the Council of Ephesus in 431. Throughout the Middle Ages Mary was venerated as first among the saints, with a special position – expressed both artistically and in writing – as intercessor for sinners on the Day of Judgement. Her feasts were specially honoured and played a large part in the medieval calendar: the feast of the Assumption on 15 August, the Annunciation or Lady Day on 25 March, the Nativity on 8 September, the Visitation on 2 July, and the Purification or Churching after the birth of Christ on 2 February (Candlemas). Dedications of churches to Mary proliferated. Her role was powerful, as one might expect, in popular piety; private prayers to her became a feature of most Christian vernacular literatures, while the Ave Maria and hymns to the Virgin became conspicuous elements in liturgy and institutional worship in both the Eastern and Western churches. Increasing emphasis on the humanity of Christ, which is a marked feature of Western Christendom from the late 11th c., coincides with increasing honour to the Madonna, the Virgin.

The cult of St Mary transcended all class boundaries, attracting chivalric elements in society as well as the peasants. Artistic representation of St Mary in Byzantium as in the West reduced the formal and stylized elements, concentrating instead on the warmth, humanity and femininity of the mother of Christ.
□ M. Warner *Alone of all her sex: the myth and cult of the Virgin Mary* (1976)

Mary of Burgundy 1477–82 (b. 1456) Heiress of Charles the Bold (d. 1477). Her marriage to Maximilian I of the house of Habsburg in August 1477 helped to safeguard some of the Burgundian state, linking it firmly to Austrian interests and preparing the realignment of European power politics, which was to culminate in the Empire of her grandson Charles V.
□ R. Vaughan *Valois Burgundy* (1975)

Masaccio (1401–*c.* 28) Florentine artist who steered Italian painting away from the decorative, linear style of his contemporaries (Ghiberti, Gentile da Fabriano) – ultimately derived from Gothic art – towards a new conception of heroic realism. His monumental, rounded figures, grouped in dramatic scenes, prefigure Alberti's artistic theories and reflect the Humanist spirit of the age, epitomized by the work of Masaccio's friends, Brunelleschi and Donatello.

His major achievement is the Brancacci Chapel fresco cycle in Sta Maria del Carmine, Florence (1425–28). This was left unfinished when he was called to Rome, where he died aged only 27.

From the prayer book of **Mary of Burgundy** (late 15th c.), showing the duchess
with her namesake – St Mary – in a sumptuous Gothic interior.

Matilda (*c*.1046–1115) Countess of Tuscany. Matilda was a devoted supporter of Pope Gregory VII throughout the Investiture Contest and continued to support the papacy after his death. In 1077 her castle at Canossa was the scene of Henry IV's absolution by Gregory. Married to the son of Welf of Bavaria, Matilda was allied with the Welf (Guelph) family in the rebellion of Conrad against his father Henry IV (1093). In 1110 she submitted to Henry V and made him heir to the lands which she had previously promised to the holy see; but at her death she left everything to the papacy. These 'Matildine' lands became another long-running cause of controversy between the Empire and the papacy.
□ H. E. J. Cowdrey *The Age of Abbot Desiderius* (1983)

Matthias I Hunyadi King of Hungary and Bohemia 1458–90 (b. 1440) Known by his humanist name, Corvinus, he was the son of János Hunyadi, powerful commander-in-chief and treasurer of Ladislas V, king of Hungary. The Hunyadi claim to the throne led Ladislas to hold Matthias hostage (1457); but on Ladislas V's death Matthias was elected king of Hungary and Bohemia (1458), his first wife being Catherine Podiebrad, daughter of the regent of Bohemia. With his adviser, János Vitéz, he pursued a policy of centralization, assisted by a staff of professional court officials and an army of mercenaries. Circumventing the Diet, he tried to introduce an absolutist regime, but was forced to compromise with a wary nobility. He established a brilliant international humanist court at Buda, founded a university (*Academia Istropolitana*) in Pozsony and engaged in much large-scale building, including his library (Corvina) and the Visegrád summer palace. He worked to build a Central European empire, launching Czech and Austrian campaigns (1468–85) to this end, with Vienna (captured 1485) at its centre. However, he did not succeed in making himself Holy Roman Emperor, and his political edifice did not survive his death.

Maximilian I of Habsburg Holy Roman Emperor 1493–1519 (b.1459) His career lies effectively well into the modern period, but he should be noted in any general work on the Middle Ages for three principal reasons: the bringing together of the Habsburg inheritance and the Burgundian lands, the attempts to stabilize the Danube frontier against the Ottoman empire, and the slow and only partial success in building up imperial institutions such as the *Reichskammergericht* (supreme court of law) in 1495. Son of the Emperor Frederick III, he married Mary of Burgundy in 1477, and on her death (1482) became regent of the wealthy Netherlands. In 1486

Relief sculpture from Innsbruck: **Maximilian I** with his jester and a councillor.

he was elected king of the Romans and became Emperor seven years later.
□G. Benecke *Maximilian I* (1982)

Mayors of the palace The office of *major palatii* developed under the Merovingians from that of *major domus* to the effective ruler of the Frankish realm, behind mere puppet kings. Conflict between Pepin II, mayor of Austrasia, and Ebroin, mayor of Neustria and Burgundy, was ended by the assassination of Ebroin (680) and the victory of Pepin over the Neustrians in 687. Thereafter, Pepin was *de facto* ruler of the three kingdoms and was succeeded by his son, Charles Martel. After deposing King Childeric III in 751, the mayor of the palace Pepin III was elected as king of the Franks.
□ J. M. Wallace-Hadrill *The Long-haired Kings* (1962); A. R. Lewis, 'The "Dukes" in the Regnum Francorum, AD 550–751', *Speculum* 51 (1976)

Medici family Florentine banking family, who during the 15th c., although claiming to be merely private citizens, became virtual rulers of Florence and princes of the Renaissance. From 1296 to 1314 the family appeared in government, declining after Salvestro de'Medici's support of the unsuccessful Ciompi uprising (1370), initiating Medici association with the People's party and rendering them suspect to other leading families. To allay suspicion Giovanni di Bicci de'Medici (1360–1429) kept out of the public eye and expanded his banking business, establishing the Medici as papal bankers and constructing the most profitable family business in

Europe. Giovanni's son, Cosimo de'Medici (1389–1464), further advanced the business and maintained involvement in government; he continued Giovanni's artistic patronage (Ghiberti, Brunelleschi, Michelozzo, Donatello, Lippi and Fra Angelico) and became a humanist, founding the Platonic Academy and establishing a magnificent library. In 1439 he arranged for Florence to host the general council of the Greek and Roman churches. Envy culminated in the Albizzi plot, leading to Cosimo's imprisonment for treason in 1433. He was exiled, but recalled in 1434 after the Albizzi fell. The Medici became the discreet ruling power of Florence, earning Cosimo the title *pater patriae*.

He was succeeded by his son Piero the Gouty (1416–69), a good diplomat who continued Cosimo's policy of French alliance. In 1466 he overcame a projected coup by the republican 'Party of the Hill', increasing his power. He too patronized the arts (della Robbia, Uccello, Pollaiuolo, Botticelli, Gozzoli, Verrocchio, and Poliziano the poet).

His son, Lorenzo the Magnificent (1449–92), was perhaps the most famous of the Medici. However, he neglected the business, and although his splendid court included Giovanni Pico, Gentile Becchi, Antonio Squarcialupi, Lippi, Ghirlandaio, Botticelli, Pollaiuolo, Michelangelo and Leonardo, the rich younger branch of the Medici, especially Lorenzo di Pierfrancesco de'Medici, commissioned more than he. He resuscitated the universities of Pisa and Florence and was an accomplished humanist and vernacular poet. Although less ostentatious than many Italian rulers, he had enemies: in 1478 an assassination attempt led by rival bankers, the Pazzi, succeeded in killing Lorenzo's brother Giuliano; Lorenzo escaped, and bloody retribution followed, leading to a bull of excommunication and attack by papal and Neapolitan forces. Disaster was only averted by Lorenzo's hazardous visit to King Ferrante of Naples to negotiate; peace was restored in 1480. In 1484 Innocent VIII, Lorenzo's friend, became pope. Lorenzo soon dictated curia policy and led most of Italy in his attempts for unity. He was no expert statesman, but maintained a period of peace during which the arts flourished.

He was succeeded in 1492 by his son, Piero di Lorenzo de'Medici (1471–1503). In 1494 Charles VIII of France attacked Tuscany on his way to claim Naples. Piero responded vigorously but the populace was paralysed by Savonarola's premonitions. Piero treated with Charles, but the Signoria of Florence repudiated his gesture and the Medici fled to Venice. Until 1498 Florence was under Savonarola's theocratic rule. The Medici wandered throughout Europe, despite attempts at reinstatement, Piero dying in French service. His brother, Cardinal Giovanni de'Medici, later Pope Leo X (1475–1521), replaced him as *paterfamilias*. In 1512, with papal and Spanish support, he ousted the government of Soderini and Machiavelli, regaining Florence for the Medici. By the time of the demise of the last Medici – Anna Maria, electress palatine (1743) – the family had become grand dukes of Tuscany and had produced another pope, Clement VII, and a queen of France, Catherine de'Medici.   MB

□ N. Rubinstein *The Government of Florence under the Medici* (1966); C. Hibbert *The Rise and Fall of the House of Medici* (1974); J. R. Hale *Florence and the Medici* (1977)

Medicine Alexandria was the great medical school of the classical world, drawing on Egyptian, Greek and Middle Eastern advances. The work of Alexandrian scholars was collected, consolidated and extended by Galen (130–201), a fine physician, anatomist and physiologist, for whom all bodily functions had a divine purpose, fitting into the Greek teleological ethos.

After Galen, the study of medicine waned – more slowly in the East than the West. An example of the resilient Eastern tradition was the encyclopaedia of Oribasius (325–403). In the West medical knowledge was confined to the monastic world, which viewed illness as a punishment for sin, therefore requiring prayer and repentance as well as medical care. Outside the monasteries, the isolated Jewish communities continued a vigorous medical practice.

Many of the classical works of the Mediterranean had been saved by translation into Arabic and they produced several leading figures. Rhazes (*c*.860–932), a Persian, was a fine physician who attempted cures for smallpox and measles with limited success; Avicenna (*c*.980–1037), another Persian, who because of his position as court physician was highly influential, produced the great *Canon of Medicine* which pervaded medieval works on drugs and chemistry; finally, Averroes (1126–98), who was principally an Aristotelian philosopher, produced his influential *Colliget*. These works were brought to Christian Europe through Jewish physicians and translators, notably through the medical school of Cordoba with its Eastern contacts at Cairo and Baghdad. Amongst this group the commentaries on Galen by Moses Maimonides were of great importance.

It was at Salerno, heir of several traditions, that in the 10th c. a lay medical school developed. It attempted to place medical practice on a sound basis and was to provide the example for later centres. Elsewhere the rise of medicine and law were intertwined, expanding notably at Montpellier, Bologna, Padua and Paris.

Treatment of head wounds: from a translation of Roger of Salerno's handbook on **medicine**, *De Chirurgia*.

Although the Second Lateran Council (1139) had forbidden the practice of medicine for temporal gain, knowledge and numbers grew. New methods and observations were made by men like Roger Bacon (c.1214–92) and Albertus Magnus (c.1190–1280). The Bolognese teacher Mondino de'Luzzi wrote his *Anothania* (1316), the first work entirely devoted to anatomy and heavily influenced by Galen and Avicenna. The re-introduction of human dissection into the medical field, a process forbidden from the time of Erastistratus (c.300) at Alexandria, quickened the pace of advance and prepared the way for future discoveries. The Renaissance artists, with their attempts to draw realistic bodies reflected improvements in anatomy and encouraged further work. Paracelsus, an eager reformer, prescribed chemical drugs for ailments. Fracastoro (1478–1553) wrote accounts of syphilis and plague infections. In 1543 Vesalius (1514–64) reflected these improvements in his *De Humani Corporis Fabrica Libri Septem*, with anatomical observations superior to Galen's, while preserving his physiological views.   CP

□ V. L. Bullough *The Development of Medicine as a Profession* (1966); C. H. Talbot *Medicine in Medieval England* (1967); P. M. Jones *Medieval Medical Miniatures* (1984)

Melfi, Council of In August 1059, Pope Nicholas II summoned the Council of Melfi as part of an attempt to reduce papal dependence on the Emperor and also in response to the Norman threat to vassal states of the papacy. At the Council Nicholas received homage and the promise of military aid from Robert Guiscard and Richard of Capua, which he used to enter Rome and remove the anti-pope Benedict X. In return, Nicholas recognized Robert as duke of Apulia, Calabria and in the future, of Sicily, and Richard as prince of Capua. With this papal recognition and encouragement, the Normans continued their conquests in south Italy, so that by 1060 the Byzantines held only their capital, Bari. The German Emperor claimed all Italy as his own, and yet the pope had recognized the position of the Normans there. The Council was thus a deliberate act of defiance, by the papacy, of the Empire.
□ J. J. Norwich *The Normans in the South* (1967)

Melisende (c.1102–61) Queen of Jerusalem. Daughter of King Baldwin II (1118–31), Melisende was married to Fulk V, count of Anjou, in 1129, and on the death of her father she and her husband were crowned queen and king of Jerusalem. After the turbulence caused by the revolt and subsequent murder of her lover Hugh de Puiset in 1132, she proved herself a capable ruler and continued to exercise direct authority, even after Fulk's death (1143), as co-ruler and regent for their son Baldwin III (1144–64). Baldwin asserted his independence in a period of civil disorder (1150–52) and Melisende was sent to exile in Nablus, where she remained a focal point of influence in the social and political life of Outremer until her death.
□ S. Runciman *A History of the Crusades* vol. 2 (1952)

Merlee, William (*fl.c.*1340) An early meteorologist and teacher at Oxford, Merlee kept monthly records, which have been preserved, of the weather in the Oxford region (1337–44). His work is a mixture of the credulous and scientific, but he shows awareness of changing weather patterns and even attempts some forecasting.

Merovingian dynasty Claiming descent from a sea god, the Salian Frankish dynasty known as the Merovingians established their authority over most of Gaul during the reign of Clovis (480–511). The civil wars of his descendants were savage and more or less endemic, though from time to time the kingdom was reunited. In the 7th c., and especially after the battle of Tertry (687), true authority passed into the hands of the mayors of the palace, ancestors of the Carolingians. But enough mystical and personal prestige remained with the Merovingians

to ensure their survival as symbolic kings (*rois fainéants*) and it was not until 751 that the last of the kings, Childeric III, was deposed and exiled to a monastery.
□ J. M. Wallace-Hadrill *The Long-haired Kings* (1962)

Michael of Cesena Minister-general of the Franciscan Order. He revolted against the Avignonese papacy, and in 1328, together with his follower William of Ockham, turned to seek protection from the Emperor Louis IV. He supported Louis in his Italian and papal ventures, even to the extent of recognizing the abortive attempt to set up an anti-pope.
□ L. K. Little *Religious Poverty and the Profit Economy in Medieval Europe* (1979)

Milan Capital of Cisalpine Gaul. It was a major Roman centre until Honorius transferred his capital to Ravenna (401). It also possessed a great religious heritage – here Constantine issued his Edict of Toleration (313) – but its religious identity stemmed from the 4th c. and St Ambrose, who gave Milan its own Ambrosian rite and ecclesiastical independence.

Milan's geographical position, in a fertile plain traversed by the major routes into Italy, rendered it commercially significant, but vulnerable to invasion. Overshadowed by Pavia, Milan was ruled successively by Lombard dukes and Carolingian counts. Its religious significance was reaffirmed by Charlemagne, and it subsequently fell increasingly under the power of its archbishop, who became principal landowner and overlord. His vassals, the nobility (*capitanei*) and gentry (*valvassores*), assumed political identities, whilst the *credenza* of St Ambrose represented the lower classes.

A 10th-c. commercial boom drew people to the city and restored its primacy. In 1035 Milan's citizenry revolted against the growing power of Archbishop Aribert (1018–45), who retained *capitanei* support. However, pro-revolutionary imperial intervention encouraged civic unity, and Milan's ensuing conflict with Conrad II became a struggle for urban liberty in which Milan triumphed (1039). The ensuing promotion of the *valvassores* (through the *de feudis* constitution) left Milan without an effective middle class.

Religious reforms again caused internal strife 1045–87, Milan's lower classes producing the pro-reformation Patarines. The resultant weakening of the archbishopric, increased civic consciousness and another economic boom enabled Milan to emerge as one of the first communes, developing a consulate by 1097. Imperial absence permitted economic expansionism until Frederick Barbarossa's intervention. In 1158 he launched a campaign against Milan

which joined the anti-imperial Lombard League (1167), eventually forcing Barbarossa into an agreement (Peace of Constance, 1183).

During the 1180s the consulate was replaced by a foreign arbitrator (*podestà*), increasingly the instrument of the ruling families. The commune's decline was hastened from the 1230s by 20 years of conflict as head of a new Lombard League against Frederick II. From 1253 to 1256 Manfred Lancia formed the first Milanese tyranny, and soon the della Torre family had established signorial government. The della Torre were replaced (*c*.1277) by the Visconti. In 1294 Matteo Visconti was appointed imperial vicar in Milan. Bonvesin da Riva's *De Magnalibus Urbis Mediolani* (*c*.1288) describes Milan as flourishing, but laments its lack of a port and civil concord. The economically disruptive della Torre/ Visconti (Guelph/Ghibelline) conflict continued into the 14th c., resulting in the Visconti's triumph. Giangaleazzo Visconti (1385–1402, duke 1395) made Milan Italy's most powerful state, its territory stretching from Piedmont to Padua and the Trevisan March. The marriage of his daughter Valentina to Louis of Orleans (1387), however, instigated French claims to Milan.

Signorial rule appears to have been beneficial. Despite high taxes, economy and industry (textiles, arms and armour) flourished, health regulations combatted plague, and canals (*Naviglio Grande*) improved communications. Giangaleazzo also patronized the arts: he began Milan cathedral in 1386. Filippo Maria, last male Visconti, died in 1447 and the free Ambrosian Republic was proclaimed (1447–50). Francesco Sforza, husband of Filippo's illegitimate daughter, effected a coup (1450) and with Medici support established the Sforza dynasty. Francesco formed a brilliant court and improved Milan in the Florentine manner. Cultural development continued under his son, Lodovico 'il Moro', whose magnificent court boasted Bramante and Leonardo. However, the Sforza suffered a severe setback under Lodovico, and Milan entered the 16th c. in French hands.
□ C. M. Ady *Milan under the Sforza* (1907); D. Muir *Milan under the Visconti* (1924)

Milan, Edict of Act of toleration issued in 313 by the co-emperors Constantine and Licinius, both of whom had monotheistic tendencies. It ostensibly resulted from discussions accompanying Licinius' marriage to Constantine's half-sister, Constantia, in Milan.

This was not the first attempt to stop persecution; an earlier Edict of Galerius (311), based upon the heathen principle that every god was entitled to worship, temporarily halted persecution, although the co-emperors Maximin Daia and Maxentius remained hostile. Constantine tolerated Christianity for political reasons and for the part which he believed it played in his victory over Maxentius (312).

The Edict, preserved in Eusebius' *Historia Ecclesiastica*, established the principle of universal toleration, though couched in terms which rendered Christianity the positive force, other religions being permitted to share its liberty. Neither emperor honoured this, Constantine attacking the Donatists and Arians, and Licinius turning against Christianity. But the notion of a state religion was abolished, until Christianity assumed this role, and toleration was the general law of the empire until Theodosius I (379–95). The church was to receive full compensation for confiscations, and Christianity became legally recognized as holding corporate property. Pagan reaction was swift: Maximin Daia, who would owe heavy compensation, entered Europe, but was forced to grant the same liberty in his Eastern provinces.

□ R.A. Markus *Christianity in the Roman World* (1974); G. Barraclough *The Christian World* (1981)

Millenarianism Millenary or Chiliastic beliefs (terms derived from the Latin and Greek words for a thousand) existed in the early church and received fresh impetus as the year 1000 approached. The main ideas involved were connected with the 'second coming of Christ', the notion of an apocalyptic period of struggle between Christ and Antichrist, between the Messiah and Satan, and the setting up of a New Jerusalem on earth. Elements of millenary thought subsisted throughout the Middle Ages on the fringe of most movements for religious revival, and were normally associated with excessive austerity, looking to a catastrophic end to existing society, and often coinciding with periods of intense economic and social upheaval.

□ N. Cohn *The Pursuit of the Millennium* (1957)

Mills The grinding of corn in hand querns was a slow and laborious business which was gradually replaced in the early Middle Ages by mills operated by water power, or in some areas by animal power. Milling could be a complex technical matter, and the most elaborate mills were normally associated with the development of a manorial economy where the lord's rights over milling became a most valuable and valued perquisite. In the drier countries of the Muslim world, where water power was not available, a technical leap forward was achieved from the 10th c. with the evolution of the windmill. First references to the use of windmills in Western

A 14th-c. English post-**mill** illustrated in the Luttrell psalter.

Christendom occur in the third quarter of the 12th c., and by the end of the 13th c. they had become a familiar feature over much of the better developed arable lands of Europe. *See* AGRICULTURE

□ J. Gimpel *The Medieval Machine* (1977); E.J. Kealey *Harvesting the Air* (1987)

Mirandola, Pico della (1463–94) Son of the prince of Mirandola, near Ferrara, this Italian philosopher was distinguished from other Florentine Platonists by his interest in the synthesis of Christian theology and diverse philosophies, particularly Jewish Cabbalism and the Arabic doctrines of Averroes. In 1486, he defended 900 *conclusiones* of various philosophers, but some theses were condemned by the papacy and he fled to France. At the intervention of Lorenzo de'Medici, he was allowed to return and stayed in Florence until his early death. His famous *Oratio de Dignitate Hominis* exalted man's dignity and his freedom to influence his own spiritual development.

□ E. Garin *Giovanni Pico della Mirandola* (1937)

Missi Dominici Term used of royal officials employed by Frankish kings and emperors to supervise their provincial administration. Initially they were appointed on ad hoc commissions, but they became a regular and integral feature of the administrative machinery. Empowered with full authority to rectify injustices and to administer oaths of allegiance, they brought a degree of centralized control and flexibility to the system of administration;

the empire was divided into *missatica* or inspection circuits, each region having two officials, usually of episcopal and comital rank, to investigate complaints. This innovation was in decline by the close of the 9th c., reflecting the decline of centralized power within the empire.

□ F. L. Ganshof *Frankish Institutions under Charlemagne* (1968)

Monasticism The word 'monk' comes from the Greek *monos*, meaning 'alone'; Christian monasticism in its earliest form was a way of life adopted by solitary ascetics or anchorites. In both Western Europe and the Byzantine East, medieval monasticism had its parentage in two distinct forms of ascetical life that appeared in Egypt early in the 4th c. One of these was the eremitical life (Greek *eremos*, 'desert') of the desert hermits, whose pioneer and leader was St Antony (*c*.251–356). The other was the cenobitical life (Greek *koinon*, 'common') of monks following a common regime in organized communities, said to have been started by St Pachomius (*c*.292–346), who established communities of men and women in the region of Egyptian Thebes *c*.320. The cenobitical life won the approval of St Basil of Caesarea, who promoted the ideal in the Eastern churches, where his Rules for monks caused him to be regarded as the father of Orthodox monasticism. The monastic lore of Egypt was transmitted to the West late in the 4th c. through the dissemination of literature about the desert fathers and the migration of individual ascetics like John Cassian, who settled in southern Gaul. Cassian's writings did much to form a Western monastic tradition.

During the 5th c. and 6th c. monasteries multiplied in Italy, Gaul, Spain and Ireland. In Gaul and Anglo-Saxon England, foundations followed in the wake of the Christian missions to the Germanic peoples. The Celtic monasticism of Ireland was imported into Europe by the mission of St Columbanus, who founded the famous centres of Luxeuil and Bobbio. One of the institutions of 7th-c. Gaul, which was reproduced in England, was the double monastery – an establishment of monks and nuns, living in separate quarters, under the direction of an abbess, usually a person of royal blood. In this early period observance varied. Rules for monks were composed by Columbanus, Caesarius of Arles and others, but no one Rule gained general acceptance to the exclusion of others. The Rule composed by the Italian abbot St Benedict of Nursia (*c*.480–*c*.550) only gradually became known in Northern Europe.

Benedict, who gained his experience from guiding his own foundation at Monte Cassino, envisaged a monastery as an isolated and self-supporting community, directed by an elected *paterfamilias* – the abbot – and bound together by the monastic virtues of obedience, personal poverty and humility. The monk's day was to be filled with a balanced round of vocal prayer (the divine office), manual work and spiritual reading. Its combination of sensible spiritual advice with attention to practical detail commended Benedict's Rule to several monastic founders of the 7th c. and 8th c. in Gaul and England; but it was in the 9th c. that it came to be regarded as the standard model for monastic observance in the West, largely through the active promotion of Charlemagne and Louis the Pious, who imposed it upon abbeys in their dominions.

Richly endowed by secular rulers, the Benedictine abbeys of the Carolingian age became centres of classical and patristic learning, and learned abbots like Hrabanus Maurus of Fulda and Walafrid Strabo of Reichenau made a significant contribution to the Carolingian renaissance. But civil war within the Empire and mounting attacks by Vikings from without made the later years of the 9th c. unpropitious for monks. Many abbeys were destroyed, communities were dispersed, and regular observance declined. The revival of regular Benedictine life in the 10th c. stemmed chiefly from two centres: Cluny, founded by Duke William of Aquitaine in 909, and the Lotharingian abbey of Gorze, restored in 933. Thanks to a rare degree of autonomy, the bequest of its founder, and a succession of remarkable abbots, the observance of Cluny spread rapidly; by the time of Abbot Hugh of Semur (1049–1109) it had acquired an empire of several hundred subordinate abbeys and priories in many parts of Europe. The usages of Gorze were adopted by several German abbeys. Both Cluny and Gorze inherited and developed the Carolingian tradition of observance, with its greatly extended choral offices, devotion to liturgical ritual and learning. Although the English monastic revival of the 10th c. was not directly sponsored by Cluny, the common customary of the English monks compiled in 970 (*Regularis Concordia*) drew heavily upon the customs of Cluny and Gorze.

The two centuries following the foundation of Cluny were the heyday of Benedictine monasticism. The abbeys had a conspicuous social role as landed corporations, centres of learning and book production, patrons of art and architecture and, as custodians of famous shrines, the foci of pilgrimage and popular religion. The ownership of great estates involved many monks in managerial tasks. It also involved abbeys in the public duties that attached to landlordship in a feudal society – seignorial jurisdiction over tenants, attendance at royal councils, and the requirement to supply quotas of knights for the royal armies.

In the 11th c. discontent with the wealth and

Monasticism: a choir of monks singing during a service, from an early 14th-c. French psalter.

A long-established belief that the Apostles were monks and that monasticism was the authentic expression of the *vita apostolica* inspired the arguments of ecclesiastical reformers that the secular clergy ought to renounce marriage and property and live in community like monks. In response to this propaganda, houses of canons regular – clerical monks – began to appear in about the mid-11th c. Later in the century they generally adopted the Rule of St Augustine, but within its very general framework their observances varied widely. Some adopted an austere life of strict enclosure modelled on the Cistercians (e.g., the canons of Arrouaise and the Premonstratensians); others followed a more moderate regime and lived in a variety of institutions: priories large and small, the chapters of some cathedrals, hospitals, castle chapels and alongside communities of nuns.

Of several orders that sought to restore the primitive observance of the Benedictine Rule, the largest and most dynamic was the Order of Cîteaux – the Cistercians. Originating in a secession from Molesme abbey led by Abbot Robert in 1098, this expanded with extraordinary speed following the arrival of St Bernard in 1112. The essence of the Cistercian reform was strict observance of the Rule, the restoration of manual work to its place in the monk's day and, at first, the rejection of such customary sources of income as rents, serfs and churches. To cultivate their lands the Cistercians used *conversi* or illiterate lay brothers, recruited from the peasantry on an unprecedented scale. The Order's most distinctive feature was its strong federal organization based upon a system of filiation and supervision by a general chapter, which all abbots had to attend annually at Cîteaux. These arrangements were set out in the *Carta Caritatis*, the first version of which, composed by Stephen Harding before 1118, was subsequently enlarged in the light of experience.

The proliferation of orders in the previous hundred years caused the Fourth Lateran Council (1215) to ban further innovations: in future would-be founders must choose an existing Rule. By this time the great age of monastic endowment was over. Numbers in many Benedictine monasteries declined, owing partly to the phasing-out of the practice (authorized by St Benedict) of donating children to be brought up as monks, and partly to the proliferation of alternative forms of religious life, especially that of the friars. The refusal of some German abbeys, like Reichenau, to accept postulants who were not of noble birth left them in the later Middle Ages with only a handful of monks. Despite the rise of some congregations of strict observance like the Olivetans in Italy and the congregation of Melk in

secular involvement of the older abbeys and of their elaborate liturgical observance began to express itself in a search for new and simpler forms of ascetical life. Fed by a growing historical sense, the quest drew its inspiration from models offered by Christian antiquity: the Lives of the desert fathers; the Life of the Apostolic brotherhood (*vita apostolica*) described in *Acts* 2, v. 42–44; and the Benedictine Rule itself. Out of this crisis arose several new orders. An eremitical movement in central Italy crystallized in the Order of Camaldoli, founded by St Romuald (*c.*1020). A similar movement in Brittany and Maine, led by the itinerant preacher Robert of Arbrissel, gave birth to the Order of Fontevrault (*c.*1100), which combined nuns and canons in double monasteries; this in turn provided a model for the double monasteries of the purely English Order of Sempringham. The most enduring plan to institutionalize the anchoritic life was the Carthusian Order, which sprang from the group hermitage in the Alps founded *c.*1082 by Bruno of Cologne, and later moved to the site of the Grande Chartreuse.

Austria, in general a more relaxed form of Benedictine life prevailed in the later Middle Ages, which received formal acknowledgment in the Constitutions of Pope Benedict XII in 1336. Monks attended the universities; and the life-style of many abbeys was barely distinguishable from that of a college of secular clergy. *See* AUGUSTINIAN CANONS; BEGUINES; CARMELITES; CARTHUSIANS; DOMINIC, ST; FRANCIS, ST; NORBERT OF XANTEN; REGULARIS CONCORDIA   CHL

□ *Western Asceticism* ed. O. Chadwick (1958); D. Knowles *Christian Monasticism* (1970); C.N.L. Brooke *The Monastic World 1000–1300* (1974); L. K. Little *Voluntary Poverty and the Profit Motive in Medieval Europe* (1978); B. Bolton *The Medieval Reformation* (1983); C. H. Lawrence *Medieval Monasticism* (1984)

Mongols Nomadic people of Central Asia whose rise to power may be attributed to Jenghiz Khan (b.*c.*1154), who united both Turkish and Mongolian tribes and was elected their supreme ruler in 1206. At his death (1227) the Mongols' influence stretched from the Adriatic to the Pacific. They spread in a wide band across northern China (1211–15), seizing Peking and all the lands north of the Hwang-Ho (Yellow) river. They turned westward 1220–21 and swept across Persia, in 1223 defeating the Russian princes at the Kalka river. These advances were later consolidated: in 1237–38 the Russian principalities were overrun, and in 1240 Kiev was sacked. The Mongols marched westwards into Poland and Hungary, destroying Cracow and a substantial German–Polish army at Legnica (1241). They occupied Baghdad in 1258, but their unbridled expansion was halted by the Mamlūk victory of Ayn Jalud.

On the death of Mongke (1258), the brittle unity of the Mongols was fractured into four main khanates: the Great khanate, Changatai khanate, the Golden Horde, and the Il-khanate.

Their social organization, based on pastoralism and a decentralized tribal structure, had facilitated their expansion; new territories had been assimilated

Persian representation of Jenghiz Khan and his **Mongol** warriors, expert horsemen and archers.

like appanages into the pre-existing structure. They depended essentially on military power, their ability to impose terror, and their skill in exacting taxes from subject populations. However, their custom of dividing inheritances created excessive fragmentation and internecine conflicts. These developments had their fullest effects contemporaneously with the rise of powerful new rivals. The Changatai khanate fell to Tamberlaine (1379). The Golden Horde, battered by Timur, was defeated and contained by the resurgent Russian princes.

Within Christendom tentative attempts were made to liaise with the Mongols against the Turks. Various emissaries were sent to treat with the khans, notably the Franciscan William of Rubruquis, but without success. Trade was opened up, however, and Eastern luxuries were an important stimulus to European travel, commerce and exchange. *See* KUBLAI KHAN

□ M. Prawdin *The Mongol Empire* (1940); G. Vernadsky *The Mongols and Russia* (1953); C. J. Halperin *Russia and the Golden Horde* (1985)

Monophysitism A schismatic and eventually heretical movement, which spread from Egypt to the Orient, originating in an exaggerated insistence on the one nature of Christ. This approach led Diodore of Tarsus to call Mary *Christokos* ('Christ-bearer'), a view followed by Nestorius. To defend orthodoxy, St Cyril had employed an Apollinarian formula, that of the one nature of the word God incarnate. His use of the phrase was strictly unheretical, but there was a problem in the use of the word 'nature' (*physis*). When the theologians of the Council of Chalcedon (451), and earlier, Nestorius spoke of two natures, they employed a traditional interpretation of the word *physis* in which it was wholly distinct from the *hypostasis* (substance), as used in the theology of the Trinity for the persons. The Monophysites rejected the Chalcedon doctrine and Cyril's argument for semantic rather than doctrinal reasons. Theologians, like Severus of Antioch, produced a solid theological foundation for the movement. They were not formal heretics for they fully maintained the integrity of the two natures in Christ after the union in the Incarnation without confusion. Only a few scattered groups held the heretical position that Christ's divinity absorbed the humanity, or vice versa. Imperial attempts were made to accommodate the dissidents, with little success. Finally, the Council of Constantinople (553) severely restricted the permissible theological position of Monophysitism; this was partially successful but provided the opportunity for new heresies.

□ W. H. C. Frend *The Rise of the Monophysite Movement* (1972)

Mid-6th-c. **mosaic** of Justinian and his court, from S. Vitale, Ravenna.

Monotheletism A 7th-c. Christological heresy which originated in attempts by the orthodox, often for political motives, to return the Monophysites to orthodoxy. They used formulae which stated that in Christ there was only one operation (*energeia*) proceeding from a unique will (*mono thelema*). Although mono-energism could denote a unique operation co-ordinating the divine and human wills in Christ, it was popularly understood as a unique source that destroyed the operation of Christ's free will. This drift towards an accommodation with the Monophysites was reflected in the Act of Union (633) of Emperor Heraclius, a document strongly influenced by the views of Sergius I, patriarch of Constantinople. The monk Sophronius of Jerusalem made this clear to Sergius, and on his elevation to the patriarchate of Jerusalem in 634, sent to Rome his *Epistola Synodica*, setting out the dangers.

His fears were realized in the imperial *Ecthesis of Heraclius* (638) which John IV (640–42) condemned in a Roman synod. In 647 Pope Theodore I excommunicated Paul, patriarch of Constantinople, for not condemning Monotheletism, and when the Emperor Constans II issued a *typos* (rule for faith), the new Pope Martin I was forced to condemn Monotheletism in the synod. The emperor responded by seizing the pope, bringing him back to Constantinople, torturing and finally exiling him. In 680–81 Constans II's successor, Constantine IV, authorized the Council of Constantinople, convoked by Pope Agatho. This removed misunderstanding by stating that two natural activities and two natural wills existed, while maintaining the free will of Christ. It stressed the inseparability, distinction and harmony of those two wills in Christ, thereby clearly refuting the tenets of Monotheletism.
□ J. Meyendorff *Christ in Eastern Christian Thought* (1975)

Montpellier One of the leading schools of medicine in Europe, Montpellier was recognized as a university by 1220. The town itself, in Languedoc, had flourished in the 12th c. and played an important part in the commercial revival attendant on the crusading movements and the general vitality of Mediterranean trade. It had close links with the kingdom of Aragon and also an influential Jewish population which proved active in the study of medicine and in the foundation of the university.
□ A. R. Lewis, 'The Development of Town Government in Twelfth-Century Montpellier', *Speculum* 22 (1947)

Mosaic The Middle Ages was the great age of mosaic production. Although mosaics had been used extensively throughout the ancient world, it was not until the early Christian period that mosaicists began to cover vast expanses of wall and vault with 'paintings' in small cubes of marble and glass. In the 14th c. mosaics were gradually supplanted by frescoes, which offered a quicker and less expensive alternative to patrons and artists of the day. As in *buon* or true fresco, the wall or vault was first covered with a medium-fine layer of plaster, which served as a base for the final layers of plaster. Both Western and Byzantine mosaicists appear to have then sketched the composition on the next layer of plaster. In Byzantium mosaicists sometimes painted a complete version of the scene in fresco on the middle layer of plaster to guide the artist in the selection and distribution of colour, a stage usually dispensed with in the West. Finally, the cubes of glass and marble were set into a fine layer of plaster, and the mosaicist worked in small sections known as *giornate*, or the amount of wall that could be covered in a day's work. Several complete cycles of mosaic still exist today, as at the cathedral of Monreale, Sicily, or the Baptistery in Florence. [*312*]
□ O. Demus *Byzantine Mosaic Decoration* (1947); H. P. L'Orange and P. J. Nordhagen *Mosaics from Antiquity to the Early Middle Ages* (1966)

Moscow Located on the waterways which linked Vladimir to Ryazan and on the land routes which avoided the impassable forest, Moscow emerged in the 12th c. as a trading community. In 1156 Yuri Dolgoruki, prince of Suzdal, built a wooden citadel – the Kremlin – to help protect traders. The attitude of the Tartars towards Moscow helped the city to rise to eminence among the East Slavonic people. Tartar tolerance towards the church and their willingness to keep open the Western trade routes was reciprocated by the Muscovite princes who acted as Mongol tax-collectors. Although ravaged by the Mongol Horde in 1238 and 1293, Moscow emerged in this harsh climate as the focus of a new centralized movement to replace Kiev. The contemporaneous decline of Vladimir, savaged by the Tartars, and the movement of the Russian metropolitan (1341) from there to Moscow further stimulated the latter's evolution.

The progressive disintegration of the Horde and Lithuania's adoption of Roman Catholicism (1386–87) provided Moscow with the opportunity to establish itself as leader of the Orthodox Slavs. In 1380 Dimitri Donskoi heavily defeated the Tartars at Kulikova on the Don, but two years later the Horde retaliated, seized Moscow and razed it. A new stone city was built which repulsed the Tartars in 1408. The Muscovite rulers continued their policy of offence as the Tartars collapsed under the onslaught of Tamberlaine though territorial expansion was piecemeal until Ivan III seized Novgorod in 1478.

Moscow's wealth depended on trade, especially in furs and manufacturing industries of specialist craftsmen, whose work revealed a pervasive Byzantine influence. As the tzar's government, his court, council and assembly settled there, the city became the proto-capital of an expanding state.
□ J. Fennell *The Crisis of Medieval Russia* (1983); H. Paskiewicz *The Rise of Moscow's Power* (1984)

Mozarabs After the Muslim triumph in the Iberian peninsula in the mid-8th c. this term was applied to those Christians and Jews who lived under Muslim rule without converting to Islam. Gradually the description was limited to Christians, as the Mozarabs were increasingly identified as guardians of the heritage of Visigothic Catholicism. From 850 onwards they faced sporadic persecution, which they bravely resisted. They were heavily concentrated in urban centres, notably Toledo, Cordoba and Seville.

Muhammad (*c.*570–632) Founder of Islam, a term which means 'submission to God'. Born in Mecca, he was soon orphaned and spent his early years as a

Muhammad and a follower flee from Mecca to Medina, watched by Christ (13th-c. miniature).

nomadic caravan-trader. In 595 his marriage to a wealthy widow, Khadija, and the expansion of his trading activities provided him with a secure income. In 610, while engaged on a meditative journey in the local countryside, he had an overwhelming spiritual experience. On Mount Hira he received his revelation from the Archangel Gabriel which he later recorded in the Koran. Muhammad stressed that his message was part of the unity of God's message that had been expressed through all his prophets at various times through history (Adam, Noah, Abraham, Moses and Jesus); the essential difference was that he had received the message in its comprehensive and final form. His prophethood was therefore the culmination of all previous revelations, and his teachings were the final word.

Initially Muhammad confined his preaching to an inner circle, and when he made it more public he was met with ridicule, hostile polemics and persecution. Mecca was an important trading centre and his preaching attacked the influential mercantile oligarchy. Eventually he was forced to flee to the cosmopolitan settlement of Medina; here he hoped his monotheistic doctrines would be more favourably received, because of its large Jewish element. Economic pressure was gradually brought to bear on Medina by the Meccans to expel him; the result was a protracted war. Finally, in a negotiated settlement Muhammad obtained permission to lead a pilgrimage to Mecca in 629. Its restraint impressed the Meccans, but in the following year the Meccan oligarchy broke its neutrality and the Muslims marched on the city, which capitulated, accepting Islam. Muhammad's authority in the Arabian peninsula was then extended, organized and consolidated: paganism was outlawed and new laws reflected the Islamic ethos. The emphasis placed by Muhammad on humanity as one family under God provided a powerful check on tribal warfare. *See* ALI
□ W. Montgomery Watt *Muhammad at Mecca* (1953)

The goddess of **music** portrayed as a noblewoman surrounded by disciples; from Boethius' *De Musica* (14th-c.).

Murād II (1404–51) He succeeded his father, Muhammad I, as sultan of the Ottoman Turks in 1421, and by 1425 had forced Constantinople to pay an annual tribute. In 1430 he seized Thessalonica, which a son of the Byzantine emperor had sold to the Venetians in 1423. Three years after his triumph Murād married the Serbian princess Mara to consolidate his European advances. His steady progress into the Balkans was halted in 1443 by a Hungarian counter-offensive led by John Hunyadi, which recaptured Sofia and Philippolis (Plovdiv). Murād stopped the Christians with his crushing victory at Varna in 1444. He retired and temporarily left political affairs to his son, Muhammad II, whose sultanate (1444–46) ended in chaos. Murād resumed control and when the Hungarians under Hunyadi launched a new offensive, he inflicted an overwhelming blow upon them at the second battle of Kosovo (1448). Before Murād could build upon this victory he died at Adrianople, but his advances provided the basis for future victories.
□ H. J. Magoulias *Decline and Fall of Byzantium to the Ottoman Turks* (1975)

Music The picture of musical activity in the Middle Ages is strongly dependent on the nature and extent of the evidence which exists for it. Systems of notation, giving indication of pitch and rhythm, were not generally in use until the 11th c., and even then, they lacked the kind of precision subsequently achieved. Further, they come primarily from the literate circles of the church, and most musical activity outside these circles – and indeed, much within them – has therefore left no direct evidence. Music was essentially created and transmitted within an oral culture, even where that culture was sophisticated and in other respects literate. In default of widespread and unequivocal notation systems, other evidence must be used to assess this rich and varied period in musical history. Information may be gleaned from literary and pictorial sources, and archaeological finds are of special value in indicating the use of musical instruments, for which notated music is almost entirely absent until the last few centuries of this period. It is also possible that within existing 'folk' or 'primitive' musics, where change is comparatively slow, elements of medieval practice are preserved.

The liturgy of the Christian church, with its relatively stable nucleus, provides most of our sources. Music was used in the Apostolic church; in the first three centuries the repertory was probably fairly unified, deriving from synagogue music. The form in which it presents itself in Europe in the earliest extant notations of the 8th c.– 10th c. is that of a developed repertory ranging in style from the 'heightened speech' of psalm-recitation to the long and melodically elaborate antiphonal and responsorial chants of mass and office. The diversity is in part a reflection of the influences which must have been brought to bear upon liturgical music during the early Middle Ages, chief among them being extra-ecclesiastical practices and individual local developments. Many characteristics of plainsong have broad parallels in primitive forms which would have been common in secular practice throughout the period. The highly developed sequence, for example, a genre sophisticated in both text and music by the mid-9th c., may well have descended from the secular practice of musicians singing songs in alternation. Local practices would have led to diversity both in repertoires and in performance methods. This was commented upon, and attempts were made to remedy the situation, a far-reaching example being the work of the Cistercian Order.

Charlemagne's introduction of Roman liturgical observance into Northern Europe is an early, documented attempt to impose an authoritative, unified practice on liturgical music. Central authority tried continually to influence Christian ritual and its music, often for wider political purposes, but probably never met with more than limited success. The employment of notation may be seen as the exercise of a kind of authority, giving to music an objective existence and a verifiable form. Some trends which initially met with resistance from conservative churchmen, became accepted practice; these include the use of polyphony (music for several simultaneous voices) and the employment of a mannered, expressive method of performance. The latter was associated with the wandering musician-entertainers sometimes called jongleurs, whose activities and life-style were strongly criticized by churchmen; the highly appealing mode of their performance was, however, exploited by the new preaching orders of the early 13th c. (Franciscans and Dominicans). The jongleurs' use of musical instruments likewise made these unacceptable in church, the exception being the organ, hallowed by long association with royal, imperial and liturgical ceremonial. Early examples of polyphony were sometimes called *organum*, which may indicate how the instrument was chiefly used. By about 1000, vocal polyphony was employed liturgically at Winchester, and in the next 250 years there are increasing numbers of notated sources from other centres, including a large repertoire associated with Notre-Dame, Paris. Polyphony's function is to add particular ceremonial importance to specific moments in the liturgy; in this it is a direct descendant of the practice, widely current in the 10th c.– 12th c., of 'troping' chants by adding to them newly composed words and/or music. It was this practice, applied to the Easter morning liturgy, which gave rise to the phenomenon of liturgical drama. In the last two centuries of this period there are extensive sources for liturgical polyphony, which after the mid-13th c. regularly shows a clear sharing of techniques and styles with contemporary secular 'art' music.

Our knowledge of extra-ecclesiastical music-making is seriously affected by the small quantity and partiality of anything stronger than inferential evidence. Notations from before *c.*1200 come primarily from literate milieux, often connected with the church. If the evidence of surviving literary texts points to a huge wealth of sung secular poetry, mixing learned, classical and biblical elements with those of vernacular and popular genres (the medieval ballad would be an example), then the strictly musical evidence for this treasure has disappeared. The oral nature of the medieval music tradition must again be recalled. The songs of the troubadours and trouvères, by no means unsophisticated or 'popular', seem to have existed in oral form for up to two centuries before they began to be written down in the 13th c. Collections of 'art' music are, however, increasingly frequent on the Continent from this period, and reflect the establishment of the role of the courtly poet-composer, and of a secular milieu which favoured the perpetuation of his work in what were sometimes sumptuously produced manuscripts. The dependence of such evidence upon its cultural context may be seen by comparing the evidence from England. Here, the establishment of secular household musicians functioned predominantly within a closed guild system, which did not make use of notation, and whose work is therefore lost.

In addition to the everyday practice of music-making, its theoretical and speculative aspects were an important part of the Quadrivium of university studies, and were developed throughout the period along the lines laid down by Boethius.   DC
□ J. Chailley *Histoire Musicale du Moyen Age* (1950); *Pelican History of Music* vol. 1, ed. A. Robertson and D. Stevens (1960); A. Harman *Man and his Music* (1962); R. H. Hoppin *Medieval Music* (1978)

Mystery plays The Christian liturgy itself contains dramatic elements of the first order, and from the 11th c. there is evidence for the elaboration of the Christian story, enacted in the form of rudimentary miracle or mystery plays at church porches or in churchyards. In succeeding centuries these playlets were given more systematic form in both a religious and corporate urban dimension. Conventions varied from area to area, but among the most popu-

lar themes were representations from both the Old and New Testaments: the story of the Creation and the Garden of Eden, Noah's Flood, the birth of Christ, the Easter story and the Passion, the Harrowing of Hell. As towns developed and guilds became more influential, the performance of cycles of mystery plays became associated with the pattern of the liturgical and urban year. In England in the later Middle Ages the writing down of plays such as those surviving from York, Beverley, Towneley or Coventry, bears eloquent testimony to the importance of regular dramatic performances, often incorporating elements of an earthy, scabrous and satiric nature, in the social life of the age.
□ R. Woolf *The English Mystery Plays* (1972); R. P. Axton *European Drama of the Early Middle Ages* (1974); W. Tydeman *The Theatre in the Middle Ages* (1978)

Mysticism A spiritual philosophy which advocates faith as its own justification and asserts the supreme validity of inner experience, attempting to grasp the divine essence or ultimate reality of things, and thereby to achieve communion with the highest.

Mysticism was not confined to Catholicism, entering the Muslim tradition via Algazel (*c.*1058–1111) and contributing to Hesychasm, but its medieval development was largely interwoven with Christian doctrine. Although mystic elements occur in early works (Pseudo-Dionysius, St Augustine), St Bernard of Clairvaux (1091–1153) is considered the founder of medieval mysticism. The growth of mysticism from the 12th c. was largely a response to that of reason (rationalization of faith by objective means, such as dialectic). Mysticism did not preclude reason, but increasingly attempted to harness it for the purposes of faith. In the 12th c. mysticism had two centres, the Cistercian abbeys and the abbey school of Saint-Victor, Paris. The principal Cistercian mystics were St Bernard of Clairvaux, William of Saint-Thierry (d. 1148) and Isaac of Stella (1147–69). St Bernard's philosophy was 'to know Jesus and Jesus crucified'. By grace one passed through humility, compassion (charity), detestation of one's sins and contemplation, to ecstasy (immediate contact with God). St Bernard's mystical theology (the practice and theory of the mystical life) was intensely personal; subsequent exponents dealt more with speculative mysticism (reflection on the mystical life and its philosophical implications).

The Victorines, notably Hugh of Saint-Victor (1096–1141) and Richard of Saint-Victor (d. 1173) attempted to incorporate reason into a process transcending it. Hugh fashioned a rationale of mysticism in which all that is open to experience is germane to the knowledge of God through contemplation.

St Bonaventura and St Gertrude continued the tradition during the 13th c.

The flowering of mystical writing (14th c.–15th c.) was again partially a response to Nominalism. Although generally speculative, it was concerned with the practical intensification of religious life, reflected in the use of the vernacular. Principal mystics of this period include Eckhart, Tauler, Suso, Ruysbroeck, St Catherine of Siena, Richard Rolle, Gerson, Denis the Carthusian (1402–71) and St Catherine of Bologna (1413–63). Their contribution was the speculative rationalization of religious experience and their conception of the relation of the soul and Creation to God. *See* GROOTE, GERHARD; JOHN SCOT ERIUGENA MB

□ G. Leff *Medieval thought* (1958); D. Knowles *The English Mystical Tradition* (1961); F. Copleston *A History of Philosophy* (1963)

N

Naples, kingdom of Often incorporating Sicily, it dominated southern Italy from the Middle Ages until 1860. Geographically it formed a strategic bridge between East and West, the resulting cross-fertilization of cultures producing many interesting developments (12th-c. southern Italian architecture; the humanism of Frederick II's court; Italian poetry, notably Boccaccio's work at the court of Robert the Wise 1309–43).

Its fortunes were closely linked with Sicily, the region being unified by Roger II of the great Hauteville family, proclaimed king of Sicily and Apulia (1130) and of Naples (1139). The Normans inherited a groundwork of Byzantine provinces, Arab amirates, Lombard principalities and free city-states, upon which they erected a new civil kingdom with a feudal base. Here the conception of an elaborate secular and enlightened monarchy evolved, with the king as head of the church (hence an influential element of religious toleration and frequent papal opposition).

The Hohenstaufen ultimately succeeded the Hautevilles, and Frederick II (king of Sicily 1198–1250) assumed authority in Naples in 1220. In 1224 he founded the university of Naples, primarily as a state institution to supply trained administrators. In 1231 he promulgated the *Liber Augustalis*, a constitution and law code for the kingdom, based upon imperial Roman codes. The state persisted under Angevin rule (1268–1442) in the French style. In 1282 the Sicilian Vespers resulted in the loss of Sicily to the Aragonese, leaving the kingdom of Naples proper: the Ausonian horn with Bari, Gaeta and Catona. For almost a century it strove, unsuccessfully, to recover Sicily, a situation in contrast to its former vitality and expansion.

The kingdom was revived by the Aragonese (1442–1504), and under Alfonso the Magnanimous (1442–58) Naples and Sicily were temporarily reunited. By the 15th c. the kingdom of Naples was the only monarchy in Italy. Its preservation was largely due to a series of able monarchs and advisers who recognized and contributed to its unique form of government, frequently placing it in the van of Western European governmental advance. The kingdom maintained a strong foreign policy, and its reputation for wealth and armed might won Ferrante I (1458–94) the title of 'arbiter of Italy'. During the late 15th c. the Neapolitan Academy became a thriving centre of humanism. In 1495 Charles VIII of France invaded the kingdom, and in 1500 it was divided between France and Spain. Conflict soon destroyed this arrangement and resulted in a Spanish victory, rendering the kingdom subject to a Spanish viceroyalty (1504–1713). *See* PONTANUS, JOVIANUS MB

□ B. Croce *History of the Kingdom of Naples* (1970); A. Ryder *The Kingdom of Naples Under Alfonso the Magnanimous* (1976)

Neoplatonism Philosophy which arose in the 3rd c., chiefly amongst the Greeks of Alexandria (Plotinus, Amelius, Porphyry). From the 5th c. until 529 its development continued in Athens (Proclus). Although pagan, it viewed knowledge and materialism as insufficient, and introduced metaphysics, thereby bringing Platonism closer to Christianity. Neoplatonism developed Plato's hierarchy of forms, translating his 'Good' into the 'One', from which emanated the first intelligence (*Logos*, word) containing the immaterial ideas (Plato's forms) of all beings. *Logos* initiated a second intelligence (World Soul) from which the individual intelligence derived, descending in a hierarchy of spiritual beings, with the human soul last.

Four Neoplatonic concepts influenced Christian thought from the start: the hierarchy of spiritual beings; the spiritual nature of reality; the return of the soul to the One through contemplation; the goodness and fullness of being. However, superficial similarities concealed essential dichotomies: Neoplatonism perceived an involuntary eternal procession of intelligences from the One to the material world, denying God's voluntary Creation; the Neoplatonic triad (the One, the Spirit, and the World Soul) was not the Trinity, and the One's omnipresence enabled pantheism to flourish. Neoplatonism was based essentially on philosophical enquiry, whilst Christianity had to reconcile nature with God. St Augustine (354–430) first fused Neoplatonic and Christian concepts, and Boethius (c.480–524) also tended towards Neoplatonism, translating certain works. Whereas St Augustine gave Neoplatonism a Christian foundation, John Eriugena (c.810–77) controversially attempted to set Christianity upon a Neoplatonic base.

Despite these attempts, the empire's division had distanced the West from the Greek philosophies. Direct knowledge of Neoplatonism was not accomplished until its reintroduction via the Arabian (Alfarabi, Avicenna) and Jewish (Avicebrol) philosophies which reached the West from the late 12th c., combining the physical (Aristotelian) and spiritual (Neoplatonic) systems to explain the universe. The translations of William of Moerbeke (1215–86) disentangled Neoplatonism and Aristotelianism, giving Neoplatonism new impetus. During the 13th c. it influenced Augustinian thought, Thomism (St Thomas Aquinas, Giles of Rome) and the Dominicans of Cologne (Albert the Great, Hugh of Strasbourg, Dietrich of Freiburg), encouraged mysticism (Eckhart) and assisted science through its light metaphysic (Witelo). MB

□ G. Leff *Medieval Thought* (1958); F. Copleston *A History of Philosophy* (1963)

Nestorian controversy A Christological schism provoked by the culmination of the Antiochene school of theology in the works of Nestorius (c.381–

451), patriarch of Constantinople 428–31. He considered that Christ had two natures (*duo physeis*), yet this did not make two Sons, for the distinct natures were united in a voluntary conjunction. This view forced Nestorius to argue against the title of 'Mother of God' (*Theotokos*, God-bearer) being attributed to Mary; the term would be inappropriate for she had begotten only a man to whom the word of God was united.

Eusebius of Doryleum, a layman, initially led the attack against Nestorius. It was continued by St Cyril of Alexandria, who in 430 persuaded a Roman synod to denounce the views of Nestorius, thereby forcing Emperor Theodosius II to call a synod to settle the matter. This Council met at Ephesus in 431, but Nestorius refused to appear when St Cyril assumed the chairmanship as Pope Clement I's legate. The Council laid down that the being (*physis*) of the word had not undergone any change in becoming flesh; the two natures were joined in a true union; their difference was not suppressed but the meeting of divinity and humanity produced one sole Christ; the word was not united to the person of a man, but had become flesh. The council deposed Nestorius as a heretic and he was removed from office by Theodosius, who further decreed that all Nestorian works be burnt.

While in banishment Nestorius produced his apologia, the *Bazaar of Heraclides*, clarifying his position and drifting back towards orthodoxy. Others developed and extended his views, helping

Antwerp and harbour in the later Middle Ages. The **Netherlands** prospered chiefly through sea-trade.

to produce the schism of the Nestorian church. Their popular base in strategic Syria and Persia ensured several attempts to accommodate their position, which were of marginal success. The Nestorians flourished and expanded, and later resisted several harsh persecutions under the Mongols and Turks. Some Nestorian churches rejoined the Roman communion in the 15th c., while others remain today.

□ A.R. Vine *The Nestorian Churches* (1937)

Netherlands The 'Low Countries', strictly speaking, comprise the areas around the Rhine, Meuse and Scheldt estuaries, lands now divided politically between Holland, Belgium, Luxembourg and small sections of France and Germany. For the greater part of the Middle Ages the Low Countries were split into numerous counties, duchies and principalities, whose chief feature after the 11th c. was a thriving urban life. The persistent language divisions between Romance-speaking (Walloon) and Germanic (Dutch, Frisian and Flemish) both reflect and exaggerate the complexity of the political structures.

In the early Middle Ages the Frisians provided an important trading element, retaining their pagan religion well into the late 8th c., until absorbed in the Frankish empire of Charlemagne. After the partition of the Carolingian empire in 843 the Low Countries were incorporated into Lothar's Middle Kingdom of Lower Lorraine; but there was much devastation caused by Viking raids at this stage. In 926 the great duchy of Lorraine became part of the kingdom of Germany, though the boundary between Germany and Capetian France remained uneasy and uncertain. In time, the counties of Flanders and Artois turned to France, while Germany and the revived Empire (after 962) received the allegiance of the three prince-bishoprics of Utrecht, Liège and Cambrai, the counties of Friesland, Holland/Zeeland (and the territories now thought of as modern Holland), Luxembourg, the county of Namur, and the duchies of Brabant and Limburg.

By the 12th c. the commercial and industrial life of the area was thriving, lying as it did along one of the main arteries of communication in Western Europe, linking the south with England and the Baltic along the river systems, notably the Rhine. Bruges became one of the 'counters' for the Hanseatic League. The cloth trade was especially powerful in Flanders and Brabant, while Liège was universally recognized as an important centre for metalworking. Urban growth in centres such as Bruges itself, Ypres, Ghent, Liège and Dinant precipitated social turbulence and violent struggles between feudal lords and towns, and between organized guilds within towns, reminiscent of the correspond-

Sigurd and Gunnar wooing Brunhilda: scene from the *Nibelungenlied* on a 13th-c. carved chair from Norway.

ing situation in the great Italian cities. Political disunity was to some extent countered, after a period of great social disorder, by the Burgundian house in the late 14th c. In 1384 Philip the Bold, duke of Burgundy, became ruler of Flanders, Artois, Nevers, Franche-Comté, Antwerp and Malines. His successors extended the heritage, which by 1433 included Holland and Zeeland. There was further intensification of urban growth at Dordrecht, Middelburg, Kampen, Zwolle and Deventer.

In the 15th c. a ship-building industry arose and commercial centres flourished, notably at Amsterdam, Haarlem, The Hague, Delft and Rotterdam. A rich cultural and religious life developed, drawing inspiration from both French and German sources. The foundation of the university of Louvain in 1423, the work of the Brethren of the Common Life and the mystical tradition (Jan van Ruysbroeck), and above all the emergence of the major 15th-c. Flemish school of art provide outstanding examples of the vitality of Netherlands society in the later Middle Ages. *See* FLANDERS; JACQUES VAN ARTEVELDE   HRL
□ *The Netherlands* ed. B. Landheer (1943); F.E. Huggett *The Modern Netherlands* (1971)

Nibelungenlied One of the greatest works of medieval German literature, the *Nibelungenlied* (or 'Song of the Nibelungs') had powerful influence on subsequent German cultural life in poetry, prose, and ultimately also in music. In its surviving literary version it puts into sophisticated early 13th-c. High German widespread popular legends of the migration age, common to much of the Germanic world, and especially well known in the North in Old Norse poetry. It tells the story of the hero, Siegfried, his slayer, Hagen, his wife and subsequent widow, Kriemhild (sister to Gunther, king of the Burgundians), of Queen Brunhilda and the treasure of the Nibelungs. The epic draws deeply on preserved traditions connected with the early history of the Burgundians and their defeat at the hands of Attila in the second quarter of the 5th c.

□ N. Thorp *The Study of the Nibelungen* (1940)

Nicaea, Council of (325) After his victory over Licinius in 323, Constantine found the Eastern province divided by the teachings of Arius, an Alexandrian priest who taught that the word was not co-eternal with the Father, and that Christ was at best an adopted son of God. Following his teacher Lucian of Antioch, he posited that the incarnate word did not have a human soul. Local attempts to stifle Arianism failed, and so did personal interventions by Constantine.

Finally, in accordance with Roman tradition, the emperor convoked a general synod, a council, which opened at Nicaea in 325. It was presided over directly by Pope Sylvester's legate, Hosius of Cordoba, and was attended by almost 300 bishops. The debates were acrimonious and lengthy. An Arian formula of faith was proposed and rejected; but Eusebius of Caesarea's optional creed was introduced and given general approval. With later additions, made specifically to exclude and denounce Arian interpretations, this became the Nicene Creed. Arianism continued to divide the Eastern church, but its influence was curtailed.

The Council also decided the vexed question of the date of the celebration of Easter, which was to be held on a Sunday, and (in line with Western tradition) on the first Sunday after the first full moon following the vernal equinox. *See* ATHANASIUS, ST

□ V.C. de Clerq *Ossius of Cordova* (1954); N.D. Kelly *Early Christian Creeds* (1960)

Nicaea, empire of After the capture of Constantinople (1204), Greek power splintered into three new Byzantine states centred on Trebizond, Epirus and Nicaea. At Nicaea the son-in-law of the Emperor Alexius III, Theodore I Lascaris (1204–22), rose to power and was crowned emperor in 1206 by the newly elected patriarch. Theodore compromised with the Latin rulers at Constantinople, the Frankish states, restrained the Bulgarian tzars and opened trading connections with the Venetians. He was succeeded by his son-in-law John III Vatatzes (1222–54), who drove the Latins from Asia Minor and seized the kingdoms of Thessalonica and Epirus. His expansion was restricted after 1242 by pressure from the Mongols. The bitter theological opposition of Gregory IX blocked *rapprochement* and eventually the patriarch excommunicated the pope. John's son Theodore II Lascaris succeeded (1254–58), but lacked the statesmanship of his father. On Theodore's death, Michael Palaeologus grasped the reins of power, ostensibly as regent for John IV (1258–61). In 1261 Michael seized power and, capitalizing on the Lascarid policy, captured Constantinople. He was crowned Emperor Michael VIII, creating the dynasty which survived until 1453. *See* PALAEOLOGI

□ D.M. Nicol *The End of the Byzantine Empire* (1979)

Niccoli, Niccolò (1364–1437) An influential Florentine humanist, who wrote little but was a passionate collector of classical manuscripts, antiquities, art and coins, as well as a keen copyist. His extensive collection of books formed the basis of the public library at S. Marco, Florence, and the sensitive elegance of his transcriptions helped to ensure that his refined version of Caroline minuscule became the standard humanistic hand.

□ G. Zippel *Niccolò Niccoli* (1890)

Nicholas II Pope 1059–61 (b.*c*.980) His short pontificate produced several highly significant measures, in anticipation of the Gregorian reform movement. Following the death of Pope Stephen IX there was a schism, with the Roman party appointing Benedict X, while the reformers elected Nicholas II, a Burgundian and former bishop of Florence. To prevent such divisions in future, in April 1059 Nicholas issued an electoral decree that popes were to be elected by cardinals on the initiative of the cardinal-bishops, and thereby reduced the influence of the Roman aristocracy and imperial interference in papal elections. Nicholas further antagonized the Emperor by establishing friendly relations with France and with the Patarines in Milan. At the Council of Melfi (August 1059) Nicholas formed an alliance with the Normans of south Italy, and his recognition of their position was a clear rejection of imperial claims to Italy. In response, a synod in Germany condemned Nicholas and declared his acts to be annulled. Thus his pontificate foreshadowed the bitter conflict between Empire and papacy. On his death a schism arose again with the election of two popes, Alexander II and Honorius II.

Nicholas Breakspear *See* **Adrian IV**

Nicholas of Cusa (d. 1464) One of the most prominent 15th-c. scholars, Cardinal Nicholas is best remembered for his metaphysical thought and skill as a collector of manuscripts in both Greek and

Latin. Born in the diocese of Trier, of German stock, he was educated at Padua and emerged as a papal supporter at the Council of Basle (1440). He was created cardinal in 1448 and later served as papal legate for Germany. He was a mathematician of some authority and held views on calendar reform in advance of his age. He believed, also, in the revolution of the earth around the sun.

□ H. Bett *Nicholas of Cusa* (1932); K. Jaspers *Anselm and Nicholas of Cusa* (1966)

Nilus of Calabria (*c.*910–1005) Born in Calabria of Greek descent, he was inspired by the Life of St Anthony and turned to a life of piety, penitence and self-sacrifice. A series of visions gained him followers, but his attempts to reconcile Benedictine and Byzantine monasteries were not successful. Late in life he impressed the young Emperor Otto III, on a visit to Rome, and the influence of his severe ascetic life at Grotaferrata did much to strengthen Western monasticism.

□ J. Décarreaux *Normands, Papes et Moines en Italie Méridionale* (1974)

Nithard (d. 844) Son of Charlemagne's daughter Bertha and Angilbert, the head of Charlemagne's chancery. In 841 Charles the Bald asked Nithard to write an account of contemporary events, and the resulting *History of the Quarrels between the sons of Louis the Pious* is invaluable as almost the only source for the wars of the period, although it is particularly biased against Lothar I. In 843 Nithard was made lay abbot of Saint-Riquier by Charles, but only a few months later he was killed in battle.

□ P. Lauer *Nithard. Histoire des fils de Louis le Pieux* (1926)

Noble English gold coin introduced by Edward III in 1344 with an initial value of 6*s* 8*d* (i.e., half a mark). From 1351 to 1412 it weighed 120 grains (7.78g). In 1412 the weight was reduced to 108 grains (7.60g). In 1465 the old weight of 120 grains was restored for the rose noble or ryal (royal), with a value of 10*s*, while a new coin, the angel, of 80 grains (5.18g), took over the value of 6*s* 8*d*.

An English **noble** (1327-77): Edward III with sword and shield standing in a ship.

Nogaret, Guillaume de (*c.*1265–1313) Teacher of law at Montpellier, Nogaret was of non-noble birth and a vigorous exponent of royal power. In 1303 Philip IV of France sent Nogaret, a member of his council, to arrest Pope Boniface VIII. Aided by the Colonna family and other enemies of Boniface, Nogaret entered Anagni; the papal residence was stormed and the pope was captured. Roused by the violence of the Colonna, the people of Anagni freed Boniface, and Nogaret fled back to France. In 1307 he was appointed keeper of the seal and was much involved in the trial of the Templars. Excommunicated in 1304 by Benedict XI, Nogaret was absolved by Clement V. He is remembered for his cruelty, ruthlessness and single-minded devotion to the French monarchy.

□ T.S.R. Boase *Boniface VIII* (1933); C.T. Wood *Philip the Fair and Boniface VIII* (1967)

Norbert of Xanten, St (*c.*1080–1134) Founder of the Premonstratensian Order, Norbert was a canon of Xanten in the Rhineland. In 1115 he was ordained a priest but, after failing to reform his fellow canons, he became a wandering preacher. He condemned the moral laxity of both clergy and laity, and followed the apostolic life with adherents of both sexes. In 1120, however, he submitted to his patron, the bishop of Laon, and agreed with papal support to found a religious community at Prémontré, near Laon. A friend of St Bernard of Clairvaux, Norbert adopted many of the Cistercian constitutions at Prémontré, but his Premonstratensian canons differed from ordinary monks in that they were encouraged to be active in society, in the mission field and also in parish life. In 1126 he became archbishop of Magdeburg and organized missionary work in eastern Germany. He was canonized in 1582.

□ E. Maire *St Norbert* (1932); P. Lefebvre *La Liturgie de Prémontré* (1957)

Normans The great conquering people of the 11th c., who in the course of 50 years (1050–1100) brought England, the southern part of the Italian peninsula and Sicily under their rule. Everywhere that aggressive war was taking place, Normans appear to have been present: on the Welsh and Scottish borders, in the Spanish *Reconquista* and the First Crusade, in the struggles of the Investiture Contest. Most scholars would, however, agree that these activities did not have the coherence of a single unified enterprise. England was the victim of a political conquest controlled by a reigning duke of Normandy, William the Conqueror. Southern Italy, which was loosely controlled by the Byzantine empire, and Islamic Sicily were slowly infiltrated by bands of warriors from the late 10th c. onwards; initial mercenary participation in the warfare of the region, in which Normans often fought on opposite sides against each other, was transformed from the 1040s into a conquest dominated by men such as Robert Guiscard and his brother Roger I 'the Great Count'. Southern Italy was not subdued until the 1070s, and Sicily not until 1091; their unification into the kingdom of Sicily did not occur until the 1130s.

The origins of these achievements must be located in the history of the duchy of Normandy, which had evolved from a territory around Rouen granted to the Viking chieftain Rollo in 911. In spite of its beginnings and considerable Scandinavian immigration up until c.950, the duchy of Normandy revealed by 11th-c. documents possesses overwhelmingly the character of a contemporary French territorial principality. The survival of Carolingian governmental institutions and the continuity of territorial boundaries over the period of Scandinavian settlement are a source of particular comment among historians; it is clear that the province's early rulers resolutely took over existing institutions. The revival of the Norman church demonstrates acceptance of Christianity. The important reign of Duke Richard II (996–1026) was widely known as a period of peace within the province and the duke himself was famed for his patronage of the church. By this time the Scandinavian language had virtually ceased to be spoken in the duchy, while Richard's decision to harbour the young Edward the Confessor, in addition to its long-term consequences, was a snub to the ambitions of Cnut and the Danish armies involved in the conquest of England. Intermarriage, several decades of relative social stability, and considerable Frankish immigration into Normandy had done much to assimilate the original Scandinavian settlers into their surroundings.

The Norman expansion of the 11th c. was therefore not a simple continuation of the Viking raids. Up to a point the Normans were merely in the van of a wider movement of conquest: there were Flemings, Bretons, Poitevins and other Frankish peoples in the army which won at Hastings; in the south, non-Norman immigration up to a ratio of one in four has been suggested, and the invaders are known to have recruited natives of the south to their cause. Greater social mobility was a feature of 11th-c. French society. The Normans' prominence within this movement derived largely from the fact that from c.1025 Normandy was convulsed by warfare within its ruling classes. This, symptomatic of a kind of 'feudal revolution', associated as in other regions of France with castle-building and the subjugation of previously free landholders, was a

particularly disturbed phase which undoubtedly fuelled the exodus to the south. The sequel, William the Conqueror's pacification of the duchy after 1050, appears to have been based on a policy of warfare against neighbouring powers; 1066 provided an opportunity which was capably taken. Subsequently, chances galore for personal aggrandizement existed for the individual Norman, through service to the Norman kings or through family connections in the south. For the more adventurous there were now frontiers to push back from bases securely under Norman rule.

To their new lands the Normans brought military methods based on cavalry and castles, which had been learnt in the hard school of contemporary northern France, and which were markedly superior to those of the people they were fighting. Everywhere the Normans took with them the moveable institutions of lordship which gave cohesion to the groups of warriors who carried out the conquests. The acquisition of land by a lord was always followed by the transfer of much of it to vassals. Thus, for instance, men from the region of Montgomery in central Normandy appear in Domesday Book holding land in Shropshire of their lord, Roger de Montgomery. The general result was the same in southern Italy, although there the lord-vassal relationships were often forged in the course of the settlement.

In their conquests the Normans encountered two of the most highly developed administrative systems in Western Europe. Anglo-Saxon institutions, such as the writ, the geld, and the hundred court, were fully exploited by the newcomers; so too were the Byzantine and Sicilian administrations. In spite of a declared respect for English law, Norman England became in many respects a colonial society, with the massive new cathedrals and castles a symbol of the newcomers' power, and Domesday Book, of their ruthlessness. In government, precisely because they came as conquerors and because they took over all crucial governmental positions, the Normans added an element of exploitation and centralization which stimulated remarkable 12th-c. developments such as the Exchequer and Henry II's legal reforms.

Also in the 12th c. the political aims of the Norman rulers and of their Angevin successors became increasingly defensive; the flow of emigrants dwindled after c.1120. In the south, where the intrusion of Normans into church and government had been less brutal, a multifarious mixture of Frankish, Byzantine, Islamic and Italian cultural and political forms evolved as the connection with Normandy faded away. The duchy of Normandy's independent existence finally came to an end when it was conquered by the French king in 1204. English kings continued to press claims to the Norman duchy, notably in the course of the Hundred Years' War, and English governors and garrisons exercised authority in the duchy with mixed success from 1415 to the end of the war in the 1450s. *See* ROGER II; WILLIAM OF VOLPIANO   DB

□ C.H. Haskins *The Normans in European History* (1915); J.J. Norwich *The Normans in the South* (1967); J. le Patourel *The Norman Empire* (1976); D. Bates *Normandy before 1066* (1982)

Northumbrian renaissance During the second half of the 7th c. and the first half of the 8th c. Anglo-Saxon Northumbria (the area north of the Humber) produced a remarkably rich culture, termed the Northumbrian renaissance. It was indeed a renaissance, in the broad sense of a rebirth of learning and art with particular reference to the classical past, but went far beyond this, fusing newly discovered elements of late antique, early Christian/Byzantine and Continental culture with more familiar Celtic and Germanic traditions, to found a British culture which has earned the title 'Insular', as one of the few such movements to have evolved totally within the British Isles.

This lively literary, artistic and religious milieu was a product of Northumbria's geographical position and political development. By the 7th c. pagan Northumbria lay between two powerful centres of Christianity. To the north-west lay Irish Dalriada and the monastery of Iona, founded by Columba *c.* 563. (Ireland had developed its own Christian culture in comparative isolation from the rest of Europe.) To the south lay the conversion-field of the Roman mission, led by Augustine at Canterbury and instigated by Pope Gregory the Great (597). Northumbria's initial conversion is attributed to the Roman Paulinus who in 625 accompanied the Christian princess Aethelberga of Kent to Northumbria, where she married its pagan King Edwin (616–32). Edwin was baptized (627), but after his death in battle, his successors Oswald (633–41) and Oswy (642–71), who had been in exile at Iona during Edwin's reign, introduced Celtic monks led by Abbot Aidan from Iona (634), who established a monastery at Lindisfarne.

Irish ascetic monasticism and preaching were ideal at this stage, but ecclesiastical unity and a formal diocesan structure were necessary to ensure strength, so in 664 at the Synod of Whitby Oswy decided to favour the Roman observance within his kingdom. Those who could not acquiesce left Northumbria, but many stayed, and it was their attempt to fuse the two traditions which was largely responsible for the Northumbrian renaissance.

There were several leading figures in this move-ment. Hild (614–80), abbess of Whitby, said to have discovered the Northumbrian poet Caedmon, conformed after 664 and was succeeded by Oswy's wife Eanfled and daughter Aelfled. Cuthbert (634–87), for whom three Northumbrian Lives survive, was the bishop of Lindisfarne who, although of Celtic training, helped to reconcile the remaining brethren to Rome. Wilfrid (634–709), commemorated by Eddius Stephanus' Life of Wilfrid (*c.*709), was a Romanophile of Celtic training who in 653 accompanied Biscop to Rome. Wilfrid was abbot of Ripon, bishop of York, founder of Hexham and the principal northern churchman (669–78), although twice deposed through disagreements with Oswy and his successor Egfrith (671–85). He was responsible for much of the building and artistic activity associated with his churches and the introduction of new styles and techniques. He was joined in this by Benedict Biscop (*c.*627–89), a Northumbrian nobleman trained at Lérins and abbot of St Peter's, Canterbury, who made five trips to Rome, bringing back numerous manuscripts, paintings and other objects for his twin Northumbrian foundations of Wearmouth (673–74) and Jarrow (*c.*681). Biscop enjoyed the patronage of the learned Northumbrian King Aldfrith (685–705). Ceolfrith (*c.*642–716) joined Biscop in ruling Jarrow and accompanied him to Rome. Upon Biscop's death he governed Wearmouth and Jarrow.

The splendid scriptorium produced, among other things, three Bibles for Ceolfrith (*c.*700), one of which he took as an offering to St Peter on his journey to Rome, where he intended to die (716). This manuscript, the *Codex Amiatinus*, represents the most thoroughly classicizing of the North-umbrian manuscripts with its uncial script and impressionistic painting. Under Ceolfrith was the monk Bede (*c.*672–735), most noteworthy of Northumbrian scholars. His works, produced during his life at Jarrow, include over 40 biblical commentaries, two Lives of St Cuthbert, a history of the abbots of Wearmouth and Jarrow, scientific works on time, the *Nature of Things*, and the *Six Ages of the World*, grammatical treatises and his masterly *Ecclesiastical History of England* (finished *c.*731), which represents the first successful medieval attempt to provide a continuous historical narrative and to interrelate events.

Perhaps the most striking visual example of Northumbrian culture is the Lindisfarne Gospels, probably produced at Lindisfarne (*c.*698) for the translation of St Cuthbert's relics. This remarkable work incorporates Celtic pelta and trumpet spirals, Germanic interlace and zoomorphic decoration, and elements of probable early Christian derivation, such as the Evangelist portraits, which are, however,

Pectoral cross of St Cuthbert: a fine product of the
Northumbrian renaissance

The Franks casket of whale-bone ivory bearing runic
inscriptions and carved scenes (early 8th c.).

subjected to a linear, calligraphic treatment which
differs from the classical painterly technique of the
Codex Amiatinus.

Monuments in other media include the humanistic sculptured crosses at Hexham, Bewcastle and
Ruthwell, St Cuthbert's incised wooden coffin and
jewelled pectoral cross, the Ormside bowl with its
classical plant forms, and the whalebone Franks
casket with its scenes from Christian, Roman and
Germanic lore.   MB
□ P. Hunter Blair *The World of Bede* (1970); H.
Mayr-Harting *The Coming of Christianity to England*
(1972); D. Wilson *Anglo-Saxon Art* (1984)

Norway The political history of Norway in the
Middle Ages is highly complicated, bound up with
its colonizing and trading ventures, and deeply
affected by its relations with the other Scandinavian
communities: Denmark and Sweden. During
the Viking Age (*c*.800–1100) Norwegian sailors,

traders, pirates and settlers established permanent
settlements in the islands around Britain (notably
and early, in Shetland and Orkney); they played a
prominent role in establishing urban centres in
Ireland and set up a long chain of predominantly
Norwegian settlers across the Atlantic on the
Faroes, Iceland (*c*.860–930) and Greenland. They
even touched the American shores, certainly Newfoundland, and possibly the mainland of the eastern
seaboard at the end of the 10th c.

It was within the context of this age of mobility
and ferment that the shape of a united kingdom of
Norway emerged. Up to that point, the tendency
appears to have been for political power to rest with
families grouped around the three distinctive
regions later associated with Trondheim in the
north, the western fjords and Bergen, and the Vik or
Oslofjord in the south. It was Harald Fairhair who,
after the decisive battle of Hafrsfjord (*c*.890), first
unified most of Norway; from that point on the idea
of a Norwegian polity never completely disappeared,
though from time to time Norway was governed
virtually as a dependent province by one or other of
its neighbours.

At the end of the 10th c. and the beginning of the
11th c. reception of Christianity strengthened both
the feeling of unity and also the potential power of
kingship under Olaf Tryggvason (995–1000) and
Olaf Haraldsson (1016–30). Olaf Haraldsson was
defeated by Cnut the Great, and killed in battle at
Stiklestad while attempting to recover his position.
Legends quickly spread about his death and he was
recognized as a saint, *perpetuus rex Norvegiae*. Cnut
(d. 1035) attempted to incorporate Norway firmly
within his empire, but a series of able rulers, Magnus,
the son of Olaf (d. 1047), Harald Hardrada (1047–66)
who died at Stamford Bridge, and Harald's son,
Olaf the Peaceful (1066–93), re-established the
native monarchic tradition.

In the 12th c. the establishment of an archbishopric at Trondheim marks an important stage in the
full acceptance of the northern kingdom within the
polity of Western Christendom. To maintain royal
authority over an area as extensive as Norway demanded constant effort and close accord with local
communities under their own laws; and violence
was never far from the Norwegian political scene.
In the reign of Sverre (1184–1202) a bitter quarrel
broke out between church and state, with the king
asserting powerful claims to control appointment to
bishoprics as a means of ensuring a degree of royal
discipline over Norwegian society. Under Haakon
IV (1217–63) the consolidation of royal political
authority reached a high point as Iceland and Greenland submitted to the Norwegian king, though the
hold on the Scottish islands slackened, the southern

group passing under the authority of the Scottish king.

The later Middle Ages proved a period of decline, partly because of a deterioration in climate and partly because of the severe ravages of the Black Death. Union with Sweden under Magnus VII (1319–43) was unsuccessful, but Norway, governed by the redoubtable Margaret, wife and then widow of Haakon VI (1343–80), was the moving force in creating the Union of Calmar (1397), by which the Scandinavian countries were to be united 'eternally' under the rule of her great-nephew and his successors. Concern over the wealth and influence of German merchants (Bergen was one of the four principal 'counters' – with London, Bruges and Novgorod – of the Hanseatic League) remained a strong element in Norwegian politics at the time. Sweden soon showed dissatisfaction with the arrangements made at Calmar, though it did not retire fully from the Union until 1523. Norway remained closely linked and subordinate to its more wealthy southern neighbour, and it was a Danish king who negotiated the transmission of Orkney and Shetland to the Scottish crown in the late 1460s.
□ T.K. Derry *A Short History of Norway* (1957).

Notker (Balbulus) the Stammerer (*c.*840–912) Librarian and then master of the school at the Benedictine monastery of St Gallen in Switzerland. His fame rests in part on his elegant and sympathetic composition of hymns and sequences, and also on his Life of Charlemagne, written in 883 or 884, which contains much anecdotal material as well as some sound historical matter about the great emperor.
□ *Two Lives of Charlemagne* ed. L. Thorpe (1969)

Novgorod Founded by Scandinavian merchants in the early 9th c. towards the head of the waterways that link the Baltic to the Black Sea, Novgorod became the centre of the new kingdom of the Rus under the leadership of King Rurik (862). His successor Oleg captured the powerful city of Kiev in 882, and the centre of power among the Scandinavian-Slavonic principalities moved south. Novgorod, though still powerful, accepted the overlordship of the Kievan princes and became increasingly Slavonic in population, language and institutional life.

In 1019 Prince Yaroslav granted the town a charter permitting a substantial degree of autonomy. As the power of Kiev declined, the Novgorod princes expanded their authority and commercial influence. Under Alexander Nevsky the city defeated the Swedes on the Neva (1240) and two years later won the great battle on the ice at Lake Paipus against

the Teutonic knights. The city paid tribute to the Tartars, but on the whole suffered less than other Russian states from Mongol and Tartar attacks.

The city's wealth was firmly rooted in trade. The easy access to the Baltic-Byzantium axis via the Volkhov, Lovat and Dnieper rivers, and to the Caspian Sea via the Volga, saw the city thrust into the role of one of the main bridges of East-West trade. The major export commodities were furs, amber, honey and wax, as well as slaves, in exchange for gold, silver and silks. The city had close links with the lucrative spice trade and growing Hanseatic League, which established one of its principal 'counters' at Novgorod.

During the 14th c. local dynastic wars enveloped the city, disturbing its trading routes. The rise of the trading rival Moscow further encouraged the city's decline as a major entrepôt. The trading supremacy of Moscow was emphatically asserted with the help of two crushing military defeats in 1456 and 1471, and Moscow's superiority was completed by its annexation of Novgorod in 1478.
□ M.W. Thompson *Novgorod the Great* (1967)

Nūr ad-Dīn (1118–74) Muslim leader in Syria, whose name means 'Light of the Faith'. He succeeded his father Zengi as ruler of Aleppo in 1146. He quickly recaptured Edessa, and taking advantage of the political opportunities offered by the Second Crusade, cautiously extended his authority. In 1154 he annexed Damascus, which became the centre of his kingdom. He captured Tripoli (1167) and in 1168 placed Egypt under his control. The disunity which had permitted the Christians to advance was now ending as Nūr ad-Dīn created a united Muslim state, though at the expense of the Shi'ite followers of the faith. His success popularized the Holy War against the crusaders and his use of temporary alliances and steady exploitation of Christian deficiencies and internecine discord produced continual success.
□ V. Eliséeff *Nūr ad-Dīn* (1966)

O

Observant Friars *See* **Dominic, St**

Odilo, St (962–1048) Appointed by his predecessor Abbot Mayeul as fifth abbot of Cluny in 994, Odilo was one of a succession of long-lived abbots. He was a leading European figure on friendly terms with the Emperor, the king of France and the papacy. He involved Cluny more closely with the feudal world by acting as an arbitrator in secular disputes and by his support of the attempts to limit warfare through the Peace and Truce of God. Under Odilo, Cluny received papal confirmation of its unique privileges and entered its greatest expansionary period, marking the full formulation of the Cluniac Order. Of his building programme at Cluny itself, Odilo said that he had found it wood and left it marble. He was succeeded by Hugh, who was chosen not only by Odilo himself, but by the brethren.

□ L. Coté *St Odilon, un Moine de l'An Mille* (1969)

Odo, St (879–942) Abbot of Cluny. After a military training Odo was converted to the religious life, but his popularity while living as a hermit forced him to go to Paris, where he studied the liberal arts and dialectic. Attracted by the fame of St Berno, Odo joined him and was made head of the school at Baume. In 927 Odo was appointed by St Berno as the second abbot of Cluny. Odo had a considerable reputation for personal sanctity and was largely responsible for establishing Cluny as the centre of Benedictine reform, and for laying the foundations of its future greatness. He did not confine himself to Cluny; with the backing of the papacy, he was active also in the reformation of numerous monasteries, including Fleury and Monte Cassino.

□ E. Amman *Odon de Cluny* (1931)

Odo (c.1030–97) Bishop of Bayeux. Half-brother of William the Conqueror, from whom he received the bishopric of Bayeux in 1049. Odo was a patron of the arts, and it is probable that he commissioned the Bayeux tapestry for the dedication of his cathedral in 1077. He played an active part in the battle of Hastings and was granted the earldom of Kent and vast estates in England, the profits from which made him one of the wealthiest men in Europe. During the king's absence in Normandy in 1067 Odo governed England, together with William FitzOsbern. He continued to be prominent in the royal council and administration up to the time of his disgrace and imprisonment (apparently for dabbling in papal politics) in 1082. After William's death (1087) he was released from captivity, but was banished from England in the following year for the part he played in the unsuccessful revolt against William II. He settled in Normandy, but died at Palermo on his way to the First Crusade.

□ D.R. Bates, 'The character and career of Odo, Bishop of Bayeux', *Speculum* 1 (1975)

Offa's dyke Forming the traditional boundary between England and Wales, this impressive earthwork runs, although not continuously, from the Dee estuary in the north to the river Wye in the south. Constructed by King Offa of Mercia (757–

96), it is a tribute to the authority he commanded from the Humber to the Channel. The old view that it was an agreed boundary is no longer held; the dyke was clearly a formidable barrier and protection against cattle theft.

□ C. Fox *Offa's Dyke* (1955); D. Hill *An Atlas of Anglo-Saxon England* (1981)

Olaf II Haraldsson, St King of Norway 1016–30 (b.c.995) A descendant of Harald Fairhair, Olaf lived as a Viking until his baptism at Rouen (c.1013). In 1015 he asserted his claim to the Norwegian throne and by 1016 was king of Norway. He built upon the work of his predecessor, Olaf I Tryggvason (c.995–1000), to promote Christianity throughout the country, but his harshness and zeal aroused great hostility. In 1028 Cnut met little opposition when he arrived at Trondheim where he was proclaimed king. Olaf fled to Russia, but returned to try to regain his kingdom with a largely foreign, heathen army; he was killed at the battle of Stiklestad. Despite his unpopularity, a far-reaching cult quickly grew up after miracles were reported following his death, and in 1164 Olaf was declared the patron saint of Norway. In 1035 his son Magnus was universally accepted as king of Norway.

□ G. Jones *The Vikings* (1968)

Omar Khayyam (c.1050–1123) Born in Nishapur, Persia, Omar Khayyam was an astronomer, mathematician and poet. On the strength of his work and reputation in algebra, he was invited by the Seljuk sultan Mālik Shah to make the astonomical observations which resulted in a reform of the calendar. He is best known, however, as the poet of the *Rubaiyat*, a collection of quatrains or *rubais*.

□ *The Rubaiyat of Omar Khayyam* trans. E. FitzGerald (1859)

Omayyads *See* **Umayyads**

Ordericus Vitalis (c.1075–1143) Born of Anglo-Norman parents near Shrewsbury, he was educated at Saint-Evroul in Normandy, where he spent much of his life busying himself with his *Ecclesiastical History* from 1109 to the time of his death. Most of his work deals with contemporary or nearly contemporary events, and provides a superb insight into the general history of the Anglo-Norman world and the local history of the abbey of Saint-Evroul.

□ M. Chibnall *The World of Ordericus Vitalis* (1982)

Oresme, Nicolas (c.1320–82) Bishop of Lisieux. While a master at the university of Paris, Oresme associated with John Buridan, rector of the university,

Miniature from **Nicolas of Oresme**'s translation of
Aristotle's *Ethics* (*c.* 1376).

in a serious attempt to examine and modify the
science of Aristotle. Concentrating on the mecha-
nics of moving bodies, their work marked an
important step towards later developments by da
Vinci, Copernicus and Galileo. Oresme also wrote
a treatise on coinage, which had great influence
on economic theory in the later Middle Ages. He
resigned to become canon, then dean of Rouen,
before being appointed as chaplain to Charles V. In
1377 he was made bishop of Lisieux.
□ *Nicholas d'Oresme, De Moneta* ed. C. Johnson
(1956)

Origen (*c.*185–*c.*254) One of the greatest of the
Eastern fathers of the Christian church, Origen
taught in Alexandria until he was banished in 232.
He founded another school in Caesarea, but in 250
during the persecution of Emperor Decius, was
arrested and tortured, and died at Tyre. His many
theological works include the *Hexapla*, a synopsis of
the Old Testament, and *Contra Celsum* (*c.*248), a
vindication of Christianity in answer to the pagan
Celsus' *True Doctrine* (*c.*168). A rigorous ascetic of
orthodox intent, Origen was accused of heresy,
as suggested by his philosophical approach to
Christian doctrine in *De Principiis* (On First Principles). His influence as a theologian persisted beyond
his denunciation by Justinian I in 543.
□ G.W. Butterworth *Origen on first principles* ed. H.
de Lubac (1966); H. Chadwick *Early Christian
Thought and the Classical Tradition* (1966)

Orleans, Council of (10 July 511) Assembly of 32
Gallic bishops (largely representing the newly
conquered south), summoned by the Merovingian

King Clovis. It sealed his new creation of Frankia,
forming a statement of the king's relations with the
church. The first ten canons dealt with matters
concerning royal authority: the right of asylum;
royal permission for ordinations; acceptable uses of
royal largesse to churches; frequenting of the royal
court by clerics seeking favours; ordination of
slaves; appropriation of Arian churches taken from
the Goths and employment of their ministers. They
delineate the scope of royal intervention, which is
not excessive, and tacitly accept the church's Roman
law (drawing upon the Theodosian *Code*). They
also promote the king's involvement in church
patronage.
□ J.M. Wallace-Hadrill *The Long-haired Kings*
(1962)

Orosius Spanish priest who fled to Hippo in 414 to
evade the barbarian invasions. Under his mentor,
Augustine, he produced several works in defence of
orthodoxy. The first, on the origin of the human
soul, made his reputation. He was sent in 415 to
debate with Pelagius before Bishop John of Jerusalem,
but the outcome was inconclusive. The episcopal
report sent to Rome questioned his orthodoxy and
drew forth his famous refutation of the charge, and
also of Pelagius, in the *Liber Apologeticus contra
Pelagianos*. Finally, Augustine asked him to produce
a historical supplement to his own *City of God*.

This work, finished in 418, set out to combat
the popular contemporary argument that Rome's
fall was directly caused by its conversion to Christianity. As the title indicates, the *Historiarum adversus
Paganos Libri Septem* was divided into seven books,
a structure which suggested biblical parallels.
The theme of beleaguered Christianity triumphant
that dominates the work explains its popularity.
□ *Seven Books of History against the Pagans* ed. I.W.
Raymond (1936); B. Lacroix *Orose et ses idées*
(1965)

Orsini family Important Roman family of nobles.
The legendary founder of the Orsini was a boy
named Orso (meaning bear) who was raised by a
domestic bear, and came to Rome *c.*425. They also
claimed ancestry from two popes, Stephen II and
Paul I, and a number of other saints and blessed persons,
such as St Benedict and his sister St Scholastica. The
family rose to prominence in the 12th c., along with
their enemies, the Colonna, another important
family in Rome. Major landholders to the north of
Rome, the most famous members of the family
were Pope Celestine III (1191–98) and Pope Nicholas
III (1277–80).
□ G.B. Colonna *Gli Orsini* (1955); J.A.F. Thompson
Popes and Princes 1417–1517 (1980)

Oseberg ship Viking ship found in 1903 at Oseberg, west of the Oslofjord. It is 21.5 m long, with 15 pairs of oars, and built of oak (c.800), but not designed for long voyages. Many grave goods survive, incuding sledges and a wagon, with fine animal carvings, as on the serpent's head at the prow. The remains of two women were found in the boat, and it is generally held that they were Queen Asa, grandmother of Harald Fairhair, and a maid-servant. The likely date of the burial is the late 9th c. *See* GOKSTAD SHIP

□ A.W. Brögger and H. Shetelig *The Viking Ships* (1951)

Ostrogoths (East Goths) One of the two main branches of the Goths who were forced to move westward under pressure from the Huns. Their empire stretched from the Don to the Dneister, bordering the shores of the Black Sea. Subjugated by the Huns c.370, they reappear in 487 marching on Constantinople. Emperor Zeno, to avert the danger, commissioned their leader Theodoric to invade Italy and subdue Odoacer, leader of the German federates who were governing Italy, ostensibly in the name of the emperor.

By 493 Theodoric had won control of Italy, ruling the peninsula capably from Ravenna and extending his influence westwards into Provence and Visi-gothic Spain. Imperial administration survived under his rule, and the Roman senate recognized him as the imperial representative. The Ostrogoths were Arian Christians, but tolerant, and they suc-ceeded by and large in giving Italy a generation of peace, by their practice of governing the Ostrogoths and the Romans separately, with little effort being made towards fusion or assimilation. At the end of Theodoric's reign the so-called Ostrogothic compromise was wearing thin and there was a series of persecutions, in the course of which the great philosopher Boethius was put to death.

By 533, under Theodoric's successors, the Ostro-goths were divided, and Justinian, the Eastern emperor, seized the opportunity to re-establish imperial authority. In 553, after a bitter and protracted struggle, the Ostrogothic kingdom collapsed. It made no permanent impression on peninsular insti-tutions or culture, but played a crucial role in the transmission of earlier structures. *See* TOTILA [*152*]

□ W. Goffart *Barbarians and Romans 418–584: The Techniques of Accommodation* (1980); T.S. Burns *A History of the Ostrogoths* (1984)

Oswald, St King of Northumbria c.633–41 (b.c.605) While Edwin was king of Northumbria (616–32), Oswald, son of Ethelfrith, Edwin's predecessor, lived in exile on Iona, where he was converted to Christianity. In 632 Edwin was killed by Cadwallon, who was in turn killed by Oswald the following year. Oswald was accepted as king by Deira and Bernicia, the two ancient divisions of Northumbria, and for most of his reign he was overlord of England south of the Humber. One of the great Christian kings, Oswald furthered the spread of Christianity by introducing Celtic missionaries from Iona, led by St Aidan. In 641 he was killed in battle by the heathen King Penda of Mercia, and his cult as a saint and martyr spread rapidly.

□ F.M. Stenton *Anglo-Saxon England* (1971)

Otto I the Great King of Germany 936–73 (b.912) Crowned Holy Roman Emperor at Rome on 2 February 962, Otto is remembered as the founder of the first *Reich*, which brought together Germany and most of Italy into one empire, and also as the virtual founder of the kingdom of Germany. His father Henry I (919–36) had prepared the way by building up a strong duchy in Saxony, safeguarding the northern frontier against the Danes; he had taken the lead in military resistance to the Slavs in the East,

Prow of the **Oseberg ship** displaying elaborate geometric and zoomorphic carving.

and above all to the Magyars who were at the height of their ravaging attacks on Western Europe. In 926 Lorraine had moved firmly into the German orbit, with the duke paying allegiance to the German king, and Otto succeeded to a kingship which nominally covered the five great stem duchies of early medieval Germany: his native Saxony, Franconia, Lorraine and the southern duchies of Swabia and Bavaria. At his coronation he emphasized the subordinate position of the dukes, who took on duties as household officers in the course of the ceremony.

His early attempts to control the duchies by appointing his kinsmen to ducal office met with only partial success. His first intervention in Italian affairs (950–51) was prompted in part by the need to prevent his brother Henry, duke of Bavaria, and his son Liudolf, duke of Swabia, from exercising an independent policy in relation to Burgundy and north Italy. The intervention proved successful in many ways: it strengthened German royal authority over the old Middle Kingdom (Lorraine, Burgundy and Lombardy), brought papal support, and in the personal field enabled Otto (a widower) to marry Adelaide, a descendant of the Carolingian house, so linking his fortunes with the tradition of Charlemagne. Further reorganization of ducal offices took place after the rebellion of Liudolf in 953, and Otto's prestige reached a high-point in 955 with his devastating defeat of the Magyars at the battle of the river Lech near Augsburg. Military ability, coupled with a strong border policy, ensured that Otto emerged as the clear leader of all the German people; the soldiers hailed him as *imperator* after the victory on the Lech.

For government he relied increasingly on churchmen who were loyal to him and whose lands were not subject to hereditary tenure. The creation of a strong German church (the Ottonian church) was dictated by necessity. Successful campaigns against the Slavs (in which Herman Billung, appointed to the Saxon duchy, was prominent) were accompanied by intense missionary efforts. Anxieties over the creation of a new archbishopric at Magdeburg were a contributory element in Otto's second, decisive intervention in Italy (961–62). A papal appeal for help against private enemies was answered and Otto marched to Rome where he was crowned Emperor. A short period of papal-imperial harmony was followed by drastic action on the new Emperor's part: the deposition of Pope John XII and the election of popes favourable to the imperial cause. Otto spent much time and energy stabilizing his position in Italy, in the course of which he arranged a marriage between his son Otto II the Red and a Byzantine princess, Theophano.

The range and nature of his activities brought

Otto I offers Magdeburg cathedral to Christ in majesty; ivory plaque *c. 970*.

Germany and Italy into long-lasting association and also cemented the close relationship between the new German kingship and the church. A cultural revival, primarily Latin and Carolingian in inspiration, sometimes called the Ottonian renaissance, brought into being a new manifestation of Western cultural life, notably in the fields of architecture, sculpture and the pictorial arts.   HRL
□ K. Leyser *Rule and Conflict in an Early Medieval Society: Ottonian Saxony* (1979), *Medieval Germany and its neighbours, 900–1250* (1982)

Otto III Holy Roman Emperor 983–1002 (b.980) Grandson of Otto the Great, and son of Otto II (973–83), the third king-emperor of that name succeeded to the throne when still a child. Two able regencies, first under the control of his mother Theophano (983–89) and then his grandmother Adelaide (990–94), testified to the intrinsic strength of the Ottonian system. The young prince was brought up under strong imperial influence and in his short life proved himself one of the most Roman of the German rulers. His candidates for the papacy, Gregory VI (996–99) and the very able and scholarly Gerbert of Aurillac, Sylvester II, encouraged his imperial ideas, but Roman intransigence and Slav political resurgence, notably in Poland, prevented the achievement of his most ambitious schemes. His active encouragement of scholars and artists brought the cultural revival of the Ottonian period to fresh heights.
□ R. Folz *The Concept of Empire in Western Europe from the Fifth to the Fifteenth Century* (1969)

Ottobono Fieschi Pope 1276. A native of Genoa, he was a nephew of Pope Innocent IV (1243–54) who elevated him to the cardinalate. Under Pope Clement IV (1265–68) Ottobono was sent to England to mediate between King Henry III and his rebellious barons. Ottobono's patience, endurance and statesmanship helped to produce the Dictum of Kenilworth (1266), which brought the baronial rebels to obedience and the royal advisers to reason, terminating the civil war. The new accord was strengthened by the Statute of Marlborough. Ottobono also preached a crusade in a well-planned campaign using the energy, zeal and skill of the mendicant friars. His programme of ecclesiastical reform culminated in his Constitutions issued at the Council of London in 1268. In 1276 Ottobono was elected to the papacy as Adrian V, but died after five weeks.
□ F.M. Powicke *The Thirteenth Century 1216–1307* (1953)

Ottoman Turks The word 'Ottoman' is derived from the founder of the dynasty, Osmān I (d.1326) who concentrated the power of the Turkish state in his own hands and harnessed the *ghāzīs* (Muslim warrior-fanatics who undertook plunderous raids, *razzia*, to fulfil the *jihād* against Christians) into a coherent policy of expansion. Initially, success was slow, but under Osmān's successor Orkhan (1326–62) the policy was continued, Nicaea falling in 1331, Nicomedia in 1337 and Gallipoli in 1354, thus providing the Ottomans with a permanent base in Europe. Internal Christian divisions eased the Ottomans' task and under Murād I (1362–89) advance quickened: Adrianople fell in 1363, and in 1371, at the battle of Cirnomen, the south Serbian states were broken. Nis and Sofia were captured by 1386, and the opposition of the north Serbian states was overcome at Kosovo in 1389. Under Bāyazīd I (1389–1403), Constantinople was placed under perpetual blockade and the Christian offensive to defend it was destroyed at Nicopolis (1396).

The Muslim administration was overburdened by the speed and scale of the gains made, and in an attempt to maintain their cultural identity in the new lands, the Muslims began a series of local wars in Turkey against other Muslim states. However, in 1402 Bāyazīd was captured and his forces heavily defeated at Ankara by Tamberlaine. The Ottoman state was temporarily fragmented by inheritance until reunited by Muhammad I (1413–21) who, with his successor Murād II, re-established the *ghāzī* ideal and the *jihād*. At Varna (1444) and Kosovo (1448) Hungarian counter-offensives were defeated and Constantinople fell to Muhammad II's forces in 1453. Muhammad II (1451–81) continued to push into Europe; Belgrade was vainly beseiged in 1456 but Athens was captured in 1458. Large areas of Asia Minor and the Black Sea coast fell to the Ottomans, as well as Serbia (1459) and Bosnia (1463–64). The size of the conquests restricted further advances, and the zeal for victory was abated and diminished.
See BEYAZET I   HRL
□ P. Sugar *South-Eastern Europe under Ottoman Rule 1354–1804* (1977)

Owain Gwynedd Prince of Gwynedd 1137–70 (b.*c.*1109) In 1137 he succeeded his father Gruffydd ap Cynan (1081–1137) to the kingdom of Gwynedd, which covered most of North Wales. While England was engaged in civil war, Owain used his skill as statesman and soldier to extend his frontiers. In 1157 Henry II led his first campaign against Owain, but it ended in a truce. Six years later, the Council of Woodstock attempted to reduce the Welsh princes from client status to that of dependent vassalage, and the subsequent uprising was led by Owain Gwynedd and Rhys ap Gruffydd of South Wales. Henry's second attempt at subduing Wales failed ignominiously and left Owain free to capture Basingwerk and Rhuddlan castles (1166–67). Having openly defied Henry in 1168 by offering help to Louis VII of France, Owain maintained his independent position until his death. He left behind him a reputation for wisdom and magnanimity.
□ R.R. Davies *Conquest, coexistence and change: Wales 1063–1415* (1987)

Oxford Town situated in the Upper Thames basin at the confluence of the Thames and Cherwell, providing fords for both, good communications and defence. It was a Saxon settlement, first mentioned in 912 (Anglo-Saxon Chronicle) when Edward the Elder took possession and probably fortified it. It appears in Domesday as a market town which fell under the jurisdiction of the d'Oilli family who built its castle, three bridges and Oseney priory (1129). Development as a prosperous borough was complicated in the later 12th c. by the appearance of the university, first mentioned in 1184, although Oxford was probably already an academic centre. The university's foundation may have been partly due to difficulty of access to Paris university during Henry II's conflict with Becket (1164–69). It was enlarged by the friars and Parisian students during the 1220s and the first colleges (Balliol, Merton and University) were founded in the second half of the century. The town did not welcome this rowdy new community. The Middle Ages witnessed the struggle for university autonomy and extended authority and civic resistance, occasioning many bloody encounters (notably 1209, 1248, 1263, 1298 and the

William of Wykeham in front of New College, **Oxford**, from the Chandler manuscript, *c.* 1460.

St Scholastica's massacre, 1355). Royal and papal support ensured the university's triumph by the mid-15th c.

In contrast to Paris, Oxford favoured the Quadrivium, becoming a centre of scientific and mathematical studies. It also exhibited conservatism, promoting Platonism and Augustinianism. Notable Oxford scholars included Edmund Rich, Robert Grosseteste, Roger Bacon, Duns Scotus, Ockham and Wycliffe.
□ C.E. Mallet *A History of the University of Oxford* vol. 1 (1968)

Oxford, Provisions of (1258) Constitutional document which the barons forced Henry III to accept after a turbulent meeting at Oxford. The barons were hostile and alarmed at the excessive favour shown to foreign favourites, the heavy demands for taxation and the apparent downgrading of the great offices of state in favour of administrators in the royal household. For the following two years England was ruled by what was virtually an oligarchic council of barons, most prominent among whom were Simon de Montfort, the king's brother-in-law, and Richard de Clare, earl of Gloucester. The detailed Provisions, aptly described

as an attempt to run a monarchy without a king, proved ultimately unworkable, but in its invocation of the spirit of Magna Carta and its general enlisting of moderate support, it helped to affirm a principle of constitutionalism in the English monarchy that outlived the subsequent civil war, and the rise to supreme power, followed by the defeat, of de Montfort.
□ R.F. Treharne *The Baronial Plan of Reform* (1932); *Documents of the Baronial Movement of Reform and Rebellion 1258–67* ed. I.J. Sanders (1973)

P/Q

Paganism (from Latin *paganus*, countryman) Term generally applied to polytheistic religions, though during the Middle Ages it was also frequently applied to non-Christian monotheistic religions (Islam and Judaism).

Classical paganism persisted until the 6th c., and other major pagan cults included the Teutonic gods of the Germanic peoples and the *Aesir* of the Vikings. The advance of Christianity fluctuated throughout Europe, with occasional pagan relapses and incursions; Lithuania was the last pagan stronghold, converted in 1386. Magic and the occult, often associated with pre-Christian religions, persisted throughout the Middle Ages, however, even within a Christian context, and Christianity often absorbed and adapted pagan sites, festivals and practices to facilitate conversion; the initial fusion frequently produced interesting hybrid cultures.

The medieval humanist introduction of the works of classical pagan authors (Plato and Aristotle) and of Jewish and Islamic writings provoked much dispute, especially during the 13th c., and significantly contributed to medieval thought.
□ *The Conflict between Paganism and Christianity in the Fourth Century* ed. A.D. Momigliano (1963); P. Brown *The World of Late Antiquity* (1971)

Painting and the minor arts For the illiterate, who during the Middle Ages constituted the majority of the population, the images painted on the walls of churches were as relevant as the sermon from the pulpit, for here were depicted vividly Heaven and Hell, Christ and his Apostles, the Virgin Mary and the Saints. The vast expanses of wall in medieval churches provided ample opportunity for large cycles of murals or mosaics, and it was only in the Gothic period that large windows filled with stained glass reduced the wall surface to a minimum.

From earliest times, the apse of a church was reserved for the most important figures, Christ in

Painting and the minor arts

Majesty or the Virgin Mary, sometimes flanked by Apostles and Saints. Biblical scenes from the Old and New Testaments were usually to be found on the walls of the nave. In Byzantium a very complex, almost rigid, iconographic system was evolved, in which the decoration of domes was symbolic of Heaven, the vaults and upper walls were devoted to the life of Christ, while the lowest zone was reserved for Saints.

In the West, where churches were predominantly of the basilican type, the arrangement was not so complex. Nevertheless, the influence of Byzantine painting was of considerable importance in Western Europe, especially during the Romanesque period. For instance, the frescoes of S. Angelo in Formis near Capua, completed by *c.*1085, are thought to reflect the style of the now destroyed mosaics of nearby Monte Cassino, decorated in the 1060s by artists from Constantinople. A very different kind of Byzantine influence is found in the frescoes of a Cluniac chapel at Berzé-la-Ville in Burgundy, in which angular, gesticulating figures express violent emotions; their bodies are modelled by means of vein-like drapery folds, thus adding to the feeling of agitation and tension. This method of modelling is ultimately of Byzantine origin, but was transmitted to Berzé by way of Italy. It is found in many regions and many media, for medieval artists were often masters of several techniques. A certain Hugo is a case in point: he painted the Bible for Bury St Edmunds, and for the same abbey cast bronze doors with biblical scenes and carved wooden statues. In his Bible, which still exists and is one of the masterpieces of Romanesque art, he too uses a Byzantine-derived method of modelling the human figure by means of so-called damp folds.

While a wall-painting was a kind of *biblia pauperum,* a book was for the clergy, scholars and for the small literate minority in general. Here the pictures were frequently made at great expense, with gold and precious lapis lazuli, simply to make the book more beautiful. The first surviving Christian books are of the early 5th c. By then the basic biblical iconography had been established, while the style employed was based on late antique art. Many of these early Christian books were brought to England and Ireland by St Augustine and his successors. They were frequently copied and, in the process, their paintings were modified by the inclusion of Anglo-Saxon and Celtic ornaments. The naturalism of the figure style of the originals sent from Italy was gradually transformed, so that the human body lost all volume and the draperies became an ornamental pattern (e.g., the Lindisfarne Gospels, late 7th c.).

The Carolingian revival stimulated book production of the highest quality. The texts were scrutinized by such scholars as Alcuin, and the decoration carried out in many centres, in one case, at the Palace School of Charlemagne's court at Aix-la-Chapelle, with the help of Greek artists. Numerous ivories and objects in precious metals were also made in these Carolingian centres. Most books were Bibles, and it was due to the Ottonian artists of the 10th c. and 11th c. that large cycles of the life of Christ were painted. Once again Greek painters were employed in Germany, and it is not surprising that Ottonian painting owes a debt to the naturalism of antique art,

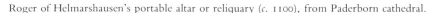

Roger of Helmarshausen's portable altar or reliquary (*c.* 1100), from Paderborn cathedral.

Details from the delicately carved ivory cover of the Lorsch Gospels (9th c.).

transmitted through Byzantine intermediaries. In England also, there was a great revival in lavish book decoration during the 10th c. and 11th c., centred on reformed Benedictine monasteries in Winchester, Canterbury, Glastonbury and others, while at the same time in northern Spain rather exotic-looking illuminations of the Apocalypse and the Bible were made by Mozarabic artists.

During the Romanesque period there was a vast production of illuminated books, sacred and secular, throughout Europe and even in the Crusading kingdom; combined with it was the carving of ivory book covers and other objects in ivory and precious metals. The work formerly carried out in monasteries gradually passed to lay workshops and even itinerant artists. England excelled in manuscript painting, and wall-paintings by English artists are found in Normandy and even distant Spain. The English were also renowned for their embroidery, the Bayeux tapestry testifying to their skill and artistry in this field. German artists were celebrated for metalwork of every kind; the goldsmith Roger of Helmarshausen, two of whose portable altars survive, employed a style similar to that of the Berzé wall-paintings. In the Mosan region (bordering the river Meuse) a very different style of painting, ivory-carving and metalwork was employed by generations of exceptionally gifted artists; it was more naturalistic and indebted to classical art. This style had a profound influence on the monumental sculpture of the Ile-de-France and thus initiated the

Transitional style. The greatest artist in the Mosan region was Nicholas of Verdun, a goldsmith and enamel-worker, whose classicizing style greatly influenced the arts at the turn of the 12th c. in France, Germany and England.

Gothic painting, metalwork and ivory-carving were dominated by the courtly art of Paris. By then the professional lay artist was well established, and some acquired great reputations, as, for instance, Maître Honoré, first mentioned in 1288, and Jean Pucelle, active in the first half of the 14th c. They were the first French Gothic painters to be influenced by Italian conceptions of pictorial space and perspective. English art of the Gothic period was much indebted to Parisian fashions. In manuscript painting the English excelled in *drôleries,* which frequently framed pages of books. By the second quarter of the 14th c. Italian elements became quite pronounced in English painting as, for example, in the Gorleston Psalter, in which the Crucifixion scene displays some knowledge of the art of Duccio. At the Bohemian court of Emperor Charles IV, all forms of painting flourished, especially murals and panel painting, with some participation by Italian artists.

Artistic development in Italy, especially from the time of Giotto, forms a separate chapter, which leads directly to the emergence of the Renaissance. The courtly International Gothic style of *c.*1400 affected only northern Italy with Milan as the main centre; and from then on artistic developments in

Italy and north of the Alps went their separate ways for the rest of the Middle Ages. *See* FRESCO; GLASS, STAINED; MANUSCRIPT ILLUMINATION; MOSAIC   GZ

□ C.R. Dodwell *Painting in Europe 800–1200* (1971); M.M. Gautier *Emaux du Moyen-Age* (1972); P. Lasko *Ars Sacra 800–1200* (1972); G. Zarnecki *Art of the Medieval World* (1975); D. Gaborit-Chopin *Ivoires du Moyen-Age* (1978); D.M. Wilson *Anglo-Saxon Art* (1984); J. Beckwith *Early Medieval Art* (1985)

Palaeologi A landed Byzantine family, prominent under the Comneni. In 1258 Michael VIII Palaeologus (1258–82) made himself co-emperor of the Nicaean empire with the minor, John IV. In 1259 he defeated a Latin coalition at Pelagonia, and in 1261 took Constantinople, installing his son Andronikos II as co-emperor. The Byzantine empire was restored after 57 years of Latin rule.

Michael VIII faced three major problems: Western plans of reconquest, the challenge of the Greek rulers of Epirus, and Turkish incursions into Nicaea. Diplomacy, including agreement to the reconciliation of the churches (ultimately rendering the dynasty immensely unpopular) and connivance at the Sicilian Vespers (1282), largely overcame the first two threats, but the Turkish problem was more intractable. Andronikos II (1282–1328) had a long and disastrous reign, except for its cultural revival. Church union was dissolved, finances floundered, Turkish incursions increased and imported Catalan mercenaries plundered. His grandson Andronikos III (1328–41) instigated civil war, forcing him to abdicate. Asia Minor was lost to the Turks in the 1330s and a new policy of European consolidation pursued.

Civil war followed Andronikos III's death until 1347, when his son John V (1354–91) and John Cantacuzenus became co-emperors. Plague broke out, the Ottoman threat grew and John V was forced to acknowledge himself as the sultan's vassal. His son Manuel II (1391–1425) sought Western aid against the Turks, but this crusade was defeated (1396), and it was the Mongol leader Tamberlaine who halted them (1402). This respite was followed by a treaty between the Byzantines, Turks, Genoa and Venice. Manuel interfered in Ottoman politics but provided no real safeguards, and by his death the empire was again subject to the Turks. His successor John VIII (1425–48) sought Western assistance, hence the healing of the schism (1439). In 1443 an abortive crusade began, soon ending in a truce. John VIII's brother Constantine XI (1448–53) died fighting when Constantinople fell to the Turks in 1453. In 1454 Scholarios was ordained patriarch under the Turks: the emperors were no more.   MB

□ D.J. Geanakoplos *Emperor Michael Palaeologus and the West* (1959); D.M. Nicol *The Last Centuries of Byzantium* (1972); R. Browning *The Byzantine Empire* (1980)

Papacy The claims of the papacy, the bishopric of Rome, to be head of the Catholic church are deeply rooted in the belief that the bishop of Rome was the successor of St Peter, chief among the Apostles, to whom Christ had entrusted the government of his church on earth. The pun implicit in the text *super hanc petram* (upon this rock I found my church) was to have great force in the Middle Ages, when the political shaping of the Mediterranean world served to bring further authority to the papacy. There were five patriarchates in the early church, and four of these (Constantinople, Antioch, Jerusalem and Alexandria) remained in the orbit of the Byzantine and Muslim worlds. Only Rome survived in the West, and the prestige of the ancient capital was transmitted to medieval society by the bishop of Rome, heir to imperial as well as Christian traditions. The part played by Pope Leo I in persuading Attila to leave Italy in the early 450s passed into legend.

It was St Gregory I the Great who firmly established the primacy of the papacy, above all in legal matters. His protection of the Roman people, his constant encouragement and exhortation of other bishops and archbishops in the West, and his initiation of the conversion of the English laid the foundation for the effective sphere of authority of the medieval papacy. Dangers that the papacy would degenerate into a mere Lombard bishopric were overcome in the 8th c. by the intervention of the Franks; and the coronation of Charlemagne as emperor by Pope Leo III, at Rome on Christmas Day 800, symbolized the new political shape achieved in the Western world. Theoretical claims to primacy continued to be current in the succeeding centuries, especially in the pontificate of Nicholas I (858–67), though for the most part the theocratic emperors of the Carolingian and Ottonian dynasties tended to be dominant.

The great crisis of the 11th c., known as the Investiture Contest, brought about dramatic change. Under the direction of the Emperor Henry III, the papacy was enabled to free itself of control by the aristocratic factions of Rome. During the minority of his son Henry IV (1056–1106) it found an ally in the Normans of south Italy to counterbalance its reliance on German military power. The affirmation of the principles of cardinal election brought its own domestic constitutional position into equilibrium. Pope Gregory VII (Hildebrand), in the course of his turbulent pontificate, set the reformed papacy on a new dynamic course. He humiliated Henry IV, forcing him to submission at Canossa. By his intense activity within the church and in relation to

Papacy: the coronation of Enea Silvio Piccolomini as Pope Pius II (1458).

the secular rulers of Europe, he moved the papacy towards the centralized and centralizing position of strength which it was to hold for the following two centuries. Pope Urban II preached the First Crusade in 1095, and the 12th c. saw papal influence and power approaching its height. A century after Canossa the Emperor Frederick Barbarossa submitted to Pope Alexander III at Venice (1177), and Pope Innocent III brought the papacy to its zenith, influencing imperial elections, acting as a universal arbiter in the West, encouraging crusades and action against heretics, and placing himself in the forefront of the move for moral reform at the great Fourth Lateran Council, held in 1215.

The very success of the papacy brought serious complications; excessive involvement in politics and finance bred resentment. Pope Boniface VIII advanced extreme claims for supremacy in the bull *Unam Sanctam* at the jubilee celebrations of 1300, but his humiliation by instruments of the French king at Anagni in 1303 showed where real power lay. Exile to Avignon (1309–78) and the Great Schism between Rome and Avignon (1378–1417) dominated papal politics in the later Middle Ages. The conflict was resolved with the election of Martin V at the Council of Constance in 1417, but reform was left (with only moderate success) in the hands of the new popes, and by the end of the 15th c. the popes bore many of the attributes of Renaissance princes. *See* CONCILIAR MOVEMENT; DONATION OF CONSTANTINE; FORGED DECRETALS; GELASIAN DOCTRINE; INDULGENCES; INQUISITION; INVESTITURE CONTEST; *see also individual Councils and popes*
□ W. Ullmann *The Growth of Papal Government in the Middle Ages* (1962); B. Tierney *The Crisis of Church and State 1030–1300* (1966); G. Barraclough *The Medieval Papacy* (1968); B. Tierney *The Origins of Papal Infallibility* (1972); W. Ullmann *A Short History of the Papacy* (1972); J. Richards *The Popes and the Papacy in the Early Middle Ages* (1979)

Papal states The lands directly under the sovereign authority of the pope were known as the papal states or the *patrimonium* of St Peter. Built up, especially by Pope Gregory I from the private possessions of bishops in Rome and its surrounding territories, it was extended with the agreement of the Frankish rulers in the later 8th c. to cover most of the territory in the old exarchate of Ravenna. These territories underwent all the vicissitudes common to European medieval society, suffering imperial intervention, border disputes, and at times violent feudal disorder. The withdrawal of the popes to Avignon in the 14th c. intensified the problems, but in the 1350s Cardinal Albornoz succeeded substantially in restoring papal authority. Much of the energy of the 15th-c. popes was taken up in maintaining their rule in Rome itself, and in the provinces of Latium, Umbria, Ancona, Ravenna and Bologna – the rich strip of land running north-east from Rome, which constituted their patrimony. See VATICAN
□ L. Duchesne *Les Origines de l'Etat Pontifical au Moyen-Age* (1912); P. Partner *The Papal State under Martin V* (1958); D.P. Waley *The Papal State in the Thirteenth Century* (1961); P. Partner *The Lands of St Peter* (1972)

Paris Town occupying an important geographical position on a fertile plain near the confluence of the rivers Oise, Marne and Yonne with the Seine, and at the junction of routes from the Mediterranean and from Aquitaine and Spain. Its nucleus, the Ile de la Cité, was settled by the Parisii and christened Lutetia when it came under Roman rule in 52 BC. Christianity was introduced by St Denis at the end of the 3rd c. and furthered by St Martin during the 4th c. Threatened attack by Attila (451) was averted by the prayers of St Geneviève, patron saint of Paris, and the actions of the Roman general Aetius.

Paris was captured by the Merovingian King Clovis, becoming his capital in 508; but following Chilperic's transfer of the capital (567) it lapsed into obscurity. In 845 it was sacked by the Vikings and in 885 withstood their prolonged siege under Bishop Gozlin and Count Eudes. In 987 Hugh Capet, duke of Paris, became king, and under him and his successors Paris became the permanent capital of France.

The 11th and 12th c. witnessed flourishing commerce, the development of luxury trades and much building activity, notably under Louis VI (1108–37), Philip Augustus and St Louis IX.

A major factor in the development of medieval Paris was the university, which grew out of the cathedral schools and was recognized by Philip Augustus in 1200. It became the great transalpine centre of orthodox theological teaching and of

The entry of Queen Isabella into **Paris** in 1389, from Froissart's chronicle (15th c.).

Thomism. From the 1220s the mendicant orders advanced its teaching, and throughout the 13th c. and 14th c. it was the most celebrated centre of learning in Christendom, its professors including Alexander of Hales, Bonaventura, Albertus Magnus and Thomas Aquinas. Medieval Paris was therefore significant in combining the functions of political capital, mercantile centre and the greatest intellectual and artistic centre in Northern Europe.

The second half of the 14th c. and first half of the 15th c. witnessed a reversal in the fortunes of Paris. From 1346 it was subject to English invasions and, despite partial recovery under Charles V, it was racked by the Burgundian/Armagnac dispute (1410–c.29). It was finally recovered from the English (1436–41) and enjoyed a period of calm followed by a restoration as a centre of the arts and letters under Francis I (1515–47).   MB

□ M. Druon *The History of Paris* (1969); M. Mollat *Histoire de l'Ile de France et de Paris* (1971)

Paris, Matthew (c.1200–59) Benedictine monk who entered the monastery of St Albans c.1217, where the large scriptorium catered for his literary interests. His earliest works were hagiographical, but his keen interest in contemporary history was reflected in the help he gave to the first great chronicler of the abbey, Roger of Wendover, whom he replaced c.1236. In 1248 he went to Norway to reform the Benedictine house on the island of Nidarholm, returning in 1249 or 1250. The rest of his life was devoted to his historical compositions.

Contemporaries, like Henry III or Haakon IV of Norway, sought out his company in the hope that posterity would receive favourable accounts. As a critical historian, Paris lacked the perception of Bede, the judicious analysis of William of Newburgh, or the synthesizing power of William of Malmesbury. Yet these failings help in part to explain his continuing popularity. His indiscriminate collection of information presented in an easy style, provides a cornucopia to be exploited by historians. His forthright prejudices, strongly expressed, give colour to his writing, whether he is fulminating against tyrannical authority, against the friars (whom he detested) or papal taxation. He was an artist of merit who delighted in illuminating his manuscripts, histories and itineraries with brilliant drawings and sketch-maps, especially valuable for their architectural and topographical details and for the information given about heraldry and costume. He emerges as something of an egoist, whose judgments are not always to be trusted. His best modern biographer refers to him as a 'crusty old gossip'. His access to places of importance, his curiosity, and above all his industry and skill as a communicator,

ensure his place amongst the foremost historians of the Middle Ages. [*204, 281*]

□ R. Vaughan *Matthew Paris* (1958)

Paris, Peace of (4 December 1259) Compacted between Henry III of England (1216–72) and Louis IX of France (1226–70). Although both kings had been bound by the truce of Chinon (1214), conflict over English possessions in France had not been settled, and sporadic warfare continued until negotiations were opened in 1257 at the insistence of Pope Alexander IV. Henry III was enmeshed by the papal offer of the Sicilian crown to his son Edmund, and the imperial crown to his brother Richard of Cornwall. Negotiations were further encouraged by pressure from Henry's barons and his need to resolve the dower of Eleanor, wife of Simon de Montfort.

Under the treaty, Henry surrendered his claims to Normandy, Maine, Anjou and Poitou, and to the dioceses of Limoges, Périgueux and Cahors; Louis acknowledged his lordship over Gascony, providing Henry became his vassal and a peer of France. Louis's other counter-concessions were mostly in expectation (promising Henry the Agenais and Quercy after the death of Alphonse), and nearly all were imprecise and open to legal obstruction. Louis also undertook to pay the cost of 500 knights for two years, and Henry agreed that Louis should deposit 15,000 marks sterling, deductable from the total sum payable to Henry under the Peace (Eleanor's dower). The Peace was a dynastic arrangement and a major piece of Western diplomacy, but also a complicated feudal instrument leading to a series of arbitrations and eventual war. Nevertheless, it brought Henry III and Edward I 35 years of untroubled peace, enabling the solution of many domestic conflicts.

□ R.F. Treharne *The Baronial Plan of Reform 1258–63* (1932); F.M. Powicke *The Thirteenth Century* (1953); J. Le Patourel, 'The Origin of the War', in *The Hundred Years' War* ed. K. Fowler (1971)

Drawing made 'from life' by **Matthew Paris** of the elephant presented to Henry III by Louis IX in 1255.

A king with his **parliament**, from the *Modus Tenendi Parliamentum* (early 14th c.).

Parliament.

From the 1230s it became common in England to describe certain important assemblies as parliaments. The word simply meant a 'parleying': a meeting between the king, his ministers, the magnates and prelates to discuss important matters of state – judicial, political and financial – and to receive and answer petitions. Parliament was the king's instrument of government; he summoned and dissolved it, and determined its agenda. Save in exceptional circumstances, he continued to do so throughout the later Middle Ages. Nevertheless, recurrent disputes between crown and magnates, and the effects of intermittent war in France and Scotland, not to mention broad social changes, profoundly influenced the way Parliament developed.

Its composition underwent some significant changes. Though the number of lay magnates varied widely at first, a stereotyped group or parliamentary peerage had evolved by the 15th c. Representatives of the lower clergy were summoned in the late 13th c. and 14th c., but their importance declined after the separation of convocation from Parliament after 1340. Furthermore, the practice of summoning representatives of the counties and boroughs to Parliament, especially when taxation was being considered, became more frequent in the late 13th c.,

and habitual after the mid-14th c. Simultaneously, Parliament was transformed from an occasional gathering at which business was transacted, into an institution with its own distinctive organization and procedures, and a recognized place in the machinery of government. From the 1330s it gradually divided into two houses, with the magnates and prelates (the upper house) deliberating separately from the representatives of the shires and boroughs (the lower house, or Commons), who after 1376 had their own spokesman or speaker. By the 15th c. Parliament had become a great national assembly whose statutes were superior to common law, and without whose agreement no valid tax could be levied.   CHK

□ *Historical Studies of the English Parliament* ed. E.B. Fryde and E. Miller (1970); G.O. Sayles *The King's Parliament of England* (1975); *The English Parliament in the Middle Ages* ed. R.G. Davies and J.H. Denton (1981)

Patrick, St (*c*.390–461) The historical Patrick is concealed in hagiographical legends, often invented to consolidate Armagh's primatial claims. Some reliable information can be gleaned from his own works: the *Confessio* was an auto-biographical account of his spiritual development and his mission; the *Letter to Coroticus* attacked the British slave trade and those clergy who tolerated it, while the *Lorica* (breastplate) was a devotional treatise. Patrick was the son of a British *decurio* (urban official) and while a youth was seized by slave-traders and sold in Ireland. He was used as a shepherd, and in his isolation underwent a profound spiritual conversion.

He escaped to the Continent with the intention of returning as a missionary, and received some training for the priesthood before being sent back to Ireland to succeed Bishop Palladius *c*.434. His missionary activity was confined to the north and west of Ireland; he established his see at Armagh near the seat of the contemporary high king, and other sees were set up as a territorial basis. His writings are inelegant but permeated with a deep sincerity. He used scripture in an individualistic way, harnessing it to attack contemporary paganism and sun-worship. Recent scholarship has diminished the more fabulous elements that have come to be attached to Patrick, revealing a devout, humble missionary who probably played a decisive, if only limited role in introducing Christianity to Ireland. *See* IRISH CHURCH [*182*]

□ K. Hughes *The Church in Early Irish Society* (1966); R.P.C. Hanson *St Patrick: His Origins and Career* (1968)

Paul the Deacon (730–99) Educated at the Lombard court of King Rachis of Pavia, he produced a celebrated poetic chronology of world history, and an important edition of *Breviarum ab Urbe Condita,* Eutropius' Roman history. When the Lombard kingdoms fell to Charlemagne he went to Monte Cassino, but was eventually enticed to Aix-la-Chapelle, where he remained 782–86.

His knowledge of Virgil, Ovid and Lucan ensured his high esteem, confirmed by his edition of Festus' *De Verborum Significatione,* an important source of archaic Latin and law. His fame rests on the uncompleted *Historia Langobardorum,* a vivid history of the Lombards 688–744. Its main aim was to emphasize the triumph of Christianity over paganism. Paul's scholarly use of earlier historical sketches, ecclesiastical documents and his own memory make it an essential source of information for Lombard culture.
□ C. Wickham *Early Medieval Italy 400–1000* (1981)

Peasants' crusade Name given to a spontaneous movement inside France as news of King Louis IX's capture on crusade (1250) filtered back. Led by a visionary the 'crusaders' took to ravaging and plundering en route and were suppressed by royal forces. Even so, the movement indicates the high regard in which the king was held.
□ A.S. Atiya *The Crusade in the Later Middle Ages* (1938)

Peasants' revolt Peasant unrest occurred sporadically throughout the Middle Ages, generally associated with existing currents of historical change. Before the 14th c. movements were localized and limited in scope, such as those for the establishment of rural communes in 11th-c. Italy and for village enfranchisement in 12th- to 13th-c. France. The concept of free status, labour services, rents, taxes, access to common rights and the administration of justice were long-established sources of dispute, but from the 14th c. to the early 16th c. popular unrest became more concentrated and violent, perhaps as a by-product of the more uniform economic difficulties and changes facing Europe. Ambitious mass movements failed fully to realize their aims, but as a factor of gradual change they assisted their ultimate attainment.

Late medieval peasant actions include the revolt in maritime Flanders (1323–27), the Jacquérie around Paris (1358), the Tuchin movement in central France (1360s-end 14th c.), the English rising (1381) and the wars of the *remensas* in Catalonia (1460s and 1480s).

The English 'Great Revolt' (1381) is one of the best documented (e. g., in the Anonimalle Chronicle and Froissart's Chronicle). Plague (1348–49) and epidemics caused a population decline, affecting

The **Peasants' crusade** was a popular movement inspired by the capture of Louis IX on crusade.

peasant-landowner relationships. The Ordinance of Labourers (reactionary labour laws attempting to freeze wages and tie labour to the lords) reversed improved peasant conditions, causing resentment, as did grievances against poor government – unpopular advisers, expenditure upon warfare, taxes, especially the new poll tax, abuses of collection and the administration of justice.

Government action against tax evasion led to uprisings in Essex and Kent at the end of May 1381. Kentish rebels took Dartford, Maidstone and Canterbury (10 June), Wat Tyler emerging as leader, whilst Essex men attacked the property of the Knights of St John, whose grand master, Sir Robert Hales, was treasurer. The Kent and Essex rebels assembled at Blackheath (12 June), John Ball addressing them with his radical preaching. A meeting with Richard II was aborted by him, and the rebels took further action against property of leading government figures. On 13 June they entered London unopposed, Londoners already destroying John of Gaunt's Savoy Palace. Richard met the rebels at Mile End (14 June) and agreed to their demands, including abolition of serfdom and seizure of traitors. The rebels occupied the Tower, beheading Sudbury and Hales, and massacred the Flemings. Richard met the remaining rebels at Smithfield (15 June) where Tyler presented further demands and was killed by the mayor of London. The rebels dispersed and Richard revoked his concessions to them (2 July). The London movement was accompanied by others in the south-east (East Anglia and the Home Counties), with sporadic outbreaks elsewhere, and artisans and gentry also participated.

The year 1381 inaugurated a century of regional uprisings (including William Cade's, 1450, and the Cornish revolt, 1497), and although the Peasants' revolt failed in the short term, it ended experimental taxation in England, curtailed military expenditure (enabling the 1394 truce with France) and triggered a resistance to serfdom which rendered it so unprofitable that it gradually faded away.   MB
□ R.H. Hilton *Bondmen made free* (1973); E.B. Fryde *The Great Revolt of 1381* (1981); R.B. Dobson *The Peasants' Revolt of 1381* (1970)

Pelagius Probably of British origin, he arrived *c*.380 in Rome where he began to teach. By 410 he had moved to Africa, where his views were opposed by Aurelius, bishop of Carthage (411). According to Pelagius, the human will is completely free, capable of good or evil. Divine grace is externally given according to one's merits, its purpose being merely to facilitate what the will can do itself; thus, Adam's sin was purely personal and had no effect on the rest of humanity. For Pelagius, death is not a punishment for sin but a necessity of human nature. His thoughts led him to attack certain practices: as all are born without sin, there is no need for infant baptism; furthermore, prayer for the conversion of others is hopeless as it cannot help them; the redemption of Christ has no effect except as an example.

His argument produced a torrent of orthodox opposition. The bishop of Carthage (411), St Augustine (412), Orosius (415) and St Jerome (415) produced works of refutation. In 417 a conference of African bishops persuaded Pope Innocent I to excommunicate Pelagius and denounce his views, though later that year Pope Zozimus I accepted him back into the church. However, Emperor Honorius, with papal support, exiled Pelagius from Rome in 418, because of renewed heretical teaching; and at the Sixteenth Council of Carthage, 214 African bishops condemned his teaching. A Council of Antioch expelled him from Palestine in the following year, and strong attack from the great figure of St Augustine of Hippo further reduced the influence of his ideas.

□ J. Ferguson *Pelagius: A historical and theological study* (1956); J.N.L. Myres, 'Pelagius and the end of Roman rule in Britain', *Journal of Roman Studies* 50 (1960)

Pelavicini, Oberto (1197–1269) A powerful landowner on the Parma-Piacenza border and from the 1230s an imperial partisan, he had important influence on the development of the Italian Signoria. He became imperial vicar of Versilia, Lunigiana and Garfagna (1243), and on Frederick II's death became leader of the local parties seeking protection from ecclesiastical victories. In 1251 King Conrad appointed him captain-general and vicar of the Empire in Lombardy, 'below the Lambro'. The centre of his power was Cremona, where he was appointed *podestà* in 1249 and 'perpetual lord and *podestà*' by 1254. His influence extended during the 1250s, as he became life-*podestà* of Piacenza, Pavia and Vercelli (1254). His power waned 1257–58 before the threat of the north Italian crusade. He was driven from Pavia and Piacenza, but manipulated the crusade to build a stronger domain (late 1250s). He held Brescia 1259–64, was associated with the della Torre rule of Milan 1259–64 and returned to Piacenza in 1261. He held a brief supremacy in Piedmont (1260–62). However, despite the support of the *popolo*, his power rested on pro-imperial alliances and waned with that of the Hohenstaufen. He lost Milan and Brescia (1264), Cremona (1266) and Piacenza (1267). His power was sporadically extremely strong, but was insecure as it had no unifying framework except Pelavicini himself. He left individual institutions unchanged, but was significant in deciding that government should rest not with temporary dictatorships, but with one ruler for life, decisively breaking with the concept of communes, and establishing that of the future Signoria.
□ J. Larner *Italy in the Age of Dante and Petrarch* (1980)

Pepin III the Short King of the Franks 751–68 (b. 714–15) Son of Charles Martel, he and his brother Carloman placed the Merovingian Childeric III on the throne of the West Franks though continuing to wield effective power as mayors of the palace. In 747 Carloman resigned, retiring to the monastery of Monte Cassino. Pepin, influenced by St Boniface's dual attack on internal discord and the barbarian threat, sought and received Pope Zacharias' (741–52) assistance in the removal of Childeric, who was forced to abdicate. Pepin was anointed as king, possibly by Boniface, thereby introducing into Gaul echoes of biblical traditions and the unctions of Visigothic Spain. In 754 Pope Stephen II (752–57), under pressure from the military advances of King Aistulf's forces, fled to Pepin's court, where he made a memorable bargain with the king. Pope Stephen bestowed on Pepin the imperial title of *patricius Romanorum*, anointed him afresh together with his two sons Charles and Carloman, and bound the Franks to choose their kings from his descendants only. In return, Pepin promised to help restore to the pope imperial lands connected with the exarchate of Ravenna and the duchy of Rome. Two campaigns (754 and 756) fulfilled these obligations and provided the basis of the papal states. Meanwhile Pepin undertook various imperial roles: he pushed the Muslims from Septimania and repelled threats from the Frisians and Saxons in the Rhineland. The basis was laid for the advances of Charlemagne, and the idea of an explicitly Christian kingship firmly established in the Frankish realm.

☐ J.M. Wallace-Hadrill *The Long-Haired Kings* (1962); E. James *The Origins of France: from Clovis to the Capetians 500–1000* (1982)

Persia Events in Persia (modern Iran) had repercussions on the history of medieval Europe, mostly of an indirect nature. The native Sāsānid dynasty, exhausted after its long struggle with Byzantium, collapsed in 641 under the impact of the first Muslim onslaught, and Persia did not recover a separate political identity until the rise of the Safavid dynasty in the early 16th c. The Persians followed a militant Shī'īte form of the Muslim religion, differentiating their community from the mass of the Muslim Sunnite observance. Reduced to the status of a province, Persia accepted Muslim dominance and conversion to the Muslim faith. Its political history was unhappy and at times disastrous under the rule of Damascus, Baghdad or the Mongols, but substantial contribution was made to world civilization by scholars, philosophers, and scientists such as Avicenna and Albiruni who, in the Arabic tongue, transmitted some of the products of the Persian heritage and that of the Hellenic world.

☐ *Cambridge History of Islam* ed. P.M. Holt, A.K.S. Lambton and B. Lewis (1970); *The World of Islam* ed. B. Lewis (1976)

Peruzzi family One of the oldest Florentine families, the Peruzzi played a key role in the political and economic life of the city of Florence from the mid-13th c. to the mid-14th c. In the second half of the 13th c., a mercantile company dedicated to a wide variety of commercial endeavours was formed by Filippo di Amideo Peruzzi. The company's influence, particularly in banking affairs, was soon felt throughout Italy and eventually in other parts of Europe, such as France and England (e.g., they provided the financial means for many of Edward III's ventures). The rise of the powerful Medici family in Florence and the collapse of the Peruzzi company in the 1340s were chiefly responsible for their loss of prestige in later years.

☐ A. Sapori *The Italian Merchant in the Middle Ages* (1970)

Peter III the Great King of Aragon 1276–85 (b. 1239) Son of James I (1213–76), he had supported his father in the *Reconquista,* but his marriage to Constance, daughter of Manfred Hohenstaufen, in 1262 gradually drew his attention towards the eastern Mediterranean. Manfred had been replaced as king of Sicily by the papal supporter Charles of Anjou, but the latter's brutal government ensured pockets of discontent which looked elsewhere for support. Peter's claim, through his wife, ensured his interest and he supported the rebels in their strife, which culminated in the Sicilian Vespers (1282), when the Angevins were expelled. Peter sailed to Sicily where he was proclaimed king, ignoring vigorous papal opposition. Pope Martin IV (1281–85) responded by excommunicating Peter, and then granted the throne to the son of the French king. Martin encouraged the Aragonese crusade which was led by Philip III, but its progress was halted by an epidemic and then further enervated by the contemporaneous deaths of Philip III and Charles of Anjou. When Peter died later in 1285 his kingdom was secure, and the division of Sicily from southern Italy an established feature of the European political scene.

☐ S. Runciman *The Sicilian Vespers* (1958); J.N. Hillgarth *The Spanish Kingdoms* vol. 1 (1976–78)

Peter Damian, St (*c.* 1007–72) A student at Parma, Modena and Faenza, he taught briefly before entering the religious life at Fonte Avellana in 1035. Eight years later he was elected prior of a congregation of hermits and there devised an eremitico-cenobitic Rule for their use. With the active encouragement of Pope Leo IX and the curia, he wrote two works of great influence: the *Liber Gratissimus,* which defended the validity of orders conferred gratis by Simonists, and the *Liber Gonorrhianus,* which attacked the moral decadence of the 11th-c. clergy.

Stephen IX made him a cardinal in 1057, but unlike Humbert of Silva Candida and Gregory VII, he believed that the reform movement ought to involve the Emperor. Nevertheless, he proved a vigorous papalist in supporting Alexander II against the anti-pope, and was used freely as a Roman ambassador in delicate cases. In 1059–60 he settled the conflict between the archbishop of Milan and the Patarines. In 1063 he upheld Cluny's exemption in its dispute with Bishop Hugh of Mâcon, while in 1069 he was at Mainz trying to settle the marital difficulties of Henry IV and his wife Bertha. He died attempting to reconcile Ravenna with the pope.

He was a prolific writer; his surviving work consists of over 170 letters, 53 sermons and 7 Lives. His theological writings emphasize the practical rather than the theoretical, preferring to teach by anecdote rather than methodical presentation.

□ A. Fliche *La Réforme Grégorienne* vol. 1 (1924); J.P. Whitney, 'Peter Damiani', *Cambridge Historical Journal* 1 (1925); B. Tierney *The Crisis of Church and State 1050–1300* (1964)

Peter of Castelnau (d. 1208) Appointed by Pope Innocent III in 1199 as papal legate to Languedoc to deal with the Albigensian heresy, Peter gained the recantation of Count Raymond VI of Toulouse, and then joined the Cistercian Order at Fontfroide *c.*1202. Further attempts to combat the heresy met initially with failure; and later success also seemed limited, even when supported by Dominic (founder of the Dominican Order) and by a strong Cistercian presence, largely because of the non-cooperation of Count Raymond. In 1207 Peter excommunicated the count and placed his lands under an interdict. A fanatical supporter of Raymond assassinated Peter, seemingly without comital complicity; and the papal response, coloured by the assassination, led to the initiation of the Albigensian crusade.

□ B. Hamilton *The Albigensian Crusade* (1974)

Peter the Hermit (*c.*1050–1115) He rose to fame as a charismatic preacher of the First Crusade in northern France. In 1096 his eloquence helped to collect a large, ill-trained and inadequately equipped force, which was annihilated by the Turks while en route for the Holy Land; the survivors escaped to Constantinople.

Peter joined the major crusading armies the following year, but played an ignominious part in the battle of Antioch (1098). After the capture of Jerusalem by the crusaders in 1099 he returned to Europe and became prior of the canons regular of St Augustine at Neufmontier in Belgium.

□ S. Runciman *History of the Crusades* vol. 1 (1951)

Peter the Lombard (d. 1160) Trained in the law schools of north Italy, Peter left Italy around 1140 and was introduced to Paris and theology by St Bernard. There, Peter taught theology for almost 20 years, becoming bishop of Paris in 1159. His *Liber Sententiarum* (four books of Sentences, *c.*1150) was for centuries the classic textbook of theology. It presents a skilful exposition of church organization and a synthesis of conflicting theological arguments, but its plan is clearly influenced by Abelard's *Sic et Non*. His Sentences were to theology what Gratian's *Decretum* was to canon law. Both works, or *Summae*, played a key role in the 12th-c. concern to consolidate past learning as the basis for new debate. *See* TWELFTH-CENTURY RENAISSANCE

□ *Renaissance and Renewal in the Twelfth Century* ed. R.L. Benson and G. Constable (1982)

Peter the Venerable (*c.*1092–1156) Abbot of Cluny and an influential figure in the monastic and literary renaissance of the 12th c., Peter succeeded Pons as the spiritual head of the Order in 1122, resisting powerful attempts to declare his succession invalid. The turbulence of his early years provoked sharp attacks on the Order, leading Peter to defend the Cluniac ethos and to initiate a series of reforms. In 1132 the heads of the daughter establishments were summoned to the mother house to hear a programme of austere regulations. In 1147 his statutes, emulating the Cistercians, further reduced luxuries in food, dress and display.

Outside the cloister, the hallmark of most of Peter's work was peace and reasonableness. In 1140 he won reconciliation for Abelard after his condemnation at Sens. Peter aimed to divert the contemporary orthodox energies against the Saracens towards fruitful dialogue and conversion – he commissioned the first Latin translation of the Koran – rather than combat and conquest. Yet even he hoped to promote an alliance against the Byzantine empire. Although eclipsed in monastic and ecclesiastical spheres by Bernard of Clairvaux, he was an esteemed counsellor and correspondent with the foremost figures in Christendom. He was called 'Venerable' by both St Bernard and Frederick Barbarossa.

□ J. Kritzeck *Peter the Venerable and Islam* (1964); G. Constable *The Letters of Peter the Venerable* (1967)

Peter's Pence Name given to a tax paid to the papacy by many of the European communities. It appears to have originated in England, where its imposition (associated initially with the creation of an English School at Rome by Ine of Wessex, reinforced by Offa of Mercia) seems to have been regularized by Alfred and his successors. It was reckoned later to consist of the exaction of 1*d* from each hearth 'from which smoke arose'. At Rome payment became associated with ideas of tribute and subjection to papal overlordship, but William the Conqueror, while sanctioning the exaction of Peter's Pence, expressly denied the payment of fealty to Rome in 1080. In spite of difficulties in assessment and collection, it continued to be paid from England throughout the Middle Ages to the time of the Reformation.

□ W.E. Lunt *Papal Revenues in the Middle Ages* (1934)

Petit, Jean (*c.*1360–1411) Born in Normandy, he was doctor of theology at the university of Paris. During his early career he seems to have produced sermons and several poems. He defended university privileges and played a leading role in its promotion of church unity during the schism of 1393–1407, acting as one of Charles VI's envoys to Rome (1407). Upon his return he became a client of the duke of Burgundy, ruining his career by defending the duke's assassination of the duke of Orleans (1407) on grounds of legitimate tyrannicide. In his *Justification du Duc de Bourgogne* (1408) he advocated, before the king's counsellors, that it was lawful, and indeed meritorious, for any subject, of his own volition, to kill a tyrant. The authorities he cited, and misused, included Aristotle, Cicero, John of Salisbury, Aquinas, Boccaccio, civil law and the scriptures. He made a poor case, and his misapplication of an acknowledged doctrine caused an outcry, Gerson denouncing his errors on behalf of the university. Petit retired in disgrace to Hesdin, where he died; but the issue of political assassination survived. Gerson secured Petit's condemnation (Council of Faith, 1414; parliament and university, 1416) whilst the Burgundians continued to defend their case, preventing another condemnation of Petit at the Council of Constance.

☐ A. Coville *Jean Petit* (1932); O. Jászi and J.D. Lewis *Against the Tyrant* (1957)

Petrarch (1304–74) Francesco Petrarca's fame rests on his re-introduction of lost or neglected texts from antiquity into European culture, and his synthesis of existing vernacular themes. Born at Arezzo, the son of a notary who had been banished from Florence, Petrarch went in 1316 to study law at Montpellier, where he produced his *Epistolae Metricae* (1318), a collection of 66 epistles in hexameters. In 1320 he moved, to continue his legal studies, to Bologna, but in 1326 he abandoned the law and entered the humanist environment of papal Avignon. The next year he had his dramatic meeting with Laura, a woman who personified his concepts of beauty and truth and whose inspiration permeated much of his work. In 1330 he took minor orders.

He was patronized by the Colonna 1330–47 and acted as a diplomat, visiting France, Flanders, Brabant and the Rhineland. He used these opportunities to collect old manuscripts, to revise earlier work and begin new enterprises. In 1338–39 he produced an epic poem, *Africa,* based on the Second Punic War and inspired by a visit to Rome in 1337. In 1341 he became poet laureate and continued his travels; he discovered Cicero's lost letters *(Ad Atticum, Ad Quintum* and *Ad Brutum)* in 1345, and the next year revised his *De Vita Solitaria,* a treatise on the advantage of the solitary life.

In 1347 he broke his Colonna connection but finished his *De Otio Religiosa,* which stressed the benefits of the monastic life. The plague of 1348 (as a result of which Laura died) forced Petrarch to leave Rome for Florence where he met Boccaccio.

Although he was present in Rome for the jubilee of 1350, bitter differences arose with the curia, and he fled to Visconti Milan, then to Padua and Venice.

In 1366 Boccaccio sent him a much desired Latin translation of Homeric poems which aided him in the production of two major works: the first was the *Familiarum Rerum Libri XXIV,* a contemplation on the world of antiquity; the second was the *Rerum Vulgarium Fragmenta,* a definitive vernacular work composed of 366 pieces in a lyrical format drawing on classical models and the ethos of the troubadours. In 1370 Urban V called Petrarch to Rome, and Petrarch revised several of his writings in these years. At his death he left works of profound spiritual contemplation as testimony of his humanism.

☐ G.H. Wilkins *The Life of Petrarch* (1961)

Philip II Augustus King of France 1180–1223 (b. 1165) Son of Louis VII and Adèle of Champagne, he merited the sobriquet Augustus because he truly augmented the Capetian realm, firstly consolidating his hold on the eastern borders with Germany, and then, helped by dissensions between Henry II and his sons, expanding westwards at the expense of the Angevin empire. In 1204 he gained full control of Normandy from King John. Further extensions into Angevin territory and support for the Albigensian crusade left the Capetian house well poised at the end of his reign to become true rulers of virtually all of France. Indeed, his son and heir, later Louis VIII (1223–26), made a serious bid for the English throne at the death of King John in 1216. Their successes were brought about partly by diplomacy and partly by warfare.

The defeat of Emperor Otto IV (ally of John and opponent of the Hohenstaufen Frederick II) at the battle of Bouvines (1214) proved decisive. France became the most powerful monarchy in the West, and Philip and his ministers established an efficient system of royal government based on the growing and prestigious heartland of Paris and the Ile-de-France, using the resources of the new university at Paris and exploiting royal authority over the great feudal nobles by means of royal officials: *baillis* in the north and seneschals in the south. It was during Philip's reign that the full force of residual monarchic authority within the feudal world became apparent and the fruits of the policy of concentric centralization were harvested.

☐ E.M. Hallam *Capetian France 937–1328* (1981); J.W. Baldwin *The Government of Philip Augustus* (1986)

Philip IV the Fair King of France 1285–1314 (b. 1268) One of the strongest rulers of France, Philip IV has left a very mixed reputation. His excessive reliance on capable servants trained in Roman law

Effigy of **Philip the Fair** in the royal abbey of Saint-Denis, Paris.

bred provincial resistance which remained a source of weakness throughout the Hundred Years' War. His opposition to the claims of the papacy under Boniface VIII was ultimately successful, but involved the rough handling of the pope and his consequent death after the Humiliation of Anagni (1303). Philip's vicious treatment of the Templars (after 1308) and the abolition of their Order resulted in financial gain to the crown, but soured responsible opinion. Long-drawn-out conflicts with England over Gascony, and with the town of Flanders led to heavy expense and to disastrous defeat at the hands of the Flemish townsmen at Courtrai (1302). Philip failed to cope with the admittedly intractable economic problems of the time, curbing the activities of Italian merchants and bankers, expelling the Jews (in 1306) and depreciating the coinage.

Nevertheless, he fostered a powerful central administration at Paris, summoned the Estates General, which encouraged the sentiment of unity in France, and exercised firm control over the Gallican church. After the election of Archbishop Bertrand of Bordeaux as Clement V and his subsequent withdrawal to the Rhone valley and Avignon, French royal influence over the papacy became powerful. Italian interests were left mostly in the hands of his brother Charles of Valois, who succeeded to the fiefs of Anjou and Maine (1302) in return for the support he had given to the French Prince Charles II, king of Naples.

The general tendency to centralize authority and government in France under Philip IV represented a culminating point in processes initiated by his grandfather Louis IX, but Philip's monarchy lacked the moral and spiritual prestige of the earlier age. □ R. Fawtier *The Capetian Kings of France* (1960); J.R. Strayer *The Reign of Philip the Fair* (1980)

Philosophy The Middle Ages are often said to have witnessed little development in philosophy (the pursuit of speculative truth), heavily subject as it was to the dictates of Christian, Jewish or Islamic faith. Autonomous philosophical reflection was severely restricted, but the imposition of a theological framework offered a fresh challenge, presenting new themes and problems for consideration, rather as in the case of the sciences in more recent times. Medieval philosophy also warrants consideration for its role in the transmission of ancient thought and the preservation of some degree of continuity, and for its influence upon later thinkers such as Descartes and Leibniz.

During the Middle Ages 'philosophy' covered a wider field than in modern times. Natural philosophy encompassed many particular sciences, such as astronomy, and philosophical methods were also applied to law and politics. Despite their close relationship and interaction, philosophy (a system of knowledge regulated by reason) and theology (a body of revealed truth held on faith) were clearly distinguished. The juxtaposition of faith and reason formed Christian philosophy, which was largely concerned with the reconciliation of God and the natural world, but there was great variation within this framework.

The sources of medieval Western thought were the Bible; patristic works; Greek and, to a lesser extent, Roman philosophies (especially Platonism and Aristotelianism); Neoplatonism; the Arabian and Jewish systems of the 10th c.–12th c. (especially those of Alfarabi, Avicenna, Averroes, Avicebrol and Maimonides); and a smattering of Greek and Arabian science (Euclid's mathematics and Alacens' astronomy). These were transmitted to the Western world at different times and in different proportions, mingling to form many different concepts. Until Arabian and Jewish works reached the West during the 12th c., it had no direct knowledge of the main body of Aristotle's works or of Neoplatonism, and Platonism was not fully rediscovered until the end of the Middle Ages. Previously, reliance was upon the Neoplatonic/Platonic writings of the church fathers, notably St Augustine. Not until the 13th c.

did a series of systems based upon a coherent body of metaphysics emerge, the growing independence of philosophy finally resulting in the dissolution of its partnership with theology and the collapse of the fabric of medieval philosophy.

Philo (1st c.) had been the first to attempt a synthesis of revealed faith and philosophic reason, followed by the Neoplatonists. St Augustine began the assimilation of Neoplatonism into Christian doctrine to provide its rational interpretation. Boethius translated some of the works of Aristotle and Porphyry (Neoplatonist) into Latin, and his *De Consolatione Philosophiae* was influential throughout the Middle Ages; John Eriugena was, however, the first to develop a full system, strongly Neoplatonic in character and based upon his translations of the Greek church fathers (Origen, Pseudo-Dionysius).

The 11th-c. cathedral schools promoted philosophical discussion, witnessing the debate over universals (the relation of genera and species to individuals) and the controversy over dialectic, advocated by Abelard and the peripatetics, opposed by Peter Damian and the mystics, and reconciled by Anselm and the School of Bec. The 12th c. saw a movement towards developed scholasticism, a broad system of knowledge within a dogmatic framework embodied in the various teachings of the new university schoolmen. The explosion of knowledge caused by the Arabian and Jewish works was utilized by schoolmen such as Robert Grosseteste and Roger Bacon in the 13th c. in an attempt to create a universal wisdom embracing all the sciences and organized by theology. Increasing philosophical independence and the eventual triumph of Aristotelianism, through the attempts of Albertus Magnus and Thomas Aquinas to assimilate the new knowledge, caused conflict, primarily in Paris university. William of Auvergne (1180–1249) and Giles of Rome (1247–1316) opposed the threat of pagan and Islamic thought and independent reason, whilst the Averroists upheld the philosopher's duty to follow human reason to its natural conclusions. The rift between philosophy and theology had begun.

During the late Middle Ages earlier philosophical methods were formalized into definite schools of thought, such as Thomism, Averroism and Scotism, promulgated by Duns Scotus, who denied philosophy's self-sufficiency. In the 14th c. Thomism and Scotism were the *via antiqua,* as opposed to the *via moderna* founded by William of Ockham, who tried to disengage and separately reinforce faith and reason. This trend away from Aristotelianism was furthered by John of Mirecourt and Nicholas of Autrecourt, and accentuated by the speculative mysticism of Eckhart. Christian thinkers such as Nicholas of Cusa turned again to Neoplatonism, leading into Renaissance Platonism. *See* ALAN OF LILLE; ALBERT OF COLOGNE; BURIDAN, JOHN; DURANDUS OF SAINT-POURCAIN; SIGER OF BRABANT; WILLIAM OF CHAMPEAUX   GE

□ E. Gilson *History of Christian Philosophy in the Middle Ages* (1955); G. Leff *Medieval Thought* (1958); F. Copleston *A History of Philosophy* (1963); E. Gilson *Medieval Philosophy* (1963); J. Marenbon *Early Medieval Philosophy 480–1150: An Introduction* (1983)

Photius (*c.*820–91) Patriarch of Constantinople. He is remembered for his part in precipitating a schism between East and West. His early career was as a layman who held high office at the Byzantine court and taught at the university of Constantinople. In 858 he was elected patriarch of Constantinople, after his predecessor, Ignatius, was deposed for rebuking Emperor Michael. Pope Nicholas I supported Ignatius, refusing Photius' request for recognition, and the question of the patriarchate became identified with that of papal jurisdiction over the Eastern church, enabling Photius to turn anti-Western feeling to his own advantage. The dispute was further aggravated by the activity of Latin missionaries in Bulgaria. Nicholas I excommunicated Photius, who in 867 convened a Council at Constantinople which anathematized and deposed the pope, and denounced Latin errors, including the *Filioque* addition to the Creed, the Saturday fast and clerical shaving of the beard. In the same year Photius lost favour at court and Ignatius was restored. Following Ignatius' death (879) Photius resumed office with Pope John VIII's recognition, but his mishandling of a Council at Constantinople lost him papal favour, causing a new schism; continuing intrigues by the Ignatian party secured his permanent exile by Emperor Leo VI (886).

□ M. Jugie *Photius et la primauté de St Pierre et du pape* (1921); F. Dvornik *The Photian Schism* (1948)

Piacenza, Synod of In March 1095 a council was convened at Piacenza by Pope Urban II as part of the consolidation of his position against Emperor and anti-pope. It passed decrees furthering the Gregorian reform programme and condemning the 'schismatics', and discussed the marital problems of King Philip of France and those of Henry IV, acting as the supreme court of Western Christendom. In accordance with newly established cordial relations with Byzantium, envoys from Emperor Alexius Comnenus were present. Alexius desired mercenary reinforcements for his campaign against the Turks. As Urban was sympathetic, the envoys reiterated Alexius' earlier requests, but overdid their appeal, stressing the threat to the whole of Christendom

from the heathen advance. They so convinced Urban and the assembly that, although Urban immediately responded by merely exhorting the aid required, it sowed the concept of a Holy War (which might incidentally fulfil his aim of uniting the Eastern and Western churches), and a few months later, at Clermont, Urban preached the First Crusade.
□ *A History of the Crusades* ed. K.M. Setton, vol I (1969); C. Erdmann *The Origin of the Idea of Crusade* (1977)

Picts People who first appear in the works of 3rd-c. Roman writers, where the term is used generically to describe the peoples of Scotland. Southern Picts spoke a Brittonic language, related to Welsh, but that of those in the north is unclear. Until the settlement of Scandinavians in the extreme north and the isles, during the 9th c. and 10th c., the Picts seem to have controlled the whole of Scotland north of the Forth and Clyde, with the exception of the west coast; the focus of their power lay in the rich farmlands of Fife. There may have been a single Pictish kingship, sometimes contested, during the 6th c. and 7th c., or a Pictish overkingship with dependent sub-kings. However, a single consolidated Pictish kingship seems to have emerged by the late 8th c., which was quick to develop institutions of government and held considerable power throughout Scotland. At that period the Pictish royal family began to intermarry with the Irish dynasty of the west coast, resulting in a series of kings with claims to both kingships, and eventually the union of the two. Scottish historiography presents this as the eclipse of the Picts, but there is good reason to think that both peoples contributed to the newly formed kingdom of Scotland, rather than that one was obliterated.

Though little is known of their societies, there are two distinctive attributes of the Picts. Their royal family recognized a principle of matrilineal succession (kings were selected from the sons of royal women, not royal men); a king's nephew or brother would therefore succeed him rather than his son. Secondly, Pictland is distinguished by the presence of many symbol stones, curiously and intricately carved monuments whose designs give very few clues to their meaning. These cluster in the east, but can be found as far north as Caithness; they clearly belong to a Christian culture and to the 6th c.–9th c.
□ *The Problem of Picts* ed. F.T. Wainwright (1955); I. Henderson *The Picts* (1967); A.A.M. Duncan *Scotland, the Making of the Kingdom* (1975)

Piero della Vigna (*c.* 1200–49) One of the ablest of the low-born servants of Emperor Frederick II, della Vigna took much responsibility for reforming

imperial administration in Sicily and south Italy. Prominent also in the affairs of the university of Naples, he was recognized as one of the great stylists of the day, and his letters and manifestoes were used as models by generations to come. He was also a poet of some note, a true precursor of the Renaissance humanists. His power was immense in the 1240s, but when found guilty of corruption, he was treated savagely, blinded, and committed suicide in S. Miniato, Florence, while awaiting execution. *See* LIBER AUGUSTALIS
□ E. Kantarowicz *Frederick II* (1931)

Pipe rolls The great financial records of the Exchequer, and the largest series of English public records. An isolated roll exists for 1129–30 and they run almost continuously from 1156 to 1832. They record the royal accounts by shire, and are thus largely shrieval accounts, although they also contain various occasional revenues, such as those from episcopal lands that might fall into royal hands *sede vacante*. They do not record all sources of royal income as these did not all pass through the Exchequer. The nature and form of the rolls provided a model for the new branches of the administration when record-keeping became necessary.

Pisa, Council of (March-August 1409) General church council convened by cardinals with the object of terminating the Great Schism which had prevailed since the death of Gregory XI (1378), when two rival popes emerged. It was attended by representatives from much of Western Christendom (including royal ambassadors and university representatives, as well as the church hierarchy). It deposed both existing popes (Gregory XII, 1406–15, and Benedict XIII, 1394–1423) and elected Alexander V (1409–10), a solution which failed, as neither of his predecessors accepted this decision. It was not until the Council of Constance (1414–18) that the first steps were taken towards an effective solution of the Schism. The authority of the Council of Pisa was open to question as it was not representative of the entire church (many supporters of the two pre-existing popes refused to take part) and was not convened by a pope. It did, however, pave the way for regular meetings by its provision for another council to discuss church reform (1412). [*187*]
□ *Councils and Assemblies* ed. G.J. Cumming and D. Baker (1971)

Pisanello (*c.*1395–*c.*1455) Medallist and painter, Antonio Pisano was born in Pisa, hence his name. He virtually invented the Renaissance medal, of which he was the greatest exponent in the mid-15th c. His masterpieces include medals of Giovanni

The Apocalyptic Christ from **Nicola Pisano**'s pulpit in Siena cathedral, *c*.1265-68.

Gonzaga, Francesco Sforza, John VIII Palaeologus and King Alfonso of Aragon. He was also a leading painter, of the International Gothic style, while his sensitive drawings reflect the naturalism of the early Renaissance.
□ G. Paccagnini *Pisanello* (1973)

Pisano, Nicola (*c*.1220–*c*.78) Italian sculptor and architect. Pisano is regarded as the founder of modern sculpture. His masterpieces include the pulpits in the Pisan baptistery (1259) and in Siena cathedral (1268), which reveal a combination of Gothic influence and classical models for Christian subjects. On the fountain at Perugia he collaborated with his son, Giovanni (*c*.1250–*c*.1314), whose work continued this revival of sculpture.
□ J. Pope-Hennessy *Italian Gothic Sculpture* (1970)

Pius II (Aeneas Sylvius Piccolomini) Pope 1458–64 (b.1405) A graduate of Siena and a notable humanist, he attended the Council of Basle (1431) as the secretary of Amadeus VIII of Savoy (later anti-pope Felix V). Several poetical works and two treatises in favour of Conciliarism added to his literary reputation and he was rewarded with the position of poet laureate by Frederick III in 1442. He entered the imperial service and produced his frivolous *Historia de Eurialo et Lucretia*. In 1445 he was reconciled to

Eugenius IV, and the next year received holy orders. In 1447, with Nicholas of Cusa, he negotiated the reconciliation of the pope and Emperor, and later that year he was elevated to the bishopric of Trieste. He produced two more humanist works, *De Viris Claris* and *De Rebus Basileae Gestis,* before being translated to Siena in 1450. Calixtus III made him a cardinal in 1456 and two years later he was elected pontiff.

As pope he did not forget his past: in 1462 the destruction of ancient monuments was forbidden. His papacy was overshadowed by the fall of Constantinople (1453), however. Pius called a council in 1460, but it was a fiasco, and he then wrote to the sultan his famous *Epistola ad Mahumetan* which aimed to convert the Muslims by argument. In an attempt to unite Europe he passed the bull *Execrabilis* which re-affirmed papal prerogatives by condemning appeals to future councils. The European response was one of indifference, and finally in 1464 Pius took the cross and set out for the East, but died at Ancona. During his period as pope he also produced his *Commentaries* – an account of his own papacy. [*255*]
□ *Memoirs of a Renaissance pope: the Commentaries of Pius II* ed. F.A. Gragg (1959); R.J. Mitchell *The Laurels and the Tiara* (1962)

Plague Pandemics in the 6th c. and 14th c. divide the Middle Ages demographically into three parts. The period 450–540 had been singularly free from severe pestilences, and the plague was to disappear again from the West by 750. It returned just before 1350, and remained endemic until after 1650.

The earlier pandemic spread from Ethiopia and reached the British Isles 541–46. The 6th-c. waves are dated *c*.542, *c*.558, *c*.572, *c*.581, *c*.590 and *c*.600. In the 7th c. the urban centres, such as Constantinople and Antioch, had been partly depopulated, and the Arabs found Damascus, a city near the desert, convenient for their capital; the caliphs left in the plague season (summer) for their desert palaces, while their armies transferred to the mountains or the deserts. The Arab elite thus suffered less than the Byzantines. Most waves of the 7th c. (*c*.618, *c*.628, *c*.640, *c*.655) affected the eastern Mediterranean, but the more severe plagues of 655–700 spread extensively in both the Islamic countries and Western Europe (northern England was affected in 664, 675–76 and *c*.687). In Ireland the last two waves were known as the Children's plagues, as they affected especially those born since the preceding epidemic. The wave of the late 680s was known as the Third plague both in Ireland and in Basra! In the first half of the 8th c. further waves affected south-east Europe and the Middle East, but north-west Europe was plague-free.

Burying victims of the **plague** at Tournai in 1349, from the annals of Gilles Le Muiset.

The advance of the **plague** as it spread across Europe from the east, 1347–50.

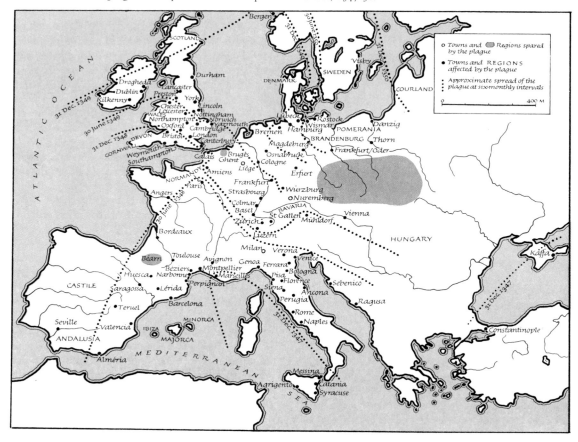

The horrors of the **plague** brought a new realism to representations of death: a plague cross from Cologne.

In the 1340s the plague spread again, this time from Central Asia, as indicated by an abnormal mortality rate recorded on dated Nestorian gravestones there in 1339. In 1346 the plague appeared at Kaffa in the Crimea from whence it spread by sea and land to most parts of Europe. By 1348 it had reached Constantinople, Italy and France; England was affected in the winter of 1348–49 and by 1350 it had swept across Germany, Poland and Scandinavia. This pandemic is now known as the Black Death. Once again there were successive waves of great severity that spread all over the West. In Europe the first six appear in c.1348, 1362, 1374, 1383, 1389 and 1400. Outbreaks recurred frequently throughout the Middle Ages, continuing for example in England until the Great Plague of 1665.

The cause of the periodicity of about 11 years is unknown. Predisposing factors appear to be meteorological. World weather patterns had been upset by volcanic darkness for 15 months in 536–37, so that by 539 famine affected Constantinople, despite the prosperity of Justinian's Graeco-Roman empire up to 535. Tree-ring analyses confirm that summers in the 540s, as in the 1340s, were abnormally cold in Scandinavia. Likewise in the 1340s even Italy was suffering economically, whereas in north-west Europe wet seasons would in any case have led to a demographic crisis had plague mortality not intervened. In north-west Europe, later urban plagues were nevertheless usually associated with cold winters, dry springs and hot dry summers, and thus with good harvests.

Population decline may have preceded the arrival of the plague; certainly there was a severe demographic crisis in the late 1310s. However, plausible estimates of population changes consistently give the population of England in 1400 as about half what it had been in 1300.

The bacillus of the plague itself was discovered in 1894; it is known to be carried by rats and communicated to man by black fleas. Violent fluctuations of rat populations in time of plague are recorded (e.g. in Spain and China 600–750). The black flea is now a tropical insect and is assumed to have attacked humans when already infected by a rat and no longer able to find living rats to bite. Certainly, the northern limit of the plague retreated gradually southeastwards in the course of the pandemic; some extinct variety of flea may have been involved in the earlier waves. The plague has two forms – bubonic and pneumonic. The former was characterized by buboes, or swellings in the armpits or groin, and frequently led to death after six days. The more unusual pneumonic form, communicated directly from one person to another, generally led to death within three days and occurred in winter in the 1340s.

The Jews, who were blamed for transmission of the disease, were persecuted and massacred – especially in Germany – whilst the fear of death also led to the growth of fanatical religious groups, such as the Flagellants. The effect of the plague on agrarian society was turbulent and complex, leading initially to attempts to reimpose feudal rights and services, and contributing to outbreaks of violence: e.g., the risings of the Jacquérie in France and the Peasants' Revolt in England. There are almost no representations of true plague in art before 1400, but the stories of the *Decameron* represent a literary response. *Pestschriften* were issued regularly with advice as to treatment, but comets, aurorae and planetary conjunctions were often blamed for the onset of an epidemic. DJS

□ P. Ziegler *The Black Death* (1969); J.F. Shrewsbury *The History of Bubonic Plague in the British Isles* (1970); W.H. McNeill *Plagues and Peoples* (1976); *The Black Death. The Impact of the 14th-Century Plague* ed. D. Williman (1982); R.S. Gottfried *The Black Death: Nature and Disaster in Medieval Europe* (1983)

Plantagenet The royal house of England 1154–1485, commonly referred to by the family name, Plantagenet. Originally a nickname of Count Geoffrey of Anjou, father of Henry II, it is usually attributed to his wearing a sprig of broom *(planta genista)* in his

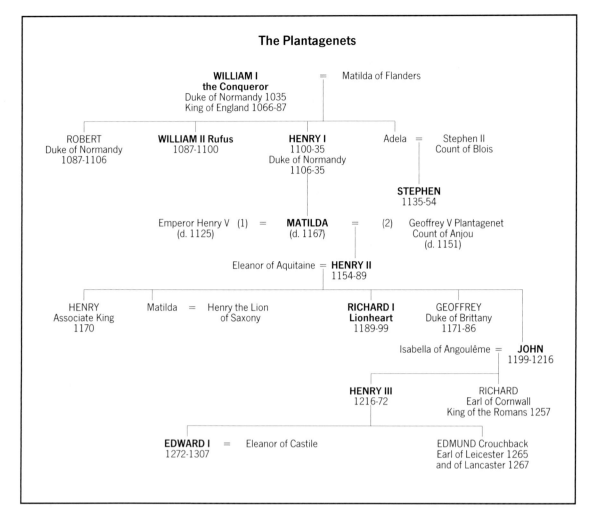

The Plantagenets

WILLIAM I the Conqueror
Duke of Normandy 1035
King of England 1066-87
= Matilda of Flanders

ROBERT
Duke of Normandy
1087-1106

WILLIAM II Rufus
1087-1100

HENRY I
1100-35
Duke of Normandy
1106-35

Adela = Stephen II
Count of Blois

STEPHEN
1135-54

Emperor Henry V (1) = **MATILDA** = (2) Geoffrey V Plantagenet
(d. 1125)   (d. 1167)   Count of Anjou
(d. 1151)

Eleanor of Aquitaine = **HENRY II**
1154-89

HENRY
Associate King
1170

Matilda = Henry the Lion
of Saxony

RICHARD I Lionheart
1189-99

GEOFFREY
Duke of Brittany
1171-86

Isabella of Angoulême = **JOHN**
1199-1216

HENRY III
1216-72

RICHARD
Earl of Cornwall
King of the Romans 1257

EDWARD I
1272-1307
= Eleanor of Castile

EDMUND Crouchback
Earl of Leicester 1265
and of Lancaster 1267

---

hat, or planting broom as cover for game. The name was not used by Geoffrey's descendants until *c*.1448, when Richard, duke of York, revived it to emphasize the superiority of his claim to the throne against the house of Lancaster.

Plotinus (*c*.204–70) Founder of the Neoplatonic system, Plotinus was born in Egypt but settled in Rome (244). His biographer, Porphyry, edited his lectures, and in the *Enneads,* Plotinus synthesized the philosophy of Plato with other philosophies. His main concern was the spiritual progress of man towards the 'One', the 'Good'. Plotinus was known indirectly in the Middle Ages through those he had influenced, including St Augustine, St Basil and Pseudo-Dionysius. In 1492 Marsilio Ficino translated the original Greek *Enneads* into Latin, which thereafter made an important contribution to Renaissance Neoplatonism.
□ A.H. Armstrong *Plotinus* (1953)

Poland It entered the historic age late, largely because of geographical factors: forests isolated it even from fellow Slavs, who formed buffers against German and Asiatic expansion. From *c*.800 internal subjections led to the hegemony of the Poles *(Polanii)* and their princes, the Piasts. Their territory around Gniezno, the first capital, and Poznan, the first bishopric, formed the nucleus of the Polish state, Great Poland. The region of Upper Vistula and Cracow was annexed, forming Little Poland. Christian influence probably appeared in the late 9th c. but political contact was delayed until the 10th c.

Medieval Poland produced two great dynasties, Piast and Jagiello. The Piasts ruled from the mid-9th c. until 1370. Their first major representative Mieszko I (*c*.960–92) acknowledged the overlordship of Emperor Otto I (963) and furthered Poland's conversion by marrying a Christian Bohemian princess (965). His son Boleslav I the Great (992–1025) promoted Mieszko's policies, fostering Poland as mis-

Grave plate in Limoges enamel (*c.*1150) for Geoffrey **Plantagenet**, count of Anjou and father of Henry II.

sionary centre to the Slavs and taking the title of king late in his reign.

The lack of a regulating succession principle among the Piasts caused conflicts during the 11th c. which permitted imperial intervention and a rise in aristocratic power. Polish territories were divided into four hereditary duchies: Silesia, Masovia, Great Poland and the Sandomierz region; the throne of Cracow, the new capital, passed to the eldest Piast in rotation. Continuing disputes enabled increasing German colonization, especially after the introduction of the Teutonic Order (1230). The promising reign of Henry II the Pious (1238–41) ended with his death at Lignica, attempting to halt the Mongols. Despite the difficulties of this period Polish integrity was preserved. Poland remained a single ecclesiastical province, developing a strong national consciousness heightened by anti-German feeling.

The 14th c. witnessed German invasions, notably in 1331 and 1332, which were checked by Casimir the Great, who isolated the Teutonic Order and, although unable to regain all western Polish territory, considerably extended Poland's eastern boundaries, rendering Polish influence in Eastern Europe of importance to Christendom. Casimir was a great and tolerant legislator, who founded Cracow university (1364) and enjoyed good standing amongst contemporary monarchs.

Casimir was the last Piast. The crown passed, via his nephew Louis of Hungary (under whom charters granted to the nobility rendered the monarchy elective), to Jadwiga of Anjou (1384–99). She married Vladislav II Jagiello of Lithuania (1386), and with Vitold of Lithuania, Jagiello's cousin, they established the Jagiello dynasty and achieved a Polish–Lithuanian union (formalized in 1413 by the Union of Horodlo). Teutonic hostilities continued despite Jagiello's victory at Grünwald (Tannenburg) in 1410.

Civil war following the deaths of Vitold (1430) and Jagiello (1434) was ended by the regent Cardinal Olesnicki, who placed Jagiello's son Ladislas upon the Hungarian throne intending an anti-Turkish crusade. This went well until Ladislas died during the defeat at Varna (1444). Casimir III Jagiello (1447–92) emerged victorious from the Thirteen-Year War with the Teutonic Order (1454–66), this and his claims to Bohemia and Hungary enabling the formation of an immense Jagiellon federation extending from Moscow to the Adriatic. Neglected threats from Moscow and the Turks were bequeathed to Casimir's sons, Ladislas (Hungary), John Albert (Poland) and Alexander (Lithuania), and to the Polish diet, a constitutional entity composed of gentry (appearing *c.*1493). Aggression from East and West caused frontier contraction, but this was not irreparable, and another son, Sigismund I (1506–48), carried Poland into her 'golden century'.

The role of Christianity in Poland's history should be noted. Poland's policy of alliance with the papacy in order to exclude imperial and Byzantine influence helped to preserve Polish independence. A strong religious identity united Poland, and its geographical position rendered it guardian of a strategic section of Christian Europe's frontier, which it not only advanced, through the conversion of outlying territories such as Pomerania and Lithuania, but also defended.   MB

□ *The Cambridge History of Poland* (1950); O. Halecki *A History of Poland* (1978); P. Jasienica *Jagiellonian Poland* (1978); N. Davies *God's Playground: a History of Poland* vol. 1 (1982)

Political thought The Middle Ages produced no books on political thought until the 14th c., although political ideas were discussed in writings on a great many other subjects. This was partly the result of the structure of the syllabus in the schools, and in the universities, which began to grow out of the schools towards the end of the 12th c. The seven liberal arts of the Trivium and, to a lesser extent, the Quadrivium were taught as a basis for more advanced studies in law, medicine or theology. But although tables of the 'divisions of philosophy' were drawn up, and politics had a place there as a branch of ethics, there was no convenient textbook from which politics could be taught; and so, along with a number of other subjects at a similar disadvantage, it failed to become a school or university subject.

When Aristotle's *Politics* was brought to the West in a Latin translation in the 13th c. this began to change. The subject became interesting as a new discipline, and one which presented a difficulty: was it to be classified as theoretical, and thus one of the superior sciences, or as an inferior practical science? The attempt to characterize politics for teaching purposes is clear in two of the first ventures into writing on political thought: Dante's *Monarchia* and Marsilius of Padua's *Defensor Pacis*. Dante tried to imitate Euclid and derive his arguments entirely from three self-evident first principles. Marsilius divided his book into Discourses; in the first he based his arguments on reason, while in the second he rested his case on the authority of the Bible, because he believed that the secular aspects of politics were best analyzed by reasoning; the place of the church in the state could only be understood from what God had revealed about his intentions for it.

These early attempts at writing on political thought were concerned in part with the fundamental questions about the nature of society which Aristotle had tried to answer in his *Politics*. Is man a social animal? What is the natural unit of society? How do societies begin? They were also prompted by a concern with contemporary issues, and in particular the question of the relationship between church and state with which Marsilius deals in his second Discourse. St Bernard had put the matter in a nutshell in the early 1150s in his serial letter to Pope Eugenius III on the duties of a pope, the *De Consideratione*. He adapted an image used in patristic times and based on the text of *Luke* 22, v.38: 'Here are two swords.' The two swords were offered to Jesus by the disciples who wanted to save him from arrest. His answer was: *Satis est* ('It is enough'). These 'two swords' were taken to represent the secular and spiritual powers respectively. It remained open to discussion whether God gave both swords to the pope, who then lent one to the emperor, or whether the temporal power belonged to the emperor by right. Bernard's view was that the emperor was the pope's subordinate.

There was also discussion of political problems and questions connected with the study of law. Legal studies had blossomed during the 12th c. with glosses on the Roman law codes which had survived, and fresh codifications of canon law. The greater part of this endeavour was directed towards the details of the laws themselves, but some general questions were raised, and the nature of law itself was defined. St Thomas Aquinas discussed law at length in his 13th-c. textbook of all theology, the *Summa Theologica*. His principal concern was to demonstrate the relationship between law and the grace of God which transcends and completes it; but in considering law itself he puts forward a division between natural law and divine law, and a further division between natural law and human law. Divine law is immutable and eternal; natural laws will last as long as the natural world endures, but human laws must change with the vagaries of human needs, and will differ from society to society.

Above all, the discussions of political theorists of the later Middle Ages, and of their predecessors (who had written on a variety of subjects involving some reflection on such matters) rested upon certain assumptions. These are clearly to be seen in Augustine's *City of God,* written in the decades after the fall of Rome (410). A number of refugees from Rome came to North Africa, where Augustine was bishop, and protested that they could not believe in a God who allowed a Christian empire to perish. Augustine replied with a series of books on the working of divine providence and a myriad other subjects, in which he distinguished between the earthly and the heavenly city. The earthly city belongs to those, alive or dead, who are not good Christians. The heavenly city is made up of all good Christians here and in the world to come, and of the good angels – all the citizens of Heaven in fact. This other-wordly dimension is present in all political thought of the next millennium. When a medieval author considers the purpose of the state, he may answer as Marsilius does, by talking in terms of peace, or by describing the happiness to be had in a community which provides a 'sufficient life'. But such notions are never merely Aristotelian, never limited to the peace or happiness to be had in this life alone. There is always something more; the state looks to a future for its citizens in which the welfare of their souls will be more important than their present comfort.

The world of real politics obtruded comparatively little upon the writing of the earlier medieval centuries in this area. John of Salisbury wrote a *Policraticus* in the 1160s, in which he makes almost no reference to the feudal state in which he lived and worked, and speaks instead of a notional *res publica,* of tyranny, and of a form of citizenship he had never known, but had read about in Cicero and other Roman authors. It was only with the rise of the Italian city-states to a new sophistication and the growth of towns all over Europe, that the idea of citizenship became a reality for a larger number of people. Dante and Marsilius of Padua wrote within an urban world. Out of that world came thoughts about the rights of citizens and their power to choose and dismiss their leaders, which was to give political thought a more modern ring after the end of the Middle Ages. *See* JOHN OF PARIS; LUCAS DE PENNA; PETIT, JEAN; WILLIAM OF OCKHAM   GE

□ A.P. d'Entrèves *The Medieval Contribution to Political Thought* (1939); *Trends in Medieval Political Thought* ed. B. Smalley (1965); W. Ullmann *A History of Political Thought: the Middle Ages* (1965), *Principles of Government and Politics in the Middle Ages* (1966); Q. Skinner *The Foundations of Modern Political Thought* vol. 1 (1978)

Pontanus, Jovianus (*c.*1422–1503) Giovanni Pontano was an Italian humanist and political leader of the kingdom of Naples. He was born at Cereto in the Spoletano, entered the service of Alfonso I of Naples and became a royal secretary (1447). Until 1495 he served the Aragonese kings of Naples holding the posts of secretary, tutor, ambassador and adviser. His acceptance of the French victory following Charles VIII's invasion (1495) led to his fall at the advent of Ferdinand II. He was a prolific writer of Latin prose and verse, the diversity of his works illustrating that of the Renaissance scene. His works included philosophical essays, humanist history *(De Bello Napoletano)*, dialogues and stories *(Asinus)* and poetry on the nature of love and on astrology *(Urania)*. Much of his work drew upon personal experience and he was prominent in establishing Renaissance Latin poetry as a genre of rich potential. He assumed the Latinized name, Jovianus Pontanus, and revived and formalized the Neapolitan Academy *(Academia Pontaniana)*.

□ J.A. Symonds *The Renaissance in Italy* (1909)

Poor Men of Lyons *See* **Waldensians**

Portugal It began as the southern part of Galicia, a region dependent on the kingdom of Asturias. By the early 10th c. it had the status of a county, and 1096–97 it was given to Henry of Burgundy when he married Teresa, the illegitimate daughter of Alfonso VI of Leon and Castile. At this time the frontier between Christian and Muslim territory ran just south of Coimbra – that is, half way between the Duero and the Tagus. Almost simultaneously Braga, restored as a diocese in 1070, had its metropolitan status recognized by the pope; it was to remain the ecclesiastical capital of medieval Portugal.

Afonso I Henriques, son of Henry and Teresa, was only five when his father died in 1112; by 1127 he was ruling in his own right, with his capital at Coimbra. In 1139, having defeated challenges from his mother (who had ruled as regent), from the Galicians and from the Almoravids, he was using the title of king, though still subject in some respects to Alfonso VII, emperor of Leon. He failed to incorporate Galicia in Portugal, but fought off Alfonso VII's invasion, and in a peace treaty of 1143 his kingship was recognized. He then concentrated his efforts on the Reconquest, and in 1147, with the help of English and German crusaders, took Lisbon. The Portuguese then began to settle the lands south of the Tagus, with the Templars defending key points; the region north of the river was entrusted to the Cistercians, whose centre was the great abbey of Alcobaça. Exploiting the wars between Almoravids and Almohads, Afonso pressed southwards, and tried to expand eastward to Badajoz (1170); but he over-reached himself, and an Almohad-Leonese coalition drove him back to the line of the Tagus. That line held; Lisbon was defended against the Almohad army and fleet, and when Afonso's long reign ended in 1185 his kingdom covered two-thirds of modern Portugal.

The Reconquest resumed in the 1220s and was completed in 1249 when the last part of the Algarve surrendered to Afonso III. The 13th c. was a time of conflict between royal and papal authority, settled in the crown's favour by a concordat in 1289. This, like the foundation of Portugal's first university (Lisbon, 1288), was an achievement of Dinis (1279–1325), who also developed foreign trade. A poet and patron of poets, he presided over the last great flowering of the Galician-Portuguese court lyric, which had been dominant in Castile as well as Portugal for a century. The last serious attempt to invade the peninsula from Morocco was defeated at the river Salado in Andalusia, by combined Portuguese and Castilian armies (1340); but this was a success within a gathering crisis. The Black Death, which struck Lisbon in 1348 and spread rapidly, caused a demographic collapse: the population of Portugal, which had reached about a million, did not rise to that level again until *c.*1450. The last years of Afonso IV (1325–57) were clouded by struggles with his son, later Peter I (1357–67); Afonso had Peter's mistress Ines de Castro murdered in 1355, and the new king took revenge on his father's ministers. In 1383 Fernando I died without male issue; his daughter was newly married to John I of Castile, and the queen mother, as regent, favoured the Castilian cause. In December 1383 a bourgeois and popular revolution broke out, and Peter I's bastard son

Portugal

João, master of Avis, assumed leadership, being proclaimed João I in 1385. The old nobility mainly took the side of the invading Castilians, and were swept away with them. With English help (João I married Philippa of Lancaster, John of Gaunt's daughter), the new regime secured its position after the decisive battle of Aljubarrota (August 1385), won by João's general Nun' Alvares Pereira, though the war dragged on until 1403, causing hardship to the people and successive debasements of the coinage. João I's long reign (until 1433) restored political stability, later to be shaken only temporarily by the battle of Alfarrobeira (1449), in which the illegitimate line of the dukes of Bragança established their predominant influence.

The 15th-c. history of Portugal is largely that of discovery and conquest in Africa and the Atlantic. The Moroccan port of Ceuta was seized in 1415, and some four years later the first voyages of exploration were undertaken to the Atlantic islands (Madeira c.1419, Azores discovered c.1439) and down the north-west African coast (Cape Bojador, long an apparently impassable barrier, was rounded in 1434). The failure to take Tangier in 1437, where the king's brother was captured by the Moors, discouraged further military expeditions and strengthened the policy of maritime exploration. Prince Henry the Navigator (1394–1460), who had urged the king to attack Tangier, now concentrated his energies on promoting the West African voyages. His motives are much debated: was he moved chiefly by the duty of spreading the Christian faith, or by the desire for Guinea gold?

The slave trade was also, from about 1440, an economic attraction for explorers. The first *feitoria* ('factory', or fortified trading-post) was established at Arguim c.1445. The discoveries continued after Henry the Navigator's death, and were given fresh impetus by the enthusiasm of João II (1481–95), whose desire both to establish contact with the legendary Prester John (thereby attacking the Muslims from the rear) and to secure the Asian spice trade, led to the exploration of East Africa, after Bartholomew Diaz rounded the Cape of Good Hope in 1487. The Treaty of Tordesillas (1494) divided the non-European world into Spanish and Portuguese spheres of influence, with what was to become Brazil on the Portuguese side of the line. For the moment, however, the Asian voyages prevailed; Vasco da Gama set out in 1497 and returned in triumph two years later. Portugal's world-wide empire was already taking shape. ADD

□ C.R. Boxer *The Portuguese Seaborne Empire* (1969); H.V. Livermore *The Origins of Spain and Portugal* (1971); A.H. de Oliveira Marques *History of Portugal* (1976)

Pound (Latin *pondus;* also *livre, lira,* etc., from Latin *libra,* whence the abbreviation *lb*). Initially a weight unit – the Roman pound of 12 oz (327.45g) – but applied subsequently to many local units containing a varying number of ounces and usually weighing between 300 and 450 oz. As a monetary unit, a money of account corresponding to 240 pennies (20 shillings of 12 pennies each) of the local coin. First struck as a coin in the form of the gold florin in 1252.

Pragmatic Sanction of Bourges On 7 July 1438 a statute of the French church was issued from Bourges in the form of a 'pragmatic', a term borrowed from old imperial rescripts and used here in a specialized sense to represent the settlement of ecclesiastical affairs by civil government. Instigated by Charles VII of France, it terminated franco-papal interim agreements following the schism and resulted from widespread Gallicanism prompted by the schism and papal fiscal abuses. Under the Sanction the French church adopted most decrees of the Council of Basle, amending some. Most sources of papal revenue in France were abolished and the monarchy established under its aegis a Gallican church. The Pragmatic was the first assertion of the rights of national churches to organize themselves, but represented a separatist policy concerned with local interests rather than those of Christendom. It was revoked by Louis XI (1461) and sporadically revived until finally replaced by the Concordat of Bologna (1516).

□ N. Valois *La Pragmatique Sanction de Bourges sous Charles VII* (1906)

Prague, university of The university of Prague was important in Czechoslovak history on political and religious, as well as cultural grounds. It was founded by Emperor Charles IV as the first Central European university. Charles published its Golden Bull of foundation twice, as king of Bohemia (1348) and as Emperor (1349), thereby constituting it as a national and imperial institution. It was modelled on its major precursors, Paris, Bologna and Oxford, adopting the Parisian constitution which entailed a division into four 'nations', with what came to be a controversial German majority. Internal schism (1372) resulted in the detachment of the law faculty which remained a separate entity until 1419.

Gradual German drift to rival universities (Vienna, Heidelberg, Cologne, Erfurt) rendered their majority even more anachronistic, and resulting conflict was heightened by the Great Schism. Finally in 1409 (Decree of Kutná Hora) King Wenceslas of Bohemia transferred three of the 'national' votes to the Czechs, causing a major German secession and nationalizing the university. The Czech assertion provoked a shift

from philosophical and theological to moral and ecclesiastical questioning, Czechs favouring Wycliffite realism against German nominalism. In 1409 John Hus became the university's rector, and until its downfall (1620) Bohemia became the militant centre of Hussitism, the university devoting itself to the service of the Czech nation in its fight to reform the church. In the ensuing conflict over universals and reform Hus led the realists and reformers, backed by 'Wiclifistae' such as Jerome of Prague, whilst Archbishop Zbynek led the conservative Czech opposition. When Prague lacked a king (1419–52), the university virtually governed the nation through the Utraquist consistory.
□ *Prague Essays* ed. R.W. Seton-Watson (1949)

Predestination In its widest sense predestination refers to God's ordination, from eternity, of all events. Theologically, with some biblical authority, it encompasses the divine decree of happiness for the elect and divine reprobation for those destined for Hell. Within Catholic dogma grace is a prerequisite of salvation, but is not arbitrarily bestowed and may be merited. Predestination for Hell is due to God foreseeing, not fore-ordaining, sin. The precise nature of predestination was discussed by many medieval authors. The heresy of predestinarianism arose in the West, attributing salvation and reprobation purely to God's will, excluding human free will and co-operation. Thus, reprobates are impelled towards sin, and the elect to righteousness through the provision of efficacious graces which destroy their free will. The heretics cited St Augustine, misinterpreting his views expressed in the *De Dono* (possibly as a refutation of Pelagianism and semi-Pelagianism, which viewed man's naturally good works as the sole determinant of predestination). The anonymous 5th-c. *Praedestinatus* was probably by a Pelagian, combatting Augustine by falsely attributing part of the work to him.

In the mid-5th c. harsh predestinarianism emerged, defended by the Gallic priest Lucidus, who submitted to Faustus of Riez and the Council of Arles (*c*.473). Conflict resumed in the 9th c., the predestinarian Gottschalk of Orbais being refuted by Hrabanus Maurus (*c*.840); Gottschalk was forced to retract and imprisoned by Hincmar, archbishop of Rheims, at the Synod of Quierzy (849). Further refutation by John Scot Eriugena merely sharpened the controversy, and under Charles the Bald the western Frankish empire was engaged in dispute, until peace was restored by the Synod of Toussy (860). Medieval teaching henceforth centred upon the repudiation of positive reprobation for Hell and assertion of divine predestination of the elect for Heaven and the co-operation of free will. This

teaching was temporarily challenged by Thomas Bradwardine (*c*.1290–1349) and the precursors of the Reformation (Wycliffe, Hus, Jerome of Prague and Johann Wessel). Predestinarianism received a vigorous impulse at the Reformation; Luther's uncompromising denial of free will in the reprobate and of merit was systematized by Calvin and variously modified. MB
□ J. Farrelly *Predestination, Grace and Free-will* (1964)

Premonstratensian Order In 1120 Norbert of Xanten founded a religious community at Prémontré, near Laon, which had been approved as an Order by 1126. The Premonstratensians, or White Canons, were reformed Augustinians, but their general organization was greatly influenced by the Cistercians. Originally, the Order was characterized by its strong element of preaching and pastoral work, and by its provision for women in double monasteries. However, the Order began to suppress its double monasteries in response to public religious opinion, and there arose internal conflict over the interpretation of the Rule of St Augustine. Gradually the more contemplative, monastic way of life gained precedence over the Apostolic functions, which were to be performed by the friars in the next century; the Dominican constitutions borrowed heavily from those of Prémontré.

Printing Although printing emerged late in the medieval period, the 15th c. witnessed vital stages in its history: the invention of the process in the West, its diffusion, and the refinement of typeface. Increased demand for books, reflected in manuscript production, was a major stimulus to printing's development.

Printing was already known in China, but probably developed independently from the West. The mechanical problems of producing 'artificial' script

The earliest illustration of a **printing**-press from the *Danse Macabre* printed at Lyons (1499).

were resolved into a workable method, which became standard for 350 years, by the Mainz goldsmith Johann Gutenberg. In 1455–56 he completed the first printed book, the Gutenberg Bible, in a 200-copy edition on paper and vellum. He had previously printed church indulgences, and woodblock printing for playing cards existed, but this was the first book. Gutenberg's lead type font was handcut in the German Gothic script of contemporary manuscripts, which persisted in Germany until the 20th c.

The technique spread rapidly, causing rival invention claims (such as Holland's Laurens Coster). Work in Mainz was continued by Johann Fust (c.1400–66) and Peter Schoeffer (c.1425–1502) who produced a psalter (1457) containing the first elaborate two-colour printed initials, date, printer's imprint and device, and colophon. Within five years German centres included Bamberg (Adolf Pfister) and Strasbourg (Johann Mentelin); by 1500 they numbered about 60. During the last quarter of the 15th c. Germany's major contribution was to the illustrated book, notably through Augsburg and Cologne, where woodcutters and printers united to develop high-quality illustrations (such as those of Albrecht Dürer).

Outside Germany Gothic type persisted for religious and law books for a century, but was replaced by a Roman type developed from 15th-c. Italian humanist script (derived from Caroline minuscule), which inspired a burgeoning of type design in Venice from 1469. Printed works were extremely diverse; printing was instrumental in the diffusion of humanism and also played a role in the Reformation.

The first English press was established (1476) by William Caxton, and the first dated English printed book (1477) was *The Dictes or Sayengis of the Philosophres*. In general, however, English printers were dependent upon the Continent. The first Basle press (1467) became the principal centre for Christian humanist printing, the printer Johann Froben (1460–1527) working with Erasmus and Holbein. In Italy the first press was established (1465) at Subiaco monastery by Conrad Sweynheym of Mainz (d.1477) and Arnold Pannartz of Cologne (d.1476), who developed a hybrid Roman/Gothic type.

The early printers were artist-craftsmen, publishers and booksellers, and therefore favoured commercial centres, especially since patrons (such as the Medici) initially withheld support. Venice therefore attracted many, founding the modern printed book. The German Johannes de Spira (d.1470) developed the first type directly inspired by Italian humanist hands, and Nicolaus Jenson's *De Evangelica Praeparatione* (1470) established the modern Roman typeface. It was adapted by Aldus Manutius (1450–1515) and Francesco Griffo (c.1450–1518), who also printed the first Greek works and developed italic (equivalent to cursive) for smaller, cheaper works.

During the first half of the 16th c. the impetus shifted to France. Printing was introduced from Germany to the Sorbonne (1470), the university recognizing the advantages of availability, cheapness and uniformity. Medieval manuscripts remained the model, despite Ulrich Gering's introduction of Roman type (c.1478), French printers evolving a type *(lettre-bâtarde)* from French legal script. Manuscript influence also led to the *éditions de luxe,* with Jean Dupré *(fl.*1481–1504) and Philippe Pigouchet *(fl.*1485–1515) producing beautifully decorated Books of Hours. It was in France that printer and engraver most closely rivalled the achievements of scribe and painter, continuing the medieval legacy. [*75, 160*]   MB

□ S.H. Steinberg *Five Hundred Years of Printing* (1966)

Procopius of Caesarea (d.562) The most illustrious of the 6th-c. Byzantine historians writing contemporary history in the tradition of Thucydides. He was secretary to Justinian's general Belisarius, whom he accompanied on several campaigns, and his *Histories of the Wars* provide an invaluable account of the Persian, Vandal and Gothic wars. His *Buildings* describes the chief public works executed under Justinian, while his *Secret History* is a notorious, critical account of the reign of Justinian.

□ *The Secret History* trans. G.A. Williamson (1966)

Prussia The Prussia which achieved fame under Frederick the Great and Bismarck bore a limited relationship to medieval Prussia. The Prussian state arose from the fusion, at the beginning of the 17th c., of the March of Brandenburg, the Hohenzollern dynasty (burgraves of Nuremberg and electors of Brandenburg) and the Baltic states founded by the Teutonic Order, from which the name 'Prussia' derived.

'Prussia' was originally applied to a small pagan Baltic people around the mouth of the Vistula. Poland had unsuccessfully attempted its conversion, but this was accomplished by the Knights of the Teutonic Order (founded 1198 in Palestine), which turned its crusading spirit upon the area in 1226 when the Golden Bull of Rimini, granted by Frederick II, empowered Grand Master Hermann of Salza to govern the area as part of the Empire. From 1226 to 1236 the Order engaged in brutal conquest and conversion. The region was subdued until the great Prussian rebellion erupted (1260) into 15 years of warfare, during which much of the original population was exterminated. The remnants were totally absorbed by the German and Slav settlers whom the Order transplanted, termed East or West Prussians according to their bank of the Vistula.

During the 14th c. Prussia flourished as a monastic republic administered by the Order (its celibacy and ban on personal property preventing feudal rule), beneath which was an economic aristocracy and affluent peasantry. As the Estates prospered the Order was increasingly viewed as alien, especially as it was replenished from the Empire. At its height in the 14th c. the Order's territory stretched from the Newmark to Estonia. Cities, such as Danzig (seat of the grand master) and Königsberg, grew, and it became an important Baltic trading power.

During the 15th c. the Order engaged in wars with Poland and Lithuania, the Prussian Estates joining the enemy. In 1466 (the Second Peace of Thorn) West Prussia became totally Polish, the Order retaining East Prussia as a Polish fief. Prussia was no longer part of the Empire.

In 1525 the last grand master, Albrecht von Brandenburg-Ansbach, used the Reformation to dissolve the Order's state, making himself temporal duke of Prussia under Poland. He was of the Hohenzollern family and through him Prussia was eventually to be allied with Brandenburg.   MB
□ F.L. Carsten *The Origins of Prussia* (1954); S. Haffner *The Rise and Fall of Prussia* (1980)

Psellus, Michael Born in Constantinople, Psellus is best known for his lively, if exaggerated, history of the Byzantine emperors and the political decadence of the period 1025–71. He was noted for his vanity, though this was apparently conventional among Byzantine authors. He was a favourite of Emperor Constantine IX (1042–55), to whom he taught rhetoric, and was genuinely interested in classical literature and philosophy, especially the work of Plato. An influential and unscrupulous court politician, he was closely involved in the intrigue which resulted in the arrest and imprisonment of Emperor Romanus, after his defeat at Manzikert (1071).

Ptolemy of Lucca (*c*.1236–1326) Bartolommeo Fiadoni was a member of the prominent Fiadoni family of Lucca and an important civic and ecclesiastical historian. He was a Dominican associate of Thomas Aquinas, first coming into contact with the great philosopher in the 1270s; thus he was able to continue the latter's book *On the Rule of Princes* (*c*.1302). He is perhaps best known for his championing of the hierocratic theory of papal power, but his work is also remarkable for its sympathetic and thoughtful analysis of the types of power structure existing in Italy in the early 14th c. Before the advent

of Marsilius of Padua, the Italian communal theory received much support from Ptolemy of Lucca.
□ B. Schmeidler *Studien zu Tholomeus von Lucca* (1908)

Quadrivium The seven liberal arts, which constituted the basis for education in the Middle Ages, were divided into two elements: the Trivium, and the more advanced studies of the Quadrivium (arithmetic, geometry, astronomy and music). In the hands of skilful teachers with access to the work of Boethius and his successors, a significant inheritance from classical culture was transmitted to the medieval Western world. To Boethius, all four branches of the Quadrivium represented different aspects of mathematics, but significant developments took place, notably from the 12th c., as clearer distinctions were made between the practice and theory of the sciences. The structure of the Quadrivium survived – though uneasily – as new knowledge accumulated. *See* EDUCATION
□ A.C. Crombie *Augustine to Galileo* (1961)

R

Ragnar Lothbrok (Ragnar Leather-breeches) Viking hero who appears frequently as a genealogical figure in the sagas. The historical evidence is sketchy, but it seems he was a major leader of the Vikings in the mid-9th c., and father of Ivar the Boneless and Hubba, Scandinavian brothers who launched a series of penetrating raids into England against Alfred's kingdom. He has also been identified with the viking who sailed up the Seine and sacked Paris in 845. He is reputed to have died by being cast into a snake-pit in Northumbria, his last words presaging filial vengeance: 'How the porklings will grunt when they hear the old boar's need.'
□ A.P. Smyth *Scandinavian Kings in the British Isles 850–880* (1977)

Rainald of Dassel (*c*.1118–67) Imperial chancellor under Frederick I Barbarossa and *éminence grise* of his policy of imperial supremacy. He was an accomplished administrator, diplomat and general, and a passionate supporter of the Empire.

Rainald studied at Paris in the 1140s and became provost of the cathedral churches of Hildesheim (1147) and Münster. His political ambitions led him into the imperial circle, and in 1156 he was appointed chancellor. Rainald was instrumental in conceiving Frederick's campaign to claim sovereignty over all Christendom, and Rome in particular, provoking a papal schism. Rainald directed a strong propaganda campaign against Pope Adrian IV and 1158–64 led troops into Italy several times. In 1159 he was elected archbishop of Cologne, and after Adrian IV's death in that year championed the imperial anti-pope Victor IV against Alexander III. The schism might have ended upon Victor IV's death (1164) had Rainald not ensured its continuance by establishing a new anti-pope, Paschal III. Rainald carefully negotiated alliances during the schism, notably with Henry II of England (from 1165), who was initially induced to support Paschal. Rainald also obtained Charlemagne's canonization by Paschal as imperial propaganda.

In 1167, during a major Italian campaign, a decisive victory over the Romans turned to disaster when Frederick's army was decimated by malaria; Rainald was one of the many who died.
□ P. Münz *Frederick Barbarossa* (1969)

Ranulf Flambard (d. 1128) Bishop of Durham and a chief minister under William Rufus (1087–1100). Ordericus Vitalis describes him as low-born, from the Bessin. By *c.*1083–85 he entered Chancery as a clerk and keeper of the royal seal, rising to prominence under the Conqueror by *c.*1087. He continued to serve William Rufus, becoming his chaplain, a justiciar and a head of the administration. He was extremely unpopular amongst chroniclers and gained a reputation as the 'lawyer of feudalism'. Little is known of his actual role, but he was generally described as a fiscal agent, and evidence connects him with the judicial side of finance. He seems to have been instrumental in extending royal authority throughout England, widening royal relations beyond mere overlord to tenant-in-chief, increasing interference in local affairs, complicating administrative offices and helping to create the Exchequer. He increased the possessions of the king, often at the church's expense.

In 1099 he became bishop of Durham while continuing his administrative role and thereby causing outcry. When Henry I ascended the throne (1100) he was imprisoned, but escaped to Normandy where he encouraged Robert's invasion of England. He was reconciled with Henry *c.*1101, but played no part in his administration, concentrating upon Durham, where he nearly completed the cathedral, fortified the town and built Norham Castle.
□ R.W. Southern, 'Ranulf Flambard and early Anglo-Norman Administration', *Transactions of the Royal Historical Society* 16 (1933)

Ranulf de Glanvill (d. 1190) Born at Stratford, Suffolk, he was a member of the lower ranks of England's landed classes. He entered royal government, rising to the rank of sheriff. His loyalty to Henry II was proved by his energetic defence of the north during the rebellion of 1173–74, in which he captured King William of Scotland at Alnwick. He succeeded Richard de Lucy as justiciar in 1180, a post he held until 1189 when Richard I removed him from office and imprisoned him. He was released on the payment of a ransom of £15,000 and accompanied Richard on the Third Crusade, dying at Acre in 1190.

His fame rests on the work commonly attributed to him, *Tractatus de Legibus et Consuetudinibus Regni Angliae* (*c.*1188), but possibly written by his nephew and secretary Hubert Walter. It was a lucid description in commentary format of the practice, procedures and principles of the royal courts. The book is structured around the forms of royal writs and their accompanying procedures, notably the recently introduced possessory assizes. The aim is effective enforcement by specific royal orders, with regal authority used to overcome conflicting jurisdictions and to ensure the efficient maintenance of the king's peace. Its popularity in judicial circles helped to consolidate the position of common law against the rapidly evolving and expanding feudal, canon and Roman legal systems.
□ G.D.G. Hall *Glanvill* (1965)

Ravenna In 402–03 Emperor Honorius and his court left Milan to take up permanent residence in Ravenna, a city that provided better protection from the barbarian tribes invading from the north. The city played a key role in the history of medieval Europe for *c.*350 years as capital, first, of the Western Roman empire and later, of Ostrogothic and Byzantine Italy. The barbarian ruler Odoacer resided there after 476, later surrendering it to the Ostrogoth Theodoric in 493. It then played an important role in the Justinianic campaigns to recapture Italy from the Goths; the Byzantine general Belisarius captured Ravenna in 540, and the city became the capital of Italy. It was subsequently made into an imperial exarchate (*c.*584–*c.*751), thereby becoming the centre of all administrative activity in Italy as well as being the principal port of entry for the Byzantines. The city was taken by the Lombards in the mid-8th c., but by 757 was under the control of the pope after the Frankish King Pepin had expelled the Lombards.

By the late Middle Ages, Venice had supplanted Ravenna as the principal port on the Adriatic. The many beautiful buildings and works of art executed in Ravenna between the 5th c. and 8th c. epitomize the strong artistic connections of the Eastern and Western Roman empire in the early Middle Ages.
□ E. Hutton *Ravenna: A Study* (1913); A. Torre *Ravenna: Storia di 3000 Anni* (1967)

Raymond IV (*c*.1041–1105) Count of Toulouse. Second son of Pons and Almodis, on the death of his elder brother William (1093), he succeeded to the whole county of Toulouse. Two years later he was the first prince to respond to Urban II's call for a crusade to the Holy Land. He left France in 1096, and when he arrived at Constantinople refused to pay homage to the Emperor Alexius. A compromise was reached whereby Raymond agreed to respect the territorial rights of the emperor, and gradually Raymond came to favour and to advocate a Greek-Latin alliance to further the aims of the crusade. Raymond was present at the siege and capture of Antioch, and argued that it should be given to the Byzantine emperor. However, Bohemond I claimed it for himself and expelled Raymond's garrison. Thereafter, Raymond appears as the true leader of the crusade, arranging the march on Jerusalem and playing a crucial role in the storming of the city in 1099. Raymond declined the royal dignity (Godfrey de Bouillon became the Defender of the Holy Sepulchre) and in 1101 founded the county of Tripoli, though he continued to campaign up to the time of his death.
□ J.H. Hill and L.L. Hill *Raymond IV of St Gilles* (1959)

Realism *See* **Scholasticism**

Reccared I King of the Visigoths 586–601 (*c*.560–602) Chiefly responsible for the conversion of the ruling Visigothic dynasty from Arianism to Catholicism, Reccared deliberately strengthened the religious ties between king and church, accepting the Old Testament custom of anointing by the bishops at his installation, cooperating with the powerful bishops at great councils and working closely with Pope Gregory I. He could not achieve complete success in the face of the diverse population and interests in the Iberian peninsula, Basque separatism, Suevi independence, Jewish difference and Arian persistence, but did much to stabilize and strengthen what became an orthodox Christian monarchy.
□ E.A. Thompson *The Goths in Spain* (1969)

Reconquest (*Reconquista*) Name given to the process by which from the 11th c. onwards the Christian communities of Spain reconquered the territories lost to the Muslims in the decades immediately following 711. The chief critical dates are the recovery of Toledo in 1085; the establishment of the kingdom of Portugal and the capture of Lisbon (1148); the battle of Las Navas de Tolosa (1212) and the subsequent extension of Christian authority to Seville and Cordoba. By the end of the 13th c. only

the kingdom of Granada was still in Muslim hands, where it remained until 1492. Literary sources tend to romanticize and oversimplify in their interpretation of Spanish history as a long crusade from the reign of Charlemagne to the end of the Middle Ages. The reality was vastly different, and the Reconquest must be interpreted in the context of a complex interaction of peoples – Christian, Muslim and Jewish – which made Spain one of the most important sources of intellectual and cultural life in the central Middle Ages. [*306*]
□ A. Mackay *Spain in the Middle Ages. From Frontier to Empire 1000–1500* (1977); D.W. Lomax *The Reconquest of Spain* (1978)

Regino (d.915) Chronicler. Of noble Frankish birth, he was successively a monk and abbot (elected 892) of Prüm, western Germany. His Chronicle, written *c*.908 and terminating at 906, renders him the historian and moralist of the internecine struggles within the Frankish empire following the death of Charles III (888). His preoccupation is with the heights achieved by the Carolingian empire, its collapse and prevailing decadence. The Chronicle was continued (*Continuatio Reginonis*) by Adalbert, archbishop of Magdeburg, after the mid-10th c., and relates the empire's recovery under the Ottonians. Regino died at St Maximin's, near Trier.
□ J. Fleckenstein *Early Medieval Germany* (1978)

Regularis Concordia Treatise on monastic customs possibly written by St Aethelwold in *c*.970, which aimed at establishing a common form of observance for English monks. The work is divided into a prologue and 12 chapters covering the religious life throughout the year. In the prologue the author informs us that King Edgar summoned a Council at Winchester and invited monks from the reforming establishments of Fleury (Cluniac) and Ghent (Lotharingian) to suggest the Rules upon which the work is based. It provides intimate details of monastic life; for example, it is the only document of the period to mention daily communion. The importance of the treatise is its place in the church reforms of the 10th c., highlighting Catholic and local aspects. By allying intimately with royal power, the reformers attempted to weaken the domination of secular and local interests. Furthermore, it strengthened the position of the monarch, permitting him to fulfil his ascribed role as Christ's vicar on earth. The widespread adoption of this Rule led to improvement in the monastic life in England.
□ *Regularis Concordia* ed. D.T. Symons (1958)

Renaissance *See* **Carolingian, Italian, Northumbrian, Twelfth-century renaissance**

Renovatio monetae (Mutatio monetae) The custom of changing the type of penny in circulation and replacing it by another, often at three-year intervals. It was widely practised in northern Germany, where it was exploited for taxation purposes, and in England between the late 10th c. and the mid-12th c.

Reynard the Fox Popular figure in a series of moralistic fables which had a great vogue in 13th-c. and 14th-c. Western Europe; the hero was represented as a clever fox, Renart or Reinhart. The composers of what is sometimes called the Reynard cycle drew ultimate inspiration from Aesop, finding the anthropomorphic device a most effective means of communicating satiric comment on the social scene.
□ J. Flinn *Le Roman de Renart* (1964)

Rheims, Council of (October 1049) Convened by Pope Leo IX. Leo employed numerous provincial councils to ensure control, greatly increasing papal power and prestige, and it was he who initiated the papal reform movement. The Council of Rheims (followed by that of Mainz) delineated his reform of the secular clergy and may be seen as the start of papal reform. Abuses were rife in France, so Leo utilized the consecration of the new abbey church of Saint-Rémy for his visit.

The Council condemned simony, clerical marriage and the sale of orders, safeguarded clerical dues, but prohibited fees for burials, Eucharist and service to the sick, and declared that bishops and abbots were to be appointed only after election by clergy and people. It was an expression of the church's corporate life, and stressed individual responsibility. Henry I of France, wary of Leo's German nationality and of papal authority, obstructed Rheims by demanding his bishops' feudal service in a well-timed campaign. Those who obeyed were excommunicated (archbishop of Sens and the bishops of Beauvais and Amiens) whilst the archbishop of Rheims and others were tried for simony; one bishop was deposed and the bishop of Langres fled.

Rhodes Principal island of the Dodecanese with the port of Rhodes at its north-eastern end. Its Greek inhabitants possessed a great classical heritage and continued to be subject to Byzantium. At the beginning of the 14th c. plans were evolved to convert the Order of Knights Hospitallers into a maritime power, to secure its independence. Rhodes and its dependencies became the target. By 1306 Rhodes was under a Byzantine governor but was in fact a pirate state and open to attack. The Order's forces landed in 1307 and possession was confirmed by Pope Clement V, but the island was not secured until 1309 in the face of resistance from the Rhodians and their Muslim allies. The Order obtained several footholds on the surrounding islands and the mainland, and for two centuries remained astride one of the major sea routes of the eastern Mediterranean. It established an independent, feudal religious republic with its own administration and modified Rhodian law. Its subjects included lay Europeans in addition to the Rhodians, who paradoxically formed a Greek Orthodox community under Roman rule, although without apparent schism.

This power presented a threat to Islam, and from 1400 attacks were directed against it. In 1453 Constantinople fell and the Turkish sultan, Mehmed the Conqueror, demanded tribute from the Order. Despite its refusal, no major Islamic attack was launched until 1479. Under Grand Master Pierre d'Aubusson, Rhodes withstood a severe siege and secured a victory (1480) which was celebrated throughout Christendom. A period of détente followed, during which the Order protected the Turkish pretender, Djem. In 1500 Turkish incursions into Italy provoked a crusade which it fell to the Order to implement. Sporadic conflict ensued until Sulaymān II the Magnificent determined to remove this thorn in his side and launched an armada (1522). Despite sophisticated fortifications and heroic defence under Grand Master Philippe de Villiers de l'Isle-Adam, the city of Rhodes was forced to an honourable surrender. The Order was allowed to leave (1523) and eventually settled in Malta. Many subjects also left and colonists were brought in. The Ottomans extended some religious tolerance to their remaining Greek subjects.   MB
□ E. Brockman *The Two Sieges of Rhodes 1480–1522* (1969)

Richard I Lionheart (Coeur de Lion) King of England 1189–99 (b.1157) Third son of Henry II, he received the duchy of Aquitaine at the age of 11. Like his brothers he had no filial loyalty and allied himself to the French king against his father in 1173–74 and 1188–89. In a series of bitter campaigns he established his authority over the refractory Poitevin barony.

On his father's death (1189) he inherited all of Henry's lands and began to prepare for the crusade. In 1190 he set out, capturing Messina and Cyprus en route before joining the crusaders at Acre (1191). The city fell within a month, and later in the year Richard's brilliant victory at Arsuf resulted in the Christian capture of Joppa. The Christians were divided and settled for an honourable truce with Saladin (1192), which allowed the Christians to have access to the holy places and to continue to hold Acre.

Richard Lionheart makes a treaty with the Saracens (Matthew Paris, *Chronica Minora*, mid-13th c.).

On his return journey Richard was captured by the followers of the Emperor Henry VI and released only after the payment of 100,000 marks. England was surprisingly well governed during his absence on crusade and his captivity. Richard's reputation as king was high among contemporaries, and he is now again well regarded after a period when it was fashionable to arraign him for neglect. He spent most of his later years in his French possessions, building the great fortress of Château-Gaillard on the Seine, and was killed at the siege of Chaluz in 1199.
□ J. Gillingham *The Life and Times of Richard I* (1978)

Richard de Clare (d. 1176) Known as 'Strongbow', Richard FitzGilbert de Clare was a leading figure in the Anglo-Norman invasion of Ireland. He was a Welsh Marcher baron, earl of Striguil and earl of Pembroke from 1148 (until the title was revoked by Henry II as a Stephen creation). In 1167 Strongbow agreed to reinstate Dermot MacMurrough, king of Leinster (expelled by High King Rory O'Conor), in return for the hand of Dermot's daughter Eva and the Leinster succession. Strongbow led a massive force to Ireland (1170), despite Henry II's disapproval. They took Waterford and Dublin, but Henry ordered them home. Strongbow countered Henry's fears of over-powerful subjects by offering to hold his Irish lands of the English crown. Henry refused, but meanwhile Dermot had died (1171); Strongbow's succession was repudiated in Leinster and he campaigned to subdue it.

Henry II prepared to visit Ireland. Strongbow met him, pledging him Dublin and its hinterland, Waterford, Wexford and the Wicklows. Henry landed (1171) and his overlordship was recognized. Strongbow and Hugh de Lacy were empowered to enfeoff Meath and Leinster, and though temporarily

recalled because of their lawlessness, Strongbow soon returned as viceroy (1173–76). An Anglo-Norman settlement was achieved and acknowledged by the Treaty of Windsor (1175), by the terms of which Rory O'Conor became Henry's vassal, three-fifths of his lands remaining Irish, with Leinster and Meath becoming Anglo-Norman. On Strongbow's death his children Gilbert and Isabella (who married William Marshall) were under age, and the earldom of Leinster temporarily passed to the crown.
□ R.H.M. Dolley *Anglo-Norman Ireland* (1972)

Rienzo, Cola di (*c.*1313–54) A Roman notary of humble birth, in 1347 Rienzo led the Popular party against the Roman aristocracy and the absentee papacy, then at Avignon. He was crowned as tribune and, dreaming of restoring the ancient Roman republic, he declared that every Italian citizen was to have Roman citizenship. He planned to unite Italy into a federation under obedience to an elected emperor in Rome. In December 1347 Rienzo was overthrown and fled from Rome. He was excommunicated and spent several years in prison before being absolved in 1352. He was killed by a mob, in October 1354, only a few months after having again assumed control of Rome.
□ I. Origo *Tribune of Rome* (1938); *Life of Cola di Rienzo* trans. J. Wright (1975)

Roads, Roman The role of Roman roads in the medieval network is debateable, as survival appears to have been sporadic and varied. The Roman system was designed to serve and unite a massive empire, while medieval authority and interests were of a more local nature. Medieval roads tended not to be engineered, but were rather rights of way. Roman roads were destroyed, abandoned, encroached upon, robbed, incorporated piecemeal into medieval routes, or maintained (as the Via Flaminia by the kings of the Goths). Major maintenance obviously depended upon the strength of central authority, and generally responsibility seems to have been shared, as in antiquity, by central government, and regional and roadside authorities, such as the *frères pontifes* and hospices.

It has been doubted that Roman roads coincided with medieval roads, as they were difficult to modify and repair, but there are instances of continued use, for example in 13th-c. Picardy and the Landes, where the Roman road was used as a pilgrim route until the 14th c. The occurrence of Roman roads as charter boundaries, settlement patterns and place-name evidence (incorporating elements such as *straet*) also imply some continuity, as do specific details, such as the English monarch's special protection of Watling Street, Ermine Street, Fosse Way and the Icknield Way. However, topography was important. New towns, such as Oxford, needed new roads and there also appears to have been a return to a pre-Roman system of communications, of improvised construction, between minor settlements.

☐ R. Chevallier *Roman Roads* (1976); B.P. Hindle *Medieval Roads* (1982)

Robert, St (1027–1111) Abbot of Molesme. During the 20 years that Robert was abbot of Molesme in Burgundy, the monastery achieved a high reputation for its sanctity, and attracted considerable endowments. This success led to the dissatisfaction of a section of the community who desired a return to a simpler life, more in keeping with the Benedictine Rule. In 1098 Robert left Molesme to settle these monks, in circumstances of extreme hardship, in a new monastery. The first abbot of the *novum monasterium*, which later became Cîteaux, Robert was forced to return to Molesme, leaving his new foundation to struggle for survival. Nevertheless, he is properly regarded as the originator of the Cistercian movement.

☐ D. Knowles *Cistercians and Cluniacs* (1955); G. Constable *Religious Life and Thought* (1979)

Robert I Bruce King of Scotland 1306–29 (b.1274) Of the Anglo-Norman Bruce family who were among the claimants to the Scottish throne upon Alexander III's death (1286). Edward I intervened, annexing Scotland (1296) and initiating the Anglo-Scottish wars of independence. In 1304 Robert Bruce became sixth lord of Annandale and head of the family. He initially supported Edward rather than his own rival claimants (Balliol and the Comyns), but sporadically supported the rebellious Scots

The great seal of **Robert Bruce**, *rex Scottorum*.

under Wallace. In 1306 he killed John Comyn and decisively entered into revolt, being crowned king at Scone. A massive English/Comyn force was mobilized. Robert was defeated at Methven and Dalry (1306) and retreated into the Western Highlands, re-emerging in 1307 to launch a campaign of guerilla warfare, defeating the English at Glen Trool and Loudon Hill. Edward I's death (1307) improved Robert Bruce's position and from 1309 he effectively ruled much of Scotland. Victories at Bannockburn (1314) and Berwick (1318) extended his rule throughout Scotland.

Hostilities, including Scottish incursions into England, continued until the Treaty of Northampton (or Edinburgh) in 1328, which confirmed Scotland's freedom and the Bruce succession, sealed by the marriage of Edward III's sister Joan and Robert's son and successor David (1329–71). *See* JOHN BALLIOL
☐ G.W.S. Barrow *Robert Bruce* (1965)

Robert Guiscard (d. 1085) Noted for his cunning as well as for his bravery (his sobriquet is cognate with the English 'wizard'), in the course of a long and colourful career he established the Norman family of Hauteville as a ruling dynasty of European importance. He joined his brothers and other Norman adventurers in south Italy in the 1140s, defeated the papal army of Leo IX at the epic battle of Civitate (1153), but emerged by the end of the decade as a defender of papal interests in the south and a counterpoise to the Germans. By the Treaty of Melfi (1059) the pope recognized him as feudal duke of Apulia and potential ruler of Sicily, still at that stage in Muslim hands. His equally glamorous young brother Roger (I) took the lead with Robert's support in the conquest of Sicily, which was not complete until *c*.1092. Robert himself concentrated on mainland politics.

His relationship with the papacy was often stormy, but when the final political crisis of Hildebrand's pontificate occurred, Robert intervened on his behalf against the Emperor Henry IV, an intervention which resulted in a savage attack on Rome by Norman troops in 1084, and the forced withdrawal of the pope to Norman protection at Salerno (where he died in 1085). Robert was also active in the politics of the eastern Mediterranean, defeating Eastern imperial schemes as well as Western. He clarified the situation in the south of Italy, removing the last Byzantine stronghold at Bari (1071) and laying the foundations for the strong feudal principality of Apulia and Sicily which was to blossom into a kingdom by 1130.

□ J.J. Norwich *The Normans in the South* (1967)

Robert le Bougre (d. before 1263) Robert le Petit acquired the name 'le Bougre' (the Bulgar) from having been a Cathar. By 1232 he was converted, becoming a Dominican. Matthew Paris (*Chronica Majora*) describes him as a well-educated and eloquent preacher. His acquaintance with Catharism rendered him valuable in its detection, and he was recruited by the founder of the medieval Inquisition, Pope Gregory IX, becoming its chief representative in northern France (where heresy was persistent if not as rampant as in the south).

In 1233 Gregory empowered the Dominicans of Besançon, led by Robert, to investigate Charité-sur-Loire. Robert's intemperate zeal provoked outcry, and in 1234 his licence was withdrawn. Nevertheless, in 1235 he was appointed inquisitor-general of France. He was particularly active in the north-east and in 1239 secured the mass execution of 183 Cathars at Mont-Aimé (Champagne). Eventually his fanaticism and false convictions led to his fall (*c*.1245) and perpetual imprisonment. He appears to have purchased a papal dispensation, leaving the Dominicans and joining several other orders before his death.

□ C.H. Haskins *Studies in Medieval Culture* (1929); B. Hamilton *The Medieval Inquisition* (1981)

Robert of Arbrissel, St (d. 1117) Founder of the Order of Fontevrault, a double order for both monks and nuns, Robert had left the household of Bishop Marbod of Rennes to become an itinerant preacher. In 1096 he was licensed by Pope Urban II to preach the First Crusade in the Loire valley. He also sought to lead a life of poverty, in imitation of Christ, and attracted many followers, particularly women. In late 1100 Robert was summoned to a Synod of Poitiers, at which he probably agreed to divide his adherents into separate convents, so founding Fontevrault, which rapidly became one of the most celebrated aristocratic monastic houses of northern France.

Robert of Sorbon (1201–74) Founder of the Sorbonne. Humbly born in Sorbon (Ardennes), he studied at Paris university in the faculties of arts and theology, where he became a master. He wrote numerous sermons and *c*.1250 became a canon of Cambrai. He subsequently wrote the treatise *De Conscientia* and *De Confessione*, and by 1256 had become Louis IX's confessor. Concern over student conditions prompted him to found the most famous Parisian college, the Sorbonne (probably officially founded 1257), for students of theology. Its role in the university's attack on the mendicant orders and in advocating Gallicanism had little to do with Robert. He secured for it many benefactors, including the king and Gérard d'Abbeville (who bequeathed his library in 1272), and continued in his roles as master, patron, priest, sermonist and courtier until his death.

□ P. Glorieux *Aux Origines de la Sorbonne* vol. 1 (1966); R.H. Rouse, 'The Early Library of the Sorbonne', *Scriptorium* 21 (1967)

Robin Hood Although he probably had some historical basis, he was not the character of popular imagination; that is to say, one who robbed the rich to pay the poor. The first reference to 'rymes of Robyn Hood' appears in *Piers Plowman* (*c*.1377). Surviving medieval legends consist of ballads such as *Robin Hood and the Monk* (*c*.1450), the late 15th-c. poem *A Gest of Robyn Hode* (probably from an earlier source) and *Robin Hood and the Potter* (*c*.1503); a fragmentary play has also survived in a manuscript of *c*.1475. In these accounts Robin is a yeoman who pursues an outlaw's existence, displays great prowess at arms and is a master of disguise and stratagem. He is no social rebel, revering the king in all matters except the ownership of deer; and his actions against authority are aimed at its abuse rather than its fundamental structure. He displays little affinity with peasants and no definite aims for redistribution of wealth. He is devoted to the Virgin, but mistrusts clerics. He can be remarkably violent, but always heroically so.

The most likely historical figure was Robert Hode, tenant of the archbishop of York, who fled from the justices in 1225. During the 13th c. a Hood family appeared around Wakefield; the legends were often set in Barnsdale, near Wakefield. By *c.*1296 Robynhod surnames appeared in Sussex and London, probably because of connections with Barnsdale brought about by the Lancaster-Lacy marriage (*c.*1294). Several later outlaws assumed the name 'Robin Hood', possibly accounting for associations with forest land, such as Sherwood.

By the late 15th c. Robin was known in Scotland: he and his men featured in the May games and plays. A 13th-c. French play, *Robin and Marion*, about totally separate characters, seems to have led to the identification of Robin with the king of the May, with Marion as his queen. Friar Tuck may have been based on Robert Stafford, 'Frere Tuk', a clerical outlaw in Sussex *c.*1417–29. The legend seems to have drawn upon, and later been confused with, real-life romances (Hereward the Wake, Eustace the Monk, Fulk FitzWarin) and other tales (*Adam Bell*, *Gamelyn*). This, and changes in audience which shifted Robin's associations from yeomen to nobles or peasants, probably led to subsequent embroidery upon the legend and contributed to its durability.

See FOREST LAW   MB

□ J.C. Holt *Robin Hood* (1982); J. Bellamy *Robin Hood: an historical enquiry* (1985)

Roderic King of the Visigoths 710–11 A figure greater in legend than in history, Roderic, duke of Andalusia, was elected king in 710, but was overwhelmingly defeated by the Muslims led by Tariq (Gibraltar = Geb-el-Tariq, or Tariq's rock) on 19 July 711. This marked the beginning of a relatively quick and successful conquest, which placed the greater part of Spain in Muslim hands.

□ R. Collins *Early Medieval Spain 400–1000* (1984)

Roger I (d.1101) Great count of Sicily and Calabria 1072–1101. The youngest son of Tancred de Hauteville, Roger went to join his brother Robert Guiscard in southern Italy in 1057. A brave warrior, he greatly aided Guiscard's conquest of Calabria and was able to capture Reggio in 1060. With the conquest of this region virtually complete, the brothers turned their attention to Sicily. Discord between the various Muslim leaders provided them with the perfect opportunity of capturing the island, although it took nearly 20 years to complete the operation.

Roger rebelled openly against his brother on several occasions: in 1062 he forced him to agree to a rule of condominium in Calabria, and in 1072 he was granted the title of count of Sicily and Calabria, though Guiscard reserved control of Palermo, half of Messina, and half of Val Demone. Roger captured Noto, the last major stronghold of the Muslims, in 1091.

Following Guiscard's death in 1085, Roger was granted his lands in Sicily. He then assumed the title of great count of Sicily and Calabria. Roger granted religious freedom to Greek Christians, Jews and Muslims, and wishing to preserve the administrative machinery, he continued to employ Muslim civil servants and accountants. He was granted the apostolic legateship for Sicily by Pope Urban II in 1099.

□ J.J. Norwich *The Normans in the South* (1967); D.M. Smith *Medieval Sicily* (1968)

Roger II King of Sicily 1130–54 (b.1095) Son of Count Roger I and Adelaide, he was driven throughout most of his reign to set up a powerful Mediterranean empire, with Sicily as its centre. For some years he was occupied with Norman territories on the mainland. Pope Honorius II, fearing his growing strength, organized a league of cities and barons in rebellion against him. Roger, however, was able to defeat the pope's forces, and was invested as duke of Salerno in 1128.

Honorius' death in 1130 was followed by a schism in the papacy: Roger supported the anti-pope Anacletus II over Innocent II. Anacletus crowned him king of Sicily, Apulia and Calabria at Palermo in 1130, but Anacletus' death in 1138 gave Innocent II greater power, and an alliance was formed between the pope and Emperor Lothar II. Once more, Roger was able to overwhelm his opposition, and Innocent recognized him as king in 1139. He then set out to subdue Naples and Capua. Not content with the mastery of these territories, Roger began to raid Byzantium and founded a short-lived empire in Tunisia.

His contribution to the building of the Sicilian state was very great. In 1140 he introduced a new code of law (the Assizes of Ariano); he also centralized finances and set up agents of the government in all districts of the mainland. His court was noted for its racial and cultural integration. In many ways an exceptional ruler, Roger was also renowned for his patronage of the arts, science and philosophy.

□ E. Curtis *Roger of Sicily* (1912); H. Wieruszowski, 'Roger of Sicily, Rex Tyrannus', *Twelfth-Century Political Thought, Speculum* 38 (1963); J.J. Norwich *The Kingdom of the Sun* (1970)

Roger Loria (*c.*1250–*c.*1305) Born in Loria, south Italy. His mother fostered Constance, queen of Aragon, and this brought him into Aragonese service,

Peter III appointing him grand admiral (1283). His career centred upon the Sicilian conflict following the Vespers (1282), in which he became a key figure. His achievements include defeating the Angevins (Malta, 1283), capturing the future Charles II (Naples, 1284), attacking Jerba (1284) and annihilating the French fleet (Las Formigas, 1285). He continued to serve Peter's son James, accompanied him to Rome to effect a settlement (1297) and was created count of Jerba by the pope. He subsequently opposed Sicilian rebels (Cape Orlando, 1299; Ponza, 1300). The Treaty of Caltabellotta (1302) ended his career and he died in retirement.
□ S. Runciman *The Sicilian Vespers* (1958)

Roger of Salisbury (d. 1139) Formerly a clerk at Avranches, Roger was Henry I's most brilliant administrator. After holding office as chancellor for about a year, he resigned in 1102 on becoming bishop of Salisbury. He introduced a new sophistication into the king's finances and is credited with the organization of the Exchequer. Patronage and family ties strengthened his control of the administration, with his son, Roger le Poer, as chancellor and his nephew Nigel, bishop of Ely, as treasurer. Roger's only recorded official title is *regni Angliae procurator*, for he governed the country in the king's absence. His fall came in 1139 when he was attacked and disgraced on grounds of treachery, and on his death that year his immense wealth was seized by King Stephen.
□ E.J. Kealey *Roger of Salisbury* (1972); J. Green *The Government of England under Henry I* (1986)

Roland Warden of the Breton March. In 778 Charlemagne, who had been campaigning against the Saracens in Spain, was forced by persistent Saxon raids to return to Germany. He left a rearguard under Roland which was attacked and killed by Basques, an incident which provided the kernel of truth for the legends which developed in northern Spain and southern France. Part of this tradition was encapsulated in the epic poem *La Chanson de Roland*, which reflects the feudal values of the period, concentrating on the relationship of master and man, on its demands and its rewards.

Rolle, Richard (1295–1349) A scholar and theologian at Oxford, he retired as a hermit to Hampole near Doncaster, where he wrote mystical works of great power in Latin and English; he also translated the psalms into the vernacular. His work is interpreted as important both for content and form: the content illustrates a strong reaction in the intellectual world against the Scholasticism of the age; the form, good vernacular prose and poetry, foreshadows the

The lover attains his prize: in a 15th-c. text of the **Roman de la Rose**.

triumph of English and its use by Wycliffe and his followers later in the century.
□ D. Knowles *The English Mystical Tradition* (1961)

Rollo (*c*.906–*c*.30) Duke of Normandy. According to Icelandic sagas, the Viking Rolf Gangr, whose name was later Gallicized as Rollo, was of noble Norwegian ancestry. After years of raiding in France, his army was defeated outside Chartres in 911. By an arrangement made at Saint-Clair-sur-Epte, Rollo did homage to Charles the Simple, king of the West Franks, and was baptized in 912. In return, Rollo was granted land of strategic importance on either side of the Seine, corresponding to Upper Normandy and marking the beginning of medieval Normandy.
□ D. Bates *Normandy before 1066* (1982)

Roman de la Rose More than 23,000 lines long, this is regarded as the greatest of the French romances. It was the work of two poets, Guillaume de Lorris (*c*.1240) and, more extensively, Jean de Meung (*c*.1275). Rich in allegory, it brings together the main characteristics of the 12th-c. and 13th-c. renaissance, at least in its vernacular manifestations: ideas of Courtly Love, and yet also of a love that is attainable; reflections on vices and virtues; on idleness, pleasure and delight; on danger, shame and jealousy. It also contains a strong element of social

Typical **Romanesque** grotesques surround a double capital in Burgos cathedral cloister, *c.* 1100.

satire, condemning abuse of power and arguing against clerical celibacy.

The poem proved immensely popular and over 200 manuscripts survive. Chaucer translated it into English, though only a portion of the surviving Middle English version appears to be by his hand. Modern critics have been known to contrast the tone of the two poets, the gentle allegory of Lorris and the satire of Meung, in terms that suggest an analogy with modern English poets, with Spenser on the one side and Pope on the other. [*106*]
□ C.S. Lewis *The Allegory of Love* (1950); *Le Roman de la Rose* ed. C.W. Dunn (1962)

Romanesque Term first used in the early 19th c. to describe a style derived, it was believed, from Roman art. The sources of Romanesque art are, however, not only Roman, but Byzantine, Islamic and even barbarian and Celtic. Its origins are closely linked with the reform of religious life in the 10th c. and 11th c., and it is therefore not surprising that this art was predominantly the result of monastic patronage and, in some cases, monastic workmanship. The copying of liturgical and other texts for worship and reading was certainly carried out in monasteries, though the decoration of books with miniatures gradually passed into professional, secular hands.

Romanesque art was evolved in the 11th c. and blossomed in the 12th c. During this period stylistic similarities exist between book illumination, goldsmithwork, ivory carving and sculpture in wood and stone. This is due to the fact that craftsmen were trained in many media. The celebrated artists' manual *De Diversis Artibus*, written *c.* 1100, demonstrates very clearly the proficiency of contemporary artists in many different fields.

It is natural that there are marked differences between Romanesque art in, for example, Spain and Norway, for each country had a different artistic tradition; yet there was a common element in all

Romanesque art: a love of simplification of forms and of decorative patterns, both of which affected even the human figure. Romanesque art was deeply religious, but it was also frequently imbued with a crude humour and a taste for fantastic and grotesque creatures. It was this aspect, so inventive and lively, which prompted the austere St Bernard of Clairvaux to exclaim when writing about the carved capitals in Romanesque cloisters: '. . . so many and so marvellous are the varieties of divers shapes on every hand, that we are more tempted to read in the marble than in our books'. *See* ARCHITECTURE   GZ
□ J. Beckwith *Early Medieval Art* (1964); G. Zarnecki *Romanesque Art* (1971)

Romans d'aventur Medieval romances form a loose genre, capable of subtle internal distinctions (such as the *roman courtois*, distinguishable by its courtly tone), but most may be termed *romans d'aventur* (chivalric romances), as adventure – the occurrence of unexpected and hazardous events – is a major component.

The romance was predominantly a French and English 12th-c. to 15th-c. genre. 'Romance' originally denoted French vernacular, but its meaning soon encompassed all works in French, and it was gradually applied specifically to tales of noble knights and ladies which arose in France. Romances were initially in verse form, but prose versions (such as the French vernacular Arthurian cycle) also arose. Romances typically consisted of a main plot with episodic amplification, generally concerning the adventures of individual noble men and women acting under the impulse of love, religious faith or mere adventure-lust; they usually ended in a happy union or the achievement of justice (save where the original model was too famous to be altered, as in the *Morte Arthure*). Combat and the 'marvellous' were common, and love played a greater part in French than English works. They were almost totally fictional (although often based on a historical core), but were embroidered with a deal of enhanced local realism (contemporary details concerning banquets, dress, etc.); this combination of the familiar and the imaginative contributed to the genre's popularity. Romance material could derive from any sources, notably classical (*The Lyfe of Alisaunder*), Eastern (*Floris and Blauncheflur*) and European history (*The Lay of Havelok* and *Morte Arthure*).

The romance had some precedent in the epic *chanson* and the *lai*, often sharing their subject matter; but it was distinguished by its breadth of view, accomplished by Chrétien de Troyes, whose *Erec* is considered the first proper romance. Chrétien transformed adventure from mere incident into meaningful human action (as in *Yvain*), which led to a stressing of the interdependence of knightly virtues (as in *Sir Gawain*) and frequently occasioned moral themes. Chrétien's approach was thoroughly absorbed in France and in England, where the greatest early romance was *King Horn*. The genre was still evinced, if not seriously employed, by Chaucer. *See* LITERATURE   MB

□ D. Everett *Essays on Middle English Literature* (1964); E. Vinaver *The Rise of Romance* (1971)

Rome Although it had no intrinsic industrial or commercial importance, Rome remained the principal city of medieval Europe both because of its classical past and because it became the focus of Christianity in the West and the seat of the pope. Political disasters in the 5th c. (the sack of the city by Alaric the Visigoth in 410 and by the Vandals in 455) caused imperial power to shift to Ravenna, but the papacy remained at Rome as a source of power and influence, with the popes drawing on their traditions as successors to St Peter. Pope Leo I (440–61) was instrumental in turning the Huns (under Attila) away from Rome, and the Christian churches became increasingly the centres of social life. The last emperor in the West, Romulus Augustulus, was deposed in 476, but Theodoric the Great ruled Italy firmly and in relative peace from Ravenna for more than 30 years (493–526), nominally in the imperial name. Justinian's policy of Western reconquest led to debilitating Gothic sieges of Rome by his generals (536–52), though subsequent Byzantine military administration led to partial recovery. From 568 the Lombards occupied northern Italy and set up powerful duchies in the south.

Throughout this troubled period – there are records of famine, epidemics and floods – the temporal power of the papacy persisted and developed, reaching a high point in the pontificate of Gregory the Great (590–604). His assertion of the primacy of Rome in all Christendom had immense impact on the future history of the city. Of more immediate moment, however, was his skill as a landlord in central Italy (and in Sicily), which formed the permanent basis for the so-called 'patrimony of St Peter', the future papal states. Missionary activity in England in the 7th c. and in Germany in the 8th c. extended Rome's importance as a pilgrimage centre. There was much church-building and setting up of national compounds such as the Saxon 'school' at Rome.

As ties with Byzantium loosened, reliance for defence came to rest with local militias, and the Lombard threat to papal independence grew greater. For protection the popes looked to the Frankish monarchy under Pepin the Short (753), and then decisively under Charlemagne (773). In return the Frankish rulers assumed the title of *patricius Romanorum*, and on Christmas Day 800, Charlemagne was crowned emperor at Rome by Pope Leo III.

In succeeding centuries emperors and popes both had vital interests in the government of the city. Real power often, however, fell into the hands of local feuding clans and aristocratic families. Alberic, 'senator of Rome', imposed strong government on the patrimony in the mid-10th c., and the revival of the Empire under Otto I (962) restored imperial discipline. For a brief period *c.*1000 Otto III and his pope, Sylvester II, seemed to fulfil the ideal of governing the Empire of the West from Otto's Roman court. After Otto's death in 1002, however, factions again proved dominant, and the succeeding century proved one of the most politically turbulent in the history of Rome, with imposed imperial reform of the papacy in 1046; initial papal defeats at the hands of the new force in Italian politics, the

View of **Rome**: woodcut from Hartmann Schedel's *Liber Chronicorum* (Nuremberg, 1493).

Normans of the south (1053), followed by the Norman alliance (1059); the formulation of proper procedures for election to the papacy (1059); and the traumatic violence of the Investiture Contest between pope and emperor (1075–1122), in the course of which Rome itself was savagely sacked by the Norman papal allies (1084).

The success of Pope Gregory VII (1073–85) and the popes who followed him in asserting papal supremacy had great consequences for the city of Rome. It became an important financial centre; the curial bankers of Pierleoni and Frangipani were Roman and did not concede their mastery of finance until overtaken by Sienese and Florentine houses in the 13th c. An artistic revival took place and can still be enjoyed in, for example, the churches of S. Clemente and Quattro Coronati. Politically the city remained turbulent, with strong papal, imperial and republican factions. Arnold of Brescia attempted to restore the republic in the mid-12th c., but failed in the face of the opposition of Pope Adrian IV, supported by the German ruler, Frederick Barbarossa (crowned Emperor at Rome in 1155). Bitter conflict later in Frederick's reign resulted in the exile of Pope Alexander III from Rome for long periods, though finally the Emperor was forced to make his submission to the pope at Venice in 1177. Within Rome itself, papal absence led to intensified communal feeling; a compromise was reached in 1188 whereby Rome retained the status of a commune, though with full recognition of the overlordship of the papacy, firmly entrenched in the so-called 'leonine city' around St Peter's.

Pope Innocent III (1198–1216), under whom the papal monarchy reached its highest point, built on this position. Expressing themes suitable to his theology of papal primacy, he restored the apse of St Peter's and protected the *confessio* with a golden bronze grille. He created two co-equal papal seats: at St Peter's, and at the Lateran, where he developed an efficient administrative centre. He established Rome as a true *caput mundi*, adorning its churches for the Fourth Lateran Council as a setting for the greatest council of the church since late antiquity.

Papal preoccupation with government and taxation led to periods of reaction in the 13th c.: Brancaleone di Andalo (1252–58) strengthened the commune, and Charles of Anjou exercised a powerful French influence on the city and the papacy, especially in the period 1266–77. At the end of the century Boniface VIII proclaimed 1300 as a holy year and Rome benefited mightily in revived finance and improved prestige from the mass pilgrimages which followed. Boniface's pontificate, however, ended in disaster at the hands of the French king, and in 1308 the papacy moved to Avignon. Rome suffered severely from the feuding of aristocratic families (the Colonna and the Orsini). Cola di Rienzo attempted to restore republican virtue to the city but was overthrown and killed in 1354. Papal rule was effectively restored by Cardinal Albornoz, and Gregory XI returned to Rome in 1378.

There followed a deeply divisive period known as the Great Schism, which was not brought to an end until 1417, when Martin V, of the Colonna family, was elected pope at the Council of Constance. Rome had fallen far behind the other great Italian cities, Florence, Venice and Milan, as a result of its troubled 14th-c. history, but the 15th c. saw some advance, initially under Martin and then increasingly with Nicholas V (1447–55). Even so, Rome at the end of the Middle Ages, for all its prestige and renown, presented an unedifying spectacle; its institutions were undeveloped in comparison with other Italian cities, and it was ruled by one of the most unscrupulous popes, in the person of the Borgia, Pope Alexander VI. *See* PAPAL STATES   HRL

□ F. Gregorovius *History of Rome in the Middle Ages* (1909); D.P. Waley *The Papal State in the Thirteenth Century* (1961); P. Llewellyn *Rome in the Dark Ages* (1971); P. Partner *The Lands of St Peter* (1972); R. Brentano *Rome before Avignon* (1974); R. Krautheimer *Rome: Profile of a city 312–1308* (1980)

Romulus Augustulus Roman emperor 475–76 Known as the last of the Western Roman emperors, Romulus was raised to the throne at Ravenna by his father Orestes, after deposing Julius Nepos. Orestes ruled on behalf of his son, who was still a minor (hence 'Augustulus', the diminutive of Augustus). In August 476 Orestes was killed by his troops who proclaimed their general, Odoacer, as king. Romulus was spared and sent to live in Campania. The year 476 conventionally marks the end of the Western Roman empire.
□ C. Wickham *Early Medieval Italy 400–1000* (1981)

Rory O'Conor High king of Connaught 1156–98 (b.1116) Son of Turlough O'Conor, he succeeded his father as king of Connaught and head of the Sil Muireadhaigh tribe. In 1166 he was recognized at Dublin as king of all Ireland, showed active support for the reforming efforts of the primate archbishop of Armagh and summoned a great public judicial assembly for the whole of Ireland at Telltown (1168). Norman political intervention proved disastrous, and though he won occasional success against the Normans and even resisted Henry II himself, the 1180s were a period of continual strife and decline in Rory's prestige, power and health. In 1191 he retired to the abbey of Cong, where he died.
□ F. Byre *Irish Kings and High Kings* (1973)

Roscelin (*c.* 1050–*c.* 1122) Philosopher and theologian. Born in Compiègne where he became a canon after studying at Soissons and Rheims, he is considered a principal nominalist, participating in the nominalist/realist controversy over universals (the relation of genera and species to individuals). His ideas survive in references by Abelard and Anselm, his only extant work being a letter to Abelard concerning the Trinity. He is said to have described universals as sounds (*flatus vocis*), signifying merely words, and only the individual as real. Application of his theories to the Trinity involved tritheism, for which he was condemned (Council of Soissons, 1092). He recanted and went to England, which he left after attacking Anselm's doctrines. He was reconciled with the church in Rome and returned to France, teaching at Tours and Loches, where Abelard was his pupil. He died a canon of Besançon.
□ F. Picavet *Roscelin, Philosophe et Théologien* (1896); G. Leff *Medieval Thought* (1958)

Rudolf I of Habsburg Holy Roman Emperor 1273–91 (b. 1218) Chiefly remembered as the founder of Habsburg greatness, he succeeded his father Albert IV, count of Habsburg, as *paterfamilias* in 1239 and gradually achieved supremacy amongst the German princes, culminating in his election as king of the Germans. His reign terminated the Interregnum and helped to restore peace to the Empire. At the Diet of Nuremberg (1274) he initiated a 'revindication' policy, by which all properties and rights controlled by the Empire under Frederick II were to be recovered. This led to conflict with Ottokar II of Bohemia, who was killed at the battle of Marchfeld (1278). Rudolf I invested his sons, Albert and Rudolf, with Ottokar's duchies of Austria and Styria (1282), establishing a Habsburg inheritance in southern Germany.

As king of the Romans, Rudolf was supported by Pope Gregory X, who planned a crusade once Rudolf had revived the Empire. Owing to changing Italian politics, however, Rudolf was not crowned Emperor and was faced with increasing French expansion. By 1291 he had strengthened the Empire as much as possible, and although Adolf of Nassau was elected his successor, Rudolf's son Albert I regained the throne in 1298.
□ E. Kleinschmidt *Herrscherdarstellung* (1974); J. Leuschner *Germany in the late Middle Ages* (1980)

Rudolf of Rheinfelden (d. 1080) Appointed to the duchy of Swabia during the minority of Henry IV, Rudolf – initially a firm supporter of the young king in his Saxon campaigns – became one of the chief figures among the magnates who in 1076 threatened withdrawal of allegiance unless the king received

Bronze effigy of **Rudolf of Rheinfelden**, anti-king of the Germans, in Merseburg cathedral.

absolution from his excommunication by Pope Gregory VII. In spite of Henry's absolution gained at Canossa (January 1077), Rudolf was elected king at Forchheim in March 1077, although it was not until the Lenten synod of 1080 that the pope finally recognized the election, prophesying publicly that Henry would be dead or deposed by the end of June. In fact, by one of the ironies of history, it was Rudolf who was killed in the October of that year.
□ G. Barraclough *Medieval Germany* (1938)

Rupert of Wittelsbach King of Germany 1400–10 (b.1352) He succeeded his father Rupert II as elector palatine in 1398. In August 1400 an assembly of princes and estates deposed King Wenceslas. Rupert was elected his successor as German king and crowned at Cologne (1401). Wenceslas did not acknowledge the deposition and until his death (1419) considered himself king of Bohemia and Germany. Rupert was unable to solve the problems he inherited. His Italian campaign, in spite of Florentine assistance, did not succeed in securing the imperial crown for Rupert. He was defeated outside Brescia and retired to Germany (1402). He did nothing to end the papal schism and failed to build up power in the north. The remainder of his reign was occupied with internal opposition. The League of Marbach (Baden, Württemberg and the Swabian towns under Archbishop John of Mainz) was formed against him in 1405 with the purpose of healing the schism; Rupert found himself isolated, and was eventually succeeded by Sigismund of Hungary (1411).

Rupert's principal achievement was his contribution to a royal administration, emerging as a specialized bureaucracy serving monarchy rather than prince. Outstanding advisers (such as Job Vener) and the allegiance of Heidelberg university contributed to the rise of a professional elite.
□ F.R.H. du Boulay *Germany in the Later Middle Ages* (1983)

Rurik Leader of the Scandinavians, mostly Swedes, known as the Rus, who established a loose lordship over the trading townships of the Russian waterways c.862. His principal settlement was at Novgorod on Lake Ladoga. Legends attributed to him and his kinsfolk portray him as the founder of historic Russia.

Russia The origins of the Russians or East Slavs are obscure. Before the arrival of the Scandinavian Varangians in the 9th c., they had spread throughout the Soviet Union, their political organization probably centring around fortified trading towns (Novgorod, Smolensk, Kiev). The Varangian conquerors became Slavicized, their Rurikovitch dynasty founding the first Russian state around Kiev. During the 9th c. the word 'Russian' (Rus, Ros) appeared, coming to denote the East Slavs as a whole. The state of Kiev expanded during the 10th c., and vital links with Byzantium were established through trade. Roman and Byzantine Christianity was known in 9th-c. Kiev, but the Byzantine tradition was officially adopted by Vladimir I (980–1015). Orthodoxy persisted throughout Russia, with Moscow replacing Constantinople as the centre of orthodoxy after 1453. Kiev reached its zenith in the mid-11th c., but during the 12th c. it was exposed to invasions by Asiatics of the Steppe (Pechenegs, Polovtsians and Mongols).

Meanwhile, a principality had emerged in the northern colonies around Suzdal, Rostov, Vladimir and Moscow. Andrei Bogoliubsky (1157–74), prince of Suzdal, sacked the enfeebled Kiev. It seemed that the commercial centre of Novgorod might succeed Kiev, Alexander Nevsky (1246–63) preserving its independence against Germans and Swedes, but a superior geographical position and military force ensured the supremacy of the principality of Vladimir-Suzdal.

During the early 13th c. south-west Russia was overrun by the Mongols, and the grand princes of Vladimir subjected to the Golden Horde; but this seems to have provided conditions beneficial to the growth of the state. Russia was now separated from the West, and the three East Slav branches were defined: Byelorussians, under Lithuanian rule; Great Russians (Novgorod and Vladimir-Suzdal), under the Golden Horde; Little Russians (Ukrainians), in the south, between the Lithuanians and Mongols.

Moscow, under the Usevolod dynasty, emerged as capital of the new Vladimir-Suzdal state, from which Ivan I Kalita (d.1341) and subsequent grand princes implemented a policy of centralization. Dmitri Donskoi (1359–89) initiated resistance to the Mongols, defeating them at Kulikovo (1380). By the end of the 15th c. the unification of central Russia under the grand prince of Moscow was complete, largely due to Ivan III the Great (1462–1505), assisted by a new aristocracy of small landowners attached to central authority, which he imposed upon the old nobility (*boyars*). The administrative and judicial code (*Sudebnik*) of 1497 attests the level of centralization achieved.

Following the decline of Kiev, the focus of Russian civilization shifted to the towns of the north-west. Byzantine artistic influence fused with indigenous tradition, Novgorod producing a typically Russian architecture. During the late 14th c. Moscow witnessed a flowering of art and literature, and experienced Italian Renaissance influence during the 15th c. Of particular note were the icon painters Theophanes the Greek, Rublev and Denis. *See* CYRIL, ST; YAROSLAV   MB

☐ G. Vernadsky *The Origins of Russia* (1959); N.V. Riasonovsky *A History of Russia* (1963); R. Portal *The Slavs* (1969); D. MacKenzie and M.W. Curran *A History of Russia and the Soviet Union* (1982); J. Fennell *The Crisis of Medieval Russia 1200–1304* (1983); R.O. Crummey *The Formation of Muscovy 1304–1613* (1987); N.S. Kollmann *Kingship and Politics: the making of the Muscovite political system 1345–1547* (1987)

Ruysbroeck, Jan van (1293–1381) One of the great mystical writers of the Middle Ages, he was born in Ruysbroeck, near Brussels, and became a priest. In 1343 he founded a small Augustinian community at Groenendael. His writings, entirely in Flemish, were extremely influential, and his criticism of abuse in the church foreshadowed the *devotio moderna*. Indeed, Gerhard Groote, founder of the Brethren of the Common Life, was one of Ruysbroeck's disciples.

☐ R. Kieckhefer *Unquiet Souls: Fourteenth-Century Souls and their Religious Milieu* (1984)

S

Sagas, Norse Some of the greatest vernacular literature of the Middle Ages was produced in Scandinavia in the 12th c. and 13th c., notably in Iceland. The name given to these writings, *saga* ('things said, a story or history'), reveals the oral base from which the literature grew. Social traditions of the North in the Viking Age and later, encouraged the storyteller to express himself in straight narrative or verse. Saga literature is divided into two main groups, the historical sagas and the family sagas. The historical group deals with the period of Scandinavian expansion (*c*.800–1050), with the settlement of Iceland and the ventures to Greenland and Vinland; it also deals with the succeeding centuries in the form of biographical accounts of the kings and (after the reception of Christianity throughout the North in the course of the 11th c.) of the bishops. The outstanding writers were Ari the Learned (Thorgilsson) who died in 1148, and Snorri Sturluson (d.1241), whose Prose Edda and *Heimskringla* represent the highest point of literary achievement in Old Norse. The family sagas reached their finest expression in the work of Snorri's nephew Sturla Thordsson (d.1284) and contemporary compilers. Most of the great sagas are available in reliable modern transla-

Islamic bronze coin of the sultan **Saladin**.

tions, including *Njálssaga*, *Laxdaelasaga*, *Egilssaga*, sagas dealing with the Orkneys and the Faroes, and the Saga of Eric the Red, which is concerned with the settlement of Greenland and with expeditions to Vinland on the American coast. *See* EDDA, THE ELDER AND THE YOUNGER

☐ J. Brönsted *The Vikings* (1965); C. Clover *The Medieval Saga* (1982)

St Andrews, university of Founded in 1410, it was the third university to be founded in Britain and the first in Scotland. A group of teachers and scholars who had been driven from France during the Great Schism came to St Andrews; best known of these was Laurence of Lindores whose lectures on Aristotle were influential in Europe. In February 1411 (or possibly 1412) the group was granted a charter by Bishop Wardlaw of St Andrews, while full university status was conferred in 1413 by Pope Benedict XIII.

Saladin (Salāh ad-Dīn) Sultan of Egypt and Syria 1175–93 (b.1138) He shared in the campaigns of his uncle Shirkuh in Egypt 1164–68, and on the latter's death in 1169 assumed control of Cairo. Conscious of Egypt's attraction to the Franks, Saladin concentrated on the economic and military build-up of the country. Between 1174 and 1186 he succeeded in bringing many important Syrian cities under his control, thereby enabling him to present a united Muslim front to the Franks. After a violation of the peace by the Franks in 1187, Saladin engaged their army at Hattin and won; he then overran Palestine and conquered Jerusalem. The princes of Europe were roused by these losses and set out on the Third Crusade, directing all their power against Acre. The siege of Acre lasted two years (1189–91), with the crusaders finally emerging as victors. Richard defeated the forces of Saladin at Arsuf (1191), but

Saladin (Salāh ad-Dīn)

was unable to recover Jerusalem, and in 1192 made peace with Saladin. A year later the Muslim leader died at Damascus.

□ M.C. Lyons and D.E.P. Jackson *Saladin: The Politics of the Holy Wars* (1982); P.H. Newby *Saladin in his time* (1983)

Saladin tithe Levied in both England and France to raise money for the Third Crusade, the 'Saladin tithe' (1188) was a tax of ten per cent of each man's revenues and moveable property. Despite general enthusiasm for the Crusade, the tax provoked bitter resentment, for many feared it would set a precedent for a new form of taxation. The collection in England by Henry II's agents went ahead, but in France Philip Augustus was forced to suspend the tax and even apologize for having proposed it.

Salerno, university of The *Studium* or School of Salerno was one of the first universities in Europe. For a long time devoted exclusively to the study of medicine, the School was already famous by the 10th c., but its fame grew, especially in the 11th c. when the celebrated physician Constantinus Africanus became a teacher there. Some of the most reasonable medical texts of the Middle Ages, derived largely from ancient, Arabic and Jewish authors, were produced at Salerno.

□ J. Décarreaux *Lombards, Moines et Normands en Italie Méridionale* (1974)

Samo (d.639) Frankish merchant who created a powerful, if transient political unit from the Slavonic tribes based on Moravia, but extending deep into territories along the Elbe. He was defeated and killed by an army drawn from the Franks and Thuringians. He is important for the tradition he established among the Moravians of a rudimentary political organization and also of regular trading contacts, notably in slaves, with the Western world.

□ J.M. Wallace-Hadrill *The Barbarian West* (1965)

Samuel Tsar of the Bulgarians (c.980–1014) After the death of Tsar Simeon in 927, the Bulgarian empire fell into decline, and much of the country passed under Byzantine rule. Samuel, son of Shishman, assumed the title of 'tsar' and, rising to power in Macedonia, soon overran Serbia and northern Bulgaria. Much of his reign was spent in conflict with Emperor Basil II. At first the emperor's troops were routed, but in 1014 he won a decisive victory. Basil then inflicted a terrible punishment on the prisoners: about 15,000 men were blinded and sent to Samuel, led by one man in each 100 who was left with one eye to guide his companions home. Samuel is said to have fallen down dead in an apoplectic fit at the sight. The state created by him broke down in 1018, and Bulgaria remained subject to Byzantium until 1185.

□ S. Runciman *A History of the First Bulgarian Empire* (1930)

San Germano, Treaty of (1230) This agreement signalled a temporary halt in hostilities between Pope Gregory IX and Frederick II. According to the terms of the Treaty, Frederick agreed to respect papal territories, and to allow freedom of election and other privileges to the Sicilian clergy; in return, the ban of excommunication was lifted. This vital act of reconciliation with the papacy gave Frederick freedom of action in the future organization of his Empire.

San Giorgio, Bank of The tremendous growth of mercantile activity in Genoa during the late Middle Ages led to the development of complex commercial and financial procedures. In 1407 the Casa di San Giorgio, a group of the state's creditors, joined together to form a municipal bank in Genoa. Certain features of the modern joint-stock company can be seen in this organization. It was dissolved in 1444, but later revived as the Bank of San Giorgio (1586).

Sancho III the Great King of Navarre 1000–35 (b. c.992) Son of King García II Sánchez, he succeeded to the throne at about the age of eight. He had the good fortune to begin his effective reign just as the long-dominant caliphate of Cordoba was disintegrating, having weakened the Christian states of the north; and he had the intelligence and will to fill the political vacuum. Establishing claims to Castile by marrying Munia, daughter of the count of Castile, he secured the border territory of La Rioja in 1016, and in the next three years turned east, incorporating the counties of Sobrarbe and Ribagorza. These provided a base, and internal dissensions the opportunity, for Sancho to intervene in Catalan politics; simultaneously, in the early 1020s, his suzerainty was recognized in Gascony, and he intervened increasingly in Castilian politics. When the young count of Castile, Sancho's brother-in-law, was assassinated in 1029 Sancho occupied the country in his wife's name, and went on to wage successful war against Leon, taking the capital in 1034 and coining money with the title of emperor.

Sancho's concentration of effort on the establishment of Navarrese hegemony in the north, at the expense of pursuing the Reconquest against a rapidly weakening Cordoba, matched his ideological and cultural attitudes: he introduced the Cluniac reform into some major monasteries, encouraged the Santiago pilgrimage and adopted French feudal

Knight of the **Order of Santiago**, from the Book of the Order at Burgos (14th c.).

ideas. It is with good reason that a Spanish historian called him Spain's first Europeanizer. Yet this ideological basis of Sancho's political success proved in the end a fatal weakness; seeing greater Navarre as his feudal patrimony, he left an expanded Navarre to one son, Castile to another, Sobrarbe and Ribagorza to a third, the county – now to become a kingdom – of Aragon to a fourth, while Leon reasserted its independence. The unity of Christian Spain, a revival of the old Visigothic ideal, was Sancho's personal creation and died with him.
□ J. Pérez de Urbel *Sancho el Mayor de Navarra* (1950)

Santiago de Compostela One of the great pilgrimage centres of the Middle Ages. The church of St James in Compostela in the far north-west of Spain was venerated from the 10th c. as the reputed burial place of James, the human brother of Christ. The routes to Compostela, bound together in the 11th c. and 12th c. by a network of hospices and religious houses, became instrumental in the dissemination of ideas, cultural, religious and architectural, throughout Christian Europe in the age of the Crusades and of the Reconquest of Spain from the Muslims. A military order, the Knights of Santiago, was founded in 1170 and played a prominent part in the wars against Islam in the west of the Iberian peninsula. St James came to be recognized as the patron saint of Spain.
□ G. Hamilton *The Routes to Compostela* (1961); J. Sumption *Pilgrimage: an image of medieval religion* (1975)

Santiago, Order of the Knights of The Order was founded in 1170, not only to fight the Almohad invaders, but also to protect and care for the pilgrims to Santiago de Compostela. Its combination of military and hospitaller functions set it apart from the other military orders of the peninsula, and it did not follow the Rule and customs of Calatrava, whose primacy it disputed. Soon after its foundation, the Order obtained a permanent seat at Uclés, and as the years passed it acquired extensive lands. Its later development was similar to that of Calatrava and it was annexed to the crown in 1493. *[23]*
□ D.W. Lomax, 'The Order of Santiago and the Kings of Leon', *Hispania* (Madrid) 18 (1958)

Saracens Term coined by classical authors of the 1st c.–3rd c. to describe an Arab tribe located in the Sinai. The name gradually came to denote the Arabs in general among the Christians, and after the rise of Islam, the Muslims. Between the 11th c. and 13th c., the term was used by the Latin crusaders to describe the Muslim peoples ranged against them. During the 9th c. the Saracens ravaged Sicily and southern Italy, and eventually gained a foothold in Sicily. They also invaded and settled parts of Spain, where they established a brilliant level of civilization.

Saxons Name given in classical times to Germans dwelling in the north-west of modern Germany, from the North Sea coastal plain to the Weser and Holstein. In the 5th c. and 6th c. migration took them to Gaul, where evidence of settlement persists in place-names around Boulogne and in Normandy, and also in large numbers to England. Bede placed them among the three powerful nations of the Germans to settle in England – Saxons, Angles and Jutes. The Saxons left on the Continent (the Old Saxons, to distinguish them from the Anglo-Saxons) continued in strong pagan independence to the time of Charlemagne. After the Frankish conquest (773–803) and forced conversion to Christianity, however, they came to form the heartland of the new Ottonian empire in the 10th c., with the Saxon duchy stretching from the Ems in the west to the Elbe in the east, and including the main territorial constituents of Westphalia, Eastphalia, Engern and Holstein.
□ L. Musset *The Germanic Invasions* (1975); K.J. Leyser *Rule and Conflict in an Early Medieval Society* (1979)

Scholasticism Term first used derisively in the 16th c. with reference to the system of philosophy practised in the medieval Schools and universities. The Scholastics sought to give theoretical substantiation to the truth of Christian doctrine, as well as to reconcile contradictory viewpoints in Christian theology, and to this end they developed an extremely sophisticated method of investigating philosophical and theoretical questions. In the early history of Scholasticism, much theological material was organized in a systematic fashion. By the 12th c., the Scholastics were collecting Sentences, which were quotations or summaries of dogma compiled from the bible and patristic literature; in interpreting them (*expositio*, *catena*, *lectio*), they gradually adopted a systematic discussion of texts and problems (*quaestio, disputatio*). This eventually gave rise to a system that attempted to provide a comprehensive view of the 'whole of attainable truth' (*summa*), a development which coincided with a clear progression toward intellectual autonomy, with thinkers such as Albertus Magnus and Thomas Aquinas.

Writings on logic had an important effect on Scholasticism; by 1200 the 'new logic' of Aristotle, based on translations of his *Analytics*, *Topics*, and *Sophistical Refutations*, had produced a 'scientific' theology in contrast to the scriptural studies of the 12th c. Aquinas, for example, believed that reason alone was necessary to understand basic truths about God and the soul, although divine revelation would expand such knowledge. The emphasis on reason was rejected to some extent in the 14th c. by men such as William of Ockham and John Duns Scotus. □ J. Pieper *Scholasticism* (1961); A. Piltz *The World of Medieval Learning* (1981)

Science In the sense that science involves the search for truth in all branches of knowledge, the Middle Ages in Europe is often held to be a relatively barren period in human history; but close examination of the main branches of human knowledge leads to a considerable modification of such a view. It is true that theology was regarded as the queen of sciences and, as such, could and did have serious impact on the free exercise of the intellect. Irrational superstition, deep-seated beliefs in magic, heathen animism thinly disguised by a Christian coating, also served to inhibit scientific investigation into natural phenomena.

Nevertheless, transmission of classical knowledge by scholars such as Boethius and Bede in the early Middle Ages, and the labours of 12th-c. and 13th-c. scholars drawing on Arabic sources, brought significant clarification and advance. From the Arabs were transmitted use of the abacus, mathematical knowledge and developments in algebra, and by the later Middle Ages Arab numerals were in common use in the West, especially in Italy among the more advanced trading communities. Gerbert of Aurillac (Pope Sylvester II, 996–1003) was a precociously outstanding mathematician, while Roger Bacon in

Richard of Wallingford, abbot of St Albans, at work with **scientific** instruments (14th c.).

England (1214–92) and Leonardo of Pisa (Fibonacci, d.*c.*1240) made significant original contributions. Astronomy was studied in depth, though with the inevitable distortions due to reliance on Ptolemy and the close relationship established with astrology. The experimental basis of alchemy, although corrupted by the search for the 'elixir of life' and the Philosopher's Stone, served to lay the foundations of chemistry. Folk remedies and interest in the healing properties of plants resulted in an accumulation of knowledge more effective in practice, perhaps, than in the fearsome form they often assumed when committed to writing. Nicolas of Oresme, bishop of Lisieux (d.1382), anticipated later discoveries in physics and the laws of planetary motion, including the proposition that the earth revolved on its axis.

In the practical scientific fields of architecture, the building of castles, cathedrals, churches and ships, the Middle Ages has an enviable record. In many practical matters associated with a predominantly agrarian society, positive and permanent advance was made: the harnessing of plough-beasts, maintenance of soil fertility, drainage, the development of efficient milling techniques. Windmills were introduced into Europe from the Muslim world in the course of the 12th c. A better grasp of mechanical techniques accumulated in the later Middle Ages, and advances were made in optics, the construction of clocks, and the elaboration of devices for the more efficient coining of money.

It is the absence of confidence in what the modern world came to recognize as scientific method that left the Middle Ages with its poor reputation; in practice, however, much slow but permanent progress was made in the understanding of natural phenomena and the use of natural resources. *See* GERARD OF CREMONA; MEDICINE [*45, 95*]

□ L. Thorndike *A History of Magic and Experimental Science* (1923–58); C.H. Haskins *Studies in the History of Medieval Science* (1926); J. Gimpel *The Medieval Machine* (1977); D.C. Lindberg *Science in the Middle Ages* (1978)

Scone, Stone of The Stone of Scone, or Stone of Destiny, was brought to Scone by Kenneth MacAlpin, who took possession of the Pictish throne in 843. He placed a royal stone of his race in the church built on the hill of Scone; for the next 500 years each new king of Scotland came here 'to be raised on the stone'. The stone was an important part of medieval Scottish coronation rites until 1296, when it was either hidden to prevent it from falling into the hands of Edward I, or, according to legend, brought to Westminster.

Scotland There were four distinct cultural groups in Scotland in the early Middle Ages – Irish, Picts, Britons and Angles – and a fifth, Scandinavians, from the late 8th c. onwards. Each group had its own distinctive language. The Irish (known as 'Scots') inhabited the western coastlands, initially sustaining close connections with northern Ireland. During the 6th c. kings of the mainland Irish Dál Riata established themselves in Argyll, founding a dynasty which was to last for centuries. In eastern Scotland, north of the Forth, and in the far north, were the Picts, the strongest group in the pre-Viking period. South of the Forth/Clyde line and in the Clyde area, there were British peoples and kingdoms, while English rulers had established a foothold on the east coast by the mid-6th c. The relationships between these peoples fluctuated, but in the long run the English were confined to Northumbria; Irish influence expanded, Pictish identity was submerged and the Britons ultimately lost political independence.

During the 7th c. both English and Irish kings raided over a wide area, with the English winning much control in Pictland. However, they were defeated at Dunnichen in 685, and although effectively expelled thereafter from present-day Scotland, they maintained contacts in religious affairs, with Pictish kings, like Nechtan (706–24), seeking advice from the English clergy at the expense of Irish clerics based in the west.

During the 8th c. Irish and Pictish royal families intermarried, resulting in heirs who had claims to both Pictish and Irish kingships; kings like Constantine and his brother Oengus II in the early 9th c. therefore held both kingdoms. In the meantime, Viking settlement was changing the character of the north and of the Northern and Western Isles, and Viking control of the seas was confining the interests of the Irish of Scotland to Scotland. Soon an Irish king, Kenneth MacAlpin, took both kingships again (843).

The union of Pictland and the Irish kingdom did not break thereafter and a patrilineal succession was established. The monarchy of Scotland had emerged, drawing on the traditions and institutions of both peoples. The British kingdoms to the south-west were effectively absorbed into the newly established kingdom of Scotland in the late 9th c., although kings of Strathclyde continued to be named until 1034. After 954 and the conquest of the Viking kingdom of York, the earldom of Northumbria became an integral part of the English kingdom, although its northern border remained indeterminate. Lothian passed firmly under Scottish control after *c.*1018.

The impact of the Norman Conquest of England on Scottish affairs proved deep and permanent. Anglo-Norman expeditions harassed Lothian, and demands for fealty from the Scottish kings were made, sometimes successfully. King Malcolm Canmore (1057–93) married Margaret, the sister of Edgar Atheling and representative of the West Saxon dynasty. Her sons ruled Scotland 1097–1153 and were followed by a succession of powerful kings (Malcolm IV, 1153–65; William the Lion, 1165–1214; Alexander II, 1214–49; and Alexander III, 1249–86). They moulded the Scottish kingdom into a true feudal monarchy. Their contacts with the Anglo-Norman feudal world were strong, both as magnates within England (the great Honour of Huntingdon) and as recruiters of able men, sometimes younger sons, willing to help the Scottish kings in return for fat fiefs north of the border; the Stewarts were the greatest of the families to rise to prominence in this way but others such as the Bruce, Balliol, Morville and Mowat families also flourished.

Claims to overlordship on the part of the English kings persisted, though from 1189 the Scottish rulers themselves regarded their homage as directed solely to their English lands and not related to the kingdom of Scotland. Within Scotland the dynasty achieved considerable success in consolidating its territories; the Western Isles were brought under its political control after the defeat of the Norwegian king at the battle of Largs (1263).

Relations with England reached a crisis point in

1290 with the disputed succession that followed the death of Queen Margaret, the Maid of Norway, last of the direct line of Malcolm Canmore. There were many claimants, and power of adjudication came to rest with King Edward I, the English king. He chose Balliol (1292–96), but the issue now became one of straight independence for Scotland, as Edward (with his Welsh successes in mind) attempted to make a reality of his overlordship. The weakness and failure of Balliol, the revolts of William Wallace, and the emergence of Robert Bruce (grandson of one of the most prominent claimants of 1290) defeated Edward's schemes and he died, a disappointed man, in 1307. The great victory at Bannockburn on 24 June 1314, in which Bruce routed the forces of Edward II, confirmed Scottish independence. English attacks were renewed after Bruce's death in 1329, but the whole question of Anglo-Scottish relations became entangled with the Hundred Years' War and the growth of the 'Auld Alliance' of Scotland and France against England.

In 1371 Robert II, grandson of Robert I through his daughter Marjory, succeeded to the Scottish throne as the first royal representative of the house of Stewart. In spite of great personal and dynastic troubles, the Stewarts maintained their hold on the throne, and a general increase in prosperity, coupled with French success in the war with England, made the later part of the 15th c. something of a golden age in Scottish history, particularly in the reign of James IV (1488–1513). Universities were founded, at St Andrews by 1414, Glasgow in 1451, and at Aberdeen in 1495. Literary life flourished (Henryson c.1430–1506; Dunbar c.1460–c.1520). Not even the military disaster at Flodden in 1513 could conceal the permanent advance made towards Scottish nationhood in the later centuries of the Middle Ages. *See* CELTIC CHURCHES; PICTS

□ G.W.S. Barrow *The Kingdom of the Scots* (1973); R. Nicholson *Scotland: The Later Middle Ages* (1974); A.A.M. Duncan *Scotland, The Making of the Kingdom* (1975)

Sculpture The exteriors of early Christian churches are plain, and this may give the false impression that sculpture played no part in Christian art at that time. This is not true, however, for even if church decoration was confined to the capitals of the interior (and these were frequently *spolia* from pagan temples), the carved sarcophagus was still much in use. Little figural sculpture survives in Byzantium from the early centuries because of its destruction during the Iconoclastic controversy (726–843). The conversion of churches into mosques after the fall of Byzantium (1453) inflicted further great losses, and so knowledge of Byzantine sculpture is confined to decorative,

non-religious carvings, predominantly capitals, friezes and panels.

In the West the sculpture of the pre-Carolingian period had undergone dramatic changes since Roman times. It had become increasingly two-dimensional, tending towards flat relief carving. As there was nobody in his empire who could undertake such works, Charlemagne used Roman capitals from Italy in his palace chapel at Aix-la-Chapelle, and brought an equestrian statue of Theodoric from Ravenna, setting it up as a monument to himself in the palace courtyard. Much of contemporary sculpture was in stucco, a technique widely used by the Romans. Documents mention narrative reliefs at Centula (Saint-Riquier), and fragments of stucco decoration survive at Germigny-des-Prés. At Cividale in northern Italy an impressive group of life-size female saints in stucco survives (early 9th c.) and testifies to the high quality of this type of sculpture during the Carolingian revival. The 9th-c. sculptures in Spain and, above all, in Britain (Ruthwell and Bewcastle crosses, Breedon-on-the-Hill frieze) can, in part, be linked to the Carolingian revival.

The pagan Vikings, who contributed so savagely to the fall of the Carolingian empire and its lively art, were themselves patrons of sophisticated wooden sculptures which employed intricate animal motifs to decorate ceremonial objects, such as those found in the Oseberg ship burial, for instance. With the Viking settlements in the British Isles, this type of art was transmitted to England and Ireland, and became one of the sources for the Christian art of the Scandinavian countries.

Ottonian sculptors produced some outstanding cult images (the Essen Madonna and the Gero cross in Cologne, both late 10th c.) which combine a naturalism inherited from classical art with a geometric stylization of forms, leading directly to the birth of the Romanesque. This style was closely linked to architecture and served to enrich it, with sculpture applied to selected features, first to capitals, then to doorways, corbels, friezes and, occasionally, to whole façades. The Romanesque sculpture of Italy and France was in the forefront of this development, with Spain, Germany and England soon following their lead. By the 12th c., the whole of Europe which recognized papal authority employed Romanesque art forms, which in isolated cases even penetrated Orthodox countries such as Serbia and Russia. Needless to say, Romanesque sculpture flourished in the Crusading kingdom.

Although some Romanesque carved capitals are masterpieces (e.g., at Cluny, Silos, Moissac, Hyde Abbey, Winchester), the glory of Romanesque sculpture is to be found in the gigantic tympana of Moissac, Autun and Vézelay and the frieze of

A cast of the magnificent Romanesque tympanum at Moissac, in which Christ is shown seated
surrounded by the twenty-four Elders and the symbols of the Evangelists.

Stone column-figures of the Prophets from the north portal of Chartres cathedral (13th c.).

Wiligelmo on the façade of Modena cathedral. During this period of great artistic activity, inspired by genuine piety, many works of outstanding quality were created and it is possible to distinguish numerous regional schools of sculpture (e.g., in Burgundy, Aquitaine, Normandy, Lombardy, Tuscany, Apulia, Herefordshire, Yorkshire and Kent).

Romanesque sculpture favoured abstract forms, and human figures were used in a totally arbitrary fashion; their size, for instance, often depended on their importance, Christ being larger than the Apostles. It was the art of a naïve faith and was dominated by the fear of damnation, depicted so vividly on many tympana.

While Romanesque architecture was superseded by the Gothic at Saint-Denis, in sculpture there was a period of some 50 years (c.1170–c.1220) when the style became more naturalistic. This was largely due to the influence of Mosan art. The great portals of Senlis, Laon, Chartres and Rheims cathedrals are the best examples of this new style, sometimes called Transitional.

Gothic sculpture emerged from this Transitional style in the first quarter of the 13th c., and the workshop responsible for the sculpture of the façade of Notre-Dame cathedral in Paris was the first to replace the gentle naturalism of the Transitional style and its gracefully flowing draperies, with more expressive faces, gestures and draperies. The statues of the Sainte-Chapelle (1243–48) are embodiments of the new style which, through the medium of ivories mass-produced in Paris at that time, was soon transmitted to the whole of Europe.

The column-figure, that is to say a statue bound to a column – a characteristic feature of early Gothic portals in France starting with Saint-Denis, which inspired subsequent similar works – gradually lost its influence, and by the late 13th c., the figure became detached from the column and eventually became free-standing. The portal of the great Dutch sculptor Claus Sluter in the Chartreuse de Champmol (1390s), the mausoleum of Philip the Bold, duke of Burgundy, is a landmark in this trend, for the dramatic figures, some kneeling, some standing, are like actors on a stage and are independent of their architectural setting.

The 14th c. witnessed the birth of portraiture in tomb sculpture. Until then effigies were, as a rule, idealized images, bearing no relation to the true physical appearance of the deceased. Taking death masks in wax or plaster led to a more faithful portrayal of the face on effigies.

During the 15th c., the Low Countries and Germany produced a number of outstanding masters, working in stone, wood and bronze: Hans Multscher, Nikolaus Gerhaert, Michael Pacher, Tilman Riemenschneider and Veit Stoss, to name a few.

As in Gothic architecture, so in sculpture the Italian contribution was very independent, and it is therefore more appropriate to consider it in relation to the birth of Renaissance art than to Gothic. *See* GOTHIC; PAINTING AND THE MINOR ARTS; PISANO, NICOLA; ROMANESQUE [286]   GZ
□ R. Salvini *Medieval Sculpture* (1969); W. Saurländer *Gothic Sculpture in France 1140-1270* (1972); L. Stone *Sculpture in Britain: the Middle Ages* (1972)

Segarelli, Gerard (d.1300) Leader of the heretical sect, the 'False Apostles' (*pseudo-apostolici*). A native of Parma, Segarelli felt drawn to a life of exemplary purity. He sold all his possessions (c.1260) and began to preach penance and Apostolic poverty. He soon attracted a large following. The sect was twice condemned by the papacy: by Honorius IV (1286), and by Nicholas IV (1290). Segarelli was finally imprisoned by the bishop of Parma, who gave him over to the secular authorities to be burnt in 1300.
□ G. Leff *Heresy in the Late Middle Ages* (1967)

Seljuk (Seljuq) Turks The Seljuks came with bands of Turkish nomads from the Central Asian steppes, making their way into Anatolia, northern Iraq and Syria, and gradually pushing the Byzantines out of Asia Minor. They occupied Jerusalem in

1071, as well as crushing the Byzantine army at the battle of Manzikert, later capturing Antioch (1085); this gave rise to the First Crusade (1096–99), with the crusaders seeking to free the Holy Land from the infidel. *See* ALP ARSLAN; TUGHRIL BEG
□ *Cambridge History of Islam* ed. P.M. Holt (1970)

Serbia In the 7th c. various groups of Slavs, the ancestors of the Serbian people, settled in the Balkans. Each tribe had its own leader or *župan* until the late 1100s, when the great warrior Stephen Nemanja formed the first united Serbian state. Several centuries later, King Stephen Dušan led the country in a series of successful wars against the Byzantine empire; however, the Serbian empire began to decline after his death in 1355.

Sergius I (d.638) Patriarch of Constantinople from 610. Born in Syria, Sergius eventually became the trusted adviser of Emperor Heraclius. In response to the split between orthodox believers and the Monophysites, Sergius formulated the doctrine of Monotheletism, claiming that Christ possessed two natures but one will. The new formula was promulgated by the emperor in 638, but unfortunately was rejected by the Monophysites and the Latin church, and condemned at the Council of Constantinople in 681.

Sforza family Northern Italian family of nobles. The descendants of the *condottiere* Muzio Attendolo (1369–1424) assumed his nickname, Sforza. Among the most famous members of the family were Francesco, ruler of Milan 1450–66, who sought to maintain peace and order in his territories; his son Galeazzo Maria (assassinated 1476); and Caterina (*c.*1462–1509), who was famous for her involvement in political and military affairs. Another Sforza, Lodovico (1451–1508), may have been partly responsible for the French invasion of Italy in 1494. The Sforza rule in Milan saw great economic growth and enlightened patronage of the arts.
□ C.M. Ady *Milan under the Sforza* (1907); J. Law *The Lords of Renaissance Italy* (1981)

The first English **shilling** (or testoon) showing Henry VII, and the royal arms on the reverse.

Shilling (from Old Norse *sciljan*, 'to cut, shear') Originally an early Germanic weight for gold, implying a piece cut from a ring or wire and weighing 20 grains (1.30g). As a money of account it was worth 12 pence, since the earliest penny (7th c.) was the same weight as the gold coin or 'shilling' of the day, and the gold:silver ratio was 1:12.

Ships and shipping Great advances were made in the maritime arts in the course of the Middle Ages, when for the most part transport by water, across the seas and along the rivers, constituted the simplest, most efficient, and often the safest means of communication. The classical inheritance remained virtually unbroken in Byzantium, and naval traditions in ship-building and weaponry contributed to the survival of Constantinople. The Arabs brought their own traditions to Mediterranean waters, but also took over the ship-building yards and expertise of Alexandria and Carthage.

In the specific European experience, the outstanding achievements of the early Middle Ages came in northern waters. Archaeologists trace a sequence of increasing technical competence from the Nydam ship of the migration period to the superb 9th-c. Gokstad and Oseberg ships, which led to the creation of ships capable of operating even in the roughest ocean conditions at acceptable risk. Gokstad represents the sensational side of ship-building techniques, the evolution of a formidable and almost irresistible weapon of war; but of equal or greater importance was the evolution of a whole complex of seaworthy trading vessels ranging from sturdy little Frisian cogs to the substantial trading vessels discovered at Skuldelev. The technical achievements of the period *c.*600–900 made possible the Viking expansion which set the cap of fortified trading centres on Northern Europe from Greenland and Iceland to the Russian waterways, Novgorod, Smolensk and Kiev.

Further advance on classical models came in the central Middle Ages in the Mediterranean, stimulated by Muslim experiment and by the needs of the crusaders. A wealth of navigational knowledge was built up and transmitted orally. The Vikings appear to have used a lodestone as a guide, but the first clear reference to a mariner's compass appears in the 12th-c. work of Alexander of Neckam, and understanding of its magnetic qualities was further extended in the later Middle Ages. Use of the compass coincided with the development of larger sailing ships and a resulting greater confidence in coping with navigation on the open seas. By the 15th c. ship-builders and navigators, notably those on the western seaboard of Europe in Portugal, were well poised for voyages of exploration to seek out new

Embarking stores and equipment onto a **ship** for a crusade; 14th-c. illumination from a text of Villehardouin.

routes to the wealth of Africa and the East. HRL

□ R.J. Lefebvre *De la marine antique à la marine moderne* (1935); A.W. Brögger and H. Shetelig *The Viking ships* (1951); B. Greenhill *Archaeology of the boat* (1975); R.W. Unger *The Ship in the Medieval Economy 600–1600* (1980); A.R. Lewis and T.J. Runyan *European Naval and Maritime History 300–1500* (1985)

Sicilian Vespers (Easter Monday 1282) Popular uprising against the rule of Charles of Anjou in Sicily. Charles, king of Sicily, had levied heavy taxes on the Sicilians for his proposed conquest of Constantinople, increasing their resentment of French rule. A riot began in Palermo on 30 March 1282 when a Sicilian woman was insulted by a French soldier, and several thousand Frenchmen were killed in a few hours. The fighting soon spread to the rest of the island.

Although the uprising may have begun as a patriotic rebellion, it then became a republican movement for municipal autonomy. A parliament was called in Palermo, and an independent republic proclaimed. The cities of western Sicily decided to form a confederation, hopefully with the pope as feudal overlord. Pope Martin IV, a Frenchman, would not accept these plans and excommunicated the rebels instead. The Hohenstaufen barons of Sicily sought the aid of Peter III of Aragon, who claimed the island as the inheritance of his wife, daughter of Manfred. On 2 September Peter was crowned king at Palermo, and the war against the Angevins began in earnest; the conflict lasted two decades. Foreign domination of Sicily cannot have been the prime reason behind the revolt of the Vespers, for in the end the Sicilians accepted yet another foreign power as master, the Aragonese.

□ S. Runciman *The Sicilian Vespers* (1958); H. Wieruszowski *Politics and Culture in Medieval Spain and Italy* (1971)

Sicily Throughout the Middle Ages Sicily was coveted by outside rulers for its riches and important strategic position in the Mediterranean. Ravaged by the Vandals and Ostrogoths in the 5th c. the island was then captured c.535 by Belisarius. The hold of the Byzantine empire was gradually weakened in the 9th c. with the advent of the Arabs, and by the end of the century Sicily was virtually an Arab province. The Normans, led by Roger I, the Great Count, reconquered the island in the Christian interest (1072–91), and his son, Roger II was crowned king in 1130. Under firm Hauteville government, drawing on Arabic, Greek, and Roman tradition the island thrived economically, financially and culturally. Late in the twelfth century the Hohenstaufens succeeded the Hautevilles and during the reign of the Emperor Frederick II (1212–50), the 'Sicilian boy', the court at Palermo became famous throughout the world for its learning and luxury. In 1268 the Angevin domination of Sicily began; they were finally overthrown in the Sicilian Vespers (1282), through which Sicily merely substituted yet another foreign master, the Aragonese, and Sicilian interests were subordinated to the needs of their Aragonese and Catalan masters. *See* CHARLES I OF ANJOU; PETER III; ROBERT GUISCARD; ROGER I; ROGER II; FREDERICK II

□ D.M. Smith *Medieval Sicily* (1969); D.C. Douglas *The Norman Achievement* (1969); D. Abulafia *Frederick the Second* (1988)

Siegfried Archbishop of Mainz 1060–84. He was appointed to the powerful see of Mainz by Agnes. He seems to have been a weak man of little character who, caught up in the struggle over lay investiture between Henry IV and Gregory VII, always backed the losing side in the conflict. He was responsible for the coronation of Rudolf of Swabia in 1077.

□ *Church and State in the Middle Ages* ed. B.D. Hill (1970).

Siger of Brabant (*c*.1235–82) Averroist philosopher. A teacher of philosophy at the university of Paris, Siger taught an Aristotelianism influenced by Averroes. His teachings were condemned in 1270 by the bishop of Paris. Six years later he was summoned to appear before the Inquisitor of France, Simon du Val, on charges of heresy and in 1277 he was again condemned by the bishop. On his way to Orvieto to seek papal absolution, he was murdered by his secretary. While accepting the truth of the Catholic faith, he insisted on man's right to follow human reason, even though, in his view, it sometimes contradicted divine revelation.
□ G. Leff *Medieval Thought from St Augustine to Ockham* (1958)

Sigismund of Luxembourg Holy Roman Emperor 1410–37 (b.1368) Ruler of Hungary, Germany and Bohemia. The son of Charles IV, Sigismund acquired the crown of Hungary in 1387. He later gained control of Germany after the death of Rupert in 1410 and the abdication of his incompetent step-

Russian icon of **St Simeon Stylites**, shown at the top of his pillar.

brother Wenceslas. Intent on healing the Great Schism of the Latin church (1378–1417), he forced John XXIII to summon a general council, which was held at Constance (1414–18). One of the key issues to be settled at Constance was the extirpation of heresy, in particular the Hussite heresy. Hus accepted an offer of safe conduct from Sigismund, and went to Constance (1415), where he was imprisoned, put on trial and burnt at the stake (6 July), thereby kindling a spirit of Bohemian nationalism and giving rise to the Hussite wars. Despite his alienation of Bohemia and his inability to reorganize political relations in Germany, Sigismund enjoyed some popularity in his lifetime for his knightly personality and initiative in promoting the Council of Constance. [*103*]
□ F.R.H. du Boulay *Germany in the Later Middle Ages* (1983)

Simeon I Tsar of Bulgaria 893–927 (b. *c*.863) Son of Boris I and the first Bulgarian ruler to assume the title 'tsar'. During his reign the Bulgarian empire was at the summit of its power. Simeon was educated at Constantinople as a monk; thus, he was deeply immersed in Greek civilization and did much to encourage an atmosphere of culture and learning at his court. However, he was largely preoccupied with the wars against the Byzantine empire, wars which grew originally out of disputes regarding trade rights, and ultimately developed into a contest for possession of the imperial throne. He failed to take Constantinople in 913 and 924; in 925 he proclaimed himself emperor of the Romans and Bulgars, drawing protests from the Byzantine emperor, Romanus Lecapenus, although the title was recognized by the pope. After his death, internal dissension did much to weaken the Bulgarian state and thus lessened the danger confronting Constantinople.
□ S. Runciman *A History of the First Bulgarian Empire* (1930)

Simeon Stylites, St (*c*.390–459) First of the 'pillar' ascetics, Simeon was born near the Syrian border of Cilicia. After some years as a monk in the monastery of Eusebona near Antioch, he retreated to a cell at Telanissos, where he began to live a life of extreme austerity. To escape from the crowds that gathered round him, he eventually mounted a pillar so that he might spend a life of peaceful contemplation. His tallest column, on which he spent more than 20 years, was about 15 m (50 ft) high, with a rail running round the top. He spent most of his life in prayer, standing on the pillar exposed to the elements; he also ate practically nothing. This novel austerity attracted to him a constant stream of pilgrims, and had many imitators.

Simon de Montfort the Elder (c.1153–1218) Fourth earl of Leicester. Simon joined the Fourth Crusade in 1199 and opposed its diversion from Palestine to Zara and Constantinople (1204); he sailed instead to the Holy Land. He inherited the earldom from his mother's brother in 1204, but his lands were seized by King John and not returned until 1215. In 1207 Innocent III had begun to preach the Albigensian Crusade, hoping that Philip Augustus would take the lead and prevent any excesses of behaviour. The latter's involvement in the war with England prevented him from taking the cross, but he did permit his barons to do so; Simon de Montfort was elected as their leader.

A soldier of great courage, he was also a skilled diplomat. He defeated Raymond VI, count of Toulouse, in 1212, and Raymond's ally Peter II of Aragon the following year. It seemed to many that de Montfort and his allies were set on dispossessing the southern nobility and seizing their lands. Provence rose in revolt against the crusaders, and Toulouse was retaken in 1217 by Raymond's son, while de Montfort was in Paris; he laid siege to the city 1217–18, and was killed in a skirmish with the enemy.
□ B. Hamilton *The Albigensian Crusade* (1974)

Simon de Montfort the Younger (c.1208–65) He came to England in 1230 to press a family claim to the earldom of Leicester. He secured his inheritance and so impressed Henry III that he rose quickly in royal favour, and married Eleanor, the king's sister, in 1238. More masterful and tenacious of his rights than other royal favourites, he soon quarrelled with the king, and over the next two decades their relations were stormy, especially after Simon's controversial period as governor of Gascony (1248–52). Yet he was not the moving spirit in the well-supported movement which forced Henry to submit to baronial control in the Provisions of Oxford (1258).

It was only after the disintegration of the baronial government that Simon became the focal point of opposition to the king. Early in 1264 he rejected the Mise of Amiens, Louis IX of France's arbitration on the dispute, and took Henry and his son (the future Edward I) prisoner at the battle of Lewes on 14 May 1264. A new scheme of government was then drawn up, with Simon the leading member of a triumvirate empowered to control the king. Though he eagerly sought a reconciliation with Henry, and in 1265 even assembled a parliament containing, for the first time, representatives of the shires and boroughs, in the hope of securing a lasting peace, the king refused to compromise on untrammelled royal rule. When Simon quarrelled with his leading colleague, Gilbert de Clare, earl of Gloucester, and the Lord Edward

escaped from custody, his position crumbled and he was defeated and killed at Evesham.
□ M.W. Labarge *Simon de Montfort* (1962); C.H. Knowles *Simon de Montfort 1265–1965* (1965)

Skanderbeg (d.1468) Leader of the Albanian revolt against the Turks, George Castriota, who had served the Turks as a janissary commander under the name of Skanderbeg, revolted against them, seized the fortress of Kroja in 1443 and declared himself a Christian. The Turks eventually triumphed in 1468, after Skanderbeg's death, but his heroic resistance, which beat back the armies of two formidable sultans, Murād II and even Muhammad II (conqueror of Constantinople, 1451–81), helped to build up a feeling of unity among the turbulent Albanians, the descendants of an ancient Illyrian people.
□ C. Chekrezi *Albania, Past and Present* (1919); H. Inalcik *The Ottoman Empire: the Classical Age* (1973)

Slavery In the early Middle Ages slavery was widespread throughout the European world, inherited as an institution both from classical and Germanic sources. The attitude of the Christian church was ambivalent, opposed to the sale of Christian slaves to non-Christians, but tending to accept slavery itself as a consequence of man's sinful nature. Attempts at legal amelioration were few and calculable; there was some move towards recognition of Christian marriage and some granting of limited rights to own small sums of money and even to acquire land. Labour was dictated by the lord's will and there was little, if any redress against his arbitrary authority.

With the evolution of a manorial economy from the 8th c. onwards came elaborate gradations of freedom and unfreedom, which make all generalizations at best tentative, and at worst positively misleading. Lords tended to find it more profitable to employ peasants better described in modern terms as serfs, than as slaves: that is to say, men possessing plots of land which they could use to maintain themselves and their families, but bound to the soil, to the disciplines of the manor, and answerable for labour of an onerous kind on the lord's demesne. Chattel slavery persisted, and in some areas of Europe Roman law caused a revival in the 12th c. The presence of the Muslim world, and indeed of the Byzantine world with its continuous classical inheritance, preserved the high theory of the *servus*, the slave as a virtually rightless man against his master.

In the West something of a turning point in attitudes to slavery can be discerned in the mid-11th c., the end of the Viking Age. The Vikings were themselves

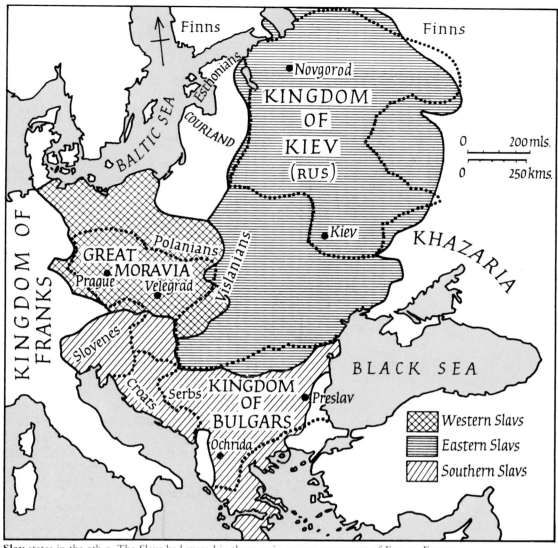

Slav states in the 9th c. The Slavs had spread in three main groups over most of Eastern Europe.

great slavers; their depredations of the Slavonic world and sale of Slavs at slave markets helped to give the term 'slave' to the Western world. England provides a clear-cut example, and its records show how the elaborate legal distinctions among the peasantry at the time of Domesday Book (1086) evolve by the 13th c. into a more uniform villeinage. In the 11th c. the two principal marks of a freeman, the right to bear arms and the right to testify on oath in public courts, were still powerful, but both diminished in significance in the highly regulated feudal society of the central Middle Ages. It is no coincidence that in the same period, the enslavement of Christians by fellow Christians (by 1100 the bulk of the Scandinavian and Slavonic peoples had been Christianized) became increasingly regarded as unethical, unprofitable and unnecessary. HRL

□ *Slavery and Serfdom in the Middle Ages: Selected Papers by M. Bloch* trans. and ed. W.R. Beck (1975); H.R. Loyn *The Free Anglo-Saxon* (1975); *The Transition from Feudalism to Capitalism* ed. R.H. Hilton (1976)

Slavs The migration and settlement of the Slavonic peoples into their familiar modern groups was as much a feature of early medieval history as the better known Germanic movements. Historically they established themselves in three powerful groups: the north-west Slavs (Poles, Czechs, Bohemians, Wends, etc.), the south-west Slavs (Serbs, Croats, 'Yugo-Slavs' generally) and the eastern Slavs (Russians). All these terms are generalized and none of the groupings is in any sense racially pure, but the basic languages were derived from the same Indo-

European stock, and the peoples themselves at the beginning of the Middle Ages dwelt principally in Eastern Europe with focal points in the Carpathians, from which they penetrated north and west to the Elbe, south and west into the Balkans, and east, straddling the great waterways of historic Russia.

They received Christianity, the symbol of settlement and acceptance into the new medieval world, at different times and from different quarters. The work of St Cyril (d. 869) from Byzantium created a liturgy in the tradition of the Eastern church and a script, which formed the basis for the modern Cyrillic script used in modern Russia and Bulgaria. Western missionaries, however, predominated on the German frontier. By the end of the 10th c. the Bohemians were Christian with a see established at Prague. The Poles were also converted from the west with a chief bishopric at Gniezno, and – in spite of the persistence of pagan practices, notably among the Wends – Western Christianity and the influence of Rome constituted the principal cultural forces among the north-west Slavs from c.1000 onwards. The picture was different in the south and east: Orthodox Byzantine Christianity predominated among the Serbs and Yugo-Slavs generally, from the last quarter of the 9th c. To the east, the decisive moves came late in the reign of Vladimir the Great (980–1015), who accepted the Orthodox faith for his eastern Slavonic peoples, the Russians.

Vastly different political experience in succeeding centuries exaggerated the divergences between the Slavonic peoples, but no force was stronger than religion in creating the special characteristics of the states of Catholic Poland and Czechoslovakia on the one hand, and of Orthodox Russia and Serbo-Croatia on the other. *See* BOHEMIA; SERBIA; WENDS; YUGOSLAVS   HRL
□ A. Florovsky *The Czechs and the Eastern Slavs* (1935); G. Vernadsky *Ancient Russia* (1943); F. Dvornik *The making of Central and Eastern Europe* (1949)

Snorri Sturluson (1179–1241) Generally regarded as the greatest of the saga writers, Snorri Sturluson, though born in Norway, spent his active political and literary life in Iceland. His greatest works include the Prose Edda, which in sophisticated literary form tells the essential outlines of Old Norse mythology, and the *Heimskringla*, which sets out the history of the kings of Norway of the Ynglinga dynasty from mythological times. Reputedly the richest man in Iceland and deeply involved in the politics of the island, Snorri met his death by what was virtually political assassination. *See* SAGAS, NORSE
□ *The Prose Edda* ed. J. Young (1954); D.M. Wilson and P. Foote *The Viking Achievement* (1968)

Gold **solidus** (613-29) of Heraclius and his son Heraclius Constantine, from Byzantium.

Solidus (Italian *soldo*, French *sou*) Originally a Roman gold coin introduced by Constantine in 309 and weighing 4.55 g. As a term for the standard gold coin the name was transferred in the 7th c. to the tremissis of reduced weight that corresponded to the Germanic shilling, so that *soldo* and cognate terms in the Romance languages became the equivalent of 12 pennies in money of account. The first silver coin to be struck having the value of a *sou* was the *gros tournois* in 1266.

Spain Roman imperial rule was swept from the Iberian peninsula when waves of barbarians – Suevi, Alans and Vandals – crossed the Pyrenees in 409. Their presence was transitory and largely destructive (hence English 'vandal'), but in 456 they were succeeded by the Visigoths, still half-savage, but Christian (albeit Arian heretics) and Latin-speaking, who settled and intermarried with the Hispano-Roman population. The Visigothic kingdom, with Toledo as its capital and the works of Isidore of Seville as its enduring cultural monument, lasted for two and a half centuries. But it was an elective monarchy; warring factions within the royal house fatally weakened it, and when in 711 one group brought Arab and Berber troops from Morocco to help them, Visigothic power collapsed. By 718 the Muslims controlled the whole peninsula except for some small mountainous regions that scarcely seemed worth occupying, and they were soon crossing the Pyrenees to threaten France.

A mountain skirmish, located by tradition at Covadonga in 718, began the Reconquest (*Reconquista*) and the kingdom of Asturias; the other nucleus of resistance was the Basque kingdom of Navarre in the Pyrenees. In the 740s civil war among the Muslims allowed a vast expansion of Asturian territory, and simultaneously the Franks drove the Muslims back across the Pyrenees, establishing the north-east of the peninsula as their Spanish March. In the March, which had such European features as the Roman rite, Carolingian script and a genuine feudal system, political power gradually crystallized around the counts of Barcelona, and the monastery of Ripoll became one of Europe's great cultural centres. During the 9th c., the advance of the Reconquest transformed the kingdom of Asturias into that of Leon. Castile was a mere county of Leon, as Aragon was of Navarre, yet Castile was already developing linguistic and politico-legal traits that set it apart as a fluid, resourceful and energetic frontier society. In the mid-10th c. Count Fernan Gonzalez, skilfully playing Navarre against Leon, won Castile's independence. Within a century, her counts had become kings, and Castile was playing a major role. Galicia (and its southern half, which became Portugal) to the west, and Aragon and Catalonia to the east, were only intermittently important to the affairs of the centre, whose politics were dominated in turn by Navarre, Leon and Castile. More than once a strong and ambitious ruler (such as Sancho III of Navarre) created a united kingdom by conquest, only to divide it among his heirs, who then fought for supremacy.

Muslim Spain, ruled for its first 40 years by governors dependent on the caliph in Damascus, had long since gone its own way, with 'Abd ar-Rahmān's establishment of the amirate of Cordoba in 756; it covered two-thirds of the peninsula, stretching north to the Duero and the Ebro. A prosperous multilingual and multiracial society developed, with large Jewish communities as well as Christian Mozarabs (indigenous Spaniards living under Arab rule), and a cultural flowering that rivalled that of the caliph's court in Damascus. The second half of the 9th c. was troubled by Norse raids and religious unrest, but 'Abd ar-Rahmān III (912–61) pacified the frontier, strengthened the central and provincial administrations, used new techniques in agriculture and irrigation to create even greater prosperity, and made Cordoba the most powerful state in Europe, with a culture whose brilliance eclipsed that of Damascus and Baghdad. In 929 he proclaimed himself caliph, spiritual as well as temporal leader; for the first time, there were two caliphs in Islam. Al-Mansūr, general (and effectively dictator) from 979, laid waste much of the Christian north, but he so weakened the power of the caliphs that on his death in 1002 the caliphate collapsed, to be succeeded by the small *taifa* kingdoms, and the Christian kingdoms became dominant.

Al-Mansūr's raids and Sancho III's hegemony broke the political dependence of Catalonia on France, and Count Ramon Berenguer I (1035–76) secured a distinctive Catalan political and legal identity. When the king of Aragon died without male heir in 1137, a loose but enduring union, the crown of Aragon, was formed under the count of Barcelona; the new kingdom included Saragossa, which had been reconquered in 1118. The successes of Alfonso VI against the *taifa* kingdoms brought about the Almoravid invasion, and despite the temporary triumph of the Cid in Valencia, the Almoravids, and after them the Almohads, effectively impeded the Reconquest for a century and a half. Yet some gains were made, and more importantly Alfonso VI's great prize, Toledo, remained in Christian hands. It was there that a school of translators fuelled the 12th-c. renaissance with Latin versions of Arabic (and hence of Greek) scientific texts. Christian Spain was strengthened demographically, economically and culturally by the intolerance of the Almohads, which sent Mozarab and Jewish refugees streaming north; Castile replaced Andalusia as the great centre of Jewish culture.

After the victory of Las Navas de Tolosa (1214), the Reconquest gained momentum under Fernando III. His conquests (Cordoba, Seville, Murcia, Jaen) were flanked by Alfonso IX of Leon's capture of Badajoz (1230), and the surrender of Valencia to James I of Aragon in 1238. Fernando's reign also marks the definitive union of Leon and Castile, under Castilian leadership. His successor Alfonso X paid the price of Fernando's spectacular success and of his own weaknesses. Acute economic and demographic problems beset Castile, and the great nobles, aided by Alfonso's heir Sancho IV, successfully challenged the central authority of the crown, causing misery to the people and delaying the Reconquest. Alfonso XI (1312–50) tamed the nobles and was making headway against Granada when he died of the plague. Disaster followed; while the Black Death ravaged the peninsula, a civil war between Alfonso's legitimate and illegitimate sons brought foreign armies into Castile and strengthened the nobles at the expense of crown and people. The Jews, prosperous and numerous, were an obvious scapegoat for Castile's miseries, and pogroms, beginning in 1391, led to semi-forced conversions (the *conversos* in turn became suspect and persecuted), to the establishment of the Spanish Inquisition (1478) and to the expulsion of the Jews from Spain (1492).

The crown of Aragon's share in the Reconquest was completed with the surrender of Valencia; Murcia, to the south, fell to Castile at about the same time. Aragon then turned its energies eastwards: Pere III seized Sicily in 1282; Corsica and Sardinia were added to the kingdom; and Catalan adventurers captured the duchy of Athens (it was held for Aragon during most of the 14th c.). Aragon's economic dominance in the Mediterranean equalled her military power, but over-expansion brought demographic problems; the economy weakened, and there were risings, first of the peasantry, then of the urban proletariat against the nobles, and finally of the nobles against the crown. In 1410 the last king in direct line of succession from the counts of Barcelona died without male issue, and after a two-year interregnum a prince of the Castilian Trastamara dynasty ascended the throne.

Alfonso V the Magnanimous achieved a temporary recovery by social reforms at home and military expansion abroad. He took Naples in 1442 and established his court there, though his attempt to secure northern Italy five years later failed. After Alfonso's death internal conflicts worsened with a series of rival and transitory monarchs, and the kingdom of Naples was divided from that of Aragon. In Castile, gradual demographic recovery in the 15th c., and the wealth created by the great sheep flocks of the Mesta and by merchantmen trading out

of Biscay and Andalusia, provided a base for further expansion; the first step towards an Atlantic empire was taken when the Canary Islands were colonized.

Only leadership was lacking, and it was provided by the Catholic Monarchs: Isabel, who ascended the disputed throne of Castile in 1474, and her husband Fernando, king of Aragon from 1479. They ruled their two kingdoms and prepared for their fusion; Navarre, long since confined to a small Pyrenean region, was added to a united Spain in 1512. They fostered education and humanistic scholarship; they finally imposed the crown's authority on the great nobles (though at the cost of giving them too much power in the realm); they supported Columbus in what was to prove (to everyone's surprise) the discovery of America; and they conquered Granada. The Nasrid kingdom had survived with almost unchanged frontiers since 1350, and was increasingly an anachronism on the edge of Christian Spain; diplomatic skill and Granadine wealth preserved it as long as Castile had no compelling motives for all-out war, but the Catholic Monarchs could no longer tolerate the reproach it offered to their vision of the countries' manifest Christian destiny.

From the 9th to the 11th c. the Muslims were pushed south, though the Reconquest of **Spain** did not end until 1492.

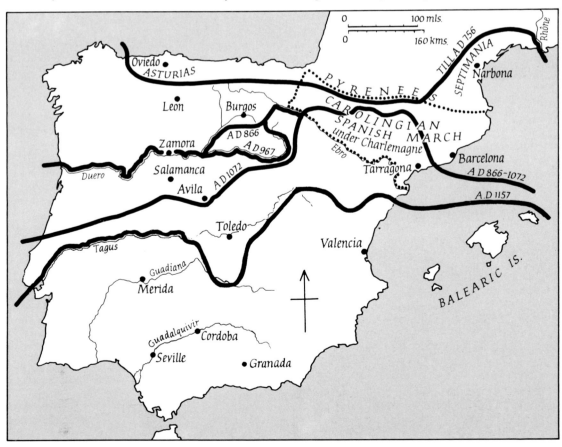

The boundary between medieval and modern culture is inevitably ill-defined, but chronological convergence gives us a startlingly precise historical boundary: in a single year (1492) Granada fell, the Jews were expelled from Spain, Antonio de Nebrija published the first serious grammar of any European vernacular, and Columbus claimed the New World for the Catholic Monarchs. By the end of the year, Spain was irrevocably transformed; the foundations of empire were laid, but with an intolerance that would ultimately weaken the entire structure. *See* 'ABBADID DYNASTY; 'ABBASID DYNASTY; CORTES; SANTIAGO, ORDER OF; TOLEDO, COUNCILS OF; UMAYYAD DYNASTY; *see also individual kings*   ADD

□ J.H. Elliott *Imperial Spain* (1963); W. Montgomery Watt and P. Cacchia *A History of Islamic Spain* (1965); H.V. Livermore *The Origins of Spain and Portugal* (1971); G. Jackson *The Making of Medieval Spain* (1972); J.F. O'Callaghan *A History of Medieval Spain* (1975); J.N. Hillgarth *The Spanish Kingdoms 1250–1516* (1976–78); A. MacKay *Spain in the Middle Ages* (1977); D.W. Lomax *The Reconquest of Spain* (1978); R. Collins *Early Medieval Spain: Unity in Diversity 400–1000* (1983)

A **stave church** in Norway, substantially *c.*1250.

Stave churches (*Stavkirken*) Distinctive type of church characteristic of Norway in the Middle Ages. Stave churches were wooden buildings, often built by the rural population, and at their best combined brilliantly the arts of the architect and carpenter. The most elaborate were supported by a series of massive wooden columns, with heavily ornamented portals and carved capitals. The outward appearance, with its succession of stepped roofs, provided a sharp contrast both to the simple stone churches and elaborate 'European' cathedrals of Trondheim and Bergen. Pagan features and echoes of heroic legend were incorporated in the carving both inside and outside the stave churches.
□ R. Hauglid *Norwegian Stave Churches* (1970)

Stephen of Blois King of England 1135–54 (b. *c.*1097) Grandson of William the Conqueror, Stephen succeeded his uncle Henry I in December 1135, thanks to his own energy combined with the political skill of his brother Henry, bishop of Winchester, and the acquiescence of the eldest of the brothers, Theobald, count of Blois. His reign was turbulent, but it is wrong to think of it as a period of perpetual anarchy. The civil war (hard fought 1141–44) between Stephen and his cousin Matilda, legitimate daughter of Henry I, brought great misery and devastation to parts of the country. The final compromise which ensured the succession of Matilda's son, Henry of Anjou (Plantagenet), to the throne after Stephen's death, was generally welcomed and inaugurated a period of strong monarchic government.

The crises of the reign helped to resolve some of the major problems of the feudal settlement of England and paved the way for a permanent legal solution to matters of succession and inheritance, not only at the royal level, but throughout the feudal order. Its reputation as a time of permanent dire distress rests largely on its portrayal in the Anglo-Saxon Chronicle (Peterborough Chronicle) as '19 winters during which Christ and his Saints slept'.
□ R.H.C. Davis *King Stephen* (1967)

Sterling (from Middle English *stere*, 'strong'; French *esterlin*) Name given to the English penny in the post-Conquest period. From the late 12th c. to the early 14th c. it circulated widely in the Low Countries, north-west Germany, Scandinavia and France, since its weight (22½ grains, or 1.46 g) and fineness (925/1000) were superior to those of most Continental deniers, making it internationally acceptable. It was much imitated, especially in the Low Countries, sometimes (e.g., by John the Blind, count of Luxembourg) in very base metal. The term is also used for silver of standard fineness (1 1oz 2dwt = 925/1000).

Stilicho, Flavius (*c*.365–408) Half-Vandal and half-Roman by birth, he was the supreme commander of the Western Roman empire 395–408. He foiled the Visigothic invasion of Italy (401–02), led by Alaric, and later destroyed another great host of invaders, led by Radagaisus, which threatened to overrun Italy (405). He had always hoped to extend his control over the prefecture of Illyricum, and in 407 he prepared its annexation. His plans failed, and he was forced to pay Alaric, an ally in the campaign, a compensation of 4000 pounds of gold. Stilicho's fortunes declined in 408: a palace revolution led to his imprisonment and execution.
□ S. Mazzarino *Stilicone: La crisi imperiale dopo Teodosio* (1942)

Strasbourg, Oaths of On the death of Louis the Pious (840) his three surviving sons continued their struggle for control of the Empire. Charles the Bald and Louis the German, who sought independent royal authority in west and east Frankia respectively, formed an alliance against Lothar, claimant to the indivisible imperial title. In recognition of this alliance against Lothar, the bilingual Oaths were sworn in February 842 by Charles and Louis, each in the other's vernacular, so that their armies could understand them. The text, as preserved in Nithard's *Histories*, provides some of the most ancient examples of the French and German languages.
□ H.R. Loyn and J. Percival *The Reign of Charlemagne: documents on Carolingian government and administration* (1975)

Subiaco Important monastic centre in the 6th c. located near Rome and providing a religious education for, among others, the great Pope Gregory I. It is Gregory who tells of the significance of Subiaco in the life of St Benedict of Nursia, who is said to have spent time as a solitary hermit in his cave there before going on to lay the foundations for a cenobitic order.
□ D.C. Butler *Benedictine Monachism* (1927)

Suger (*c*.1085–1151) Abbot of Saint-Denis. An important patron of the arts and trusted friend and adviser to two French kings, Louis VI and Louis VII. Of humble birth, he was given as oblate to the royal abbey of Saint-Denis at the age of ten, and 1094–1104 was educated at the Prieuré de l'Estrée with the future King Louis VI. By 1107 he had proved himself a skilled advocate and diplomat. At the request of King Louis VI, he was twice sent to Rome (1122, 1123) on special missions; he remained an intimate of the royal family for the rest of his life. In 1123 he was elected abbot of Saint-Denis, where he later instituted a programme of reform, influenced by his friend Bernard of Clairvaux. Suger seems to have had two main ambitions in life: in addition to his desire to aggrandize the abbey of Saint-Denis, he also sought to strengthen the power of the crown of France. When King Louis VII set out on the Second Crusade (1147), he appointed Suger regent of France. The abbot's excellent management of the country's finances at this time helped to establish Louis as the most powerful ruler in France.

Suger began to rebuild Saint-Denis in the late 1130s, and the result is traditionally regarded as one of the first examples of the Gothic style in art and architecture. His many writings, such as his Life of Louis VI, reveal his skill as a historian. Suger died at the abbey in January 1151; his epitaph read: 'Small of body and family, constrained by a twofold smallness / He refused, in his smallness, to be a small man.'
□ M. Aubert *Suger* (1950); *Abbot Suger: On the Abbey Church of Saint-Denis and its Art Treasures* ed. E. Panofsky (1979); S. Crosby *The Royal Abbey of Saint-Denis from its Beginnings to the Death of Suger* (1987)

Suso, Heinrich (*c*.1296–1336) Dominican preacher and mystic. Suso studied at Cologne (*c*.1322 and 1325) under Master Eckhart, whom he greatly admired. His principal work, *The Little Book of Eternal Wisdom* (*c*.1328), is one of the classics of German mysticism. It was widely read in the 14th c. and 15th c. and included Thomas à Kempis among its admirers. Suso also preached widely and effectively in Switzerland and the Upper Rhine area.
□ J.M. Clark *The Great German Mystics* (1949)

Sutri, Synod of (1046) Faced with an intolerable situation at Rome, where no fewer than three men (Benedict IX, Sylvester III and the respectable Gregory VI) had some claim to be pope, the reforming Emperor Henry III had a synod summoned to Sutri, and afterwards at Rome, where the three claimants were deposed and the succession passed to the German bishop of Bamberg, Clement II, who then crowned Henry as Emperor (Christmas 1046).
□ *Hildebrandine Essays* ed. J.P. Whitney (1932)

Sweden The medieval Swedish kingdom first took recognizable form in the 4th c. around Lake Malar, but its continuous political history did not become possible until the 9th c. when its chief centre lay at Uppsala. The southern part of modern Sweden, Scania, was at this stage under Danish control. The rich grave goods discovered in the aristocratic cemeteries at Välsgarde and Vendel give some impression of the wealth and potential of Scandinavian society even before the dramatic outburst of the Viking Age. The Swedes played a full part in the

Stained-glass window showing the arms of the **Swiss** canton of Uri.

Viking ventures, dominant in the expansion to the east, but with a presence also in the movement west over sea.

At home, however, they were slow to consolidate royal authority and to accept fully conversion to Christianity. The result was a sense of subordination in affairs to Denmark and to the Hanseatic merchants who, from the 13th c., entrenched themselves firmly in the island of Gotland. Some permanent Swedish settlement occurred in Finland in the 14th c., but in 1397, by the Union of Calmar, Sweden accepted the lordship of Queen Margaret of Denmark, who inaugurated a period of uneasy unified rule over the Scandinavian kingdoms.

□ L. Musset *Les peuples scandinaves au Moyen-Age* (1951); M. Stenburger *Sweden* (1962); D.M. Wilson *The Vikings and their Origins: Scandinavia in the First Millennium* (1970)

Switzerland The origins of Switzerland as a political unit can be traced to 1291, when the three German-speaking cantons of Uri, Schwyz and Unterwalden united to withstand pressure from the Habsburg dynasty. Their success was associated in legend with stories of William Tell of Uri, forced to endanger his own son's life by shooting an apple off his head at the whim of a tyrannical Habsburg official. Historical credit should rather be given to the tenacity and bravery of the mountain folk, the difficulty of terrain, and the rather half-hearted efforts at repression. Further cantons joined the federation in the 14th c., Lucerne, Zürich, Bern and Zug, and accretions in the later Middle Ages included Freiburg and Soleure. Basle was not a full member until the early 16th c., and indeed, it was not until Napoleonic days that the confederation took complete shape. The special interest of Switzerland in the Middle Ages comes from its success in establishing a permanent polity on a non-monarchic basis.

□ E. Bonjour, H. Offler and G.R. Potter *Short History of Switzerland* (1952); J. Steinberg *Why Switzerland?* (1976)

Syagrius (464–86) Gallo-Roman general who exercised control over a number of towns between the Somme and the Loire until his defeat at the hand of Clovis at Soissons (486). Syagrius had inherited his right to military protection over the towns from his father Aegidius, a former *magister militum* of the Roman empire. With the collapse of the western half of the empire in 476, Syagrius adopted a position of independent authority: indeed, Gregory of Tours describes him as *rex Romanorum* (king of the Romans), which suggests that he ruled in the manner of a barbarian king. Following his defeat in battle, he was handed over to Clovis who had him secretly put to death.

□ J.M. Wallace-Hadrill *The Barbarian West 400–1000* (1952); A.H.M. Jones *The Later Roman Empire 284–602* (1964)

Sylvester II (Gerbert of Aurillac) Pope 999–1003 (b. *c*.940) Of humble birth, Gerbert was educated at the Benedictine monastery of Aurillac. An encounter in Rome (970) with the Emperor Otto I was decisive, for Gerbert was to spend much of his life within the orbit of the German Empire. About 972 he went to Rheims to study, and eventually lectured there for many years. In 997 he left France for the court of Otto III.

The Emperor welcomed him as an old supporter of the imperial family and soon procured his appointment to the archbishopric of Ravenna (998). A year later, he elevated Gerbert to the papacy. The first Frenchman to hold this office, Gerbert (as Pope Sylvester II) is generally credited with having encouraged Otto's glorious vision of a restored Roman empire. He also opposed simony and upheld clerical celibacy, and did much to strengthen the church in Eastern Europe. Besides being a distinguished statesman, Gerbert was an accomplished scholar. The teaching methods devised by him were extremely influential in Northern Europe; he enlarged the

Sylvester II (Gerbert of Aurillac)

scope of the study of logic and raised mathematics to a new position of importance. He was also a devoted collector of ancient manuscripts.

□ J. Leflon *Gerbert: Humanisme et Chrétienté au Xe siècle* (1946)

Synods In the early history of the church, the words 'synod' and 'council' were often interchangeable. However, by the early 4th c. large ecumenical gatherings such as Nicaea (325) were called councils, and a meeting of bishops from a province or region, as well as of the bishop and clergy of a particular diocese, were usually referred to as synods.

T

Tamberlaine (1336–1403) Mongol khan from 1370, also known as Timūr-i Lang or Timur the Lame. Of noble Turkish origin, though claiming descent from Jenghiz Khan, he succeeded in his ambition to reconstruct the 13th-c. Mongol empire. With Samarkand as his capital, by 1400 he had mastered all the Mongol-ruled territories of Central Asia, overrun Persia, Mesopotamia and Syria, and extended his rule as far north as Moscow and as far south as northern India. The savagery of his campaigns did not prevent both the West and Byzantium from regarding him briefly as a possible ally against the Ottomans, and both Christians and Turks died at the great battle of Ankara (1402), where Tamberlaine defeated and captured Bāyazīd, the Ottoman sultan. Completing his conquest of Anatolia, he successfully besieged the last Christian city of Asia Minor, Smyrna, in the same year.

On his death, which occurred as he was advancing on China, his empire disintegrated, the dynasty only being preserved by the great moghuls of Delhi. The crumbling Byzantine empire was never strong enough to take advantage of the disruption of Ottoman power in Asia, although Tamberlaine's intervention did allow it another 50 years of life.

□ H. Hookham *Tamburlaine the Conqueror* (1962); D.M. Nicol *The Last Centuries of Byzantium* (1972)

Tancred de Hauteville Minor Norman baron from near Coutances, notable only for the careers of his many sons, all of whom journeyed to southern Italy in the mid-11th c. to seek their fortunes. Of the five sons born to Tancred's first wife Muriella – William (d. 1046), Drogo (d. 1051), Humphrey (d. 1057), Geoffrey and Serlo – the first three, each in turn, became counts of Apulia. His second marriage to Fredesendis produced seven sons – Robert Guiscard

Tamberlaine and his men capture the fortress of the knights of St John at Smyrna (*c.*1490).

(d. 1085), Mauger, William, Aubrey, Tancred, Humbert and Roger (d. 1101) – and both the eldest and youngest of these had spectacular careers; they were involved in the conquest of Sicily (completed 1091), which Roger ruled as the 'Great Count'. Robert Guiscard, after recognition by the pope as duke of Apulia and Calabria (1059), became involved in papal and Byzantine politics and was responsible in 1084 for the sack of Rome. *See* ROBERT GUISCARD; ROGER I

□ J.J. Norwich *The Normans in the South* (1967); D.C. Douglas *The Norman Achievement* (1969)

Tannenburg, battle of (1410) This marked the end of the influence and prestige of the Teutonic knights, in confrontation with the rising nationalism of Poland. The conflict centred on the province of Samogitia on the Baltic coast which separated the Teutonic colonies of Prussia and Livonia, and which Poland and Lithuania (united since 1386) had ceded to the Order in exchange for the province of Dobrzyn in 1404. In 1410, suspecting Lithuanian complicity in revolts in Samogitia, the Teutonic knights invaded Dobrzyn and were heavily defeated at

Tannenburg by the Polish nobility. The Peace of Thorn (1411) provided an intermediate settlement, but war broke out again and the Teutonic knights were compelled to renounce Samogitia in 1422.

Tari (pl. *taris* or *tareni*) From an Arabic word meaning 'fresh', in the sense of newly struck. A name given originally to the quarter-dinars (1.06g) of the Arabs in Sicily and to the imitations of these struck at Amalfi and Salerno (11th c.–13th c.) and in Sicily by the Normans and their successors down to 1278. After the mid-12th c. the coins, while remaining of the same fineness, ceased to be struck to a uniform weight, though the *trappeso* (tari-peso) remained as weight equivalent to 1/30th of an ounce.

Tariq ibn Ziyād Berber commander from North Africa who initiated the Muslim conquest of Spain. In 711 he attacked the Spanish coast with a force of 7000 Berbers somewhere near Gibraltar (from *Gebel-Tariq*, 'Rock of Tariq'), then proceeded inland to a site near Sidonia where, in the same year, reinforced with a further 5000 men sent by his superior, Mūsā, he defeated the usurper Roderic, last king of Visigothic Spain. Tariq and Mūsā together continued the conquest, overrunning most of the Iberian peninsula, much of which remained in Muslim hands throughout the Middle Ages. In 713 they quarrelled, possibly over the disposition of booty, and were recalled to Damascus, where Mūsā was accused of dishonesty and Tariq's loyalty questioned. Both died in obscurity shortly afterwards.
□ H.V. Livermore *The Origins of Spain and Portugal* (1971)

Tassilo Duke of Bavaria 748–88 (b. *c*.742) After a disputed minority, he was restored to the ducal throne at the age of 15 by Pepin the Short, king of the Franks, to whom he submitted as a vassal in 757. The 8th-c. *Annales Regni Francorum* report the solemnity of the occasion, the first known mention of the vassalic oath of allegiance and submission with the hands (*per manus*). In Charlemagne's reign he twice defected from his oath, eventually submitting and offering his son Theodo as a hostage when faced with military attack in 787. The following year, after the sentence of death demanded by the general assembly at Ingelheim was commuted by Charlemagne to life imprisonment, he entered a monastery. In 794, on Charlemagne's order, he emerged to renounce publicly his family rights in Bavaria, and control of the province passed to the Franks.
□ D. Bullough *The Age of Charlemagne* (1965); *Carolingian Chronicles* ed. B.W. Scholz and B. Rogers (1970)

Tauler, Johann (*c*.1300–61) With Eckhart and Suso, one of the three great Rhineland mystics of the 14th c. A native of Strasbourg, where he spent most of his active life, he became a Dominican friar at an early age and devoted himself to preaching. His central theme was the method by which the soul can be made ready for union with God, and was expressed in both mystical and homely terms appropriate to the Dominican nuns and pious laity whom he addressed. His surviving works consist of vernacular sermons and one letter, and were widely read during his lifetime. Luther knew and admired his works, though 16th-c.. Catholic theologians suspected him of quietism. Interest in Tauler was revived in the 19th c. by both Protestant and Catholic theologians.
□ J.M. Clark *The Great German Mystics* (1949)

Teutonic knights (Knights of the Sword) Founded in 1198 as a religious and military order in imitation of the Hospitallers, the Teutonic knights soon acquired lands in Germany and Syria. They supported Frederick II's crusade and were granted East Prussia by him in 1226. From that year on, initially as auxiliaries of the Polish duke of Masovia, they began to subdue and convert the Prussians, building their first fortified centre at Thorn in 1231. Gradually, their Baltic possessions (which by the 14th c. extended as far as the Gulf of Finland) dominated their activities and, after the fall of Acre (1291), which they helped to defend, they ended their association with the Crusades. By 1283 Prussia had been ruthlessly subjugated; natives were uprooted to make way for new German settlers, revolts severely dealt with, and many of the indigenous population reduced to serfdom. By 1410 the Order had established 1400 villages and 93 new towns on its Prussian lands and had come into conflict with Poland, who defeated it at the battle of Tannenburg. Prussia became a fief of the Polish crown under the terms of the Second Peace of Thorn (1466). In 1525 the grand master of the Teutonic knights accepted the doctrines of Luther; the Order became secularized and the grand master became the first duke of Prussia.
□ S. Runciman *A History of the Crusades* vol. 3 (1954); G. Barraclough *The Origins of Modern Germany* (1966); O. Halecki *A History of Poland* (1978)

Theodora (d. 548) Wife of Justinian I. The beautiful daughter of the keeper of the bears in the amphitheatre of Constantinople, Theodora married Justinian after he had raised her to the patriciate and persuaded his uncle, the Emperor Justin I, to abrogate the law which forbade the marriage of senators and actresses. She became empress on

The Empress **Theodora**: detail from the superb mosaic at S. Vitale, Ravenna (6th c.).

Justinian's accession in 527, though she was despised by some of the aristocracy because of her disreputable background.

She was attracted to the Monophysite heresy, unlike her intensely orthodox husband, and used her influence to protect its adherents, setting up a Monophysite monastery in the palace of Hormisdas, protecting refugee bishops and being instrumental in the deposition of Pope Sylverius and his replacement by the more amenable Vigilius. Her influence, however, was limited; she was not able to affect Justinian's religious policy and, in spite of her strong personal hatred of John of Cappadocia (Justinian's praetorian prefect in the East), it took her ten years to engineer his downfall.

Much of what is known of Theodora is coloured by the scandalous and biased writings of Procopius, though even he was able to recognize her strength of character. This was demonstrated most clearly on the occasion of the Nika revolt (532), when the normally inimical circus factions, the Greens and the Blues, joined forces in an attempt to depose Justinian. Procopius reports Theodora's words: 'For an emperor to become a fugitive is a thing not to be endured . . . the purple makes a fine winding sheet.' These rallied the faint-hearted Justinian when he was on the point of flight, and inspired him to stay and crush the revolt.

□ Procopius *The Secret History* trans. G.A. Williamson (1966); C. Diehl *Theodora of Byzantium* (1972)

Theodore of Tarsus (602–90) Archbishop of Canterbury from 668. Although 66 years old at the time of his appointment and requiring instruction in the ways of the English church, he proved to be a great ecclesiastical statesman responsible for the organization of a regular diocesan episcopate. Called by Bede 'the first archbishop whom the entire church of the English obeyed', he presided over two important church councils (Hertford 672, and Hatfield 679). Under his rule, Canterbury became a centre of Latin and Greek learning. His *Poenitentiale*, collected after his death, had great influence on future penitential discipline in the churches of England and Germany.

□ H. Mayr-Harting *The Coming of Christianity to Anglo-Saxon England* (1972)

Theodoric the Great King of the Ostrogoths 490–526 (b. *c*.455) Theodoric the Amal, called Dietrich of Bern in the *Nibelungenlied*, ruled much of the Western Roman empire, including Italy, Sicily, Dalmatia, Noricum and Rhaetia; he was also suzerain in his grandson's name of the Visigothic kingdom of Spain and Septimania. His childhood and youth were spent in Constantinople, and it was in the name of the Emperor Zeno that he invaded Italy and in 493 defeated Odoacer (who had in 476 deposed the last Western emperor, Romulus Augustulus). Theodoric made no imperial claim and was content to rule as king in his realm, a position tacitly recognized by the Eastern emperors, who returned to him the imperial regalia which Odoacer had delivered to Zeno.

He admired Roman civilization and is quoted as saying, 'an able Goth wants to be like a Roman; only a poor Roman would want to be like a Goth'. In Italy he followed a conciliatory policy, respecting the senate and Roman institutions, and permitting both his Roman and Gothic subjects to keep their own laws and officials. At his court in Ravenna he employed Romans as his civilian officials, reserving military positions for the Goths. Even the allotment of lands made to his followers after his conquest seems to have been achieved without incident.

Although Theodoric was an Arian, he remained on good terms with the Catholic church and on occasions acted as an arbiter in church matters, most notably in the Laurentian schism of 498, when two popes were elected simultaneously. However, in 523 Justin I, the Eastern emperor, proscribed Arianism throughout the empire, an event which undermined Theodoric's authority in Italy and led to senatorial conspiracies against him. His reprisals were severe, the philosopher Boethius being the most noted victim. Theodoric died before his counter-measures against the Catholics could be put fully into force. The ensuing struggle for succession

The mausoleum of **Theodoric** the Ostrogoth at Ravenna.

set in motion Justinian's campaign of reconquest.
□ W. Ensslin *Theoderich der Grosse* (1947); A.H.M. Jones *The Later Roman Empire 284–602* (1964); C. Wickham *Early Medieval Italy* (1981)

Theodosian Code (438) Collection of all imperial constitutions issued from the reign of Constantine onwards and promulgated in the names of Theodosius II and Valentinian III, the Eastern and Western emperors. This official publication superseded two earlier private collections, the Gregorian and Hermogenian Codes. Theodosius' commissioners, under the presidency of Antiochus, the praetorian prefect, spent eight years on the task, searching provincial archives and private law collections to produce a permanent record of imperial legislation. The *Code* is of great value as source material for a sparsely documented period of Roman history, and, with the addition of new decrees published after the *Code* (Novels or *Novellae*), influenced the law code of the Visigoths and formed the foundation for the *Code* of Justinian (529).
□ *The Theodosian Code and Novels, and the Sirmondian Constitutions* trans. C. Pharr (1952)

Theodulf (*c.*750–821) Bishop of Orleans and abbot of Fleury. By birth a Spanish Visigoth, he became a leading theological and literary figure at Charlemagne's court, serving as a royal legate in the south of France (798) and taking part in the trial of Pope Leo III in Rome (800). Suspected of complicity in the

revolt (817) of Bernard of Italy against Charlemagne's successor Louis the Pious, he was deposed in 818 and exiled to Angers.

He is now generally believed to have been the author of the *Libri Carolini*, a scholarly statement of the official Carolingian position with regard to the Iconoclastic controversy then dividing the Eastern and Western churches. His works include a version of the Vulgate, the poem *Ad Judices*, which gives advice to judges based on his own experience, and other poems, some satirical, which give a lively picture of court life. His episcopal statutes, containing advice for both clergy and laity, were popular and influential in his own lifetime.
□ A. Freeman, 'Theodulf of Orleans and the *Libri Carolini*', *Speculum* 32 (1957), 40 (1965) and 46 (1971); H. Liebeschütz, 'Theodulf of Orleans and the problem of the Carolingian Renaissance', *Fritz Saxl 1890–1948* ed. D.J. Gordon (1957)

Theophano (d.991) Wife of Otto II. A strong-willed Greek princess, kinswoman to the Byzantine emperor, John Tzimisces (969–76). Her marriage to

Ivory relief of Christ blessing the Emperor Otto II and his wife, **Theophano** (late 10th c.).

the German Emperor Otto II in 972 implied a recognition of the Saxon dynasty as emperors in the West. With Adelaide, her mother-in-law, she became joint regent for her son Otto III after Otto II's death in 983. Both women took the title of *Augusta*, but Theophano proved to be the dominant partner, giving herself on occasions the masculine title of *imperator augustus*. Her presence, though not greatly affecting relations between the two empires, opened new avenues for Byzantine influence in Germany. Otto III introduced Greek ceremonial and offices in his court, but died before his planned marriage to a Greek princess could take place.
□ K. Hampe *Germany under the Saxon and Salian Kings* (1973)

Thierry of Chartres (d.1151) One of the most powerful of the intellectuals and teachers of the 12th c., Thierry, brother of Bernard of Chartres, taught in Paris and its suburbs in the 1130s, and possibly earlier. He became chancellor and archdeacon at Chartres in 1142. He wrote voluminously, his range extending over commentaries on Cicero, *Genesis*, cosmology and above all on Boethius. He played a special role in the transmission of Platonic thought in the West, and his *Heptateuchon* became recognized as a standard textbook on the liberal arts.
□ C.N.L. Brooke *The Twelfth-Century Renaissance* (1969)

Third Order of St Francis Founded originally by the saint as the Order of Penitence, to enable pious lay men and women to participate in the regulated religious life of the Franciscans whilst continuing to live in their own homes and to earn their own living. Organized under their own Rule, first given them by Ugolino (c.1221) and later expanded and authorized by Pope Nicholas IV, the Tertiaries held chapters, shared devotions and practised charitable works. By the 14th c. the Order had split into two groups: the 'secular Tertiaries' and a new, cloistered Third Order Regular. Most active in Italy, the Tertiaries attracted mainly members of the artisan class. Notable Tertiaries include St Elizabeth of Hungary, Raymond Lull, and (possibly) Christopher Columbus.
□ J.R.H. Moorman *A History of the Franciscan Order* (1968)

Thomas, earl of Lancaster (c.1278–1322) Holder of five earldoms, royal councillor and a powerful defender of the controversial Ordinances of 1311, he earned the hatred of Edward II for his involvement in the murder of Piers Gaveston, the king's favourite. Edward's defeat at Bannockburn (1314) increased Lancaster's influence, but he was never able to gather a united party around himself. Unable to come to terms with the 'moderate' magnates or the Court party, it was in alliance with the Marcher lords – angered by the behaviour of Hugh Despenser, Edward's new favourite – that he was defeated by the royal forces at Boroughbridge (1322). He was executed after a summary trial.
□ J.R. Maddicott *Thomas of Lancaster* (1970)

Three Chapters The controversy over the Three Chapters, as certain writings suspected of Nestorianism came to be called, was connected with the larger split between Monophysite and Chalcedonian Christians. Possibly hoping to reconcile the two groups, the Emperor Justinian denounced the Three Chapters in 544 and forced a reluctant Pope Vigilius and the Fifth Ecumenical Council to do the same. No reconciliation resulted; instead, although the Eastern church accepted the decision, there was outrage in the West (especially in Africa), schism between Vigilius' successor Pelagius I and some of the Italian churches, and considerable damage done to papal prestige.

Timur the Lame *See* **Tamberlaine**

Toledo, Councils of These general councils of the Spanish Catholic church of the 6th c. and 7th c. grew in importance when Reccared, the Visigothic king, was converted from Arianism to Catholicism. He announced his conversion at the Third Council of Toledo (589), and from then on a series of important general councils was held until the end of the Visigothic kingdom of Spain in 711.

As well as dealing with ecclesiastical affairs, the councils involved the bishops in the secular rule of the kingdom, although their role does not seem to have been to initiate legislation, but merely to discuss and then to confirm measures presented to them by the king. From the Eighth Council (653) royal officials also appear to have taken part. Canons issued by the councils covered such matters as the discipline of the clergy, the enforcement of the uniformity of religious practice, the punishment of heresy and the extirpation of paganism. Nearly every council passed severe anti-Semitic measures, regularly forbidding intermarriage between Jews and Christians and participation in Jewish religious rites, with heavy penalties for disobedience.

Councils were convoked only at the command of the king and were largely under his control. The 75th canon of the Fourth Council (633), called by E.A. Thompson 'the most famous canon ever agreed by the Spanish church', decreed that the royal succession should be determined by the magnates and bishops of the kingdom sitting in common council; it imposed anathema on anyone who should break his oath of allegiance or attempt to usurp the throne, and called upon the king to rule moderately and piously.

☐ R. Collins *Early Medieval Spain 400–1000* (1984)

Totila King of the Ostrogoths 541–52 The last great Ostrogothic king, Totila revived Gothic resistance to Justinian's reconquest of Italy. Recruiting slaves and peasants to augment his force of 5000 Goths, he reconquered the south of Italy and outmatched the limited and mutinous troops of Justinian's general Belisarius. In 550 he captured Rome and advanced upon Sicily. Eventually he was defeated by Belisarius' replacement, Narses, who arrived with reinforcements and sufficient funds to pay the arrears due to the imperial troops. Totila was killed at the battle of Busta Gallorum, and a few months later his successor Teias was also defeated by Narses, thus bringing to an end the Ostrogothic kingdom of Italy.

☐ T. Hodgkin *Italy and her Invaders* vol. 5 (1916)

Towns The development of a distinctive town life is an important feature of medieval Europe. In the last centuries of the ancient world the civilization of the Greeks and Romans, in its fullest forms, was urban, and its literature and institutions reflected urban values. The Roman empire was, indeed, the greatest of the ancient city-states, with a common citizenship enjoyed by its privileged subjects. The final collapse of centralized government in the 5th c. and the piecemeal settlement of the West by Germanic invaders effaced the empire's urban economy and its culture together. The subsequent re-coalescence of urban populations is a significant aspect of the new culture of the Middle Ages, which arose on the ruins of Rome.

No such change is ever precise and complete. Over a large part of Continental Europe the Christian church maintained traditions of Roman government, and therefore something of urban life, on such foundations as remained to support them. The Roman *diocesis* became an ecclesiastical institution; the *civitas* tribal and cantonal capitals of Gaul, such as Paris, Rheims and Tours, became the seats of bishops. The transition in Italy from Antiquity to Middle Ages was briefer and more ambiguous than in the rest of Europe, and in Rome itself and the larger towns, concentrated populations suggest some continuity of institutions. Even north of the Alps, in such places as Bordeaux, and in Spain and North Africa before the Arab invasions, vestiges of the Roman legal and administrative system survived in the new age, with schools to support them.

These survivals had only slight effects upon northern Gaul, Britain and the Rhine basin, where Roman influence had always been attenuated by remoteness from the Mediterranean. In Britain some Roman towns were abandoned entirely, such as Silchester (*Calleva Atrebatum*) in Hampshire and *Venta Icenorum* in Norfolk. In general, however, the strategic importance of prime sites ensured some continuity of occupation, and the question for debate is to what extent, and when, the communities there can be considered urban. A town is characterized by a certain density of settlement, which goes beyond the community's ability to grow its own food; a pattern of occupations including the regular exchange of goods and services; and a distinctive civil status. The population of medieval towns was dense by contemporary standards, but never very large. In England only London approached 50,000, whilst the largest provincial cities of Bristol, Norwich and York remained close to 10,000. The smallest rural boroughs numbered craftsmen and traders by scores, and their whole communities only in hundreds. On the Continent, although the biggest centres were larger than London, the scale from city to market town was correspondingly extended. All had in common a dependence on the countryside for much of their food, and for immigration to maintain their numbers.

Civil status is an elusive concept in early times, and can easily be over-emphasized. Nevertheless, the common interest of kings and bishops gave some places a particular prominence. Royal households and religious communities alike had to be supported, and where their estates were widely scattered, transport and a system of exchange produced and sustained markets on both old and new sites. The church in particular needed incense and other materials which Western Europe could not supply, and both spices from the East and furs from the North found buyers at all times. Although such long-distance trade never ceased, it was for some centuries in the hands of merchants and carriers who frequented fairs and other seasonal sites rather than permanent settlements. The Frisians were one people who maintained such a commerce, until they were eventually eclipsed by the Vikings. The crisis of the Scandinavian invasions of the West, which destroyed early entrepôts like Dorestadt, later helped to drive trade and a more ordered administration into defensible and populous towns.

From the 10th c. European society was sustained by a network of urban settlements, though their size and condition varied greatly. In England, where the power of the kings was precociously consolidated, towns were characterized by a degree of licensed dependence and uniformity. Damaging as the Scandinavian incursions had been, the reaction against them produced a relatively well-contrived system. The Old English name for a fort, *burh*, came gradually to mean an urban settlement. For a century before the Norman Conquest fortified boroughs were commonly centres of administration, with their own courts, protected markets and a privileged tenure for their inhabitants. They also housed mints, which produced a coinage of exceptional quality under tight royal control.

Elsewhere in Europe towns reflected the prevailing political conditions by the degree of their autonomy or subjugation. In France the authority of the kings rested more lightly on their subjects outside their own domains, but if towns and cities were free of royal control, they had counts and local lords to reckon with. The larger German cities benefited from the decline in the emperors' strength, and those which eventually expressed their power in the Hanseatic League already enjoyed a substantial independence on their own ground. In Italy, Pisa, Genoa and Venice deployed fleets more powerful than those of the Hanse, whilst inland centres of trade and communications, such as Milan, Florence and Siena, could raise armies to protect themselves and their hinterlands.

For every one of the new city-states, however, there were many thousands of small settlements, approximated to larger neighbours in their functions and pretensions, and essential to the existence, not only of the greatest towns, but also to the sovereign lords, lay and ecclesiastical, with whom the few cities like Venice treated and vied. Although in the formative time of the 11th c. and 12th c. burgesses and citizens sparred with, and were usually overawed by, kings, prelates and noblemen, their quarrels concealed an ineradicable interdependence. Towns and merchants aspired to control of their own affairs at home, but needed and sought protection when they were at large. Kings and lords disliked the assertiveness of townsmen and were alarmed by their propensity to form sworn associations, notably the communes of the 12th c. Such manifestations seemed subversive and threatening, but at the same time lords looked to the towns not only for supplies, but also for the tolls and taxes which paid for political protection, and for the loans which traders, unlike farmers, could produce at any season of the year.

Trade, with some industries, maintained the towns; the administration of laws ensured their independence. In an age in which communities of all kinds were distinguished by their customs, the customs of towns were marked (amongst usages that might be found in any rural community) by provision for a relative degree of personal liberty, the free disposition of property, often including its devise by testament, the ready enforcement of contracts, and the recovery of debt. Despite the forms in which they were expressed, such customs were not of uniform antiquity, but were a convenient means of safeguarding and developing the rules which defined and protected the community. Towns readily exchanged information on such matters; the earliest letter between two municipalities in England describes the terms of Northampton's royal charter for the benefit of the burgesses of Lancaster, who in 1200 were seeking a similar grant. The customs of the Norman borough of Breteuil (Eure) were granted to scores of places in England, Wales and Ireland by Anglo-Norman lords, and the customs of Magdeburg spread to hundreds of towns in Eastern Europe as German knights, merchants and craftsmen moved towards the plains of the Vistula and the Dneister.

Sheltered by their walls and defined by their customs, the townsmen lived in distinct but not isolated communities. Subject, except for a minority of true city-states, to their sovereign lords, they administered law in their own courts and raised their own taxes. They founded and patronized churches and chapels; maintained schools and hospitals, roads and bridges. Their clerks kept court rolls, registers, act-books and cartularies, and wrote chronicles in which they celebrated the myths and the history of the locality. The audiences they addressed were self-conscious and self-regarding, but they were not unaware of a wider world. Noblemen had town houses, and successful townsmen acquired country estates. Both patronized the same artists and craftsmen. Towns themselves took on some of the embellishments of aristocratic society. The men of the Cinque Ports, whose ships made up the king's standing naval force, and the citizens of London were collectively styled barons on state occasions. Municipalities came to display coats of arms and other heraldic devices.

One of the earliest occasions for such displays came with the use of a common seal to authenticate acts made in the name of the town. Municipal seals appear in Northern Europe in the 12th c. and were quickly established as one of the marks of urban privilege. As civic business became more complex, there were seals for specialized courts and for individual officials. Devices on the early seals drew on religious, as often as heraldic symbols, on views of the town with its gates and walls, and occasionally on portraiture. The seal of Doullens (Somme) depicts the heads of the *Scabini*, or senior councillors, for example.

The seal was one expression of the unity of the townsmen; ceremonial was another, especially the rituals of the fraternity or guild. Guilds, with their sworn brotherhood and the sanction of a special peace between the brethren, were particularly well

A German **town**-scene: from the altarpiece in the Jakobskirche at Rothenburg.

suited to the conditions of town life. They were only briefly associated with the winning and exercise of self-government, but they provided all classes of society with a means of formal association. Religious and social guilds provided clubs for the magistracy and benefit societies for the townsmen at large. Craft guilds under general municipal supervision regulated admissions and working conditions, and provided for the welfare of artisans. All public and most private guilds had a focus in a church or chapel and retained priests as their chaplains. From the 14th c. onward, and particularly with the rise of the cult of Corpus Christi, guild plays on biblical themes were orchestrated by the municipalities in the ritual of the civic year.

The economic crisis of the later Middle Ages brought severe problems to the towns. Under the pressure of a rising population, from the 11th c. to the later 13th c. many new urban settlements were established and enfranchised, often marked today only by place-names such as Newton, in England, and its equivalent Villeneuve, Neumarkt and the like elsewhere. In a stationary or contracting economy they were not all viable and some decayed. At the same time new centres of cloth-making flourished in southern England, though a specialized population ran the risk of cyclical unemployment, which was a serious problem in the Flemish cities of Ghent, Bruges and Ypres by the early 16th c. Yet towns continued to lure immigrants from the countryside, and side by side with decay in some quarters there is evidence of the sub-division and more intensive building of other plots, and the development of specialized buildings such as inns. The chimney-stack, discharging the smoke of ground-floor rooms around rather than through upper storeys, was a feature of town-houses at least from the 12th c., as was the narrow street frontage of shop-space and carriage-entry giving onto a long and variously occupied courtyard, of which many examples survive today all over Europe.

The image of the medieval town as walled, compact and closely built is not a misleading one, though the reality was more complex. The walls and gates served to regulate traffic and facilitate the collection of tolls more often than they defended the town from assault. There were gardens and orchards inside the walls, and even the largest towns had fields and common ground outside. These were tokens that the rural community was dominant in

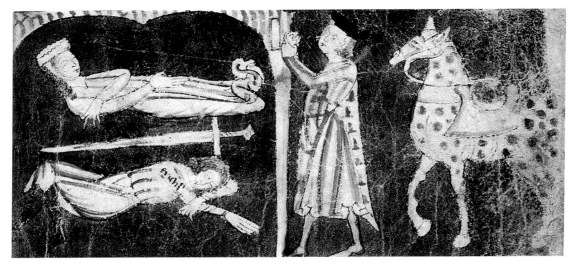

Tristan and Isolde lie asleep with a sword between them, watched by King Mark (13th c.).

medieval, just as the urban community is in modern society. The towns nevertheless performed vital functions in concentrating people and skills, and in realizing wealth. The universities, which displaced monastic houses as centres of learning and became vital to church and state as training-grounds for administrators, were products of the medieval town. So too, in another sense, were the voyages of exploration which opened a wider world to the European powers in the age of the Renaissance. *See* COMMERCE; FAIRS; GUILDS; UNIVERSITIES; WOOL TRADE; *See also individual towns* GM
□ M.W. Beresford *New towns of the Middle Ages* (1967); P. Dollinger *The German Hansa* (1970); S. Reynolds *An introduction to the history of English medieval towns* (1977)

Trebizond, empire of (1204–1461) Founded on the south-east coast of the Black Sea by the brothers Alexius and David, grandsons of the Byzantine emperor, Andronicus I, the empire survived as an independent Christian state until its conquest by Muhammad II in 1461, being the last of the Greek states to resist him. Its rulers, from the Comnenus family, used the title of 'Emperors of all the East', and the empire became famous for its riches and the beauty of its princesses; its metropolitan was accorded great honour at the Council of Florence (1439).

The empire's geographical position on the East/West trade routes attracted both Genoese and Venetian traders, who each had separate quarters within the city; the Genoese, in particular, proved to be very turbulent guests. But its isolated situation – a thin coastal strip surrounded by Muslim states separating it from the Greek empire – made complete indepen-

dence impossible, and the emperors of Trebizond protected themselves by submitting at various times to the Latin empire of Constantinople (1204–61), to local Muslim amirs, and to the Ottomans and Mongols. Marriage alliances with the Greek imperial house and the surrounding amirs were also part of this pattern.

The Comnenus family survived dynastic wars and palace revolutions, especially during the 14th c., and the empire maintained its Greek character in spite of intermarriage and a mixed population. Many religious foundations were made by its rulers, including the monastery of Dionysion on Mount Athos; the best preserved today is the monastery church of St Sophia, dating from the 13th c. and rich in sculptural decoration and wall paintings. The fall of Constantinople to the Ottomans in 1453 made the collapse of Trebizond inevitable. After its allies from the surrounding amirates had fallen one by one, it surrendered in 1461, and the last emperor was executed by Muhammad II in 1463.
□ W. Miller *Trebizond, the Last Greek Empire* (1926); A.A.M. Bryer *The Empire of Trebizond and the Pontos* (1980)

Tribonian (d. 542) Nominated quaestor by Justinian in 529, Tribonian was largely responsible for the vast body of legal codification associated with the reign. He served on the commission of eight which prepared the first *Codex Justinianus*, a collection of valid imperial edicts since the time of Hadrian, and with Dorotheus, a professor at Berytus, and three eminent lawyers he was responsible for the revision of the *Code* issued in 534. He was in charge of the preparation of the *Digest* (*Pandects*) of 533, the first attempt ever to bring the rulings of Roman jurists into an orderly system, making use of extracts from 200–300 treatises by about 40 writers, with Ulpian and Paulus predominating. He was further commissioned to produce a handbook for students, the *Institutes*, also published in 533. Although a great scholar and administrator, Tribonian acquired a reputation for venality and was one of the officials of Justinian whose dismissal was demanded by the crowds during the Nika rebellion of 532. He was re-appointed quaestor in 535 and retained the office until his death.

□ A.M. Honore *Tribonian* (1978); C. Mango *Byzantium: The Empire of New Rome* (1981)

Tribur, Diet of (1076) Convoked during the Investiture Contest, at a time when Emperor Henry IV and Pope Gregory VII had mutually excommunicated each other. Henry was confronted with a united German opposition and called upon, either to free himself from excommunication within four months, or to accept deposition and to live as a private citizen until the pope's decision on the matter should be announced. A second meeting was planned, to be held at Augsburg with the pope presiding, but before it could take place, Henry made his famous secret journey to Canossa, where he was temporarily reconciled with Gregory. This was seen as a breach of the Tribur agreement on the part of both parties by many of the German princes intent on Henry's deposition, and led them, in the following year at Forchheim, to elect Rudolf of Swabia as their new king, so ushering in many years of civil war.

□ G. Barraclough *The Origins of Modern Germany* (1966)

Tristan (Tristram) and Isolde (Iseult) One of the great love stories of the Middle Ages. The romance of Tristan and Isolde, rooted in traditions which probably date back to the period of Viking rule in Ireland in the 10th c., was given complete artistic form in the Ango-Norman world in the 12th c. It was written in French, translated into German by the great poet Gottfried von Strassburg, and also rendered into English and Old Norse. A lengthy prose version incorporates much Arthurian material, comparing the skill and reputation of Tristan and Lancelot as knights and as lovers. Cornwall, and especially Tintagel, provides the central location for the story, which ranges around the Celtic world from Cumbria to Ireland, and to Brittany. The principal characters are Tristan himself, King Mark of Cornwall (Tristan's uncle), Isolde of Ireland and Isolde of Brittany. The ingredients of the story, variously mixed in the different versions, constitute the quintessence of medieval romance: a lost nephew, a trusting lord and husband whose

trust is betrayed, love potions forcing hopeless love in impossible circumstances, poisoned cups and poisoned weapons, mysterious remedies, dragons and disasters, inevitable and also contrived tragic death, and the survival of love after death.

□ R. Curtis *Tristan Studies* (1969)

Trivium The seven liberal arts formed the basis of education in the Middle Ages, and were divided, from about the Carolingian period, into the Trivium and Quadrivium. The three arts of the Trivium – Latin grammar, rhetoric and dialectic – were defined by Hugh of Saint-Victor thus: 'Grammar is the knowledge of how to speak without error; dialectic is clear-sighted argument which separates the true from the false; rhetoric is the discipline of persuading to every suitable thing.'

By the 12th c. more emphasis was placed upon dialectic (or logic), and there was considerable controversy between defenders of the old logic and proponents of the new logic, largely created by the re-discovery of Aristotle. Dialectic, with its rational and speculative emphasis, was at first seen as dangerous when applied to theology, but nevertheless it grew

Grammar, part of the **Trivium**, holding a book, writing implements and a whip (*c.* 1110).

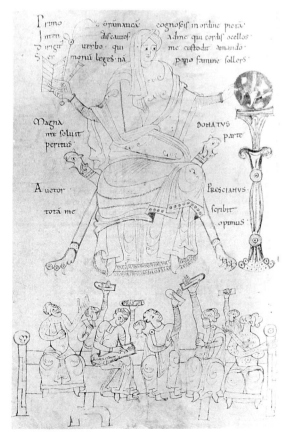

in importance as the full Trivium lost some ground, though grammar remained a necessary basis of medieval education, and rhetoric kept an important place in the Italian universities. *See* EDUCATION

☐ A. Piltz *The World of Medieval Learning* (1981)

Troubadours Beginning with the songs of William IX of Aquitaine (1071–1127), which range from the bawdy through the sensual to the refined, and ending with Guiraut Riquier (d.1292), who rejects profane love and sings in praise of the Virgin Mary, the troubadour poet-musicians of the courts of southern France left a rich and varied literary legacy. Other well-known exponents include Marcabru, Jaufre Rudel, Bernart de Ventadorn, Arnaut Daniel, Bertran de Born, Peire Cardenal and Guiraut de Bornelh. They celebrated the doctrine of *fin' amors*, the ritual glorification of the female sex and the cult of true love, both earthly and heavenly. Their songs – some of the melodies have survived – were composed in a variety of styles, from the 'clear' (*leu*) to the 'obscure' (*clus*) and covered a gamut of forms of varying degrees of technical complexity (*canso, tenso, planh, sirventes,* etc.). They exerted a profound influence not only on the lyric poetry of Western Europe, but also more generally on its literature, and eventually perhaps even on social attitudes. *See* COURTLY LOVE

☐ A. Jeanroy *Histoire Sommaire de la Poésie Occitane* (1945); C. Camproux *Histoire de la Littérature Occitane* (1953); L.T. Topsfield *Troubadours and Love* (1975)

Tughril Beg (*c*.993–1063) A grandson of the semi-legendary Seljuk, ruler of the Ghuzz tribesmen near the Aral sea, Tughril Beg is regarded as the founder of the Turkish Seljuk dynasty. With his brother, Chagri Beg, his conquests took him across Persia to Baghdad, where he defeated the Būyid general Basasiri after a protracted struggle, and was invested as sultan by the 'Abbāsid caliph in 1058. He died childless and was succeeded by Alp Arslan, Chaghri's son, under whom the Seljuks and their undisciplined followers, the Turkomans, continued to press forward. At the battle of Manzikert (1071), they inflicted a crushing defeat upon the Byzantine empire, an event which led indirectly to the preaching of the First Crusade.

☐ J.J. Saunders *A History of Medieval Islam* (1965)

Turks *See* **Ottoman, Seljuk Turks**

Twelfth-century renaissance In learning and artistic creativity, as well as in political order and the comforts of life, the centuries between the fall of the Roman empire in the West (5th c.) and the beginnings of economic and cultural revival in the 10th c.

Twelfth-century renaissance: the first page of Gratian's *Decretum*.

and 11th c. have often been considered the 'dark' ages. Whether the label is appropriate or not, there is no doubt of the power of the revival which followed: between the 11th c. and 13th c. it transformed the face of Western Europe, and in learning and culture it forms a large stepping-stone between the minor revivals of the 8th c.–10th c. and the Italian Renaissance of the 15th c. To this cultural revival the phrase 'Twelfth-century renaissance' has come to be attached. Although R. W. Southern has acclaimed its 'sublime meaninglessness', he and many others have meanwhile attempted to define its content: it embraced art, architecture and vernacular literature, but its special character was its ecclesiastical centre and inspiration, in the Schools, where logic and grammar, theology and canon law were taught, and in religious organizations. Such movements cannot be closely confined in limits of time, but by any reckoning the 12th-c. renaissance must include at least the period *c*.1050–*c*.1250.

The word 'renaissance' has commonly been taken to imply a deliberate rebirth and revival of ancient culture. Twelfth-century scholars were indeed backward-looking: they revered ancient authorities; in the celebrated phrase attributed by John of Salisbury to Bernard of Chartres, they claimed to be dwarfs on the shoulders of giants. Classical learning revived, and with it 'humanism' in at least two senses of the term; devotion to Latin literature and interest in human individuality and emotion. But attitudes to ancient Rome were ambivalent, and many scholars thought all learning should subserve the study of the Bible and theology. This helps to explain the rhythm of the 'renaissance' in Northern Europe, where the marked revival in the study of Latin and rhetoric, and in creative Latin writing in prose and verse, crumbled in the 13th c., giving rise to a desiccated but finely tuned scholastic Latin which provided the vehicle for the impressive and highly specialized theological structures of the schoolmen.

This specialization was also a product of the growth of the Schools. One marked feature of the 11th c. and 12th c. was a love of travel, issuing in pilgrimages and crusades, and the wanderings of students and scholars in search of distant masters. It was partly this which made possible the *succès fou* of a few great masters and centres of learning – and which in turn enabled these centres to develop their academic prowess and repute, and to become universities. In Northern Europe Paris was the undisputed centre, and its greatest attraction in the early 12th c. was the brilliant teacher, philosopher-theologian and lover, Peter Abelard. The intellectual stimulus of his teaching and the brilliance of his technique in applying logic (dialectic in medieval usage) to theology, was a major force in 12th-c. thought. But Abelard was only one of many teachers in Paris; their disciple John of Salisbury lists over a dozen major masters under whom he studied grammar, rhetoric, dialectic, other forms of philosophy, and above all, theology.

From this time forward Paris was the foremost centre of theological study in Europe and the chief intellectual centre of Northern Europe; in the course of the 12th c. it acquired a structure of institutions which converted it into a formal 'university', and by 1250 there were universities in Oxford, Cambridge and Montpellier, and several in Italy. The two English universities were, however, modest competitors to Paris as centres of theological study.

As a major intellectual discipline, the chief alternative to theology was law, Roman and canon. The 12th c. witnessed a radical transformation in the study and practice of canon law, whose central focus was the production of the *Concordance of Discordant Canons*, or *Decretum*, of Gratian in Bologna (*c.* 1140). It was no chance that it was written in Bologna, which for two generations had been the centre of the revival of Roman law, and a place where its study and practice both flourished. Gratian himself was apparently not a teacher or a practising lawyer, and he had little personal liking for Roman law. But his book was a catalyst, and by the time he and his disciples had finished with it, it was both a corpus of authorities and a stimulating texbook, which was to become the basic aid to canon law studies from the 12th c. to the 20th c. The attempt to reconcile discordant authorities lies at the base of much 12th-c. teaching and scholarship, from the canonist bishop Ivo of Chartres (d.1115), through Abelard the theologian to Gratian the lawyer and Peter the Lombard, the theologian who became professor and bishop in Paris and provided, in his

Sentences (*c.* 1150), a textbook of theological authorities as fundamental as Gratian's for law. It was on these foundations that the faculties of higher studies most characteristic of medieval universities – theology and law – were built. One marked feature of the 12th c. was the revival of interest in science, much influenced by Islamic and Jewish learning, and of this the chief centres in Christian Europe lay at Montpellier and Salerno.

In the 10th c. and 11th c. the monasteries lay at the centre of learning and craftsmanship in Western Europe. It is at first sight a paradox to find that in the 12th c., when the religious orders grew enormously both in size and variety, this dominance ceased – but in essence it is an illustration of the growing variety and richness of 12th-c. culture. The centres of learning came to lie in non-monastic schools like those of Paris and Bologna; the crafts came increasingly to be the work of lay professionals – never exclusively, but predominantly so. Yet monasteries remained, alongside cathedrals and other major churches, the principal channels of patronage in the arts. It was a great age of building, which witnessed the heyday of Romanesque and the birth of Gothic architecture. Gothic spread from Saint-Denis (Paris), through northern France to England and over much of Western Europe; the 12th c. saw flourishing schools of sculpture, especially in France and northern Italy, and local schools in book illumination and the minor crafts scattered over much of the face of Christendom.

The religious orders and Christian art and learning gave their mark and character to the 'renaissance'; yet its quality can only be savoured through appreciation of the rich vernacular literature, especially French and German, so characteristic of the 11th c.–13th c. In origin an oral literature, the crusading epics of the 11th c.–12th c., the *Song of Roland* and the other *chansons de geste* made bloodshed and war the typical theme of surviving French and German literature down to *c.*1150; thereafter Arthurian romance, knightly prowess and Courtly Love take front of stage, culminating in the rich, sophisticated *Parzival* of Wolfram von Eschenbach, shortly after 1200. The *Parzival* is a devout layman's version of the Grail story; one limb of a very rich and varied vernacular culture, in which men of learning like Chrétien de Troyes and Gottfried von Strassburg (author of the best-known version of the Tristan legend) mingled with poets and minstrels of much less sophisticated mind. The vernacular literature shows how the culture of the age spread widely among the unlearned as well as in the Schools, and developed secular as well as spiritual themes. *See* ADELARD OF BATH; ALAN OF LILLE; THIERRY OF CHARTRES; VICTORINES   CB
□ C.H. Haskins *The Renaissance of the Twelfth Century*

(1927); C.N.L. Brooke *The Twelfth-Century Renaissance* (1969); R.W. Southern *Medieval Humanism and other studies* (1970); C.R. Dodwell *Painting in Europe 800–1200* (1971); C. Morris *The Discovery of the Individual* (1972); *The Flowering of the Middle Ages* ed. J. Evans (1966)

Tyler, Wat One of the principal leaders of the Peasants' Revolt of 1381. Wat Tyler, a soldier who had served in France, led the revolt of the men of Kent and Essex who overran the city of London. Dramatic events included the execution of Archbishop Sudbury on Tower Hill and the burning of the great palace of John of Gaunt at the Savoy. In what proved to be a decisive confrontation at Smithfield, Tyler was struck down and killed in the presence of the young King Richard II by William Walworth, mayor of London.
□ R.H. Hilton *The English Rising of 1381* (1985)

Tyre A flourishing industrial and commercial port on the Syrian coast, it passed into crusader hands in 1124 after a siege of five months. Strongly defended by its walled isthmus, it was one of the few Latin-held territories to survive Saladin's campaigns; on the point of surrender in 1188, it rallied successfully under the determined leadership of Conrad of Montferrat. Conrad was murdered by the Assassins shortly after being chosen as the next king of Jerusalem, and control of Tyre became a matter of dispute between various Latin princes until it was abandoned without struggle to Sultan al-Ashraf in 1291, when Latin rule in Syria came to an end.

Uccello, Paolo (1397–1475) In his long career Uccello emerged as one of the masters of the Florentine school of painting. His surviving frescoes and panels illustrate a distinct technical advance, from the more purely decorative attributes of Gothic art to an increasingly scientific attitude towards perspective and naturalism.
□ J. Pope-Hennessy *Paolo Uccello* (1969)

Ugolino *See* **Gregory IX**

Umayyad (Omayyad) dynasty Based in Damascus, the Umayyads became the dominant ruling family in the Muslim world from 660 to 750, when major revolts led to their overthrow and the emergence of the 'Abbāsids. A remnant led by 'Abd ar-Rahmān fled to Spain and there established a Muslim dynasty

Wat Tyler is cut down by William Walworth, mayor of London, in the presence of Richard II.

with its centre at Cordoba, which flourished in the 9th c. and 10th c. *See* ABD AL-MALIK
□ B. Lewis *The Arabs in History* (1960)

Universities As institutions, universties are a medieval creation. The word *universitas*, meaning 'autonomous institution', was regularly applied to guilds and even communes, and it is indicative of the original character of the universities that they first adopted and then appropriated this name. The first universities were in fact guilds, bodies of masters responsible for granting degrees and admitting men to the profession, or bodies of students. Gradually, the whole of what would now be called the university – the *studium*, as it was termed – came under external control; but the initial impetus was an independent one.

The first signs that higher education was becoming institutionalized appear in the 12th c. C.H. Haskins observed that 'In 1100 the school followed the teacher; by 1200 the teacher followed the school.' In Paris the fame of Abelard, Hugh of Saint-Victor and others had attracted an increasing number of students, and when there were more than the cathedral school could hold, rival schools were set up on the Left Bank. Masters banded together in an attempt to control the quality and type of teaching, and in this met their first opponent, the chancellor of Notre-Dame cathedral, traditionally awarder of the licence to teach. Their struggle was echoed in relations between town and gown, and culminated in the Carnival riots of 1228–29 and the closure of the university for two years.

The masters emerged from this with much greater control over the licence; an important step had been taken in weaning bishops from the notion that they held a monopoly of control over education. But another controversy followed which was to dominate the 13th c. (and to push the university onto a sounder constitutional footing), with the arrival in Paris of the friars, and their attempts to have their students exempted from the 'foundation' arts course. The reason for this was at least partly the friars' mistrust of the Aristotle-orientated arts course; and so controversy over the structure of universities was paralleled by a controversy over the absorption of Aristotle into the Christian system.

The Parisian structure rapidly became the model for other universities of northern Europe. An important variant was Oxford, and soon after, Cambridge; here the foundation of residential colleges where instruction took place encouraged the development of the tutorial system which continues to this day (most European colleges were basically boarding-houses).

At Bologna, organization was very different. Bologna's reputation as a centre of law (Irnerius, Gratian, Accursius, etc.) grew at the same time as that of Paris for theology, and attracted older, lay and, in the main, wealthier students, who were less inclined to accept the masters' control. The disturbed political climate of Italy with its endemic urban conflict also put foreign citizens at a disadvantage, and before 1200 there developed associations of students, by subject and within that, by nation, who used their collective bargaining power to gain extensive control over their employees, the teachers. The statutes of these 'student universities' indicate that the students were in control of the teaching programme, fining those who failed to teach as desired or to the minimum audience required, and exacting an oath of obedience from the doctors, as well as from stationers and even landlords.

Several pressures ensured that this system did not last long. In their growth and in the establishment of their constitutions and rights, both Paris and Bologna had benefited considerably from papal and imperial support. The Emperor, eager to protect the development of Roman law, had granted all-important privileges in the *Authentica Habita* (1155), while the pope, who traditionally saw himself as guardian of education, supported the autonomy of both universities (and in particular the regulation of degrees). As the number of universities increased and the constitutional influence of Paris and Bologna spread, the system was gradually but fundamentally transformed. It was then the turn of local forces. In Italy universities founded by communes had teachers on the commune's payroll; Bologna soon followed suit. 'Student power', deprived of much of its *raison d'être*, declined and in many places remained only as a formality. Elsewhere, too, universities were founded through local, often princely initiative and

organized as branches of local government. Of the *c*.70 universities founded by 1500, only the oldest and most powerful retained much independence. The university system was already largely 'tamed' within 200 years of its inception.

Universities came to play a crucial role in the intellectual, political and social life of Europe. Their political influence is apparent in the way that the growth of Paris university and of the town as capital in the 13th c. go hand in hand; in the way that universities were widely consulted for legal opinions during the Great Schism; and in the way that the university of Prague acted as a centre for the nascent Bohemian reform movement at the time of Hus. This was natural as the universities dominated several professional fields. University training was overwhelmingly vocational: an arts degree was preliminary to a higher degree in theology, law or medicine, and the syllabus reflected this. For example, there was a predominance of logic at Paris, where the arts course was most frequently a preliminary to theology, while at Bologna 'philosophy', a preliminary to medicine, consisted mainly of Aristotle's medical texts. The university's intellectual influence of course extended beyond formal teaching; the myth that the universities stood in opposition to the humanist movement of the early Renaissance, for example, is being demolished as historians realize how many humanists were university-trained, how many taught there, and how their interests crept into and gradually altered

Relief carving from the façade of Notre Dame, showing scenes of **university** life at Paris.

Urban II consecrates the great abbey of Cluny (III) in 1095, from the late 12th-c. Book of Offices.

both the range of courses on offer and the way in which traditional subjects were taught.

The greatest contrasts with the modern system relate to the character of medieval universities as guilds for professional training. A degree was, at least initially, a licence to teach, and this fact is reflected in the kind of training universities provided – with public disputation and apprentice-teaching playing prominent roles – and in the length of degree courses (16 years for a doctorate of theology in addition to the initial arts degree). This meant that comparatively few students took their studies all the way to degree stage. A consequence was great flexibility with regard to attendance, and great mobility between universities. As the importance of degrees as professional qualifications increased, this mobility was sustained by intense competition between the universities. The old tradition of the wandering scholar was thus given a new lease of life. The concept of the community of scholarship combined with local traditions of university ceremonial and ritual to create a powerful myth about academic traditions and freedoms, which provided some compensation for the increasingly tight control and professional orientation of the universities. *See* EDUCATION; ROBERT OF SORBON   PD
□ H. Rashdall *The Universities of Europe in the Middle Ages* (1936); L. Thorndike *University Records and Life in the Middle Ages* (1944); G. Leff *Paris and Oxford Universities in the 13th and 14th centuries* (1968); A.B. Cobban *The Medieval Universities: their Development and Organization* (1975); *The University in Society* vol. 1, ed. L. Stone (1975)

Urban II (Odo of Châtillon) Pope 1088–99 (b. *c*.1040) A former Cluniac prior and supporter of Pope Gregory VII, Urban continued the basic reforming programme of Gregory while avoiding extremes of confrontation with the secular powers. Even so there was from time to time great friction with the Emperor Henry IV over his continued recognition of the anti-pope Clement III and with the French King Philip I over marital problems. Archbishop Anselm, in exile as a result of his quarrel with William Rufus, turned to Urban for support and was present at his councils, when decrees against lay investiture were reiterated (1098). Urban's pontificate is chiefly remembered, however, for his positive steps towards moral reform and for the preaching of the First Crusade at Clermont (1095). French by blood and an orator by temperament, he roused the people of Western Europe, notably the French-speaking community, to attempt to recover Jerusalem, but died before that objective was achieved.
□ H.G.J. Cowdrey *The Age of Abbot Desiderius* (1983)

Urban VI (Bartolomeo Prignano) Pope 1378–89 (b. *c*.1318) A native of Naples, Urban was elected pope on the death of Gregory XI, partly to meet the strong popular current of opinion that demanded an Italian pope after the long exile in Avignon. His autocratic temper and resort to violence led almost immediately to a reaction, as a result of which the French cardinals, supported by some Italians, elected an anti-pope (Clement VII) and withdrew again from Rome to Avignon. The resulting schism greatly harmed the church, and Urban's energies were taken up almost completely in political struggles against Clement.
□ W. Ullmann *The Origins of the Great Schism* (1948)

V

Vacarius the Glossator (*c*.1120–*c*.1200) Active and learned in Roman law, Vacarius was trained at Bologna and spent time in the 1140s and 1150s in England. It was here that he produced his most important work, the *Liber Pauperum*, which has been described as a poor man's guide to Justinian's *Code* and *Digest*. Through this work and later writings he had a powerful influence on the teaching of law in England in the late 12th c. and 13th c., though the view that designated him as the first known teacher of law at Oxford is no longer held. Among other important works attributed to him are a tract on marriage and theological studies upholding the orthodox view of the human nature of Christ.
□ *The Liber Pauperum of Vacarius* ed. F. de Zulueta (1927)

Vagantes Wandering scholars, poets, clerics, students and 'hangers-on' were characteristic of the central Middle Ages, and particularly of the urban element in the time of population expansion (12th c. and 13th c.). Most information about them comes from the disapproving, stabler side of the literate world. They left a body of characteristic poetry, overlapping with Goliardic verse and best represented in the *Carmina Burana*.
□ H. Waddell *The Wandering Scholars* (1961)

Valla, Lorenzo (1407–57) Most famous for his application of the new humanist standards of criticism to documents used by the papacy in support of its temporal power. In 1440 he published his tract against the Donation of Constantine, which effectively proved that the famous document, under the terms of which imperial authority had been transmitted to the papacy, was spurious. Valla was also a considerable philosopher, anxious, with his linguistic mastery, that old errors arising from faulty translations of Aristotle or the Bible should not be perpetuated.
□ S.I. Camporeale *Lorenzo Valla, umanesimo e teologia* (1972)

Vandals One of the most prominent groups of East German barbarians who overran the Western Roman empire in the 5th c. and 6th c. Notorious for their ruthlessness, they were nevertheless substantially Christian, though of Arian beliefs. After 406 they crossed the Rhine frontier and swept through Gaul into Spain, where, in alliance with the Alans, they settled temporarily in Andalusia. In 429 they crossed to North Africa and in the course of the following ten years subdued the whole prosperous province, capturing Hippo in 431 and Carthage in 439. Their King Gaiseric (428–77) was one of the great figures of the migration age. One of the few German leaders to turn to sea-power, he came to control the western Mediterranean and in 455 sacked Rome itself.

The Vandals preserved their integrity as a minority ruling group in a Roman province only by a rigorous process of religious segregation. Intermittent persecutions of the native Catholic population emphasized the dichotomy within the kingdom, and in a short, sharp campaign in 533 Belisarius, the principal general of the Emperor Justinian, defeated the Vandals and utterly overthrew the kingdom. North Africa, though harassed by Moors and Berbers, passed back into imperial hands until the capture of Carthage by the Muhammadans in 698.

Although relatively short-lived (little more than a century), the Vandal kingdom proved of great importance in the history of the decline of the Western empire, because of the decisive break it made in sea communications between Rome, North Africa and the western Mediterranean generally.
□ J.M. Wallace-Hadrill *The Barbarian West 400–1000* (1952); L. Musset *The Germanic Invasions* (1975)

Vatican The Vatican palace in Rome has been the home of the popes since their return from Avignon in 1377. In earlier days it had been a papal palace, built on the Vatican hill immediately to the north of the basilica of St Peter, though the Lateran palace had been the chief papal residence. Parts of the existing palace date from the 13th c., but the overwhelming mass is the result of the building activities of the Renaissance popes. It contains the papal archives, one of the greatest repositories of historical records in the world. *See* PAPAL STATES
□ A.A. de Marco *The Tomb of St Peter* (1964); J.A.F. Thomson *Popes and Princes 1417–1517* (1980)

Venice City created in the 6th c. as a refuge from the wars of Ostrogoths and imperial forces, on the islands to the north of the Po estuary in north-east Italy. By the 10th c. it had become an important commercial element in the Adriatic, preserving a precious link between the Eastern empire and the Western world. Strong state control of naval building and of the basic organization of trade led to a great expansion of prosperity and power in the 11th c. and 12th c. Venice gained important commercial privileges at Constantinople in 1081, extended her territorial authority over Istria and parts of Dalmatia, and benefited greatly from the success of the crusading movement, winning privileges notably in Tyre and Acre. Their break with the Eastern empire in the later 12th c. had disastrous effects on the politics of the whole Near East. Venice directed the Fourth Crusade to its own ends, capturing Zara in Dalmatia in 1202 and Constantinople itself in 1204.

For much of the early part of the 13th c. Venice was virtually supreme in the eastern Mediterranean, but rivalry with Genoa, particularly after the Greek recovery of Constantinople in 1261, led to a more balanced situation, with Venetian power and influence still immensely important throughout the Greek islands. Genoa eventually declined after heavy naval defeats in the late 14th c., and the Venetian republic was thereafter chiefly involved in building up a strong principality in north-eastern Italy and in preserving as much as it could of its Greek possessions (Crete, the Ionian Isles and Naxos) in the face of overwhelming Ottoman pressures in the Balkans.

The constitution of Venice was very complex,

An elaborate 14th-c. illumination of **Venice** showing the Doge's palace, St Mark's cathedral, and ships departing.

with an elected duke (doge), a council, a senate and an elaborate interlocking system of courts and provincial governorships. Effective power remained in the hands of a wealthy group of aristocratic families, exercising (after 1310) supreme power through a secret and much feared Council of Ten. Partly because of its wealth and experience in business and government, Venice avoided the fate of other great Italian cities and did not fall into the hands of tyrants. In the 15th c. Venice became famous as the centre of a new printing industry. *See* CONTARINI; FOSCARI, FRANCESCO

□ D.S. Chambers *The Imperial Age of Venice 1380–1580* (1970); F.C. Lane *Venice, a maritime republic* (1973), *Studies in Venetian social and economic history* ed. B.G. Kohl and R.C. Müller (1987)

Verdun, Treaty of (843) Drawn up to settle the dynastic civil war which had sprung up among the grandsons of Charlemagne. Under its terms the empire was divided into three kingdoms. Charles the Bald was granted the kingdom of the West Franks, Neustria, Aquitaine and the Spanish March, with its eastern frontier roughly along the Schildt, the Saône, and the Rhône; this territory was mostly Romance-speaking and became the historic kingdom of France. Louis the German obtained the eastern Frankish kingdom, consisting essentially of the four stem duchies of Franconia, Saxony, Bavaria and Swabia, the nucleus of the historic kingdom of Germany. Lothar, the eldest of the grandsons, retained the imperial title and the territory known as the Middle Kingdom, a long, incoherent block of land running from the North Sea to south of Rome, containing Lorraine (as it came to be known), Burgundy and the greater part of Italy. In spite of the artificial nature of the arrangements, the Treaty established the basis for the future political pattern of the territories contained in the Carolingian empire.

□ R. McKitterick *The Frankish Kingdoms under the Carolingians 751–987* (1983)

Victorines Members of a theological school who represent an important aspect of the 12th-c. monastic revival. Founded by William of Champeaux in 1106, they came to adopt a modification of the Augustinian Rule which enabled them to concentrate as regular canons on intellectual work coupled with some pastoral activity. They were closely associated with the theological teaching at Notre-Dame in Paris during one of its most influential periods in the 12th c. Thoroughly orthodox, they brought new life into efforts to reconcile mysticism with the rational scholasticism that was dominant in that age, and their work had a great influence on later medieval theology, notably among some of the Franciscans.
□ G. Constable *Religious Life and Thought* (1979); B. Bolton *The Medieval Reformation* (1983)

Vienne, Council of (1311–12) Summoned by the first of the Avignonese popes, Clement V, this Council, held at Vienne in the Rhone valley, was strongly influenced by the French king Philip the ·Fair. The Council abolished the Order of the Templars, but resisted attempts to condemn posthumously Boniface VIII, Philip's old opponent, on charges of blasphemy.

Vikings Term probably derived from the Vik (Oslofjord) and used indiscriminately to describe the inhabitants of Scandinavia. The Viking Age, *c.*800–*c.*1100, represents a period of great outburst from the North into the more settled lands to the south-west and south-east. To the inhabitants of Europe the Vikings appeared as a permanent, if sporadic, affliction for the best part of three centuries. In fact, there were two separate Viking Ages, with marked regional and chronological subdivisions.

First Viking Age: Raiding began seriously in the early 9th c., and settlements were made in the northern islands of Orkney and Shetland, in Ireland and off the coast of France. In 851 a Viking army made the first attempt to winter in England, in Kent. A climactic point was reached *c.*860, when in the space of a few years there occurred the first Viking raids in the Mediterranean (859), the beginnings of the settlement of Iceland (860), the establishment of the powerful principality of Kiev under Rurik (862) and the massive onslaughts against England under the sons of Ragnar Lothbrok in 865. The succeeding 60 years placed the bounds to effective permanent Viking settlement – intensification was quite another matter – with the setting up of fortified townships along the trade routes of the Russian waterways, the establishment of the Danelaw in England (880s) and the settlement in Normandy (911). The completion of the settlement of the Atlantic islands and Iceland (930); the intrusion of an Irish/Norwegian element into north-west England; the absorption of the Danes in the West Saxon policy and their expulsion from Brittany, brought the first Viking Age to an end.

Second Viking Age: Viking success was limited to some extent by sheer lack of manpower and resources. In Western Europe the native communities learned how to cope with Viking onslaughts, and in the 10th c. the increasing power of Christian kingship and the shaping of the feudal order owed much to success against pagan, barbarian aggression. Within Scandinavia itself, the establishment of permanent dynasties and the slow acceptance of Christianity dominate the scene. Denmark is rich in archaeological remains from the period, and elaborate fortified settlements such as those at Trelleborg and Fyrkat testify to the organizing power of the dynasty of Gorm the Old, to Sweyn Forkbeard and his son Cnut, conquerors of England. Cnut was king of England (1016–35), of Denmark (from 1019), and intermittently (firmly after 1030) king of Norway.

There was some deepening of settlement, and Scandinavian merchants continued to affect the whole process of European urbanization. To the West there was even further colonization on the fringes, in Greenland and temporarily (*c.*1000) on the North American coast, in Vinland 'the good'. To the east, Russia became increasingly and solidly Slav. Vladimir the Great, ruler of Kiev, adopted the Christianity of the Greek Orthodox church in 988, decreeing that the language of the new church was to be Slavonic – neither Greek, nor Scandinavian. His conversion coincided with similar moves elsewhere in the Slav and Hungarian worlds, and towards the end of the 10th c. Scandinavia itself began to be drawn into the mesh of Christendom. Olaf Tryggvason (998–1000) and Olaf Haraldsson (St Olaf the Stout, 1016–30), in the face of some bitter hostility, forced conversion on the Norwegians, while Iceland accepted Christianity *c.*1000.

Viking characteristics remained strong: fortitude, physical bravery, harsh common sense, laconic understatement. St Olaf's half-brother, Harald Hardrada enjoyed an archetypal Viking career: he served as captain of the Varangian guard at Constantinople, amassed great wealth, contended successfully for the throne of Norway in 1047, and died at Stamford Bridge in battle against Harold II of England in 1066. Yet his exploits take on a Norwegian, as much as a Viking air. There is much in the view that a Scandinavian ceased to be a Viking when he became a Christian. *See* GOKSTAD; OSEBERG   HRL
□ G. Jones *The Vikings* (1968); D.M. Wilson *The Vikings and their Origins* (1970); P.G. Foote and

D.M. Wilson *The Viking Achievement* (1970); P.H.
Sawyer *The Age of the Vikings* (1971); H.R. Loyn
The Vikings in Britain (1977)

Villani, Giovanni (*c.*1275–1348) Best remembered
for his *History of Florence*, Villani was also a merchant,
administrator and soldier. After a long public career
which involved travel abroad and office as a super-
visor of fortifications, he suffered heavy financial
loss in his old age from the failure of the great
banking houses of Bardi and Peruzzi, and died of the
Black Death. His *History*, which was continued by
other members of the family, attempted to cover the
whole period from biblical times. Written in clear
direct Latin, it remains one of the principal sources
for the history of Florence in the days of Dante.
□ L. Green *Chronicle into History* (1972)

Villon, François (1431–after 1463) Remembered
for his *ballades* and *rondeaux* and above all for his
Grand Testament, a string of ironic and satiric
bequests, Villon represents an attempt to express a
new, intensely personal feeling in French vernacular

poetry. After graduating from the university of
Paris, his name became a by-word for violence and
debauchery, and the known facts of his life involve
at least one killing, many robberies and imprisonment. Conversely, his expression of remorse, of
regret for a wasted life and lost opportunities, and of
wonder and terror at the shortness of human life
produced his finest poetry: *Où sont les neiges d'antan?*
('Where are the snows of yesteryear?').
□ *The Complete Works of François Villon* trans. A.
Bonner (1960)

Vincent of Beauvais (*c.*1190–*c.*1264) An outstanding scholar, and almost certainly an early member of
the Dominican house at Paris and Beauvais, Vincent
made his reputation at Paris in close contact with
members of the Capetian dynasty during the reign
of St Louis IX. He is chiefly remembered for his
encyclopaedic work, the *Speculum Maius*, in which
he attempted to gather together all knowledge under
the headings of natural history, doctrine (including
philosophy, the humanities, law, mathematics and
medicine) and history (both sacred and secular), up

Viking settlements in Iceland and Greenland, and possible landfall in Vinland.

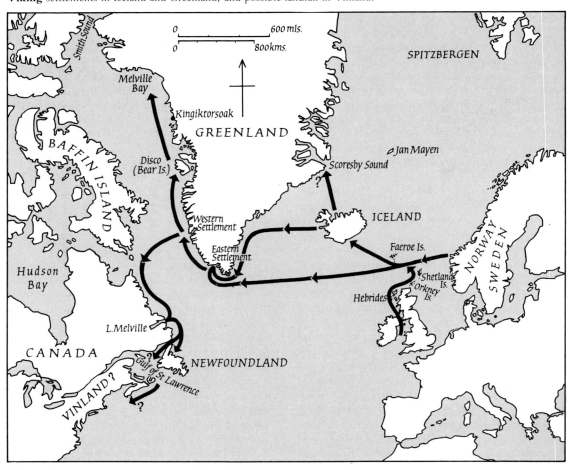

to the time of St Louis's First Crusade in 1250.
□ A.L. Gabriel *The Educational Ideas of Vincent of Beauvais* (1962)

Vinland Region somewhere on the east coast of America, possibly Newfoundland or the coast of Maine, explored by Vikings operating from Greenland in the late 10th c. and early 11th c. Unsuccessful attempts were made by Leif and Thorvald, the sons of Eric the Red, to effect a settlement, and a slightly later attempt by Thorfinn Karlsefni also failed. Hostility of the natives seems to have been the principal immediate cause, though it must also be recognized that Greenland already represented an astonishing extension of settlement by what were, after all, the limited manpower resources of Viking Age Scandinavia.
□ G. Jones *The Norse Atlantic Saga* (1964)

Visconti family The most prominent family in Milan 1277–1447. Tracing their antecedents back to supporters of the imperial cause during the Investiture Contest, the Visconti maintained successfully a pro-imperial and anti-papal stance throughout the 14th c. The powerful Giangaleazzo bought the title of duke from the Emperor Wenceslas IV of the Luxembourg house late in the century, and at the height of his power was ruling most of north Italy and threatening Florence itself. Dynastic divisions and bitter urban rivalries prevented the building up of a permanent Lombard duchy, and on the death of Filippo Maria in 1447 Milan passed under the control of his son-in-law, the great mercenary captain, Francesco Sforza.
□ D. Muir *Milan under the Visconti* (1924); H. Baron *The Crisis of the Early Italian Renaissance* (1955)

Visigoths (Western Goths) A significant and coherent part of the East Germanic Gothic peoples. Converted to Arian Christianity in the 4th c., they played a leading part in the move which, under Hunnic pressure, led to the crossing of the Danube frontier in 376 and the subsequent imperial defeat at Adrianople in August 378, in the course of which the Emperor Valens was killed. The Visigoths then settled uneasily as federate troops of the empire in the Balkans, but under their powerful leader Alaric they turned their attention to Italy. After a long series of diplomatic moves and campaigns they sacked Rome (23–27 August 410), though Alaric himself died in the same year.

The psychological effects of the sack of Rome were universal, but the immediate political consequences relatively unimportant. The Visigoths continued to exercise a curious duality as federates, and on occasion as plunderers, of the Roman population.

Vincent of Beauvais in his study – from a late 15th-c. translation of the *Speculum Historiale*.

They moved into Gaul and fought as allies of the Romans in the great battle of Châlons (451) against Attila and his Huns. Under their King Euric (466–84) they consolidated their hold in Gaul south of the Loire, and moved their sphere of influence steadily south into Spain. Their Arianism created distrust and permanent disharmony with the Romanic population, and in the first decade of the 6th c. they lost control of most of Gaul, except for the provinces along the Mediterranean shore, to the newly converted Catholic Franks.

The Visigothic kingdom in Spain was more long-lasting. Religious dissension ravaged the political life of the kingdom, but in 589 Reccared I called a Council at Toledo where the decision was taken to accept Catholicism. A dissident Arian minority among the Visigoths and persecution of the Jews in the 7th c. weakened the fabric of society in Spain, preparing the ground for the Arab conquest of the early decades of the 8th c. Nevertheless the Visigothic kingdom lasted longer than any other East German political structure and left a permanent heritage to the West in its art, culture and influence on theories of kingship and ecclesiastical law. *See* RODERIC; WULFILA [*152*]   HRL
□ E.A. Thompson *The Goths in Spain* (1969); L. Musset *The Germanic Invasions* (1975); *Visigothic Spain: New Approaches* ed. E. James (1980)

St Vladimir the Great, prince of Kiev, portrayed on a painted banner.

Vitold (Vitout) King of Poland 1386–1434 Nephew of Jagiello, founder of the great Polish dynasty, Vitold won recognition as grand duke of a greater Lithuania in 1401 and built up a formidable principality, which at its widest extent stretched from the Baltic to the Black Sea. He is chiefly remembered for his leadership in the decisive battle at Tannenburg in 1410, when the Lithuanians and Poles in alliance crushed the Teutonic knights and put a temporary end to German expansion in the East. He was not as successful against the Mongols, but maintained a powerful and virtually independent Lithuanian principality noted for its tolerance of the various races (mostly Slav but with a Lithuanian ruling element) and religions (Catholic and Orthodox).
□ G. Vernadsky *The Mongols and Russia* (1953)

Vlad the Impaler Prince of Wallachia 1456–62 and 1476–77 A figure greater in legend than in history, his by-name was given him on account of his ferocious execution of literally thousands of Turks and Bulgars in 1461. Within Wallachia he stands as a supporter of the Hungarians and an enemy of the Turks, though he was imprisoned for some 12 years in the Hungarian capital by Matthias Corvinus. His brother, who succeeded him, was completely subservient to the Turk, and hope of Rumanian independence passed into the keeping of the Moldavian dynasty.
□ R.W. Seton-Watson *A History of the Roumanians* (1934); H. Inalcik *The Ottoman Empire: the Classical Age 1300–1500* (1973)

Vladimir I the Great, St Prince of Kiev 980–1015 (b.955) He left a reputation for ferocity and boundless ambition. His chief importance lies in a firm accord made with the Byzantine Emperor Basil II in 988–89 under the terms of which he married the emperor's sister, received baptism and pledged himself to support the Greek missionaries active in Kievan Russia. He forced Christianity on many of his people and established enduring links between the Byzantine empire and the Russian peoples in religious, cultural and social matters.
□ G. Vernadsky *Kievan Russia* (1948)

Vladislav II Jagiello King of Poland 1386–1434 (b.c.1351) Statesman-king who succeeded in holding together during his lifetime a huge principality which at its highest point stretched from the Baltic to the Crimea. The support of his nephew Vitold,

St Jerome distributes the text of the **Vulgate** at Jerusalem.

who exercised virtually autonomous control of Lithuania, was essential for the success of his political schemes. Facing formidable problems in the East (Tartars and Turks) and in the West (the hostility and suspicion of his brother-in-law, the Emperor Sigismund, anxious for his own position in Hungary and Bohemia), Vladimir had also to steer a very careful path through the religious complications exacerbated by the Hussite reformation.

Within Poland he relied heavily on the support of the great magnates, but the powers of the king were great, and the hold of the Jagiello dynasty was strengthened (in spite of the elective quality of the monarchy). Traditions of tolerance and freedom were well established in Poland during the long reign of this remarkable monarch, though the disruptive social patterns of the kingdom were never far from the surface.

Vulgate Accepted by the Council of Trent (1546) as the only authentic Latin text of the scriptures, the Vulgate – so called because it was the version in most common (*vulgus*) use in the West throughout the Middle Ages – was based essentially on the work of St Jerome (*c*.342–420). Jerome was instructed in 383 by Pope Damasus to revise the Latin New Testament using Greek models. Later in the 380s he withdrew to a cave near Bethlehem and translated the greater part of the Old Testament directly from the Hebrew. In the course of the 6th c. his work, together with the Gallican psalter, was collected into one book, the *Vulgata*. Revisions were made, notably by Alcuin and Theodulf of Orleans in the 8th c. and early 9th c., at the court of Charlemagne. Scholars at the university of Paris attempted further standardization of the text in the 12th c. and 13th c. The strength of the Latinity and the integrity of the text helped to ensure the continued force of Latin as a more or less universal scholarly language throughout the West in the Middle Ages. *See* ANSELM OF LAON

☐ B. Smalley *The Study of the Bible in the Middle Ages* (1952), *The Gospels in the Schools* (1985); *The Bible in the Medieval World* ed. K. Walsh and D. Wood (1985)

Wace A Jersey man resident in Normandy where he became a canon of Bayeux. Master Wace (only his forename survives) was the author of three vernacular hagiographic texts and, more importantly, two extensive rhymed chronicles in French: the *Roman de Brut* (1155) and the *Roman de Rou* (left unfinished *c*.1170–75). The former, an imaginative reworking of Geoffrey of Monmouth's *Historia Regum Britanniae*, may have been instrumental in popularizing Arthurian legend on the Continent. The latter was a history of the dukes of Normandy, also based principally on Latin sources. Wace had undoubted literary talent which is seen to best advantage in his vivid descriptive passages.

☐ *Le Roman de Rou* ed. A.J. Holden (1970–73)

Waiblingen *See* **Ghibellines**

Walafrid Strabo (*c*.808–49) Monk of Reichenau. Student of Hrabanus Maurus and a noted theologian and poet of his day, Strabo was tutor to the young Charles the Bald 829–38. Apart from two years in exile (840–42) he spent the rest of his life as abbot of Reichenau. His commentary on the scriptures, the *Glossa Ordinaria*, survived as an enduring and influential text throughout the Middle Ages. He was also responsible for revising Einhard's biography of Charlemagne.

☐ E.S. Duckett *Carolingian Portraits* (1969)

Waldemar I the Great King of Denmark 1157–82 (b.1131) A warrior of renown, he ended the civil wars in his country, crushed the power of the Wends and made Denmark the leading power of Scandinavia. His half-brother Absalon, bishop of Roskilde, was his closest aid and helped to establish his dynasty on the Danish throne.

Waldensians Followers of Waldo, later erroneously known as Peter Valdes (d.*c*.1216), a rich merchant of Lyons who gave up his wealth and position in the 1170s to become a wandering preacher, living a life of Apostolic poverty. He and his followers were examined by Pope Alexander III at the Third Lateran Council (1179), and although their way of life found approval, they were forbidden to preach without permission from the local episcopate. This they failed to obtain, and in 1182 they were excommunicated and expelled from Lyons. In 1184 they were named as heretics in the papal bull *Ad Abolendam*, and became victims of persecution.

The Waldensians or Poor Men of Lyons bore many similarities to the Franciscans, whom Pope Innocent III was to accept and use for the church. In the later 12th c. the French Midi was home of the growing Cathar heresy, however, and the powerful Waldensian message based on Apostolic poverty, preaching and teaching the scriptures in the vernacular alarmed the authorities – despite its success against the Cathars. The consequent outlawing and persecution of the sect did not lead to its disappearance. The Waldensian preachers and the followers or 'friends' who supported them with alms, spread into

Waldensian heretics were associated with witchcraft and devil worship (15th c.).

Lombardy, Spain, Germany and Austria, and later into Bohemia, Poland and Hungary.

Their congregations were drawn largely from the peasantry and inhabited isolated rural areas. Of the two earliest groups, those in France remained relatively close to orthodox beliefs, some rejoining the Catholic church, others surviving the persecutions which followed the Albigensian Crusade and sustaining a precarious existence until the Reformation. The second group, the Vaudois of northern Italy, split away from the Lyons group in 1205 and adopted a more radical and aggressive form of the heresy, strongly influenced by Donatist beliefs. In the isolated valleys of the Piedmont they survived spasmodic bouts of persecution and a crusade launched against them in 1497. In 1532 most of them were reunited with their *confrères* from Saxony and Dauphiné, who were heavily influenced by the teachings of Luther and Zwingli, and drawn into the mainstream of the Reformation.
□ W.L. Wakefield *Heresy, Crusade and Inquisition in Southern France 1100–1250* (1974)

Wales Although included in the Roman provinces of Britain, apart from the south-east Wales was little touched by Roman material culture and therefore relatively little affected by the end of formal contact with central Roman administration in the early 5th c. In the next century, however, a number of kingdoms emerged; one of these, Dyfed, occupied the area and took the name of an earlier tribal unit, the Demetae; others had a different relationship with the past.

Until the 9th c. only the broadest lines of development are discernible: Gwynedd in the north-west had kings whose pretensions were always wide-ranging, and who may have been acknowledged by others; in the south-east a new kingdom of Glywysing (later known as Morgannwg) replaced and absorbed a number of smaller kingdoms in the course of the 7th c. This pattern of the expansion of some kingdoms at the expense of others, with little consolidation, may be typical of other areas.

English raiding intermittently upset the stability of local life, although it had few lasting effects, except in the north-east. Here, constant pressure effectively undermined the lowland base of the kingdom of Powys, confining the Welsh to the upland and allowing the lowland to be absorbed by England. This was clearly so by 823, when the English took the stronghold of Degannwy on the north coast, but it may have been effectively completed by the late 8th c., when King Offa of Mercia appears to have constructed the dyke which bears his name. This drew a clear border line between Wales and England. The strangled Powys was left to be absorbed by Gwynedd in 855.

Meanwhile, Welsh horizons and Welsh politics were changing. Viking attacks were heavy during the second half of the 9th c., especially on the two western peninsulas, and the English King Alfred sent military assistance to Gwynedd, asking for submission from the kings of Wales. The Viking problem remained a serious one through much of the 10th c. and 11th c. Although no long-term Viking effects are apparent, except in toponymy, it is more than possible that Gwynedd was at times in the 11th c. controlled by Dublin Vikings. English demands for submission continued, and Welsh kings appeared at English courts in the mid-10th c., witnessing transactions as sub-kings. English influence on some aspects of Welsh law may well be a result of these contacts.

Within Wales, while the 9th c. was dominated by the expansion of Gwynedd, the 10th c. was dominated by conflict and interaction between Gwynedd and Dyfed, whose kings were then drawn from the same dynasty, but whose kingships remained separate. In the south-east affairs remained unconnected until the 11th c., but even as some consolidation of the kingdom was effected, new dynasties were establishing themselves within Morgannwg, undermining the power of the main line. This anarchic trend was intensified when kings of the Dyfed and Gwynedd line began to intrude and brought the south-east at last into the main arena of Welsh politics.

Gruffydd ap Rhydderch and Gruffydd ap Llywelyn contended for control of all Wales in the mid-11th c., using Viking and English mercenaries to aid their own plans. The attempts re-awakened English interest, and shortly after Gruffydd ap Llywelyn's victory in 1055, the English fought back and killed him in 1063. The North Welsh kings were then appointed by the English, whose influence was soon overtaken by that of the Normans. From 1070 they set about the conquest of Wales, benefiting from the 11th-c. anarchy and limited development of governmental institutions; by 1093 they had conducted successful military campaigns in many parts of Wales and effectively won control of the south.

The early 12th c. was a period of relative calm. In Stephen's reign, however, the disputed succession and civil wars weakened Anglo-Norman control and resulted in a resurgence of Gwynedd, Powys and Deheubarth. In 1171 Henry II made a pact with Rhys ap Gruffydd of Deheubarth (1153–97), thereby winning the alliance and support of a leading political figure. There was nevertheless a strong spirit of independence in the Welsh church and among the Welsh people, and tensions between the Normans and the Welsh are well exemplified in the career and writings of Gerald of Wales (c.1146–1223).

Ascendance among the Welsh princedoms was wrested from Deheubarth by Llywelyn ab Iorwerth of Gwynedd, who also became a leading figure in English politics. His grandson Llywelyn ap Gruffydd further built up authority in alliance with Simon de Montfort; a measure of his power is that even after de Montfort's fall, Henry III recognized and confirmed him as prince of Wales and overlord of the other Welsh princes (1267). A dispute between Llywelyn and Edward I arose in 1276, leading to conflict and Llywelyn's defeat, and to a drastic curbing of his powers. He was involved in another rising in 1282, which resulted in the conquest and subjugation of Wales. Edward I was in 1301 to create his own son Edward II prince of Wales, a title which henceforth was normally given to the king's male heirs.

By the Statute of Wales (1284) the principality of Gwynedd was brought under the direct rule of the English crown and divided into three shires: Caernarvon, Merioneth and Anglesey. Further south the ancient shires of Cardigan and Carmarthen were reorganized, and on the Cheshire border the shire of Flint was created. Castles were built and boroughs founded in strategic places, but the Marcher lordships were consolidated and extended.

The 14th c. saw isolated revolts in Wales but also a growing prosperity under English rule. In 1400, however, Owain Glyndwr, a descendant of Rhys ap Gruffydd, rebelled to uphold his rights which he found were threatened, and went on to become the leader of widespread resistance. The English failed to crush him, and he came to exercise the powers of a prince; later he became a great Welsh national hero. His power collapsed c.1410, ushering in a long period of disorder, resolved only after 1485 when Henry Tudor, a Welshman, became king of England.

See CELTIC CHURCHES   WD

□ J.E. Lloyd *History of Wales from the Earliest Times to the Edwardian Conquest* (1911); W. Rees *South Wales and the March* (1924); G. Williams *The Welsh Church from Conquest to Reformation* (1962); R. Griffiths *The Principality of Wales in the Later Middle Ages* (1972); W. Davies *Wales in the Early Middle Ages* (1982); R.R. Davies *Conquest, Coexistence and Change: Wales 1063–1415* (1987)

Wallace, William (c.1270–1305) Leader of Scots resistance to Edward I of England. Elected guardian of the kingdom in 1297 for the imprisoned King John Balliol, he was defeated by the English king at Falkirk in 1298. In 1305 he was captured and hanged by the English. Although his career was stained by violence and his immediate political success was limited, he retains importance as a symbol of resistance and as a Scottish national hero.
□ A. Fisher *William Wallace* (1986)

Walsingham, Thomas (c.1360–c.1422) Historian and monk at St Albans for his entire career (apart from a period as prior at the subordinate house of Wymondham), Thomas wrote the *Chronica Majora*, a continuation of the work of Matthew Paris, a *Gesta Abbatum* and also, in his later days, a *Chronica Sancti Albani* which told the story of St Albans Abbey down to 1419. His work is a primary source of special importance for the reigns of Richard II and Henry IV, and is characterized by a strong degree of bitterness against John Wycliffe, dismissed in one of his purple passages as 'that limb of Satan, idol of heretics, mirror of hypocrites and fabricator of lies'.
□ *The St Albans Chronicle* ed. V.H. Galbraith (1937)

Walter of Brienne (d.1356) Count of Lecce and duke of Athens. Born of an important French family, he was raised at the court of the king of Naples. In 1331 he tried unsuccessfully to regain the duchy of

War: Normans set fire to the wooden buildings on the motte at Dinant (Bayeux tapestry).

Athens, lost by his father to the Grand Company of Catalan in 1311. He next went to France to fight with Philip VI in his wars against the English (1339–40); and in 1342 he was made *signore* of Florence, which was suffering in its wars against Pisa. His rule was not a success, and his despotic behaviour led to his expulsion and abdication in 1343. He returned to France and the service of King John, and was killed at the battle of Poitiers.
□ N. Cheetham *Medieval Greece* (1981); G. Dennis *Byzantium and the Franks 1350–1420* (1982)

Walter the Penniless (d. 1096) Leader of the French popular contingent of the First Crusade. He and his 2000–3000 peasant followers were the first crusaders to reach Constantinople (July 1096) and formed the vanguard of the great pilgrim army of Peter the Hermit. Walter died fighting the Turks at Civetot.

Walworth, William (d. 1385) Wealthy London merchant who was first elected mayor of London in 1374. Again mayor in 1381, he raised an army to defend the city and King Richard II against Wat Tyler and his forces. He was present with his men at the confrontation between the king and the peasants' army at Smithfield on 15 June 1381, when he took part in killing Wat Tyler, and was knighted by the king as a reward. [322]
□ R.B. Dobson *The Peasants' Revolt of 1381* (1983)

War A crucial dynamic factor in economic, social and political developments in the Middle Ages. A number of pitched battles, such as the defeat of the Muslims at Poitiers (732) or the campaigns of the crusaders in the Holy Land, stand out as events with clear and immediate consequences. Less immediately obvious, but similarly of importance, were the effects of the kind of localized warfare waged by the castellans of Poitou in the 10th c. and 11th c., or of the Anglo-French conflict 1294–1303, which

brought about crises in the financial administration of both kingdoms and concomitant political problems. It is true that medieval armies were small, and that campaigns were limited in scope and did not invariably produce devastation in the countryside. Nevertheless, the rest of society had to support those fighting men, whether through the tenurial arrangements often described as feudal, or later through taxation, which allowed the armies to be paid directly. Throughout the Middle Ages, secular society was geared to the needs of warfare.

The medieval church sought constantly to limit and control conflict. Lay Christian rulers were traditionally the protectors and guarantors of ecclesiastical exemption from the effects of war, but in the early Middle Ages the church suffered from invasions and from the breakdown of political authority in many regions. Some ecclesiastics met force with force, an example being the Celtic monastic communities in Ireland. In other places the church acted as a peacemaking influence. The disturbed conditions of Burgundy and Aquitaine in the later 10th c. brought into being the Peace and Truce of God, by which priests and the poor were given protection and acts of violence outlawed on many days of the year. The movement spread widely and had a profound influence on lay society. The military religious orders were the result of a different approach: the sanctification of aggression and its organization against the infidel.

The cult of chivalry, which grew out of the tradition of Courtly Love, reinforced the idea of a Christian code of conduct for the knight, and combat in the later Middle Ages was generally preceded by mass and confession. The theory of 'just war' developed by the canonists laid down that war must be fought by laymen for a just and necessary cause which could be achieved in no other way. Such concepts gradually gained ground over earlier feudal customs which allowed anyone of knightly status to wage war.

Public authority as well as ecclesiastical sanctions were brought to bear on illicit combat, as a complex series of laws and customs came to regulate the conduct of war. Different criteria applied in the case of wars against heathen and infidel, however, most of which were waged with savage ferocity. Charlemagne laid Saxony waste in order to bring Christianity to it, and many campaigns in the Crusades were punctuated by acts of violence, such as the massacre of the Muslims and Jews at Jerusalem in 1099. In the West, also, ideal standards were not always followed: the Brabançon mercenaries employed by the English, French and German kings in the later 12th c. were notoriously barbaric, while during the Hundred Years' War, the English armies inflicted widespread damage on the French population, often on the instructions of their leaders.

The enduring symbols of medieval warfare from the 11th c. onwards are the knight and the castle. The holder of a castle could both dominate and protect an area, and only when he recognized the authority of an overlord could his power be kept in check. In the later Middle Ages, fortified towns gained a significant strategic importance as well. The fighting vassal or retainer of the early Middle Ages gave way to the *miles* or knight, supported by a land or money fee, from about the 10th c. He was heavily armed and mounted on a powerful horse, giving him a great advantage over lighter troops. Trained in the private wars and tournaments which the clergy so much opposed, he was encouraged to hold to his chivalrous ideals of courage, virtue and duty. Footsoldiers were no real match for heavy cavalry, as the Anglo-Saxon thegns, armed with axes, found at Hastings in 1066. From the 13th c., however, specialized troops fighting on foot, many as mercenaries, achieved some important victories. The Welsh archers with their longbows gave Edward III a considerable advantage in the Hundred Years' War, as in the battle of Crécy (1346); while the Flemish communal armies with their heavy hand arms proved a match for Philip IV of France at Courtrai (1302). Ships played an important part in the transportation of fighting men, as in the Viking raids; and some pitched battles were fought at sea, such as the English defeat of the French at Sluys in 1340. The navies of the Italian communes, and in particular those of the Genoese, were respected and powerful forces.

Many medieval commanders had an appreciation of strategy. They tried to avoid pitched battles where possible, preferring to manoeuvre and to besiege their opponents' castles using specialized equipment. The appearance of gunpowder in the later Middle Ages presaged major developments in siege warfare. Battles were rare, but often decisive,

Early use of the cannon in warfare, from Froissart's chronicle (15th c.).

as when in 1288 the duke of Brabant defeated the count of Limburg and the archbishop of Cologne at Worringen. Carefully worked out tactics made a considerable difference to their outcome, and a feigned flight could at times bring victory. *See* ARMOUR; CASTLES; CHIVALRY; KNIGHTHOOD   EMH
□ R.C. Smail *Crusading Warfare 1097–1193* (1956); J.F. Verbrüggen *The Art of Warfare in Western Europe during the Middle Ages* (1977)

Wardship Exercised over a fief when the heir was a minor. The king, feudal lord or relative administered the estates on the heir's behalf until he reached majority, fulfilling the services due and often taking considerable profits from the lands in his charge.

Wars of the Roses Name given to the English civil wars waged *c.*1455–89. Their underlying causes included economic recession and the diminishing prosperity of the landowning classes; the ending of the Hundred Years' War in 1453; problems arising from 'bastard feudalism'; and the escalation of private feuds between great families such as the Percys and the Nevilles. The central and immediate reason for their outbreak was, however, the ineffectiveness of Henry VI and the corruption of his advisers. The warring factions fought at first for control of the king and then, after *c.*1460, for the crown itself. A complicating factor was the chance of inheritance, which had thrown up a great many contenders for the throne, all descended from Edward III.

The 1450s saw the attempts of Richard, duke of York, with the backing of Warwick (the Kingmaker), to gain control of Henry VI at the expense of Queen Margaret and her followers. In 1459 the Yorkist leaders fled abroad, only to return in 1460 to capture the king at Northampton. It was then that Duke Richard claimed the throne; but his own followers did not support him and he had to be content with the promise of succession. The queen regrouped the Lancastrian forces, however, and won two major victories, at Sandal in 1460, where York lost his life, and St Albans in 1461. She failed to gain the support of London and was forced to retreat to the north, allowing York's son Edward, fresh from defeating another Lancastrian army at Mortimer's Cross, to proclaim and install himself as king with the backing of Warwick. At Towton Edward IV's forces won a major victory in the largest pitched battle of the war. Edward consolidated his position, but during the 1460s he and Warwick were gradually estranged. Warwick failed to bring off a coup d'état, joined the Lancastrians and with French backing re-installed Henry VI on the throne (1470). With the support of the Burgundians and Hansards, Edward IV invaded

England in 1471 and defeated the Lancastrians at the battles of Barnet and Tewkesbury. Warwick was killed, Henry VI died in the Tower in mysterious circumstances, and Queen Margaret was imprisoned and then exiled. Here the direct dynastic struggle ended, but in 1485 Henry Tudor, a distant Lancastrian connection, was to profit from the dissensions of Richard III's reign. He invaded England, defeated Richard, and took the throne for himself.

Recent studies of the Wars suggest that they were as much a symptom of the general violence and lawlessness of English society as its cause. The pillage and devastation involved have been exaggerated; only 1459–61 and 1469–71 did law and order apparently collapse altogether. Although seven high-ranking families died out completely, there were fewer extinctions of the male lines of noble houses through the Wars than through lack of male heirs. The dangers of allowing the local aristocracy to abrogate untrammelled local power was, however, a lesson not to be lost on Henry VII.   EMH
□ J.R. Lander *Conflict and Stability in Fifteenth-Century England* (1974); C. Ross *The Wars of the Roses: A Concise History* (1977); A. Goodman *The Wars of the Roses, Military Activity and English Society 1452–97* (1981)

Warwick, earl of (Richard Neville) (1428–71) Later known as 'the Kingmaker', he was a man of great ambition, whose pursuit of power dominated English politics for almost two decades and helped to fuel the conflict in the Wars of the Roses. He succeeded to the Warwick title through his wife in 1449, and in the 1450s became an adherent of Richard, duke of York, whose attempts to gain and retain power over Henry VI he strongly backed. In 1461 he succeeded to the Salisbury earldom and supported the seizure of the crown by Richard of York's heir, Edward IV. During the next few years Warwick and the young king were gradually estranged, and after several abortive attempts at rebellion, Warwick fled abroad to join the Lancastrians. In 1470 he returned to England and put Henry VI back on the throne, only to be defeated in his turn and killed at the battle of Barnet (1471) by Edward IV.
□ R.A. Griffiths *The Reign of Henry VI* (1981)

Wazo (*c.*980–1048) Appointed bishop of Liège in 1042, he was an early defender of the independence of the church from lay control, and reproached the Emperor Henry III for his interference in ecclesiastical elections. Although brought up in conservative imperial episcopal traditions, he represents the early stages in church reform movements that were to culminate in the Investiture Contest.
□ E. Hörschelmann *Bischof Wazo von Lüttich* (1955)

Weights and measures: relief showing scales, from the public weigh-house at Nuremberg (late 15th c.).

Weights and measures Until the creation and general adoption of the metric system, these varied enormously in detail, since they were standardized differently in every country or region, and some almost in every village. They have nonetheless a strong family resemblance, since they were for the most part based on either natural (inch, foot), or Roman and Germanic units (ounce, pound; grain, mark); these categories were of course not mutually exclusive, since 'natural' units often lay behind the Roman and Germanic units. There were even a few pre-Roman survivals, such as the French league and *arpent*.

Units from these varied sources had initially no natural relation with each other, and modifications came about when some public authority adopted one of them as a standard and defined others as exact multiples or fractions of it, making, for example, the foot exactly 12 inches, although the average human foot falls short of this. Even what at first sight appear to be eccentric and quite arbitrary units, like the 16½-ft perch and the 7-lb stone, usually have some rational explanation. Much confusion was caused by the application of Latin terms to measures which might be of the same nature and order of magnitude as their Roman counterparts, but which were neither derived from these nor in fact identical with them.

Standards were initially arrived at either by averaging – this was the principle behind the various kinds of 'grain' and was often used for establishing a local 'foot' – or through the arbitrary preference of some public authority. The standards themselves, of stone or metal, were usually kept under lock and key in some government office, while certified copies were made available to the public in marketplaces or affixed to the walls of churches or guildhalls. Measures of land in 9th-c. Salernitan charters are sometimes expressed in terms of a metal standard fixed in the wall of Naples cathedral, and the measure known as 'St Paul's foot', widely used in England in the later Middle Ages, was incised on a pillar in St Paul's Cathedral.

The first documented distribution of metal standards in England dates from 1196–97, but the earliest surviving ones (at Winchester) date from a distribution carried out in 1357; only from the 16th c. are complete sets of the units of length, volume and weight available. The same is generally true elsewhere. Even when a standard existed, there was a constant tendency for it to be disregarded in favour of some traditional local measure, or to be modified in use through the operation of what may be termed the 'baker's dozen' principle. Cloth would be sold *cum pollicibus*, a thumb being placed at the end of the metal yard, and measuring started again on its other side; the pan of the balance containing goods that were sold by weight would by custom be allowed to sink downwards instead of the two pans being maintained exactly even. Such intrusive discounts might eventually be incorporated in the standards themselves, resulting in the 37-inch Scottish yard and the 112-lb cwt.

The metric equivalents given in modern works of reference for medieval units are not usually based on surviving medieval standards but on those used in each locality in the early 19th c. The dimensions of these were ascertained with great precision as different parts of Europe went over to the metric system and metrologists assume rather hopefully that the standards had not changed, at least appreciably, since medieval times. There is only one extensive set of earlier figures, those derived in the 1760s by Mathieu Tillet on behalf of the French Académie des Sciences, though much help can be got from 18th-c. merchants' manuals. The many figures given in the medieval equivalents of these, notably in Pegolotti's *La Pratica della Mercatura* (*c.*1340), have to be treated with caution, for their figures are not always self-consistent and the possibility of copyists' errors has to be taken into account.

The following list includes the more common units, with explanations of how they were arrived at, where this is known or can be plausibly conjectured. Where metric equivalents are given, English units are intended except where the contrary is indicated.

Length Inch (2.54 cm): *uncia*, from *unguis*, the breadth of the thumb-nail; hence its name of thumb, tomme, etc. in Scotland, Holland and Scandinavia. Foot (12 ins, 30.48 cm): Roman *pes* (29.45 cm); French *pied* (32.48 cm). Ell: French *aune*; both from *ulna*, a measure of quite unpredictable dimensions sometimes equated with 2 ft (*c*.60 cm) but often much larger, with the cloth ell in 15th-c. England measuring 45 inches (114 cm). Yard (3 ft, 91.44 cm): from Old English *gerd*, cognate with *verga*, 'rod', introduced as a cloth measure by Henry I; according to William of Malmesbury it was the distance from his nose to the end of his outstretched arm – the traditional way of measuring cloth. Fathom (6 ft, 1.82 m): the length of the outstretched arms, as French *toise*, from *tensa*, 'stretched'. Perch: from *pertica*, also 'rod' or 'pole', the actual measure used; standardized for arable at 16½ ft, probably 20 'natural' ft of 10 ins, but about 25 ft for woodland and with many local variants. Furlong (40 perches or 220 yds, 201.6 m); 'furrow length'. Mile (standardized as 1760 yards or 8 furlongs, 1.61 km); originally imprecise and up to *c*.2200 yds in the Middle Ages; the term is from *mille pasuum*, though the Roman mile of 1000 paces or 5000 ft was only 1.47 km. League: from Gallic *leuga*: like the Germanic *rasta*, basically imprecise, being the distance one could walk before needing to stop and 'rest'; standardized by the Romans as 1½ miles, but much longer (2 or 3 English miles) in the Middle Ages.

Area Important mainly for land; since fields and woods are usually irregular in shape, the units tend to be back-formations from units involving use. The English acre, from *ager*, 'field', was not a precise unit (4840 [22 × 220] sq. yds or 40.46 ares) and was defined in terms of a furlong, but probably originated as the amount of land that could be ploughed in a morning, like the German *Morgen* (30–40 ares). Other units for arable land were derived from the amount of seed required for sowing it, e.g. the French *setier* (*c*. 34 ares), from Latin *sextarius*, *c*.30 litres. The more widely used *arpent* (from *arepenna*) was a Gallic survival, usually about the same, but larger (*c*.50 ares) for woodland.

Volume Like area, this is difficult to measure directly, and units are usually back-formations from more easily ascertained weights. The basic unit in England was the pint (0.57 litres), having as its multiples the quart (2 pints), gallon (8 pints), peck (2 gallons) and bushel (8 gallons, 36.35 litres; larger than the old Winchester bushel of 35.24 litres). The smaller units were mainly liquid measures and the higher ones dry measures, though above the bushel there were still larger ones for liquids again (e.g., for wine, the tun = 2 pipes = 4 hogsheads = 252 gallons). The Anglo-Saxon *pund* was both a pound and a pint of water, as is shown by the medical handbook known as the *Leechdoms*. The later and

much smaller 'pint', which became the standard, was apparently derived from the weight of a pound of grain (wheat or peas). Where grain was concerned there were constant problems arising from the fact that 'heaped' as distinct from 'straked' measure would vary according to the shape of the receptacle employed as the standard.

Weights These are easy to compare with each other, since the balance makes doubling and halving simple, but are without obvious large units. Most medieval terminology is borrowed from that of Rome. The basic 'grains' used originally for weighing gold, are throughout Europe *c*.0.05 g (usually 0.048 g, but Paris grain 0.052 g) or 0.065 (English Troy grain used for precious metals) i.e., a standardized wheatgrain and barleycorn respectively, which, save in a few places (such as Venice), replaced the classical carat of 0.189 g. These units, as medieval metrological texts regularly note, were conveniently related to each other, for 1 carat = 3 barleycorns = 4 wheatgrains. The ounce went back to the Roman *uncia* of 27.29 g and was everywhere between *c*.28 g and *c*.32 g, being related in various ways to the grain. The English Troy ounce (31.10 g) was 20 pennyweights of 24 grains each. The mark, an early Germanic unit, was very early equated with 8 ounces (oz), and the pound was sometimes 12 oz, as in the Roman system, which was carried on for the weighing of gold and silver in the Troy(es) pound. The pound of everyday life was 15 or (more usually) 16 oz (avoirdupois lb, or double mark), but other figures occur, the multiples varying according to local practice and the merchandise being weighed.

Higher weights, required for agricultural produce, metals, etc., were either peculiar to the material (fothers of lead, chaldrons of coal) or were fractions or multiples of the hundredweight, originally 100 lbs or for a few goods 120 lbs ('long hundred'). The English units of 104 lbs (for spices) and 112 lbs (wool and most other commodities) were fixed after a violent dispute between Edward I and the Grocers' Company on weighing procedures, to allow for the inclusion in the measure of allowances customarily made on the principle of the 'baker's dozen'. The 112-lb cwt made possible the replacement of the inconvenient 6¼-lb sixteenth, called a nail or clove, by the more convenient 7-lb unit that remained in use in the wool trade to the end of the 18th c. *See* CARAT; MARK; POUND   PG

□ H. Duursther *Dictionnaire universel des poids et mesures anciens et modernes* (1840); P. Grierson *English linear measures: a study in origins* (1972); R.D. Connor *The weights and measures of England* (1987)

Welf *See* **Guelph**

Wenceslas, St (*c*.907–29) Duke of Bohemia. He was instrumental in spreading Christianity in his lands. Murdered by his brother Boleslav, he was soon venerated as a martyr and became patron saint of his country in the early 11th c. His assassination was a direct result of his pro-German policy, a curious irony in the light of later Czech history.
□ F. Dvornik *Life of St Wenceslas* (1929)

Wends Name given by the Scandinavians and Germans to the West Slav peoples who occupied the Baltic coast between Kiel and the Vistula. Relatives of the Bohemians and Poles, the Wends had migrated from the south-east between the 1st c. and 6th c., and by *c*.900 had established fairly stable frontiers. There were a number of different tribes: in the East the Pomeranians, in the West the Wagrians, Polabians and Abotrites, and between them, in the lands between the rivers Warnow and Oder, a group of tribes known as the Liutizians or Wolf people; north of these, on the coast, were the Rugians. The western and central tribes spoke West Lechic languages, but the Pomeranian tongue was East Lechic, a linguistic relative of Polish. The Wendish social structure bore many similarities to that of Scandinavia, with powerful princes and a small military elite ruling a predominantly peasant society. On the coast a number of urban trading and fishing communities such as Szczecin and Oldenburg flourished in sheltered inlets from the 11th c. onwards. Such new ports were excellent bases for piracy as well as commerce, and the fleets from the ports and the light cavalry armies of the princes were a powerful combination in time of war.

In the early 12th c. the Wends were for the most part heathen and idol-worshipping peoples. Their paganism was an intrinsic part of their social organization, and their priests had formidable powers. Their conquest and conversion had first been attempted in the 10th c. with the establishment of bishoprics such as Oldenburg, but a pagan reaction had followed and in *c*.1100 there were only a few small Christian communities in some coastal towns. The continuation of missionary efforts resulted in the conversion of some of the Pomeranian and Abotrite princes in the 1120s and the destruction of temples in their lands by German priests. In the early 1140s, moreover, the Saxons dispossessed some of the Wendish rulers of western Wagria.

Finally, in 1147 the Saxon nobility, with the encouragement of St Bernard of Clairvaux and Pope Eugenius III, launched a crusade against the Wends. Two Saxon armies joined by two Danish fleets attacked the Abotrites with some modest success; but although some of Prince Nyklot's followers accepted baptism, and the prince became a tributary of the Saxons, it was only a token surrender and no land was captured. In the next half-century the episcopate and the monastic orders began to colonize the region and, in conjunction with the local rulers, to organize warfare against the heathen Wends, and their conversion. Bern, a Cistercian monk from Amelungsborg, converted the Abotrite Prince Pribislav of Mecklenburg; and in 1169 King Waldemar I of Denmark and his half-brother Absalon, bishop of Roskilde, broke the power of the Rugians, whose piracy had ravaged the Danish coast. In the 1160s and 1170s Waldemar had allied himself with Henry the Lion, duke of Saxony, but rivalry between the Danes and Saxons became intense, as both sought territory and tribute. (Waldemar's work was continued by Cnut and Waldemar II, but was still not complete by the death of the latter in 1241.) Despite papal blessing for the wars, the conversion of the Wends and their absorption into Western society thus owed as much to land hunger as to crusading ideals. EMH
□ A.P. Vlasto *The Entry of the Slavs into Christendom* (1970); E. Christiansen *The Northern Crusades* (1980)

Wessel, Johann (*c*.1420–89) Alias Wessel Gansfort, a Dutch theologian working in Paris and Italy, whose views on the papacy and ecclesiastical authority prefigured those of Martin Luther. His knowledge of Hebrew and Old Testament studies illustrate one side of the humanist activities of the later Middle Ages, conservative in concentration on the Bible and the Fathers, yet potentially revolutionary compared with existing circumscribed scholarly tastes.
□ C. Ullmann *Reformers before the Reformation* (1854)

Wessex According to later West Saxon tradition, the kingdom of Wessex was founded by Germanic chieftains who landed near Southampton and then travelled north across Salisbury Plain in the late 5th c. and early 6th c. This version, however, takes no account of the Jutes, who on Bede's evidence had already occupied the Isle of Wight and neighbouring coastal lands. A series of victories by the West Saxons over the British culminated in King Ceawlin's capture of Aylesbury and the Upper Thames valley (571) and of Gloucester, Cirencester and Bath (577). Thus he extended his authority from the south coast to the Bristol Channel and as far east as Selwood forest. The first West Saxon bishopric was established by Birinus, a missionary, at Dorchester-on-Thames (635), but in 662 it was displaced as the ecclesiastical centre of Wessex by Winchester, which became the political capital as well.

The next two centuries saw a fluctuation in the fortunes of the kingdom. Although from the 650s the kings gradually extended their rule into Devon and Cornwall, the Upper Thames fell to Wulfhere and the Mercians in 661. Ine's reign in Wessex (688–726) saw the conquest of Cornwall as far as the river Hayle and the rebuilding of West Saxon power on the south coast. After his death royal control was again weak until Egbert (802–39) subjugated the whole of Cornwall (825) and overran Mercia (829). Although his kingdom stretched from Cornwall to Kent it was probably far less strong than later chroniclers suggested, and its cohesion was soon to be severely tested by the Scandinavian raids and later invasions.

In 870 the Danes based at Reading mounted their first major campaign against Wessex, but were beaten back by King Aethelred (d.871) and his brother and successor, Alfred, a man of vision and learning as well as a great leader. Two more attacks were made in 876 and 878, and Alfred was forced to retreat to Athelney (Somerset) to consolidate his forces. Later that year, in a dramatic reversal of fortunes, he decisively defeated the Danes at Edington (Wiltshire) and compelled their leader Guthrum to accept baptism and to retreat to East Anglia. Thereafter he built up the defences of his kingdom by land and by sea, and in 880 occupied London, which became, by agreement with Guthrum, an eastern outpost on the borders of Wessex and the Danelaw. Alfred's son, Edward the Elder (899–925), and his grandsons Athelstan (925–39), Edmund (939–46) and Eadred (946–55) gradually extended West Saxon rule by capturing strongholds west of Watling Street from the Danes and by successful campaigns in Northumbria and Scotland. At *Brunanburh*, a battle fought by the West Saxons and their Mercian allies in 937, King Athelstan defeated his Scandinavian, British and Scottish opponents and paved the way for the expulsion of the Danish kings of York by Eadred and the coronation of Edgar as king of all England at Bath in 973. Military prowess and the backing of the English church had brought the West Saxon dynasty to pre-eminence in the English kingdom.   EMH
□ F.M. Stenton *Anglo-Saxon England* (1970); H.R. Loyn *Anglo-Saxon England and the Norman Conquest* (1962)

Westminster Abbey Site with monastic associations reaching back to the early 7th c. It was refounded for 12 Benedictine monks by St Dunstan in *c*.959, and again on a far greater scale by Edward the Confessor, who had the church magnificently rebuilt in the Norman style from 1045. In 1161 the Confessor, whose tomb was here, was canonized, and from 1245 Henry III, in devotion to his growing cult, financed the early stages of another reconstruction of the church in the Gothic style. The project never gained popular support and was shelved after his death, not to be resumed until 1376. The church was completed in the early 16th c. with the Henry VII chapel.

As the English coronation church from 1066 and the principal royal mausoleum from the 13th c., Westminster Abbey fostered its connections with the English kings. The royal palace nearby became the principal site of the Exchequer in the reign of Henry II and remained the centre of the financial and legal operations of government throughout the Middle Ages. The Abbey's chapter-house became a store for royal jewels and records. The monks supported a flourishing school, but the Abbey never became a major centre of royal historiography on the lines of Saint-Denis in France. The Abbey possessed substantial estates with an income of almost £3500 each year at the Dissolution; they were concentrated in Middlesex and Essex but took in 22 counties in all. Westminster's dependencies included Great Malvern Priory and a hospital in Knightsbridge. Its wealth and royal connections gave the Abbey a leading place among the religious houses of medieval England.
□ R.A. Brown, H.M. Colvin and A.J. Taylor *The History of the King's Works: The Middle Ages* HMSO (1963); B. Harvey *Westminster Abbey and its Estates in the Middle Ages* (1977)

Whitby, Synod of Called in 664 to reconcile the clergy of two different traditions, both of which had helped to convert Northumbria: the Celtic church, represented by Colman and Cedd, and the Roman church, represented by Wilfrid. The differences in their practices included methods of tonsure and procedures at baptism, but the central point at issue was the method of computing the date of Easter. King Oswy's decision in favour of Rome provoked some Celtic hostility but paved the way for the unification of the English church under Archbishop Theodore of Tarsus.
□ H. Mayr-Harting *The Coming of Christianity to Anglo-Saxon England* (1972)

White Friars *See* **Carmelites**

Widukind (d. after 785) He led the resistance to Charlemagne's attempts to conquer and dominate Saxony from the mid-770s. After bitter fighting he was subjugated, and accepted baptism in 785. Although he took no part in later Saxon revolts against Charlemagne, legends accreted around him and he became a Saxon folk hero.

Widukind (d.*c*.1004) Monk of Corvey. Author of the chronicle, the *Res Gestae Saxonicae*, a valuable

The funeral of Edward the Confessor, showing the newly consecrated, but unfinished **Westminster Abbey**.

historical source for the deeds and court life of Emperor Otto I of Saxony.
□ *Sächsische Geschichten* trans. P. Hirsch (1931)

Wilfrid, St (634–709) Bishop of York and one of the leading figures in the English church. A man of vigour and vision, he played an important role as bishop, church-builder and missionary in the English kingdoms, especially Sussex. His stay in Rome (653–58) had influenced him strongly in favour of the customs of the Roman church, which he represented at the Synod of Whitby (664). His appeals to Rome over the division of his see of York (677 and 704) brought him into conflict with successive archbishops and with the Northumbrian ruling house; he spent long periods in exile from his native Northumbria. Contemporary records portray him as a type of masterful political bishop.
□ *The Life of Bishop Wilfrid by Eddius Stephanus* ed. B. Colgrave (1927)

William I the Conqueror Duke of Normandy, and king of England 1066–87 (b.*c*.1028) A man of remarkable ability whose political and military skills earned him a dominant place in Western Europe. The Anglo-Saxon chronicler portrayed him as wise, powerful and 'gentle to the good men who loved God', but 'stern beyond all measure to those people who resisted his will'. The illegitimate son of Robert I of Normandy and Herlève, supposedly a tanner's daughter from Falaise, he became duke in 1035 while still a child. He depended for political survival on a faction of the nobility, on the church, and on King Henry I of France who helped him to crush his enemies in 1047. In the early 1050s he gained a valuable ally from his marriage with Matilda of Flanders, but his growing power brought him into conflict with his Capetian overlord.

In the 1060s William embarked upon dramatic territorial expansion which was greatly to enrich his followers and himself. Maine was captured, campaigns were mounted on the Breton frontier, and in 1066 came the climax with the battle of Hastings, the defeat and death of King Harold, and the conquest of England. With its wealth and crown, the last was a prestigious and much sought-after prize, and the Conqueror and his followers consolidated their victory only with considerable difficulty. When a major rebellion broke out in the north in 1069, it was violently suppressed. Most of the English land-owners were replaced with William's men, all owing strict feudal obedience to the king; and as high posts in the church fell vacant, they too went to the French. Landholding was organized for the support of the mounted knight, and large numbers of strong castles, symbolic of the new order, were constructed. The Old English governmental and judicial machinery was developed to suit Norman needs. The Domesday survey of 1086 is a striking illustration of the administrative capabilities of William's regime.

William the Conqueror died while campaigning to maintain his hold on Maine. He was buried in his own monastic foundation of Saint-Etienne at Caen.
□ D.C. Douglas *William the Conqueror* (1964)

William I the Lion King of Scotland 1165–1214 (b.1143) He successfully consolidated royal power in his lands by extending feudal tenures into the far north and by building up the royal administration. He fought hard against the territorial ambitions of the English kings, but was defeated and forced into vassalage by Henry II, and later by John. Even so he claimed with some success that the ties of vassalage applied to his English lands and not to his position as king of Scotland.

□ G.W.S. Barrow *The Kingdom of the Scots* (1973)

William (Guilhem) IX (1071–1127) Duke of Aquitaine from 1086, he was an influential patron of the troubadours and himself one of the earliest troubadour poets. Under his patronage the court at Poitiers became a leading cultural centre. He interrupted his long-standing feud with the count of Toulouse to go on crusade in 1101, but his forces suffered severe defeat at Heraclea.

□ H. Davenson *Les Troubadours* (1964)

William of Champeaux (*c*.1070–1121) Theologian who taught at the cathedral schools in Paris, but was driven out in 1108 by Peter Abelard's mockery of his views on universals. He later became the leading master at the School of Saint-Victor in Paris. Prominent politically in his attempts, as an emissary to the Emperor Henry V (1106–25), to bring an end to the Investiture Contest, he also made significant contribution to medieval philosophy by his tract *De Origine Animae*, in which he emphasized the creative act of God in the making of each and every human soul.

□ R.W. Southern *Medieval Humanism and other studies* (1970)

William of Malmesbury (*c*.1095–*c*.1143) Modelling his work on Bede and intent on filling the historiographical gap between Bede's day and his own, William spent his active life as monk and librarian at the Benedictine monastery of Malmesbury, and left two historical works of outstanding merit: the *Gesta Regum*, or 'Deeds of the kings of England', which took the story from 449 to 1120, and the *Gesta Pontificum*, which, though concentrating on the Anglo-Saxon period, also brought much vital information to notice concerning the more recent history of the English ecclesiastical sees up to the 1120s. His *Historia Novella* provided a valuable, strictly contemporary account of parts of the reign of Henry I and the early years of Stephen. He also wrote a Life of St Dunstan, translated Coleman's Life of St Wulfstan of Worcester, and produced influential work on the history of Glastonbury. His good Latin style, his desire to reveal historical truth (though he was not above accepting dubious evidence in support of the antiquity of Glastonbury or Malmesbury, for example), and his eye for a good story ensured the continued popularity of his work; he ranks among the leading 12th-c. historians.

□ H. Farmer, 'William of Malmesbury's life and works', *Journal of Ecclesiastical History* 13 (1962); R.M. Thomson *William of Malmesbury* (1987)

William of Ockham (*c*.1285–1349) English Franciscan theologian who studied at Oxford. His principal works, the *Sentences* and *Quodlibeta*, were probably complete in 1324 when he answered heresy charges at the papal court in Avignon. Condemned in 1326, he took the part of the Spiritual Franciscans in their disputes with Pope John XXII, and had to flee to the protection of the Emperor Louis of Bavaria. He stayed in Munich, from where he issued powerful treatises denouncing the temporal authority of the papacy. A powerful and influential thinker, his stress on the vast divide between man and the all-powerful and unknowable God divided faith from reason and pointed the way towards advances in the natural sciences.

□ G. Leff *William of Ockham* (1975)

William of Rubruquis (Roebruck) (b. *c*.1215) Franciscan friar sent in 1253 by Louis IX of France on a diplomatic mission to the Mongols. His account of his journey and of the court of the great khan at Karakorum made it clear that hope of a large-scale conversion of the Mongols to Christianity was illusory.

□ I. de Rachewiltz *Papal Envoys to the Great Khan* (1971)

William of Volpiano (William of Dijon) (964–1031) Italian monk of Cluny who became abbot of Saint-Bénigne at Dijon in 990. Under the auspices of Cluny, he provided the inspiration and organization for a major revival of the flagging monastic life in Normandy, the Paris region and other parts of northern France.

William of Wykeham (1324–1404) He rose to high office in England: he was bishop of Winchester from 1366, and chancellor of England 1367–71 and 1389–91. He is best remembered for his major educational foundations of New College, Oxford (built 1380–86) and Winchester College (1382–94). [*251*]

Alabaster effigy of **William of Wykeham** in Winchester cathedral (late 14th c.).

William Tell The character of fully developed legend, as in the 16th-c. *Chronicon Helveticum*, was a peasant from Bürglen in the canton of Uri, Switzerland, who in the late 13th c. or early 14th c. defied the authority of the Austrian governor of Altdorf, Gessler. As a penalty, he was compelled to shoot with his bow and arrow at an apple placed on the head of his young son. He was successful, but his threats to the governor led to his arrest. On his way to prison he escaped and later killed Gessler in an ambush near Küssnacht. The Swiss subsequently rose up against their Austrian rulers. The historical basis of the story remains a matter of debate, as there are no references to Tell in sources written before the 1470s; but there are clear connections between the story of William Tell and other medieval mythical and heroic tales.

Wills and testaments A will is a legal instrument whereby the owner of land makes arrangements for its disposal after his death; a testament similarly distributes his assets. Such transactions were common among the wealthier classes in the Roman world, but in Western Europe in the earlier Middle Ages they were generally precluded by the practice of disposing of land and assets amongst members of the kin, and by feudal and customary law. From the 11th c. wills and testaments began to appear more frequently as churchmen familiar with Roman law encouraged the free disposal of land and established ecclesiastical control over the legal processes involved.
□ *Anglo-Saxon Wills* ed. D. Whitelock (1930); S. Epstein *Wills and Wealth in Medieval Genoa 1150–1250* (1984)

Winchester Bible In two splendid volumes (now rebound into four) the Winchester Bible, though incomplete, represents some of the finest products of the 12th-c. book illuminator's art. The work of five distinctive, first-class artists can be discerned: the Master of the Leaping Figures, the Apocrypha Drawings Master, the Master of the Morgan Leaf (all active 1155–60), the Master of the Genesis Initial and the Gothic Majesty Master (both active *c.*1170–85). The Bible provides a source of delight and information for the general historian as well as for the historian of art. Influence from Byzantium and the Mediterranean world is present, but increasingly the emphasis is on more naturalistic elements, in the facial expressions and active movements of men and women, and in the portrayal of beasts, draperies and foliage.
□ W.F. Oakeshott *The Artists of the Winchester Bible* (1945); C.M. Kaufmann *Romanesque Manuscripts 1066–1190* (1975)

Wine trade The Romans brought the cultivation of vines with them into northern Italy, Gaul, the Rhineland and England, but wine was never produced on a large scale on the northern fringes of the empire and remained an expensive, aristocratic drink. Its consumption by the aristocracy continued into the Middle Ages, but its use by the Christian church in the Eucharist made it a universal necessity. As a result, much wine, often of poor quality, was grown locally; Domesday Book mentions 38 vineyards in England. There is evidence that a long-distance wine trade was also established early. By the early 7th c. there was a wine fair held annually at Saint-Denis, and in Charlemagne's time Rouen was a busy centre for wine imports to England from the Ile de France, Burgundy and the Loire. German wine from the Rhine and Moselle was also brought to England, probably by the same route. The Norman Conquest further strengthened these links, and the process was profitable to the king, who levied *prisage*, a tax in kind, on imported wines.

It was probably improved climatic conditions in the 11th c. and 12th c. which brought about an expansion in the number of vineyards in Northern Europe. Long-distance trade, increasingly subject to price regulation and taxation, was still centred at Rouen in the 12th c., but when in 1152 King Henry II married Eleanor, duchess of Aquitaine, direct trading links were established with her lands, and wine ships began to make direct runs between Bordeaux, La Rochelle and the Loire, and London, Bristol and Sandwich. Bordeaux wine was considered a superior commodity, and the English loss of Normandy, Anjou and parts of Poitou to the French in the early 13th c. brought about a reduction in imports of wine from and via northern France and a growth in the Gascon trade.

The upper Rhineland and the Moselle also appear to have been exporters of wine in the later Middle Ages, but are far less well documented than the Bordeaux region, which dominated the market from the 13th c. to the mid-14th c. More than half of the Bordeaux wines went to Brittany and the Low Countries, but England, too, took a sizeable share, and English merchants handled most of this trade. In a typical year in the 14th c., England imported some 30–40,000 tuns from Gascony, and imports from other sources (Greece, Portugal, the Moselle and Lorraine) were a mere fraction of the total. The Hundred Years' War and the Black Death disrupted Gascon exports, however, and the capture of Bordeaux by the French in 1453 proved a further blow to the region. The shortfall in demand in Northern Europe was made up by wines from Italy, the Iberian peninsula and various regions of France.

A new rival to the Bordeaux vintage emerged in

ſ̨ e nus ne ſoffeꝛꝛoit ſi grans cops longement *D ar ſo*

Collecting and treading the grapes for the preparation of **wine** (*c.* 1340).

the later 14th c. in the shape of the sweeter, more potent and more durable wines from the Levant, such as Malmsey from Crete and Romeney from the Ionian islands. They were imported first by the Genoese and the Venetians, and from the early 15th c. by English merchants. The Spanish and Portuguese, already wine producers and exporters, also began to make similar wines in the 15th c. They came only in small quantities, however, and the bulk of the trade in this period was concerned with more bitter, short-lived vintages. EMH
□ A.D. Francis *The Wine Trade* (1972); M.K. James *Studies in the Medieval Wine Trade* ed. E.M. Veale (1972)

Winfrith *See* **Boniface, St**

Witchcraft In the later Middle Ages there was a widespread belief in Europe in covens of cannibalistic, devil-worshipping witches who worked evil by magical means. The increasing intensity of the persecution of supposed witches eventually led to the great witch crazes of the 16th c. and 17th c., when thousands of people were put to death. Nevertheless, there were areas, such as England, where the stereotype of the witch made little progress either in educated circles or in popular consciousness. Moreover, even where the stereotype had become established orthodoxy, there were often important people who rejected it. Witchcraft continued to mean different things to different people throughout the Middle Ages.

In classical times the idea of magic (that is, causing events through outward but non-natural means) was well established, and it was believed that magic could be used for good as well as evil purposes. From the first, the Christian church attacked all magic as evil, heretical and diabolically inspired. Yet in the age of its triumphant advance the church did not fear magic and came to perceive it as an illusion devised by the devil to deceive man. On the other hand, the limits to the church's influence in this matter in society at large were demonstrated by the continuing distinction made in secular law between so-called white magic and black magic. White magic, with its myriad manifestations across Europe, was often, ironically enough, associated with the sacred symbols and magical powers of the church, and its ministers persisted well into the age of Enlightenment.

Attitudes began to alter in the central Middle Ages. In educated circles there was increasing interest in ideas of ritual magic or invocation. Inevitably, the detailed theological investigation by the Scholastics of the heavenly hosts, their degrees, relations and powers encouraged speculation about the members of the demonic legions. The notion became current that those with knowledge, or magi, could invoke spirits, control them by spells, and use them for their own devices. This development was strongly attacked by the church: Pope John XXII in the bull *Super Illius Specula*, issued in the 1320s, condemned ritual magic as diabolism and heresy. Western society was increasingly prone to self-doubt and anxiety about the powers of evil and, as evidence invoked in the trial and suppression of the Templars (1307–14) showed, less inclined to dismiss magic as unreal. As it proved, the clerical attack on magic was a major factor in the formation of later ideas about witchcraft. Popular beliefs had always existed about magic, ranging from white magic to sorcery. In attempting to make sense of this amorphous body of popular ideas during the 14th c., the church gradually came to the conclusion that all sorcery involved an implicit pact with the devil. In 1398 the university of Paris condemned sorcery as idolatry and heresy, and thus linked sorcery ineluctably with diabolism.

The idea has long been widely held that medieval witchcraft was a cult or sect with its roots in the Roman cult of Janus and in folk practices and fertility rites. It is said that the heretical sects of the 12th c. and 13th c. were the proponents of this cult and were linked directly to the witches of the later Middle Ages. Recent research has discarded such notions and cast serious doubts on the theory that the stereotype of the witch emerged as early as the 13th c. in heresy trials against Catharism. Nevertheless, the demonization by society of the heretical sects, at first a by-product of persecution, later began to stimulate it. Further, these persecutions brought with them a new inquisitorial legal procedure in which the charge was laid not by an individual, as in the normal accusatory procedures, but by the authorities. The accused was interrogated in secret, allowed little or no defence, and his confession was extracted by torture. Gradually the various elements of sorcery, ritual magic and diabolism merged into the concept of devil-worshipping witchcraft. The crucial period in this fusion appears to have been the early 15th c., when those accused of sorcery and magic were treated as heretics and diabolists, and were tried using inquisitorial procedures. From this time on, each round of witch trials producing its batch of manipulated confessions reinforced and elaborated the developing stereotype. The process was encouraged by a growing corpus of learned literature on the subject, two of the most influential works being John Nider's *Formicarius* (1435) and Jacob Sprenger and Henry Institoris' *Malleus Maleficarum* (1486).

Through extensive persecution in the Valais region of Switzerland in 1428, the fully-fledged stereotype of the witch made an early appearance. Here, in France and Germany, and to a lesser extent in Italy, there were a large number of witch trials during the rest of the 15th c., with persecution and burnings reaching a peak 1455–60 and 1480–85. In 1459, for example, a mass trial in Arras led to a virtual reign of terror in the city. In England, by contrast, witch trials were virtually unknown in the Middle Ages, a result perhaps in part of the legal system, with its base in common law, and in part of English resistance to many of the ideas about witches which had wide acceptance in the rest of Europe.   TSS
□ N. Cohn *Europe's Inner Demons* (1975); R. Kieckhefer *European Witch Trials: their Foundation in Learned and Popular Culture* (1976)

Wolfram von Eschenbach (d. after 1220) The most celebrated German poet of the Middle Ages. From the lesser nobility of Bavaria, he apparently served a number of Franconian lords. His surviving work consists of eight fine lyric poems, most of which are *Tagelieder* or dawn songs, the fragments of one epic poem, *Titurel*, and the complete texts of two others. *Parzifal* is a vast epic cycle, based in part on earlier romance sources, such as the works of Chrétien de Troyes; its substance revolves around Percival, King Arthur and the Holy Grail. The later *Willehalm* is a religious epic about the crusader William of Toulouse, written to instruct Christian knights in virtue and duty.
□ M. Wynn *Wolfram's 'Parzifal'* (1984)

Women They emerge from medieval sources in a multitude of guises. An enduring image is the *grande dame* worshipped from afar by her knight, as depicted from the 12th c. onwards in tales of chivalry. Its antithesis is the view of women in marriage treaties – as commodities, to be valued according to the inheritance or dowries they brought with them. The cult of the Virgin Mary, popular throughout society from the 11th c., was a less exclusive ecclesiastical equivalent of Courtly Love, which singled out Christ's mother as a figure at once divine and maternal. Its obverse was the strong mysogynist tradition inherited from St Paul and patristic writings, which portrayed woman as Eve, the ultimate temptress and obstacle to salvation; it was better to marry than burn – but only just – and a man intent on a holy life should enter a religious order. These changing and often contradictory ideas about women are symptomatic of the complex and

These images of **witches** riding their broomsticks (*c.*1451) show how early the stereotype was established.

Working **women** alongside men in the fields; from the *Très Riches Heures* (15th c.).

varying nature of their status and functions in medieval society.

The great majority of women lived and died wholly unrecorded, as they laboured in the field, the farm and the home. It is probable that in the early Middle Ages in much of Western Europe life expectancy for women was lower than that for men, and women as labourers and bearers of children could therefore be a valued commodity. By the 11th c., however, the imbalance was reversed. Popular religious movements were one outlet for the surplus females, but the majority worked to support themselves. Many women in the Middle Ages were agricultural labourers, and the harshness of their lives is captured in Langland's *Piers Plowman*. Domestic work could be an equally oppressive burden on poor women, yet to the 15th-c. French poetess Christine of Pisa, the life of peasants bowed down with toil might give them 'greater sufficiency than some that be of high estate'. Other women worked in trades such as selling food or drink, in clothmaking, or in crafts. The wives of merchants and traders were often involved in their husbands' businesses and might choose to carry on with them as widows. The ladies of wealthy burgesses, of knights and of the nobility were responsible for organizing not only the functioning of their households but also their domestic economy, which could be a demanding charge.

Among the nobility marriage was a critical factor in the transmission of land and fiefs, and was arranged by families with great care, often with little consideration for the preferences of the parties involved, one or both of whom might be children. Only in periods and places where women had personal rights over land did they exercise much independence. Late Roman law had placed the unmarried woman in tutelage, but the constraints gradually broke down, and by the 10th c. in Spain and south-

ern France women were succeeding to land on equal terms with men. By contrast, in 13th-c. Germany, female inheritance of land, though common, was still regarded as a privilege rather than a right. Feudal customs tended to dismiss women as too weak to carry out military services, and male guardians normally carried them out instead; they might be husbands or overlords, and the latter would have control over the marriages of their wards. In societies where male primogeniture was a commonly accepted pattern of inheritance, women were undesirable as heirs, a notion taken to extremes in 14th-c. France, where by the elaboration of the so-called Salic law, they were excluded from succession to the throne.

At the very summit of society, however, some women managed to wield very great power, and a few became empresses or queens in their own right. As Urraca, who became queen of Castile in 1109, and the Empress Matilda, heiress of Henry I (1100–35) in England and Normandy, both found, the rule of a woman often led to opposition and rebellion. Mélisende, queen of Jerusalem in her own right, however, was successful in defending her crown and kingdom, and acted as co-ruler with her son Baldwin III in the 1140s. Queen regents were also to be reckoned with. Two Merovingian queens of the late 6th c. and 7th c., Brunhild and Bathild, acted effectively in this capacity for their sons and ensured the continued succession of their dynasty. In the 13th c. Blanche of Castile became regent for her young son Louis IX of France and retained control of the kingdom in the face of determined opposition. A century before that, Eleanor, duchess of Aquitaine, brought her lands to two successive husbands, the French and English kings, thereby dramatically altering the balance of power between them. Many queens consort exercised considerable authority; a very few, such as Isabella of France, wife of Edward II of England, were instrumental in the deposition of their husbands. On occasion women led armies or, like Joan of Arc, provided inspiration and direction. Their reward was to be described by contemporary writers in unflattering terms such as 'manlike' and 'Jezebel'; Joan of Arc was burned at the stake for heresy and sorcery.

The religious life provided a calling or an honourable refuge from the world for men and women alike, but far more opportunities were offered to the men. Before the 12th c. women's monasticism was centred on a few wealthy and aristocratic nunneries such as Whitby in Northumbria or Quedlinburg in Saxony. Here, the abbesses had much independence and authority, but their communities were in a minority; in pre-Conquest England, for example, there was only one nunnery for every four monas-

The lady of leisure: from a late 15th-c. tapestry, *A mon seul désir*.

teries. The monastic reform movements of the 11th c. and 12th c. brought scant encouragement for religious women: the Cistercian nuns were kept at a distance, yet firmly confined by their brethren. In the 13th c. the Franciscans, a preaching mendicant order, were to cloister their nuns equally closely. The tradition of wealthy royal and aristocratic foundations, of which the Order of Fontevrault is an outstanding example, continued throughout the Middle Ages; but there was mounting pressure from women in all ranks of society to be accepted into the religious life. The result was the foundation of many small nunneries in the later 12th c. and 13th c., the growth of the Béguine movement, and the creation of other orders of women, such as the Brigettines. Heresies which allowed females a significant role (such as Waldensianism and, later, Lollardy) also proved popular. Women mystics and hermits such as Christina of Markyate in the 12th c. returned, in their solitary existence, to the earliest roots of the monastic life in the desert. Their rigour and asceticism contrasts with the rather comfortable way of life in many nunneries in the later Middle Ages, symbolized by Chaucer's prioress, but both forms of religious life offered women an equally honourable refuge from the world. EMH

□ E. Power *Medieval Women* ed. M.M. Postan (1975); *Medieval Women . . . Dedicated to Professor Rosalind M.T. Hill* ed. D. Baker (1978); P. Stafford *Queens, Dowagers and Concubines* (1983); M.W. Labarge *Women in Medieval Life* (1986); S.M. Stuard *Women in medieval history and historiography* (1987)

Sheep-shearing: from a late 15th-c. Hours of the Virgin belonging to Henry VII.

Wool trade.

Wool trade. From Roman times there was a flourishing trade in wool and finished woollen cloth in Western Europe. As with all long-distance trade, there were changes in the main areas of wool production and centres of the woollen industry during the course of the Middle Ages. Under the Romans, the skills of cloth-making on a large scale were brought from the Middle East and flourished in Italy. Wool was imported from Spain and southern Gaul, regions which produced little finished cloth, while in northern Gaul a vigorous woollen industry developed; by the 4th c. the region was exporting high-grade cloth and fashionable clothing to Italy.

The collapse of the empire clearly disrupted such long-distance trade, but there is some evidence that it continued on a reduced scale and began to revive in the 7th c. Charlemagne's preference for native woollen garments rather than exotic silks must have helped the manufacturers. The Frisian cloaks which he is said to have worn may well have been products of the already growing Flemish cloth industry, which emerges in 11th- and 12th-c. sources as well established, well organized, and as a market for the excess labour of the region; its products went as far afield as Novgorod.

By the 9th c. England, too, was exporting cloth, a commodity much valued and often plundered by the Vikings. The expansion of Viking settlements and the establishment of trading links between them did much to stimulate the wool trade here as elsewhere around the North Sea. The Domesday survey reveals substantial flocks of sheep in late 11th-c. England, and the seizure of wool crops by a predatory crown was by the 13th c. an established expedient.

As the northern woollen industry became increasingly organized, its techniques improved, and in place of the woad and madder used in previous centuries it began to require exotic dyes imported from the East. In return, cloth was exported to southern Europe and then on to the East; Italian merchants, who transported it, regularly visited the Champagne cloth fairs from the mid-12th c.

In the 13th c. the Flemish woollen industry reached its apogee, and adjoining areas of northern France, as well as parts of central and eastern England, also produced high-quality cloth. Among the particularly valued English products was the red cloth of Lincoln, in demand by the royal wardrobe and for presents to foreign rulers. The trade was controlled by merchant entrepreneurs such as the late 13th-c. Jean Boine Broke of Douai. He used wool from his own estates, supplemented by that purchased from English abbeys such as Holmcultram (Cumbria); he stored it in his own premises, sent it to be made into cloth in his own workshops or in the homes of independent craftsmen, and marketed the finished products through his own agents. Such men formed guilds, which exercised a powerful and often minute control over their industry. They devised detailed regulations and appointed inspectors to maintain quality and to take part in wage negotiations with employees. Such associations were formed by foreign as well as native merchants; in England the foreign guilds were known as *Hansae*, and were regulated and given important privileges by the crown.

Flanders produced some of its own raw wool, but the principal supplier in the later Middle Ages was England. Much of this crop was of the highest quality; most was produced on large demesne estates and was frequently sold directly to foreign merchants. The great entrepreneurs might also act as middlemen for smaller producers. During the 14th c. the crown imposed an increasingly heavy tax on wool exports, and permitted a merchant company known as the Staple to hold a monopoly on the trade, so that profits might be levied more easily; one result was the increasing expense of raw wool. England was not the only supplier: from the mid-13th c. Spain emerged as a producer of wool and exported to Flanders and England, where stringent regulations were drawn up to forbid its mixing with the native equivalent. Another area exporting wool on a small scale was Germany. The hegemony of Flanders and England was challenged from the 12th c. by the Italian towns, whose merchants handled much of the trade in woollen cloth with the East. Communities such as Genoa and Florence specialized in dying and finishing northern cloth. In Florence, the Calimala guild controlled the purchase of northern wool at the Champagne fairs, arranged for its transport to Italy, negotiated a reduction in tolls, and stringently regulated the dyeing and finishing of the cloth. The manufacture of woollen cloth on a commercial scale also became increasingly widespread, and in the mid-14th c. was the principal industry of many areas of Lombardy and Venezia. The high-quality raw wool was imported largely from England, its purchase helped by the special status enjoyed there by Italian merchants, many of whom were papal tax-collectors. In 14th-c. Florence, the *Arte della Lana*, the clothmaking guild, displaced the *Arte di Calimala* in importance and influence.

As the Italian industry grew, the Flemish woollen manufacturers were beset by many problems: trade disputes culminating in popular unrest in Bruges and other cities in 1280; a dearth of raw wool from England and its high price; and the disruption of trade routes as a result of Franco-Flemish hostility. The duchy of Brabant, where conditions were more stable, managed to maintain its trade by such expedients as establishing direct links with Genoa. In England the woollen industry was hampered for a time by the restrictive regulations of the trade guilds in the urban centres, but the introduction of the spinning wheel and of the fulling mill, requiring a constant supply of running water, revolutionized the industry, which gradually moved out to rural areas. The abundant supply of wool, the lack of a Staple to restrict and control the export of cloth, the lightness of the export duties imposed by the crown

Woolworking as one of the seven mechanical arts, showing a hand loom and treadle loom.

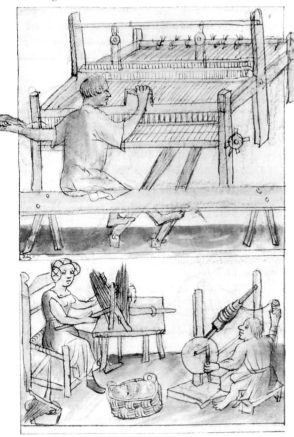

in the early 14th c., all helped to bring about a dramatic expansion in the cloth-making industry. Its centres were the west of England, East Anglia and the West Riding of Yorkshire, from where the cloth was transported to ports such as Bristol or Hull. Thus, by the 15th c. England was the leading producer of woollen cloth in Western Europe, her clothiers relatively free from the stringent regulations which hampered their foreign competitors. The great wool churches of the Cotswolds and East Anglia provide a striking illustration of the power and wealth of these wool barons.   EMH

□ E. Power *The Wool Trade in English Medieval History* (1941); *The Cambridge Economic History of Europe* vol. 2, ed. M.M. Postan and E.E. Rich (1952); T.H. Lloyd *The English Wool Trade in the Middle Ages* (1977)

Worms, Concordat of (1122) At the German episcopal city of Worms on the left bank of the Rhine the Emperor Henry V reached an agreement with Pope Calixtus II which technically brought the Investiture Contest to an end. The Concordat was expressed by means of an imperial charter, granted to God and St Peter, and a papal bull, granted to the Emperor. Henry V conceded the technicalities of election to spiritual office to the ecclesiastical hierarchy, promising support for canonical election to bishoprics and abbacies, and renouncing investiture with ring and staff.

In return the pope conceded the right of the Emperor to be present at elections and to invest the German prelates with their regalia by the lay sceptre *before* their consecration to spiritual office. This ensured imperial control of the dues and duties owed to him by bishops and abbots, who were also, in the society of the day, powerful feudal magnates. An exception was made even here, on grounds of geography and common sense, for Italian and Burgundian prelates, who were empowered to be invested by the sceptre and pay their dues within six months of their consecration. In practice the Emperor retained great influence, amounting in most cases to control over the appointment of his prelates; but the church also gained a significant victory in establishing beyond a shadow of doubt its right to invest to spiritual office.

□ *Sources for the History of Medieval Europe* ed. B. Pullan (1971)

Worms, Synod of (24 January 1076) Council of German bishops, convoked in haste by the Emperor Henry IV in response to Pope Gregory VII's prohibition of lay investiture and the subsequent dispute over the election to the archbishopric of Milan. Two archbishops and twenty-four bishops accused

Gregory of immorality, perjury, misuse of his powers in Germany, and of usurping his office; the Emperor supported their castigation and called on him to resign. In response Gregory VII excommunicated Henry and declared him deposed, and the Emperor, rapidly losing support, submitted to the pope at Canossa in 1077.

□ *The Correspondence of Gregory VII* ed. E. Emerton (1945)

Writ Brief written instruction issued on behalf of the English king in execution of his will. Surviving Anglo-Saxon writs generally notify grants of land or rights on land, and after *c.*1070 such documents were usually in Latin. All had seals affixed and protocols naming the sender and recipients, and greeting them. This basic form later developed into a variety of letters and writs, in French as well as Latin, which were the staple executive instruments of the medieval English administration. Short written instructions on a similar pattern were also issued by other medieval rulers, including kings of France and Germany.

□ F.E. Harmer *Anglo-Saxon Writs* (1952); R.C. van Caenegem *Royal Writs in England from the Conquest to Glanvill* (1959)

Wulfila (Ulfilas) (*c.*311–*c.*83) Apostle of the Goths. An Arian Christian missionary to the Visigoths, for whom he invented the Gothic alphabet and translated the Bible. He constructed his alphabet from a mixture of Greek and Latin letters, and his work proved decisive in the transmission of the literate heritage of the Mediterranean world to the Germanic peoples at the time of the great migrations.

□ G.W.S. Friedrichsen *The Gothic Version of the Gospels* (1926), *The Gothic Version of the Epistles* (1939); *The Conflict between Paganism and Christianity in the Fourth Century* ed. A.D. Momigliano (1963)

Wulfstan (d. 1023) Archbishop of York from 1002. He is noted for his homilies, especially the *Sermo Lupi ad Anglos* (1014), an appeal to the English to repent and reform. He also drafted law codes for Aethelred the Unready and Cnut, and produced treatises on government and the reform of the church. Politically he proved to be a key figure in ensuring the succession of Cnut as Christian king of England.

□ D. Whitelock, 'Archbishop Wulfstan, Homilist and Statesman', *Transactions of the Royal Historical Society* (1942)

Wycliffe, John (*c.*1330–84) Academic philosopher of distinction who influenced a major popular heretical movement. By the 1370s he had become the leading philosopher at the university of Oxford, noted for his treatises in defence of universals. A royal clerk by 1371–72, he was involved in politics until 1378 as part of John of Gaunt's anti-clerical movement, and during this period his interests turned towards church doctrine. In *On the Church* (1378), he rejected the ecclesiastical hierarchy and put forward the idea of the true church as a community of believers; in *On the Eucharist* (1379), he more radically denied the doctrine of transubstantiation. Condemned by the pope in 1377, he had to leave Oxford (1381) and retired to his rectory in Lutterworth, from where, under Gaunt's protection, he issued numerous openly unorthodox treatises. His writings were to prove a vital formative influence on the Lollard movement.

□ K.B. MacFarlane *John Wycliffe and the Beginnings of English Non-Conformity* (1952); *Wyclif in his times* ed. A. Kenny (1986)

Y/Z

Yaroslav the Wise Grand prince of Russia 1035–54. Son of Vladimir the Great (d. 1015), Yaroslav faced a long struggle with his elder brother Svyatopolk before finally becoming great prince of Kiev (1019). It was not until 1035 and the childless death of another brother, Mstislav, that he won sole control of his father's dominions. This heralded a thriving period for Kievan Russia, much encouraged by strong links with Byzantium, despite a Russo-Byzantine war (1043–46). Christianity strengthened its hold; the church's position was regulated and Ilarion became the first native metropolitan of Kiev. Building activity flourished, culminating in the cathedral of St Sophia (1037), and the laws were clarified. Prosperity at home was matched by progress abroad: Russian frontiers were extended and consolidated, especially in the Baltic region, while relations with the West were maintained, often through dynastic marriages. After Yaroslav's death, when authority was again distributed among the family, a decline in Kiev's fortunes began.

□ G. Vernadsky *The Origins of Russia* (1959)

Yolande of Brienne (*c.*1212–28) Given the name Isabella, but more usually known as Yolande, she was heiress to the kingdom of Jerusalem through her mother Mary (d. 1212). Her father, John of Brienne, acted as regent during her minority. In August 1225 she was married by proxy to Emperor Frederick II, a match promoted by Pope Honorius III who thus hoped to speed the Emperor on a crusade to the

Holy Land. After being crowned queen of Jerusalem she travelled to Brindisi. Here the marriage was solemnized, a ceremony seen as Frederick's pledge of his commitment to the crusade. He immediately dispossessed John of Brienne and assumed the rights and title of king consort. In April 1228 Yolande bore a son, Conrad. She died a few days later, leaving her infant as child king of Jerusalem. Neither he nor his son Conradin ever visited the Holy Land to be crowned; and with Conradin's death (1268) the line of Yolande came to an end.
□ S. Runciman *A History of the Crusades* vol. 3 (1954)

Yugoslavs Their original homeland lay beyond the Carpathian mountains. During the period of mass migration, these South Slavs (*Jugo* meaning south) moved into a region around the Lower Danube. They began raiding the Balkan peninsula in the reign of Emperor Justinian I (527–65), whose attempts to regain lost imperial territory weakened the frontiers here. By the early 7th c. settlement had begun. Tribal divisions were exacerbated by conversion to Christianity, for the Serbs and Macedonians accepted Byzantine orthodoxy, while the Croats and Slovenes received the faith from Rome. Many Bosnians came to adopt heretical Bogomil beliefs.

Throughout the Middle Ages the South Slavs faced pressure from foreign powers. At times individual states established effective independence and enjoyed periods of success, but unity was never achieved. Croatia emerged earliest, with Tomislav becoming the first Balkan ruler to assume the title of king (925). Later, however, the Croats accepted union with Hungary (1102). Slovenia succumbed to Germanic control, ultimately wielded by the Habsburgs. Both Serbia and Bosnia dominated in turn, but both eventually fell before a new outside threat: the Ottoman Turks. Although parts of Dalmatia survived under Venetian protection, the early 16th c. found most Yugoslavs living under Muslim subjugation.
□ V. Dedijer *History of Yugoslavia* (1974)

Zabarella, Francesco (1360–1417) Italian canonist who advocated a conciliarist solution to the Great Schism. He studied canon law at the university of Bologna, taught in Florence and later Padua, and served three popes as legal adviser. His reputation among contemporaries was high. In 1410 he was made bishop of Florence and the following year cardinal-deacon. He acted as one of the negotiators for Pope John XXIII in talks with Emperor Sigismund concerning a general council, and participated in the resulting Council of Constance (1414–18). It was during the sessions here that he died. In his *Tractatus de Schismate* Zabarella's proposals for

A well-armed **Yugoslav** foot-soldier adorns a bronze bellplate of the early Middle Ages.

resolving the Great Schism became a synthesis of the conciliar approach to ecclesiastical government. He sought, and often found, justification for this approach in earlier canonistic thought. *See* CONCILIAR MOVEMENT
□ W. Ullmann *The Origins of the Great Schism* (1948); B. Tierney *Foundations of Conciliar Theory* (1955)

Zacharias, St Pope 741–52. A Greek by birth, whose translation of Gregory the Great's *Dialogues* was widely read in the East. His diplomatic skills restrained Lombard expansion for nearly ten years. He strengthened papal links with Frankia by agreeing that the Frankish crown belonged to the person who in reality exercised its authority (751). After the subsequent deposition of Childeric III, he sanctioned the anointing of the new king, Pepin. This decision was reached at a time when the Lombards were causing fresh difficulties, unopposed by the iconoclastic Byzantine emperor. Zacharias' role in the transfer of Frankish royal power was later often cited by upholders of papal supremacy.
□ H.K. Mann *The Lives of the Popes in the Early Middle Ages* (1902)

BIBLIOGRAPHICAL NOTE

There is as yet no single, easily accessible general work of reference on the Middle Ages in Europe that can be recommended. When complete, Scribner's *Dictionary of the Middle Ages* (ed. J.R. Strayer, 1982-), planned in 12 volumes, will provide such a guide. For up-to-date information on scholarly output, consult the *Annual Bulletin of Historical Literature*, published by the Historical Association, London.

The following specialist encyclopaedias and works of reference are especially helpful and reliable:

Cambridge Medieval History ed. J.B. Bury, 8 vols. (1911-36); *Shorter Cambridge Medieval History* ed. C.W. Previté-Orton, 2 vols. (1952)

Lexicon des Mittelalters ed. L. Lutz et al, planned in 5 vols. (1977-)

Reallexicon der germanischen Altertumskunde ed. J. Hoops, 4 vols. (1911-19); new edition, ed. R. Wenskus, planned in 20 vols. (1968-)

A. Potthast *Bibliotheca Historica Medii Aevi* 2 vols. (1896; revised edition 1962-68)

L.J. Paetow *A Guide to the Study of Medieval History* (1931; revised edition 1980)

R.C. van Caenegem *Guide to the Sources of Medieval History* 2 vols. (1978)

Oxford History of the Christian Church planned in 20 vols. (1976-); in particular, J.M. Wallace-Hadrill *The Frankish Church* (1983)

Oxford Dictionary of the Christian Church ed. F.L. Cross and E.A. Livingstone (1974)

New Catholic Encyclopaedia ed. W.J. McDonald, 17 vols. (1967-79)

Cambridge History of the Bible vol. 2, ed. G.W.H. Lampe (1969)

Encyclopaedia Judaica ed. J. Klatzkin, 16 vols. (1928-)

New Standard Jewish Encyclopaedia ed. C. Roth and G. Wigoder (1970; revised edition 1975)

Encyclopaedia of Islam (1913-38); new edition in 5 vols., ed. H.A.R. Gibb et al (1960-86)

Encyclopaedia of World Art ed. M. Pallottino, 16 vols. (1959-83)

New Oxford History of Music vols. 1 and 2, ed. J.A. Westrup et al, planned in 10 vols. (1954-)

A History of Technology vol. 2, ed. C. Singer et al (1956)